Rick

W9-AHR-163

# VIENNA
## SALZBURG
## & TIROL

# CONTENTS

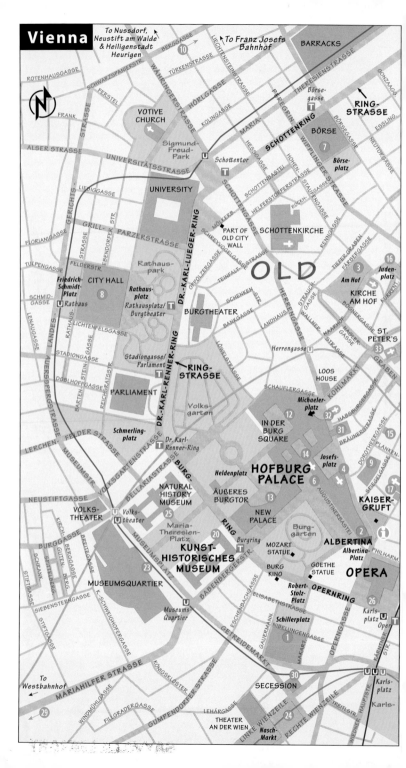

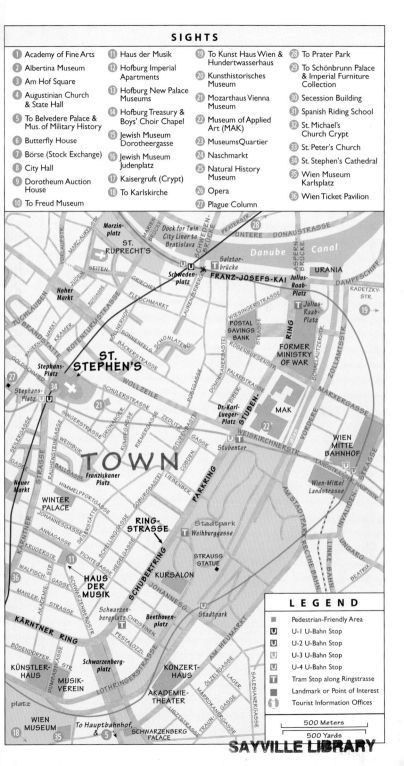

## SIGHTS

1. Academy of Fine Arts
2. Albertina Museum
3. Am Hof Square
4. Augustinian Church & State Hall
5. To Belvedere Palace & Mus. of Military History
6. Butterfly House
7. Börse (Stock Exchange)
8. City Hall
9. Dorotheum Auction House
10. To Freud Museum
11. Haus der Musik
12. Hofburg Imperial Apartments
13. Hofburg New Palace Museums
14. Hofburg Treasury & Boys' Choir Chapel
15. Jewish Museum Dorotheergasse
16. Jewish Museum Judenplatz
17. Kaisergruft (Crypt)
18. To Karlskirche
19. To Kunst Haus Wien & Hundertwasserhaus
20. Kunsthistorisches Museum
21. Mozarthaus Vienna Museum
22. Museum of Applied Art (MAK)
23. MuseumsQuartier
24. Naschmarkt
25. Natural History Museum
26. Opera
27. Plague Column
28. To Prater Park
29. To Schönbrunn Palace & Imperial Furniture Collection
30. Secession Building
31. Spanish Riding School
32. St. Michael's Church Crypt
33. St. Peter's Church
34. St. Stephen's Cathedral
35. Wien Museum Karlsplatz
36. Wien Ticket Pavilion

### LEGEND

- Pedestrian-Friendly Area
- U  U-1 U-Bahn Stop
- U  U-2 U-Bahn Stop
- U  U-3 U-Bahn Stop
- U  U-4 U-Bahn Stop
- T  Tram Stop along Ringstrasse
- Landmark or Point of Interest
- Tourist Information Offices

500 Meters
500 Yards

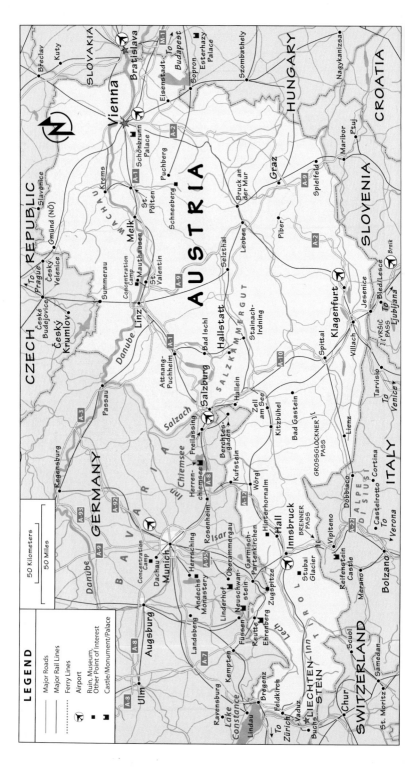

*Schönbrunn Palace and Gardens in Vienna*

*Salzburg at sunset*

*Vienna's St. Stephen's Cathedral*

*Welcome to Austria!*

*Hallstatt in the Salzkammergut*

# Rick Steves®

# VIENNA
# SALZBURG
# & TIROL

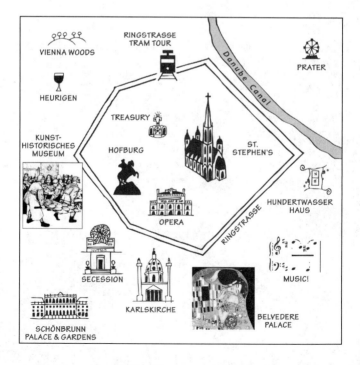

VIENNA WOODS

RINGSTRASSE
TRAM TOUR

Danube Canal

PRATER

HEURIGEN

TREASURY

KUNST-
HISTORISCHES
MUSEUM

HOFBURG

ST.
STEPHEN'S

HUNDERTWASSER
HAUS

OPERA

RINGSTRASSE

SECESSION

MUSIC!

KARLSKIRCHE

BELVEDERE
PALACE

SCHÖNBRUNN
PALACE & GARDENS

# INTRODUCTION

Austria offers alpine scenery, world-class museums, cobbled quaintness, and Wiener schnitzel. Unlike Germany, its industrious neighbor to the northwest, Austria is content to bask in its good living and opulent past as the former head of one of Europe's grandest empires. Austrians are relaxed, gregarious people who love the outdoors as much as a good cup of coffee in a café.

This book focuses on Vienna and all of its cultural offerings, as well as the Danube Valley, Salzburg, Hallstatt (the gem of the Salzkammergut Lake District), and the mountainous Tirol region. Because some sights just across the border are so scenic and interesting, this book also ducks into Germany (Berchtesgaden and Bavarian sights) and Slovakia (Bratislava).

I'll give you all the information and opinions necessary to wring the maximum value out of your limited time and money. If you plan three weeks or less in Austria and have a normal appetite for information, this book is all you need. If you're a travel-info fiend, this book sorts through all the superlatives and provides a handy rack upon which to hang your supplemental information.

Experiencing Europe's culture, people, and natural wonders economically and hassle-free has been my goal for three decades of traveling, tour guiding, and travel writing. With this new edition, I pass on to you the lessons I've learned.

The destinations covered in this book are balanced to include a comfortable mix of cities and villages, mountaintop hikes and medieval castles, sleepy river cruises and sky-high gondola rides. While you'll find the predictable biggies (such as Mozart's house and the Vienna Opera), I've also mixed in a healthy dose of Back Door intimacy (thrilling mountain luges, a beer with monks, and a lakeside town reachable by boat). I've been selective, including only the most exciting sights. For example, there are dozens of quaint

INTRODUCTION

## Map Legend

| | | | | | |
|---|---|---|---|---|---|
| 𝟁 Viewpoint | ✈ Airport | ) ( Tunnel |
| ↑ Entrance | Ⓣ Taxi Stand | Pedestrian Zone |
| ⊕ Tourist Info | 🅣 Tram Stop | ----- Railway |
| WC Restroom | Ⓑ Bus Stop | ........... Ferry/Boat Route |
| 🏰 Castle | Ⓜ Metro Stop | ⊢──⊣ Tram |
| ⛪ Church | Ⓟ Parking | Stairs |
| ▪ Statue/Point of Interest | ) ( Mtn. Pass | • • • • • Walk/Tour Route |
| ⊠ Elevator | ⬡ Park | ------- Trail |

*Use this legend to help you navigate the maps in this book.*

villages in Austria's Salzkammergut Lake District. I take you to only the most charming: Hallstatt.

The best is, of course, only my opinion. But after spending a third of my adult life exploring and researching Europe, I've developed a sixth sense for what travelers enjoy. The places featured in this book will make anyone want to slap-dance and yodel.

## ABOUT THIS BOOK

*Rick Steves Vienna, Salzburg & Tirol* is a personal tour guide in your pocket. Each recommended destination is a mini-vacation on its own, filled with exciting sights, strollable neighborhoods, affordable places to stay, and memorable places to eat.

The first half of this book focuses on Vienna and contains the following chapters:

**Austria** offers an introduction to this delightful country.

**Orientation to Vienna** includes specifics on public transportation, helpful hints, local tour options, easy-to-read maps, and tourist information. The "Planning Your Time" section suggests a schedule for how best to use your limited time.

**Sights in Vienna** describes the top attractions and includes their cost and hours.

The **Self-Guided Walks** and **Tours** lead you through interesting neighborhoods and must-see sights. In Vienna, these include a city walk, St. Stephen's Cathedral, the Hofburg Imperial Apartments and Treasury, and the Kunsthistorisches Museum. A breezy tram tour takes you around Vienna's Ringstrasse.

**Sleeping in Vienna** describes my favorite hotels, from good-value deals to cushy splurges.

**Eating in Vienna** serves up a range of options, from inexpensive cafés to fancy restaurants, clustered by neighborhood.

# Key to This Book

## Updates
This book is updated regularly—but things change. For the latest, visit www.ricksteves.com/update.

## Abbreviations and Times
I use the following symbols and abbreviations in this book:

Sights are rated:

| | |
|---|---|
| ▲▲▲ | Don't miss |
| ▲▲ | Try hard to see |
| ▲ | Worthwhile if you can make it |
| No rating | Worth knowing about |

Tourist information offices are abbreviated as **TI**, and bathrooms are **WC**s. To categorize accommodations, I use a **Sleep Code** (described on page 476).

Like Europe, this book uses the **24-hour clock.** It's the same through 12:00 noon, then keeps going: 13:00, 14:00, and so on. For anything over 12, subtract 12 and add p.m. (14:00 is 2:00 p.m.).

When giving **opening times,** I include both peak season and off-season hours if they differ. So, if a museum is listed as "May-Oct daily 9:00-16:00," it should be open from 9 a.m. until 4 p.m. from the first day of May until the last day of October (but expect exceptions).

If you see a ✪ symbol near a sight listing, it means that sight is described in far greater detail elsewhere—either with its own self-guided tour, or as part of a self-guided walk.

For **transit** or **tour departures,** I first list the frequency, then the duration. So, a train connection listed as "2/hour, 1.5 hours" departs twice each hour, and the journey lasts an hour and a half.

---

**Entertainment in Vienna** is your guide to evening fun, including classical concerts, opera, and things to do after dark.

**Vienna Connections** has information on Vienna's airport and how to get to nearby destinations by train, car, and boat.

The **Danube Valley,** just west of Vienna, covers tiny **Melk,** with its hulking riverside monastery, and the concentration-camp memorial in **Mauthausen.** Just east of Vienna is **Bratislava,** the Slovakian capital.

The **Salzburg** section covers this touristy but charming town, as well as nearby **Berchtesgaden** (home to Hitler's Eagle's Nest) and beautiful lakeside **Hallstatt.**

The **Tirol** section describes my favorite stops in this mountainous region: **Innsbruck** and its little sister just downriver, **Hall.**

INTRODUCTION

The section also covers the top sights in **Western Tirol** and southern **Bavaria,** including the famous castles of "Mad" King Ludwig.

The **Vienna: Past and Present** chapter introduces you to some of the key people and events in this city's complicated past, making your sightseeing more meaningful.

**Practicalities** is a traveler's tool kit, with my best travel tips and advice about money, sightseeing, sleeping, eating, staying connected, and transportation (trains, car rentals, driving, and flights). There's also a list of recommended books and films.

The **appendix** has nuts-and-bolts information, including useful phone numbers and websites, a festival list, a climate chart, a handy packing checklist, and German survival phrases.

Browse through this book, choose your favorite destinations, and link them up. Then have a *wunderbar* trip! Traveling like a temporary local, you'll get the absolute most out of every mile, minute, and dollar. As you visit places I know and love, I'm happy that you'll be meeting some of my favorite Austrians.

# Planning

This section will help you get started on planning your trip—with advice on trip costs, when to go, and what you should know before you take off.

## TRAVEL SMART

Your trip to Austria is like a complex play—it's easier to follow and really appreciate on a second viewing. While no one does the same trip twice to gain that advantage, reading this book in its entirety before your trip accomplishes much the same thing.

Design an itinerary that enables you to visit sights at the best possible times. Note festivals, holidays, specifics on sights, and days when sights are closed (all covered in this book). To get between destinations smoothly, read the tips in Practicalities on taking trains and buses, or renting a car and driving. A smart trip is a puzzle—a fun, doable, and worthwhile challenge.

When you're plotting your itinerary, strive for a mix of intense and relaxed stretches. To maximize rootedness, minimize one-night stands. It's worth taking a long drive after dinner (or a train ride with a dinner picnic) to get settled in a town for two nights. Every trip—and every traveler—needs slack time (laundry, picnics, people-watching, and so on). Pace yourself. Assume you will return.

Reread this book as you travel, and visit local tourist information offices (abbreviated as TI in this book). Upon arrival in a new town, lay the groundwork for a smooth departure; get the schedule for the train, bus, or boat that you'll take when you depart. Drivers can figure out the best route to their next destination.

Update your plans as you travel. You can carry a small mobile device (phone, tablet, laptop) to find out tourist information, learn the latest on sights (special events, tour schedules, etc.), book tickets and tours, make reservations, reconfirm hotels, research transportation connections, and keep in touch with loved ones. If you don't want to bring a pricey device, you can use guest computers at hotels and make phone calls from landlines.

Enjoy the friendliness of the Austrian people. Connect with the culture. Set up your own quest for the best Baroque building, Sacher-Torte, wine garden, or whatever. Slow down and be open to unexpected experiences. Ask questions—most locals are eager to point you in their idea of the right direction. Keep a notepad in your pocket for noting directions, organizing your thoughts, and confirming prices. Wear your money belt, learn the currency, and figure out how to estimate prices in dollars. Those who expect to travel smart, do.

## TRIP COSTS

Five components make up your trip costs: airfare, surface transportation, room and board, sightseeing and entertainment, and shopping and miscellany.

**Airfare:** A basic round-trip flight from the US to Vienna can cost, on average, about $1,000-2,000 total, depending on where you fly from and when (cheaper in winter). Consider saving time and money by flying into one city and out of another; for instance, into Vienna and out of Munich). Overall, Kayak.com is the best place to start searching for flights on a combination of mainstream and budget carriers.

**Surface Transportation:** For a two-week whirlwind trip of this book's destinations by public transportation, allow $300 per person. If you'll be renting a car, allow $200 per week not including tolls, tolls, gas, and supplemental insurance. If you'll be keeping the car for three weeks or more, look into leasing, which can save you money on insurance and taxes for trips of this length. Car rentals and leases are cheapest if arranged from the US. Train passes normally must be purchased outside of Europe but aren't necessarily your best option—you may save money by simply buying tickets as you go. Don't hesitate to consider flying, as budget airlines can be cheaper than taking the train (check www.skyscanner.com for intra-European flights). For more on public transportation and car rental, see "Transportation" in Practicalities.

**Room and Board:** You can manage comfortably in Austria on $120 a day per person for room and board (less in small towns, more in big cities such as Vienna and Salzburg). This allows $10 for

# Vienna, Salzburg & Tirol:
# Best Two-Week Trip by Train

| Day | Plan | Sleep in |
|---|---|---|
| 1 | Fly into Vienna | Vienna |
| 2 | Vienna | Vienna |
| 3 | Vienna | Vienna |
| 4 | Vienna | Vienna (or head to Melk in evening if biking or cruising Danube on Day 5) |
| 5 | Danube Valley (Melk to Krems and back) | Melk |
| 6 | To Salzburg via Mauthausen | Salzburg |
| 7 | Salzburg | Salzburg |
| 8 | Salzburg | Salzburg |
| 9 | To Hallstatt | Hallstatt |
| 10 | Hallstatt and surroundings | Hallstatt |
| 11 | To Innsbruck | Hall or Innsbruck |
| 12 | Innsbruck; to Bavaria | Füssen or Reutte |
| 13 | Bavaria and castles | Füssen or Reutte |
| 14 | Fly out of Innsbruck or Munich (or train back to Vienna) | |

**With more time:** Depending on your interests, you could easily spend several more days in Vienna (for museums, the music scene, going to cafés and wine gardens, day-tripping to Bratislava) and a couple more days in Salzburg (for the music scene, nearby sights, day-tripping to Berchtesgaden). The countryside

lunch, $25 for dinner, $5 for beer and *Eis* (ice cream), and $80 for lodging (based on two people splitting the cost of a $160 double room that includes breakfast). Students and tightwads can enjoy Austria for as little as $60 a day ($30 per hostel bed, $30 for meals and snacks).

**Sightseeing and Entertainment:** In big cities, figure about $15 per major sight (Vienna's Kunsthistorisches Museum-$20, Mozart's Residence in Salzburg-$14), $6 for minor ones, and $25-50 for bus tours and splurge experiences (such as concert tickets and alpine lifts). An overall average of $30 a day works for most people. Don't skimp here. After all, this category is the driving force behind your trip—you came to sightsee, enjoy, and experience Austria.

**Shopping and Miscellany:** Figure $5 per stamped postcard, coffee, beer, and ice-cream cone. Shopping can vary in cost from nearly nothing to a small fortune. Good budget travelers find that

of southern Bavaria and western Tirol are great places to linger and explore (consider a day or two of car rental).

**With a car:** Pick up your car when you leave Vienna. After Melk (in the Danube Valley), drive to Hallstatt, with a stop at Mauthausen en route. After Hallstatt, head to Salzburg. From Salzburg, you can drive (via Berchtesgaden, if you're interested) through southern Bavaria en route to Füssen or Reutte. Then drive eastward through Tirol's Inn Valley to Innsbruck to drop off your car.

this category has little to do with assembling a trip full of lifelong and wonderful memories.

## SIGHTSEEING PRIORITIES

So much to see, so little time. How to choose? Depending on the length of your trip, and taking geographic proximity into account, these are my recommended priorities:

|  |  |
|---|---|
| 3 days: | Vienna |
| 5 days, add: | Salzburg |
| 7 days, add: | Hallstatt |
| 10 days, add: | Danube Valley, Tirol, and Bavaria |
| 14 days, add: | Innsbruck, Hall, and day-trip to Bratislava |
| 16 days, add: | More time in Vienna |

For a suggested itinerary, see the sidebar above. If you don't have time to see it all, prioritize according to your interests. The

"Vienna, Salzburg & Tirol a Glance" sidebar can help you decide where to go.

## WHEN TO GO

The "tourist season" runs roughly from May through September. Summer has its advantages: best weather, snow-free alpine trails, very long days (light until after 21:00), and the busiest schedule of tourist fun.

Travel during "shoulder season" (late April-June and Sept-early Oct) is easier and a bit less expensive. Shoulder-season travelers get minimal crowds, decent weather, the full range of sights and tourist fun spots, and the ability to grab a room almost whenever and wherever they like—often at a flexible price. Also, in fall, fun harvest and wine festivals enliven many towns and villages, while forests and vineyards display beautiful colors.

Winter travelers find concert seasons in full swing, with absolutely no tourist crowds, but some accommodations and sights are either closed or run on a limited schedule. Confirm your sightseeing plans locally, especially when traveling off-season. The weather can be cold and dreary, and nightfall draws the shades on sightseeing well before dinnertime. But dustings of snow turn Austrian towns and landscapes into a wonderland, and December offers the chance to wander through traditional Christmas markets.

You may find the climate chart in the appendix helpful.

## KNOW BEFORE YOU GO

Your trip is more likely to go smoothly if you plan ahead. Check this list of things to arrange while you're still at home.

You need a **passport**—but no visa or shots—to travel in Austria. You may be denied entry into certain European countries if your passport is due to expire within three months of your ticketed date of return. Get it renewed if you'll be cutting it close. It can take up to six weeks to get or renew a passport (for more on passports, see www.travel.state.gov). Pack a photocopy of your passport in your luggage in case the original is lost or stolen.

**Book rooms well in advance** if you'll be traveling during peak season (May-Sept) or any major holidays (see page 516).

Call your **debit- and credit-card companies** to let them know the countries you'll be visiting, to ask about fees, request your PIN code (it will be mailed to you), and more. See page 468 for details.

Do your homework if you want to buy **travel insurance.** Compare the cost of the insurance to the likelihood of your using it and your potential loss if something goes wrong. Also, check whether your existing insurance (health, homeowners, or renters) covers you and your possessions overseas. For more tips, see www.ricksteves.com/insurance.

# Vienna, Salzburg & Tirol at a Glance

These attractions are listed (as in this book) roughly from east to west.

▲▲▲**Vienna** Austria's regal capital city, rich with swirling architecture and world-class museums; impressive Habsburg sights (Schönbrunn Palace, in-city royal apartments, treasury, crypt, and Lipizzaner stallions); massive St. Stephen's Cathedral; and a grand classical-music tradition, from its renowned Opera house to its famous Boys' Choir.

▲**Danube Valley** Romantic, bikeable valley west of Vienna, dotted with ruined castles, adorable villages and vineyards, and highlighted by the glorious Melk Abbey and somber Mauthausen concentration camp memorial.

▲**Bratislava, Slovakia** Once-depressed communist town, now a thriving capital city, less than an hour from Vienna and bursting with colorfully restored buildings; a quirky traffic-free old town; and a people-friendly Danube riverfront area.

▲▲**Salzburg** Austrian musical mecca for fans of Mozart and *The Sound of Music,* offering a dramatic castle, Baroque churches, near-nightly concerts, and an old town full of winding lanes.

**Berchtesgaden, Germany** Alpine town across the border from Salzburg, famous for incredible views, a pristine lake—and as the site of Hitler's mountaintop retreat.

▲▲**Hallstatt and the Salzkammergut** Scenic lake district, home to the halcyon village of Hallstatt, with its medieval town center, fun salt mine, plentiful hiking opportunities, and placid swan-filled lake.

▲**Tirol** Austria's panhandle region and mountain-sports capital, centering around the distinctive city of Innsbruck and little neighboring Hall, with its quaint and colorful old town.

▲▲▲**Bavaria and Western Tirol** Pair of Alps-straddling regions boasting the fairy-tale castles of Neuschwanstein, Hohenschwangau, and Linderhof; inviting villages such as the Austrian retreat of Reutte and German towns of Füssen and Oberammergau; the towering Zugspitze and its high-altitude lifts; and hiking, luge, and other mountain activities.

INTRODUCTION

## Rick Steves Audio Europe

If you're bringing a mobile device, be sure to check out **Rick Steves Audio Europe,** where you can download free audio tours and hours of travel interviews (via the Rick Steves Audio Europe app, www.ricksteves.com/audioeurope, Google Play, or iTunes).

My self-guided **audio tours** are user-friendly, easy-to-follow, fun, and informative, covering the major sights and neighborhoods in Vienna and Salzburg (Vienna's Ringstrasse, historic city center, and St. Stephen's Cathedral, as well as Salzburg's Old Town). Compared to live tours, my audio tours are hard to beat: Nobody will stand you up, the quality is reliable, you can take the tour exactly when you like, and they're free.

Rick Steves Audio Europe also offers a far-reaching library of intriguing **travel interviews** with experts from around the globe. The interviews are organized by destination, including many of the places in this book.

Consider buying a **rail pass** after researching your options (see page 500 and www.ricksteves.com/rail for all the specifics).

If you're planning on **renting a car** in Austria, bring your driver's license and an International Driving Permit (see page 504).

I don't reserve ahead for events, but if you do, note that in Vienna and Salzburg (especially during its festival), major **musical events** can be sold out for weeks—though there are plenty of live music options available without advance booking. Planning ahead of time will guarantee you a seat to see the **Lipizzaner Stallions** (see page 49), **Vienna Boys' Choir** (page 197), and performances at the **Opera** (page 198); though again, I prefer cheap, on-the-spot experiences (such as same-day standing-room tickets for the Opera).

To get tickets to **Neuschwanstein Castle** (in Bavaria) during peak season, go online, email, or phone ahead to avoid the long lines (see page 404 for tips).

If you plan to hire a **local guide,** reserve ahead by email. Popular guides can get booked up.

If you're bringing a **mobile device,** download any apps you might want to use on the road, such as translators, maps, and transit schedules. Check out **Rick Steves Audio Europe,** featuring audio tours of major sights, hours of travel interviews on Austria, and more (see sidebar above).

Check the **Rick Steves guidebook updates** page for any recent changes to this book (www.ricksteves.com/update).

Because airline **carry-on restrictions** are always changing, visit the Transportation Security Administration's website (www.

> ## How Was Your Trip?
>
> Were your travels fun, smooth, and meaningful? If you'd like to share your tips, concerns, and discoveries, please fill out the survey at www.ricksteves.com/feedback. To check out readers' hotel and restaurant reviews—or leave one yourself—visit my travel forum at www.ricksteves.com/travel-forum. I value your feedback. Thanks in advance—it helps a lot.

tsa.gov) for an up-to-date list of what you can bring on the plane and for the latest security measures (including screening of electronic devices, which you may be asked to power up).

# Traveling as a Temporary Local

We travel all the way to Europe to enjoy differences—to become temporary locals. You'll experience frustrations. Certain truths that we find "God-given" or "self-evident," such as cold beer, ice in drinks, bottomless cups of coffee, and bigger being better, are suddenly not so true. One of the benefits of travel is the eye-opening realization that there are logical, civil, and even better alternatives. A willingness to go local ensures that you'll enjoy a full dose of Austrian hospitality.

Europeans generally like Americans. But if there is a negative aspect to the Austrian image of Americans, it's that we are loud, wasteful, ethnocentric, too informal (which can seem disrespectful), and a bit naive.

While Austrians look bemusedly at some of our Yankee excesses—and worriedly at others—they nearly always afford us individual travelers all the warmth we deserve.

Judging from all the happy feedback I receive from travelers who have used this book, it's safe to assume you'll enjoy a great, affordable vacation—with the finesse of an independent, experienced traveler.

Thanks, and *gute Reise!*

*Rick Steves*

# Back Door Travel Philosophy

### From *Rick Steves Europe Through the Back Door*

Travel is intensified living—maximum thrills per minute and one of the last great sources of legal adventure. Travel is freedom. It's recess, and we need it.

Experiencing the real Europe requires catching it by surprise, going casual..."through the Back Door."

Affording travel is a matter of priorities. (Make do with the old car.) You can eat and sleep—simply, safely, and enjoyably—anywhere in Europe for $125 a day plus transportation costs. In many ways, spending more money only builds a thicker wall between you and what you traveled so far to see. Europe is a cultural carnival, and time after time, you'll find that its best acts are free and the best seats are the cheap ones.

A tight budget forces you to travel close to the ground, meeting and communicating with the people. Never sacrifice sleep, nutrition, safety, or cleanliness to save money. Simply enjoy the local-style alternatives to expensive hotels and restaurants.

Connecting with people carbonates your experience. Extroverts have more fun. If your trip is low on magic moments, kick yourself and make things happen. If you don't enjoy a place, maybe you don't know enough about it. Seek the truth. Recognize tourist traps. Give a culture the benefit of your open mind. See things as different, but not better or worse. Any culture has plenty to share.

Of course, travel, like the world, is a series of hills and valleys. Be fanatically positive and militantly optimistic. If something's not to your liking, change your liking.

Travel can make you a happier American, as well as a citizen of the world. Our Earth is home to seven billion equally precious people. It's humbling to travel and find that other people don't have the "American Dream"—they have their own dreams. Europeans like us, but with all due respect, they wouldn't trade passports.

Thoughtful travel engages us with the world. In tough economic times, it reminds us what is truly important. By broadening perspectives, travel teaches new ways to measure quality of life.

Globetrotting destroys ethnocentricity, helping us understand and appreciate other cultures. Rather than fear the diversity on this planet, celebrate it. Among your most prized souvenirs will be the strands of different cultures you choose to knit into your own character. The world is a cultural yarn shop, and Back Door travelers are weaving the ultimate tapestry. Join in!

# AUSTRIA

During the grand old Habsburg days, Austria was Europe's most powerful empire. Its royalty built a giant kingdom (*Österreich* means "Eastern Empire") of more than 50 million people by making love, not war—having lots of children and marrying them into the other royal houses of Europe.

Today, this small, landlocked country clings to its elegant past more than any other nation in Europe. The waltz is still the rage. Music has long been a key part of Austria's heritage. The giants of classical music—Haydn, Mozart, Beethoven—were born here or moved here to write and perform their masterpieces. Music lovers flock to Salzburg every summer to attend its famous festival. But traditional folk music is also part of the Austrian soul. The world's best-loved Christmas carol, "Silent Night," was written by Austrians with just a guitar for accompaniment. Don't be surprised if you hear yodeling for someone's birthday—try joining in.

Austrians are very sociable—it's important to greet people in the breakfast room and those you pass on the streets or meet in shops. The Austrian version of "Hi" is a cheerful *"Grüss Gott"* (for more on the language, see "Hurdling the Language Barrier" on page 488 and "German Survival Phrases for Austria" on page 521).

While Austria has gained notoriety for electing racist right-wingers, that attitude does not prevail everywhere. Large parts of the country may be conservative, but its capital city, Vienna, is extremely liberal. In fact, for 80 years (except for the Nazi occupation), Vienna has had a socialist government with progressive, people-oriented programs. After the fall of the Soviet Union, the leading political party changed its name to "Social Democrat"... but its people-oriented agenda is still the same. When the Austrian drag actor Conchita Wurst won the Eurovision song contest

AUSTRIA

# Austria Almanac

**Official Name:** Republik Österreich ("Eastern Empire"), or simply Österreich.

**Population:** Of Austria's 8.3 million people, 91 percent are ethnic Austrians; 4 percent are from the former Yugoslavia. Three out of four Austrians are Catholic; about one in 20 is Muslim. German is the dominant language (though there are a few Slovene- and Hungarian-speaking villages in border areas).

**Latitude and Longitude:** 47°N and 13°E. The latitude is the same as Minnesota or Washington state.

**Area:** With 32,400 square miles, Austria is similar in size to South Carolina or Maine.

**Geography:** The northeast is flat and well-populated; the less-populated southwest is mountainous, with the Alps rising up to the 12,450-foot Grossglockner peak. The 1,770-mile-long Danube River meanders west-to-east through the upper part of the country, passing through Vienna.

**Biggest Cities:** One in five Austrians lives in the capital of Vienna (1.7 million in the city; 2.4 million in the greater metropolitan area). Graz has 265,000 people; Linz has 191,000.

**Economy:** Austria borders eight other European countries and is well-integrated into the EU economy. The Gross Domestic Product is $350 billion (similar to that of Massachusetts). Its per-capita GDP of $40,000 is among Europe's highest. One of its biggest moneymakers is tourism. Austria produces wood, paper products (nearly half the land is forested)...and Red Bull Energy Drink. The country's aging population increasingly collects social security—a situation that will strain the national budget in years to come.

**Government:** Austria has been officially neutral since 1955, and its citizens take a dim view of European unity. Although right-leaning parties made substantial gains in recent elections, the government continues to be a center-left coalition, currently headed by Federal President Heinz Fischer and Chancellor Werner Faymann (both Social Democrats). Austria is the only EU nation that lets 16- and 17-year-olds vote.

**Flag:** Three horizontal bands of red, white, and red.

**The Average Austrian:** A typical Austrian is 43 years old, has 1.41 children, and will live to be 79. He or she inhabits a 900-square-foot home, and spends leisure time with a circle of a few close friends. Chances are high that someone in that closely knit circle is a smoker—Austrians smoke more cigarettes per day than any other Europeans.

in 2014, many saw it as a vote of confidence for tolerance and openness.

While Vienna sits in the flat Danube valley, much of Austria's character is found in its mountains. Austrians excel in mountain climbing and winter sports such as alpine skiing. Innsbruck was twice the site of the Winter Olympics, and Salzburg was a finalist for the 2014 games. When watching ski races, you'll often see fans celebrating with red-and-white flags at the finish line—Austria has won more Olympic medals in alpine skiing than any other country.

Austria lost a piece of its mountains after World War I, when the Tirol was divided between Austria and Italy. Many residents of Italy's South Tirol still speak German, and it's the first language in some of their schools. Though there was bitterness at the time of the division, today, with no border guards and a shared currency, you can hardly tell you're in a different country.

While Austrians talked about unity with Germany long before Hitler ever said *"Anschluss,"* they cherish their distinct cultural and historical traditions. They speak German, but are not Germans—just as Canadians are not Americans. Austria is mellow and relaxed compared to Deutschland. *Gemütlichkeit* is the word most often used to describe this special Austrian cozy-and-easy approach to life. It's good living—whether engulfed in mountain beauty or bathed in lavish high culture. People stroll as if every day were Sunday, topping things off with a cheerful visit to a coffee or pastry shop.

It must be nice to be past your prime—no longer troubled by being powerful, able to kick back and celebrate life in the clean, peaceful mountain air.

# VIENNA
## *Wien*

# ORIENTATION TO VIENNA

Vienna is the capital of Austria, the cradle of classical music, the home of the rich Habsburg heritage, and one of Europe's most livable cities. The city center is skyscraper-free, pedestrian-friendly, dotted with quiet parks, and traversed by electric trams. Many buildings still reflect 18th- and 19th-century elegance, when the city was at the forefront of the arts and sciences. Compared with most modern European urban centers, the pace of life is slow.

For much of its 2,500-year history, Vienna (*Wien* in German—pronounced "veen") was on the frontier of civilized Europe. Located on the south bank of the Danube, it was threatened by Germanic barbarians (in Roman times), marauding Magyars (today's Hungarians, 10th century), Mongol hordes (13th century), Ottoman Turks (the sieges of 1529 and 1683), and encroachment by the Soviet Empire after World War II.

Vienna reached its peak in the 19th century, when it was on a par with London and Paris in size and importance. It became one of Europe's cultural capitals, home to groundbreaking composers (Beethoven, Mozart, Brahms, Strauss), scientists (Doppler, Boltzmann), philosophers (Freud, Husserl, Schlick, Gödel, Steiner), architects (Wagner, Loos), and painters (Klimt, Schiele, Kokoschka). By the turn of the 20th century, Vienna was one of the world's most populous cities and sat on the cusp between stuffy Old World monarchism and subversive modern trends.

After the turmoil of the two world wars and the loss of Austria's empire, Vienna has settled down into a somewhat sleepy, pleasant place where culture is still king. Classical music is everywhere. People nurse a pastry and coffee over the daily paper at small cafés. It's a city of world-class museums, big and small. Anyone with an interest in painting, music, architecture, beauti-

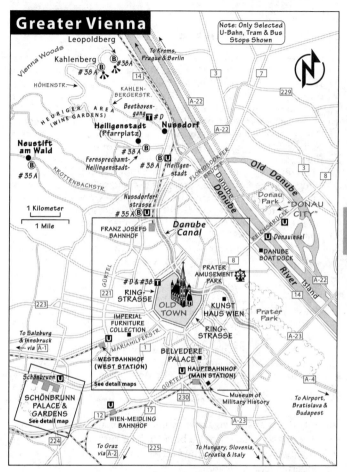

# Greater Vienna

Note: Only Selected
U-Bahn, Tram & Bus
Stops Shown

Leopoldberg

Vienna Woods

Kahlenberg  ®#38A

#38A

HÖHENSTR.

KAHLEN-
BERGERSTR.

A-22

Beethoven-
gang   T #D

HEURIGER  AREA
(WINE GARDENS)

Heiligenstadt
(Pfarrplatz)  ●

Nussdorf  ●

A-22

Neustift
am Wald  ●

#38A  ®

Old Danube

Fernsprechamt-
Heiligenstadt-  ®U  "Heiligen-
#35A  #38A  stadt"

® #35A

KROTTENBACHSTR.

Danube

Donau
Park

"DONAU
CITY"

Nussdorfer-
strasse  ®U

● Donauinsel

1 Kilometer

1 Mile

FRANZ JOSEFS
BAHNHOF

Danube
Canal

● DANUBE
BOAT DOCK

River Island

GÜRTEL

221

223

#D & #38  T

RING-
STRASSE

OLD
TOWN

8

PRATER
AMUSEMENT
PARK

KUNST
HAUS WIEN

Prater
Park

A-22

14

A-23

IMPERIAL
FURNITURE
COLLECTION

RING-
STRASSE

To Salzburg
& Innsbruck
← via A-1

MARIAHILFERSTR.  1

WESTBAHNHOF
(WEST STATION)

BELVEDERE
PALACE  ■

See detail maps

HAUPTBAHNHOF
(MAIN STATION)

A-4

To Airport,
Bratislava &
Budapest

GÜRTEL

■ Museum of
Military History

Schönbrunn  U

SCHÖNBRUNN
PALACE &
GARDENS
See detail map

230

224

12  17

WIEN-MEIDLING
BAHNHOF

A-23

To Graz
via A-2  225

To Hungary, Slovenia,
Croatia & Italy

To Krems,
Prague & Berlin

ful objects, or Sacher-Torte with whipped cream will feel right at home.

## VIENNA: A VERBAL MAP

Vienna sits between the Vienna Woods (Wienerwald) and the Danube (Donau). To the southeast is industrial sprawl. The Alps, which arc across Europe from Marseille, end at Vienna's wooded hills, providing a popular playground for walking and sipping new wine. This greenery's momentum carries on into the city. More than half of Vienna is parkland, filled with ponds, gardens, trees, and statue-maker memories of Austria's glory days.

Think of the city map as a target with concentric sections: The bull's-eye is St. Stephen's Cathedral, the towering cathedral south of the Danube. Surrounding that is the old town, bound tightly by

ORIENTATION

# Vienna Past and Present

Vienna is a head without a body. The capital of the once-grand Habsburg Empire for 640 years, Vienna started and lost World War I and, with it, the empire's far-flung holdings. Culturally, historically, and touristically, this city is the sum of its illustrious past, ranking right up there with Paris, London, and Rome.

Vienna has often been the easternmost city of the West. In Roman times, it was Vindobona, on the Danube facing the barbarians. In the Middle Ages, Vienna was Europe's bastion against the Ottomans—a Christian breakwater against the rising tide of Islam (armies of up to 200,000 were repelled in 1529 and 1683). During this period, as the Ottomans dreamed of conquering what they called "the big apple" for their sultan, Vienna lived with a constant fear of invasion (and the Habsburg court ruled from safer Prague). You'll notice none of Vienna's great palaces were built until after 1683, when the Turkish threat was finally over.

The Habsburgs, who ruled the enormous Austrian Empire from 1273 to 1918, shaped Vienna. Some ad agency has convinced Vienna to make Elisabeth, wife of Emperor Franz Josef—with her narcissism and struggles with royal life—the darling of the local tourist scene. You'll see images of "Sisi" (SEE-see) all over town. But stay focused on the Habsburgs who mattered: Maria Theresa (ruled 1740-1780, see page 55) and Franz Josef (ruled 1848-1916, see page 142).

After Napoleon's defeat, the Congress of Vienna in 1815 shaped the political landscape of 19th-century Europe. Over the next 100 years, Vienna enjoyed its violin-filled belle époque, giv-

the circular road known as the Ringstrasse, marking what used to be the city wall. The Gürtel, a broader, later ring road, contains the rest of downtown. Outside the Gürtel lies the uninteresting sprawl of modern Vienna.

Addresses start with the *Bezirk* (district) number, followed by the street and building number. The Ringstrasse (a.k.a. the Ring) circles the first district. Any address higher than the ninth *Bezirk* is beyond the Gürtel, far from the center. The address "7, Lindengasse 4" is in the seventh district, #4 on Linden street. Its postal code would be 1070 (the middle two digits of the postal codes show the district).

Much of Vienna's sightseeing—and most of my recommended restaurants—are located in the Old Town (the first district, inside the Ringstrasse). Walking across this circular area takes about 30 minutes. St. Stephen's Cathedral sits in the center, at the intersection of the two main (pedestrian-only) streets: Kärntner Strasse and the Graben.

Several sights sit along, or just beyond, the Ringstrasse: To

ing us our romantic image of the city: fine wine, chocolates, cafés, waltzes, and the good life.

In 1900, Vienna's 2.2 million inhabitants made it the world's fifth-largest city—after New York, London, Paris, and Berlin. The empire itself encompassed more than 50 million people, of whom only 12 million spoke German as their mother tongue. Emigration from the provinces to Vienna was common, and a true Viennese person today is a Habsburg cocktail, with ancestors from the distant corners of the old empire: not just from the Czech Republic, Slovakia, and Hungary, but also Slovenia, Serbia, Croatia, Bosnia, Italy, Transylvania, Ukraine, and Poland.

While Vienna's old walls had held out would-be invaders (including the Ottomans), they were no match for WWII bombs, which destroyed nearly a quarter of the city's buildings. In modern times, neutral Austria extended deep into the USSR's Warsaw Pact buffer zone. Today, Vienna is not an outpost, but rather the center of a dynamic area that includes Brno, Bratislava, and Budapest. The university students you'll see were born after the fall of the Iron Curtain and think nothing of zipping across borders for lunch.

Vienna's population has dropped to 1.7 million, with dogs being the preferred "child" and the average Viennese mother having only 1.3 children. Vienna, once the capital of a far-flung realm, now feels oversized for Austria's 8.3 million residents—but its reduced political weight makes it easier to enjoy the Habsburg grandness and elegance that it never lost.

ORIENTATION

the southwest are the Hofburg and related Habsburg sights, and the Kunsthistorisches Museum; to the south is a cluster of intriguing sights near Karlsplatz; to the southeast is Belvedere Palace. A branch of the Danube River (*Donau* in German, DOH-now) borders the Ring to the north.

As a tourist, concern yourself only with this compact old center. When you do, sprawling Vienna suddenly becomes manageable.

## PLANNING YOUR TIME

For a big city, Vienna is pleasant and laid-back. Packed with sights, it's worth two days and two nights on even the speediest trip. If you have more time, Vienna can easily fill it; art and music lovers in particular won't regret adding a third or fourth day.

If you're visiting Vienna as part of a longer European trip, you could sleep on the train on your way in and out—Berlin, Prague, Kraków, Venice, Rome, and the Rhine Valley are each handy night trains away.

**Palace Choices:** The Hofburg and Schönbrunn are both world-class palaces, but seeing both is redundant—with limited time or money, I'd choose just one. The Hofburg comes with the popular Sisi Museum and is right in the town center, making for an easy visit. With more time, a visit to Schönbrunn—set outside town amid a grand and regal garden—is also a great experience. (For efficient sightseeing, drivers should note that Schönbrunn Palace is conveniently on the way out of town toward Salzburg.)

## Vienna in One to Four Days

Below is a suggested itinerary for how to spend your time. I've left the **evenings** open for your choice of activities. The best options are taking in a concert, opera, or other musical event; enjoying a leisurely dinner (and people-watching) in the stately old town or atmospheric Spittelberg Quarter; heading out to the *Heuriger* wine pubs in the foothills of the Vienna Woods; or touring the Haus der Musik interactive music museum (open nightly until 22:00). Plan your evenings based on the schedule of musical events while you're in town. If you've downloaded my audio tours (see "Rick Steves Audio Europe" sidebar on page 10), both the Vienna City Walk and Ringstrasse Tram Tour work wonderfully in the evening. Whenever you need a break, linger in a classic Viennese café.

**Day 1**

| | |
|---|---|
| 9:00 | Circle the Ringstrasse by tram (following my self-guided tram tour). |
| 10:30 | Drop by the TI for planning and ticket needs. |
| 11:00 | Take the Opera tour (schedule varies, confirm at TI). |
| 14:00 | Follow my Vienna City Walk, including Kaisergruft visit and St. Stephen's Cathedral Tour (nave closes at 16:30, or 17:30 June-Aug). |
| 18:00 | Take the 1.5-hour Red Bus City Tour for a look at greater Vienna (evening bus runs April-Oct only). |

**Day 2**

| | |
|---|---|
| 9:00 | Browse the colorful Naschmarkt. |
| 11:00 | Tour the Kunsthistorisches Museum. |
| 14:00 | Tour the Hofburg Palace Imperial Apartments and Treasury. |

**Day 3**

| | |
|---|---|
| 10:00 | Visit Belvedere Palace, with its fine collection of Viennese art and great city views. |
| 15:00 | Tour Schönbrunn Palace to enjoy the royal apartments and grounds. |

# Daily Reminder

**Sunday:** All sights (except the Postal Savings Bank) and most tourist shops are open, but department stores and other shops are closed, including the Naschmarkt open-air market and the Dorotheum auction house. Most churches have restricted hours for sightseers, and there are no tours of the crypt at St. Michael's Church. In spring and fall, the Spanish Riding School's Lipizzaner stallions usually perform at 11:00.

**Monday:** Most of the major sights are open (such as St. Stephen's Cathedral, Opera, Hofburg Imperial Apartments and Treasury, Schönbrunn Palace, and Belvedere Palace), but many sights are closed, including the New Palace museums, Wien Museum Karlsplatz, Secession, Academy of Fine Arts, Imperial Furniture Collection, Museum of Applied Art (MAK), Otto Wagner exhibit, and the Opera Museum. The Kunsthistorisches Museum is closed except in summer. The Kunst Haus Wien is half-price.

**Tuesday:** All sights are open, except the Hofburg Treasury, New Palace museums, and Natural History Museum. The Leopold Museum (at the MuseumsQuartier) is closed except in summer. The Museum of Applied Art (MAK) is free after 18:00 and stays open until 22:00. The Haus der Musik is half-price after 20:00.

**Wednesday:** All sights are open. The Albertina, Natural History Museum, and Belvedere Lower Palace stay open until 21:00.

**Thursday:** All sights are open. The Kunsthistorisches and MuseumsQuartier museums (Leopold and Modern Art) stay open until 21:00.

**Friday:** All sights are open.

**Saturday:** All sights are open, except the Jewish Museum Vienna (both locations) and the Postal Savings Bank, and there are no tours of the crypt at St. Michael's Church. The Spanish Riding School's Lipizzaner stallions usually perform at 11:00 in spring and fall. The Third Man Museum is open only today (14:00-18:00).

ORIENTATION

## Day 4

10:00   Enjoy (depending on your interest) the engaging Karlsplatz sights (Karlskirche, Wien Museum, Academy of Fine Arts, and The Secession).

12:00   Tour the Albertina Museum.

15:00   Shoppers can stroll Mariahilfer Strasse. Non-shoppers can rent a bike and head out to the modern Donau City "downtown" sector, Danube Island (for fun people-watching), and the Prater amusement park.

## With More Time...

Vienna itself can easily fill a longer visit. But a day trip can be more rewarding than spending extra time in town. For rustic pastoral beauty, head for Melk and the Danube Valley; for an exciting detour into the Slavic world, hit the up-and-coming Slovak capital of Bratislava.

# Vienna Overview

## TOURIST INFORMATION

Vienna's main TI is a block behind the Opera at Albertinaplatz (daily 9:00-19:00, free Wi-Fi, theater box office, tel. 01/211-140, www.vienna.info). There's also an airport TI (daily 7:00-22:00, run by a private company). At either TI, confirm your sightseeing plans, and pick up two copies of the free and essential city map with a list of museums and hours (also available at most hotels). Rip up one copy of the Vienna map—reducing it down to just the city-center inset—and keep it in your pocket for ready reference. (Stuff the other copy in your backpack in case you need it.) Also look for the monthly program of concerts (called *Wien-Programm*) and the *Vienna from A to Z* booklet (both described below), and the annual city guide (called *Vienna Journal*). Ask about their program of guided walks (€14 each). While hotel and ticket-booking agencies at the train station and airport can answer questions and give out maps and brochures, I'd rely on the official TI.

*Wien-Programm:* This monthly entertainment guide is particularly important, listing all sorts of events, including music, theater, walks, expositions, and museum exhibits. It's organized this way: First you see the current month's festivals and live music (jazz, rock, and more). Next come the schedules for the Spanish Riding School and the Vienna Boys' Choir, followed by listings for museums and exhibitions, theater options, and the opera (noting which performances are projected on the big screen outside the Opera house). The next section lists classical concerts (also organized by date, with phone numbers to call direct to check seat availability and to save the 20 percent booking fees that you pay if you buy tickets through an agency). Last is a list of guided walks offered (*E* means "in English"). Note the key for abbreviations on the inside cover, which helps make this dense booklet useful even for non-German speakers.

*Vienna from A to Z:* Consider this handy booklet, sold by the main TI for €3.60. Every major building in Vienna sports a numbered flag banner that keys into this booklet and into the TI's city map. If you get lost, find one of the "famous-building flags" and match its number to your map. If you're at a famous building, check the map to see what other key numbers are nearby, then check the

*A to Z* book description to see if you want to go in. This system is especially helpful for those just wandering aimlessly among Vienna's historic charms.

## Sightseeing Passes and Combo-Tickets

The much-promoted €22 **Vienna Card** (www.wienkarte.at) is not worth the mental overhead for most travelers. It gives you a 72-hour transit pass (worth €16.50) and minor discounts (usually 10-25 percent) at the city's museums. It might save the busy sightseer a few euros (though seniors and students will do better with their own discounts). The 48-hour version (€19) is an even worse deal.

Some sights offer **combo-tickets** that cover several venues at a single price. If you're seeing those sights anyway, a combo-ticket can save money and let you skip ticket-buying lines at your next sight. Buy these combo-tickets at any of the participating sights.

**Sisi Ticket:** This €25.50 ticket covers the Hofburg Imperial Apartments (with its Sisi Museum and Porcelain Collection) as well as Schönbrunn Palace's Grand Tour and the Imperial Furniture Collection. When used at Schönbrunn, the ticket lets you enter the palace immediately, without a reserved entry time. The ticket saves €0.50 off the combined cost of the Hofburg Apartments and Schönbrunn, making the good Imperial Furniture Collection effectively free.

**Hofburg Treasury and Kunsthistorisches Museum/New Palace:** If you're seeing the Hofburg Treasury (royal regalia and crown jewels) and the Kunsthistorisches Museum (world-class art collection), this €20 combo-ticket is well worth it (and you get the New Palace as a bonus).

**Haus der Musik and Mozarthaus:** The Haus der Musik (mod museum with interactive exhibits) has a combo deal with Mozarthaus Vienna (exhibits and artifacts about the great composer) for €17—a €5 savings for music lovers.

## ARRIVAL IN VIENNA

For a comprehensive rundown on Vienna's various train stations and its airport, as well as tips on arriving or departing by car or boat, see the Vienna Connections chapter.

## HELPFUL HINTS

**Teens Sightsee Free:** Those under 19 get in free to state-run museums and sights.

**Music Sightseeing Priorities:** Be wary of Vienna's various music sights. Many "homes of composers" are pretty disappointing. My advice to music lovers is to concentrate on these activities: Take in a concert, tour the Opera house, snare cheap standing-room tickets to see an opera there (even just part of a perfor-

ORIENTATION

mance), enjoy the Haus der Musik, and scour the wonderful Collection of Ancient Musical Instruments in the Hofburg's New Palace. If in town on a Sunday, don't miss the glorious music at the Augustinian Church Mass (see page 51).

**Skip This:** The highly advertised experience called Time Travel Vienna (just off the Graben on Habsburgergasse) promises "history, fun, and action." In reality, it's €18 and 45 minutes wasted in a tacky succession of amusement-park history vignettes with much of the information in German only.

**Internet Access:** You'll find free Wi-Fi hotspots around town, including at the TI, Westbahnhof, Stephansplatz, Naschmarkt, City Hall Park, Prater Park, and Donauinsel. If you need a computer, **Netcafe** is inside a Persian restaurant at the Hotel Capricorno, near the Danube Canal (€4/hour or free with drink, daily 11:00-21:00, Schwedenplatz 3). **Netcafe-Refill** is at Mariahilfer Strasse 103, close to many recommended hotels (€4.50/hour, Mon-Fri 9:00-21:00, Sat 10:00-20:00, closed Sun, tel. 01/595-5558).

**Post Offices:** The main post office is near Schwedenplatz at Fleischmarkt 19 (Mon-Fri 7:00-22:00, Sat-Sun 9:00-22:00). Convenient branch offices are at the Westbahnhof (Mon-Fri 7:00-21:00, Sat 9:00-18:00, Sun 9:00-14:00) and near the Opera (Mon-Fri 7:00-19:00, closed Sat-Sun, Krugerstrasse 13).

**English Bookstore:** Stop by the woody and cool **Shakespeare & Co.,** in the historic and atmospheric Ruprechtsviertel district near the Danube Canal (Mon-Fri 9:00-21:00, Sat 9:00-20:00, closed Sun, north of Hoher Markt at Sterngasse 2, tel. 01/535-5053, www.shakespeare.co.at). See the map on page 41.

**Keeping Up with the News:** Don't buy newspapers. Read them for free in Vienna's marvelous coffeehouses. It's much classier.

**Laundry:** **Schnell & Sauber Waschcenter** is big, open long hours, close to Mariahilfer Strasse accommodations, and easily reached from downtown by U-Bahn (self-serve-€9/load, free Wi-Fi; daily 6:00-24:00, Westbahnstrasse 60, U-6: Burggasse/Stadthalle, or take tram #49 to Urban-Loritz-Platz, see map on page 173, mobile 0660-760-4546, www.schnellundsauber.at).

**Travel Agency:** Conveniently located on Stephansplatz, **Ruefa** sells tickets for flights, trains, and boats to Bratislava. They'll waive the €8 service charge for train and boat tickets for my readers (Mon-Fri 9:00-18:00, closed Sat-Sun, Stephansplatz 10, tel. 01/513-4000, Gertrude and Sandra speak English).

**Drinking Water:** The Viennese are proud of their perfectly drinkable tap water from alpine springs. You'll spot locals refilling their little bottles at fountains all over town. In response to—and anticipation of—global warming, the city has installed shiny public water fountains with signs reminding people to stay hydrated (one is on the Graben at the corner of Spiegelgasse). Some restaurants even serve *Leitungswasser* (tap water), though they'll often charge a nominal fee (about €0.40) for the service.

**Updates to This Book:** For updates to this book, check www.ricksteves.com/update.

## GETTING AROUND VIENNA
### By Public Transportation

Take full advantage of Vienna's efficient transit system, which includes trams (a.k.a. streetcars), buses, U-Bahn (subway), and S-Bahn (faster suburban) trains. It's fast, clean, and easy to navigate. The free Vienna city map, available at TIs and hotels, includes a small schematic transit map.

I generally stick to the tram to zip around the Ring (trams #1, #2, and #D) and take the U-Bahn to outlying sights, hotels, and

Vienna's train stations (see map on page 28). There are five color-coded U-Bahn lines: U-1 red, U-2 purple, U-3 orange, U-4 green, and U-6 brown. Two useful trams (#D and #O) have letters instead of numbers (a relic from long ago). If you see a bus number that starts with *N* (such as #N38), it's a night bus, which

operates after other public transit stops running. Transit info: tel. 01/790-9100, www.wienerlinien.at.

**Tickets and Passes:** Trams, buses, the U-Bahn, and the S-Bahn all use the same tickets. Except on days spent entirely within the Ring, buying a single- or multi-day pass is usually a good investment (and pays off if you take at least four trips). Many people find that once they have a pass, they end up using the system more.

Buy tickets from vending machines in stations (marked *Fahrkarten/Ticket*, easy and in English), from *Vorverkauf* offices in stations, from *Tabak-Trafik* shops, or as a last resort for trams or buses—on board (single tickets only, more expensive). You have lots of choices:

- Single tickets (€2.20, €2.30 if bought on tram or bus, good for one journey with necessary transfers)
- 24-hour transit pass (€7.60)
- 48-hour transit pass (€13.30)
- 72-hour transit pass (€16.50)
- 7-day transit pass (*Wochenkarte*, €16.20—the catch is that the

# Vienna's Public Transportation

ORIENTATION

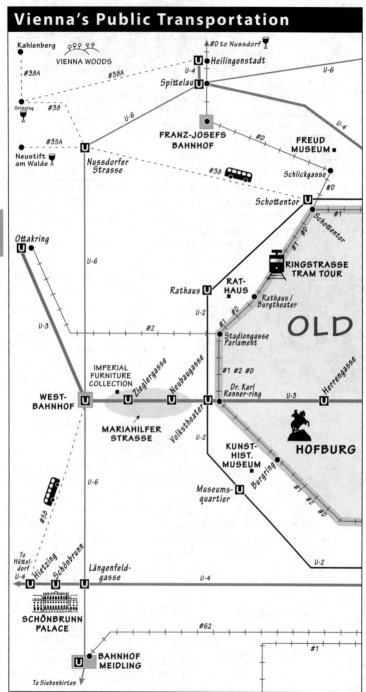

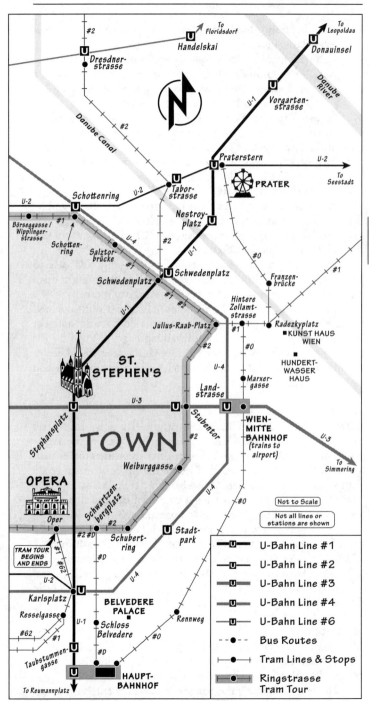

ORIENTATION

To Floridsdorf

To Leopoldau

Handelskai

Donauinsel

Danube River

Dresdner-strasse

U-1

Vorgarten-strasse

Danube Canal

#2

N

Praterstern

U-2

To Seestadt

PRATER

Schottenring

U-2

Tabor-strasse

U-2

Nestroy-platz

U-1

Börsegasse / Wipplinger-strasse

#1

Schotten-ring

Salztor-brücke

U-4

#2

#1

#0

#1

Franzen-brücke

Schwedenplatz

U-1

Schwedenplatz

#1

#2

Julius-Raab-Platz

Hintere Zollamt-strasse

Radezkyplatz

#1

KUNST HAUS WIEN

#2

#0

HUNDERT-WASSER HAUS

ST. STEPHEN'S

U-4

Marxer-gasse

Land-strasse

Stephansplatz

U-3

Stubentor

WIEN-MITTE BAHNHOF (trains to airport)

U-3

To Simmering

TOWN

Weiburggasse

#2

U-4

Not to Scale

Not all lines or stations are shown

OPERA

Schwartzen-bergplatz

Oper

#2 #D

#2

Schubert-ring

Stadt-park

TRAM TOUR BEGINS AND ENDS

#1

#62

#D

U-2

Karlsplatz

BELVEDERE PALACE

Resselgasse

U-1

Schloss Belvedere

Rennweg

#62

#1

#0

#D

Taubstummen-gasse

HAUPT-BAHNHOF

To Reumannplatz

| | |
|---|---|
| U | U-Bahn Line #1 |
| U | U-Bahn Line #2 |
| U | U-Bahn Line #3 |
| U | U-Bahn Line #4 |
| U | U-Bahn Line #6 |
| --•-- | Bus Routes |
| ⊢•⊣ | Tram Lines & Stops |
| | Ringstrasse Tram Tour |

pass runs from Monday to Monday, so you may get less than seven days of use)
- 8-day "Climate Ticket" (*Acht-Tage-Klimakarte*, €38.40, can be shared—for example, four people for two days each). With a per-person cost of €4.80/day (compared to €7.60/day for a 24-hour pass), this can be a real saver for groups.

**Transit Tips:** To get your bearings on buses, trams, the U-Bahn, and the S-Bahn, you'll want to know the end-of-the-line stop in the direction that you're heading. For example, if you're in the city center at Stephansplatz and you want to take the U-Bahn to the main train station (Hauptbahnhof), you'd take U-1 going in the direction "Reumannplatz."

You must stamp your ticket at the barriers in U-Bahn and S-Bahn stations, and in the machines on trams and buses (stamp it only the first time for a multiple-use pass). Cheaters pay a stiff €70 fine, plus the cost of the ticket.

On trams, stop announcements are voice-only and easy to miss—carry a map. Rookies miss stops because they fail to open the door. Push buttons, pull latches—do whatever it takes.

Before you exit a U-Bahn station, study the wall-mounted street map. Choosing the right exit—signposted from the moment you step off the train—saves lots of walking.

Cute little electric buses wind through the tangled old center (from Schottentor to Stubentor). Bus #1A is best for a joyride—hop on and see where it takes you.

## By Taxi

Vienna's comfortable, civilized, and easy-to-flag-down **taxis** start at €2.50. You'll pay about €10 to go from the Opera to the Westbahnhof. Pay only what's on the meter—any surcharges (other than the €2 fee for calling a cab or €11 fee for the airport) are just crude cabbie rip-offs. Rates are legitimately higher at night.

Consider the luxury of having your own **car and driver.** Johann (a.k.a. John) Lichtl is a gentle, honest, English-speaking cabbie who can take up to four passengers in his car (€27/1 hour, €25/hour for 2 hours or more, €27 to or from airport, mobile 0676-670-6750). Consider a custom-tailored city driving tour (2 hours), a day trip to the Danube Valley (€160, see Danube Valley chapter), or a visit to the Mauthausen concentration camp memorial with a little Danube sightseeing en route (€200).

## By Bike

With more than 600 miles of bike lanes (and a powerful Green Party), Vienna is a great city on two wheels. Bikes ride the U-Bahn for free (but they aren't allowed during weekday rush hours).

The bike path along the Ring is wonderfully entertaining (in fact, my Ringstrasse Tram Tour works even better by bike than by tram)—you'll enjoy the shady park-like ambience of the boulevard while rolling by many of the city's top sights. Besides the Ring, your best sightseeing by bike is through Stadtpark (City Park), across Danube Island, and out to the modern Donau City business district (for more on biking on Danube Island and to Donau City, see page 88). These routes are easy to follow on the free tourist city map available from the TI. Pedestrians should stay out of red-colored pavement (the usual marking for bike lanes), but also watch out for bike lanes just marked with white lines.

**Borrowing a Free/Cheap Bike: Citybike Wien** lets you borrow bikes from public racks all over town (toll tel. 0810-500-500, www.citybikewien.at). The three-speed bikes are heavy and clunky—and come with a basket, built-in lock, and ads on the side—but they're perfect for a short, practical joyride in the center (such as around the Ringstrasse).

While bike programs in many other European cities are difficult for tourists to take advantage of, Vienna's system is easy to use. Bikes are locked into more than 100 stalls scattered through the city center. To borrow a bike, use the computer terminal at any rack: Press the credit card button, insert and pull out your card, register your name and address, and select a username and password for future rentals (you can also register online at www.citybikewien.at). Then, unlock the bike you want by punching in its number. First-time registration is €1, and they'll place a refundable €20 hold on your card while you're using the bike (only one bike per credit card—couples must use two different cards). Since the bikes are designed for short-term use, it costs more per hour the longer you keep it (first hour-free, second hour-€1, third hour-€2, €4/hour after that). When you're done, drop off your bike at any stall, and make sure it's fully locked into the rack to avoid being charged for more time.

**Renting a Higher-Quality Bike:** If you want to ride beyond the town center—or you simply want a better set of wheels—check out **Pedal Power,** with a handy central location near the Opera house. The local authority on bike touring in town and to points along the Danube, Pedal Power rents bikes and provides good biking info (€5/hour, €17/4 hours, €27/24 hours, daily May-Sept 8:30-18:00, Elisabethstrasse 13—see map on page 41, tel. 01/729-7234, www.pedalpower.at). For a better selection and better gear, it's smart to use their main office by Prater Park. While less central,

ORIENTATION

it's very easy to get to (U-1 or U-2: Praterstern, then walk 100 yards to Ausstellungsstrasse 3). They can also deliver a bike to your hotel and pick it up when you're done (€32/day including delivery, service available year-round), and they organize bike tours (described later). Pedal Power offers a 10 percent discount to anyone with this book.

# Tours in Vienna

To sightsee on your own, download my series of free audio tours that illuminate some of Vienna's top sights and neighborhoods (see sidebar on page 10).

### Walking Tours
The *Walks in Vienna* brochure (available at the TI) and the TI website describe many guided walks. A basic 1.5-hour "Vienna at First Glance" introductory walk is offered daily throughout the summer (€14, leaves at 14:00 from in front of the main TI, just behind the Opera, in both English and German, just show up, tel. 01/774-8901, mobile 0664-260-4388, www.wienguide.at).

### Bike Tours
**Pedal Power** runs a three-hour tour twice daily from May to September, covering the central district. The morning tour is English-only, while the afternoon tour is bilingual (€29/tour includes bike, €10 extra to keep bike for the day, departs at 10:00 and 14:30 from the statue in Schillerplatz in front of the Academy of Fine Arts, across the Ring from the Opera, tel. 01/729-7234, www.pedalpower.at). They also rent bikes and offer Segway tours daily in summer (www.segway-vienna.at).

For a private bike tour, contact guide **Wolfgang Höfler** (€150/3 hours, bike not included, mobile 0676-304-4940, www.vienna-aktivtours.com, office@vienna-aktivtours.com; also leads walking tours—see listing, later, under "Local Guides").

### Bus Tours
**Red Bus City Tours'** convertible buses do a 1.5-hour loop, hitting the highlights of the city with a 20-minute shopping break in the middle. They cover the main first-district attractions as well as a big bus can, along with the entire Ringstrasse. But the most interesting part of the tour is outside the center—zipping through Prater Park, over the Danube for a glimpse of the city's Danube Island playground, and into the "Donau City" skyscraper zone. If the weather's good, the bus goes topless and offers great opportunities for photos. Tours start one block behind the Opera at the main TI—see the map on page 41 for the location (€14 ticket from driver, €2 discount with this book if purchased from "office" in

the souvenir shop at Operngasse 2—right by where the tour begins; departs hourly April-Oct 10:00-18:00, Nov-March at 11:00, 13:00, and 15:00; pretty good recorded narration in any language, your own earbuds are better than the beat-up headphones they provide, tel. 01/512-4030, www.redbuscitytours.at, Gabriel).

**Vienna Sightseeing** offers a three-hour city tour, including a tour of Schönbrunn Palace (€39, 3/day April-Oct, 2/day Nov-March). They also run hop-on, hop-off bus tours with recorded commentary. The schedule is posted curbside (three different one-hour routes, €13/1 route, €16/2 routes, €20/all day, departs from the Opera 4/hour July-Aug 10:00-20:00, runs less frequently and stops earlier off-season, tel. 01/7124-6830, www.viennasightseeing.at). Given the city's excellent public transportation and mostly walkable sights, I'd skip this tour; if you just want a quick guided city tour, take the Red Bus tours recommended earlier.

### Ring Tram Tour

The **Vienna Ring Tram,** a yellow made-for-tourists streetcar, runs clockwise along the entire Ringstrasse (€8 for 30-minute loop, 2/hour 10:00-17:30, recorded narration, includes a good set of earbuds you can keep and reuse, www.wienerlinien.at). The 25-minute tour starts every half-hour at Schwedenplatz. At each stop, you'll see an ad for this tram tour (look for *VRT Ring-Rund Sightseeing*). The schedule clearly notes the next departure time.

To save money, follow my self-guided tram tour using city trams that circle the Ring. You'll need to make one transfer, but the trams run frequently and you'll sit alongside real *Wiener*s (◐ see Ringstrasse Tram Tour chapter).

### Horse-and-Buggy Tour

These traditional horse-and-buggies, called *Fiakers,* take rich romantics on clip-clop tours lasting 20 minutes (Old Town-€55), 40 minutes (Old Town and the Ring-€80), or one hour (all the above, but more thorough-€110). You can share the ride and cost with up to five people. Because it's a kind of guided tour, talk to a few drivers before choosing a carriage, and pick someone who's fun and speaks English (tel. 01/401-060).

### Local Guides

You'll pay about €140-150 for two hours. Get a group of six or more together and call it a party. The tourist board's website (www.vienna.info) has a long list of local guides with their specialties and contact information.

My favorite private Vienna guides are: **Lisa Zeiler** (€150/2 hours, mobile 0699-1203-7550, lisa.zeiler@gmx.at); **Wolfgang Höfler** (a generalist with a knack for having psychoanalytical fun with history, enjoys the big changes of the 19th and 20th centuries, €150/2 hours, mobile 0676-304-4940, www.vienna-aktivtours.com, office@vienna-aktivtours.com, also leads bike tours—described earlier); **Adrienn Bartek-Rhomberg** (€150/half-day, see website for tour topics, mobile 0650-826-6965, www.experience-vienna.at, office@experience-vienna.at); and **Gerhard Strassgschwandtner** (who runs the Third Man Museum and is passionate about history in all its marvelous complexity, €140/2 hours, mobile 0676-475-7818, www.special-vienna.com, gerhard@special-vienna.com). If these folks are booked, any of them can set you up with another good guide.

ORIENTATION

# SIGHTS IN VIENNA

Vienna has a dizzying number of sights and museums—from paintings to history to music to furniture to prancing horses. Just perusing the list on your TI-issued Vienna city map can be overwhelming. To get you started, I've tried to select the sights that are most essential and user-friendly, and arranged them by neighborhood for handy sightseeing.

When you see a ✪ in a listing, it means the sight is covered in much more depth in my Vienna City Walk or one of my self-guided tours. This is why Vienna's most important attractions get the least coverage in this chapter—we'll explore them later in the book.

While most major sights should take credit cards, a few lesser sights may be cash only—be prepared. For more tips on sightseeing, see page 473.

## IN THE OLD TOWN, WITHIN THE RING
These sights are listed roughly from south to north. For a self-guided walk connecting many of central Vienna's top sights—including some of the ones below—✪ see the Vienna City Walk chapter.

### ▲▲▲Opera (Wiener Staatsoper)
The Opera house, facing the Ring and near the TI, is a central point for any visitor. Vienna remains one of the world's great cities for classical music, and this building still belts out some of the finest opera, both classic and cutting-edge. While the critical reception of the building 130 years ago led the architect to commit suicide, and though it's been rebuilt since its destruction by WWII bombs, it's still a sumptuous place. The interior has a chandeliered lobby and carpeted staircases perfect for making the scene. The theater

itself features five wraparound balconies, gold-and-red decor, and a bracelet-like chandelier.

Depending on your level of tolerance for opera, there are several different ways to experience the Opera house. You can simply admire the Neo-Renaissance building from the outside (and maybe slip inside the lobby for a peek when the box office opens around 17:00). You could take a guided tour of the lavish interior (see below), or visit the nearby Opera Museum to learn about the company's history. Best of all, attend a performance of Vienna's opera company, which can be surprisingly easy and cheap to do—and doesn't have to take up a whole evening (get details in the Entertainment in Vienna chapter).

## Opera House Tours

The only way to see the Opera house interior (besides attending a performance) is with a guided 45-minute tour in English. You'll see the chandeliered halls where operagoers gather at intermission, enjoying elaborate spaces with coffered ceilings, gold trim, and iron-work lamps. You'll learn about the opera's history (see the Opera Museum description, next), and to compare the old parts of the building (such as Emperor Franz Josef's ornate reception room) with the post-war reconstruction. The highlight is the 2,000-seat theater itself—where the main floor is ringed by box seating, under a huge sugar-doughnut chandelier. You may see workers on the stage erecting sets for that evening's performance, and learn the ingenious ways they load and unload the elaborate equipment so quickly. Certain tours (marked with an asterisk on the tour schedule) take you onto the wings of the stage itself.

To take a tour, just show up at the tour entrance, located at the southwest corner of the building. Be there 20 minutes before your tour starts and buy a ticket. No reservations are taken, and they don't sell out.

**Cost and Hours:** €6.50, includes modest Opera Museum. Tours generally run several times a day at the top of each hour between 10:00 and 16:00, but the schedule is different every day, as it's determined by rehearsals and performances. There are lots of tours in July and August (when there are no performances), and fewer tours September through June and on Sundays year-round. Find the monthly schedule online, in the Opera's monthly *Prolog* magazine, or posted at the tour entrance; tel. 01/514-442-606, www.wiener-staatsoper.at)

## Opera Museum (Staatsopernmuseum)

This exhibit traces the illustrious history of the Vienna State Opera (not opera in general), highlighting its most famous singers, directors, and performances. You'll peruse old posters and photos, costumes, models of set designs, a musical score by Wagner, and one of

Margot Fonteyn's ballet slippers. It's all in a single room, with lots of English information and a soundtrack of choice arias.

**Cost and Hours:** €3, included in Opera tour ticket; Tue-Sun 10:00-18:00, closed Mon; a block west of the Opera (near the Albertina Museum), tucked down a courtyard at Hanuschgasse 3, tel. 01/514-442-100).

**Visiting the Museum:** Circle clockwise and hit these high notes:

It's 1869. Vienna is the center of European music, and the brand-new Opera opens with local boy Mozart's dramatic *Don Giovanni*. The Opera quickly establishes itself as the northern rival of La Scala in Milan, mounting lavish productions of Verdi's *Aida*, Wagner's over-the-top Ring, and Strauss Junior's *Die Fledermaus*.

By 1900, the world was changing fast, and the Opera was in the hands of a revolutionary new director/composer—Gustav Mahler. (Mahler is so important that his story is told, not on the wall, but on placards nearby.) Mahler introduced the avant-garde values of The Secession: provocative Art Nouveau sets, dramatic lighting effects to express the unseen, a serious atmosphere (talking during the show was now *verboten*), and new works by Vienna's own Richard Strauss. Mahler's innovations were controversial, and he eventually resigned.

When Nazi Germany annexed Austria (1938), many artists quit rather than take a loyalty oath. The Opera declined through the war years. In 1945—not long after the curtain fell on the conflagration scene in Wagner's *Gotterdammerung*—the Opera house was blasted in an air raid and went up in flames.

In 1955, the rebuilt Opera opened. The once-staid organization committed itself to a more modern, international approach under the photogenic, charismatic director Herbert von Karajan (who also merits his own info placards). Through the 1960s and beyond, Vienna was a magnet for the world's biggest names: Maria Callas, Leonard Bernstein, Luciano Pavarotti, and on and on. Today, the Opera maintains a balance of mounting both classic warhorses and avant-garde productions.

### ▲▲Haus der Musik

Vienna's "House of Music" is a high-tech experience that celebrates this hometown specialty. The museum, spread over five floors and well-described in English, is unique for its effective use of interactive touch-screen computers and headphones to explore the physics of sound. One floor is dedicated to the heavyweight Viennese composers

**SIGHTS**

(Mozart, Beethoven, etc.) who virtually created classical music as we know it. Really experiencing the place takes time. It's open late and makes a good evening activity.

**Cost and Hours:** €12, includes audioguide for third floor only, half-price after 20:00, €17 combo-ticket with Mozarthaus, daily 10:00-22:00, last entry 30 minutes before closing, two blocks from the Opera at Seilerstätte 30, tel. 01/513-4850, www.hdm.at.

**Visiting the Museum:** The first floor highlights the Vienna Philharmonic Orchestra, known the world over for their New Year's Eve concerts. See Toscanini's baton, Mahler's cap, and Bernstein's tux. Throw the dice to randomly "compose" a piece of music.

The second floor explores the physics of sound. Wander through the "sonosphere" and marvel at the amazing acoustics. Interactive exhibits explore the nature of sound and music; I could actually hear what I thought only a piano tuner could discern. You can twist, dissect, and bend sounds to make your own musical language, merging your voice with a duck's quack or a city's traffic roar. A tube filled with pebbles demonstrates the power of sound waves...watch them bounce. The "instrumentarium" presents various tools of the trade, new and old.

The third floor celebrates the famous hometown boys. (You'll need the included audioguide to fully explore this section.) **Haydn** established the four-movement symphony, and pioneered the "sonata form" technique of repeating a brief melody throughout a longer work. **Mozart** was music's first charismatic rock star. See the picture of the famous performing Mozart family, with little Wolfgang and his sister at the keyboard, their father on violin, and (a portrait of) their mom behind. **Beethoven** (see his "square piano," a letter to his brother, and depictions of his many Vienna apartments) turned mere entertainment into serious art. His nine symphonies amped up the size of the orchestra and the emotional wattage, anticipating the powerful Romantic style. **Schubert,** who died in obscurity at 31, wrote 600 songs that are sung today and the brilliant *Unfinished Symphony.* **Strauss** (father and son) created the dance craze that defines Vienna—the waltz. **Mahler** expanded the orchestra to its fullest range, and paved the way for atonal modernists like **Schönberg, Webern,** and **Berg.**

Before leaving, pick up a virtual baton to conduct the Vienna Philharmonic. If you screw up, the musicians put their instruments down and ridicule you; make it through the piece, and you'll get a rousing round of applause.

### ▲Dorotheum Auction House (Palais Dorotheum)

For an aristocrat's flea market, drop by Austria's answer to Sotheby's. The ground floor has shops, an info desk with a schedule of upcoming auctions, and a few auction items. Some pieces are available for immediate sale (marked *VKP*, for *Verkaufpreis*—"sales price"), while others are up for auction (marked *DIFF. RUF*). Labels on each item predict the auction value.

The upstairs floors have antique furniture and fancy knickknacks (some for immediate sale, others for auction), many brought in by people who've inherited old things and don't have room for them. The top floor has a fancy antique gallery with fixed prices. Wandering through here, you feel like you're touring a museum with exhibits you can buy. Afterward, you can continue your hunt for the perfect curio on the streets around the Dorotheum, which are lined with many fine antique shops.

**Cost and Hours:** Free, Mon-Fri 10:00-18:00, Sat 9:00-17:00, closed Sun, classy little café on second floor, between the Graben pedestrian street and Hofburg at Dorotheergasse 17, tel. 01/51560, www.dorotheum.com.

## ▲St. Peter's Church (Peterskirche)

Baroque Vienna is at its best in this gem, tucked away a few steps from the Graben.

**Cost and Hours:** Free, Mon-Fri 7:00-20:00, Sat-Sun 9:00-21:00; free organ concerts Mon-Fri at 15:00, Sat-Sun at 20:00; just off the Graben between the Plague Monument and Kohlmarkt, tel. 01/533-6433, www. peterskirche.at.

**Visiting the Church:** Admire the rose-and-gold, oval-shaped Baroque interior, topped with a ceiling fresco of Mary kneeling to be crowned by Jesus and the Father, while the dove of the Holy Spirit floats way up in the lantern. Taken together, the church's elements—especially the organ, altar painting, pulpit, and coat of arms (in the base of the dome) of church founder Leopold I—make St. Peter's one of the city's most beautiful and ornate churches.

To the right of the altar, a dramatic golden statue shows the martyrdom of St. John Nepomuk (c. 1340-1393). The Czech saint defied the heretical King Wenceslas, so he was tossed to his death off the Charles Bridge in Prague. In true Baroque style, we see the dramatic peak of his fall, when John has just passed the point of no return. The Virgin Mary floats overhead in a silver cloud.

The present church (from 1733) stands atop earlier churches

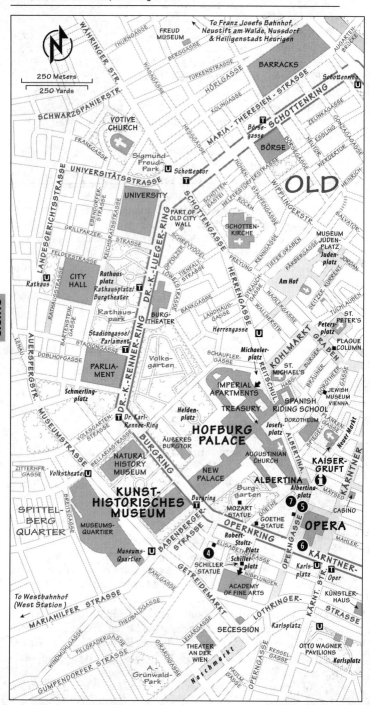

SIGHTS

SIGHTS

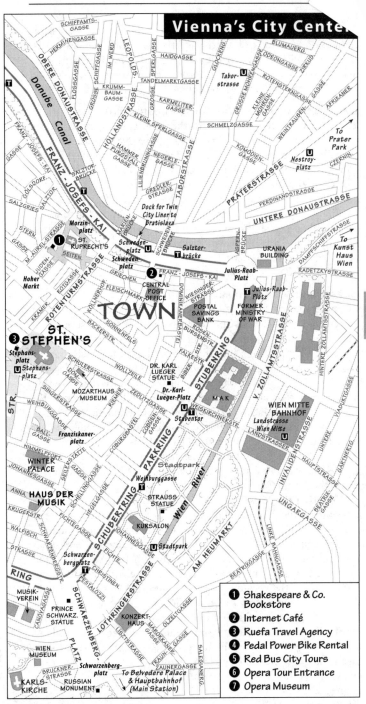

**Vienna's City Center**

1 Shakespeare & Co. Bookstore
2 Internet Café
3 Ruefa Travel Agency
4 Pedal Power Bike Rental
5 Red Bus City Tours
6 Opera Tour Entrance
7 Opera Museum

dating back 1,600 years. On either side of the nave are glass cases containing skeletons of Christian martyrs from Roman times. Above the relic on the left is a painting of the modern saint Josemaría Escrivá, founder of the conservative Catholic organization Opus Dei, of *Da Vinci Code* notoriety.

### ▲▲▲St. Stephen's Cathedral (Stephansdom)

This massive Gothic church with the skyscraping spire sits at the center of Vienna. Its highlights are the impressive exterior, the view from the top of the south tower, a carved pulpit, and a handful of quirky sights associated with Mozart and the Habsburg rulers.

**Cost and Hours:** Church foyer—free, Mon-Sat 6:00-22:00, Sun 7:00-22:00; main nave—€4, Mon-Sat 9:00-11:30 & 13:00-16:30, Sun 13:00-16:30, until 17:30 June-Aug; audioguide-€1; cathedral's other sights, including the south and north towers, catacombs, and treasury, have varying costs and hours; tel. 01/515-523-526, www.stephanskirche.at.

○ See the St. Stephen's Cathedral Tour chapter.

### Mozarthaus Vienna Museum

In September of 1784, 27-year-old Wolfgang Amadeus Mozart moved into this spacious apartment with his wife Constanze and their week-old son Karl. For the next three years, this was the epicenter of Viennese high life. It was here that Mozart wrote *Marriage of Figaro* and *Don Giovanni* and established himself as the toast of Vienna. Today, the actual apartments are pretty boring (mostly bare rooms), but the museum does flesh out Mozart's Vienna years with paintings, videos, and a few period pieces.

**Cost and Hours:** €10, includes audioguide, €17 combo-ticket with Haus der Musik, daily 10:00-19:00, last entry 30 minutes before closing, a block behind the cathedral, go through arcade at #5a and walk 50 yards to Domgasse 5, tel. 01/512-1791, www.mozarthausvienna.at.

**Visiting the Museum:** Start on the third floor, working your way down through museum displays to the actual apartment on the first floor. Exhibits set the scene: **Vienna in the 1780s,** population 50,000, was a blossoming music capital. It supported more than just the traditional church and court music. Mozart played piano for packed houses in nearby restaurants, and he wrote crowd-pleasing pieces for the theater. Antonio Salieri, the emperor's musical director, was supposedly jealous of Mozart's God-given talent, but in reality he probably fostered the young man's career (and Mozart eventually succeeded him). Mozart joined the Freemasons, whose symbolism would appear in his opera *The Magic Flute.* Mozart loved the good life—nice clothes, gambling at cards, even peepshows—and the three years he spent in this house were his champagne years.

The second floor delves into **Mozart's Musical World.** There are displays on his friendship with fellow-genius Haydn and his successful operas. But after 1787, the money dried up: He and 'Stanze moved to a cheaper place outside the city center, Wolfgang hit the road to raise money, and his health suffered. He died just four years later at age 35.

The first-floor **apartment** consists of a half-dozen nondescript rooms, sparsely decorated with period pieces (but none of them Mozart's). See the portraits of him and Constanze, and picture them here: raising their kids, playing billiards, perhaps jamming with Haydn (though there's no evidence of that), or just gazing out the window as Mozart composed another masterpiece. Unfortunately, the bare rooms don't quite succeed in capturing the joie de vivre of the exuberant young genius in his prime.

### Jewish Museum Vienna (Jüdisches Museum Wien)

The museum operates two buildings a 10-minute walk apart; the main museum is on Dorotheergasse (near the Hofburg), and a smaller, more archeological exhibit is at Judenplatz (near Am Hof).

**Cost and Hours:** €10 ticket includes both museums; Dorotheergasse location, at #11—Sun-Fri 10:00-18:00, closed Sat; Judenplatz location, at #8—Sun-Thu 10:00-18:00, Fri 10:00-14:00, closed Sat; tel. 01/535-0431, www.jmw.at.

**Visiting the Museums:** The **Jewish Museum Dorotheergasse** fills a four-story downtown building with exhibits, a bookstore, and a small, reasonably priced café serving Middle Eastern fare. It documents Vienna's Jewish community from earliest times to the present. The collection is well-described in English, and you only need the €4 videoguide if you want more detail (such as interviews and films).

The main part of the exhibit is on the second floor, covering Vienna's Jews up to World War II. A ground-floor exhibit carries the story forward to the present day. The evocative third floor is a "visible storage" archive with stacks of Judaica and works of art that once ornamented synagogues.

Jews settled in Vienna in the early Middle Ages, only to be brutally expelled in 1420 (similar events took place in other German-speaking towns). Another community formed in the 17th century, but was broken up in 1670. Even during the years when Jews were forbidden to live in Vienna, many settled in the small towns and cities of the Habsburg empire, and in the parts of Poland that the Habsburgs took over in the 1770s. In 1782, Josef II partially eased restrictions on his Jewish subjects, allowing them to own property, attend university, and even (if they paid a special tax) to live in Vienna. Still, it was not until the 1850s that the Jewish community in Vienna was allowed to build a synagogue, and it

# Vienna at a Glance

**▲▲▲Opera** Dazzling, world-famous opera house. **Hours:** By guided tour only, July-Aug generally Mon-Sat at the top of each hour 10:00-16:00; fewer tours Sept-June and Sun. See page 35.

**▲▲▲St. Stephen's Cathedral** Enormous, historic Gothic cathedral in the center of Vienna. **Hours:** Foyer—Mon-Sat 6:00-22:00, Sun 7:00-22:00; main nave—Mon-Sat 9:00-11:30 & 13:00-16:30, Sun 13:00-16:30, until 17:30 June-Aug. See page 42.

**▲▲▲Hofburg Imperial Apartments** Lavish main residence of the Habsburgs. **Hours:** Daily July-Aug 9:00-18:00, Sept-June 9:00-17:30. See page 47.

**▲▲▲Hofburg Treasury** The Habsburgs' collection of jewels, crowns, and other valuables—the best on the Continent. **Hours:** Wed-Mon 9:00-17:30, closed Tue. See page 48.

**▲▲▲Kunsthistorisches Museum** World-class exhibit of the Habsburgs' art collection, including works by Raphael, Titian, Caravaggio, Rembrandt, and Bruegel. **Hours:** June-Aug daily 10:00-18:00; Sept-May Tue-Sun 10:00-18:00, closed Mon; Thu until 21:00 year-round. See page 58.

**▲▲▲Schönbrunn Palace** Spectacular summer residence of the Habsburgs, rivaling the grandeur of Versailles. **Hours:** Daily July-Aug 8:30-18:30, April-June and Sept-Oct 8:30-17:30, Nov-March 8:30-17:00. See page 82.

**▲▲Haus der Musik** Modern museum with interactive exhibits on Vienna's favorite pastime. **Hours:** Daily 10:00-22:00. See page 37.

**▲▲Hofburg New Palace Museums** Uncrowded collection of armor, musical instruments, and ancient Greek statues, in the elegant halls of a Habsburg palace. **Hours:** Wed-Sun 10:00-18:00, closed Mon-Tue. See page 48.

**▲▲Albertina Museum** Habsburg residence with decent apartments and world-class temporary exhibits. **Hours:** Daily 10:00-18:00, Wed until 21:00. See page 53.

**▲▲Kaisergruft** Crypt for the Habsburg royalty. **Hours:** Daily 10:00-18:00. See page 54.

**▲▲Belvedere Palace** Elegant palace of Prince Eugene of Savoy, with a collection of 19th- and 20th-century Austrian art (including

Klimt). **Hours:** Daily 10:00-18:00, Lower Palace only until 21:00 on Wed. See page 69.

▲**St. Peter's Church** Beautiful Baroque church in the old center. **Hours:** Mon-Fri 7:00-20:00, Sat-Sun 9:00-21:00. See page 39.

▲**Spanish Riding School** Prancing white Lipizzaner stallions. **Hours:** Spring (Feb-June) and fall (mid-Aug-Dec) only, performances usually Sat-Sun at 11:00, plus less-impressive training sessions generally Tue-Fri 10:00-12:00. See page 49.

▲**St. Michael's Church Crypt** Final resting place of about 100 wealthy 18th-century Viennese. **Hours:** By tour Mon-Fri at 11:00 and 13:00, no tours Sat-Sun. See page 57.

▲**Natural History Museum** Big building facing the Kunsthistorisches, featuring the ancient *Venus of Willendorf*. **Hours:** Wed-Mon 9:00-18:30, Wed until 21:00, closed Tue. See page 58.

▲**Karlskirche** Baroque church offering the unique (and temporary) chance to ride an elevator up into the dome. **Hours:** Mon-Sat 9:00-18:00, Sun 13:00-19:00. See page 61.

▲**Academy of Fine Arts** Small but exciting collection by 15th- to 18th-century masters. **Hours:** Tue-Sun 10:00-18:00, closed Mon. See page 63.

▲**The Secession** Art Nouveau exterior and Klimt paintings in situ. **Hours:** Tue-Sun 10:00-18:00, closed Mon. See page 64.

▲**Naschmarkt** Sprawling, lively outdoor market. **Hours:** Mon-Fri 6:00-18:30, Sat 6:00-17:00, closed Sun, closes earlier in winter. See page 67.

▲**Museum of Military History** Huge collection of artifacts tracing the military history of the Habsburg Empire. **Hours:** Daily 9:00-17:00. See page 78.

▲**Kunst Haus Wien Museum** Modern art museum dedicated to zany local artist/environmentalist Hundertwasser. **Hours:** Daily 10:00-19:00. See page 79.

▲**Imperial Furniture Collection** Eclectic collection of Habsburg furniture. **Hours:** Tue-Sun 10:00-18:00, closed Mon. See page 81.

SIGHTS

was only in 1867 that reforms allowed freedom of movement and residence for everyone in the empire.

After that, Jews moved from the small towns to Vienna in large numbers, attracted by educational and economic opportunities in the rapidly expanding and industrializing capital. Psychologist Sigmund Freud, writers Arthur Schnitzler and Stefan Zweig, and journalist Theodor Herzl were among the prominent Austrian Jews of the pre-WWI period. In 1910, almost 10 percent of Vienna's two million inhabitants were Jewish. But the officially Catholic city was a hostile, anti-Semitic environment for them, with pressure to assimilate or emigrate, especially under the Christian Socialist Karl Lueger, who was mayor from 1897 to 1910. After the Nazi annexation of Austria in 1938, Jews were once again persecuted, expelled, or forced to emigrate. Those who did not were mostly sent to their deaths in the concentration camps in Poland. After the war, only a handful returned to their homes, and today the local Jewish community numbers just a few thousand.

The smaller, less interesting **Museum Judenplatz** was built around the scant remains of the medieval synagogue that served Vienna's 1,500 Jewish residents up until their massacre in 1420. Its main exhibit is an underground hall where you see the synagogue's foundations. The museum also has brief displays on medieval Jewish life and a well-done video re-creating the neighborhood as it looked five centuries ago.

The classy square above the ruins, called Judenplatz, is now dominated by a blocky **memorial** to the 65,000 Viennese Jews killed by the Nazis. (It's a slightly incongruous location—by WWII, the center of Viennese Jewish life had long since moved to the city's Second District.) The memorial—a library turned inside out—invokes Jewish identity as a "people of the book" and asks viewers to ponder the huge loss

of culture, knowledge, and humanity that took place between 1938 and 1945.

### Winter Palace of Prince Eugene of Savoy

In the early 1700s, the diplomat-soldier Prince Eugene of Savoy lived in this "winter" mansion in the center of town, while spending his summers in the airy Belvedere Palace on the outskirts (see page 69). Today, it mostly houses temporary exhibits, plus a room of giant paintings showing the layout of major early 18th-century Habsburg army battles (helpful for military strategists like Eugene). The grand building's ornate, gilded rooms are nice (with chandeliers, ceiling frescoes, and damask walls), but there are better palaces in town, and it's probably not worth your time and money unless you have a special interest in whatever temporary exhibit is showing.

**Cost and Hours:** €9, €25 Prinz Eugen Ticket includes Belvedere Palace, daily 10:00-18:00, Himmelpfortgasse 8, www.belvedere.at.

## THE HOFBURG PALACE

The complex, confusing, and imposing Imperial Palace, with 640 years of architecture, demands your attention. This first Habsburg residence grew with the family empire from the 13th century until 1913, when the last "new wing" opened. The winter residence of the Habsburg rulers until 1918, it's still home to the Austrian president's office, 5,000 government workers, and several important museums. For an overview of the palace layout, see page 135.

**Planning Your Time:** Don't get confused by the Hofburg's myriad courtyards and many museums. Focus on three sights: the Imperial Apartments, the Treasury, and the museums at the New Palace (Neue Burg). With more time, consider the Hofburg's many other sights, covering virtually all facets of the imperial lifestyle: Watch the famous Lipizzaner stallions prance at the Spanish Riding School; visit the Augustinian Church, which holds the Habsburgs' hearts—in more ways than one (as the site of royal weddings, and the crypt with the actual Habsburg hearts); peruse the Habsburgs' book collection at the Austrian National Library; stroll through the inviting imperial-turned-public Burggarten park; ogle the great Habsburg art collection at the Albertina Museum (or, better yet, the Kunsthistorisches Museum—described later); or see the Vienna Boys' Choir at the Imperial Music Chapel (described on page 197).

**Eating at the Hofburg:** Down the tunnel to Heldenplatz is a tiny but handy sandwich bar called **Hofburg Stüberl.** It's ideal for a cool, quiet sit and a drink or snack (same €3 sandwich price whether you sit or go, Mon-Fri 7:00-18:00, Sat-Sun 10:00-16:00). The recommended **Soho Kantine,** off the Burggarten near the butterfly house, is a cheap-but-not-cheery option.

### ▲▲▲Hofburg Imperial Apartments (Kaiserappartements)

These lavish, Versailles-type, "wish-I-were-God" royal rooms are the downtown version of the grander Schönbrunn Palace. If you're rushed and have time for only one palace, make it this one. Palace visits are a one-way romp through three sections: a porcelain and silver collection, a museum dedicated to the enigmatic and troubled Empress Sisi, and the luxurious apartments themselves.

The Imperial Apartments are a mix of Old World luxury and modern 19th-century conveniences. Here, Emperor Franz Josef I lived and worked along with his wife Elisabeth, known as Sisi. The Sisi Museum traces the development of her legend, analyzing how her fabulous but tragic life created a 19th-century Princess Diana. You'll read bits of her poetic writing, see exact copies of her now-lost jewelry, and learn about her escapes, dieting mania, and chocolate bills.

**Cost and Hours:** €11.50, includes well-done audioguide; €25.50 Sisi Ticket also covers Schönbrunn Palace (where you can skip the line) and Imperial Furniture Collection; daily July-Aug 9:00-18:00, Sept-June 9:00-17:30, last entry one hour before closing; enter from under the rotunda just off Michaelerplatz, through the Michaelertor gate; tel. 01/533-7570, www.hofburg-wien.at.

○ See the Hofburg Imperial Apartments Tour chapter.

### ▲▲▲Hofburg Treasury
### (Weltliche und Geistliche Schatzkammer)

One of the world's most stunning collections of royal regalia, the Hofburg Treasury shows off sparkling crowns, jewels, gowns, and assorted Habsburg bling in 21 darkened rooms. The treasures, well-explained by an audioguide, include the crown of the Holy Roman Emperor, Charlemagne's saber, a unicorn horn, and more precious gems than you can shake a scepter at.

**Cost and Hours:** €12, €20 combo-ticket with Kunsthistorisches Museum and New Palace museums, Wed-Mon 9:00-17:30, closed Tue, last entry 30 minutes before closing, audioguide-€4; from the Hofburg's central courtyard pass through the black, red, and gold gate, then follow *Schatzkammer* signs to the Schweizerhof; tel. 01/525-240, www.kaiserliche-schatzkammer.at.

○ See the Hofburg Treasury Tour chapter.

### ▲▲Hofburg New Palace Museums:
### Armor, Music, and Ancient Greek Statues

The New Palace (Neue Burg) houses three separate collections—an armory (with a killer collection of medieval weapons), historical musical instruments, and classical statuary from ancient Ephesus. The included audioguide brings the exhibits to life and lets you hear the collection's fascinating old instruments being played. An added bonus is the chance to wander alone among the royal Habsburg halls, stairways, and painted ceilings.

**Cost and Hours:** €14 ticket covers all three collections and the Kunsthistorisches Museum across the Ring, €20 combo-ticket adds the Hofburg Treasury, Wed-Sun

SIGHTS

10:00-18:00, closed Mon-Tue, last entry 30 minutes before closing, almost no tourists, tel. 01/525-240, www.khm.at.

**Visiting the Museums:** Start on the second floor with the **Arms and Armor Collection,** where you're welcomed by colorful mannequins of knights on horseback. The adjoining rooms display weapons from all over the vast Habsburg Empire, including exotic Turkish suits of armor. Long after gunpowder had rendered medieval weaponry obsolete, the Habsburgs staunchly maintained the knightly code of chivalry and celebrated family events with tournaments and jousts.

The **Ancient Musical Instruments Collection** shows instruments through the ages, especially the rapid evolution from harpsichord to piano. In the 19th century, Vienna was the world's musical capital. In the large entry hall, admire Beethoven's (supposed) clarinet and a strange keyboard perhaps played by Mozart. Browse around to find Leopold Mozart's violin (Room XIII) and a piano owned by Robert and Clara Schumann and later by Brahms (Room XVI).

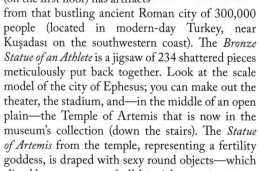

The **Ephesus Museum** (on the first floor) has artifacts from that bustling ancient Roman city of 300,000 people (located in modern-day Turkey, near Kuşadası on the southwestern coast). The *Bronze Statue of an Athlete* is a jigsaw of 234 shattered pieces meticulously put back together. Look at the scale model of the city of Ephesus; you can make out the theater, the stadium, and—in the middle of an open plain—the Temple of Artemis that is now in the museum's collection (down the stairs). The *Statue of Artemis* from the temple, representing a fertility goddess, is draped with sexy round objects—which may have symbolized breasts, eggs, or bulls' testicles.

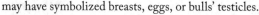

### ▲Spanish Riding School (Spanische Hofreitschule)

This stately 300-year-old Baroque hall at the Hofburg Palace is the home of the renowned Lipizzaner stallions. The magnificent building was an impressive expanse in its day. Built without central pillars, it offers clear views of the prancing horses under lavish chandeliers, with a grand statue of Emperor Charles VI on horseback at the head of the hall.

Lipizzaner stallions were a creation of horse-loving Habsburg Archduke Charles, who wanted to breed the perfect animal. He imported Andalusian horses from his homeland of Spain, then mated them with a local line to produce an extremely intelligent and easily trainable breed. Italian and Arabian bloodlines were later added to tweak various characteristics. The name "Lipizzaner" comes from Lipica in Slovenia, where the stud farm was located until 1920 (when Slovenia became part of Yugoslavia and the horses were moved to the Austrian city of Graz). Lipizzaner stallions are known for their noble gait and Baroque profile. These regal horses have changed shape with the tenor of the times: They were bred strong and stout during wars, and frilly and slender in more cultured eras. But they're always born black, fade to gray, and turn a distinctive white in adulthood.

The school offers three ways to see the horses: performances, morning exercises, and guided tours of the stables. To see what the options are during your visit, go to www.srs.at and enter your dates under "Event Search" or call 01/533-9031. Photos are not allowed, nor are children under age 3.

At any time of day and at no cost, you can just walk by the stables (there's a big window from the covered passageway along Reitschulgasse) and usually see the horses poking their heads out of their stalls.

**Performances:** The Lipizzaner stallions put on great 80-minute performances in spring and fall. Each performance is packed, but with just a few rows of seats and standing-room spots that are right there, there's not a bad view in the house. The formal emcee thoughtfully introduces each number in German and English as horses do their choreographed moves to jaunty recorded Viennese classical music (in 4:4 meter rather than 3:4—I guess the horses don't waltz). The pricey seats book up months in advance, but standing room is usually available the same day (seats-about €50-160, standing room-about €25, prices can vary depending on the show; Feb-late June and mid-Aug-Dec usually Sat-Sun at 11:00, no shows in Jan or late June-mid-Aug; box office opens at 9:00 and is located inside the Hofburg—go through the main Hofburg entryway from Michaelerplatz, then turn left into the first passage; tel. 01/533-9031, www.srs.at). If buying tickets online, look for the tiny English flag at the top of the page when you're redirected to the ticket purchase site.

**Morning Exercises:** For a less expensive, more casual experience, morning exercises with music take place on weekday mornings in the same hall and are open to the public. Don't have high expectations, as the horses often do little more than trot and warm up. Tourists line up early at Josefsplatz (the large courtyard between Michaelerplatz and Albertinaplatz), at the door marked *Spanische Hofreitschule*. But there's no need to show up when the doors open at 10:00, since tickets never really "sell out." Only the horses stay for the full two hours. As people leave, new tickets are

## Sunday-Morning Culture in Vienna

Sunday morning in Vienna can provide a cultural thrill for visitors. Three wonderful events take place within 200 yards of each other on most Sunday mornings. The Vienna Boys' Choir sings at the 9:15 Mass in the Hofburg's Imperial Music Chapel (mid-Sept-June, see page 197). Without reservations, you'll stand in the lobby craning your neck to see the church service, though you can easily watch the boys on the video monitor while you listen to them live. At 11:00, choose between two other Viennese high-culture experiences. At the Hofburg's Spanish Riding School, nab a standing-room spot for the performance of the Lipizzaner stallions (spring and fall only, see page 49). Or, easiest of all, sit down in the Augustinian Church for the 11:00 Mass, with a glorious orchestra and choir leading the music (see below).

printed, so you can just prance in with no wait at all. You can also buy tickets for the training sessions at the box office, described earlier (€14 at the door, family discounts, generally March-late June and early-Aug-Dec Tue-Fri 10:00-12:00, occasionally also on Mon).

**Guided Tours:** One-hour guided tours are given almost every afternoon year-round. You'll see the Winter Riding School with its grand Baroque architecture, the Summer Riding School in a shady courtyard, and the stables (€16; tours usually daily at 14:00, 15:00, and 16:00; in English and German, purchase tickets online or at the box office, described earlier).

### ▲Augustinian Church (Augustinerkirche)

Built into the Hofburg, this is the Gothic and Neo-Gothic church where the Habsburgs got latched (weddings took place here), then later dispatched.

**Cost and Hours:** Free, open long hours daily, Augustinerstrasse 3—facing Josefsplatz, with its statue of the great reform emperor Josef II and the royal library next door.

**Visiting the Church:** In the front, notice the windows above on the right, from which royals witnessed the Mass in private. Don't miss the exquisite, pyramid-shaped memorial (by the Italian sculptor Antonio Canova) to Maria Theresa's favorite daughter, Maria Christina, with its incredibly sad white-marble procession. Left of that is a chapel dedicated to Charles I, the last Habsburg emperor (r. 1916-1918). Pushed by Habsburg royalists who worship here, Charles is on a dubious road to sainthood. (The Catholic Church requires that you perform a miracle before they'll make you a saint. Charles I's miracle: He healed the varicose veins of a nun.)

**Sunday Mass:** The church's 11:00 Sunday Mass is a hit with music lovers—both a Mass and a concert, often with an orchestra accompanying the choir (acoustics are best in front). Pay by contributing to the offering plate and buying a CD afterwards. Check posters by the entry, or www.hochamt.at (click on "Programm"), to see what's on—typically you'll hear one of Mozart or Haydn's many short Masses.

**Royal Hearts:** The hearts of 54 Habsburg nobles are in urns in a vault off the church's Loreto Chapel (on the right beyond the Maria Christina memorial). The earliest dates from 1618; the last is the heart of Franz Josef's father, who died in 1878. On Sunday mornings after Mass (at about 12:45), the chapel is

opened and visitors, after listening to a 15-minute lecture in German, can peer through a tiny grate at the rows of urns (suggested donation €2.50).

## State Hall (Prunksaal) and Austrian National Library Museums

The National Library (Österreichische Nationalbibliothek) runs four museums in different parts of the Hofburg complex. The most worthwhile is the **State Hall** (Prunksaal), a postcard-perfect Baroque library entered from Josefplatz, next to the Augustinian Church (see map on page 135). In this former royal library, with a statue of Charles VI in the center, you'll find yourself whispering. The setting takes you back to 1730 and gives you the sense that, in imperial times, knowledge of the world was for the elite—and with

that knowledge, the elite had power. More than 200,000 old books line the walls, but patrons go elsewhere to read them—the hall is just for show these days.

The entrance to the National Library's main, modern reading area—with crowds of students at exam times—is on Heldenplatz. The public isn't really allowed in, except to walk through to visit the **Papyrus Museum** in the basement. This little collection tells the story of writing in Egypt from 3000 B.C. to A.D. 1000, with scant English descriptions.

A couple blocks north of the Hofburg, in the building at Herrengasse 9 (across from the Herrengasse U-Bahn station), the library also runs the **Globe Museum** (the world's largest, with 250

SIGHTS

terrestrial and celestial spheres) and a modest two-room museum on **Esperanto** and other artificial languages.

**Cost and Hours:** €7 for State Hall; €4 combo-ticket for Papyrus, Globe, and Esperanto museums; daily 10:00-18:00, Thu until 21:00; tel. 01/53410, www.onb.ac.at.

## Burggarten (Palace Garden) and Butterfly House

This greenbelt, once the backyard of the Hofburg and now a people's park, welcomes visitors to loiter on the grass. On nice days, it's lively with office workers enjoying a break. The statue of Mozart facing the Ringstrasse is popular. The iron-and-glass pavilion (c. 1910 with playful Art Nouveau touches) now houses the recommended Café Restaurant Palmenhaus and a small but fluttery butterfly exhibit. The butterfly zone is delightfully muggy on  a brisk off-season day, and trippy any time of year. If you tour it, notice the butterflies hanging out on the trays with rotting slices of banana. They lick the fermented banana juice as it beads, and then just hang out there in a stupor...or fly giddy loop-de-loops.

**Cost and Hours:** €6; April-Oct daily 10:00-16:45, Sat-Sun until 18:15; Nov-March daily 10:00-15:45.

## ▲▲Albertina Museum

This charming museum has three highlights: impressive staterooms of the former palace, a permanent collection of art from Impressionist to modern, and excellent temporary exhibits. The building, at the southern tip of the Hofburg complex (near the Opera), was the residence of Maria Theresa's favorite daughter, Maria Christina, who was the only one allowed to marry for love rather than political strategy. Her many sisters were jealous. (Marie-Antoinette had to marry the French king...and lost her head over it.) Maria Christina's husband, Albert of Saxony, was a great collector of original drawings and amassed an enormous assortment of works by Dürer, Rembrandt, Rubens, Schiele, and others. As it's Albert and Christina's gallery, it's cleverly called the "Albertina."

**Cost and Hours:** €12, daily 10:00-18:00, Wed until 21:00, helpful audioguide-€4, overlooking Albertinaplatz across from the TI and Opera, tel. 01/534-830, www.albertina.at.

**Visiting the Museum:** Begin on the first floor with the State Rooms and Batliner Collection.

**State Rooms** *(Prunkräume):* Wander freely under chandeliers and across parquet floors through a couple-dozen rooms of imperial splendor, unconstrained by velvet ropes. It's a kaleidoscope of colors, as each room's damask walls and curtains are a different rich shade of red, yellow, or green. You'll see the billiard room, the tea salon, the bedrooms, and the tiny Goldkabinett, with walls plated in 23-carat gold. (The rooms themselves are nice, but they're virtually empty of period furnishings.) Most impressive is the large Hall of Muses (in pastel lavender and yellow), lined with statues of the graceful demi-goddesses (plus Apollo) who inspire the arts.

**Batliner Collection:** This manageable collection sweeps you quickly through modern art history, featuring minor works by major artists. Though the collection is permanent, you'll see only about 100 works selected from the 300 in the archives.

Start with a room of classic Impressionism: Monet's water lilies, Degas' dancers, and Renoir's cute little girls. By 1900, the modern world was approaching, as seen in Munch's moody landscapes and (Vienna's own) Gustav Klimt, with his eerie femme fatales.

The next few rooms illustrate how art transitioned from Impressionist to abstract. The Fauves (Matisse, Vlaminck, Derain) amped up the colors of Impressionism to surreal levels. Expressionists (Nolde, Kirchner) used their trademark thick paint, clashing colors, black outlines, and grotesque figures to capture the unsettled atmosphere of the World War I era. The subject matter becomes increasingly flat and two-dimensional, eventually dissolving into a pattern of paint that would become purely abstract art.

The Russian Gallery has a few classic Chagalls, with his fiddler-on-the-roof village scenes and bouquets of flowers.

The Picasso room has canvases from various periods of his life: early brown Cubist experiments, portraits of the women in his life, and exuberant colorful works from his last years on the sunny Riviera. Paintings by Francis Bacon and big Abstract Expressionist canvases bring art up to the cusp of the 21st century.

**Temporary Exhibits:** A highlight of the museum is their special exhibitions, which often feature works from the Albertina's world-renowned collection of drawings and paintings.

## CHURCH CRYPTS NEAR THE HOFBURG
Two churches near the Hofburg offer starkly different looks at dearly departed Viennese: the Habsburg coffins in the Kaisergruft, and the commoners' graves in St. Michael's Church.

### ▲▲Kaisergruft (Imperial Crypt)
Visiting the imperial remains of the Habsburg family is not as easy as you might imagine. These original organ donors left their bodies—about 150 in all—in the unassuming Kaisergruft, their hearts in the Augustinian Church (viewable Sun after Mass—see page

# Empress Maria Theresa (1717-1780) and Her Son, Emperor Josef II (1741-1790)

Maria Theresa was the only woman to officially rule the Habsburg Empire in that family's 640-year reign. She was a strong and effective empress (r. 1740-1780). People are quick to remember Maria Theresa as the mother of 16 children (10 survived into adulthood). Ponder the fact that the most powerful woman in Europe either was pregnant or had a newborn for most of her reign. Maria Theresa ruled after the Austrian defeat of the Ottomans, when Europe recognized Austria as a great power. (Her rival, the Prussian king, said, "When at last the Habsburgs get a great man, it's a woman.") For an abridged Habsburg family tree, see page 455.

The last of the Baroque imperial rulers, and the first of the modern rulers of the Age of Enlightenment, Maria Theresa marked the end of the feudal system and the beginning of the era of the grand state. She was a great social reformer. During her reign, she avoided wars and expanded her empire by skillfully marrying her children into the right families. For instance, after daughter Marie-Antoinette's marriage into the French Bourbon family (to Louis XVI), a country that had been an enemy became an ally. (Unfortunately for Marie-Antoinette, Maria Theresa's timing was off.)

To stay in power during an era of revolution, Maria Theresa had to be in tune with her age. She taxed the Church and the nobility, provided six years of obligatory education to all children, and granted free health care to all in her realm. Maria Theresa also welcomed the boy genius Mozart into her court.

The empress' legacy lived on in her son, Josef II, who ruled as emperor himself for a decade (1780-1790). He was an even more avid reformer, building on his mother's accomplishments. An enlightened monarch, Josef mothballed the too-extravagant Schönbrunn Palace, secularized the monasteries, established religious tolerance within his realm, freed the serfs, made possible the founding of Austria's first general hospital, and promoted relatively enlightened treatment of the mentally ill. Josef was a model of practicality (for example, reusable coffins à la *Amadeus*, and no more than six candles at funerals)—and very unpopular with other royals. But his policies succeeded in preempting the revolutionary anger of the age, largely enabling Austria to avoid the turmoil that shook so much of the rest of Europe.

**SIGHTS**

51), and their entrails in the crypt below St. Stephen's Cathedral (described on page 42). Don't tripe.

**Cost and Hours:** €5.50, daily 10:00-18:00, last entry 20 minutes before closing, €0.50 map includes Habsburg family tree and a chart locating each coffin, crypt is in the Capuchin Church at Tegetthoffstrasse 2 at Neuer Markt; tel. 01/512-6853, www. kaisergruft.at.

**Visiting the Kaisergruft:** Descend into a low-ceilinged crypt full of gray metal tombs. Start up the path, through tombs ranging from simple caskets to increasingly big monuments with elaborate metalwork ornamentation. **Josef I** (the tomb midway along on the right, with the trumpeting angel) was the Holy Roman Emperor who battled France's Louis XIV to a standstill. **Karl VI** (a few steps farther along) was Josef's little brother, best known for failing to father a male heir, but who arranged for his daughter to take the throne—Maria Theresa.

You soon reach the massive pewter tomb under the dome of **Maria Theresa.** The only female Habsburg monarch, she had to be granted special dispensation to rule. Her 40-year reign was en-lightened and progressive. She and her husband, **Franz I,** recline Etruscan-style atop their fancy coffin, gazing into each other's eyes as a cherub crowns them with glory. They were famously in love (though Franz was less than faithful) and their numerous children were married off to Europe's royal houses. Maria Theresa outlived her husband by 15 years, which she spent in mourning. Old and fat, she installed a special lift to transport herself down into the Kai-sergruft to visit her dear, departed Franz. At the four corners of the tomb are the Habsburgs' four crowns: the Holy Roman Empire, Hungary, Bohemia, and Jerusalem. At his parents' feet lies **Josef II,** the patron of Mozart and Beethoven. Compare the Rococo splendor of Maria Theresa's tomb with the simple coffin of Josef, who was known for his down-to-earth ruling style during the Age of Enlightenment.

Continuing to the right of Maria Theresa's tomb, you'll pass the tombs of **Franz II** (a.k.a. Francis I) and his son **Ferdinand I.** These two rulers were forced to relinquish some of the Habsburg power in the face of Napoleon's armies and democratic revolutions.

Down three steps, the next room illustrates the Habsburgs' fad-ing 19th-century glory. There's the appropriately austere military tomb of the long-reigning **Franz Josef** (see sidebar on page 142). Alongside is his wife, **Elisabeth**—a.k.a. "Sisi" (see page 137)—who always wins

the "Most Flowers" award. Their son was Crown Prince **Rudolf.** Rudolf and his teenage mistress supposedly committed suicide to-gether in 1889 at Mayerling hunting lodge...or was it murder? It took considerable legal hair-splitting to win Rudolf this hallowed burial spot: After examining his brain, it was determined that he was mentally disabled and therefore incapable of knowingly killing himself and his girl.

In the final room (with humbler copper tombs), you reach the final Habsburgs. **Karl I** (see his bust, not a tomb) was the last of the Habsburg rulers, and was deposed in 1918. His son was Crown Prince **Otto,** who is buried near his mother, **Zita.** When Otto was laid to rest here in 2011, it was probably the last great Old Regime event in European history. The monarchy died hard in Austria. Today there are about 700 living Habsburg royals, mostly living in exile. When they die, they will be buried in their countries of exile, not here.

Body parts and ornate tombs aside, the real legacy of the Habsburgs is the magnificence of this city. Step outside. Pan up. Watch the clouds glide by the ornate gables of Vienna.

### ▲St. Michael's Church Crypt (Michaelerkirche)

St. Michael's Church, which faces the Hofburg on Michaelerplatz, offers a striking contrast to the imperial crypt. Regular tours take visitors underground to see a typical church crypt—filled with the rotting wooden coffins of well-to-do commoners.

**Cost and Hours:** €7 for 45-minute tour, Mon-Fri at 11:00 and 13:00, no tours Sat-Sun, mostly in German but with enough English, wait at the sign that advertises the tour at the church en-trance and pay the guide directly, mobile 0650-533-8003, www. michaelerkirche.at.

**Visiting the Crypt:** Climbing below the church, you'll see about a hundred 18th-century coffins and stand on three feet of debris, surrounded by niches filled with stacked lumber from de-cayed coffins and countless bones. You'll meet a 1769 mummy in lederhosen and a wig, along with a woman who is clutching a cross and has flowers painted on her high heels. You'll learn about death in those times—from how the wealthy didn't want to end up in standard shallow graves, instead paying to be laid to rest below the church, to how, in 1780, the enlightened emperor Josef II ended the practice of cemetery burials in cities but allowed the rich to become the stinking rich in crypts under churches. You'll also dis-cover why many were buried with their chin strapped shut (because when the muscles rot, your jaw falls open and you get that ghostly skeleton look that nobody wants).

St. Michael's Church itself has an interesting history. In 1791, a few days after Mozart's death, his *Requiem* was performed here for the first time. (See the small monument just inside the door on the right.) In the rear of the nave, to the right as you enter, is a small memorial to Austrian victims of the concentration camp at Dachau. The cross was made in 1945 at Dachau by newly freed inmates and is dedicated to Austrian martyrs.

## KUNSTHISTORISCHES MUSEUM AND NEARBY

In the 19th century, the Habsburgs planned to link their palace and museum buildings with a series of arches across the Ringstrasse. Although that dream was never fully realized, the awe-inspiring museums still face off across Maria-Theresien-Platz, with a monument to Maria Theresa at its center (for more on this monument, see page 107 of the Vienna City Walk chapter).

### ▲▲▲Kunsthistorisches Museum

This exciting museum, across the Ring from the Hofburg Palace, showcases the grandeur and opulence of the Habsburgs' col-

lected artwork in a grand building (built in 1888 to display these works). While there's little Viennese art here, you will find world-class European masterpieces galore (including canvases by Raphael, Caravaggio, Velázquez, Dürer, Rubens, Vermeer, Rembrandt, and a particularly exquisite roomful of Bruegels), all well-displayed on one glorious floor, plus a fine display of Egyptian, classical, and applied arts. Another highlight, filling a wing of the ground floor, is the Habsburg "Chamber of Wonders" *(Kunstkammer)*, showing off the imperial collection of exquisite fine-art objects and exotic curios.

**Cost and Hours:** €14 (free for kids under 19), ticket also covers New Palace museums across the Ring, €20 combo-ticket also includes the Hofburg Treasury; June-Aug daily 10:00-18:00; Sept-May Tue-Sun 10:00-18:00, closed Mon; Thu until 21:00 year-round, last entry 30 minutes before closing, audioguide-€4, on the Ringstrasse at Maria-Theresien-Platz, U-2 or U-3: Volkstheater/Museumsplatz, tel. 01/525-240, www.khm.at.

○ See the Kunsthistorisches Museum Tour chapter.

### ▲Natural History Museum (Naturhistorisches Museum)

In the twin building facing the Kunsthistorisches Museum, you'll find moon rocks, dinosaur stuff, and the fist-sized *Venus of Willendorf*—at 25,000 years old, the world's oldest sex symbol. Even though the museum is not glitzy or high-tech, it's a hit with children and scientifically curious grown-ups. Of the museum's 20 million objects, you're sure to find something interesting. The collection's presentation is almost charming in its old school-ness.

**Cost and Hours:** €10, Wed-Mon 9:00-18:30, Wed until 21:00, closed Tue, on the Ringstrasse at Maria-Theresien-Platz, U-2 or U-3: Volkstheater/Museumsplatz, tel. 01/521-770, www.nhm-wien.ac.at.

**Visiting the Museum:** For a quick visit, head first to the *Venus of Willendorf*—she's on the mezzanine level, in Room 11 (from the entrance lobby, climb the first 12 steps, then swing around to the left at the first landing to reach the mezzanine level). The four-inch-tall, chubby stone statuette, found in the Danube Valley (see page 212), is a generic female (no face or feet) resting her hands on her ample breasts. The statue's purpose is unknown, but she may have been a symbol of fertility for our mammoth-hunting ancestors. In Room 10 nearby are big dinosaur skeletons. Also on this floor is an impressive exhibit of rocks, including one of the largest collections of meteorites in the world (mezzanine, Rooms 1-5, to the right of the entrance lobby).

For a more chronological visit, start upstairs on the first floor (in Room 21), and follow hundreds of millions of years of evolution—from single cells to sea creatures, reptiles, birds, mammals, and primates. If hall after hall of stuffed animals gets you down, seek out the "vivarium" downstairs, with live animals. Finish with the hairless primate—man—also downstairs, in Rooms 11-14.

## MuseumsQuartier

The vast grounds of the former imperial stables now corral a cutting-edge cultural center for contemporary arts and design, including several impressive museums; the best are the Leopold Museum and the Museum of Modern Art. For many, the MuseumsQuartier is most enjoyable not for its galleries but as a youthful gathering spot in the evening for light, fun meals and cocktails.

**Cost and Hours: Leopold Museum**—€12; June-Aug daily 10:00-18:00; Sept-May Wed-Mon 10:00-18:00, closed Tue; Thu until 21:00 year-round, last entry 30 minutes before closing; audioguide-€3.50 but worth it only for enthusiasts, tel. 01/525-700, www.leopoldmuseum.org; **Museum of**

**Modern Art**—€10, Mon 14:00-19:00, Tue-Sun 10:00-19:00, Thu until 21:00, good audioguide-€3, tel. 01/52500, www.mumok.at.

**Information:** At the visitors center, various combo-tickets are available for those interested in more than just the Leopold and Modern Art museums. You can also rent a €4 audioguide that explains the complex (behind Kunsthistorisches Museum, U-2 or U-3: Volkstheater/Museumsplatz, tel. 01/525-5881, www.mqw.at).

**Visiting the MuseumsQuartier:** Walk into the complex from the Hofburg side, where the main entrance (with visitors center, shop, and ticket office) leads to a big courtyard with cafés, fountains, and ever-changing "installation lounge furniture," all surrounded by the quarter's various museums.

The **Leopold Museum** features several temporary exhibits of modern Austrian art. The top floor holds the largest collection of works by Egon Schiele (1890-1918; these works make some people uncomfortable—Schiele's nudes are *really* nude) and a few paintings by Gustav Klimt, Kolo Moser, and Oskar Kokoschka. While this is a great collection, you can see even better works from these artists in the Belvedere Palace, described later.

The **Museum of Modern Art** (Museum Moderner Kunst, a.k.a. "MUMOK") is Austria's leading gallery for international modern and contemporary art. It's the striking lava-paneled building—three stories tall and four stories deep, offering seven floors of far-out art that's hard for most visitors to appreciate. This state-of-the-art museum shows off its huge and rotating collection of works by "classical" modernists (Paul Klee, Pablo Picasso, Pop artists) and more contemporary art.

Rounding out the sprawling MuseumsQuartier are an architecture center, Electronic Avenue, design forum, children's museum, "Quartier 21" (with gallery space and shops), and the **Kunsthalle Wien**—two halls with temporary exhibits of contemporary art (about €8 for one, €12 for both; daily 10:00-19:00, Thu until 21:00, tel. 01/521-8933, www.kunsthallewien.at).

## KARLSPLATZ AND NEARBY

These sights cluster around Karlsplatz, just southeast of the Ringstrasse (U-1, U-2, or U-4: Karlsplatz). If you're walking there from central Vienna, use the U-Bahn station's passageway (at the Opera) to avoid crossing busy boulevards. Once at Karlsplatz, allow about 30 minutes walking time to connect the various sights: the Karlskirche, Secession, and Naschmarkt.

### Karlsplatz

This picnic-friendly square, with its Henry Moore sculpture in the pond, is ringed with sights. The massive, domed Karlskirche and its twin spiral columns dominate the square. The small green, white, and gold pavilions that line the street across the square from the church are from the late 19th-century municipal train system *(Stadtbahn)*. One of Europe's first subway systems, this precursor to today's U-Bahn was built with a military purpose in mind: to move troops quickly in time of civil unrest—specifically, out to Schön-brunn Palace. With curvy iron frames, decorative marble slabs, and painted gold trim, these are pioneering works in the *Jugendstil* style, designed by Otto Wagner, who influenced Klimt and the Se-cessionists. One of the pavilions has a sweet little exhibit on **Otto Wagner** that illustrates the Art Nouveau lifestyle around 1900. It also shows models for his never-built dreams and the grand ex-pansion of Vienna (€4, described in English, April-Oct Tue-Sun 10:00-18:00, closed Mon and Nov-March, near the Ringstrasse, tel. 01/5058-7478-5177, www.wienmuseum.at).

## ▲Karlskirche (St. Charles' Church)

Charles Borromeo, a 16th-century bishop from Milan, inspired his parishioners during plague times. This "votive church" was dedi-

cated to him in 1713, when an epidemic spared Vienna. The church offers the best Baroque in the city, with a unique combination of columns (showing scenes from the life of Charles Bor-romeo, à la Trajan's Column in Rome), a classic pediment, and an elliptical dome.

**Cost and Hours:** €8, ticket covers church interior, elevator ride, and skippable one-room museum; Mon-Sat 9:00-18:00, Sun 13:00-19:00, last entry 30 minutes before closing; el-

evator runs until 17:30, last ascent at 17:00; audioguide-€2; www. karlskirche.at. The entry fee may seem steep, but remember that it helps to fund the restoration. There are often classical music con-certs performed here on period instruments (usually Thu-Sat; ask about Rick Steves discount, see www.concert-vienna.info).

**Visiting the Church:** The dome's colorful 13,500-square-foot fresco—painted in the 1730s by Johann Michael Rottmayr—shows

Signor Borromeo (in red-and-white bishops' robes) gazing up into heaven, spreading his arms wide, and pleading with Christ to spare Vienna from the plague.

The church is especially worthwhile for the chance to ride an **elevator** (installed for renovation work) up into the

cupola. The industrial lift takes you to a platform at the base of the 235-foot dome (if you're even slightly afraid of heights, skip this trip). Consider that the church was built and decorated with a scaffolding system essentially the same as this one. Once up top, you'll climb stairs to the steamy lantern at the extreme top of the church.

At that dizzying height, you're in the clouds with cupids and angels. Many details that appear smooth and beautiful from ground level—such as gold leaf, paintings, and fake marble—look rough and sloppy up close. It's surreal to observe the 3-D figures from an unintended angle—check out Christ's leg, which looks dwarf-sized up close. Give yourself a minute to take it in: Faith, Hope, and Charity triumph and inspire. Borromeo lobbies heaven for relief from the plague. Meanwhile, a Protestant's Lutheran Bible is put to the torch by angels. At the very top, you'll see the tiny dove representing the Holy Spirit, surrounded by a cheering squad of nipple-lipped cupids.

## Wien Museum Karlsplatz

This underappreciated city history museum, worth ▲ for those intrigued by Vienna's illustrious past, walks you through the story of Vienna with well-presented artifacts.

**Cost and Hours:** €8, free first Sun of the month, open Tue-Sun 10:00-18:00, closed Mon, Karlsplatz 8, tel. 01/505-8747, www.wienmuseum.at.

**Visiting the Museum:** Work your way up chronologically. The ground floor exhibits prehistoric and Roman fragments, along with a fine digital reconstruction of the Roman city of Vindobona. Compare that to the model of medieval Vienna (c. 1420), looking much as it does today (but notice the castle at the location of today's Hofburg and the city wall tracing the Ringstrasse). Also dating from this period are some original statues from St. Stephen's Cathedral (c. 1350),

with various Habsburgs showing off the slinky hip-hugging fashion of the day. You'll also enjoy a rare close-up look at original stained glass (circa 1500) from the cathedral.

The first floor focuses on the Renaissance and Baroque eras, including suits of armor, old city maps, booty from an Ottoman siege, and an 1850 city model showing the town just before the wall was replaced by the Ring. Finally, the second floor picks up after 1815. Look for architect Adolf Loos' minimalist living room (while you might imagine this less-is-more pioneer—described on page 100—lived in an empty cardboard box, his cozy home has more decoration than you might expect). The city model from 1898 shows off the new Ringstrasse. There's also a modest, eclectic art collection, including sentimental Biedermeier paintings and objets d'art, and early 20th-century paintings (including four by Klimt, as well as works by Schiele, Kokoschka, and other Secessionists). Look for the model of a never-built new home for the Academy of Fine Arts—an Art Nouveau design by Otto Wagner.

### ▲Academy of Fine Arts (Akademie der Bildenden Künste)

Few tourists make their way to Vienna's art academy to see its small but impressive collection of paintings, starring Botticelli, Guardi, Rubens, Van Dyck, and other great masters. The highlight is a triptych by the master of medieval surrealism, Hieronymus Bosch. The collection's location in a working art academy gives it a certain sense of realness.

**Cost and Hours:** €8 includes permanent collection and special exhibits, Tue-Sun 10:00-18:00, closed Mon; audioguide-€2, photography fee-€5; 3 blocks from the Opera at Schillerplatz 3, tel. 01/588-162-222, www.akbild.ac.at.

**SIGHTS**

**Visiting the Museum:** The *Gemäldegalerie* is upstairs, on the school's first floor. The first room, dedicated to the Academy itself, is dominated by a portrait of the school's founder, Empress Maria Theresa, in an aqua-blue dress (see photo at left). The fine portrait (from 1750) is by the Swedish painter Martin Meytens, whose self-portrait looks on approvingly from the right. On the left wall is a scene depicting the Academy in action: a nude model sits center stage while professors paint, draw, and sculpt him. Go through the door to the right of Maria Theresa, and work your way counterclockwise through the exhibit.

The next section of 18th-century Italian works includes a series of "postcard" scenes of Venice by **Francesco Guardi** in his proto-Impressionistic style.

In the long hall, among the still lifes and landscapes, find **Rembrandt's** *Portrait of a Young Woman*, wearing a ruff collar that was all the rage (c. 1632). See **Peter Paul Rubens'** typical fleshy nudes, such as his voluptuous *Three Graces*. The small sketchy cartoons were used to create giant canvases for a church in Belgium; it later burned down, leaving only these rare sketches. Nearby, Rubens' talented protégé, **Anthony van Dyck,**

shows his prowess in a small-but-famous self-portrait painted at the age of 15 (pictured on previous page).

The Italian Renaissance is represented by Titian and—one of the museum's prize pieces—a round **Botticelli** canvas. Recently cleaned to show off its vivid reds and blues, it depicts the Madonna tenderly embracing the Baby Jesus while angels look on.

The last room holds the captivating, harrowing *Last Judgment* triptych by **Hieronymus Bosch** (c. 1482, with some details

added by Lucas Cranach). This is the polar opposite of Bosch's most famous work, *The Garden of Earthly Delights* (in Madrid's El Prado). Read the altarpiece from left to right, following the pessimistically medieval narrative about humankind's fall from God's graces: In the left panel, at the bottom, God pulls Eve from Adam's rib in the Garden of Eden. Just above that, we see a female (representing the serpent) hold out the forbidden fruit to tempt Eve. Above that, Adam and Eve are being shooed away by an angel. At the top of this panel, God sits on his cloud, evicting the fallen angels (who turn into insect-like monsters). In the middle panel, Christ holds court over the living and the dead. Notice the jarring contrast between Christ's serene expression and the grotesque scene playing out beneath him, where mutant demons slice-and-dice the damned. These disturbing images crescendo in the final (right) panel, showing an unspeakably horrific vision of hell that few artists have managed to top in the more than half-millennium since Bosch.

On your way out of the academy, ponder how history might have been different if the school had accepted a student who applied to study here twice but was always rejected—Adolf Hitler.

## ▲The Secession

This little building, strategically located behind the Academy of Fine Arts, was created by the Vienna Secession movement, a group

of nonconformist artists led by Gustav Klimt, Otto Wagner, and friends. (For more on the art movement, see the sidebar on page 66.)

The young trees carved into the walls and the building's bushy "golden cabbage" rooftop are symbolic of a renewal cycle. Today, The Secession continues to showcase cutting-

SIGHTS

edge art, as well as one of Gustav Klimt's most famous works, the *Beethoven Frieze*.

**Cost and Hours:** €9 includes special exhibits, Tue-Sun 10:00-18:00, closed Mon, audioguide-€3, Friedrichstrasse 12, tel. 01/587-5307, www.secession.at.

**⊃ Self-Guided Tour:** Start in the basement, home to the museum's highlight: Gustav Klimt's classic *Beethoven Frieze*. One of the masterpieces of Viennese Art Nouveau, this 105-foot-long fresco (now somewhat cracked and faded) was the multimedia centerpiece of a 1902 exhibition honoring Ludwig van Beethoven. Klimt's still-powerful work was inspired by Beethoven's *Ninth Symphony*. Klimt em-

bellished the work with painted-on gold (aided by his brother, a goldsmith) and by gluing on reflective glass and mother-of-pearl for the ladies' dresses and jewelry. Working clockwise around the room, follow Klimt's story:

**Left Wall:** Floating female figures drift and weave and search—like we all do—for happiness. Unfortunately, their aspirations are dashed and brought to earth, leaving them kneeling and humble. They plead for help from heroes stronger than themselves—represented by the firm knight in gold, who revives their hopes and helps them carry on.

**Center Wall:** The women encounter many obstacles in their pursuit of happiness—the three dangerous Gorgons (naked ladies with snake hair), the gorilla-faced monster of fear, and the three seductive women of temptation. These obstacles can leave us bent over with grief (like the woman on the right) while our hopes pass by overhead.

**Right Wall:** But we can still find happiness through art, thanks to Lady Poetry (with the lyre) and the great hero of the arts: Beethoven. In the original 1902 exhibition, a statue of Beethoven appeared at this crucial turning point in the narrative, where the blank space is today.

Beethoven's presence inspires the yearning souls to carry on. Swept up in a column of fire, they finally reach true happiness. At the climax of the frieze, a heavenly choir serenades a naked couple embracing in ecstasy, singing the "Ode to Joy"—Friedrich Schiller's poem incorporated into the Ninth Symphony: "Joy, you beautiful spark of the gods...under thy gentle wings, all men shall become brothers."

# Art Nouveau (a.k.a. *Jugendstil* or the Vienna Secession), c. 1896-1914

As Europe approached the dawn of a new *(nouveau)* century, it embraced a new art: Art Nouveau. Though the movement began in Paris and Belgium, each country gave it its own spin. In German-speaking lands (including Austria), Art Nouveau was called *Jugendstil* (meaning "youth style").

## Background

Art Nouveau was forward-looking and modern, embracing the new technology of iron and glass. But it was also a reaction against the sheer ugliness of the mass-produced, boxy, rigidly geometrical art of the Industrial Age. Art Nouveau artists returned to nature (which abhors a straight line) and were inspired by the curves of plants. Art Nouveau street lamps twist and bend like flower stems. Ironwork fountains sprout buds that squirt water. Dining rooms are paneled with leafy garlands of carved wood. Advertising posters feature flowery typefaces and beautiful young women rendered in pure, curving lines. Art Nouveau was a total "look" that could be applied to furniture, jewelry, paintings, and the building itself.

Imagine being a cutting-edge artist in late-19th-century Vienna, surrounded not by creativity, but by conformity. Take, for example, the Ringstrasse, with its Neo-Greek, Neo-Gothic, Neo-Baroque architecture. There was nothing daring or new—it was simply redoing what had already been done (Historicism). This drove Vienna's impatient young generation of artists (Gustav Klimt, Otto Wagner, Egon Schiele, Oskar Kokoschka, and company) to escape, or "secede," from all this conventionalism. They established "The Secession" (Vienna's own *Jugendstil* movement) and transcended into a world of pure beauty, hedonism, eroticism, and aesthetics.

The Secession preferred buildings that were simple and geometrically pure, decorated with a few unadulterated Art Nouveau touches. Architects, painters, and poets had no single unifying style, except a commitment to what was new. The Secessionist motto was: "To each age its art, and to art its liberty."

## Secession Sights

The TI has a free brochure (*Architecture from Art Nouveau to the*

**The Rest of the Secession:** There's a small exhibit of scale models and photos about the construction of the influential Secession building. Finally, don't overlook the interesting temporary exhibits (included in your ticket). An association of 350 members chooses a dozen or so special exhibits each year to highlight local art happenings. They illustrate how the free spirit of Vienna's Secession survives a century after its founding.

*Present*) that lays out Vienna's 20th-century architecture. Here are some of the best *Jugendstil* sights:

**The Secession:** This clean-lined building was the headquarters of The Secession and where young artists first exhibited their "youth-style" art in 1897. It's nicknamed the "golden cabbage" for its bushy gilded rooftop (actually, those are the laurel leaves of Apollo, the God of Poetry) designed by Klimt.

**Belvedere Palace:** This museum's collection includes work by Klimt, who gained fame painting slender young women entwined together in florid embraces, exploring the same highly charged erotic terrain as his contemporary, Sigmund Freud. Klimt took the decorative element of Art Nouveau to extremes (for more about the palace, see page 69).

**The Anchor Clock on Hoher Markt:** This mosaic-decorated clock (1911-1917) was actually an advertisement for a life insurance company. Spanning two buildings, it's full of symbolism, stretching from the butterfly on the left to the Grim Reaper on the right. The clock honors 12 great figures from Vienna's history, from Marcus Aurelius to Joseph Haydn. While each gets his own top-of-the-hour moment, all parade by at high noon in a musical act. A plaque on the left names each figure. Notice the novel way to mark the time.

**Karlsplatz:** Wagner, Vienna's premier *Jugendstil* architect, designed several structures for Vienna's subway system, including these original arched entrances (see page 60).

**Austrian Postal Savings Bank:** This early-20th-century building is a key example of Wagner's modern work (see page 77).

## ▲Naschmarkt

In 1898, the city decided to cover up its Vienna River. The long, wide square they created was filled with a lively produce market that still bustles most days (closed Sun). It's long been known as *the* place to get exotic faraway foods. In fact, locals say, "From here start the Balkans."

**Hours and Location:** Mon-Fri 6:00-18:30, Sat 6:00-17:00,

closed Sun, closes earlier in winter; between Linke Wienzeile and Rechte Wienzeile, U-1, U-2, or U-4: Karlsplatz.

**Visiting the Naschmarkt:** From near the Opera, the Naschmarkt (roughly, "Nibble Market") stretches along Wienzeile street.

This "Belly of Vienna" comes with two parallel lanes—one lined with fun and reasonable eateries, and the other featuring the town's top-end produce and gourmet goodies. This is where top chefs like to get their ingredients. At the gourmet vinegar stall, you can sample the vinegar as you would perfume—with a drop on your wrist (see photo). Farther from the center, the Naschmarkt becomes likably seedy and surrounded by sausage stands, Turkish *Döner Kebab* stalls, cafés, and theaters. At the market's far end is a line of buildings with fine Art Nouveau facades. Each Saturday, the Naschmarkt is infested by a huge flea market where, in olden days, locals would come to hire a monkey to pick little critters out of their hair (flea market sets up west of the Kettenbrückengasse U-Bahn station).

Picnickers can pick up their grub in the market and head over to Karlsplatz (described earlier) or the Burggarten. In recent years, some stalls have been taken over by hip new eateries and bars, bringing a youthful vibe and fun new tastes to the market scene.

### Mariahilfer Strasse

While there are more stately and elegant streets in the central district, the best opportunity to simply feel the pulse of workaday Viennese life is a little farther out, along Mariahilfer Strasse. An easy plan is to ride the U-3 to the Zieglergasse stop, then stroll and browse your way downhill to the MuseumsQuartier U-Bahn station. If you're interested in how Austria handles its people's appetite for marijuana, search out two interesting stores along the way: Bushplanet Headshop (at Esterhazygasse 32, near the Neubaugasse U-Bahn stop) and Bushplanet Growshop (set back in a courtyard off Mariahilfer Strasse at #115, both locations Mon-Fri 10:00-19:00, Sat 10:00-18:00, closed Sun, www.bushplanet.at; see map on page 173).

## MORE SIGHTS BEYOND THE RING

The following museums are located outside the Ringstrasse but inside the Gürtel, or outer ring road.

### South of the Ring
#### ▲▲Belvedere Palace (Schloss Belvedere)

This is the elegant palace of Prince Eugene of Savoy (1663-1736), the still-much-appreciated conqueror of the Ottomans. Eugene, a

Frenchman considered too short and too ugly to be in the service of Louis XIV, offered his services to the Habsburgs. While he was indeed short and ugly, he became the greatest military genius of his age, the savior of Austria, and the toast of Viennese society. When you conquer cities, as Eugene did, you get really rich. With his wealth he built this palace complex. Only Eugene had the cash to compete with the Habsburgs, and from his new palace he looked down on the Hofburg—both literally and figuratively. He lived in the lower palace and entertained in the upper one, which he built to rival Schönbrunn with its similar layout and feel.

Prince Eugene had no heirs, so the state got his property, and Emperor Josef II established the Belvedere as Austria's first great public art gallery. Today you can tour Eugene's lavish palace, see sweeping views of the gardens and the Vienna skyline, and enjoy world-class art starring Gustav Klimt, French Impressionism, and a grab bag of other 19th- and early-20th-century artists. While Vienna's other art collections show off works by masters from around Europe, this has the city's best collection of homegrown artists.

**Cost and Hours:** €12.50 for Upper Belvedere Palace only, €19 for Upper and Lower Palaces (generally not worth it), €25 Prinz Eugen Ticket includes Winter Palace in city center, gardens free except for the Orangerie (included in big tickets); daily 10:00-18:00, Lower Palace only until 21:00 on Wed, grounds open until dusk; audioguide-€4 or €6/2 people, no photos allowed inside; entrance at Prinz-Eugen-Strasse 27, tel. 01/7955-7134, www.belvedere.at.

**Eating at the Belvedere:** There's a charming little café on the ground floor of the Upper Palace, where you can dine with portraits of the emperor and empress looking down upon you; in summer you can sit outdoors in the garden.

**Getting There:** The palace is a 15-minute walk south of the Ring. To get there from the center, catch tram #D at the Opera (direction: Hauptbahnhof). Get off at the Schloss Belvedere stop

## *The Third Man:*
## Movie, Museum, and Fans

Released in 1949 and voted one of the greatest films of all time by the British Film Institute, *The Third Man* is still screened several times a week at Vienna's Burg Kino cinema, and has inspired one of the city's most fascinating museums.

With a screenplay by British novelist Graham Greene, the European *noir* thriller *The Third Man* takes place in post-World War II Vienna—a time when the city was divided, like Berlin, among the four victorious Allies. Rife with intrigue, with a dramatic cemetery scene, coffeehouse culture surviving amid the rubble, and Orson Welles being chased through the sewers, this tale of a divided city afraid of falling under Soviet rule is an enjoyable two-hour experience.

You can catch *The Third Man* in Vienna at the Burg Kino cinema (€7-9, in English; about 2 showings weekly—usually Sun afternoon, and Tue early evening; a block from the Opera at Opernring 19, tel. 01/587-8406, www.burgkino.at).

**The Third Man Museum** (Dritte Mann Museum) is the life's work of Karin Höfler and Gerhard Strassgschwandtner. They have lovingly curated a vast collection of artifacts about the film, postwar Vienna, and the movie's popularity around the world. *Third Man* fans will love the quirky movie artifacts, but even if you're just interested in Vienna in the pre- and postwar years, the museum is worthwhile. Displays cover the 1930s, when Austria was ripe for the *Anschluss* (annexation with Germany); the plight of 1.7 million displaced people in Austria after the war; the challenges of de-Nazification after 1945; and candid interviews with soldiers. As a bonus, the museum takes a fascinating look at moviemaking and marketing around 1950.

Don't be shy about asking for a personal tour from Gerhard or Karin (€7.50, Sat only 14:00-18:00, or by appointment for *Third Man* nuts; also some guided tours on summer Wed at 14:00—confirm on website; private showings for groups, U4: Kettenbrückengasse, a long block south of the Naschmarkt at Pressgasse 25, tel. 01/586-4872, www.3mpc.net).

(just below the Upper Palace gate), cross the street, walk uphill one block, go through the gate (on left), and look immediately to the right for the small building with the ticket office.

**◒ Self-Guided Tour:** The Belvedere Palace is actually two grand buildings—the Upper Palace and Lower Palace—separated by a fine garden. For our purposes, the **Upper Palace** is what matters. Buy your ticket at the office behind the palace, then go around to the front to enter. Once inside, the palace's eclectic collection is tailor-made for browsing. There are two grand floors, set around impressive middle halls.

**Ground Floor:** The main floor displays a collection of Austrian

Baroque (on the left) and medieval art (on the right). The Baroque section includes a fascinating room of grotesquely grimacing heads by **Franz Xaver Messerschmidt** (1736-1783), a quirky 18th-century Habsburg court sculptor who left the imperial life to follow his own, somewhat deranged muse. After his promising career was cut short by mental illness, Messerschmidt relocated to Bratislava and spent the rest of his days sculpting a series of eerily lifelike "character heads" *(Kopfstücke)*. Their most unusual faces are contorted by extreme emotions. They're not just smiling but guffawing; not just frightened but terrified; not just in pain but in agony; not just angry but furious. Strolling through this collection made my cheeks hurt. Messerschmidt served as his own model for these works, pinching himself to create a pain reaction he could replicate in stone. Stroll around the circle.

• *From the entrance, climb the staircase to the **first floor** and enter the grand red-and-gold, chandeliered...*

**Marble Hall:** This was Prince Eugene's party room. The ceiling fresco shows Eugene (in the center, wearing blue and pink) about to be crowned with a laurel wreath for his military victories and contributions to Vienna. While it's easy to think of the palace as a museum, see it also as a monument to a military hero. It's strewn with images of war in which the adversaries wear lots of turbans, as some of Austria's enemies were Muslims. Look for small copper engravings that show the rooms as they looked in Eugene's day.

*Belvedere* means "beautiful view," and the **view from the Marble Hall** is especially spectacular. Look over the Baroque gardens,

the mysterious sphinxes (which symbolized solving riddles and the finely educated mind of your host, Eugene), the Lower Palace, and the city. Left to right, find the green dome of St. Peter's Church, the spire of St. Stephen's (where Eugene is buried, see page 115), and much nearer, the black dome of the Silesian Church. St. Stephen's spire is 400 feet tall, and no other tall buildings are allowed inside the Ringstrasse. The hills beyond—covered with vineyards—are where the Viennese love to go to sample new wine. Behind the spire you can see Kahlenberg, from where you can walk down to several recommended *Heurigen* (wine gardens—

SIGHTS

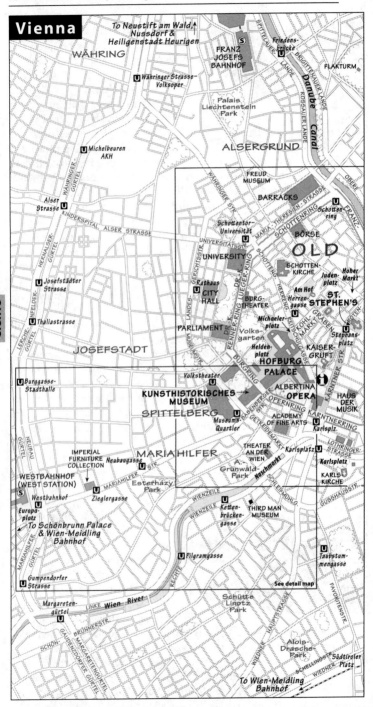

# Vienna

To Neustift am Wald,
Nussdorf &
Heiligenstadt Heurigen

WÄHRING

FRANZ
JOSEFS
BAHNHOF

Friedens-
brücke

FLAKTURM

Danube Canal

Währinger Strasse-
Volksoper

Palais
Liechtenstein
Park

Michelbeuren
AKH

ALSERGRUND

FREUD
MUSEUM

BARRACKS

Schotten-
ring

Alser
Strasse

Schottentor-
Universität

BÖRSE

OLD

Josefstädter
Strasse

UNIVERSITY

SCHOTTEN-
KIRCHE

Juden-
platz

Hoher
Markt

Thaliastrasse

Rathaus
CITY
HALL

BURG-
THEATER

Am Hof
Herren-
gasse

ST.
STEPHEN'S

JOSEFSTADT

PARLIAMENT

Michaeler-
platz

Volks-
garten

Stephans-
platz

Helden-
platz

HOFBURG
PALACE

KAISER-
GRUFT

Burggasse-
Stadthalle

Volkstheater

KUNSTHISTORISCHES
MUSEUM

ALBERTINA

OPERA

HAUS
DER
MUSIK

SPITTELBERG

Museums
Quartier

ACADEMY
OF FINE ARTS

Karlspl.

IMPERIAL
FURNITURE
COLLECTION

Neubaugasse

MARIAHILFER

THEATER
AN DER
WIEN

Karlsplatz

Karlsplatz

WESTBAHNHOF
(WEST STATION)

MARIAHILFER

A.
Grünwald-
Park

Naschmarkt

KARLS
KIRCHE

Westbahnhof

Esterházy
Park

Zieglergasse

WIENZEILE

Europa-
platz

WIENZEILE

Ketten-
brücken-
gasse

THIRD MAN
MUSEUM

To Schönbrunn Palace
& Wien-Meidling
Bahnhof

Gumpendorfer
Strasse

Pilgramgasse

Taubstum-
mengasse

See detail map

Margareten-
gürtel

LINKE Wien Rivet

Schütte
Linotz
Park

To Wien-Meidling
Bahnhof

Alois-
Drasche-
Park

Südtiroler
Platz

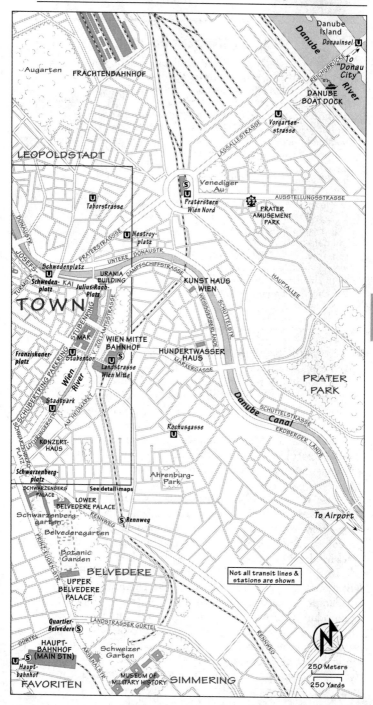

**SIGHTS**

Danube Island
*Donauinsel* U

To "Donau City"

Danube River

Augarten  FRACHTENBAHNHOF

DANUBE BOAT DOCK

*Vorgarten-strasse* U

LEOPOLDSTADT

LASSALLESTRASSE

AUSSTELLUNGSSTRASSE

*Taborstrasse* U

S U
*Praterstern Wien Nord*

Venediger Au

PRATER AMUSEMENT PARK

*Nestroy-platz* U

PRATERSTRASSE
UNTERE DONAUSTR.

DONAUSTR.

*Schwedenplatz* U
JOSEFS

*Schweden-platz* U
TURMR.
KAI
*Julius-Raab-Platz*

URANIA BUILDING
DAMPFSCHIFFSTRASSE

KUNST HAUS WIEN

HAUPTALLEE

TOWN

WEISSGERBERLÄNDE

SCHÜTTELSTR.

STUBENRING

MAK

WIEN MITTE BAHNHOF

HUNDERTWASSER HAUS

*Franziskaner-platz*

*Stubentor* U

Wien River

ZOLLAMTSSTRASSE

S
*Landstrasse Wien Mitte*

MARKERGASSE

PRATER PARK

*Stadtpark* U

SCHUBERTRING PARKING

AM HEUMARKT

*Rochusgasse* U

SCHÜTTELSTRASSE

Danube Canal

ERDBERGER LÄNDE

KONZERT-HAUS

LOTHRINGERSTR.

SCHWARZENBERG-PLATZ

*Schwarzenberg-platz*

Ahrenburg-Park

See detail maps

SCHWARZENBERG PALACE

LOWER BELVEDERE PALACE

*Schwarzenberg-garten*

RENNWEG

S *Rennweg*

To Airport

Belvederegarten

Botanic Garden

PRINZ-EUGEN-STR.

BELVEDERE

Not all transit lines & stations are shown

UPPER BELVEDERE PALACE

*Quartier-Belvedere* S

LANDSTRASSER GÜRTEL

N

GÜRTEL

HAUPT-BAHNHOF (MAIN STN)

ARSENALSTR.

RENNWEG

U S
*Haupt-bahnhof*

Schweizer Garten

250 Meters

FAVORITEN

MUSEUM OF MILITARY HISTORY

SIMMERING

250 Yards

## Gustav Klimt (1862-1918)

Klimt, a noted womanizer, made a career painting the female form as beautiful, seductive, and dangerous. His erotic paintings scandalized official Vienna, and he was a founder of the Secessionist art group, whose members "seceded" from bourgeois constraints. He dedicated his later years to works commissioned by the liberal elite.

Klimt explored multimedia. Besides oil paints, he painted with gold leaf or applied bright objects to the canvas/panel for decorative effect. He often worked in a square-frame format. (Occasionally he and his brother, a gold engraver, made the frames as well.) There's no strong perspective in his paintings; the background and foreground are merged together into a flat decorative pattern. His women are clearly drawn, emerging from the complex design. With their come-hither looks and erotic poses, they capture the overripe beauty and edgy decadence of turn-of-the-century Vienna.

SIGHTS

see page 192). These hills are the beginnings of the Alps, which stretch from here all the way to France.

The square you're overlooking was filled with people on May 15, 1955, as city leaders stood on the balcony just in front of you and proclaimed the famous words "Austria is free"—heralding Austrian independence after the decade-long Allied occupation following World War II. The Allied powers—France, Great Britain, the US, and the Soviet Union—signed the treaty re-establishing Austria as a sovereign country right here in the Marble Hall.

• Facing the garden, to the right is the...

**East Wing:** Alongside Renoir's ladies, Monet's landscapes, and Van Gogh's rough brushstrokes are similar works by their lesser-known Austrian counterparts. Around 1900, Austrian artists come to the fore, soaking up Symbolism, Expressionism, and other Modernist trends.

In the two rooms full of sumptuous paintings by **Gustav Klimt,** you can get caught up in his fascination with the beauty and danger he saw in women. To Klimt, all art was erotic art. He painted during the turn of the century, when Vienna was a splendid laboratory of hedonism. For him, Eve was the prototypical woman; her body, not the apple, provided the seduction. Frustrated by the censorship of his age, Klimt refused every form of state support. Even fully clothed, his women have a bewitching eroticism in a world full of pollen and pistils.

The famous painting of *Judith I* (1901) shows no biblical hero-ine—Klimt paints her as a high-society Vienna woman with an os-tentatious dog-collar necklace. With half-closed eyes and slightly parted lips, she's dismissive...yet mysterious and bewitching. Hold-ing the head of her biblical victim, she's the modern femme fatale.

In what is perhaps Klimt's best-known painting, *The Kiss*, two lovers are wrapped up in the colorful gold-and-jeweled cloak of bliss. Klimt's woman is no longer dominating, but submissive, abandoning herself to her man in a fertile field and a vast universe. In a glow emanating from a radiance of desire, the body she press-es against is a self-portrait of the artist himself. Look at it with your partner and search for meaning. Don't miss the later but also hauntingly beautiful Klimt paintings that hang nearby.

Klimt nurtured the next generation of artists, especially **Egon Schiele.** While Klimt's works are mystical and other-worldly, Schiele's tend to be darker and more introspective. One of Schiele's most recognizable works, *The Embrace*, shows a couple engaged in an erotically charged, rippling moment of passion. Striking a darker tone is *The Family*, which depicts a crouching couple. This family portrait from 1918 is especially poignant be-cause his wife died while he was still working on it. (Schiele and his child were soon taken by the influenza epidemic that swept through Europe after World War I.) There's also a room of Schiele portraits, including *Mother with Two Children*.

**The Rest of the Upper Palace:** The Belvedere's collection goes through the whole range of 19th- and 20th-century art: Histori-cism, Romanticism, Impressionism, Realism, tired tourism, Ex-pressionism, Art Nouveau, and early Modernism. In the west wing of the first floor are some **Max Oppenheimer** portraits, famous for the way they almost comically exaggerate the subjects' features to demonstrate their personality traits.

The **second floor** shows off early 19th-century paintings in the Biedermeier style. This was the period (1815-1848) when conser-vative elements in Central Europe clamped down on Napoleon's revolutionary ideas. The paintings here are realistic portraits, land-scapes, and scenes from everyday life and from history, as well as Romanticism. The style is soft-focus, hypersensitive, super-sweet, and sentimentally Romantic—the poor are happy, things are lit impossibly well, and folk life is idealized. (Then came the demo-cratic revolutions of 1848, the invention of the camera, Realism and Impressionism...and all hell broke loose.)

**Grounds and Gardens:** The delightfully manicured grounds are free and fun to explore. The only area with an entry fee is the **Orangerie garden,** along the west side of the Lower Palace (and accessed through that palace).

**Lower Palace:** Covered by a separate ticket, this is the home where Prince Eugene actually hung his helmet. Today it contains a small stretch of three of his private apartments (relatively uninteresting compared to the sumptuous Habsburg apartments elsewhere in town). The Lower Palace also houses some generally good special exhibits, as well as the entrance to the Orangerie, privy

garden, and stables (until 12:00). If the special exhibits intrigue you, it's worth buying the combo-ticket to get in here; otherwise, I wouldn't bother to visit.

## East of the Ring
### Museum of Applied Arts (Museum für Angewandte Kunst)

Facing the Old Town from across the Ring, the MAK, as it's called, is a design museum best known for its collection of furniture and decorative art from Vienna's artistic golden age (around 1900).

**Cost and Hours:** €8, free Tue after 18:00; open Wed-Sun 10:00-18:00, Tue 10:00-22:00, closed Mon; Stubenring 5, U-3: Stubentor, tel. 01/711-360, www.mak.at.

**Visiting the Museum:** There are three floors. The permanent "Vienna 1900" exhibit on the top floor is usually most visitors' main destination, and the MAK Design Lab (MAK Design Labor in German) in the basement is also worth seeing. The ground-floor collections (Asian, Baroque, and carpets) are skippable for most. The unique gift shop makes for a fun diversion.

Fans of the graphic arts and furniture design will want to see the three-room **Vienna 1900** exhibit. The walls are lined with a fine collection of period posters. Check out Joseph von Storck's 1889 bound book for the anniversary of a local museum (in a glass cabinet). The "less-is-more" approach is represented by Josef Hoffman's functional chairs and desks, and a complete bedroom installation by Margaret Schütte-Lihotsky. A wooden relief of the goddess Diana, by Carl Otto Czeschka, is impressive. You'll also find nine sketches by Gustav Klimt for a frieze on the wall of a mansion in Belgium (incorporating a version of *The Kiss*). The collection follows local designers as they moved from Historicism through Art Nouveau and on to Modernism and Internationalism.

The **MAK Design Lab** is a big, up-to-date exhibit that's partly conventional (you look at lots of old stuff)—but presented in a way that strives to engage visitors with the design challenges of everyday life, such as sitting, reading, eating, sorting and holding things, clothing ourselves, and using resources sustainably. Daringly constructed, it takes a bit of time to appreciate, as you walk from station to station devoted to each of these themes.

# Restitution of Art Stolen by Nazis

The Austrian government has worked to fairly reimburse victims of the Nazis, whose buildings, businesses, personal belongings, and art were taken after the 1938 *Anschluss* (when Germany annexed Austria).

A fund of more than $200 million was established by the Austrian government and corporations that profited through collaboration with the Nazis. Surviving locals (mostly Jews) who paid a *Reichsfluchtsteuer* ("tax for fleeing the country") were located and given some money. Former slave laborers were also tracked down and given €5,000 each.

Most significantly for sightseers, great art was restored to its rightful owners. The big news for the Vienna art world was the return of several Gustav Klimt paintings to their former owners, most notably Klimt's portrait of Adele Bloch-Bauer, which for years was part of Vienna's Belvedere Palace collection. The painting was restored to Adele's heirs living in America, who in 2006 sold the portrait for $135 million—one of the highest prices ever paid for a painting. The Austrian government had an opportunity to buy back the portrait, but decided against it. Fortunately for art viewers visiting Vienna, the most famous Klimt *(The Kiss)* remains in the Belvedere Palace. And the Adele portrait? It is now in the collection of the Neue Galerie, a New York City museum devoted to early-20th-century German and Austrian art and design.

**SIGHTS**

**Eating:** The **Restaurant Österreicher im MAK,** accessed through the gift shop, is named not for the country but for its renowned chef (Helmut Österreicher). Classy and mod, it's trendy for locals, if even a bit pretentious (€10 weekday lunches, €10-23 main dishes, pricier fixed-price meals, food served 11:30-15:00 & 18:00-23:00, reserve for evening, tel. 01/714-0121, www. oesterreicherimmak.at).

## Austrian Postal Savings Bank
### (Die Österreichische Postsparkasse)

Built between 1904 and 1912, the Postal Savings Bank was one of the key buildings in the development of modern architecture.

Today it's a pilgrimage site for architects from all over the world (for whom it's a ▲▲▲ sight). It's still a bank (though private now). You can enter the atrium for free, and visit a pleasant, small museum that tells the building's story in both German and English.

**Cost and Hours:** Foyer and atrium—free, museum—€6 (get tickets from counter 14 in the atrium); open Mon-Fri 10:00-17:00, closed Sat-Sun; just inside the Ringstrasse at Georg-Coch-Platz 2, tel. 059-9053-3825, www.ottowagner.com.

**Visiting the Postal Savings Bank:** The postal savings system was intended for working-class people, who didn't have access to the palatial banks of the 19th century—but could walk to a post office. Secessionist architect Otto Wagner believed "necessity is the master of art," and he declared that "what is impractical can never be beautiful." Everything about his design—so gray, white, and efficient—is practical. It's so clean that the service provided here feels almost sacred. This is a textbook example of form following function, and the form is beautiful.

The product of an age giddy with advancement, the **building** dignifies the technological and celebrates it as cultural. Study the sleek, yet elegantly modern exterior: Angles high above—made of an exciting new material, aluminum—seem to proclaim the modern age. The facade and its unadorned marble siding panels, secured by aluminum bolts, give the impression that the entire building is a safe-deposit box. The interior is similarly functionalist. The glass roof lets in light; the glass floor helps illuminate the basement. Fixtures, vents, and even the furniture fit right in—all bold, geometrical, and modern.

The **museum** goes into considerable detail on the building, including plans, photos, and news reports, and preserves the original bank-teller counters.

## ▲Museum of Military History (Heeresgeschichtliches Museum)

While much of the Habsburg Empire was built on strategic marriages rather than the spoils of war, a big part of Habsburg history is military. And this huge place, built about 1860 as an arsenal by Franz Josef, tells the story well with a thoughtful motto (apparently learned from the school of hard knocks): "War belongs to museums."

**Cost and Hours:** €6, includes good audioguide, free first Sun of the month, open daily 9:00-17:00, on Arsenalstrasse, tel. 01/795-610, www.hgm.or.at. It's a 5-minute walk from the Hauptbahnhof, or a 10-minute walk behind the Belvedere Palace.

**Visiting the Museum:** You'll wander the wings of this vast museum nearly all alone. Its two floors hold a rich collection of artifacts and historic treasures from the times of Maria Theresa to Prince Eugene to Franz Josef. The particularly interesting 20th-century section includes exhibits devoted to Sarajevo in 1914 (with the car Franz Ferdinand rode in and the uniform he wore when he was assassinated), Chancellor Dolfuss and the pre-Hitler Austrian Fascist party, the *Anschluss*, and World War II.

## ▲Kunst Haus Wien Museum and Hundertwasserhaus

This "make yourself at home" museum and nearby apartment complex are a hit with lovers of modern art, mixing the work and phi-

losophy of local painter/environmentalist Friedensreich Hundertwasser (1928-2000), a.k.a. "100H$_2$O."

**Cost and Hours:** €10 for museum, €12 combo-ticket includes special exhibitions, half-price on Mon, open daily 10:00-19:00, extremely fragrant and colorful garden café, tel. 01/712-0491, www.kunsthauswien.com.

**Getting There:** It's located at Untere Weissgerberstrasse 13, near the Radetzkyplatz stop on trams #O and #1 (signs point the way). By U-Bahn, take U-3 or U-4 to Landstrasse and either walk 10 minutes downhill (north) along Untere Viaduktgasse (a block east of the station), or transfer to tram #O (direction: Praterstern) and ride three stops to Radetzkyplatz.

**Visiting the Museum and Apartments:** Stand in front of the colorful checkerboard building that houses the **Kunst Haus Wien Museum.** Consider Hundertwasser's style. He was against "window racism": Neighboring houses allow only one kind of window, but 100H$_2$O's windows are each different—and he encouraged residents in the Hundertwasserhaus (a 5-10 minute walk away, described later) to personalize them. He recognized "tree tenants" as well as human tenants. His buildings are spritzed with a forest and topped with dirt and grassy little parks—close to nature and good for the soul.

Floors and sidewalks are irregular—to "stimulate the brain" (although current residents complain it just causes wobbly furniture and sprained ankles). Thus 100H$_2$O waged a one-man fight—during the 1950s and 1960s, when concrete and glass ruled—to save the human soul from the city. (Hundertwasser claimed that "straight lines are godless.")

Inside the museum, start with his interesting biography. His fun paintings are half psychedelic *Jugendstil* and half just kids' stuff. Notice the photographs from his 1950s days as part of Vienna's bohemian scene. Throughout the museum, keep an eye out for the fun philosophical quotes from an artist who believed, "If man is creative, he comes nearer to his creator."

The Kunst Haus Wien provides by far the best look at Hundertwasser, but for an actual lived-in apartment complex by the green master, walk 5-10 minutes to the one-with-nature **Hunder-**

**SIGHTS**

twasserhaus (at Löwengasse and Kegelgasse). This complex of 50 apartments, subsidized by the government to provide affordable housing, was built in the 1980s as a breath of architectural fresh air in a city of boring, blocky apartment complexes. While not open to visitors, it's worth visiting for its fun and colorful patchwork exterior and the Hundertwasser festival of shops across the street. Don't miss the view from Kegelgasse to see the "tree tenants" and the internal winter garden that residents enjoy.

Hundertwasser detractors—of which there are many—remind visitors that $100H_2O$ was a painter, not an architect. They describe the Hundertwasserhaus as a "1950s house built in the 1980s" that was colorfully painted with no real concern for the environment, communal living, or even practical comfort. Almost all of the original inhabitants got fed up with the novelty and moved out.

## North of the Ring
### Sigmund Freud Museum

Freud enthusiasts (and detractors) enjoy seeing the apartment and home office of the man who fundamentally changed our understanding of the human psyche. Dr. Sigmund Freud (1856-1939), a graduate of Vienna University, established his practice here in 1891. For the next 47 years, he received troubled patients who hoped to find peace by telling him their dreams, life traumas, and secret urges. It was here that he wrote his influential works, including the landmark *Interpretation of Dreams* (1899). The museum is narrowly focused on Freud's life. If you're looking for a critical appraisal of whether he was a cocaine-addicted charlatan or a sincere doctor groping toward an understanding of human nature, you won't find it here.

**Cost and Hours:** €9, includes audioguide, daily 10:00-18:00, tiny bookshop, half a block from the Schlickgasse stop on tram #D, Berggasse 19, tel. 01/319-1596, www.freud-museum.at.

**Visiting the Museum:** Freud's three-room office has been turned into a permanent display on his life, while the larger apartment (where he lived with his family) is used for temporary exhibits. Freud, who was Jewish, fled Vienna for England when the Nazis came to power. He took most of his possessions with him, including the famous couch that patients reclined on (now in a

London museum), so the museum doesn't really give you a feel for how he lived.

In the office entryway, you can see Freud's cane, hat, pocket flask, and a few other objects. The waiting room is the most furnished, with original furniture, his books, and his collection of primitive fertility figurines. The consulting room and study are lined with old photos and documents that trace Freud's fascinating life: a happy childhood (first in a small Moravian town, then in Vienna); medical school in the then-pioneering field of psychology; research into the effects of cocaine; a happy marriage, large family, and wholesome middle-class lifestyle; use of hypnosis as therapy; years of self-analysis and first patients in analysis; publication of controversial works on dreams and sexuality; association with other budding psychologists such as the Swiss Carl Jung; and, finally, his hard-earned recognition and worldwide fame. A binder, loaned to visitors, complements the more general audioguide with detailed (if tedious) descriptions.

### West of the Ring, on Mariahilfer Strasse
#### ▲Imperial Furniture Collection (Hofmobiliendepot)
Bizarre, sensuous, eccentric, or precious, this collection (on four fascinating floors) is your peek at the Habsburgs' furniture—from the empress's wheelchair ("to increase her fertility she was put on a rich diet and became corpulent") to the emperor's spittoon—all thoughtfully described in English. Evocative paintings help bring the furniture to life. The Habsburgs had many palaces, but only the Hofburg was permanently furnished. The rest were done on the fly—set up and taken down by a gang of royal roadies called the "Depot of Court Movables" (Hofmobiliendepot). When the monarchy was dissolved in 1918, the state of Austria took possession of the Hofmobiliendepot's inventory—165,000 items. Now this royal storehouse is open to the public in a fine and sprawling museum. Don't go here for the *Jugendstil* furnishings. The older Baroque, Rococo, and Biedermeier pieces are the most impressive and tied most intimately to the royals. Combine a visit to this museum with a stroll down the lively shopping boulevard, Mariahilfer Strasse.

**Cost and Hours:** €8.50, covered by Sisi Ticket (see page 25), Tue-Sun 10:00-18:00, closed Mon, Mariahilfer Strasse 88, main entrance around the corner at Andreasgasse 7, U-3: Zieglergasse, tel. 01/5243-3570, www.hofmobiliendepot.at.

SIGHTS

## ▲▲▲SCHÖNBRUNN PALACE (SCHLOSS SCHÖNBRUNN)

Among Europe's palaces, only Schönbrunn rivals Versailles. This former summer residence of the Habsburgs is big, with 1,441 rooms. But don't worry—only 40 rooms are shown to the public. Of the plethora of sights at the vast complex, the highlight is a tour of the palace's Royal Apartments—the chandeliered rooms where the Habsburg nobles lived. You can also stroll the gardens, tour the coach museum, and visit a handful of lesser sights nearby.

Schönbrunn is sprawling and can be mobbed with tourists. Here's how I'd plan my time for an efficient visit: First, see the Royal Apartments with the Grand Tour ticket, reserved in advance to avoid crowds (details below). After the Royal Apartments, wander the gardens, which are free. With more time and energy, pick-and-choose among the other sightseeing options and buy tickets as you go. Allow at least three hours (including transit time) for your excursion to Schönbrunn.

**Getting There:** While on the outskirts of Vienna, Schönbrunn is an easy 10-minute subway ride from downtown. Take U-4 (which conveniently leaves from Karlsplatz) to Schönbrunn (direction: Hütteldorf) and follow signs for *Schloss Schönbrunn*. Exit bearing right, then cross the busy road and continue to the right, to the far, far end of the long yellow building. There you'll find the visitors center, where tickets are sold.

**Hours:** Royal Apartments—daily July-Aug 8:30-18:30, April-June and Sept-Oct 8:30-17:30, Nov-March 8:30-17:00, last entry 30 minutes before closing; gardens—generally open 6:30-20:00.

**Cost:** The Royal Apartments offer two tour options: The best is the 40-room **Grand Tour** (€14.50, 50 minutes, includes audioguide), which covers both the rooms of Franz Josef and Sisi, as well as the (more-impressive) Rococo rooms of Maria Theresa. The **Imperial Tour** (€11.50, 35 minutes, includes audioguide) covers only the less-interesting first 22 rooms.

If venturing beyond the apartments, consider a combo-ticket: The **Classic Pass** includes the Grand Tour, as well as other sights on the grounds—the Gloriette viewing terrace, maze, and privy garden (€18.50, available April-Oct only). The **Classic Pass Plus** adds on an *Apfelstrudel* demo and tasting (€21.50, available April-Oct only). Note that the **Sisi Ticket** (€25.50; see page 25) gives you the Schönbrunn Grand Tour (with no waiting in line), plus the

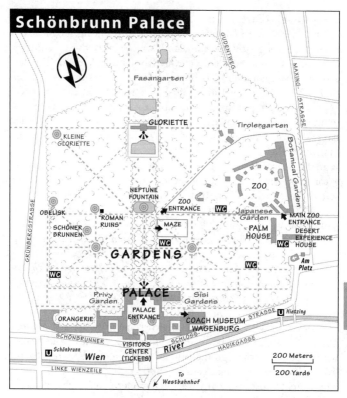

**Schönbrunn Palace**

Fasangarten

GLORIETTE

Tirolergarten

KLEINE
GLORIETTE

Botanical Garden

MAXINGSTRASSE

GUDENTWEG

NEPTUNE
FOUNTAIN

ZOO

ZOO
ENTRANCE

WC

Japanese
Garden

OBELISK

"ROMAN
RUINS"

MAZE

SCHÖNER
BRUNNEN

WC

PALM
HOUSE

MAIN ZOO
ENTRANCE

DESERT
EXPERIENCE
HOUSE

WC

GRÜNBERGSTRASSE

G A R D E N S

WC

Am
Platz

WC

SIGHTS

Privy
Garden

PALACE

Sisi
Gardens

ORANGERIE

PALACE
ENTRANCE

COACH MUSEUM
WAGENBURG

SCHLOSS STRASSE

Hietzing

SCHÖNBRUNNER

VISITORS
CENTER
(TICKETS)

River

HADIKGASSE

Schönbrunn

Wien

To
Westbahnhof

LINKE WIENZEILE

200 Meters

200 Yards

Hofburg Imperial Apartments (in town) and the Imperial Furniture Collection.

**Reservations:** In summer and good-weather weekends, definitely make a reservation. Otherwise, you'll likely have to wait in line at the ticket desk, and then wait again until your assigned entry time—which could be hours later. Book your ticket at www.schoenbrunn.at, where you reserve an entry time, then print your ticket (or ask your hotel to print it for you). Tickets can also be reserved by phone and picked up at the visitors center (tel. 01/8111-3239). Those with a Sisi Ticket can enter without a reserved entry time.

**Other Crowd-Beating Tips:** Even with a reserved entry time, the palace can be a jam-packed sauna of shoulder-to-shoulder mobs shuffling through. It's busiest from 9:30 to 11:30. Crowds start to subside after 14:00. Without a reservation, come late in the day. If you have time to kill before your entry time, spend it exploring the gardens or Coach Museum.

**Information:** Tel. 01/8111-3239, www.schoenbrunn.at. No photos in the Royal Apartments.

### ▲▲▲Royal Apartments

In the 1500s, the Habsburgs built a small hunting lodge near a beautiful spring (*schön-brunn*), and for the next three centuries, they made it their summer getaway from stuffy Vienna. The palace's exterior (late-1600s) is Baroque, but the interior was finished under Maria Theresa (mid-1700s) in let-them-eat-cake Rococo. As with the similar apartments at the Hofburg (the Habsburgs' winter home), these apartments give you a sense of the quirky, larger-than-life personalities who lived here. It's the place where matronly Maria Theresa raised her brood of 16 kids...where six-year-old Mozart played his first big gig...and where Maria Theresa's great-great-grandson Franz Josef (r. 1848-1916) tried to please his self-absorbed wife Elisabeth, a.k.a. Sisi.

**◑ Self-Guided Tour:** Your tour of the apartments, accompanied by an audioguide, follows a clearly signed one-way route. Think of the following mini-tour as a series of bread crumbs, leading you along while the audioguide fills in the details.

• *With your ticket in hand, approach the palace. Follow signs to the entrance gate stamped on your ticket (A, B, C, etc.). When your entry time arrives, don't be shy: Politely push your way through the milling crowds to get to the ticket taker.*

Begin in the **Guards' Room,** where jauntily dressed mannequins of Franz Josef's bodyguards introduce you to his luxurious world. Continue through the Billiard Room to the **Walnut Room.** Wow. Rococo-style wood paneling and gilding decorate this room where Franz Josef—a hard-working modern monarch—received official visitors. Nearby is the **Study**—Franz Josef (see his mustachioed portrait) worked at this desk, sometimes joined by his beautiful, brown-haired wife Sisi (see her portrait). In the **Bedroom,** there are a praying stool, iron bed, and little toilet, which attest to Franz Josef's spartan lifestyle.

• *As you turn the corner, you enter...*

**Empress Sisi's Study and Dressing Room:** See her portrait in a black dress, as well as (a reconstruction of) the spiral staircase that once led down to her apartments. The long-haired mannequin and makeup jars in the dressing room indicate how obsessive Sisi was about her looks.

• *Pass through this room to reach...*

**Franz Josef's and Sisi's Bedroom:** The huge wood-carved double bed suggests marital bliss, but the bed is not authentic—and as for the bliss, history suggests otherwise. Nearby is **Sisi's Salon.** Though this was Sisi's reception room, the pastel paintings show her husband's distinguished ancestors—the many children of Maria Theresa (including Marie-Antoinette, immediately to the left as you enter).

Follow along to the **Dining Room.** The whole family ate here at the huge table; today it's set with dinnerware owned by Maria Theresa and Sisi. Next is the **Children's Room,** with portraits of Maria Theresa (on the easel) and some of her 11 (similar-looking) daughters. The bathroom was installed for the last Habsburg empress, Zita.

• *Turning the corner, pass through two rooms, until you reach the...*

**Hall of Mirrors:** In this room, six-year-old Mozart performed for the family (1762). He amazed them by playing without being able to see the keys, he jumped playfully into Maria Theresa's lap, and he even asked six-year-old Marie-Antoinette to marry him.

• *Pass through the next three rooms, which lead to the large, breathtaking, white-and-gold...*

**Great Gallery:** Imagine the parties they had here: waltzers spinning across the floor, lit by chandeliers reflecting off the mirrors, beneath stunning ceiling frescoes, while enjoying views of the gardens and a decorative monument called the Gloriette (described later). When WWII bombs rained on Vienna, the palace was largely spared. It took only one direct hit—crashing through this ballroom—but, thankfully, that bomb was a dud. In 1961, President Kennedy and Soviet Premier Khrushchev met here.

• *Pass through the final three rooms (pausing at a painting of Maria Theresa riding a Lipizzaner horse) until you reach the...*

**Hall of Ceremonies:** Wedding receptions were held here, beneath a regal portrait of Maria Theresa in a pink lace dress.

• *If you've bought the Grand Tour ticket, you can continue on. As you prepare to exit, look to the left of the doorway to find a crowded painting with (supposedly) a picture of the child Mozart (sitting next to a priest in grey). The next room is the...*

**Blue Chinese Salon:** It was here, in 1918, that the last Habsburg emperor made the decision to relinquish power. The nearby black-lacquer **Vieux-Laque Room** may convince you the Grand Tour ticket was worth it. Continue to the **Napoleon Room.** When Napoleon conquered Austria, he took over Schönbrunn and made this his bedroom. He dumped Josephine and took a Habsburg princess as his bride, and they had a son (cutely pictured holding a wreath of flowers).

• *Turn the corner through the Porcelain Room and enter the stunning...*

**Millions Room:** Admire the rosewood paneling inset with little painted scenes, and see how the mirrors reflect to infinity.

• *We're nearing the end. Pass through three (admittedly gorgeous) rooms, and turn the corner into the...*

**Rich Room:** This darkened room has what may have been Maria Theresa's wedding bed, where she and her husband Franz produced 16 children. Then comes the **Study,** with a fitting end to this palace tour—a painting showing the happy couple who left their mark all over Schönbrunn. Maria Theresa and Franz are surrounded by their brood. Imagine these kids growing up here, riding horses, frolicking in the gardens, and preparing to marry fellow royals in order to bring peace and prosperity to the happy house of Habsburg.

### ▲▲Palace Gardens and Nearby Sights

The large, manicured grounds fill the palace's backyard, dominated by a hill-topping monument called the Gloriette. Unlike the gardens of Versailles, meant to shut out the real world, Schönbrunn's park was opened to the public in 1779 while the monarchy was in full swing. It was part of Maria Theresa's reform policy, making the garden a celebration of the evolution of civilization from autocracy into real democracy.

Today it's a delightful, sprawling place to wander—especially on a sunny day. You can spend hours here, enjoying the views and the people-watching. And most of the park is free, as it has been for more than two centuries (open daily sunrise to dusk, entrance on either side of the palace).

**Getting Around the Gardens:** A **tourist train** makes the rounds all day, connecting Schönbrunn's many attractions (€6, 2/hour in peak season, none Nov-mid-March, one-hour circuit). Unfortunately, there's no bike rental nearby.

**Visiting the Gardens:** The gardens are laid out on angled, tree-lined axes that gradually incline, offering dramatic views back to the palace. The small side gardens flanking the palace are the most elaborate: to the left of the palace is the **Privy Garden/Crown Prince Garden** (*Kronprinzengarten*, €3); to the right are the free **Sisi Gardens.** Better yet, just explore, using a map (such as the one in this book, or pick one up at the palace). Highlights include several whimsical **fountains,** such as the faux "Roman ruins," the obelisk, and the Neptune Fountain (straight back from the palace). Next to the Neptune Fountain is a kid-friendly **maze** *(Irrgarten)* and playground area (€4.50).

If the weather is good, huff up the zigzag path above the Neptune Fountain to the **Gloriette,** a purely decorative monument celebrating an obscure Austrian military victory. You can pay for a pricey drink in the café, shell out €3 to hike up to the viewing terrace, or skip the whole thing, as views are about as good from the lawn in front (included in Schönbrunn passes described earlier, daily April-Sept 9:00-18:00, July-Aug until 19:00, Oct 9:00-17:00, closed Nov-March).

*Nearby Sights:* To the right of the palace is a large zoo complex and several affiliated sights. Europe's oldest **zoo** *(Tiergarten)*  was built by Maria Theresa's husband for the entertainment and education of the court in 1752 (€16.50, daily April-Sept 9:00-18:30, closes earlier off-season, tel. 01/877-9294, www.zoovienna.at). Nearby are two skippable sights. The **palm house** *(Palmenhaus)*, with its stately green ribcage on the outside, is disappointing inside (€4, daily May-Sept 9:30-18:00, Oct-April 9:30-17:00, last entry 30 minutes before closing). Likewise, the **Desert Experience House** *(Wüstenhaus)*, featuring desert flora and fauna in an arid climate, is nothing special (€4, same hours as palm house).

### ▲Coach Museum Wagenburg

The Schönbrunn coach museum is a 19th-century traffic jam of 50 impressive royal carriages and sleighs. Highlights include silly sedan chairs, the death-black hearse carriage (used for Franz Josef in 1916, and most recently for Empress Zita in 1989), and an extravagantly gilded imperial carriage pulled by eight Cinderella horses. This was rarely used other than for the coronation of Holy Roman Emperors, when it was disassembled and taken to Frankfurt for the big event. You'll also get a look at one of Sisi's impossibly narrow-waisted gowns, and (upstairs) Sisi's "Riding Chapel," with portraits of her 25 favorite horses.

**Cost and Hours:** €6, daily May-Oct 9:00-18:00, Nov-April 10:00-16:00, audioguide-€2, 200 yards from palace, walk through right arch as you face palace, tel. 01/525-243-470.

# Activities in Vienna

These activities allow you to take it easy and enjoy the Viennese good life.

### ▲▲Cafés

A break for *Kaffee und Kuchen* (coffee and cake) in one of the city's historical cafés is a must on any Viennese visit (see my recommended cafés in the Eating in Vienna chapter).

### ▲*Heuriger* Wine Gardens

Locals and tourists alike enjoy lingering in these rustic wine gardens in rural neighborhoods, easily accessible by public transporta-

SIGHTS

tion from downtown Vienna (see listings in the Eating in Vienna chapter).

## ▲Stadtpark (City Park)

Vienna's major park, along the eastern edge of the Ring, is a waltzing world of gardens, memorials to local musicians, ponds, peacocks, music in bandstands, and Viennese escaping the city. Notice the *Jugendstil* entrance at the Stadtpark U-Bahn station. The faux-Renaissance Kursalon hall, where Johann Strauss was the violin-toting master of waltzing ceremonies, hosts daily touristy concerts in three-quarter time (for details, see page 200). Find the famous golden statue of Strauss with his violin (next to the Kursalon, straight in from the Weihburggasse tram stop).

## ▲Prater Park (Wiener Prater)

Since the 1780s, when the reformist Emperor Josef II gave his hunting grounds to the people of Vienna as a public park, this place has been Vienna's playground. For the tourist, the "Prater" is the sugary-smelling, tired, and sprawling amusement park (Wurstelprater). For locals, the "Prater" is the vast, adjacent green park with its three-mile-long, tree-lined main boulevard (Hauptallee). The park still tempts visitors with its huge 220-foot-tall, famous, and lazy Ferris wheel *(Riesenrad)*, roller coaster, bumper cars, Lilliputian railroad, and endless eateries. Especially if you're traveling with kids, this is a fun, goofy place to share the evening with thousands of Viennese.

**Cost and Hours:** Rides cost €1.50-€5 and run May-Sept 9:00-24:00—but quiet after 22:00, March-April and Oct 10:00-22:00, Nov-Dec 10:00-20:00, grounds always open, U-1: Praterstern, www.prater.at. For a local-style family dinner, eat at Schweizerhaus (good food, great Czech Budvar—the original "Budweiser"—beer, classic conviviality).

## Danube Island (Donauinsel)

In the 1970s, as part of a flood protection program, the city dug a channel (the so-called Neue Donau—New Danube) parallel to the Danube River. With the dredged-out dirt, the engineers formed 12-mile-long Danube Island. Originally just an industrial site, it's evolved into a much-loved idyllic escape from the city (easy U-Bahn access on U-1: Donauinsel).

The skinny island provides a natural wonderland. All along the pedestrianized, grassy park, you'll find locals—especially immigrants and those who can't afford their own cabin or fancy vacation—at play. The swimming comes tough, though, with rocky entries rather than sand. The best activity here is a bike ride. If you venture far from the crowds, you're likely to encounter nudists on inline skates.

## Shopping in Vienna

**Traditional Austrian Clothing:** If you're interested in picking up a classy felt suit or dirndl, you'll find shops all over town. Most central is the fancy **Loden-Plankl** shop, with a vast world of traditional Austrian formalwear upstairs (across from the Hofburg, at Michaelerplatz 6). The **Tostmann Trachten** shop is the ultimate for serious shopping. Frau Tostmann powered the resurgence of this style. Her place is like a shrine to traditional Austrian and folk clothing (called Tracht)—handmade and very expensive (Schottengasse 3A, 3-minute walk from Am Hof, tel. 01/533-5331).

**Artsy Gifts:** Vienna's museum shops are some of Europe's best. The design store in the Museum of Applied Art (MAK) is a delight; the shops of the Albertina Museum, Kunsthistorisches Museum, Belvedere Palace, Kunst Haus Wien, Sigmund Freud Museum, and the MuseumsQuartier museums are also particularly good.

**Window Shopping:** The narrow streets north and west of the cathedral are sprinkled with old-fashioned shops that seem to belong to another era, carrying a curiously narrow range of items for sale (old clocks, men's ties, gloves, and so on). Dedicated window-shoppers will enjoy the Dorotheum auction house (see page 38).

**SIGHTS**

**Biking Danube Island:** For a simple, breezy joyride, bike up and down the traffic-free and people-filled island. Weather permitting, you can rent a bike from the shop at the **Reichsbrücke,** the bridge spanning the island (€5/hour, €25/day, May-Aug daily 9:00-21:00, shorter hours in spring and fall, closed off-season, 70 yards from U-1: Donauinsel, tel. 01/263-5242, www.fahrradverleih.at).

### Donau City (Donaustadt)

This modern part of town, just beyond Danube Island, is the skyscraping "Manhattan" of Austria. It was laid out as a potential Vienna-Budapest expo site in the 1990s. But Austrians voted down the fair idea, and eventually the real estate became today's modern planned city: It's quiet and traffic-free, with inviting plazas and a small church dwarfed by towering places of business. The high-rise DC Towers are the tallest office buildings in Austria. With business, residential, and shopping zones surrounded by inviting parkland, this corner of the city is likely to grow as Vienna expands. Its centerpiece is the futuristic UNO City, one of four United Nations headquarters worldwide. While it lacks the Old World character, charm, and elegance of the rest of Vienna, Donau City may interest travelers who are into contemporary glass-and-steel architecture (U-1: Kaisermühlen VIC).

**Biking to Donau City and Beyond:** Sightseers on bikes can cross the Danube to Donau City. From the Opera, it's pretty much a straight pedal around the center via the Ringstrasse, past Prater Park, and across the river. The way is easy enough to find with the help of the basic tourist map from the TI. (Recommended local guide Wolfgang Höfler leads tours along this route, which he shared with me; see page 32).

The route will take you over four stretches of water: the Danube Canal, the actual Danube, the New Danube, and the Old Danube. Along the way, you'll gain a better understanding of the massive engineering done over the years to contain and tame the river.

As you leave the city center, you'll first pedal over the Danube Canal, an arm of the river that brings river traffic into the city; then you hit the main part of the river and the man-made Danube Island (itself a part of the city's flood barriers). From the Reichsbrücke bridge over the island, survey the river's traffic. The cruise industry is booming, and Vienna's river cruise port is hosting more boats than ever. Many of them sail from here all the way to Romania and the Black Sea coast. You may also be inspired by the entire Austrian navy: Look for the two tiny camouflaged gunboats moored in the shade of the bridge.

In the distance, across the river, are the skyscrapers of Donau City. To reach it, continue across the bridge over Danube Island and cross the New Danube. From Donau City, the bike path leads across the Old Danube (Alte Donau), an old arm of the river but now a lake, which hosts a frolicking park with all the water fun a hot-and-tired city could hope for, including lakeside cafés and boat rentals. From here you can simply retrace your route, or you can make a big circle by following the delightful bike path southeast along the Old Danube to the next bridge (Praterbrücke). This leads to the vast Prater Park, where you'll follow the breezy main boulevard (Hauptallee) back to the big Ferris wheel and ultimately to downtown.

### A Walk in the Vienna Woods (Wienerwald)

For a quick side-trip into the woods and out of the city, catch the U-4 subway line to Heiligenstadt, then bus #38A to Kahlenberg, where you'll enjoy great views and a café overlooking the city. From there, it's a peaceful 45-minute downhill hike to the *Heurigen* of Nussdorf or to enjoy some new wine (see page 190). Your free TI-produced city map can be helpful...just go downhill.

For the very best views, stay on bus #38A to Leopoldsberg (if your #38A bus goes only to Kahlenberg—see the destination marked on the front of the bus or ask the driver—hop off in Kahlenberg and wait for the next bus to Leopoldsberg, 2/hour). There you'll find a lovely Baroque church and shady tables with expansive panoramas of the city and the Danube. While it seems like a long way to go for a big view, buses are cheap (or free with a transit pass) and run frequently (2/hour to Leopoldsberg, last bus around 17:30; buses that end at Kahlenberg run 4-8/hour, last bus around midnight). For an overview of this area, see the map on page 19.

**Naschmarkt**
Vienna's busy produce market is a great place for people-watching (see page 67).

SIGHTS

# VIENNA CITY WALK

Vienna, one of Europe's grandest cities of the past, is also a vibrant city of today. Here in Vienna's urban core, where old meets new, you'll get the lay of the land as you stroll between the city's three most important landmarks: the Opera, St. Stephen's Cathedral, and the Hofburg Palace. Along the way, we'll drop into some of the smaller sights that help make this city so intriguing (many of which are covered in greater detail elsewhere in the book): the poignant monuments that subtly cobble together this proud nation's often-illustrious, sometimes-tragic history; the genteel stores, cafés, and pastry shops where the Viennese continually perfect their knack for fine living; the unassuming churches where the remains of the Habsburg monarchs are entombed; and the defiantly stern architectural styles that emerged to counteract all that frilly Habsburg excess. Use this walk as a springboard for exploring this fine city—and, along the way, get an overview of Vienna's past and present.

## Orientation

**Length of This Walk:** Allow one hour and more time if you plan to stop at any of the major sights along the way.

**Opera House:** A visit is possible only with a 45-minute guided tour—€6.50, July-Aug generally daily at the top of each hour 10:00-16:00; Sept-June fewer tours; tel. 01/514-442-606. For information on attending a performance, see page 198.

**Café Sacher:** Daily 8:00-24:00, Philharmoniker Strasse 4, tel. 01/51456.

**Albertina Museum:** €12, daily 10:00-18:00, Wed until 21:00, overlooking Albertinaplatz across from the TI and the Opera, tel. 01/534-830, www.albertina.at.

**Kaisergruft:** €5.50, daily 10:00-18:00, last entry at 17:40,

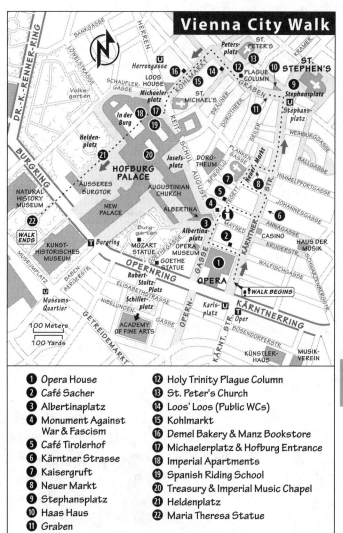

**Vienna City Walk**

1 Opera House
2 Café Sacher
3 Albertinaplatz
4 Monument Against War & Fascism
5 Café Tirolerhof
6 Kärntner Strasse
7 Kaisergruft
8 Neuer Markt
9 Stephansplatz
10 Haas Haus
11 Graben
12 Holy Trinity Plague Column
13 St. Peter's Church
14 Loos' Loos (Public WCs)
15 Kohlmarkt
16 Demel Bakery & Manz Bookstore
17 Michaelerplatz & Hofburg Entrance
18 Imperial Apartments
19 Spanish Riding School
20 Treasury & Imperial Music Chapel
21 Heldenplatz
22 Maria Theresa Statue

Tegetthoffstrasse 2, off Neuer Markt, tel. 01/512-6853, www.kaisergruft.at.

**St. Stephen's Cathedral:** Church foyer—free, Mon-Sat 6:00-22:00, Sun 7:00-22:00; main nave—€4, Mon-Sat 9:00-11:30 & 13:00-16:30, Sun 13:30-16:30, until 17:30 June-Aug; tel. 01/515-52-3526, www.stephanskirche.at. The cathedral's other sights, including the south and north towers, catacombs, and treasury, have varying costs and hours—for details, see page 109.

**St. Peter's Church:** Free; Mon-Fri 7:00-20:00, Sat-Sun 9:00-21:00; free organ concerts Mon-Fri at 15:00, Sat-Sun at 20:00; just off the Graben between the Plague Monument and Kohlmarkt, tel. 01/533-6433, www.peterskirche.at.

**St. Michael's Church Crypt:** €7 for 45-minute tour, Mon-Fri at 11:00 and 13:30, mobile 0650-533-8003, www.michaelerkirche.at.

**Hofburg Imperial Apartments:** €11.50, covered by €25.50 Sisi Ticket (see page 25); daily July-Aug 9:00-18:00, Sept-June 9:00-17:30, last entry one hour before closing; tel. 01/533-7570, www.hofburg-wien.at.

**Hofburg Treasury:** €12, €20 combo-ticket with Kunsthistorisches Museum, Wed-Mon 9:00-17:30, closed Tue, last entry 30 minutes before closing, tel. 01/525-240, www.kaiserliche-schatzkammer.at.

**Starring:** Vienna's "big three" (Opera house, cathedral, palace), plus an array of sights, squares, and shops tucked between them.

## The Walk Begins

• *Begin at the square outside Vienna's landmark Opera house. (The entrance faces the Ringstrasse; we're starting at the busy pedestrian square that's to the right of the entrance as you're facing it.)*

### ❶ Opera House

If Vienna is the world capital of classical music, this building is its throne room, one of the planet's premier houses of music. It's typical of Vienna's 19th-century buildings in that it features a revival style—Neo-Renaissance—with arched windows, half-columns, and the sloping, copper mansard roof typical of French Renaissance *châteaux* (see sidebar on page 131).

Since the structure was built in 1869, almost all of the opera world's luminaries have passed through here. Its former musical directors include Gustav Mahler, Herbert von Karajan, and Richard Strauss. Luciano Pavarotti, Maria Callas, Placido Domingo, and many other greats have sung from its stage.

In the pavement along the side of the Opera (and all along Kärntner Strasse, the bustling shopping street we'll visit shortly), you'll find star plaques forming a Hollywood-style walk of fame. These represent the stars of classical music—famous composers,

singers, musicians, and con-
ductors.

Looking up at the Opera,
notice the giant outdoor screen
onto which some live performances are projected (as noted
in the posted schedules).

If you're a fan, take a guided tour of the Opera (see page
35). If you're not, you still might consider springing for an evening performance (standing-room tickets are surprisingly cheap;
see page 198). Regular opera tickets are sold at various points near
here: The closest ticket office is the small one just below the screen,
while the main one is on the other side of the building, across the
street on Operngasse. For information about other entertainment
options during your visit, check in at the Wien Ticket kiosk in the
booth on this square.

The Opera house marks a busy intersection in Vienna, where
Kärntner Strasse meets the Ring. The Karlsplatz U-Bahn station in
front of the Opera is an underground shopping mall with fast food,
newsstands, and lots of pickpockets.

• *Walk behind the Opera and across the street toward the dark-red
awning to find the famous...*

### ❷ Café Sacher

This is the home of the world's classiest chocolate cake, the Sacher-Torte: two layers of cake separated by apricot jam and cov-

ered in dark-chocolate icing, usually served
with whipped cream. It was invented in a fit
of improvisation in 1832 by Franz Sacher,
dessert chef to Prince Metternich (the mas-
termind diplomat who redrew the map of
post-Napoleonic Europe). The cake became
world famous when the inventor's son served
it next door at his hotel (you may have noticed
the fancy doormen). Many locals complain
that the cakes here have gone downhill, and
many tourists are surprised by how dry they
are—you really need that dollop of *Schlagobers*.

Still, coffee and a slice of cake here can be €8 well invested for the
historic ambience alone (daily 8:00-24:00). While the café itself is
grotesquely touristy, the adjacent Sacher Stube has ambience and
natives to spare (same prices, daily 10:00-24:00). For maximum
elegance, sit inside.

• *Continue past Hotel Sacher. At the end of the street is a small, triangular, cobbled square adorned with modern sculptures.*

### ❸ Albertinaplatz

As you approach the square, to the right you'll find the **TI** (see page 24).

On your left, the tan-and-white Neoclassical building with the statue alcoves marks the tip of the Hofburg Palace—the sprawling complex of buildings that was long the seat of Habsburg power (we'll end this walk at the palace's center). The balustraded terrace up top was originally part of Vienna's defensive rampart. Later, it was the balcony of Empress Maria Theresa's daughter Maria Christina, who lived at this end of the palace. Today, her home houses the **Albertina Museum,** topped by a sleek, controversial titanium canopy (called the "diving board" by critics). The museum's plush, 19th-century staterooms are hung with facsimiles from its choice collection of prints, watercolors, and drawings (the originals are too light-sensitive to be displayed continuously), and a modern addition is dedicated to classical modern art, covering each artistic stage from Impressionism to the present day (see page 53).

Albertinaplatz itself is filled with sculptures that make up the powerful, thought-provoking ❹ **Monument Against War and Fascism,** which commemorates the dark years when Austria came under Nazi rule (1938-1945).

The memorial has four parts. The split white monument, *The Gates of Violence,* remembers victims of all wars and violence.

Standing directly in front of it, you're at the gates of a concentration camp. Then, as you explore the statues, you step into a montage of wartime images: clubs and WWI gas masks, a dying woman birthing a future soldier, and chained slave laborers sitting on a pedestal of granite cut from the infamous quarry at Mauthausen concentration camp (see page 226). The hunched-over figure on the ground behind is a Jew forced to scrub anti-Nazi graffiti off a street with a toothbrush. Of Vienna's 200,000 Jews, more than 65,000 died in Nazi concentration camps. The sculpture with its head buried in the stone is Orpheus entering the underworld, meant to remind Austrians (and the rest of us) of the victims of Nazism...and the consequences of not keeping our governments on track. Behind that, the 1945 declaration that established Austria's second republic—and enshrined human rights—is cut into the stone.

Viewing this monument gains even more emotional impact when you realize what happened on this spot: During a WWII bombing attack, several hundred people were buried alive when the cellar they were using as shelter was demolished.

Austria was led into World War II by Germany, which annexed the country in 1938, saying Austrians were wannabe Germans anyway. But Austrians are not Germans—never were, never will be. They're quick to proudly tell you that Austria was founded in the 10th century, whereas Germany wasn't born until 1870. For seven years just before and during World War II (1938-1945), there was no Austria. In 1955, after 10 years of joint occupation by the victorious Allies, Austria regained total independence on the condition that it would be forever neutral (and never join NATO or the Warsaw Pact). To this day, Austria is outside of NATO (and Germany).

Behind the monument is ❺ **Café Tirolerhof,** a classic Viennese café full of things that time has passed by: chandeliers, marble tables, upholstered booths, waiters in tuxes, and newspapers. For more on Vienna's cafés, see page 187.

Often parked nearby are the Red Bus City Tour buses, offering a handy way to get a quick overview of the city (see page 32).

• *From the café, turn right on Führichsgasse, passing the cafeteria-style Rosenberger Markt Restaurant. Walk one block until you hit...*

## ❻ Kärntner Strasse

This grand, traffic-free street is the people-watching delight of this in-love-with-life city. Today's Kärntner Strasse (KAYRNT-ner SHTRAH-seh) is mostly a crass commercial pedestrian mall—its famed elegant shops long gone. But locals know it's the same road Crusaders marched down as they headed off from St. Stephen's Cathedral for the Holy Land in the 12th century. Its name indicates that it leads south, toward the region of Kärnten (Carinthia, a province divided between Austria and Slovenia). Today it's full of shoppers and street musicians.

Where Führichsgasse meets Kärntner Strasse, note the city **Casino** (across the street and a half-block to your right, at #41)—once venerable, now tacky, it exemplifies the worst of the street's evolution. Turn left to head up Kärntner Strasse, going away from the Opera. As you walk along, be sure to look up, above the modern storefronts, for glimpses of the street's former glory. Near the end of the block, on the left at #26, **J & L Lobmeyr Crystal** ("Founded in

1823") still has its impressive brown storefront with gold trim, statues, and the Habsburg double-eagle. In the market for some $400 napkin rings? Lobmeyr's your place. Inside, breathe in the classic Old World ambience as you climb up to the glass museum (free entry, Mon-Fri 10:00-19:00, Sat 10:00-18:00, closed Sun).

• *At the end of the block, turn left on Marco d'Aviano Gasse (passing the fragrant flower stall) to make a short detour to the square called Neuer Markt. Straight ahead is an orange-ish church with a triangular roof and cross, the Capuchin Church. In its basement is the...*

### ❼ Kaisergruft

Under the church sits the Imperial Crypt, filled with what's left of Austria's emperors, empresses, and other Habsburg royalty. For centuries, Vienna was the heart of a vast empire ruled by the Habsburg family, and here is where they lie buried in their fancy pewter coffins. You'll find all the Habsburg greats, including Maria Theresa, her son Josef II (Mozart's patron), Franz Josef, and Empress Sisi. Before moving on, consider paying your respects here (see page 54).

• *Stretching north from the Kaisergruft is the square called...*

### ❽ Neuer Markt

A block farther down, in the center of Neuer Markt, is the **four rivers fountain** showing Lady Providence surrounded by figures

symbolizing the rivers that flow into the Danube. The sexy statues offended Empress Maria Theresa, who actually organized "Chastity Commissions" to defend her capital city's moral standards. The modern buildings around you were rebuilt after World War II. Half of the city's inner center was intentionally destroyed by Churchill to demoralize the Viennese, who were disconcertingly enthusiastic about the Nazis.

• *Lady Providence's one bare breast points back to Kärntner Strasse (50 yards away). Before you head back to the busy shopping street, you could stop for a sweet treat at the heavenly, rec-*

*ommended Kurkonditorei Oberlaa (to get there, disobey the McDonald's arrows—it's at the far-left corner of the square).*

*Leave the square and return to Kärntner Strasse. Turn left and continue down Kärntner Strasse. As you approach the cathedral, you're likely to first see it as a reflection in the round-glass windows of the post-modern Haas Haus. Pass the U-Bahn station (which has WCs) where the street spills into Vienna's main square...*

## ❾ Stephansplatz

The cathedral's frilly spire looms overhead, worshippers and tourists pour inside the church, and shoppers and top-notch street entertainers buzz around the outside. You're at the center of Vienna.

The Gothic **St. Stephen's Cathedral** (c. 1300-1450) is known for its 450-foot south tower, its colorful roof, and its place in Viennese history. When it was built, it was a huge church for what was then a tiny town, and it helped put the fledgling city on the map. At this point, you may want to take a break from the walk to tour the church (❂ see the St. Stephen's Cathedral Tour chapter). Even if you don't go inside, check out the old facade and World War II-era photos that show the destruction during the war (across the square to the right of the church, next to the door marked *3a Stephansplatz*).

Where Kärntner Strasse hits Stephansplatz, the grand, soot-covered building with red columns is the **Equitable Building** (filled with lawyers, bankers, and insurance brokers). It's a fine example of Neoclassicism from the turn of the 20th century—look up and imagine how slick Vienna must have felt in 1900.

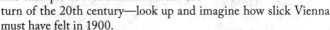

Facing St. Stephen's is the sleek concrete-and-glass ❿ **Haas Haus,** a postmodern building by noted Austrian architect Hans Hollein (finished in 1990; see photo at left). The curved facade is supposed to echo the Roman fortress of Vindobona (its ruins were found near here). Although the Viennese initially protested having this stark modern tower right

# Adolf Loos (1870-1933)

"Decoration is a crime," wrote Adolf Loos, the turn-of-the-20th-century architect who was Vienna's answer to Frank Lloyd Wright. Foreshadowing the Modernist style of "less is more" and "form follows func-tion," Loos stripped buildings down to their structural skele-ton.

In his day, most build-ings were plastered with fake Greek columns, frosted with Baroque balustrades, and studded with statues. Even the newer buildings featured flow-ery Art Nouveau additions. Loos' sparse, geometrical style stood out at the time—and it still does more than a century later. Loos was convinced that unnecessary ornamentation was a waste of workers' valuable time and energy, and was a symbol of an unevolved society. (He even went so far as to compare decoration on a facade with a lavatory wall smeared with excrement.) On this walk, you'll pass four examples of his work:

**American Bar** (a half-block off Kärntner Strasse, on the left just before Stephansplatz at Kärntner Durchgang 10): Built in 1908, the same year that Loos published his famous essay "Ornament and Crime," this tiny bar features Loos' special-ties—and fine cocktails. The facade is cubical, with square col-umns and crossbeams (and no flowery capitals). The interior is elegant and understated, with rich marble and mirrors that appear to expand the small space. As they have little patience with gawkers, the best way to admire the interior is to sit down and order a drink.

**Public WCs on Graben:** These are some of the classiest bathrooms in town (see page 102).

**Manz Bookstore:** The facade is a perfect cube, divided into other simple, rectangular shapes.

**Loos House on Michaelerplatz:** This boldly stripped-down facade (pictured above) peers defiantly across the square at the over-the-top Hofburg. Compare it with the Hof-burg's ornate, Neo-Rococo look (done only a few decades earlier) to see how revolutionary Loos was (see page 104).

next to their beloved cathedral, since then, it's become a fixture of Vienna's main square. Notice how the smooth, rounded glass reflects St. Stephen's pointy architecture, providing a great photo opportunity—especially at twilight. The café and pricey restaurant on the rooftop offer a nice perch, complete with a view of Stepha-nsplatz below—though not necessarily of the cathedral (take the elevator up to the sixth floor, which has a glassed-in lounge; walk up one flight to reach the terrace and restaurant).

• *Exit the square with your back to the cathedral. Walk past the Haas Haus, and bear right down the street called...*

## ⓫ Graben

This was once a *Graben*, or ditch—originally the moat for the Roman military camp. Back during Vienna's 19th-century heyday,

there were nearly 200,000 people packed into the city's inner center (inside the Ringstrasse), walking through dirt streets. Today this area houses 20,000. Graben was a busy street with three lanes of traffic until the 1970s, when it was turned into one of Europe's first pedestrian-only zones. Take a moment to absorb the scene—you're standing in an area surrounded by history, postwar rebuilding, grand architecture, fine cafés, and people enjoying life...for me, quintessential Europe.

As you stroll down the Graben from Stephansplatz, after about 50 yards, you'll reach a modern water dispenser. Vienna has suffered fiercely hot summers lately, leading the city government to install watering stations and shady benches for its citizens and visitors.

In another fifty yards, you reach Dorotheergasse, on your left, which leads (after two more long blocks) to the **Dorotheum** auction house. Consider poking your nose in here later for some fancy window-shopping (see page 38). Also along this street are two recommended eateries: the sandwich shop Buffet Trześniewski—one

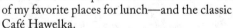

of my favorite places for lunch—and the classic Café Hawelka.

In the middle of the Graben pedestrian zone is the extravagantly blobby ⓬ **Holy Trinity plague column** *(Pestsäule)*. The 60-foot pillar of clouds sprouts angels and cherubs, with the wonderfully gilded Father, Son, and Holy Ghost at the top (all protected by an anti-pigeon net).

In 1679, Vienna was hit by a massive epidemic of bubonic plague. Around 75,000 Viennese died—about a third of the city. Emperor Leopold I dropped to his knees (something emperors never did in public) and begged God to save the city. (Find Leopold about a quarter of the way up the monument, just above the brown banner. Hint: The typical inbreeding of royal families left him with a gaping underbite.) His prayer was heard by Lady Faith (the statue below Leopold, carrying a cross). With the help of a heartless little cupid, she tosses an old naked woman—symbolizing the plague—into the abyss and saves the city. In gratitude, Leopold vowed to erect this monument, which became a model for other cities ravaged by the same plague.

• *Thirty yards past the plague monument, look down the short street to the right, which frames a Baroque church with a stately green dome.*

### ⓭ St. Peter's Church

Leopold I ordered this church to be built as a thank-you for surviving the 1679 plague. The church stands on the site of a much older church that may have been Vienna's first (or second) Christian church. Inside, St. Peter's shows Vienna at its Baroque best (see page 39). Note that the church offers free organ concerts (Mon-Fri at 15:00, Sat-Sun at 20:00).

• *Continue west on Graben, where you'll immediately find some stairs leading underground to...*

### ⓮ Loos' Loos

In about 1900, a local chemical-maker needed a publicity stunt to prove that his chemicals really got things clean. He purchased two wine cellars under Graben and had them turned into classy WCs in the Modernist style (designed by Adolf Loos—see sidebar on page 100), complete with chandeliers and finely crafted mahogany. While the chandeliers are gone, the restrooms remain a relatively appealing place to do your business—in fact, they're so inviting that they're used for poetry readings. Locals and tourists happily pay €0.50 for a quick visit.

• *Graben dead-ends at the aristocratic supermarket Julius Meinl am Graben (see listing on page 183). From here, turn left. In the distance is the big green-and-gold dome of the Hofburg, where we'll head soon. The street leading up to the Hofburg is...*

### ⓯ Kohlmarkt

This is Vienna's most elegant and unaffordable shopping street, lined with Cartier, Armani, Gucci, Tiffany, and the emperor's palace at the end. Strolling Kohlmarkt, daydream about the edible window displays at ⓰ **Demel,** the ultimate Viennese chocolate shop (#14, daily 9:00-19:00, www.demel.com). The room is filled with Art Nouveau boxes of Empress Sisi's choco-dreams come true: *Kandierte Veilchen* (candied violet petals), *Katzenzungen* (cats' tongues), and so on. The cakes here are moist (compared to the dry Sacher-Tortes). The enticing window displays change monthly, reflecting current happenings in Vienna. Wander inside. There's an impressive cancan of Vienna's most beloved cakes—displayed to tempt visitors into springing for the €10 cake-and-coffee deal (point to the cake you want). Farther in, you can see the bakery in action. Sit inside, with a view of the cake-making, or outside, with the street action (upstairs is less crowded). Shops like this boast "K.u.K."—signifying that during the Habsburgs' heyday, it was patronized by the *König und Kaiser* (king and emperor—same guy). If you happen to be looking through Demel's window at exactly 19:01, just after closing, you can witness one of the great tragedies of modern Europe: the daily dumping of its unsold cakes.

Next to Demel, the **Manz Bookstore** has a Loos-designed facade (see sidebar on page 100). By the way, across the street (and back a few steps) is a fine travel book and map shop (Freytag & Berndt, which carries most of my guidebooks).

• *Kohlmarkt ends at the square called...*

## ⓱ Michaelerplatz

This square is dominated by the **Hofburg Palace.** Study the grand Neo-Baroque facade, dating from about 1900. The four heroic giants illustrate Hercules wrestling with his great challenges (Emperor Franz Josef, who commissioned the gate, felt he could relate).

In the center of this square, a scant bit of **Roman Vienna** lies exposed just beneath street level.

**Spin Tour:** Do a slow, clockwise pan to get your bearings, starting (over your left shoulder as you face the Hofburg) with **St. Michael's Church,** which offers fascinating tours of its crypt (see page 57). To the right of that is the fancy **Loden-Plankl shop,** with traditional Austrian formalwear, including dirndls. Farther to the right, across Augustinerstrasse, is the wing of the palace that houses the **Spanish Riding School** and its famous white Lipizzaner stallions (see page 49). Farther down this street lies **Josefsplatz,** with the Augustinian Church (see page 51), and the Dorotheum auction house. At the end of the street are Albertinaplatz and the Opera (where we started this walk).

Continue your spin: Two buildings over from the Hofburg

# Michaelerplatz:
# Where New Faces Down Old

It's fascinating to think of Michaelerplatz as the architectural embodiment of a fundamental showdown that took place at the dawn of the 20th century, between the old and the new.

Emperor Franz Josef came to power during the popular revolution year of 1848 (as an 18-year-old, he was locked in his palace for safety). Once in power, he saw that the real threat to him was not from without, but from within. He dismantled the city wall and moved his army's barracks to the center of the city. But near the end of his reign, the modern world was clearly closing in.

Franz Josef's Neo-Rococo design for the Hofburg, featuring huge statues of Hercules in action at the gate, represents a desperate last stand of the absolutism of the emperor. Hercules was a favorite of emperors—a prototype of the modern ruler. The only mythical figure that was half-god, Hercules earned this half-divinity with hard labors. Like Hercules, the emperor's position was a combination of privileged birth and achievement—legitimized both by God and by his own hard work.

A few decades after Franz Josef erected his celebration of divine right, Loos responded with his starkly different house across the street. Although the Loos House might seem boring today, in its time, this anti-Historicist, anti-Art Nouveau statement was shocking. Inspired by Frank Lloyd Wright, it was considered to be Vienna's first "modern" building, with a trapezoidal footprint that makes no attempt to hide the awkwardly shaped street corner it stands on. Windows lack the customary cornice framing the top—a "house without eyebrows."

And so, from his front door, the emperor had to look at the modern world staring him rudely in the face, sneering, "Divine power is B.S. and your time is past." The emperor was angered by the bank building's lack of decor. Loos relented only slightly by putting up the 10 flower boxes (or "moustaches") beneath the windows.

But a few flowers couldn't disguise the notion that the divine monarchy was beginning to share Vienna with new ideas. As Loos worked, Stalin, Hitler, Trotsky, and Freud were all rattling about Vienna. Women were smoking and riding bikes. It was a scary time...a time ripe with change. And, of course, by 1918, after a Great War, the Habsburgs and the rest of Europe's imperial families were history.

(to the right), the modern **Loos House** (now a bank) has a facade featuring a perfectly geometrical grid of square columns and windows. Compared to the Neo-Rococo facade of the Hofburg, the stern Modernism of the Loos House appears to be from an entirely different age. And yet, both of these—as well as the Eiffel Tower and Mad Ludwig's fairy-tale Neuschwanstein Castle—were built in the same generation, roughly around 1900. In many ways, this jarring juxtaposition exemplifies the architectural turmoil of the turn of the 20th century, and represents the passing of the torch from Europe's age of divine monarchs to the modern era (see sidebar).

• *Let's take a look at where Austria's glorious history began—at the...*

## Hofburg

This is the complex of palaces where the Habsburg emperors lived

(except in summer, when they lived out at Schönbrunn Palace). Enter the Hofburg through the gate, where you immediately find yourself beneath a big rotunda (the netting is there to keep birds from perching). The doorway on the right is the entrance to the ⓲ **Imperial Apartments,** where the Habsburg emperors once lived in chandeliered elegance. Today you can tour its lavish rooms, as well as a museum about Empress Sisi, and a porcelain and silver collection (✪ see the Hofburg Imperial Apartments Tour chapter). To the left is the ticket office for the ⓳ **Spanish Riding School** (see page 49).

Continuing on, you emerge from the rotunda into the main courtyard of the Hofburg, called **In der Burg.** The Caesar-like statue is of Habsburg Emperor Franz II (1768-1835), grandson of Maria Theresa, grandfather of Franz Josef, and father-in-law of Napoleon. Behind him is a tower with three kinds of clocks (the yellow disc shows the phase of the moon tonight). To the right of Franz are the Imperial Apartments, and to the left are the offices of Austria's mostly ceremonial president (the more powerful chancellor lives in a building just behind this courtyard).

Franz Josef faces the oldest part of the palace. The colorful red, black, and gold gateway (behind you), which used to have a drawbridge, leads over the moat and into the 13th-century Swiss Court (Schweizerhof), named for the Swiss mercenary guards once stationed there. Study the gate. Imagine the drawbridge and the chain. Notice the Habsburg coat of arms with the imperial eagle above and the Renaissance painting on the ceiling of the passageway.

As you enter the Gothic courtyard, you're passing into the historic core of the palace, the site of the first fortress, and, historically, the place of last refuge. Here you'll find the ⓴ **Treasury** (Schatzkammer; ✪ see the Hofburg Treasury Tour chapter) and the **Imperial Music Chapel** (Hofmusikkapelle, see page 197), where the Boys' Choir sings Mass. Ever since Joseph Hayden and Franz Schubert were choirboys here, visitors have gathered like groupies on Sundays to hear the famed choir sing.

Returning to the bigger In der Burg courtyard, face Franz and turn left, passing through the **tunnel,** with a few tourist shops and restaurants, to spill out into spacious ㉑ **Heldenplatz** (Heroes' Square). On the left is the impressive curved facade of the **New Palace** (Neue Burg). This vast wing was built in the early 1900s to be the new Habsburg living quarters (and was meant to have a matching building facing it). But in 1914, the heir to the throne, Archduke Franz Ferdinand—while waiting politely for his long-lived uncle, Emperor Franz Josef, to die—was assassinated in Sarajevo. The archduke's death sparked World War I and the eventual end of eight centuries of Habsburg rule.

Today the building houses the **New Palace museums,** an eclectic collection of weaponry, suits of armor, musical instruments, and ancient Greek statues (see page 48). The two equestrian statues depict Prince Eugene of Savoy (1663-1736), who battled the Ottoman Turks, and Archduke Charles (1771-1847), who battled Napoleon. Eugene gazes toward the far distance at the prickly spires of Vienna's City Hall.

**Spin Tour:** Make a slow 360-degree turn, and imagine this huge square filled with people.

In 1938, 300,000 Viennese gathered here, entirely filling vast Heroes' Square, to welcome Adolf Hitler and celebrate their annexation with Germany—the *"Anschluss."* The Nazi tyrant stood on the balcony of the New Palace and declared, "Before the face of German history, I declare my former homeland now a part of the Third Reich. One of the pearls of the Third Reich will be Vienna." He never said "Austria," a word that was now forbidden.

When pondering why the Austrians—eyes teary with joy and vigorously waving their Nazi flags—so willingly accepted Hitler's rule, it's important to remember that Austria was already a fascist nation. Austrian Chancellor Engelbert Dollfuss, though pro-Catholic, pro-Habsburg, and anti-Hitler, was a fascist dictator who silenced any left-wing opposition. Also, memories of the grand Habsburg Empire were still fresh in the collective psyche. The once vast and mighty empire of 50 million at its 19th-century peak came out of World War I a tiny landlocked land of six million that now suffered terrible unemployment. The opportunistic Hitler promised jobs along with a return to greatness—and the Austrian people gobbled it up.

Standing here, it's fascinating to consider Austrian aspirations for grandeur. In fact, the Habsburgs envisioned an Imperial Forum stretching from here across the Ringstrasse.

• *Walk on through the Greek-columned passageway (the Äusseres Burgtor), cross the Ringstrasse, and stand between the giant Kunsthistorisches and Natural History Museums, purpose-built in the 1880s to house the private art and history collections of the empire and to celebrate its culture and power. The emperor planned to tie these grand buildings and the palace together with two mighty triumphal arches spanning the Ringstrasse, connecting them into an awe-inspiring ensemble. And today, while the emperor's vision died with his empire, a huge statue of perhaps the greatest of the Habsburgs, Maria Theresa, stands in the center of it all.*

## ㉒ Maria Theresa Monument

Vienna's biggest monument shows the empress holding a scroll from her father granting the right of a woman to inherit his throne.

The statues and reliefs surrounding her speak volumes about her reign: Her four top generals sit on horseback while her four top advisors stand. Behind them, reliefs celebrate cultural leaders of her day, including little Wolfie Mozart with mentor "Papa" Joseph Haydn (with his hand on Mozart's shoulder, facing the Natural History Museum). The moral of this propaganda: a strong military and a wise ruler are prerequisites for a thriving culture—attributes that characterized the 40-year rule of the woman who was perhaps Austria's greatest monarch.

• *Our walk is finished. You're in the heart of Viennese sightseeing. Surrounding this square are some of the city's top museums. And the Hofburg Palace itself contains many of Vienna's best sights and museums. From the Opera to the Hofburg, from chocolate to churches, from St. Stephen's to Sacher-Tortes—Vienna waits for you.*

# ST. STEPHEN'S CATHEDRAL TOUR

This massive church is the Gothic needle around which Vienna spins. According to the medieval vision of its creators, it stands like a giant jeweled reliquary, offering praise to God from the center of the city. The church and its towers, especially the 450-foot south tower, give the city its most iconic image. (Check your pockets for €0.10 coins; those minted in Austria feature the south tower on the back.) The cathedral has survived Vienna's many wars and today symbolizes the city's spirit and love of freedom.

## Orientation

**Cost:** It's free to enter the foyer and north aisle of the church, but it costs €4 to get into the main nave, where most of the interesting items are located (more for special exhibits). The towers, catacombs, treasury, and audioguide cost extra (all described later). The €16 combo-ticket—covering entry, both towers, catacombs, treasury, and audioguide—is overkill for most visitors.

**Hours:** The church doors are open daily 6:00-22:00 (Sunday opens at 7:00), but the main nave is open for tourists Mon-Sat 9:00-11:30 & 13:00-16:30, Sun 13:00-16:30, until 17:30 June-Aug. During services, you can't enter the main nave (unless you're attending Mass) or access the north tower elevator or catacombs, but you can go into the back of the church.

**Information:** Tel. 01/515-523-526, www.stephanskirche.at.

**Tours:** The €4.50 tours in English are entertaining (daily at 15:45, check information board inside entry to confirm schedule; price includes main nave entry). The €1 audioguide is helpful.

**Treasury:** Consider riding the elevator (just inside the cathedral's entry) to the treasury. Tucked away in a loft in the oldest part

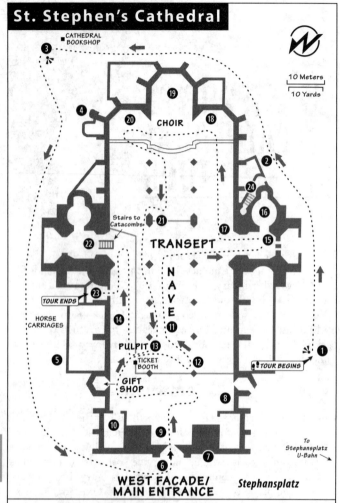

# St. Stephen's Cathedral

1. South Side View & Old Photos
2. Reliefs, Memorials & Former Tombstones
3. North Tower View
4. Pulpit with Vanquished Turk
5. Stonemason's Hut
6. West Facade & Main Entrance
7. 05 Sign
8. Maria Pócs Icon
9. Organ & Treasury
10. Chapel of Prince Eugene of Savoy
11. Main Nave
12. Pillar Statues (Madonna with the Protective Mantle)
13. Pulpit with Self-Portrait
14. Similar Self-Portrait
15. Mozart Plaque
16. Mozart Baptistery
17. Madonna of the Servants
18. Tomb of Frederick III
19. High Altar
20. Wiener Neustädter Altar
21. Plaque of Rebuilding
22. Catacombs Entry
23. North Tower (Elevator)
24. South Tower (Stairs)

of the church, it offers precious relics, dazzling church art, a portrait of Rudolf IV (considered the earliest German portrait), and wonderful views down on the nave (€4 admission includes audioguide, daily 10:00-18:00).

**Catacombs:** The catacombs are open to the public only by guided tour (€5, daily 10:00-11:30 & 13:30-16:30, tours generally depart on the half-hour and are in German and English). Just be at the stairs in the left/north transept to meet the guide—you'll pay at the end. You'll see a crypt for bishops and archbishops, and Crock-Pots of Habsburg guts filling dusty shelves.

**Towers:** The iconic **south tower** rewards a tough climb up a claustrophobic, 343-step staircase with dizzying views. You can reach it via the entrance outside the church, around the right as you face the west facade (€4, daily 9:00-17:30, last entry at 17:00).

The shorter **north tower** holds the famous "Pummerin" bell and is easier to ascend (no stairs, elevator), but it's much lower and not as exciting, with lesser views (€5, daily 9:00-17:30 & 19:00-21:30, entrance inside the church on the left/north side of the nave; you can access this elevator without buying a ticket for the main nave).

**English Service:** There's a Mass in English each Saturday at 19:00.

**Theft Alert:** All the commotion in and around the church makes it a favorite for pickpockets. Be on guard.

**Starring:** The cathedral's mighty exterior and evocative interior, including an ornately carved pulpit and various bits and pieces of Austrian history.

# The Tour Begins

## CATHEDRAL EXTERIOR

Before we go inside, let's circle around the cathedral for a look at its impressive exterior. We'll stop at several points along the way to take it all in.

### ❶ South Side

• *As you face the church's main entry, go to the right across the little square, and find the old-time photos next to the door marked* 3a Stephansplatz *(see map). From here, you can take in the sheer magnitude of this massive church, with its skyscraping spire.*

The church we see today is the third one on this spot. It dates mainly from 1300 to 1450, when builders expanded on an earlier structure and added two huge towers at the end of each transept. When it was built, St. Stephen's—covering almost an acre of land—was a huge church for what was then just a modest town of 10,000. The ruler who built the church was competing with St. Vitus Cathedral, which was being built at the same time in Prague; he made sure that Vienna's grand church was bigger than Prague's. This helped convince the region's religious authorities that Vienna deserved a bishop, thus making St. Stephen's a "cathedral." Politically, this helped Vienna become a city to be reckoned with, and it soon replaced Prague as the seat of the Holy Roman Empire.

The impressive 450-foot **south tower**—capped with a golden orb and cross—took two generations to build (65 years) and was finished in 1433. The tower is a rarity among medieval churches in that it was completed before the Gothic style—and the age of faith—petered out.

Find the Turkish **cannonball** stuck in a buttress (above the low, green roof on the middle buttress, marked with the date *1683*)—a remnant of one of several Ottoman sieges of the city.

The half-size **north tower** (223 feet), around the other side of the church, was meant to be a matching steeple. But around 1500, it was abandoned in mid-construction, when the money was needed to defend the country against the Ottomans rather than to build church towers.

The nave's sharply pitched **roof** stands 200 feet tall and is covered in 230,000 colorful ceramic tiles. The zigzag pattern on the south side is purely decorative, with no special symbolism.

The cathedral was heavily damaged at the end of World War II. Near where you are standing are **old photos** showing the destruction. In 1945, Vienna was caught in the chaos between the occupying Nazis and the approaching Soviets. Allied bombs sparked fires in nearby buildings, and the embers leapt to the cathedral rooftop. The original timbered Gothic roof burned, the cathedral's huge bell crashed to the ground, and the fire raged for two days. Civic pride prompted a financial outpouring, and the roof was rebuilt to its original splendor by 1952—doubly impressive considering the bombed-out state of the country at that time. Locals who contributed to the postwar reconstruction each had a chance to "own" one tile for their donation. Inside, we'll see a plaque honoring the rebuilding of the cathedral.

The little buildings lining the church exterior are **sacristies** (utility buildings used for running the church).

• *Circle the church exterior counterclockwise, passing the* **entrance to the south tower.** *If you're up for climbing the 343 stairs to the top, you could do it now, but it's better to wait until the end of this tour (tower climb described at the end of this chapter).*

Near the tower entrance, look for the carved ❷ **reliefs and memorials** and former **tombstones** now decorating the church wall. These are a reminder that the area around the church was a graveyard until 1780.

Look high above at the colorful **roof tiles,** with the double-headed Habsburg eagle, the date 1831, and the initials *FI* (for Emperor Franz I, who ruled when the roof was installed).

• *As you hook around behind the church, look for the cathedral bookshop (Dombuchhandlung) at the end of the block. Pause in front of that shop.*

### ❸ North Tower View

This spot provides a fine, wide-angle view of the stubby north tower and the apse of the church. From this vantage point, you can see the exoskeletal fundamentals of **Gothic architecture:** buttresses shoring up a very heavy roof, allowing for large windows that could be filled with stained glass to bathe the interior in colorful light. A battalion of storm-drain gargoyles stands ready to vomit water during downpours. Colored tiles on the roof show not the two-headed eagle of Habsburg times (as on the other side), but two distinct eagles of modern times (1950): the state of Austria on the left and the city of Vienna on the right.

Just above street level, notice the marble ❹ **pulpit** under the golden starburst. The priest would stand here, stoking public opinion against the Ottomans, in front of crowds far bigger than could fit into the church. Above the pulpit (in a scene from around 1700), a saint stands victoriously atop a vanquished Turk.

• *Continue circling the church, passing a line of horse carriages waiting to take tourists for a ride. Watch for the blocky, modern-looking building huddled next to the side of the cathedral. This is the...*

**ST. STEPHEN'S CATHEDRAL**

### ❺ Stonemason's Hut

There's always been a stonemason's hut here, as workers must keep the church in good repair. Even today, the masonry is maintained in the traditional way—a never-ending task. Unfortunately, the local limestone used in the Middle Ages is quite porous and absorbs modern pollution. Until the 1960s, this was a very busy traffic circle, and today's acidic air still takes its toll. Each winter, when rainwater soaks into the surface and then freezes, the stone corrodes—and must be repaired. Your church entry ticket helps fund this ongoing work.

Across the street (past the horse carriages) is the **archbishop's palace,** where the head of this church still lives today (enjoying a very short commute).

• *Around the corner is the cathedral's front door. Stand at the back of the square, across from the main entrance, to take in the entire...*

## ❻ West Facade

The Romanesque-style main entrance is the oldest part of the church (c. 1240—part of a church that stood here before). Right

behind you is the site of Vindobona, a Roman garrison town. Before the Romans converted to Christianity, there was a pagan temple here, and this entrance pays homage to that ancient heritage. Roman-era statues are embedded in the facade, and the two **octagonal towers** flanking the main doorway are dubbed the "heathen towers" because they're built with a few recycled Roman stones (flipped over to hide the pagan inscriptions and expose the smooth sides).

To the right of the main doorway is a reminder of the time the city was under Nazi rule. Anti-Nazi rebels carved **"O5"** into the wall, about chest high (❼ behind the Plexiglas, under the first plaque). The story goes that Hitler—who'd actually grown up in Austria—spurned his roots. When he attained power, he refused to call the country "Österreich," its native name, insisting on the Nazi term "Ostmark." Austrian patriots wrote the code "O5" to keep the true name alive: The "5" stands for the fifth letter of the alphabet (E), which often stands in for an umlaut, giving the "O" its correct pronunciation for "Österreich."

Before entering, study the details of the **main doorway.** Christ—looking down from the tympanum over the door—is triumphant over death. Flanked by angels with dramatic wings, he welcomes all. Ornate, tree-like pillars support a canopy of foliage and creatures, all full of meaning to the faithful medieval worshipper. The fine circa-1240 carvings above the door were once brightly painted. The paint was scrubbed off in the 19th century, when pure stone was more in vogue.

• *Enter the church.*

## CATHEDRAL INTERIOR

Find a spot to peer through the gate down the immense nave—more than a football field long and nine stories tall. It's lined with

clusters of slender pillars that soar up-
ward to support the ribbed crisscross
arches of the ceiling. Stylistically, the
nave is Gothic with a Baroque overlay.
It's a spacious, glorious venue that's often
used for high-profile concerts (there's a
ticket office outside the church, to the
right as you face the main doorway).

• *We'll venture down the nave soon, but first
take some time to explore the area at the...*

### Cathedral Foyer

To the right as you enter, in a gold-and-silver sunburst frame, is a
crude Byzantine-style ➑ **Maria Pócs Icon** (Pötscher Madonna),

brought here from a humble Hungarian village church. The picture of Mary and Child is
said to have wept real tears in 1697, as Central
Europe was once again being threatened by
the Turks. Prince Eugene of Savoy (described
below) saved the day at the stunning Battle of
Zenta in modern-day Serbia—a victory that
broke the back of the Ottoman army. If you
see crowds of pilgrims leaving flowers or lighting candles around the icon, they're most likely
Hungarians thanking the Virgin for helping
Prince Eugene drive the Ottomans out of their homeland.

Over the main doorway is the choir loft, with the 10,000-pipe
➒ **organ,** a 1960 replacement for the famous one destroyed during
World War II. This organ is also one of Europe's biggest, but it's
currently broken and sits unused...too large to remove. Architects
aren't sure whether it serves a structural purpose and adds support
to the actual building.

Along the left wall is the **gift shop.** Step in to marvel at the
14th-century statuary decorating its wall—some of the finest carvings in the church.

To the left of the gift shop is the gated entrance to the ➓
**Chapel of Prince Eugene of Savoy.** Prince Eugene (1663-1736), a
teenage seminary student from France, arrived in Vienna in 1683
as the city was about to be overrun by the Ottoman Turks. He
volunteered for the army and helped save the city, launching a brilliant career as a military man for the Habsburgs. His specialty was
conquering the Ottomans. When he died, the grateful Austrians
buried him here, under this chapel, marked by a tomb hatch in the
floor.

• *Nearby is the entrance to the main nave. Buy a ticket and walk to the
center of the...*

**ST. STEPHEN'S CATHEDRAL**

## ⓫ Main Nave

• *Looking down the nave, note the statues on the columns (about 30-40 feet above the ground).*

## ⓬ Pillar Statues

The nave's columns are richly populated with 77 life-size stone statues, making a saintly parade to the high altar.

Check out the first pillar on the right. Facing the side wall is the **Madonna with the Protective Mantle,** shown giving refuge to people of all walks of life (notice all the happy people of faith tucked under her cape). Also on that same pillar, find Moses with the Ten Commandments. On other columns, Bible students can find their favorite characters and saints—more Madonnas, St. George (killing the dragon), St. Francis of Assisi, arrow-pierced St. Sebastian, and so on.

• *Start down the nave toward the altar. At the second pillar on the left is the...*

## ⓭ Pulpit

The Gothic sandstone pulpit (c. 1500) is a masterpiece carved from three separate blocks (see if you can find the seams). A spi-

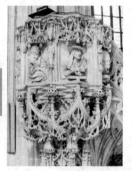

ral stairway winds up to the lectern, surrounded and supported by the four church "fathers," whose writings influenced early Catholic dogma. Each has a very different and very human facial expression (from back to front): Ambrose (daydreamer), Jerome (skeptic), Gregory (explainer), and Augustine (listener).

The pulpit is as crammed with religious meaning as it is with beautifully realistic carvings. The top of the stairway's railing swarms with lizards (animals of light)

and toads (animals of darkness). The "Dog of the Lord" stands at the top, making sure none of those toads pollutes the sermon. Below the toads, wheels with three parts (the Trinity) roll up, while wheels with four spokes (the four seasons and four cardinal directions, symbolizing mortal life on earth) roll down.

Find the guy peeking out from under the stairs. This may be a **self-portrait** of the sculptor. In medieval times, art was done for the glory of God, and artists worked anonymously. But this pulpit was carved as humanist Renaissance ideals were creeping in from Italy—and individual artists were becoming famous. So the artist included what may be a rare self-portrait bust in his work. He leans out from a window, sculptor's compass in hand, to observe the world and his work. The artist's identity, however, is disputed. Long thought to be Hungarian mason Anton Pilgram, many scholars now believe it's Dutch sculptor Nicolaes Gerhaert van Leyden; both worked extensively on the cathedral.

A few steps past the next column, look through the fence and find on the left wall a ⑭ **similar self-portrait** of Pilgram (or is it Gerhaert?) in color, taken from the original organ case. He holds a compass and L-square and symbolically shoulders the heavy burden of being a master builder of this huge place.

• *Continue up the nave. We'll visit several sights at the front of the church, moving in a roughly counterclockwise direction.*

*When you reach the gate that cuts off the front of the nave, turn right and enter the south transept. Go all the way to the doors, then look left to find the...*

### ⑮ Mozart Plaque

Wolfgang Amadeus Mozart (1756-1791) was married in St. Stephen's, attended Mass here, and had two of his children baptized here.

Mozart spent most of his adult life in Vienna. Born in Salzburg, Mozart was a child prodigy who toured Europe. He performed for Empress Maria Theresa's family in Vienna when he was eight. At age 25, he left Salzburg in a huff (freeing himself from his domineering father) and settled in Vienna. Here he found instant fame as a concert pianist and freelance composer, writing *The Marriage of Figaro, Don Giovanni,* and *The Magic Flute.* He married Constanze Weber in St. Stephen's, and they set up house in a lavish apartment a block east of the church (this house is now the lackluster Mozarthaus museum—see page 42). Mozart lived at the heart of Viennese society—among musicians, actors, and aristocrats. He played in a string quartet with Joseph Haydn. At church, he would have heard Beethoven's teacher playing the organ. (Mozart may have met the star-struck young Beethoven in Vienna—or maybe not; accounts vary.)

After his early success, Mozart fell on hard times, and the couple had to move to the suburbs. When Mozart died at age 35 (in 1791), he was not buried at St. Stephen's, because the cemetery that once surrounded the church had been cleared out a decade earlier as an anti-plague measure. Instead, his remains (along with most Viennese of his day) were dumped into a mass grave outside of

town. But he was honored with a funeral service in St. Stephen's—
held in the Prince Eugene of Savoy Chapel, where they played his
famous (unfinished) *Requiem.*

Look into the adjacent chapel at the fine ⓰ **baptistery** (stone bottom, matching carved-wood top,
from around 1500). This is where Mozart's children
were baptized.

On the right-hand column near the entrance to
the south transept, notice the fine carved statue of the
⓱ **Madonna of the Servants** (from 1330). This remains a favorite of working people, such as the house-
keepers who clean your hotel room.

• *Now walk down the right aisle to the front. Dominating
the chapel at the front-right corner of the church is the...*

### ⓲ Tomb of Frederick III

This imposing, red-marble tomb is like a big king-
size-bed coffin with an effigy of Frederick lying on top (not vis-

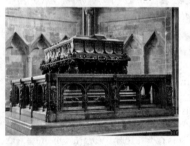

ible—but there's a photo of
the effigy on the left). The
top of the tomb is decorated
with his coats of arms, representing the many territories
he ruled over. It's likely by
the same Nicolaes Gerhaert
van Leyden who may have
done the pulpit.

Frederick III (1415-
1493) is considered the "father" of Vienna for turning the small village into a royal town with a cosmopolitan feel. Frederick secured
a bishopric, turning the newly completed St. Stephen's church into
a cathedral. The emperor's major contribution to Austria, however,
was in fathering Maximilian I and marrying him off to Mary of
Burgundy, instantly making the Habsburg Empire a major player
in European politics. The lavish tomb (made
of marble from Salzburg) is as long-lasting as
Frederick's legacy. To make sure it stayed that
way, locals saved his tomb from damage during
World War II by encasing it, like the pulpit, in
a shell of brick.

• *Walk to the middle of the church and face the...*

### ⓳ High Altar

The tall, ornate, black marble altarpiece (1641,
by Tobias and Johann Pock) is topped with a
statue of Mary that barely fits under the towering vaults of the ceiling. It frames a large

painting of the stoning of St. Stephen, painted on copper. Stephen (at the bottom), having refused to stop professing his faith, is pelted with rocks by angry pagans. As he kneels, ready to die, he gazes up to see a vision of Christ, the cross, and the angels of heaven. The stained glass behind the painting—some of the oldest in the church—creates a kaleidoscopic jeweled backdrop.

• *To the left of the main altar is the...*

### ⑳ Wiener Neustädter Altar

The triptych altarpiece—the symmetrical counterpart of Frederick III's tomb—was commissioned by Frederick in 1447. Its gilded wooden statues are especially impressive.

• *Walk back up the middle of the nave, toward the gate. When you reach the gate, look immediately to the right (on the third column—with the gate attached). About 10 feet above the ground is the...*

### ㉑ Plaque of Rebuilding

St. Stephen's is proud to be Austria's national church. The plaque explains in German how each region contributed to the rebuilding after World War II: *Die Glocke* (the bell) was financed by the state of Upper Austria. *Das Tor* (the entrance portal) was from Steiermark, the windows from Tirol, the pews from Vorarlberg, the floor from Lower Austria, and so on.

During World War II, many of the city's top art treasures were stowed safely in cellars and salt mines—hidden by both the Nazi occupiers (to protect against war damage) and by citizens (to protect against Nazi looters). The stained-glass windows behind the high altar were meticulously dismantled and packed away. The pulpit was encased in a shell of brick. As the war was drawing to a close, it appeared St. Stephen's would escape major damage. But as the Nazis were fleeing, the bitter Nazi commander in charge of the city ordered that the church be destroyed. Fortunately, his underlings disobeyed. Unfortunately, the church accidentally caught fire during Allied bombing shortly thereafter, and the wooden roof collapsed onto the stone vaults of the ceiling. The Tupperware-colored glass on either side of the nave dates from the 1950s. Before the fire, the church was lit mostly with clear Baroque-era windows.

• *Head back toward the main entrance. Along the north side of the nave, you have two options, both described on the next page: Tour the catacombs or ascend the north tower. Or you can head outside for the pulse-raising climb up the south tower.*

## OTHER CATHEDRAL SIGHTS

• *Near the middle of the church, at the left/north transept, is the entrance to the...*

### ❷ Catacombs *(Katakomben)*

The catacombs (viewable by guided tour only) hold the bodies—or at least the innards—of 72 Habsburgs, including that of Rudolf IV, the man who began building the south tower. This is where Austria's rulers were buried before the Kaisergruft was built (see page 54), and where later Habsburgs' entrails were entombed. The copper urns preserve the imperial organs in alcohol. I touched Maria Theresa's urn and it wobbled.

• *Also in the north nave, but closer to the cathedral's main door (look for the Aufzug zur Pummerin sign), is the entrance for the...*

### ❸ North Tower

The cramped north tower elevator takes you to a mediocre view and a big bell. Nicknamed "the Boomer" (Pummerin), it's old (first cast in 1711), big (nearly 10 feet across), and very heavy (21 tons). By comparison, the Liberty Bell is four feet across and weighs one ton. It's supposedly the second-biggest bell in the world that rings by swinging. A physical symbol of victory over the Ottomans in 1683, the Pummerin was cast from cannons (and cannonballs) captured from the Ottomans when the siege of Vienna was lifted. During the WWII fire that damaged the church, the Pummerin fell to the ground and cracked. It had to be melted down and recast. These days, locals know the Pummerin as the bell that rings in the Austrian New Year. You'll see its original 1,700-pound clapper in the catacombs if you take that tour.

• *Exit the church. Make a U-turn to the left if you're up for a climb up the...*

### ❹ South Tower

The 450-foot-high south tower, once key to the city's defense as a lookout point, is still dear to Viennese hearts. (It's long been affectionately nicknamed "Steffl," Viennese for "Stevie.") No church spire in (what was) the Austro-Hungarian Empire is taller—by Habsburg decree. It offers a far better view than the north tower, but you'll earn it by hiking 343 tightly wound steps up the spiral staircase (this hike burns about one Sacher-Torte worth of calories). From the top, use your city map to locate the famous sights. There are great views of the colorful church roof, the low-level Viennese skyline (major skyscrapers are regulated in the city center), and—in the distance—the Vienna Woods.

• *Your tour is over. You're at the very center of Vienna. Explore.*

ST. STEPHEN'S CATHEDRAL

# RINGSTRASSE TRAM TOUR

In the 1860s, Emperor Franz Josef had the city's ingrown medieval wall torn down and replaced with a grand boulevard 190 feet wide. The road, arcing nearly three miles around the city's core, predates all the buildings that line it. Those buildings are very "Neo": Neoclassical, Neo-Gothic, and Neo-Renaissance—an approach called Historicism (see sidebar on page 131). One of Europe's great streets, the Ringstrasse is lined with many of the city's top sights.

This self-guided tram tour gives you a fun orientation and a ridiculously quick glimpse of some major sights as you glide by. Vienna's red trams (a.k.a. streetcars) circle the Ring. Most of them are sleek and modern, with a few lovably clickety-clackety older ones still running. Neither tram #1 nor #2 makes the entire loop around the Ring, but you can see it all by making one transfer between them (at the Schwedenplatz stop). It's a no-stress way to sit shoulder-to-shoulder with ordinary *Wiener*s and see their city. In fact, my hope is that you'll feel like a *Wiener* yourself as you make this big loop.

If you have a transit pass (instead of a ticket), you can—and should—jump on and off as you go, seeing sights that interest you. Some of the best stops are: Weihburggasse (Stadtpark), Stubentor (Museum of Applied Art, a.k.a. MAK), Rathausplatz (City Hall and its summertime food circus), and Burgring (Kunsthistorisches Museum and Hofburg Palace).

You'll find that the tram goes faster than you can read. It's best to look through this chapter ahead of time, then ride with an eye out for the various sights described here. As you go, use time spent waiting at red lights and tram stops to catch or read the next segment to better anticipate what's coming up.

Or, to do this tour at your own pace, consider renting a **bike.** This allows you to easily stop at sights or to detour to nearby points of interest. The grassy median strip has excellent bike paths that run along almost the entire circuit of the Ring (except for a few blocks after the votive church, near the end of this tour). The City-bike Wien rental program is cheap and easy (for details, see page 30).

# Orientation

**Cost:** €2.20 (one transit ticket), €2.30 if bought on tram. A single ticket can be used to cover the whole route, including the transfer between trams (but you're not otherwise allowed to interrupt your trip, except to transfer). With a transit pass, you're free to hop off whenever you like, then hop back on another tram (they come along every few minutes). For more on riding Vienna's trams, see page 27.

**When to Go:** While this tour works fine in the daylight, the tram ride is also pleasant after dark, when nearly every sight on the route is well-lit.

**Pricier Option:** A yellow just-for-tourists streetcar circles the Ring without requiring a transfer—but it costs more and runs less frequently (€8 for one 30-minute loop, 2/hour 10:00-17:00, see page 33).

**Length of This Tour:** About an hour; allow more time if you hop off along the way.

**Starring:** Vienna's grandest boulevard, major landmarks, and a dizzyingly quick, once-over-lightly look at the city.

# The Tour Begins

To help you keep your bearings, this tour includes the name of each tram stop you'll pass, and tells you which way to look along the way. Stop names are announced in German as you approach and labeled (in small, sometimes hard-to-read lettering) at the stops themselves. Be aware that if no one requests a particular stop, the tram may zip on through.

Catch tram #2 in the middle of the street in front of the Opera house (from the underpass next to the Opera, follow signs to *Oper-nring;* the tram stop, called **Oper,** is to your right when you emerge at street level). You want the tram going against the direction of car traffic (direction Friedrich-Engels-Platz)—that is, to the right, as you face the Opera. If you can, grab a seat on the right-hand side of the tram. On many trams, annoying advertisements blur the window views; try to find a seat with a view clear of these.

Again, this commentary is ridiculously fast. With a transit pass, feel free to hop off to get a closer look at anything that

# The Birth of Modern Vienna

This tour quickly passes a statue of Dr. Karl Lueger (1844-1910), the influential mayor of Vienna during the pivotal period around the turn of the 20th century. Although controversial for his anti-Semitic and anti-immigrant rhetoric, Lueger worked together with architect Otto Wagner (1841-1918) to shape the modern Vienna you see today. Read this information during any down time (or before you board the tram), so you can recognize Lueger when you see him (at stop #5).

While Lueger was mayor (1897-1910), Vienna was in the midst of an incredible growth spurt: In 1850, the city had 500,000 residents; at its peak, around 1900, the population was 2.2 million—about 20 percent more than the city's current population of 1.7 million.

Emperor Franz Josef put Lueger and Wagner (the "Father of Modern Vienna") to work with a staff of 60 architects to turn the city into a capital befitting the grandiose Habsburg Empire. Consider the dramatic changes this team oversaw in a relatively short time: In the previous generation, Roman-style aqueducts still brought fresh spring water into the city from the Alps. By the 20th century, the city had modern plumbing. Thomas Edison supervised the electrical lighting of Schönbrunn Palace, and shortly after that, gas lighting brightened the entire Ringstrasse. The Danube was tamed by building solid banks, along with other flood-control projects. In the 1870s, engineers even began an artificial island that took a century to complete.

As Vienna grew and sprawled, it became decentralized, as with "city centers" all over the place. To tie it all together, the new Vienna needed a fine tram and subway system. Consequently, much of the city's subway infrastructure also dates from this era. Around town, you'll notice that some of the older U-Bahn stops are still Art Nouveau in design. Also during this time (in 1898), the horse-drawn tramline around the Ringstrasse was converted to electric power.

In so many ways, the Vienna of today was created during this brief spurt of architectural and engineering energy a century ago. Lueger himself has fallen into disrepute because of his racist politics (Hitler cited him as an inspiration in *Mein Kampf*). After decades of controversy, the part of the Ring named after Lueger in 1934 was rechristened the Universitätsring in 2012, and many would like to see his statue removed as well.

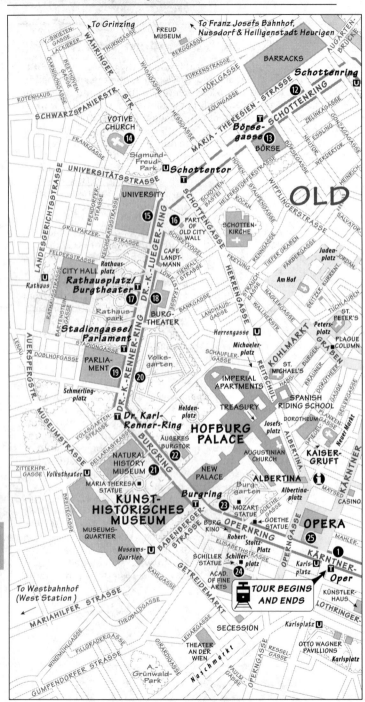

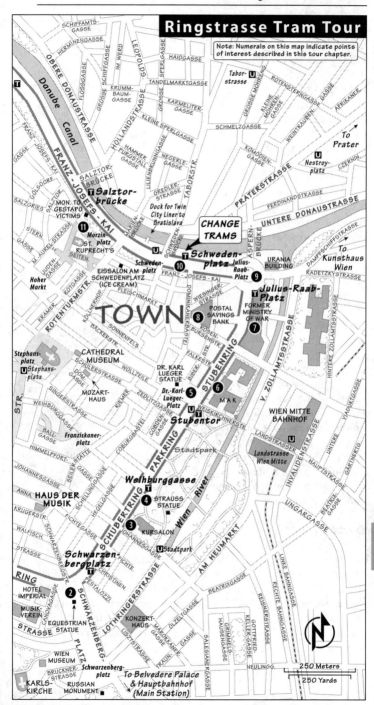

# Ringstrasse Tram Tour

Note: Numerals on this map indicate points of interest described in this tour chapter.

Danube Canal

OBERE DONAUSTRASSE

FRANZ-JOSEFS-KAI

SCHIFFAMTSGASSE
HERMINENGASSE
GROSSE SCHIFFGASSE
KLEINE PFARRGASSE
IM WERD
LEOPOLDS
GROSSE SPERLGASSE
HAIDGASSE
TANDELMARKTGASSE
KARMELITER-GASSE
GROSSE MOHRENG
ROTENSTERNGASSE
WEINTRAUBENG
AFRIKANER

Tabor-strasse U

To Prater

KOMÖDIEN-GASSE

Nestroy-platz U

CZERNIN

FERDINANDSTRASSE

PRATERSTRASSE

UNTERE DONAUSTRASSE

ASPERN-BRÜCKE

URANIA BUILDING

DAMPFSCHIFFSTRASSE

RADETZKYSTRASSE

To Kunsthaus Wien

Salztorbrücke

MON. TO GESTAPO VICTIMS

**11**

Morzin-platz

ST. RUPRECHT'S

SEITENST.

Schweden-platz

U

Schweden-brücke

**10** Schweden-platz

T CHANGE TRAMS

Dock for Twin City Liner to Bratislava

Julius-Raab-Platz

**9**

Julius-Raab-Platz

U

FORMER MINISTRY OF WAR **7**

V. ZOLLAMTSSTRASSE

HINTERE ZOLLAMTSSTRASSE

Hoher Markt

Stephans-platz U Stephansplatz

TOWN

CATHEDRAL MUSEUM

MOZART-HAUS

POSTAL SAVINGS BANK **8**

DR. KARL LUEGER STATUE

Dr.-Karl-Lueger-Platz **5**

**6**

MAK

Stubentor U

STUBENRING

WIEN MITTE BAHNHOF

Landstrasse Wien Mitte U

INVALIDENSTRASSE

UNGARGASSE

Franziskaner-platz

HAUS DER MUSIK

Weihburggasse

**4** STRAUSS STATUE

Wien River

Stadtpark

**3** KURSALON

U Stadtpark

Schwarzen-bergplatz

T

HOTEL IMPERIAL

MUSIK-VEREIN

**2**

EQUESTRIAN STATUE

SCHWARZENBERG-PLATZ

KONZERT-HAUS

WIEN MUSEUM

KARLS-KIRCHE

RUSSIAN MONUMENT

Schwarzenberg-platz

To Belvedere Palace & Hauptbahnhof (Main Station)

N

250 Meters
250 Yards

RINGSTRASSE TRAM

intrigues you, or just to catch your breath—trams come by every few minutes.

• *Let's go. Before you leave the* **Oper stop**...

### ❶ Look Left

Just next to the Opera house, the city's main pedestrian drag, Kärntner Strasse, leads to the zigzag-mosaic roof of **St. Stephen's Cathedral**. This tram tour makes a 360-degree circle around the cathedral, staying about this same distance from the great church that marks the center of Vienna.

• *As the tram sets off...*

### ❷ Look Right

Along this stretch, you'll pass a string of Vienna's finest five-star hotels, including **Hotel Imperial**—the choice of nearly every visiting big shot, from The Rolling Stones to Queen Elizabeth.

Just after the hotel, at Schwarzenberg-platz, an **equestrian statue** honors Prince Charles Schwarzenberg, who fought Napoleon. From the end of World War II until 1955, Austria and its capital were occupied by foreign troops, including Russian forces; during that time the square was named Stalinplatz after the Soviet dictator.

In the distance beyond the prince, at the far end of the long square, look for a fountain with a big colonnade just behind it. This **Russian monument** was built in 1945 as a forced thank-you to the Soviets for liberating Austria from the Nazis. Formerly a sore point, now the monument is just ignored.

• *Coming up soon is the* **Schwarzenbergplatz** *stop. When you pass it...*

### ❸ Look Right

Three blocks beyond the Schwarzenbergplatz stop is the huge **Stadtpark** (City Park). This inviting green space honors many great Viennese musicians and composers with statues. At the beginning of the park, the gold-and-cream concert hall behind the trees is the **Kursalon,** opened in 1867 by the Strauss brothers, who directed many waltzes here. Touristy Strauss concerts are held in this building (for details, see page 200). If the weather's nice, hop off at the next stop (Weihburggasse) for a stroll in the park.

• *Right at the* **Weihburggasse stop**...

### ❹ Look Right

In the park but barely visible from the tram (squint through the park gate near the stop), the gilded statue of "Waltz King" **Johann Strauss** holds a violin as he did when he conducted his orchestra, whipping his fans into a three-quarter-time frenzy.

• *The next several sights pass quickly, so read about them while you're waiting at the next stop (Stubentor). Just after the tram sets off again...*

### ❺ Look Left

Centered in a public square, a bronze statue (now turned green) of **Dr. Karl Lueger** honors the popular mayor who shaped Vienna into a modern city (see sidebar on page 123).

• *Immediately after the Lueger statue...*

### ❻ Look Right

The big, red-brick building across the street is the **Museum of Applied Art** (MAK), showing furniture and design through the ages (also has good café and gift shop; see page 76).

• *A block after the museum...*

### ❼ Look Right

The long, white building used to be the **Austrian Ministry of War**—back when that was a major operation. Above its oval windows, you can see busts of soldiers wearing Stratego-style military helmets. The equestrian statue at the entrance is Field Marshal Radetzky, a military big shot in the 19th century under Franz Josef.

• *Now...*

### ❽ Look Left

Radetzky is pointing across the street toward the **Postal Savings Bank** (set back on a little square; see page 77). Designed by Otto Wagner, it's one of the rare Secessionist buildings facing the Ring. (For more on The Secession, see the sidebar on page 66.)

• *Immediately after the **Julius-Raab-Platz stop**, the tram makes a sharp left turn, when you should...*

## ❾ Look Right

The white-domed building on your right is the **Urania,** Franz Josef's 1910 observatory. On the horizon behind the Urania, visually

trace the canal and squint to get a glimpse of the huge red cars of the giant hundred-year-old Ferris wheel in Vienna's **Prater amusement park** (fun and characteristically Viennese, described on page 88).

• *At the next stop,* ***Schwedenplatz...***

## ❿ Prepare to Get Off and Transfer

Hop off tram #2 at the Schwedenplatz stop and wait for tram #1 (heading in the same direction you've been going; trams come along every 5-10 minutes). Gelato fans may want to prolong the wait a little with a break at Eissalon am Schwedenplatz (daily 10:00-23:00). Before venturing away, check the electronic board at the stop to see how many minutes until the next tram arrives.

### While You Wait...

Notice the waterway next to you, and how blue it isn't: It's the **Danube Canal** (a.k.a. the "Baby Danube"), one of the many small

arms of the river that once made up the Danube at this location. The rest have been gathered together in a mightier modern-day Danube, farther away. This area was once the center of the original Roman town, Vindobona, located on the banks of the Danube—beyond which lay the barbarian Germanic lands.

The modern boat station is for the fast boat to Bratislava, Slovakia, about an hour downstream.

If some of the buildings across the canal seem a bit drab, that's because this neighborhood was thoroughly bombed in World War II. These postwar buildings were constructed on the cheap and are now being replaced by sleek, futuristic buildings.

By the way, this is called Schwedenplatz ("Sweden Square") because after World War I, Vienna was overwhelmed with hungry orphans. The Swedes took several thousand in, raised them, and finally sent them home healthy and well-fed.

• *Get ready—here comes tram #1. This time, grab a seat on the left if you can. Keep an eye toward the old city center. After three blocks, opposite the gas station (be ready—it passes fast)...*

## ⓫ Look Left

You'll see the ivy-covered walls and round Romanesque arches of **St. Ruprecht's** (Ruprechtskirche), the oldest church in Vienna. It was built in the 11th century on a bit of Roman ruins.

The low-profile, modern-looking, concrete **monument** in the corner of the park (close to the tram, on the left) commemorates the victims of the Gestapo, whose headquarters were here.

• *Take a breather for a bit—there's not much to see until after the next two stops (**Salztorbrücke** and **Schottenring**).*

## In the Meantime...

It's interesting to remember that the Ringstrasse replaced the mighty walls that once protected Vienna from external enemies.

Imagine the great imperial capital contained within its three-mile-long wall, most of which dated from the 16th to 18th century. As was typical of city walls, it was lined with cannons (2,200, in Vienna's case) and surrounded by a "shooting field" or "cannonball zone." This swath of land, as wide as a cannonball could fly (about 400 yards), was clear-cut so no one could approach without being targeted.

After the popular unrest and uprisings of 1848, the emperor realized the real threat against him was from within. He rid the city of its walls in about 1860, built this boulevard and transportation infrastructure (good for moving both citizens in good times and soldiers in bad), and, as you'll see in a moment, moved his army closer at hand. Napoleon III's remodel of Paris demonstrated that wide boulevards make it impossible for revolutionaries to erect barricades to block the movement of people and supplies. That encouraged Franz Josef to implement a similarly broad street plan for his Ring. A straight stretch of boulevard may seem just stately, but for an embattled emperor, it's an easy-to-defend corridor.

When the emperor had the walls taken down, the shooting field was wide open and ripe for development. Hence, the wonderful architecture that lines the outer edge of the Ringstrasse is all from the same era (post 1860).

• *The tram leaves the canal after the **Schottenring stop**, and turns left. But you should...*

## ⓬ Look Right

Through a gap in the buildings, on the right, you'll get a glimpse of a huge, red-brick castle—actually high-profile **barracks** built here at the command of a nervous Emperor Franz Josef (who found himself on the throne as an 18-year-old in 1848, the same year people's revolts against autocracy were sweeping across Europe).

• *When you pull into the **Börsegasse stop**...*

### ⓭ Look Left

The orange-and-white, Neo-Renaissance temple of money—the **Börse**—is Vienna's stock exchange. The next block is lined with banks and insurance companies—the financial district of Austria.

• *At the next stop **(Schottentor)**...*

### ⓮ Look Right

The huge, frilly, Neo-Gothic church across the small park is a **"votive church,"** a type of church built to fulfill a vow in thanks for God's help—in this case, when an 1853 assassination attempt on Emperor Franz Josef failed.

If you have an extra moment at the Schottentor stop, look ahead and left down the long, straight stretch of boulevard and imagine the city's impressive wall and that vast swath of no-man's land that extended as far as a cannonball could fly.

• *Just after the **Schottentor stop**...*

### ⓯ Look Right

You're looking at the main building of the **University of Vienna** (Universität Wien). Established in 1365, the university has no real campus, as its buildings are scattered around town. It's considered the oldest continuously operating university in the German-speaking world.

• *Immediately opposite the university...*

### ⓰ Look Left

A chunk of the old **city wall** is visible (behind a gilded angel). Beethoven lived and composed in the building just above the piece of wall.

• *As you pull into the **Rathausplatz/Burgtheater stop**, first...*

### ⓱ Look Right

The Neo-Gothic **City Hall** (Rathaus) flies both the flag of Austria and the flag of Europe. The square in front (Rathausplatz) is a festive site in summer, with a thriving food circus and a huge screen

RINGSTRASSE TRAM

## Historicism

Most of the architecture along the Ring is known as "Historicism" because it's all Neo-this and Neo-that. It takes design elements from the past—Greek columns, Renaissance arches, Baroque frills—and plasters them on the facade to simulate a building from the past.

Generally, the style fits the purpose of the particular building. For example, the Neoclassical parliament building celebrates ancient Greek notions of democracy. The Neo-Gothic City Hall recalls when medieval burghers ran the city government in Gothic days. Neo-Renaissance museums, such as the Kunsthistorisches and Natural History Museums, celebrate learning. And the Neo-Baroque National Theater recalls the age when opera and theater flourished.

showing outdoor movies, operas, and concerts (mid-July–mid-Sept 11:00-late; see pages 185 and 202). In December, the City Hall becomes a huge Advent calendar, with 24 windows opening—one each day—as Christmas approaches.
• *And then...*

#### ⓲ **Look Left**
Immediately across the street from City Hall is the **Burgtheater,** Austria's national the-
ater. Locals brag it's the "leading theater in the German-speaking world." Next door (on the left) is the recommended **Café Landtmann** (the only café built with the Ringstrasse buildings, and one of the city's finest).

• *Just after the **Stadiongasse/Parlament stop**...*

#### ⓳ **Look Right**
The Neo-Greek temple of democracy houses the **Austrian Parliament.** The lady with the golden helmet is Athena, goddess of wisdom.
• *And then swivel to...*

#### ⓴ **Look Left**
Across the street from the Parliament is the imperial park called the **Volksgarten,** with a fine public rose garden.
• *The next stop is **Dr. Karl-Renner-Ring**. When the tram pulls away...*

RINGSTRASSE TRAM

### ㉑ Look Right

The vast building is the **Natural History Museum** (Naturhistorisches Museum), which faces its twin, the **Kunsthistorisches Museum,** containing the city's greatest collection of paintings. The **MuseumsQuartier** behind them completes the ensemble with a collection of mostly modern art museums. A hefty statue of Empress Maria Theresa squats between the museums, facing the grand gate to the Hofburg Palace.

• *Now...*

### ㉒ Look Left

Opposite Maria Theresa, the arched gate (the Äusseres Burgtor, the only surviving castle gate of the old town wall) leads to the **Hofburg,** the emperor's palace. Of the five arches, the center one was used only by the emperor.

Your tour is nearly finished, so consider hopping off here to visit the Hofburg, the Kunsthistorisches Museum, or one of the museums in the MuseumsQuartier.

• *Fifty yards after the **Burgring** stop...*

### ㉓ Look Left

Until 1918, the appealing **Burggarten** was the private garden of the emperor. Today locals enjoy relaxing here, and it's also home to a famous statue of **Mozart** (pictured here; hard to see from the tram).

A hundred yards farther (also on the left, just out of the park, but also difficult to see), the German philosopher **Goethe** sits in a big, thought-provoking chair.

• *Now it's time to...*

### ㉔ Look Right

Goethe seems to be playing trivia with German poet **Schiller** across the street (in the little park set back from the street). Behind the statue of Schiller is the **Academy of Fine Arts** (described on page 63); next to it (on the right, facing the Ring) is the Burg Kino, which plays the movie *The Third Man* three times a week in English (see page 203).

• *Get ready to...*

### ㉕ Look Left...and Get Off

Hey, there's the **Opera** again. Jump off the tram and see the rest of the city. (To join me on a walking tour of Vienna's center, which starts here at the Opera, ❂ see the Vienna City Walk chapter.)

# HOFBURG IMPERIAL APARTMENTS TOUR

In this tour of the Hofburg Imperial Apartments, see the lavish, Versailles-like rooms that were home to the hardworking Emperor Franz Josef I and his reclusive, eccentric empress, known as "Sisi." From here, the Habsburgs ruled their vast empire.

Franz Josef was (for all intents and purposes) the last of the Habsburg monarchs, and these apartments straddle the transition from old to new. You'll see chandeliered luxury alongside office furniture and electric lights.

Franz Josef and Sisi were also a study in contrasts. Where Franz was earnest, practical, and spartan, Sisi was poetic, high-strung, and luxury-loving. Together, they lived their lives in the cocoon of the Imperial Apartments, seemingly oblivious to how the world was changing around them.

## Orientation

**Cost:** €11.50, includes well-done audioguide; also covered by €25.50 Sisi Ticket (see page 25), which includes the Schönbrunn Palace Grand Tour and the Imperial Furniture Collection.

**Hours:** Daily July-Aug 9:00-18:00, Sept-June 9:00-17:30, last entry one hour before closing.

**When to Go:** It can be crowded mid-mornings, so go either right at opening time or after 14:00.

**Getting There:** Enter from under the rotunda just off Michaelerplatz, through the Michaelertor gate.

**Information:** You'll find some helpful posted information in English, and the included audioguide brings the exhibit to life. With those tools and this chapter, you won't need the €9

*Imperial Apartments/Sisi Museum/Silver Collection* guidebook.
Tel. 01/533-7570, www.hofburg-wien.at.

**Length of This Tour:** If you listen to the entire audioguide, allow
40 minutes for the silver collection, 30 minutes for the Sisi
Museum, and 40 minutes for the apartments.

# The Tour Begins

Your ticket grants you admission to three
separate exhibits, which you'll visit on a
pretty straightforward one-way route.
The first floor holds a collection of precious porcelain and silver knickknacks
*(Silberkammer).* You then go upstairs to
the Sisi Museum, which has displays
about her life. This leads into the 20-odd
rooms of Imperial Apartments *(Kai-
serappartements),* starting in Franz Josef's rooms, then heading into the dozen
rooms where his wife Sisi lived.

## IMPERIAL PORCELAIN AND SILVER COLLECTION

Your visit (and the excellent audioguide) starts on the ground floor,
with the Habsburg court's vast tableware collection, which the audioguide actually manages to make fairly interesting. Browse the
collection to gawk at the opulence and to take in some colorful
Habsburg trivia. (Who'd have thunk that the court had an official
way to fold a napkin—and that the technique remains a closely
guarded secret?) Still, I wouldn't bog down here, as there's much
more to see upstairs.

• *Once you're through all those rooms of dishes, climb the stairs—the same
staircase used by the emperors and empresses who lived here. At the top
is a timeline of Sisi's life. Swipe your ticket to pass through the turnstile,
consider the (rare) WC, and enter the room with the...*

### Model of the Hofburg

Circle to the far side to find where you're standing right now, near
the smallest of the Hofburg's three domes. That small dome tops
the entrance to the Hofburg from Michaelerplatz.

The Hofburg was the epicenter of one of Europe's great political powers—600 years of Habsburgs lived here. The Hofburg
started as a 13th-century medieval castle (near where you are right
now) and expanded over the centuries to today's 240,000-square-
meter (60-acre) complex, now owned by the state.

To the left of the dome (as you face the facade) is the steeple

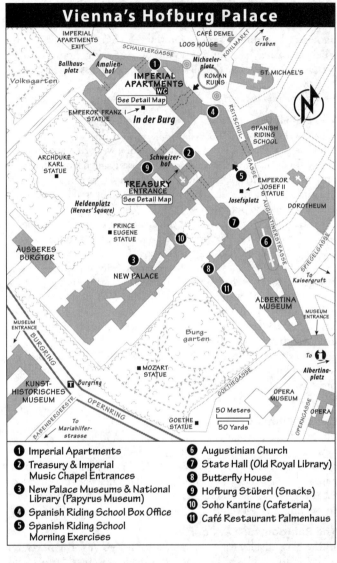

**Vienna's Hofburg Palace**

❶ Imperial Apartments
❷ Treasury & Imperial Music Chapel Entrances
❸ New Palace Museums & National Library (Papyrus Museum)
❹ Spanish Riding School Box Office
❺ Spanish Riding School Morning Exercises
❻ Augustinian Church
❼ State Hall (Old Royal Library)
❽ Butterfly House
❾ Hofburg Stüberl (Snacks)
❿ Soho Kantine (Cafeteria)
⓫ Café Restaurant Palmenhaus

of the Augustinian Church. It was there, in 1854, that Franz Josef married 16-year-old Elisabeth of Bavaria, and their story began.
• *Now enter a darkened room at the beginning of the...*

## SISI MUSEUM

Empress Elisabeth (1837-1898)—a.k.a. "Sisi" (SEE-see)—was Franz Josef's mysterious, beautiful, and narcissistic wife. This museum traces her fabulous but tragic life.

## Sisi's Death

The exhibit starts with Sisi's sad end, showing her **death mask,** photos of her **funeral procession** (by the Hercules statues facing Michaelerplatz), and an **engraving** of a grieving Franz Josef. It was at her death that the obscure, private empress' legend began to grow.

• *Continue into the corridor.*

## The Sisi Myth

**Newspaper clippings** of the day make it clear that the empress was not a major public figure in her lifetime. She was often absent from public functions, and the censored press was gagged from reporting on her eccentricities. After her death, however, her image quickly became a commodity and began appearing on everyday items such as **candy tins** and **beer steins.**

The plaster-cast **statue** captures the one element of her persona everyone knew: her beauty. Sisi was nearly 5'8" (a head taller than her husband), had a 20-inch waist (she wore very tight corsets), and weighed only about 100 pounds. (Her waistline eventually grew...to 21 inches. That was at age 50, after giving birth to four children.) This statue, a copy of one of 30 statues that were erected in her honor in European cities, shows her holding one of her trademark fans. It doesn't show off her magnificent hair, however, which reached down to her ankles.

Sisi-mania really got going in the 1950s with a series of **movies** based on her life (starring Romy Schneider), depicting the empress as beautiful and innocent.

• *Round the corner into the next room.*

## Sisi's Childhood

Sisi grew up on a country estate in Bavaria, amid horses and woods, far from sophisticated city life. (See her **baby shoes** in a box and the picture of her **childhood palace.**) At 15, Franz Josef—who'd been engaged to someone else—spied Sisi and fell in love. They married. At the wedding reception, Sisi burst into tears, the first sign that something was not right.

## The Ballroom: Sisi at Court

In the glass display cases are replicas of her **gowns. Big portraits** of Sisi and Franz Josef show them dressed to the nines. **Jewels** (also replicas) reproduce some of the finery she wore as empress—but to her, they were her "chains." She hated official court duties and the constraints of public life, and hated being the center of attention. Sisi's mother-in-law dominated her child-rearing, her first-born died, and she complained that she couldn't sleep or eat. However, she did participate in one political cause—championing rights

# Sisi (1837-1898)

Empress Elisabeth—Franz Josef's beautiful wife—was the 19th-century equivalent of Princess Diana. Known as "Sisi" 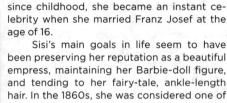 since childhood, she became an instant celebrity when she married Franz Josef at the age of 16.

Sisi's main goals in life seem to have been preserving her reputation as a beautiful empress, maintaining her Barbie-doll figure, and tending to her fairy-tale, ankle-length hair. In the 1860s, she was considered one of the most beautiful women in the world. But, despite severe dieting and fanatical exercise, age took its toll. After turning 30, she refused to allow photographs or portraits, and was generally seen in public with a delicate fan covering her face (and bad teeth).

Complex and influential, Sisi was adored by Franz Josef, whom she respected. Although Franz Josef was supposed to have married her sister Helene (in an arranged diplomatic marriage), he fell in love with Sisi instead. It was one of the Habsburgs' few marriages for love.

Sisi's personal mission and political cause was promoting Hungary's bid for autonomy within the empire. Her personal tragedy was the death of her son Rudolf, the crown prince, in an apparent suicide (an incident often dramatized as the "Mayerling Affair," named after the royal hunting lodge where it happened). Disliking Vienna and the confines of the court, Sisi traveled more and more frequently. (She spent so much time in Budapest, and with Hungarian statesman Count Andrássy, that many believe her third daughter to be the count's.) As the years passed, the restless Sisi and her hardworking husband became estranged. In 1898, while visiting Geneva, Switzerland, she was murdered by an Italian anarchist.

Sisi's beauty, bittersweet life, and tragic death helped create her larger-than-life legacy. However, her importance is often inflated by melodramatic accounts of her life. The Sisi Museum seeks to tell a more accurate story.

for Habsburg-controlled Hungary (see her **bust** and **portrait as Queen of Hungary**).

• *Head into the next, darkened room.*

## Sisi's Beauty

Sisi longed for the carefree days of her youth. She began to withdraw from public life, passing time riding horses (see **horse** statuettes and pictures) and tending obsessively to maintaining her physical beauty. In the glass case on the right wall, you'll see some of her **menus,** and a **bill from Demel.** Her **recipes** for beauty preparations included creams and lotions as well as wearing a raw-meat face mask while she slept. Sisi weighed herself obsessively on her gold-trimmed **scale** and tried all types of diets, including bouillon made with a **duck press.** (She never gave up pastries and ice cream, however.) After she turned 30, Sisi refused to appear in any portraits or photographs, preferring that only her more youthful depictions be preserved. Appreciate the **white gloves,** the **ivory fan,** and the **white nightgown** (displayed nearby)...because her life was about to turn even more dark.

• *Then enter the darkest room.*

### Death of Sisi's Son

A mannequin wears a replica of Sisi's **black dress,** and nearby you'll see **black jewels** and accessories. In 1889, Sisi's and Franz Josef's son, Prince Rudolf—whose life had veered into sex, drugs, and liberal politics—apparently killed his lover and himself in a suicide pact. Sisi was shattered and retreated further from public life.

• *Stroll through several more rooms.*

### Escape

Sisi consoled herself with **poetry** (the museum has quotes on the walls) that expresses a longing to escape into an ideal world. As you continue through the exhibit, you'll see she also consoled herself with travel. There's a reconstruction of her **rail car**—a step above a *couchette.* A **map** shows her visits to Britain, Eastern Europe, and her favorite spot, Greece.

### Final Room: Assassination

Sisi met her fate while traveling. While walking along a street in Geneva, Sisi was stalked and attacked by an Italian anarchist who despised royal oppressors and wanted notoriety for his cause. (He'd planned on assassinating a less-famous French prince that day—whom he'd been unable to track down—but quickly changed plans when word got out that Sisi was in town.) The **murder weapon** was this small, crude, knife-like file. It made only a small wound, but it proved fatal.

• *After the Sisi Museum, a one-way route takes you through a series of royal rooms. The first room—as if to make clear that there was more to the Habsburgs than Sisi—shows a family tree tracing the Habsburgs from 1273 (Rudolf I at upper left) to their messy WWI demise (Karl I, lower right). From here, enter the private apartments of the royal family (Franz Josef's first, then Sisi's). Much of the following commentary complements the information you'll hear listening to the audioguide.*

## IMPERIAL APARTMENTS

These were the private apartments and public meeting rooms for the emperor and empress. Franz Josef I lived here from 1857 until his death in 1916. (He had hoped to move to new digs in the New Palace, but that was not finished until after his death.)

Franz Josef was the last great Habsburg ruler. (For an abridged Habsburg family tree, see page 455.) In these rooms, he presided over defeats and liberal inroads as the world was changing and the monarchy becoming obsolete. Here he met with advisors and welcomed foreign dignitaries, hosted lavish, white-gloved balls and stuffy formal dinners, and raised three children. He slept (alone) on his austere bed while his beloved wife Sisi retreated to her own rooms. He suffered through the execution of his brother, the suicide of his son and heir, the murder of his wife, and the assassination of his nephew, Archduke Ferdinand, which sparked World War I and spelled the end of the Habsburg monarchy.

### The Emperor's Rooms
#### Waiting Room for the Audience Room

**Mannequins** from the many corners of the Habsburg realm illustrate the multiethnic nature of the vast empire. (Also see the **map** of the empire, by the window.) Every citizen had the right to meet privately with the emperor, and people traveled fairly far to do so. While they waited nervously, they had these **three huge paintings** to stare at—propaganda showing crowds of commoners enthusiastic about their Habsburg rulers.

The painting on the right shows an 1809 scene of Emperor Franz II (Franz Josef's grandfather) returning to Vienna, celebrating the news that Napoleon had begun his retreat.

In the central painting, Franz II makes his first public appearance to adoring crowds after recovering from a life-threatening illness (1826).

In the painting on the left, Franz II returns to Vienna (see the Karlskirche in the background) to celebrate the defeat of Napoleon. The 1815 Congress of Vienna that followed was the greatest assembly of diplomats in European history. Its goal: to establish peace by shoring up Europe's monarchies against the rise of democracy and nationalism. It worked for about a century, until a colossal war—World War I—wiped out the Habsburgs and other European royal families.

This room's **chandelier**—considered the best in the palace—is Baroque, made of Bohemian crystal. It lit things until 1891, when the palace installed electric lights.

# Hofburg Imperial Apartments Tour

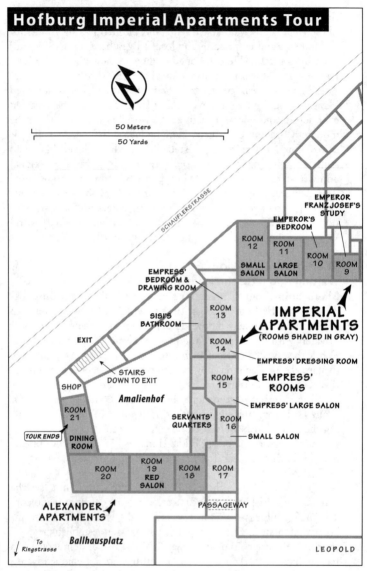

## Audience Chamber

This is the room where Franz Josef received commoners from around the empire. Imagine you've traveled for days to have your say before the emperor. You're wearing your new fancy suit—Franz Josef required that men coming before him wear a tailcoat, women a black gown with a train. You've rehearsed what you want to say. You hope your hair looks good.

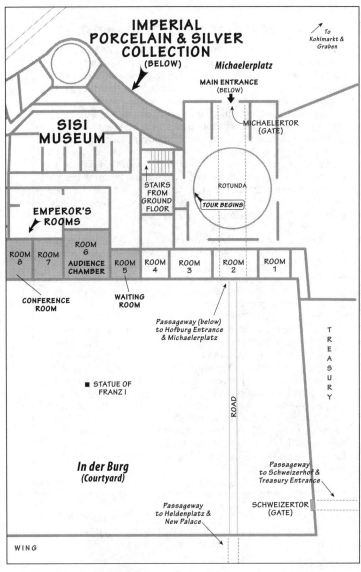

Suddenly, you're face-to-face with the emp himself. (The **portrait** on the easel shows Franz Josef in 1915, when he was more than 80 years old.) Despite your efforts, you probably weren't in this room long. He'd stand at the **lectern** (far left) as the visiting commoners had their say. (Standing kept things moving.) You'd hear a brief response from him (quite likely the same he'd given all day), and then you'd back out of the room while bowing (also

# Emperor Franz Josef (1830-1916)

Franz Josef I—who ruled for 68 years (1848-1916)—was the embodiment of the Habsburg Empire as it finished its six-century-long ride. Born in 1830, Franz Josef had a stern upbringing that instilled in him a powerful sense of duty and—like so many men of power—a love of all things military.

His uncle, Ferdinand I, suffered from profound epilepsy, which prevented him from being an effective ruler. As the revolutions of 1848 rattled royal families throughout Europe, the Habsburgs forced Ferdinand to abdicate and put 18-year-old Franz Josef on the throne. Ironically, as one of his first acts as emperor, Franz Josef—whose wife would later become closely identified with Hungarian independence—put down the 1848 revolt in Hungary with bloody harshness. He spent the first part of his long reign understandably paranoid, as social discontent continued to simmer.

Franz Josef was very conservative. But worse, he wrongly believed that he was a talented military tactician, leading Austria into catastrophic battles against Italy (which was fighting for its unification and independence) in the 1860s. As his army endured severe, avoidable casualties, it became clear: Franz Josef was a disaster as a general.

Wearing his uniform to the end, Franz Josef never saw what a dinosaur his monarchy was becoming, and never thought it strange that the majority of his subjects didn't even speak German. Franz Josef had no interest in democracy and pointedly never set foot in Austria's parliament building. But, like his contemporary Queen Victoria, he was a microcosm of his empire—old-fashioned but sacrosanct. His passion for low-grade paperwork earned him the nickname "Joe Bureaucrat." Mired in these petty details, he missed the big picture. In 1914, he helped start a Great War that ultimately ended the age of monarchs. The year 1918 marked the end of Europe's big royal families: Hohenzollerns (Prussia), Romanovs (Russia), and Habsburgs (Austria).

required). On the lectern is a partial **list** of 56 appointments he had on January 3, 1910 (three columns: family name, meeting topic, and *Anmerkung*—the emperor's "action log").

## Conference Room

The emperor and his cabinet sat at this long Empire-style table to discuss policy. An ongoing topic was what to do with unruly Hungary. After 1867, Franz Josef granted Hungary a measure of independence (thus creating the "Austro-Hungarian Empire"). Hungarian diplomats attended meetings here, watched over by **paintings** on the wall showing Austria's army suppressing the popular Hungarian uprising...subtle.

## Emperor Franz Josef's Study

This room evokes how seriously the emperor took his responsibilities as the top official of a vast empire. Famously energetic, Franz Josef lived a spartan life dedicated to duty. The **desk** was originally positioned in such a way that Franz Josef could look up from his work and see the **portrait** of his lovely, long-haired, tiny-waisted Empress Elisabeth reflected in the mirror. Notice the **trompe l'oeil paintings** above each door, giving the believable illusion of marble relief. Notice also all the **family photos**—the perfect gift for the dad/uncle/hubby who has it all.

The walls between the rooms are wide enough to hide servants' corridors (the hidden door to his valet's room is in the back-left corner). The emperor lived with a personal staff of 14: "three valets, four lackeys, two doormen, two manservants, and three chambermaids."

## Emperor's Bedroom

Franz Josef famously slept on this no-frills **iron bed** and used the **portable washstand** until 1880 (when the palace got running water). He typically rose at 3:30 and started his day in prayer, kneeling at the **prayer stool** against the far wall. After all, he was a "Divine Right" ruler. While he had a typical emperor's share of mistresses, his dresser was always well-stocked with **photos** of Sisi. Franz Josef lived here after his estrangement from Sisi. An **etching** shows the empress—a fine rider and avid hunter—sitting side-saddle while jumping a hedge.

## Large Salon

This red-walled room was for royal family gatherings and went unused after Sisi's death. The big, ornate **stove** in the corner was fed from behind (this remained a standard form of heating through the 19th century).

## Small Salon

This room is dedicated to the memory of Franz Josef's brother (see the **portrait with the weird beard**), the Emperor Maximilian I of Mexico, who was overthrown and executed in 1867. It was also a smoking room. This was a necessity in the early 19th century, when smoking was newly fashionable for men, and was never done in the presence of women.

After the birth of their last child in 1868, Franz Josef and Sisi began to drift further apart. Left of the door is a small **button** the emperor had to buzz before entering his estranged wife's quarters. You, however, can go right in.

• *Climb three steps and enter Sisi's wing.*

## Empress' Rooms
### Empress' Bedroom and Drawing Room

This was Sisi's room, refurbished in the Neo-Rococo style in 1854. There's the red **carpet,** covered with oriental rugs. There were always lots of fresh flowers. She not only slept here, but also lived here—the bed was rolled in and out daily—until her death in 1898. The **desk** is where she sat and wrote her letters and poems.

### Empress' Dressing/Exercise Room

Servants worked three hours a day on Sisi's famous hair, while she passed the time reading. She'd exercise on the **wooden structure** and on the **rings** suspended from the doorway to the left. Afterward, she'd get a massage on the red-covered **bed.** You can psychoanalyze Sisi from the **portraits and photos** she chose to hang on her walls. They're mostly her favorite dogs, her Bavarian family, and several portraits of the romantic and anti-monarchist poet Heinrich Heine. Her infatuation with the liberal Heine, whose family was Jewish, caused a stir in royal circles.

### Empress' Lavatory and Bathroom

Detour into the behind-the-scenes palace. In the narrow passageway, you'll walk by Sisi's hand-painted porcelain, dolphin-head **WC** (on the right). In the main bathroom, you'll see her huge copper tub (with the original wall coverings behind it), where servants washed her hair. Sisi was the first Habsburg to have running water in her bathroom (notice the hot and cold faucets). Beneath the carpet you're walking on is the first linoleum ever used in Vienna (c. 1880).

### Servants' Quarters (Bergl Rooms)

Next, enter the servants' quarters, with hand-painted **tropical scenes.** Take time to enjoy the playful details. As you leave these rooms and re-enter the imperial world, look back to the room on the left.

### Empress' Large Salon

The room is **painted** with Mediterranean escapes, the 19th-century equivalent of travel posters. The **statue of Polyhymnia** (the mythical Muse of poetry) is by the great Neoclassical master Antonio Canova. It has the features of Elisa, Napoleon's oldest sister, who hobnobbed with the Habsburgs. A **print** shows how Franz Josef and Sisi would—on their good days—share breakfast in this room.

### Small Salon

The portrait is of **Crown Prince Rudolf,** Franz Josef's and Sisi's only son. On the morning of January 30, 1889, the 30-year-old Rudolf and a beautiful baroness were found shot dead in his hunting lodge in Mayerling. An investigation never came up with a complete explanation, but Rudolf had obviously been cheating on his wife, and the affair ended in an apparent murder-suicide. The scandal shocked the empire and tainted the Habsburgs; Sisi retreated further into her fantasy world, and Franz Josef carried on stoically with a broken heart. The mysterious "Mayerling Affair" has been dramatized in numerous movies, plays, an opera, and even a ballet.

• *Leaving Sisi's wing, turn the corner into the white-and-gold rooms occupied by the czar of Russia during the 1814-1815 Congress of Vienna. Sisi and Franz Josef used the rooms for formal occasions and public functions.*

## Alexander Apartments
### Red Salon

The Gobelin wall hangings were a 1776 gift from Marie-Antoinette and Louis XVI in Paris to their Viennese counterparts.

### Dining Room

It's dinnertime, and Franz Josef has called his extended family together. The settings are modest...just silver. Gold was saved

for formal state dinners. Next to each name card was a menu listing the chef responsible for each dish. (Talk about pressure.) While the Hofburg had tableware for 4,000, feeding 3,000 was a typical day. The cellar was stocked with 60,000 bottles of wine. The kitchen was huge—50 birds could be roasted at once on the hand-driven spits.

The emperor sat in the center of the long table. "Ladies and gentlemen" alternated in the seating. The green glasses were specifically for Rhenish wine (dry whites from the Rhine valley). Franz Josef enforced strict protocol at mealtime: No one could speak without being spoken to by the emperor, and no one could eat after he was done. While the rest of Europe was growing democracy and expanding personal freedoms, the Habsburgs preserved their ossified worldview to the bitter end.

In 1918, World War I ended, Austria was created as a modern nation-state, the Habsburgs were tossed out...and Hofburg Palace was destined to become a museum.

• *Drop off your audioguide, zip through the shop, go down the stairs, and you're back on the street. Two quick lefts take you back to the palace square (In der Burg), where the Treasury awaits just past the black, red, and gold gate on the far side (see the next chapter).*

# HOFBURG TREASURY TOUR

The Hofburg Palace's "Treasure Room" contains the best jewels on the Continent. Slip through the vault doors and reflect on the glitter of 21 rooms filled with secular and religious ornaments: scepters, swords, crowns, orbs, weighty robes, double-headed eagles, gowns, gem-studded bangles, and a unicorn horn.

There are plenty of beautiful objects here—I've highlighted those that have the most history behind them. But you could spend days in here marveling at the riches of the bygone empire.

Use this chapter to get the lay of the land, but rent the excellent audioguide to really delve into the Treasury (and to make up for the lack of written English descriptions).

## Orientation

**Cost:** €12, €20 combo-ticket with Kunsthistorisches Museum and New Palace museums.

**Hours:** Wed-Mon 9:00-17:30, closed Tue, last entry 30 minutes before closing.

**Getting There:** The Treasury is tucked away in the Hofburg Palace complex. From the Hofburg's central courtyard (In der Burg), salute the Caesar-esque statue and turn about-face. Pass through the black, red, and gold gate (Schweizertor), following *Schatzkammer* signs, which lead into the Schweizerhof courtyard; the Treasury entrance is in the far-right corner. Follow signs to a stairway that climbs up to the Treasury (see map on page 135).

**Information:** Tel. 01/525-240, www.kaiserliche-schatzkammer.at.

**Tours:** The €4 audioguide describes 100 stops—well worth it to

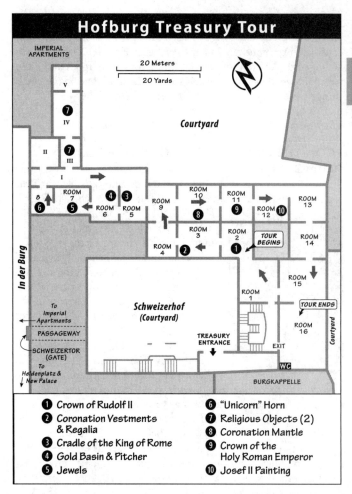

# Hofburg Treasury Tour

- ❶ Crown of Rudolf II
- ❷ Coronation Vestments & Regalia
- ❸ Cradle of the King of Rome
- ❹ Gold Basin & Pitcher
- ❺ Jewels
- ❻ "Unicorn" Horn
- ❼ Religious Objects (2)
- ❽ Coronation Mantle
- ❾ Crown of the Holy Roman Emperor
- ❿ Josef II Painting

get the most out of this dazzling collection. (The longer €7 audioguide is gilding the lily.)

**Starring:** The Imperial Crown and other accessories of the Holy Roman Emperors, plus many other crowns, jewels, robes, and priceless knickknacks.

# The Tour Begins

The Habsburgs saw themselves as the successors to the ancient Roman emperors, and they wanted crowns and royal regalia to match the pomp of the ancients. They used these precious objects for coronation ceremonies, official ribbon-cutting events, and their own personal pleasure. You'll see the prestigious crowns and accoutrements of the rulers of the Holy Roman Empire (a medieval alliance of Germanic kingdoms so named because it wanted to be considered the continuation of the Roman Empire). Other crowns belonged to Austrian dukes and kings, and some robes and para-phernalia were used by Austria's religious elite. And many costly things were created simply for the enjoyment of the wealthy (but not necessarily royal) Habsburgs.

• *Skip through Room 1 to where we'll begin, in Room 2.*

## FROM THE FIRST HABSBURG TO NAPOLEON
### Room 2

The personal **crown of Rudolf II** (1602) occupies the center of the room along with its accompanying scepter and orb; a bust of Rudolf

II (1552-1612) sits nearby. The crown's design symbolically merges a bishop's miter ("Holy"), the arch across the top of a Roman emperor's helmet ("Roman"), and the typical medieval king's crown ("Emperor"). Accompanying the crown are the matching **scepter** (made from the ivory tusk of a narwhal) and **orb** (hold-ing four diamonds to symbolize the four corners of the world, which the emperor ruled). Orbs have been royal symbols of the world since ancient Roman times. They seem to indicate that, even in pre-Columbus days, Europe's intelligentsia assumed the world was round.

This crown was Rudolf's personal one. He wore a different crown (which we'll see later) in his official role as Holy Roman Em-peror. In many dynasties, a personal crown like this was dismantled by the next ruler to custom-make his own. But Rudolf's crown was so well-crafted that it was passed down through the generations, even inspiring crown-shaped church steeples as far away as Am-sterdam (when that city was under Habsburg control).

Two centuries later (1806), this crown and scepter became the official regalia of Austria's rulers, as seen in the large **portrait of Franz I** (the open-legged guy behind you). Napoleon Bonaparte had just conquered Austria and dis-solved the Holy Roman Empire. Franz (ruled 1792-1835) was allowed to remain in power, but he had to downgrade his title from "Franz II, Holy Roman Emperor" to "Franz I, Em-peror of Austria."

## Rooms 3 and 4

These rooms contain some of the **coronation vestments and regalia** needed for the new Austrian (not Holy Roman) Emperor. There was a different one for each of the emperor's subsidiary titles, e.g., King of Hungary or King of Lombardy. So many crowns and kingdoms in the Habsburgs' vast empire! Those with the white ermine collars are modeled after Napoleon's coronation robes.

• *For more on how Napoleon had an impact on Habsburg Austria, pass through Room 9 and into...*

## Room 5

Ponder the **Cradle of the King of Rome,** once occupied by Napoleon's son, who was born in 1811 and made King of Rome. The lit-

tle eagle at the foot is symbolically not yet able to fly, but glory-bound. Glory is symbolized by the star, with dad's big *N* raised high. While it's fun to think of Napoleon's baby snoozing in here, this was a ceremonial "throne bed" that was rarely used.

Napoleon Bonaparte (1769-1821) was a French commoner who rose to power as a charismatic general in the Revolution. While pledging allegiance to democracy, he in fact crowned himself Emperor of France and hobnobbed with Europe's royalty. When his wife Josephine could not bear him a male heir, Napoleon divorced her and married into the Habsburg family.

**Portraits** show Napoleon and his new bride, Marie Louise, Franz I/II's daughter (and Marie-Antoinette's great-niece). Napoleon gave her a **jewel chest** decorated with the bees of industriousness, his personal emblem. With the birth of the baby King of Rome, Napoleon and Marie Louise were poised to start a new dynasty of European rulers... but then Napoleon met his Waterloo, and the Habsburgs remained in power.

## MISCELLANEOUS WONDERS
## Room 6

For Divine Right kings, even child-rearing was a sacred ritual that needed elaborate regalia for public ceremonies. The 23-pound **gold basin and pitcher** were used to baptize noble children, who were dressed in the **baptismal dresses** displayed nearby.

## Room 7

These jewels are the true "treasures," a cabinet of wonders used by Habsburgs to impress their relatives (or to hock when funds got

low). The irregularly shaped, 2,680-karat **emerald** is rough-cut, as the cutter wanted to do only the minimum to avoid making a mistake and shattering the giant gem. Check out the milky **opal,** the "**hair amethyst,**" and a 492-karat **aquamarine.** The helmet-like, jewel-studded **crown** (left wall) was a gift from Muslim Turks supporting a Hungarian king who, as a Protestant, was a thorn in the side of the Catholic Habsburgs (who eventually toppled him).

## Room 8

The eight-foot-tall, 500-year-old **"unicorn horn"** (actually a narwhal tusk), was considered to have magical healing powers bestowed from on high. This one was owned by the Holy Roman Emperor—clearly a divine monarch. The huge **agate bowl,** cut from a single piece, may have been made in ancient Roman times and eventually found its way into the collection of their successors, the Habsburgs.

## Religious Rooms

After Room 8, you enter several rooms of **religious objects**—crucifixes, chalices, mini-altarpieces, reliquaries, and bishops' vestments. Habsburg rulers mixed the institutions of church and state, so these precious religious accoutrements were also part of their display of secular power.

• *Browse these rooms, then backtrack, passing by the Cradle of the King of Rome, and eventually reaching...*

## REGALIA OF THE HOLY ROMAN EMPIRE
## Room 10

The next few rooms contain some of the oldest and most venerated objects in the Treasury—the robes, crowns, and sacred objects of the Holy Roman Emperor.

The big red-silk and gold-thread **mantle,** nearly 900 years old, was worn by Holy Roman Emperors at their coronations.

Notice the oriental imagery: a palm tree in the center, flanked by lions subduing camels. The hem is written in Arabic (wishing its wearer "great wealth, gifts, and pleasure"). This robe, brought

back from the East by Crusaders, gave the Germanic emperors an exotic look that recalled great biblical kings such as Solomon. Many Holy Roman Emperors were crowned by the pope himself. That fact, plus this Eastern-looking mantle, helped put the "Holy" in Holy Roman Emperor.

## Room 11

The collection's highlight is the 10th-century **crown of the Holy Roman Emperor.** It was probably made for Otto I (c. 960), the first king to call himself Holy Roman Emperor.

The Imperial Crown swirls with symbolism "proving" that the emperor was both holy and Roman: The cross on top says the HRE

ruled as Christ's representative on earth, and the jeweled arch over the top is reminiscent of the parade helmet of ancient Romans. The jewels themselves allude to the wearer's kinghood in the here and now. Imagine the impression this priceless, glittering crown must have made on the emperor's medieval subjects.

King Solomon's portrait on the crown (to the right of the cross) is Old Testament proof that kings can be wise and good. King David (next panel) is similar proof that they can be

just. The crown's eight sides represent the celestial city of Jerusalem's eight gates. The jewels on the front panel symbolize the 12 apostles.

On the forehead of the crown, notice that beneath the cross there's a pale-blue, heart-shaped sapphire. Look a little small for the prime spot? That's because this is a replacement for a long-lost opal said to have had almost mythical, magical powers.

Nearby is the 11th-century **Imperial Cross** that preceded the emperor in ceremonies. Encrusted with jewels, it had a hollow compartment (its core is wood) that carried substantial chunks thought to be from *the* **cross** on which Jesus was crucified and *the* **Holy Lance** used to pierce his side (both pieces are displayed in the same glass case). Holy Roman Emperors actually carried the lance into battle in the 10th century. Look behind the cross to see how it was a box that could be clipped open and shut, used for holding

# Charlemagne (Karl der Grosse) and the Holy Roman Empire

The title Holy Roman Emperor conveyed three important concepts:

**Holy** = The emperor ruled by divine authority (and not as a pagan Roman).

**Roman** = He was a successor to the empire that fell in A.D. 476.

**Emperor** = He was a ruler over many different nationalities.

Charlemagne (747-814) briefly united much of Western Europe—that is, the former Roman Empire. On Christmas Eve in the year 800, he was crowned "Roman Emperor" by the pope in St. Peter's Basilica in Rome. After Charlemagne's death, the empire split apart. His successors (who ruled only a portion of Charlemagne's empire) still wanted to envision themselves as inheritors of Charlemagne's greatness. They took to calling themselves Roman Emperors, adding the "Holy" part in the 11th century to emphasize that they ruled by divine authority.

The Holy Roman Emperorship was an elected, not necessarily hereditary, office. Traditionally, the rulers of four important provinces would gather with three powerful archbishops to pick the new ruler; these seven "kingmakers" each held the prestigious title of Elector. The practice lasted through medieval and Renaissance times to the Napoleonic Wars, with most of the emperors hailing from the Habsburg family.

At the empire's peak around 1520, it truly was great. Emperor Charles V ruled Spain in addition to the HRE, so his realm stretched from Vienna to Spain, from Holland to Sicily, and from Bohemia to Bolivia in the New World. But throughout much of its existence, the HRE consisted of little more than petty dukes, ruling a loose coalition of independent nobles. It was Voltaire who quipped that the HRE was "neither holy, nor Roman, nor an empire."

Napoleon ended the title in 1806. The last Habsburg emperors (including Franz Josef) were merely Emperors of Austria.

holy relics. You can see bits of the "true cross" anywhere, but this is a prime piece—with the actual nail hole.

The other case has additional objects used in the coronation ceremony: The **orb** (orbs were modeled on late-Roman ceremonial objects, then topped with the cross) and **scepter** (the one with the oak leaves), along with the sword, were carried ahead of the emperor in the procession. In earlier times, these objects were thought to have belonged to Charlemagne himself, the greatest ruler of medieval Europe, but in fact they're mostly from 300 to 400 years later (c. 1200).

Yet another glass case contains more objects said to belong

to Charlemagne. Some of these may be authentic, since they're closer to his era. You'll see the jeweled, purse-like **reliquary of St. Stephen** and the **saber of Charlemagne**. The gold-covered **Book of the Gospels** was the Bible that emperors placed their hands on to swear the oath of office. On the wall nearby, the **tall painting** depicts Charlemagne modeling the Imperial Crown—although the crown wasn't made until a hundred years after he died.

## Room 12

Now picture all this regalia used together. The **painting** shows the coronation of Maria Theresa's son Josef II as Holy Roman Emperor in 1764. Set in a church in Frankfurt (filled with the bigwigs—literally—of the day), Josef is wearing the same crown and royal garb that you've just seen.

Emperors followed the same coronation ritual that originated in the 10th century. The new emperor would don the mantle. The entourage paraded into a church for Mass, led by the religious authorities carrying the Imperial Cross. The emperor placed his hand on the Book of the Gospels and swore his oath. Then he knelt before the three archbishop Electors, who placed the Imperial Crown on his head (sometimes he even traveled to Rome to be crowned by the pope himself). The new emperor rose, accepted the orb and scepter, and—dut dutta dah!—you had a new ruler.

• *The tour is over. Pass through Rooms 13-16 to reach the exit, browsing relics, portraits, and objects along the way.*

# KUNSTHISTORISCHES MUSEUM TOUR

The Kunsthistorwhateveritis Museum—let's just say "Koonst"—houses the family collection of Austria's luxury-loving Habsburg rulers. Their joie de vivre is reflected in this collection—some of the most beautiful, sexy, and fun art from two centuries (c. 1450-1650). At their peak of power in the 1500s, the Habsburgs ruled Austria, Germany, northern Italy, the Netherlands, and Spain—and you'll see a wide variety of art from all these places and beyond.

The building itself is worth notice—a lavish textbook example of Historicism. Despite its palatial feel, it was originally designed for the same purpose it serves today: to showcase its treasures in an inviting space while impressing visitors with the grandeur of the empire.

This chapter gives just a taste of the Kunst. Hit these highlights—mainly large canvases in the large halls—then explore the smaller side rooms for more delights.

## Orientation

**Cost:** €14, includes New Palace museums at the Hofburg; free for kids under age 19, €20 combo-ticket also includes the Hofburg Treasury.

**Hours:** June-Aug daily 10:00-18:00; Sept-May Tue-Sun 10:00-18:00, closed Mon; Thu until 21:00 year-round, last entrance 30 minutes before closing.

**Getting There:** It's on the Ringstrasse at Maria-Theresien-Platz, U-2 or U-3: Volkstheater/Museumsplatz (exit toward *Burgring*).

**Information:** Tel. 01/525-240, www.khm.at.

**Tours:** The excellent €4 audioguide, covering nearly 600 items, is worthwhile if you want an in-depth tour beyond the items covered in this chapter.

**Services:** There's a free cloakroom. The restaurant is on the first floor.

**Starring:** The world's best collection of Bruegel, plus Titian, Caravaggio, a Vermeer gem, and Rembrandt self-portraits.

# The Tour Begins

Of the museum's many exhibits, we'll tour only the Painting Gallery (Gemäldegalerie) on the first floor. Italian-Spanish-French art

is in one half of the building, and Northern European art in the other. On our tour, we'll get a sampling of each. Note that the museum labels the largest rooms with Roman numerals (Saal I, II, III) and the smaller rooms around the perimeter with Arabic (Rooms 1, 2, 3). The museum seems to constantly move paintings from room to room, so be flexible.

• *Climb the main staircase, featuring Antonio Canova's statue of Theseus clubbing a centaur. Bear right when you reach Theseus. At the top of the staircase, make a U-turn to the left. Enter Saal I and walk right into the High Renaissance.*

• *Start in Saal I.*

## ITALIAN RENAISSANCE

About the year 1500, Italy was in the midst of a 100-year renaissance, or "rebirth," of interest in the art and learning of ancient Greece and Rome. In painting, that meant that ordinary humans and Greek gods joined saints and angels as popular subjects.

### Titian—*Danae* and *Ecce Homo*

In the long career of Titian the Venetian (it rhymes), he painted portraits, Christian Madonnas, and sexy Venuses with equal ease.

Titian captured Danae—a luscious nude reclining in bed—as she's about to be seduced. Zeus, the king of the gods, descends as a shower of gold to consort with her—you can almost see the human form of Zeus within the cloud. Danae is helpless with rapture, opening her legs to receive him, while her servant tries to catch the heavenly spurt with a golden dish. Danae's rich, luminous flesh is set off by the dark servant at right and the threatening sky above. The white sheets beneath her make her glow even more. This is not just a classic nude—it's a Renaissance Miss August. How could ultra-conservative Catholic emperors have tolerated such a downright pagan and erotic painting? Apparently, without a problem.

# Kunsthistorisches Museum—First Floor

KUNSTHISTORISCHES

ROOM 17
VERMEER

ROOM 16

ROOM 15

ROOM 14

SAAL
TEMPORARY

WC

STAIRS TO
SECOND FLOOR

ROOM 18

SAAL XI

SAAL X

BRUEGEL

SAAL IX

THESEUS STATUE

ROOM 19

SAAL XII

NORTHERN
EUROPEAN
ART

STAIRS FROM
GROUND FLOOR

ROOM 20

SAAL XIII

SAAL XIV

RUBENS

SAAL XV
DÜRER

ROOM 21
REMBRANDT

TOUR ENDS

ROOM 22

ROOM 23

ROOM 24

MAIN

*Maria-Theresien-*

In the large canvas *Ecce Homo*, a crowd mills about, when suddenly there's a commotion. They nudge each other and start to point. Follow their gaze diagonally up the stairs to a battered figure entering way up in the corner. "Ecce Homo!" says Pilate. "Behold the man." And he presents Jesus to the mob. For us, as for the unsym-

pathetic crowd, the humiliated Son of God is not the center of the scene, but almost an afterthought.

• *Continue to Saal III.*

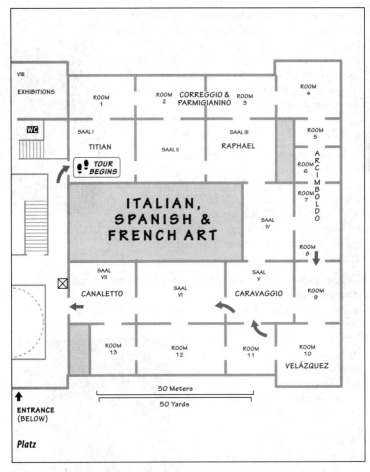

Map labels:
VIII EXHIBITIONS
WC
ROOM 1
ROOM 2
CORREGGIO & PARMIGIANINO
ROOM 3
ROOM 4
ROOM 5
ROOM 6
ROOM 7
ROOM 8
ROOM 9
ROOM 10 VELÁZQUEZ
ROOM 11
ROOM 12
ROOM 13
SAAL I TITIAN
SAAL II
SAAL III RAPHAEL
SAAL IV
SAAL V
SAAL VI
SAAL VII CANALETTO
CARAVAGGIO
ARCIMBOLDO
TOUR BEGINS

**ITALIAN, SPANISH & FRENCH ART**

50 Meters
50 Yards

ENTRANCE (BELOW)
*Platz*

### Raphael—*Madonna of the Meadow*

Young Raphael epitomized the spirit of the High Renaissance, combining symmetry, grace, beauty, and emotion. This Madonna is a mountain of motherly love—Mary's head is the summit and her flowing robe is the base—enfolding Baby Jesus and John the Baptist. The geometric perfection, serene landscape, and Mary's adoring face make this a masterpiece of sheer grace—but then you get smacked by an ironic fist: The  cross the little tykes play with foreshadows their gruesome deaths.

• *Before moving on, be aware that the Kunst displays excellent small* *canvases in the smaller side rooms. For example, in Rooms 1-3, you may find **Correggio's** Jupiter and Io, showing Zeus seducing another female, this time disguised as a cloud. **Parmigianino's** Self-Portrait in a Convex Mirror depicts the artist gazing into a convex mirror and perfectly reproducing the curved reflection on a convex piece of wood. Amazing.*

*Farther along, through the small rooms along the far end of this wing (likely Rooms 6-7), find...*

### Arcimboldo—Portraits of the Seasons

These four cleverly deceptive portraits by the Habsburg court painter depict the four seasons (and elements) as people. For example, take *Summer*— a.k.a. "Fruit Face." With a pickle nose, pear chin, and corn-husk ears, this guy literally is what he eats. Its grotesque weirdness makes it typical of Mannerist art.

• *Find Caravaggio in Saal V.*

### Caravaggio—*Madonna of the Rosary* and *David with the Head of Goliath*

Caravaggio shocked the art world with brutally honest reality. Compared with Raphael's super-sweet *Madonna of the Meadow,* Caravaggio's *Madonna of the Rosary* (the biggest canvas in the room) looks perfectly ordinary, and the saints kneeling around her have dirty feet.

In *David with the Head of Goliath,* Caravaggio turns a third-degree-interrogation light on a familiar Bible story. David shoves the dripping head of the slain giant right in our noses. The painting, bled of color, is virtually a black-and-white crime-scene photo—slightly overexposed. Out of the deep darkness shine only a few crucial details. This David is not a heroic Renaissance man like Michelangelo's famous statue, but a homeless teen that Caravaggio paid to portray God's servant. And the severed head of Goliath is none other than Caravaggio himself, an in-your-face self-portrait.

• *Move into Room 10, in the corner of the museum.*

### Velázquez—Habsburg family portraits

When the Habsburgs ruled both Austria and Spain, cousins kept in touch through portraits of themselves and their kids. Diego Velázquez was the greatest of Spain's "photojournalist" painters—heavily influenced by Caravaggio's realism, capturing his subjects without passing judgment, flattering, or glorifying them.

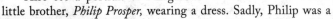

For example, watch little Margarita Habsburg grow up in three different portraits, from age two to age nine. Margarita was destined from birth to marry her Austrian cousin, the future Emperor Leopold I. Pictures like these, sent from Spain every few years, let her pen pal/fiancé get to know her.

Also see a portrait of Margarita's little brother, *Philip Prosper,* wearing a dress. Sadly, Philip was a

sickly boy who would only live two years longer. The amulets he's wearing were intended to fend off illness. His hand rests limply on the back of the chair—above an adorable puppy who seems to be asking, "But who will play with me?"

The kids' oh-so-serious faces, regal poses, and royal trappings are contradicted by their natural precociousness. No wonder Velázquez was so popular.

Also notice that all of these kids are quite, ahem, homely. To understand why, find the portrait of their dad, Philip V, which shows the defects of royal inbreeding: weepy eyes and a pointed chin (sorry, that pointy moustache doesn't hide anything).

• *Return to the main Saals and continue on, past glimpses of Baroque art, featuring large, colorful canvases showcasing over-the-top emotions and pudgy, winged babies (the surefire mark of Baroque art). In Saal VII, find paintings of the Habsburg summer palace, Schloss Schönbrunn, by* **Canaletto,** *one of which also shows the Viennese skyline in the distance.*

*Exit Saal VII. Cross the stairwell and enter Saal XV, in the part of the museum dedicated to Northern Art.*

## NORTHERN ART

The "Northern Renaissance," brought on by the economic boom of Dutch and Flemish trading, was more secular and Protestant than Catholic-funded Italian art. We'll see fewer Madonnas, saints, and Greek gods and more peasants, landscapes, and food. Paintings are smaller and darker, full of down-to-earth objects. Northern artists sweated the details, encouraging the patient viewer to appreciate the beauty in everyday things.

## Dürer—Landauer Altarpiece

As the son of a goldsmith and having traveled to Italy, Albrecht Dürer combined meticulous Northern detail with Renaissance symmetry. So this altarpiece may initially look like a complex hog pile of saints and angels, but it's perfectly geometrical. The crucified Christ forms a triangle in the center, framed by triangular clouds and flanked by three-sided crowds of people—appropriate for a painting about the Trinity. Dürer

practically invented the self-portrait as an art form, and he included himself, the lone earthling in this heavenly vision (bottom right), with a plaque announcing that he, Albrecht Dürer, painted this in 1511.

• *Now enter the big-canvas, bright-colored world of Baroque in Saals XIII and XIV.*

## Peter Paul Rubens

Stand in front of Rubens' *Self-Portrait* and admire the darling of Catholic-dominated Flanders (northern Belgium) in his prime: famous, wealthy, well-traveled, the friend of kings and princes, an artist, diplomat, man about town, and—obviously—confident. Rubens' work runs the gamut, from realistic portraits to lounging nudes, Greek myths to altarpieces,

from pious devotion to violent sex. But, can we be sure it's Baroque? Ah yes, I'm sure you'll find a pudgy, winged baby somewhere.

In the large *Ildefonso Altarpiece,* a glorious Mary appears (with her entourage of p.w.b.'s) to reward the grateful Spanish St. Ildefonso with a chasuble (priest's smock).

The 53-year-old Rubens married Hélène Fourment, a dimpled girl of 16 (find her portrait nearby). She pulls the fur around her ample flesh, simultaneously covering herself and exalting her charms. Rubens called this painting *The Little Fur*—and used the same name for his young bride. Hmm. Hélène's sweet cellulite was surely an inspiration to Rubens—many of his female figures have Hélène's gentle face and dimpled proportions.

How could Rubens paint all these enormous canvases in one lifetime? He didn't. He kept a workshop of assistants busy painting backgrounds and minor figures, working from his own small sketches. Then the master stepped in to add the finishing touches. For example, the giant canvas *The Miracles of St. Ignatius of Loyola* was painted partly by assistants, guided by Rubens' sketches (displayed nearby).

• *In the corner room (Room 21), find dark, brooding works by Rembrandt.*

### Rembrandt van Rijn

Rembrandt became wealthy by painting portraits of Holland's upwardly mobile businessmen, but his greatest subject was himself. In the *Large Self-Portrait* we see the hands-on-hips, defiant, open-

stance determination of a man who will do what he wants, and if people don't like it, tough.

In typical Rembrandt style, most of the canvas is a dark, smudgy brown, with only the side of his face glowing from the darkness. (Remember Caravaggio? Rembrandt did.) Unfortunately, the year this was painted, Rembrandt's fortunes changed.

Looking at the *Small Self-Portrait* from 1657, consider Rembrandt's last years. His wife died, his children died young, and commissions for paintings dried up as his style veered from the common path. He had to auction off paintings to pay his debts, and he died a poor man. Rembrandt's numerous self-portraits painted from youth until old age show a man always changing—from wide-eyed youth to successful portraitist to this disillusioned, but still defiant, old man.

• *Pass through several rooms until you reach Room 17, with a small jewel of a canvas by Jan Vermeer.*

### Jan Vermeer

In his small canvases, the Dutch painter Jan Vermeer quiets the world down to where we can hear our own heartbeat, letting us appreciate the beauty in common things.

The curtain opens and we see *The Art of Painting*, a behind-the-scenes look at Vermeer at work. He's painting a model dressed in blue, starting with her laurel-leaf headdress. The studio is its own little dollhouse world framed by a chair in the foreground and the wall in back. Then Vermeer fills this space with the few gems he wants us to focus on—the chandelier, the map, the painter's costume. Everything is lit by a crystal-clear light, letting us see these everyday items with fresh eyes.

The painting is also called *The Allegory of Painting*. The model has the laurel leaves, trumpet, and book that symbolize the muse of history and fame. The artist—his back to the public—earnestly tries to capture fleeting fame with a small sheet of canvas.

• *The nearby Saal X contains the largest collection of Bruegels in captivity. Linger. If you like it, linger longer.*

**KUNSTHISTORISCHES**

### Pieter Bruegel the Elder

The undisputed master of the slice-of-life village scene was Pieter Bruegel the Elder (c. 1525-1569)—think of him as the Norman Rockwell of the 16th century. His name (pronounced "BROY-gull") is sometimes spelled *Brueghel*. Don't confuse Pieter Bruegel the Elder with his sons, Pieter Brueghel the Younger and Jan Brueghel, who added luster and an "h" to the family name (and whose works are also displayed in the Kunst). Despite his many rural paintings, Bruegel was actually a cultivated urbanite who liked to wear peasants' clothing to observe country folk at play (a trans-fest-ite?). He celebrated their simple life, but he also skewered their weaknesses—not to single them out as hicks, but as universal examples of human folly.

*The Peasant Wedding*, Bruegel's most famous work, is less about the wedding than the food. It's a farmers' feeding frenzy, as the barnful of wedding guests scrambles to get their share of free eats. Two men bring in the next course, a tray of fresh pudding. The bagpiper pauses to check it out. A guy grabs bowls and passes them down the table, taking our attention with them. Everyone's going at it, including a kid in an oversized red cap who licks the bowl with his fingers. In the middle of it all, look who's  been completely forgotten—the demure bride sitting in front of the blue-green cloth. According to Flemish tradition, the bride was not allowed to speak or eat at the party, and the groom was not in attendance at all. (One thing: The guy carrying the front end of the food tray—is he stepping forward with his right leg, or with his left, or with...all three?)

Speaking of two left feet, Bruegel's *Peasant Dance* shows a celebration at the consecration of a village church. Peasants happily clog to the tune of a lone bagpiper, who wails away while his pit crew keeps him lubed with wine. Notice the over-exuberant guy in the green

hat on the left, who accidentally smacks his buddy in the face. As with his other peasant paintings, Bruegel captures the warts-and-all scene accurately—it's neither romanticized nor patronizing.

Find several Bruegel landscape paintings. These are part of an original series of six "calendar" paintings, depicting the seasons

of the year. *Gloomy Day* opens the cycle, as winter turns to spring... slowly. The snow has melted, flooding the distant river, the trees are still leafless, and the villagers stir, cutting wood and mending fences. We skip ahead to autumn in *The Return of the Herd*—still sunny, but winter's storms are fast approaching. We see the scene from above, emphasizing the landscape as much as the people. Finally, in *Hunters in Snow* it's the dead of winter, and three dog-tired hunters with their tired dogs trudge along with only a single fox to show for their

efforts. As they crest the hill, the grove of bare trees opens up to a breathtaking view—they're almost home, where they can join their mates playing hockey. Birds soar like the hunters' rising spirits—emerging from winter's work and looking ahead to a new year.

The *Tower of Babel*, modeled after Rome's Colosseum, stretches into the clouds, towering over the village. Impressive as it looks, on closer inspection the tower is crooked—destined eventually to tumble onto the village. Even so, the king (in the foreground) demands further work.

• *Our tour is over. Linger among the Bruegels. Then consider...*

KUNSTHISTORISCHES

## THE REST OF THE KUNST

We've seen only the *Kunst* (art) half of the Kunsthistorisches ("art history") Museum. The museum's ground floor has several world-class collections of Greek, Roman, Egyptian, and Near Eastern antiquities. You can see a statue of the Egyptian pharaoh Thutmosis III and the Gemma Augustea, a Roman cameo thought to be kept by Augustus on his private desk. Or view the *Kunstkammer*—the personal collections of the House of Habsburg. Amassed by 17 emperors over the centuries, the

*Kunstkammer* ("art cabinet") is a dazzling display of 2,000 ancient treasures, medieval curios, and *objets d'art* from 800 B.C. to 1891. The highlight is Benvenuto Cellini's famous $60 million, gold-plated salt cellar, in Room XXIX, (pictured), stolen in 2003 and recovered from its burial spot in the woods in 2005.

# SLEEPING IN VIENNA

## Contents

Accommodations in Vienna are cheap and plentiful—a €100 double here might go for €150 in Munich and €200 in Milan. Within the Ring, you'll need to shell out over €100 for a double room with bath. But around Mariahilfer Strasse, two people can stay comfortably for €70. The prices I've listed are for high season—generally April through June and September, October, and December. Expect them to spike higher for conventions (most frequent in Sept-Oct), dip in July and August, and drop in November and from January to March.

Many of the smaller places I've listed occupy a single upper floor of a traditional apartment building, with a shared entryway that is often dingier and darker than the pension itself. Don't let this give you the wrong impression—most pensions can't afford to maintain the entrance without their not-always-cooperative neighbors chipping in.

While few accommodations in Vienna are air-conditioned, you can generally get fans on request. Viennese elevators can be confusing: In most of Europe, 0 is the ground floor, and 1 is the first floor up (our "second floor"). But in Vienna, elevators can also have floors like P, U, M, and A before getting to 1—so floor 1 can actually be what we'd call the fourth or fifth floor.

## Sleep Code

**Abbreviations**       €1 = about $1.40, country code: 43, area code: 01
**S** = Single, **D** = Double/Twin, **T** = Triple, **Q** = Quad, **b** = bath-room, **s** = shower only, **t** = toilet only.
**Price Rankings**
  **$$$  Higher Priced**—Most rooms €130 or more.
    **$$  Moderately Priced**—Most rooms between €75-130.
      **$  Lower Priced**—Most rooms €75 or less.
English is spoken at each place. Unless otherwise noted, credit cards are accepted, rooms have no air-conditioning, breakfast is included, and Wi-Fi is generally free. Prices change; verify current rates online or by email. For the best prices, always book directly with the hotel.

For more tips on accommodations, see the "Sleeping" section in the Practicalities chapter. And for guidance on reaching your hotel upon arrival in Vienna, see the Vienna Connections chapter.

# Accommodations

## WITHIN THE RING, IN THE OLD CITY CENTER

You'll pay extra to sleep in the atmospheric old center, but if you can afford it, staying here gives you the classiest Vienna experience and enables you to walk to most sights.

**$$$ Hotel Schweizerhof** is classy, with 55 big rooms, all the comforts, shiny public spaces, and a formal ambience. It's centrally located midway between St. Stephen's Cathedral and the Danube Canal (Sb-€86-103, Db-€120-160, Tb-€143-188, fourth bed-€35, 10 percent discount with this book if you pay cash, grand break-fast, fans on request, elevator, Wi-Fi, Bauernmarkt 22, U-1 or U-3: Stephansplatz, tel. 01/533-1931, www.schweizerhof.at, office@schweizerhof.at).

**$$$ Pension Aviano** is a peaceful, family-run place and is the best value among my pricier listings. It has 17 rooms, all comfort-able and some beautiful, with flowery carpets and other Baroque frills. It's high above the old-center action on the third and fourth floors of a typical downtown building (Sb-€112, Db-€155-177 de-pending on size, extra bed-€25-33, 5 percent discount if you book directly with the hotel and mention Rick Steves, non-smoking, fans, elevator, guest computer, Wi-Fi, between Neuer Markt and Kärntner Strasse at Marco d'Avianogasse 1, tel. 01/512-8330, www.secrethomes.at, aviano@secrethomes.at, Frau Kavka).

**$$$ Hotel am Stephansplatz** is a four-star business hotel with 56 rooms. It's plush but not over-the-top, and reasonably priced for its sleek comfort and incredible location facing the cathe-

# Hotels in Central Vienna

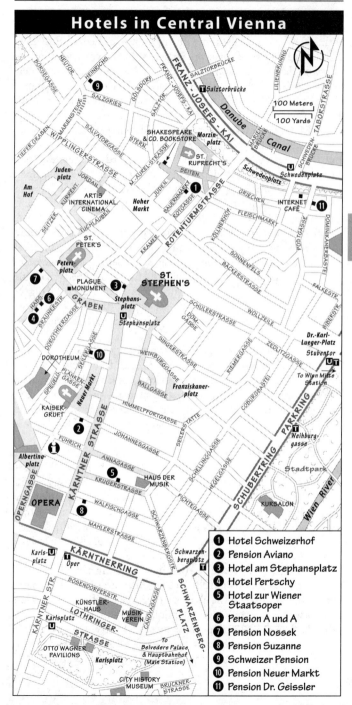

1 Hotel Schweizerhof
2 Pension Aviano
3 Hotel am Stephansplatz
4 Hotel Pertschy
5 Hotel zur Wiener Staatsoper
6 Pension A und A
7 Pension Nossek
8 Pension Suzanne
9 Schweizer Pension
10 Pension Neuer Markt
11 Pension Dr. Geissler

SLEEPING

dral. Every detail is modern and quality, and breakfast is superb, with a view of the city waking up around the cathedral (Sb-€159-209, Db-€179-299, also has pricier suites that can be triples, prices vary with demand and room size, air-con, elevator, guest computer, Wi-Fi, gym and sauna, Stephansplatz 9, U-1 or U-3: Stephansplatz, tel. 01/534-050, www.hotelamstephansplatz.at, office@hotelamstephansplatz.at).

**$$$ Hotel Pertschy,** circling an old courtyard, is big and hotelesque. Its 56 huge rooms are elegantly creaky, with chandeliers and Baroque touches. Those on the courtyard are quietest (Sb-€90-130, Db-€140-200 depending on size, extra bed-€36, non-smoking rooms, elevator, guest computer, Wi-Fi, Habsburgergasse 5, U-1 or U-3: Stephansplatz, tel. 01/534-490, www.pertschy.com, info@pertschy.com).

**$$$ Hotel zur Wiener Staatsoper,** run by the same family as the Schweizerhof, is quiet, with a more traditional elegance. Its 22 tidy rooms come with high ceilings, chandeliers, and fancy carpets on parquet floors (tiny Sb-€98, Db-€150, extra bed-€25, fans on request, elevator, Wi-Fi, a block from the Opera at Krugerstrasse 11; U-1, U-2, or U-4: Karlsplatz; tel. 01/513-1274, www.zurwienerstaatsoper.at, office@zurwienerstaatsoper.at, manager Claudia).

**$$ Pension A und A,** a friendly nine-room B&B run by Andreas and Andrea, offers a sleek, mod break from crusty old Vienna. This place, wonderfully located just off the Graben, has a nice entryway and period elevator—but open the door and you'll find white minimalist hallways and contemporary style in the rooms (Db-€120-150 depending on size, air-con, Wi-Fi, Habsburgergasse 3, tel. 01/890-5128, www.aunda.at, office@aunda.at).

**$$ At Pension Nossek,** an elevator takes you above any street noise into Frau Bernad and Frau Gundolf's world, tastefully decorated with lace and flowers, and with a small guest sitting room. With 32 rooms right on the wonderful Graben, this is a particularly good value (S-€60-67, Ss-€70, Sb-€90, Db-€130, Db suite-€165, extra bed-€37, air-con, elevator, guest computer, Wi-Fi, Graben 17, U-1 or U-3: Stephansplatz, tel. 01/5337-0410, www.pension-nossek.at, reservation@pension-nossek.at).

**$$ Pension Suzanne,** as Baroque and doily as you'll find in this price range, is wonderfully located a few yards from the Opera. It's small, but run with the class of a bigger hotel. The 26 rooms are packed with properly Viennese antique furnishings and paintings (Sb-€90, Db-€118-139 depending on size, 4 percent discount with this book if you pay cash, extra bed-€25, spacious apartment for up to 6 also available, fans on request, elevator, guest computer, Wi-Fi, Walfischgasse 4; U-1, U-2, or U-4: Karlsplatz and follow signs

for Opera exit; tel. 01/513-2507, www.pension-suzanne.at, info@
pension-suzanne.at, delightfully run by manager Michael).

**$$ Schweizer Pension** has been family-owned for four gen-
erations. Anita and her son Gerald offer lots of tourist info and 11
homey rooms (four with shared facilities) for a great price, with
parquet floors. It does feel kind of Swiss—tidy and well-run (S-
€56, big Sb-€82, D-€79, Db-€99, Tb-€125, cash only, entirely
non-smoking, elevator, Wi-Fi, full-service laundry-€18/load,
Heinrichsgasse 2, U-2 or U-4: Schottenring, tel. 01/533-8156,
www.schweizerpension.com, schweizer.pension@chello.at). They
also rent a quad with bath (€139—too small for 4 adults but great
for a family of 2 adults/2 kids under age 15).

**$$ Pension Neuer Markt** is family-run and perfectly central,
with 37 comfy but faded rooms, and hallways with a cruise-ship
ambience (Ss-€70-80, Sb-€90-100, Db-€120, prices vary with season and room size, extra bed-€20, in hot weather request a quiet
courtyard-side room when you reserve, fans, elevator, guest computer, Wi-Fi, Seilergasse 9, tel. 01/512-2316, www.hotelpension.
at, neuermarkt@hotelpension.at, Wolfgang).

**$$ Pension Dr. Geissler,** a respectable budget option, has
23 plain-but-comfortable rooms on the eighth floor of a modern,
nondescript apartment building just off Schwedenplatz, about 10
blocks northeast of St. Stephen's near the Bratislava ferry terminal
(S-€48, Ss-€68, Sb-€76, D-€65, Ds-€77, Db-€95, elevator, Wi-Fi
in most rooms, Postgasse 14, U-1 or U-4: Schwedenplatz—Post-
gasse is to the left as you face Hotel Capricorno, tel. 01/533-2803,
www.hotelpension.at, dr.geissler@hotelpension.at).

## ON OR NEAR MARIAHILFER STRASSE

Lively Mariahilfer Strasse connects the Westbahnhof (West Sta-
tion) and the city center. The U-3 subway line runs underneath
the street on its way between the Westbahnhof and St. Stephen's
Cathedral. This vibrant, inexpensive area is filled with stores, cafés,
and even a small shopping mall. It's a great neighborhood to stay
in, and a glut of hotel rooms keeps prices low and competition keen.
Its smaller hotels and pensions are generally immigrant-run, often
by well-established Hungarian families. Most of these listings are
within a five-minute walk of a U-Bahn stop. If you're driving, your
hotel may provide discounted parking at a local garage for €13-19
per day. As you'd expect, the far end of Mariahilfer Strasse (around
and past the Westbahnhof) is rougher around the edges, while the
section near downtown is more gentrified.

### Closer to Downtown

**$$$ NH Atterseehaus Suites,** part of a Spanish chain, is a stern,
stylish-but-passionless business hotel on Mariahilfer Strasse.

It rents 73 "suites" that are ideal for families, each with a living room, two TVs, bathroom, desk, and kitchenette (rack rate: Db-€99-200, but going rate usually closer to €110-125, extra bed-€35, 1 kid under age 12 stays free, breakfast-€17/person, non-smoking rooms, air-con, elevator, Wi-Fi, parking-€19/day, Mariahilfer Strasse 78, U-3: Zieglergasse, tel. 01/524-5600, www.nh-hotels. com, nhatterseehaus@nh-hotels.com).

**$$ Hotel Pension Corvinus** is bright, modern, and proudly and warmly run by a Hungarian family: parents Miklós and Judit and sons Anthony and Zoltán. Its 15 comfortable rooms are spacious, and some are downright sumptuous (Sb-€69-79, Db-€99-109, Tb-€119-129, these prices promised to Rick Steves readers who book by email or phone, 2 percent discount if you pay cash, extra bed-€26, ask about family rooms and apartments with kitchens, air-con, elevator, guest computer, Wi-Fi, parking-€15/day, on the third floor at Mariahilfer Strasse 57, U-3: Neubaugasse, tel. 01/587-7239, www.corvinus.at, hotel@corvinus.at).

**$$ Hotel Kugel** is run with pride and attitude by the gentlemanly, hands-on owner, Johannes Roller. Its 25 fine rooms have Old World charm and are a good value, especially for families (Db-€90, nicer Db with canopy bed-€100, family Qb-€150, Quint/b available, these prices if you book directly with the hotel, guest computer, Wi-Fi, free minibar, some tram noise, Siebensterngasse 43, at corner with Neubaugasse, U-3: Neubaugasse, tel. 01/523-3355, www.hotelkugel.at, office@hotelkugel.at).

**$$ Hotel Pension Mariahilf**'s 12 rooms are clean, well-priced, and good-sized (if a bit outmoded), with a slight Art Deco flair (Sb-€66, twin Db-€80, Db-€90, Tb-€105, 5-person apartment with kitchen-€159, these prices if you book directly with the hotel and mention Rick Steves, elevator, Wi-Fi, parking-€18/day, Mariahilfer Strasse 49, U-3: Neubaugasse, tel. 01/586-1781, www. mariahilf-hotel.at, info@mariahilf-hotel.at, Babak).

**$$ K&T Boardinghouse** rents five modern, spacious rooms on the first floor of a quiet building a block off Mariahilfer Strasse (Db-€79, Tb-€99, Qb-€119, 2-night minimum, no breakfast, air-con-€8/day, cash or PayPal only but reserve with credit card, coffee in rooms, guest computer, Wi-Fi; Chwallagasse 2, U-3: Neubaugasse; tel. 01/523-2989, mobile 0676-553-6063, www.ktboardinghouse.at, kt2@chello.at, run by Tina, who

also guides day-trips to Hungary and Slovakia). From Mariahilfer

Strasse, turn left at Café Ritter and walk down Schadekgasse one short block; tiny Chwallagasse is the first right.

**$$ Haydn Hotel** is a formal-feeling business hotel one floor below Hotel Corvinus, with 21 bland, spacious, modern rooms (Sb-€90, Db-€120, extra bed-€30, suites and family apartments, 10 percent Rick Steves discount off these prices if you pay cash, all rooms non-smoking, air-con, elevator, guest computer, Wi-Fi, parking-€17/day, Mariahilfer Strasse 57, U-3: Neubaugasse, tel. 01/5874-4140, www.haydn-hotel.at, info@haydn-hotel.at, Nouri).

**$$ Pension Kraml** is a charming, 17-room place tucked away on a small street between Mariahilfer Strasse and the Naschmarkt. It's family-run and feels classic, with breakfast served in the perfectly preserved family restaurant (no longer in operation) that the owner's grandmother ran in the 1950s. The rooms are big and quiet, with a homey, Old World ambience (S-€45, D-€58, Ds or Dt-€68, Db-€78, T-€78, Tb-€99, Qb-€120, Quint/b-€135, family apartment available, these prices for guests who book directly with the hotel, guest computer, Wi-Fi, lots of stairs and no elevator, Brauergasse 5, midway between U-3: Zieglergasse and U-4: Pilgramgasse, tel. 01/587-8588, www.pensionkraml.at, pension.kraml@chello.at, Stephan Kraml).

**$ Pension Hargita** rents 24 bright and attractive rooms (mostly twins) with woody Hungarian-village decor. While the pension is directly on bustling Mariahilfer Strasse, its windows block noise well. Don't let the dark entryway put you off—this spick-and-span, well-located place is a great value (S-€40, Ss-€47, Sb-€57, D-€54, Ds-€60, tiny Db-€65, Db-€68, Ts-€75, Tb-€82, Qb-€114, cash preferred, extra bed-€10, breakfast-€5, completely non-smoking, lots of stairs and no elevator, air-con in common areas, guest computer, Wi-Fi, bike parking, corner of Mariahilfer Strasse at Andreasgasse 1, right at U-3: Zieglergasse, tel. 01/526-1928, www.hargita.at, pension@hargita.at, Erika and Tibor).

**$ Pension Lindenhof** rents 19 very basic, very worn but clean and very inexpensive rooms. It's a dark and mysteriously dated time warp filled with plants (and a fun guest-generated postcard wall); the stark rooms have outrageously high ceilings and teeny bathrooms (S-€30, Sb-€37, D-€40, Db-€54, T-€60, Tb-€81, Q-€80, Qb-€108, hall shower-€2, breakfast-€3, cash only, elevator, no Internet access, next door to a harmless strip bar at Lindengasse 4, U-3: Neubaugasse, tel. 01/523-0498, www.pensionlindenhof.at, pensionlindenhof@yahoo.com, run by Gebrael family).

## Near the Westbahnhof (West Station)

**$$ Motel One,** a German chain that seems ready to take on the hotel world, surveyed business customers and offers only what they want to pay for. The result is what the chain calls a "low-budget

SLEEPING

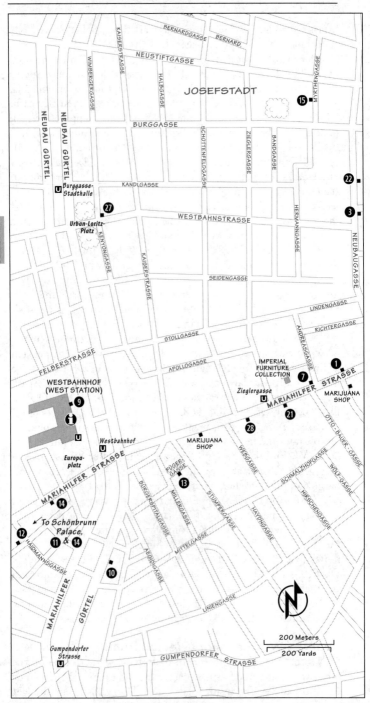

JOSEFSTADT

BERNARDGASSE
BERNARD
NEUSTIFTGASSE
KAISERSTRASSE
WIMBERGERGASSE
HALBGASSE
MYRTHENGASSE
15

BURGGASSE
SCHOTTENFELDGASSE
ZIEGLERGASSE
BANDGASSE
NEUBAU GÜRTEL
NEUBAU GÜRTEL
Burggasse-
Stadthalle
KANDLGASSE
HERMANNGASSE
22

Urban-Loritz-
Platz
27
WESTBAHNSTRASSE
NEUBAUGASSE
3

KENYONGASSE
KAISERSTRASSE
SEIDENGASSE

LINDENGASSE
RICHTERGASSE

STOLLGASSE
APOLLOGASSE
ANDREASGASSE
IMPERIAL
FURNITURE
COLLECTION
7
1

FELBERSTRASSE

WESTBAHNHOF
(WEST STATION)
9
Zieglergasse
MARIAHILFER STRASSE
Marijuana
Shop

21
Westbahnhof
28
MARIJUANA
SHOP
WEBGASSE
OTTO-BAUER-GASSE
WOLF-GASSE

Europa-
platz
MARIAHILFER STRASSE
FUGER-
GASSE
13
STUMPERGASSE
HAYDNGASSE
SCHMALZHOFGASSE
HIRSCHENGASSE

To Schönbrunn
Palace, &
14
BÜRGERSPITALGASSE
MILLERGASSE
AEGIDIGASSE
MITTELGASSE

12
11
14
HAIDMANNSGASSE
10
LINIENGASSE

MARIAHILFER
GÜRTEL

N

Gumpendorfer
Strasse
GUMPENDORFER STRASSE

200 Meters
200 Yards

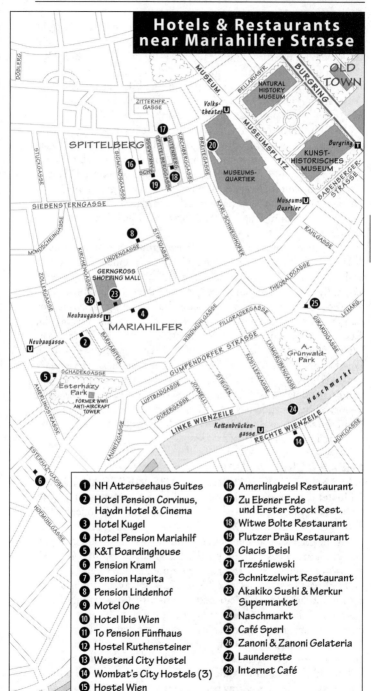

# Hotels & Restaurants near Mariahilfer Strasse

1. NH Atterseehaus Suites
2. Hotel Pension Corvinus, Haydn Hotel & Cinema
3. Hotel Kugel
4. Hotel Pension Mariahilf
5. K&T Boardinghouse
6. Pension Kraml
7. Pension Hargita
8. Pension Lindenhof
9. Motel One
10. Hotel Ibis Wien
11. To Pension Fünfhaus
12. Hostel Ruthensteiner
13. Westend City Hostel
14. Wombat's City Hostels (3)
15. Hostel Wien
16. Amerlingbeisl Restaurant
17. Zu Ebener Erde und Erster Stock Rest.
18. Witwe Bolte Restaurant
19. Plutzer Bräu Restaurant
20. Glacis Beisl
21. Trześniewski
22. Schnitzelwirt Restaurant
23. Akakiko Sushi & Merkur Supermarket
24. Naschmarkt
25. Café Sperl
26. Zanoni & Zanoni Gelateria
27. Launderette
28. Internet Café

SLEEPING

design hotel": 441 sleek and modern rooms, built cruise-ship tight with quality materials but no frills, a 24-hour reception but minimal service, and refreshingly straightforward pricing (Sb-€71, Db-€86, no triples but you can slip in a child under age 16 for free, breakfast-€7.50, Wi-Fi, air-con, parking-€13/day, attached to the Westbahnhof at Europaplatz 3, tel. 01/359-350, www.motel-one.com, wein-westbahnhof@motel-one.com).

**$$ Hotel Ibis Wien,** a modern high-rise hotel with American charm, is ideal for anyone tired of quaint old Europe. Its 341 cookie-cutter rooms are bright, comfortable, and modern, with all the conveniences (Sb-€69-75, Db-€87-93, Tb-€106, breakfast-€11, air-con, elevator, guest computer, Wi-Fi, parking garage-€13/day; exit Westbahnhof to the right and walk 400 yards, Mariahilfer Gürtel 22, U-3: Westbahnhof; tel. 01/59998, www.ibishotel.com, h0796@accor.com).

**$ Pension Fünfhaus** is plain, clean, and bare-bones—almost institutional—with tile floors and 47 rooms. The neighborhood is, well...improving (you might see a few ladies loitering late at night), but really not that bad, and this "pension" does the job if you want rock-bottom prices and few services—but try Hargita, Kraml, or Lindenhof first (S-€35, Sb-€44, D-€51, Db-€62, Tb-€87-95, 4-person apartment-€106, cash only, includes very basic breakfast, Wi-Fi in breakfast room, closed mid-Nov-Feb, Sperrgasse 12, U-3: Westbahnhof, tel. 01/892-3545, www.pension5haus.at, vienna@pension5haus.at, Frau Susi Tersch). Half the rooms are in the main building and half are in the annex at Grandgasse 8, which has good rooms, but its location near the train tracks is a bit sketchy at night. From the station, walk five minutes on Mariahilfer Strasse to #160, then turn right on Sperrgasse.

## CHEAP DORMS AND HOSTELS NEAR MARIAHILFER STRASSE AND THE WESTBAHNHOF

**$ Hostel Ruthensteiner** is your smallest and coziest option, with 100 beds in four- to eight-bed dorms and lots of little touches (€17 dorm beds, D-€48, Db-€70, includes lockers and sheets, includes towels in private rooms, towel rental in dorms-€1, breakfast-€3-4, non-smoking, guest computer, Wi-Fi, kitchen, laundry-€6/load, comfy common areas with piano and guitars, bike rental; Robert-Hamerling-Gasse 24; tel. 01/893-4202, www.hostelruthensteiner.com, info@hostelruthensteiner.com). From the Westbahnhof, follow Mariahilfer Strasse away from the center to #149, and turn left on Haidmannsgasse. Go one block, then turn right.

**$ Westend City Hostel,** just a block from the Westbahnhof and Mariahilfer Strasse, is well-run and well-located in a residential neighborhood, so it's quiet after 20:00. It has a small lounge, high-ceilinged rooms, a tiny back courtyard, and 180 beds in 4- to

12-bed dorms, each with its own bath (€19-28/person depending on day of week and how many in the room, Db-€70-92, cheaper Nov-mid-March—except around New Year's; includes sheets and locker, towel purchase-€4, breakfast included when you book directly with the hostel, cash only, elevator, pay guest computer, Wi-Fi, laundry-€7/load, Fügergasse 3, tel. 01/597-6729, www. westendhostel.at, info@westendhostel.at).

**$ Wombat's City Hostel** has three well-run locations—each with about 250 beds and four to six beds per room (€18-22 dorm beds, D-€60-70, lockers, bar, Wi-Fi, generous public spaces; near tracks behind the Westbahnhof at Grangasse 6, even closer to the station at Mariahilfer Strasse 137, and near the Naschmarkt at Rechte Wienzeile 35; tel. 01/897-2336, www.wombats-hostels. com, office@wombats-vienna.at).

**$ Hostel Wien** is your classic, huge and well-run official youth hostel, with 260 beds (€19-22/person in 2- to 6-bed rooms, price depends on season, includes sheets and breakfast, towel purchase-€3, nonmembers pay €3.50 extra, pay guest computer, Wi-Fi in lobby, always open, no curfew, lockers and lots of facilities, coin-op laundry, Myrthengasse 7, take bus #48A from Westbahnhof, tel. 01/523-6316, hostel@chello.at, www.1070vienna.at).

## MORE HOTELS IN VIENNA

If my top listings are full, here are some others to consider. Rates vary with season and demand.

Near City Hall, the cordial **$$ Theaterhotel** is a shiny gem of a hotel on a fun shopping street (Db-€110-190, Josefstädter Strasse 22, tel. 01-405-3648, www.cordial.at, chwien@cordial.at).

A stone's throw from Stephensplatz, **$$$ Hotel Domizil**'s 40 rooms are light, bright, and neat as a pin (Db-€135-185, Schulerstrasse 14, tel. 01-513-3199, www.hoteldomizil.at, info@ hoteldomizil.at).

A few steps from Schwedenplatz, **$$$ Hotel Marc Aurel** is an affordable, plain-Jane business-class hotel with rare air-conditioning (Db-€159 but sometimes as low as €99, Marc Aurel Strasse 8, tel. 01-533-5226, www.hotel-marcaurel.com, marcaurel@chello. at).

Just off Kärntner Strasse, **$$ Hotel Astoria** is a turn-of-the-century Old World hotel with 128 classy rooms (Db-€105-130, Kärntner Strasse 32, tel. 01-515-771-00, www.austria-trend.at/ hotel-astoria/en/, reservierung.astoria@austria-trend.at).

# EATING IN VIENNA

## Contents

The Viennese appreciate the fine points of life, and right up there with waltzing is eating. The city has many atmospheric restaurants. As you ponder the Hungarian and Bohemian influence on many menus, remember that Vienna's diverse empire may be no more, but its flavors linger. In addition to restaurants, this chapter covers two uniquely Viennese institutions: the city's classic café culture, and its unique *Heuriger* wine pubs nestled in the foothills of the Vienna Woods.

The Viennese word for a pub that serves food—or an informal restaurant—is *Beisl* (BYE-zul). You'll find these in each neighborhood, filled with poetry teachers and their students, couples loving without touching, housewives on their way home from cello lessons, and waiters who enjoy serving hearty food and drinks at an affordable price. Ask at your hotel for a good *Beisl.* (Beware: Because of Austria's lax smoking laws, pubs may be quite smoky; fortunately, most have outdoor seating.)

Most restaurants offer a *"menu"*—a fixed-price meal—at lunchtime on weekdays (typically around €10 for a main course plus soup or salad). Besides price, consider the season when choosing a restaurant in Vienna. In winter, indoor dining has great appeal, but in summer the crowds move onto the street, and balmy evenings drive people into the hills to enjoy wine gardens *(Heurigen)* surrounded by fields of grapevines. Consider the weather and then review this list of recommended restaurants with indoor or outdoor dining in mind.

To read up on Austrian cuisine, see the Practicalities chapter.

## Restaurants in Vienna

### NEAR ST. STEPHEN'S CATHEDRAL
Each of these eateries is within about a five-minute walk of the cathedral (U-1 or U-3: Stephansplatz).

**EATING**

**Gigerl Stadtheuriger** offers a fun, near-*Heuriger* wine cellar experience without leaving the city center. Just point to what looks good. As in other *Heurigen* (see page 192), food is sold by the piece or weight; 100 grams *(10 dag)* is about a quarter-pound (cheese and cold meats cost about €4 per 100 grams, salads are about €2 per 100 grams; price sheet posted on wall to right of buffet line). The *Karree* pork with herbs is particularly tasty and tender. They also have entrées, spinach strudel, quiche, *Apfelstrudel,* and, of course, casks of new and local wines (sold by the *Achtel,* about 4 oz). Meals run €8-12 (daily 15:00-24:00, indoor/outdoor seating, behind cathedral, a block off Kärntner Strasse, a few cobbles off Rauhensteingasse on Blumenstock, tel. 01/513-4431).

**Zu den Drei Hacken,** a fun and typical *Weinstube* (wine pub), is famous for its local specialties (€13-19 main courses, €9-13 weekday lunches, Mon-Sat 11:00-23:00, closed Sun, indoor/outdoor seating, Singerstrasse 28, tel. 01/512-5895).

**Trześniewski** is an institution—justly famous for its elegant open-face finger sandwiches (€1.20) and small beers (€1 each). Three different sandwiches and a *kleines Bier (Pfiff)* make a fun, light lunch. Point to whichever delights look tasty (or grab the English translation sheet and take time to study your 22 sandwich options). The classic favorites are *Geflügelleber* (chicken liver), *Matjes mit Zwiebel* (herring with onions), and *Speck mit Ei* (bacon and eggs). Pay for your sandwiches and a drink. Take your drink tokens to the lady on the right. Sit on the bench and scoot over to

EATING

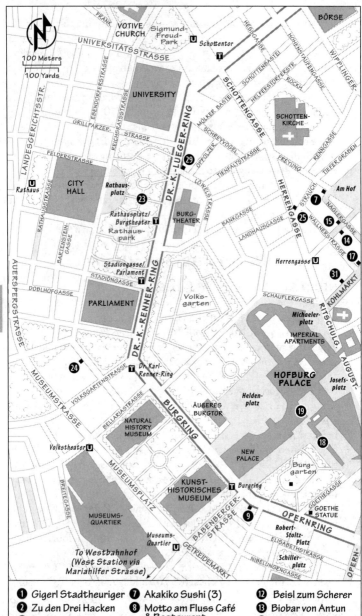

1. Gigerl Stadtheuriger
2. Zu den Drei Hacken
3. Trześniewski
4. Reinthaler's Beisl & Café Hawelka
5. Cantinetta La Norma
6. Gyros
7. Akakiko Sushi (3)
8. Motto am Fluss Café & Restaurant
9. Zanoni & Zanoni Gelateria (2)
10. Rest. Ofenloch
11. Brezel-Gwölb
12. Beisl zum Scherer
13. Biobar von Antun
14. Esterhazykeller
15. Hopferl Bierhof
16. Zum Schwarzen Kameel Rest. & Wine Bar

# Restaurants in Central Vienna

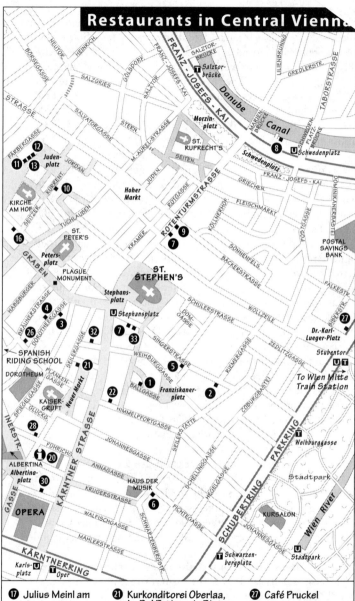

EATING

a tiny table when a spot opens up. In the fall, try their fancy grape juices—*Most* or *Traubenmost* (described on page 484). Started by a Polish cook who moved to Vienna, Trześniewski (chesh-NEFF-ski) has been a Vienna favorite for more than a century...and many of its regulars seem to have been here for the grand opening. You can grab an early, quick dinner here, but the selection can get paltry by the end of the day, and filling up here isn't cheap (Mon-Fri 8:30-19:30, Sat 9:00-17:00, closed Sun; 50 yards off the Graben, nearly across from brooding Café Hawelka, Dorotheergasse 2; tel. 01/512-3291). Their other locations serve the same sandwiches with the same menu but without the historic ambience: at Mariahilfer Strasse 95 (near many recommended hotels, Mon-Fri 8:30-19:00, Sat 9:00-18:00, closed Sun, U-3: Zieglergasse, tel. 01/596-4291) and in the Westbahnhof train station (near track 9, Mon-Fri 7:00-23:00, Sat-Sun 8:00-23:00, U-3: Westbahnhof, tel. 01/982-2975).

**Reinthaler's Beisl** is a time warp that serves simple, traditional fare all day. It's handy for its location (a block off the Graben, across the street from Trześnicwski) and because it's a rare restaurant in the center that's open on Sunday. Its fun, classic interior winds way back, and it also has a few tables on the quiet street outside (use the handwritten daily menu rather than the printed English one, €8-13 main courses, daily 11:00-22:30, at Dorotheergasse 4, tel. 01/513-1249).

**Cantinetta La Norma,** a short walk from the cathedral, serves fresh, excellent Italian dishes amid a cozy yet energetic ambience. Even on weeknights the small dining area is abuzz with friendly chatter among its multinational, loyal regulars (€8-11 pizzas and pastas, €14-20 main courses, weekday lunch specials, daily 11:00-24:00, outdoor seating, Franziskaner Platz 3, tel. 01/512-8665, run by friendly Paco and Hany).

**Gyros** is a humble little Greek/Turkish joint (more sit-down than takeout) run by Yilmaz, a fun-loving Turk from Izmir. He simply loves to feed people—the food is great, the prices are decent, and you almost feel like you took a quick trip to Istanbul (€9-13 plates, Mon-Sat 11:00-23:00, closed Sun, a long block off Kärntner Strasse at corner of Fichtegasse and Seilerstätte, mobile 0699-1016-3726).

**Akakiko Sushi** is a local chain of pan-Asian restaurants with a Japanese emphasis. They serve sushi, of course, but also €9-11 noodle soups, rice dishes, and more. The €10-13 bento box meals are a decent value. There are several convenient locations: Singerstrasse 4 (a block off Kärntner Strasse near the cathedral), Rotenturmstrasse 6 (also near the cathedral), Heidenschuss 3 (near other recommended eateries just off Am Hof, U-3: Herrengasse), and Mariahilfer Strasse 42 (fifth floor of Kaufhaus Gerngross, near many recommended hotels, U-3: Neubaugasse). Though they lack

## *Wieners* in Wien

For hard-core Viennese cuisine, drop by a *Würstelstand.* The local hot-dog stand is a fixture on city squares throughout the old center, serving a variety of hot dogs and pickled side dishes with a warm corner-meeting-place atmosphere. The *Wiener* we know is named for Vienna, but the guy who invented the weenie studied in Frankfurt. Out of nostalgia for his school years, he named his fun fast food for that city...a Frankfurter. Only in Vienna are *Wieners* called *Frankfurters.* (Got that?) When it comes to wieners, there's no pretense of being healthy. When Viennese eat at a *Würstelstand,* their friends will know it for the rest of the day by their burps.

Explore the fun menus. Be adventurous. The many varieties of hot dogs cost €3-4 each. Check out the sausage terms on page 485. Convenient stands are on Hoher Markt, the Graben, and in front of the Albertina Museum—a fun place to hang out after an opera performance as musicians and local opera buffs drop by. (By the way, the sleek modern design of the Albertina Museum stand is by famous local architect Hans Hollein, who also did the "diving board" entrance of the museum—look up).

**EATING**

charm, these are fast, modern, air-conditioned, and reasonable (all open daily 10:30-23:30).

**Motto am Fluss Café and Restaurant,** on the upper floors of the Bratislava riverboat terminal, is good for a bite or drink overlooking the Danube Canal. The classy café, on the top floor, has indoor and outdoor tables (€10-13 main courses, €9-10 weekday lunch specials, daily 8:00-24:00, tel. 01/252-5511); the pricey and elegant restaurant is one floor down and serves modern cuisine (indoor seating only but with great canal-perch tables, €18-26 main courses, extensive wine-by-the-glass list, €21 three-course lunches, daily 11:30-14:30 & 18:00-24:00, tel. 01/252-5510).

*Ice Cream!:* **Zanoni & Zanoni** is a *gelateria* run by an Italian family, with several branches around town. They're mobbed by happy Viennese hungry for their €2 two-scoop cones to go. The downtown branch has a fun outdoor area where you can people-watch while licking your gelato (daily 7:00-24:00, 2 blocks up Rotenturmstrasse from cathedral at Lugeck 7, tel. 01/512-7979). There's another location behind the Kunsthistorisches Museum, facing the Ring (at Burgring 1, U-2 or U-3: Volkstheater/Museumsplatz) and another along the side of the Gerngross mall (at Kirchengasse 1, off Mariahilfer Strasse).

## NEAR AM HOF SQUARE

The streets around the square called Am Hof (U-3: Herrengasse) hide atmospheric medieval lanes with both indoor and outdoor eating action. The following eateries are all within a block or two of the square.

**Restaurant Ofenloch** serves good, old-fashioned Viennese cuisine with formal service, both indoors and out. This 300-year-old eatery, with great traditional ambience, is dressy (with white tablecloths) but intimate and woodsy (€13-16 lunch specials, €16-20 main courses, €3 cover charge, Mon-Sat 11:00-23:00, closed Sun, Kurrentgasse 8, tel. 01/533-8844).

**Brezel-Gwölb,** a Tolkienesque nook with tight indoor tables and outdoor dining on a quiet little square, serves fine but forgettable food in an unforgettable atmosphere. It's ideal for a romantic late-night glass of wine (€9-16 main courses, €11 three-course weekday lunches, daily 11:30-24:00; leave Am Hof on Drahtgasse, then take first left to Ledererhof 9; tel. 01/533-8811).

**Beisl zum Scherer,** around the corner, is untouristy and serves traditional main dishes for €9-16. Outside tables face a stern Holocaust memorial on a pretty square. Inside seating comes with a soothing woody atmosphere and intriguing decor. It's named for a pre-WWI satirical newspaper that was published here. In the evening, let friendly Sakis explain the daily specials—which don't show up on the English menu (Mon-Sat 11:30-24:00, closed Sun, Judenplatz 7, tel. 01/533-5164).

**Biobar von Antun** is an earthy little place that serves three-course vegan meals (soup, salad, and main course) for €9-12 weekdays at lunch, and €13-15 at other times. They also have hearty €10-11 salads and fancy juices (Mon-Fri 11:30-14:30 & 17:30-22:30, Sat-Sun 12:00-22:30, on Judenplatz at Drahtgasse 3, tel. 01/968-9351, Antun Peskovic).

**Esterhazykeller,** both ancient and popular, has traditional fare in two serving areas. For a cheap and sloppy buffet, descend to the subbasement, a wine cellar that dates back to 1683. While the food is self-serve from the deli counter (a meal-sized plate costs around €10), you'll order drinks at your table (Mon-Fri 16:00-23:00, Sat-Sun 11:00-23:00). For table service from an only slightly pricier menu on a pleasant square, sit upstairs or outside (€10-12 main courses, €7 weekday lunches, daily 11:00-23:00, may close for lunch in Aug-Sept and/or in bad weather, just below Am Hof at Haarhof 1, tel. 01/533-3482).

The outdoor seating at **Hopferl Bierhof** on the same square might be a better option if it's hot and you're in the mood for a beer. It has a large, meaty menu and nice ambience, with Ottakringer beer on tap (€10-20 main courses, daily 11:30-24:00, Naglergasse 13, tel. 01/533-4428).

**Zum Schwarzen Kameel Wine Bar** ("The Black Camel") is filled with a professional local crowd enjoying small plates from the same kitchen as their fancy restaurant, but at a better price. This is *the* place for horseradish and thin-sliced ham (*Beinschinken mit Kren*, €10/plate, *Achtung*—the horseradish is *hot*). Stand, grab a stool, find a table on the street, or sit anywhere you can—it's customary to share tables in the wine-bar section. Fine Austrian wines are sold by the *Achtel* (eighth-liter glass) and listed on the board. They also have a buffet of tiny €1.25 open-face finger sandwiches. Prices are the same inside or at their streetside outdoor tables (daily 8:00-24:00, Bognergasse 5, tel. 01/533-8125).

For a splurge, the adjacent **Zum Schwarzen Kameel Restaurant** is a tiny, elegant alternative. The dark-wood, 12-table, Art Nouveau restaurant serves fine gourmet Viennese cuisine (€23-36 main courses, €68 and €86 five-course set-price meals, pricey wine, €3 cover charge, daily 12:00-24:00, tel. 01/533-8125).

*Gourmet Supermarket:* **Julius Meinl am Graben,** a posh supermarket with two floors of temptations right on the Graben, has been famous since 1862 as a top-end delicatessen with all the gourmet fancies. Assemble a meal from the picnic fixings on the shelves. There's also a café, with light meals and great outdoor seating; a stuffy and pricey restaurant upstairs; and a takeout counter with good benches for people-watching while you munch (shop open Mon-Fri 8:00-19:30, Sat 9:00-18:00, closed Sun; restaurant open Mon-Sat until 24:00, closed Sun; Am Graben 19, tel. 01/532-3334).

## NEAR THE OPERA

These eateries are within easy walking distance of the Opera (U-1, U-2, or U-4: Karlsplatz).

**Café Restaurant Palmenhaus** overlooks the Palace Garden (Burggarten—see page 53). Tucked away in a green and peaceful corner two blocks behind the Opera in the Hofburg's backyard, this is a world apart. If you want to eat modern Austrian cuisine surrounded by palm trees rather than tourists, this is the place. And, since it's at the edge of a huge park, it's great for families. They specialize in fresh fish with generous vegetables—options are listed on the chalkboard (€10 weekday lunches, €18-26 main courses; daily 10:00-24:00, Sun until 23:00; Nov-Feb daily from 11:00 except Jan-Feb closed Mon-Tue; extensive fine-wine list, indoors in greenhouse or outdoors, Burggarten 1, tel. 01/533-1033).

**Soho Kantine** is a cave-like, government-subsidized cantina, serving the National Library staff but open to all, and offering unexciting, institutional sit-down lunches in the Hofburg. Pay for your meal—your choice of bland meat or bland vegetarian—and a drink at the bar, take your token to the kitchen, and then sit down

EATING

and eat with the locals. Wednesday is schnitzel day and Friday is fish day (€6.50-7 two-course lunch, Mon-Fri 11:30-15:00, closed Sat-Sun and Aug, hard to find—just past the butterfly house in a forlorn little square, look for *Soho* sign in entry corridor, Burggarten, mobile 0676-309-5161).

**Rosenberger Markt Restaurant** is mobbed with tour groups. Still, if you're OK with a freeway-cafeteria ambience in the center of the German-speaking world's classiest city, this self-service eatery is fast and easy. It's just a block toward the cathedral from the Opera. The best cheap meal here is a small salad or antipasto plate stacked high (daily 11:00-22:00, lots of fruits, veggies, fresh-squeezed juices, addictive banana milk, ride the glass elevator downstairs, Maysedergasse 2, tel. 01/512-3458).

**Kurkonditorei Oberlaa** may not have the royal and plush fame of Demel (see page 103), but this is where Viennese connoisseurs serious about the quality of their pastries go to get fat. With outdoor seating on Neuer Markt, it's particularly nice on a hot summer day. Upstairs has more temptations and good seating (€12 three-course weekday lunches—€15 Sat-Sun, great selection of cakes, daily 8:00-20:00, Neuer Markt 16, other locations about town, including the Naschmarkt, tel. 01/5132-9360).

**Le Bol Patisserie Bistro** (next to Oberlaa) satisfies your need for something French. The staff speaks to you in French, serving fine €10-14 salads, baguette sandwiches, and fresh croissants (Mon-Sat 8:00-22:00, Sun 10:00-20:00, Neuer Markt 14).

**Danieli Ristorante** is your best classy Italian bet in the old town. White-tablecloth dressy, but not stuffy, it has reasonable prices. Dine in their elegant back room or on the street (€11-19 pastas, €9-15 pizzas, €17-26 main courses, daily 12:00-24:00, 30 yards off Kärntner Strasse opposite Neuer Markt at Himmelpfortgasse 3, tel. 01/513-7913).

**Supermarkets: Billa Corso** is a top-end version of the Billa supermarket chain, and sells hot, gourmet, ready-made meals (by weight). You're welcome to sit and enjoy whatever you've purchased in either eating area: inside (air-conditioned) and out on the square. They also have a great deli selection of salads, soups, and picnic items (warm food-€2/100 grams, WC on ground floor, Mon-Fri 8:00-20:00, Sat 8:00-19:00, closed Sun, Neuer Markt 17, on the corner where Seilergasse hits Neuer Markt, tel. 01/961-2133). A non-gourmet **Billa** is on a side street around the corner from St. Stephen's Church (Mon-Fri 7:15-19:30, Sat 7:15-18:00, closed Sun, Singerstrasse 6).

## JUST WEST OF THE RING

**Justizcafe,** the cafeteria serving Austria's Supreme Court of Justice, offers a fine view, great prices, and a memorable breakfast or

## City Hall Food Circus

During the summer, scores of outdoor food stands and hundreds of picnic tables are set up in the park in front of the City Hall (Rathausplatz). Local mobs enjoy mostly ethnic meals for decent-but-not-cheap prices and classical entertainment on a big screen (see page 202). The fun thing here is the energy of the crowd and a feeling that you're truly eating as the Viennese do...not schnitzel and quaint traditions, but trendy "world food" with young people out having fun in a fine Vienna park setting (July-Aug daily from 11:00 until late, in front of City Hall on the Ringstrasse, U-2: Rathaus).

lunchtime experience—even if the food is somewhat bland. Your goal is the black boxy structure on the top of the Palace of Justice. To reach it, enter the building through its grand front door, pass through tight security (no guns; Swiss Army knives OK but better to leave them in your room), say "wow" to the eye-popping Historicist courtyard, head to the very back of the building and ride the elevator to the fifth floor, then walk back to the front past rows of judges' chambers. You can sit behind the windows inside or dine outside on the roof, enjoying one of the best views of Vienna while surrounded by legal beagles—go early or late to miss the crush (€6.50 breakfasts, €8-12 two- and three-course lunches, Mon-Fri 7:00-10:00 & 11:00-14:30, closed Sat-Sun, Schmerlingplatz 10, U-2 or U-3: Volkstheater/Museumsplatz, mobile 0676-755-6100).

EATING

### SPITTELBERG

This charming cobbled grid of traffic-free lanes is a favorite dining neighborhood for the Viennese. It's handy, set between the MuseumsQuartier and Mariahilfer Strasse (near many recommended hotels, or wander over here after you close down the Kunsthistorisches Museum; U-2 or U-3: Volkstheater/Museumsplatz). Tables tumble down sidewalks and into breezy courtyards; the charming buildings here date mostly from the early 1800s, before the Mariahilfer neighborhood was built. It's only worth a special trip on a balmy summer evening, as it's dead in bad weather. Stroll Spittelberggasse, Schrankgasse, and Gutenberggasse, then pick your favorite. Don't miss the vine-strewn wine garden at Schrankgasse 1. To locate these restaurants, see the map on page 173.

**Amerlingbeisl,** with a charming, casual atmosphere both on the cobbled street and in its vine-covered courtyard, is a great value, serving a mix of traditional Austrian and international dishes (check the board with daily specials—some vegetarian—for €7-10, €14 main courses, daily 9:00-2:00 in the morning, Stiftgasse 8, tel. 01/526-1660).

**Zu Ebener Erde und Erster Stock** (loosely translated as "Downstairs, Upstairs") is a charming little restaurant with a mostly traditional Austrian menu. Filling a cute 1750 building, it's true to its name, with two dining rooms: casual and woody downstairs (traditionally for the poor); and a fancy Biedermeier-style dining room with red-velvet chairs and violet tablecloths upstairs (where the wealthy convened). There are also a few al fresco tables along the quiet side street. Reservations are smart (€10-18 main courses, €29 traditional three-course fixed-price meal, seasonal specials, €3 cover charge, Mon-Fri 7:30-21:30, last seating at 20:00, closed Sat-Sun, Burggasse 13, tel. 01/523-6254, www.zu-ebener-erde-und-erster-stock.at).

**Witwe Bolte** is classy. The interior is tight, but its tiny square has a wonderful leafy ambience (€12-20 main courses, €2 cover charge, daily 11:45-23:30 except closed 15:00-17:30 mid-Jan-mid-March, Gutenberggasse 13, tel. 01/523-1450).

**Plutzer Bräu,** next door to Amerlingbeisl, feels a bit more commercial. It's a big, sprawling, impersonal brewpub serving stick-to-your-ribs pub grub (€8-9 meatless dishes, €10-20 main courses, ribs, burgers, traditional dishes, Tirolean beer from the keg, also brew their own, daily 11:00-2:00 in the morning, food until 23:00—22:00 on Sun, Schrankgasse 4, tel. 01/526-1215).

**Glacis Beisl,** at the top edge of the MuseumsQuartier just before Spittelberg, is popular with locals. A gravelly wine garden tucked next to a city fortification, its outdoor tables and breezy ambience are particularly appealing on a balmy evening (€10-19 main courses, €10 weekday lunch specials, daily 11:00-24:00, Breitegasse 4, tel. 01/526-5660).

## MARIAHILFER STRASSE AND THE NASCHMARKT

Mariahilfer Strasse (see map on page 173) is filled with reasonable cafés serving all types of cuisine. For a quick yet traditional bite, consider the venerable **Trześniewski** sandwich bar's branch at Mariahilfer Strasse 95 (see page 177), or its imitators (one is at #91).

**Schnitzelwirt** is an old classic with a 1950s patina and a mixed local and tourist clientele. In this smoky, working-class place, no one finishes their schnitzel (notice the self-serve butcher paper and plastic bags for leftovers). Walk to the no-smoking section in the back, passing the kitchen piled high with breaded cutlets waiting for the deep fryer. The €9-11 schnitzels are served with a starch or salad; if you order the €6 version, you may want to add a €3 side. They also serve Austrian standards including *Szegediner Gulasch*. You'll find no tourists, just cheap schnitzel meals (Mon-Sat 10:00-23:00, closed Sun, Neubaugasse 52, U-3: Neubaugasse, tel. 01/523-3771).

*Supermarket*: **Merkur,** in the basement of the Gerngross shopping mall at Mariahilfer Strasse 42, is big and open fairly late (Mon-Wed 8:00-20:00, Thu-Fri 8:00-21:00, Sat 8:00-18:00, closed Sun, U-3: Neubaugasse).

*Naschmarkt:* For a picnic or a trendy dinner, try the **Naschmarkt,** Vienna's sprawling produce market. This thriving Old World scene comes with plenty of fresh produce, cheap local-style eateries, cafés, kebab and sausage stands, and the best-value sushi in town (Mon-Fri 6:00-18:30, Sat 6:00-17:00, closed Sun, closes earlier in winter; U-1, U-2, or U-4: Karlsplatz, follow *Karlsplatz* signs out of the station). Picnickers can buy supplies at the market and eat on nearby Karlsplatz (plenty of chairs facing the Karlskirche) or pop into the Burggarten behind the famous Mozart statue.

In recent years, the Naschmarkt has become fashionable for dinner (or cocktails), with an amazing variety of local and ethnic eateries to choose from. Prices are great, the produce is certainly fresh, and the dinners are as local as can be. The best plan: Stroll through the entire market to survey the options, and then pick the place that appeals. For more on the Naschmarkt, see page 67.

# Vienna's Café Culture

In Vienna, the living room is down the street at the neighborhood coffeehouse. This tradition is just another example of the Viennese expertise in good living. Each of Vienna's many long-established (and sometimes even legendary) coffeehouses has its individual character (and characters). These classic cafés can be a bit tired, with a shabby patina and famously grumpy waiters who treat you like an uninvited guest invading their living room. Yet these spaces somehow also feel welcoming, offering newspapers, pastries, sofas, quick and light workers' lunches, elegant ambience, and "take all the time you want" charm for the price of a cup of coffee. Rather than buy the *International New York Times* ahead of time, spend the money on a cup of coffee and read the paper for free, Vienna-style, in a café.

## VIENNESE COFFEE TERMS
As in Italy and France, Viennese coffee drinks are espresso-based. Obviously, *Kaffee* means coffee and *Milch* is milk; *Obers* is cream, while *Schlagobers* is whipped cream. Beyond those basics, here are some uniquely Viennese coffee terms (use them elsewhere, and you'll probably get a funny look):

- *Schwarzer, Mokka:* straight, black espresso; order it *kleiner* (small) or *grosser* (big)

- *Verlängeter* ("lengthened"): espresso with water, like an Americano
- *Brauner:* with a little milk
- *Schale Gold* ("golden cup"): with a little cream
- *Melange:* like a cappuccino
- *Franziskaner:* a *Melange* with whipped cream rather than foamed milk, often topped with chocolate flakes
- *Kapuziner:* strong coffee with a dollop of sweetened cream (oddly, not a cappuccino, which derives its name from the same word)
- *Verkehrt* ("incorrect"), *Milchkaffee:* with lots and lots of milk—similar to a *caffè latte*
- *Einspänner* ("buggy"): with lots and lots of whipped cream, served in a glass with a handle (as it was the drink of horse-and-buggy drivers, who only had one hand free)
- *Fiaker* ("horse-and-buggy driver"): black, with kirsch liqueur or rum, served with a cherry
- *(Wiener) Eiskaffee:* coffee with ice cream
- *Maria Theresia:* coffee with orange liqueur

Americans who ask for a "latte" are mistaken for Italians and given a cup of hot milk.

## CAFÉS

These are some of my favorite Viennese cafés. All of them, except for Café Sperl, are located inside the Ring (see map on page 179).

**Café Central,** while a bit touristy, remains a classic place, lavish under Neo-Gothic columns and celebrated by 19th-century Austrian writers. They serve fancy coffees (€4-7), breakfasts (€7-17), two-course weekday lunch specials (€10), and traditional main dishes (€13-19), and entertain guests with live piano—schmaltzy tunes on a fine, Vienna-made Bösendorfer each evening from 17:00-22:00 (Mon-Sat 7:30-22:00, Sun 10:00-22:00, free Wi-Fi, corner of Herrengasse and Strauchgasse, U-3: Herrengasse, tel. 01/533-3764).

**Café Sperl** dates from 1880 and is still furnished identically to the day it opened—from the coat tree to the chairs (Mon-Sat 7:00-23:00, Sun 11:00-20:00 except closed Sun July-Aug, just off Naschmarkt near Mariahilfer Strasse, Gumpendorfer 11, U-2: MuseumsQuartier, tel. 01/586-4158; see map on page 173).

**Café Bräunerhof,** between the Hofburg and the Graben, offers classic ambience with few tourists and live music on weekends (light classics, no cover, Sat-Sun 15:15-18:00), along with €7 lunches on weekdays (Mon-Fri 8:00-20:00, Sat-Sun 8:00-18:30, no hot food after 15:00, Stallburggasse 2, U-1 or U-3: Stephansplatz, tel. 01/512-3893).

**Café Hawelka** has a dark, "brooding Trotsky" atmosphere,

# Viennese Coffee: From Ottomans to Starbucks

The story of coffee in Vienna is steeped in legend. In the 17th century, the Ottomans (invaders from the Turkish Empire) were laying siege to Vienna. A spy working for the Austrians who infiltrated the Ottoman ranks got to know the Turkish life-style...including their passion for a drug called coffee. After the Austrians persevered, the ecstatic Habsburg emperor offered the spy anything he wanted. The spy asked for the Ottomans' spilled coffee beans, which he gathered up to start the first coffee shop in town. (It's a nice story. But actually, there was already an Armenian in town running a coffeehouse.)

In the 18th century, coffee boomed as an aristocratic drink. In the 19th-century Industrial Age, people were expected to work 12-hour shifts, and coffee became a hit with the working class, too. By the 20th century, the Vienna coffee scene became so refined that old-timers remember when waiters brought a sheet with various shades of brown (like paint samples) so customers could make clear exactly how milky they wanted their coffee.

In 2003, Vienna's first Starbucks boldly opened next to the Opera—across the street from the ultimate Old World coffeehouse, the Café Sacher. (Their goal was 27 branches. They managed nine before stalling out.) The locals like the easy-chair ambience and quality of Starbucks coffee, but think it's overpriced. Viennese coffee connoisseurs aren't impressed by quantity, can't relate to flavored coffee, and think drinking out of a paper cup is really trashy. The consensus: For the same price, you can have an elegant and traditional experience in an independent, Vienna-style coffee shop instead. While the "coffee-to-go" trend has been picked up by many bakeries and other joints, the Starbucks invasion has stalled, with no-where near as many outlets as the Seattle-based coffee empire had planned.

**EATING**

paintings by struggling artists who couldn't pay for coffee, a saloon-wood flavor, chalkboard menu, smoked velvet couches, an international selection of newspapers, and a phone that rings for regulars. Frau Hawelka died just a couple weeks after Pope John Paul II did. Locals suspect the pontiff wanted her much-loved *Buchteln* (marmalade-filled doughnuts) in heaven. The café, which doesn't serve hot food, remains family-run (daily 8:00-24:00, just off the Graben, Dorotheergasse 6, U-1 or U-3: Stephansplatz, tel. 01/512-8230).

*Other Classics in the Old Center:* All of these places are open long hours daily: **Café Pruckel** (at Dr.-Karl-Lueger-Platz, across from Stadtpark at Stubenring 24); **Café Tirolerhof** (2 blocks from the Opera, behind the TI on Tegetthoffstrasse, at Führichgasse 8); and **Café Landtmann** (directly across from the City Hall on the Ringstrasse at Dr.-Karl-Lueger-Ring 4). The Landtmann is unique, as it's the only grand café built along the Ring with all the other grand buildings. **Café Sacher** (see page 95) and **Demel** (see page 103) are famous for their cakes, but they also serve good coffee drinks.

# *Wein* in Wien: Vienna's Wine Gardens

The *Heuriger* (HOY-rih-gur), a uniquely Viennese institution, dates back to the 1780s, when Emperor Josef II decreed that vintners needed no special license to serve their own wines and juices to the public in their own homes. Many families grabbed this opportunity and opened *Heurigen* (HOY-rih-gehn)—wine-garden restaurants. (The name comes from the fact that they served *heurig*—new—wine from the most recent vintage.)

A tradition was born. Today, *Heurigen* are licensed, but do their best to maintain the old-village atmosphere, serving each fall's vintage until November 11 of the following year, when a new vintage year begins. To go with your wine, a *Heuriger* serves a variety of prepared foods that you choose from a deli counter. This is the most intimidating part of the *Heurigen* experience for tourists, but it's easily conquerable—see the sidebar for tips. Some *Heurigen* compromise by offering a regular menu that you can order from. At many establishments, strolling musicians entertain—and ask for tips.

Most *Heurigen* are decorated with enormous antique presses from their vineyards. Some places even have play zones for kids. The experience is best in good weather, but you can eat indoors, too. Many places are open irregularly, closing in winter or during the grape-picking season, so call or check websites before heading out.

I've listed three good *Heuriger* neighborhoods, all on the northern outskirts of town (see the map on page 19). To get here from downtown Vienna, it's best to use public transit (cheap, 30 minutes, runs late in the evening, directions given per listing below), or take a 15-minute taxi ride from the Ring (about €15-20). Keep in mind that there are more than 1,700 acres of vineyards within Vienna's city limits and countless *Heuriger* taverns. Every Viennese has their favorite and will be only too glad to tell you about it.

Choose a neighborhood rather than a particular place. The ambience at any single *Heuriger* can change depending on that evening's clientele (locals, tour groups, workplace parties, birthdays). Each neighborhood I've described is a square or hub with two or three recommended spots and many other wine gardens worth considering. Wander around, then choose the *Heuriger* with the best atmosphere. (And for a near-*Heuriger* experience without leaving downtown Vienna, drop by Gigerl Stadtheuriger—see page 177—which has the same deli-counter system as a *Heuriger*, but not the semirural atmosphere.)

## NEUSTIFT AM WALDE

This district is farthest from the city but is still easy to reach by public transit. It feels a little less touristy than other places, and is the only one of the neighborhoods I list where you'll actually see the vineyards.

**Fuhrgassl Huber,** which brags it's the biggest *Heuriger* in Vienna, can accommodate 1,000 people inside and just as many outside. You can lose yourself in its sprawling backyard, with vineyards streaking up the hill from terraced tables. Musicians stroll most nights after 19:00 (open Mon-Sat 14:00-24:00, Sun 12:00-24:00, Neustift am Walde 68, tel. 01/440-1405, family Huber).

**Das Schreiberhaus Heurigen-Restaurant** is a popular, family-owned place right at the bus stop. Its creaky, old-time dining rooms are papered with celebrity photos. There are 600 spaces inside and another 600 outside, music nightly after 19:00 unless it's slow, and a cobbled backyard that climbs in steps up to the vineyards. Alone among my listings, this place offers a €9 all-you-can-eat lunch buffet on weekdays until 15:00 (open daily 11:00-24:00, Rathstrasse 54, tel. 01/440-3844).

**Weinhof Zimmermann,** a 10-minute uphill walk from the bus stop, is my favorite. It's a sprawling farmhouse where the green tables on patios echo the terraced fields all around. While dining, you'll feel like you're actually right in the vineyard. The idyllic setting comes with rabbits in petting cages, great food, no city views but fine hillside vistas, and wonderful peace (Tue-Sat 15:00-24:00, Sun 13:00-24:00, closed Mon, tel. 01/440-1207, www.weinhof-zimmermann.at). Get off bus #35A at the Agnesgasse stop (at the corner of Rathstrasse and Agnesgasse—one stop before the Neustift am Walde stop), then hike a block uphill on Agnesgasse and turn left on Mitterwurzergasse to #20.

*Getting to the Neustift am Walde* **Heurigen:** Ride bus #35A to the Neustift am Walde stop. To pick up the bus, either take tram D to Liechtenwerder Platz, or the U-6 subway to Nussdorfer Strasse.

## NUSSDORF

An untouristy district, characteristic and popular with the Viennese, Nussdorf has plenty of *Heuriger* ambience. This area feels very real, with a working-class vibe, streets lined with local shops, and characteristic *Heurigen* that feel a little bit rougher around the edges.

**Schübel-Auer Heuriger** is my favorite here—the back en-

**EATING**

## The *Heuriger* Experience

To understand how a *Heuriger* works, think of a full-service prepared-foods counter at an American supermarket, and imagine a seating section with tables nearby. You choose from the array of deli items and hot dishes at the counter, and the staff arranges them nicely on a plate and brings it to your table. Then a waiter appears and takes your drink order. You'll pay at the counter for your food, and pay your waiter for your drinks.

Food is generally sold by weight, often in *"10 dag"* units (that's 100 grams, or about a quarter-pound). The buffet has several sections: The core of your meal is a warm dish, generally meat (such as ham, roast beef, roast chicken, roulade, or meat loaf) carved off a big hunk. There are also warm sides *(Beilagen),* such as casseroles and sauerkraut, and a wide variety of cold sides—various salads and spreads. Rounding out the menu are bread and cheese (they'll slice it off for you).

Unfortunately only one of the *Heuriger* I've listed (Schübel-Auer) labels its dishes (and only in German). But many *Heuriger* staff speak English, and pointing also works. Here's a menu decoder of items to look for...or to avoid:

| | |
|---|---|
| *Aufstrich* | spread |
| *Backhühner* | roasted chicken |
| *Blunzen* | black pudding (sausage made from blood) |
| *Bohnen* | big white beans |
| *Bratlfett* | gelatinous jelly made from fat drippings |
| *Fleckerl* | noodles |
| *Fleischlaberln* | fried ground-meat patties |
| *Kartoffel* | potato |

trance is right at the tram stop, and it offers a big and user-friendly buffet (most dishes are labeled and the patient staff speaks English). Its rustic ambience can be enjoyed indoors or out (Tue-Sat 16:00-24:00, closed Sun-Mon, closed mid-Dec-mid-Feb, Kahlenberger Strasse 22, tel. 01/370-2222).

**Heuriger Kierlinger,** next door, is also good, with a particularly rollicking, woody room around its buffet (Mon-Sat 15:30-24:00, Sun 15:30-23:00, Kahlenberger Strasse 20, tel. 01/370-2264).

**Bamkraxler** ("Tree-Climber") is not a *Heuriger,* but rather a

| | |
|---|---|
| *Kernöl* | vegetable oil |
| *Knoblauch* | garlic |
| *Knödl* | dumpling |
| *Kornspitz* | whole-meal bread roll |
| *Krapfen* | donut |
| *Kräuter* | herbs |
| *Kren* | horseradish |
| *Kummelbraten* | crispy roast pork with caraway |
| *Lauch* | leek |
| *Leberkäse* | meat loaf |
| *Liptauer* | spicy cheese spread |
| *Presskopf* | jellied brains and innards |
| *Roastbeef* | roast beef |
| *Schinken* | ham |
| *Schinkenfleckerln* | pasta with cheese and ham |
| *Schmalz* | a spread made with pig fat |
| *Spanferkel* | suckling pig |
| *Speck* | fatty bacon |
| *Specklinsen* | lentils with bacon |
| *Stelze* | grilled knuckle of pork |
| *Sulz* | gelatinous brick of meaty goo |
| *Waldbauernflade* | rustic bread |
| *Zwiebel* | onion |

Pay for your food at the buffet, then find a table. Once seated, order your wine (or other drinks) from a server. A quarter-liter (*Viertel*, FEER-tehl, 8 oz) glass of new wine costs about €2-3. *Most* (mohst) is lightly alcoholic grape juice—wine in its earliest stages. Once it gets a little more oomph, it's called *Sturm* (shtoorm). Teetotalers can order *Traubenmost* (TROW-behn-mohst), grape juice. For more on Austrian wines, see page 484.

EATING

*Biergarten* with a regular menu and table service—which some prefer to the *Heuriger* cafeteria line. It's a fun-loving, family-oriented place with fine keg beer (tapped daily at 17:00) and a big kids' playground (€10-15 main courses, €7-10 wurst plates, Tue-Sat 16:00-24:00, Sun 11:00-24:00, closed Mon, open all year, Kahlenberger Strasse 17, tel. 01/318-8800). To get here from the tram, walk all the way through either of the other listings, pop out on Kahlenberger Strasse, and walk 20 yards uphill.

**Getting to the Nussdorf Heurigen:** Take tram #D from the Ringstrasse (stops include the Opera, Hofburg/Kunsthistorisches

Museum, and City Hall) to its endpoint, the Beethovengang stop (despite what it says on the front of the tram, the Nussdorf stop isn't the end—stay on for one more stop). Exit the tram, cross the tracks, go uphill 40 yards, and look for Schübel-Auer and Kierlinger on your left.

## HEILIGENSTADT (PFARRPLATZ)
A 5- to 10-minute walk from Nussdorf is Pfarrplatz, a tiny village square watched over by a church. Beethoven lived—and began work on his Ninth Symphony—here in 1817; he'd previously written his Sixth Symphony *(Pastorale)* while staying in this then-rural district. He hoped the local spa would cure his worsening deafness. (Confusingly, though Pfarrplatz is the historic center of Heiligenstadt; today the name "Heiligenstadt" is more often associated with a big train and U-Bahn station some blocks away, near the river. If you're lost, ask for Pfarrplatz.)

**Mayer am Pfarrplatz** (a.k.a. Beethovenhaus), right next to the church, is famous and touristy. It feels more polished compared to the other *Heurigen* I list, which is not necessarily a good thing. The inner courtyard, under cozy vines, has a California vibe and often an accordion player, and the sprawling backyard has a big children's play zone. You can order €12-18 main courses from the menu (daily 16:00-24:00 except April-Oct Sat-Sun from 12:00, Pfarrplatz 2, tel. 01/370-1287).

**Weingut and Heuriger Werner Welser** is a block uphill (go up Probusgasse). It's traditional, with dirndled waitresses and lederhosened waiters. It feels a bit crank-'em-out, but it's still lots of fun, with music nightly from 19:00 (open daily 15:30-24:00, Probusgasse 12, tel. 01/318-9797).

***Getting to the Heiligenstadt* Heurigen:** Take the U-4 line to its last station, Heiligenstadt, then transfer to bus #38A. Get off at Fernsprechamt/Heiligenstadt, walk uphill for a minute or two, and take the first right onto Nestelbachgasse, which leads to Pfarrplatz and the Beethovenhaus. You can also walk from the Nussdorf *Heuriger* (at the end station of tram #D); bring one of the free city maps to guide you.

**Sightseeing Hint:** From here, you can continue on bus #38A uphill to the Kahlenberg and Leopoldsberg viewpoints (see page 90).

# ENTERTAINMENT IN VIENNA

Vienna—the birthplace of what we call classical music—still thrives as Europe's music capital. On any given evening, you'll have your choice of opera, Strauss waltzes, Mozart chamber concerts, and lighthearted musicals. The Vienna Boys' Choir lives up to its worldwide reputation.

Besides music, you can spend an evening enjoying art, watching a classic film, or sipping Viennese wine in a village wine garden. Save some energy for Vienna after dark.

## Music

As far back as the 12th century, Vienna was a mecca for musicians—both sacred and secular (troubadours). The Habsburg emperors of the 17th and 18th centuries were not only generous supporters of music, but fine musicians and composers themselves. (Maria Theresa played a mean double bass.) Composers such as Haydn, Mozart, Beethoven, Schubert, Brahms, and Mahler gravitated to this music-friendly environment. They taught each other, jammed together, and spent a lot of time in Habsburg palaces. Beethoven was a famous figure, walking—lost in musical thought—through the Vienna Woods. In the city's 19th-century belle époque, "Waltz King" Johann Strauss and his brothers kept Vienna's 300 ballrooms spinning.

This musical tradition continues into modern times, leaving many prestigious Viennese institutions for today's tourists to enjoy: the Opera, the Boys' Choir, and the great Baroque halls and churches, all busy with classical and waltz concerts. As you poke into churches and palaces, you may hear groups practicing. You're welcome to sit and listen.

In Vienna, it's music *con brio* from October through June,

ENTERTAINMENT

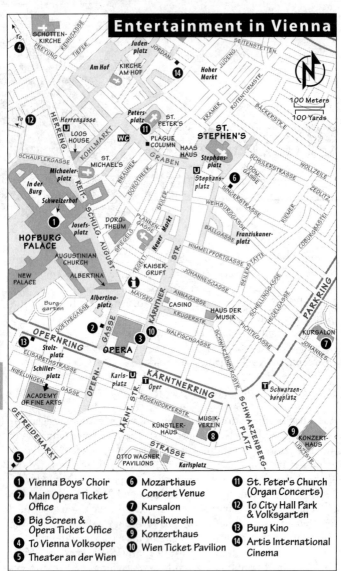

# Entertainment in Vienna

100 Meters
100 Yards

1 Vienna Boys' Choir
2 Main Opera Ticket Office
3 Big Screen & Opera Ticket Office
4 To Vienna Volksoper
5 Theater an der Wien
6 Mozarthaus Concert Venue
7 Kursalon
8 Musikverein
9 Konzerthaus
10 Wien Ticket Pavilion
11 St. Peter's Church (Organ Concerts)
12 To City Hall Park & Volksgarten
13 Burg Kino
14 Artis International Cinema

reaching a symphonic climax during the Vienna Festival each May and June. Sadly, in summer (generally July and August), the Boys' Choir, Opera, and many other serious music companies are—like you—on vacation. But Vienna hums year-round with live classical music; touristy, crowd-pleasing shows are always available.

For music lovers, Vienna is also an opportunity to make pilgrimages to the homes (now mostly small museums) of favorite composers. If you're a fan of Schubert, Brahms, Haydn, Beethoven, or Mozart, there's a sight for you. But I find these homes inconveniently located and generally underwhelming. The centrally located Haus der Musik (see page 37) is my favorite setting for celebrating the great musicians and composers who called Vienna home.

**Venues:** Vienna remains the music capital of Europe, with 10,000 seats in various venues around town mostly booked with classical performances. The best-known entertainment venues are the Staatsoper (a.k.a., "the Opera"), the Volksoper (for musicals and operettas), the Theater an der Wien (opera and other performances), the Wiener Musikverein (home of the Vienna Philharmonic Orchestra), and the Wiener Konzerthaus (various events). Schedules for these venues are listed in the monthly *Wien-Programm* (available at TI, described on page 24). You can also check event listings at www.viennaconcerts.com.

**Buying Tickets:** Most tickets run from €45 to €60 (plus a stiff booking fee when purchased in advance by phone or online, or through a box office like the one at the TI). A few venues charge as little as €30; look around if you're not set on any particular concert. While it's easy to book tickets online long in advance, spontaneity is also workable, as there are invariably people selling their extra tickets at face value or less outside the door before concert time. If you call a concert hall directly, they can advise you on the availability of (cheaper) tickets at the door. Vienna takes care of its starving artists (and tourists) by offering cheap standing-room tickets to top-notch music and opera (generally an hour before each performance).

## VIENNA BOYS' CHOIR (WIENER SÄNGERKNABEN)

The boys sing (from a high balcony, heard but not seen) at the 9:15 Sunday Mass from mid-September through June in the Hofburg's **Imperial Music Chapel** (Hofmusikkapelle). The entrance is at Schweizerhof; you can get there from In der Burg square or go through the tunnel from Josefsplatz.

Reserved seats must be booked in advance (€5-29; reserve by fax, email, or mail: fax from the US 011-431-533-992-775, send email to office@hofburgkapelle.at, or write Wiener Hofmusikkapelle, Hofburg-Schweizerhof, 1010 Wien; call 01/533-9927 for information only—they can't book tickets at this number; www.hofburgkapelle.at).

Much easier, standing room inside is free and open to the first 60 who line up. Even better, rather than line up early, you can simply swing by and stand in the narthex just outside, where you can hear the boys and see the Mass on a TV monitor.

The Boys' Choir also performs at the new concert hall, **MuTh**, on Fridays at 17:30 in September and October (€39-89, Am Augartenspitz 1 in Augarten park, U-2: Taborstrasse, tel. 01/347-8080, www.muth.at, tickets@muth.at).

They're talented kids, but, for my taste, not worth all the commotion. Remember, many churches have great music during Sunday Mass. Just 200 yards from the Hofburg's Boys' Choir chapel, the Augustinian Church has a glorious 11:00 service each Sunday (see page 51).

## OPERA
### Vienna State Opera (Staatsoper)

The Vienna State Opera puts on 300 performances a year, featuring the "Orchestra of the Opera" in the pit. (Any musician aspiring to join the Vienna Philharmonic Orchestra must put in three years here before even being considered.) In July and August the singers rest their voices (or go on tour). Since there are different operas nearly nightly, you'll see big trucks out back and constant action backstage—all the sets need to be switched each day. Even though the expensive

seats normally sell out long in advance, the opera is perpetually in the red and subsidized by the state, so affordable seats are often available. The excellent "electronic libretto" translation screens help make the experience worthwhile for opera newbies. (Press the button to turn yours on; press again for English.)

**Opera Tickets:** Main-floor seats go for €80-100; bargain-hunters get limited-view seats for €20-30. You can book tickets in advance by phone (tel. 01/513-1513, phone answered daily 10:00-21:00) or online (www.wiener-staatsoper.at). In person, you can head to one of the Opera's two box offices: on the west side of the building (across Operngasse and facing the Opera), or the smaller one just under the big screen on the east side of the Opera (facing Kärntner Strasse; both offices open Mon-Fri 9:00 until two hours before each performance, Sat 9:00-12:00, closed Sun).

Unless Placido Domingo is in town, it's easy to get one of 567 **standing-room tickets** (*Stehplätze*, €3 up top or €4 downstairs, can purchase one ticket/person, tickets sold until 20 minutes after curtain time). While the front doors open one hour before the show starts, a side door (middle of building, on the Operngasse side) opens 80 minutes before curtain time, giving those in the know an early grab at standing-room tickets. Just walk straight in, then head right until you see the ticket booth marked *Stehplätze*. If fewer than 567 people are in line, there's no need to line up early. If you're one of the first 160 in line, try for the "Parterre" section and you'll end up dead-center at stage level, directly under the Emperor's Box (otherwise, you can choose between the third floor—*Balkon*, or the fourth floor—*Galerie*). Dress is casual (but do your best) at the standing-room bar. Locals save their spot along the rail by tying a scarf to it.

**Rick's Crude Tips:** For me, three hours is a lot of opera. But just to see and hear the Opera in action for half an hour is a treat. And if you go, you'll get the added entertainment of seeing Vienna all dressed up. I'd buy a standing-room ticket and plan to just watch the first part of the show. Unfortunately if you buy a ticket but show up after the performance has started, you may be forced to watch it on a closed-circuit TV instead. While most will not want to stand through the entire performance, there are some spots that offer a wall for leaning. Regulars prefer the *Balkon* or *Galerie* sections because each ticket holder gets a section of railing along with a digital screen to read the libretto. Once you've saved your spot with your scarf, you can leave to check your belongings.

**"Live Opera on the Square":** Demonstrating its commitment to bringing opera to the masses, each spring and fall the Vienna Opera projects several performances live on a huge screen on its building, puts out chairs for the public to enjoy...and it's all free. (These projected performances are noted as *Oper live am Platz* in the official Opera schedule—posted all around the Opera building; they are also listed in the *Wien-Programm* brochure.)

### Vienna Volksoper

For less-serious operettas and musicals, try Vienna's other opera house, located along the Gürtel, west of the city center (see *Wien-Programm* brochure or ask at TI for schedule, Währinger Strasse 78, tel. 01/5144-43670, www.volksoper.at).

### Theater an der Wien

Considered the oldest theater in Vienna, this venue was designed in 1801 for Mozart operas—intimate, with just a thousand seats. It treats Vienna's music lovers to a different opera every month—generally Mozart with a contemporary setting and modern interpretation. Although Vienna now supports three opera companies, this is the only company playing through the summer (facing the Naschmarkt at Linke Wienzeile 6, tel. 01/58885, www.theater-wien.at).

## TOURISTY MOZART AND STRAUSS CONCERTS

If the music comes to you, it's touristy—designed for flash-in-the-pan Mozart fans. Powdered-wig orchestra performances are given almost nightly in grand traditional settings (€25-50). Pesky wigged-and-powdered Mozarts peddle tickets in the streets. They

rave about the quality of the musicians, but you'll get second-rate chamber orchestras, clad in historic costumes, performing the greatest hits of Mozart and Strauss. (The musicians are usually quite good—often Hungarians, Poles, and Russians working a season here to fund music studies back home—but often haven't performed much together, so aren't "tight.") These are casual, easygoing concerts with lots of tour groups. While there's not a Viennese person in the audience, the tourists generally enjoy the evening.

To sort through your options, check with the ticket office in the TI (same price as on the street, but with all venues to choose from). Savvy locals suggest getting the cheapest tickets, as no one seems to care if cheapskates move up to fill unsold pricier seats.

## Mozarthaus Concert Venue

Of the many fine venues in Vienna, the Sala Terrena at Mozarthaus might be my favorite. Intimate chamber-music concerts take place in a small room richly decorated in Venetian Renaissance style (€43-49, Thu-Fri and Sun at 19:30, Sat at 18:00, near St. Stephen's Cathedral at Singerstrasse 7, tel. 01/512-3457, www.viennaconcerts.com/mozarthaus.php). Don't confuse this with the Mozarthaus Vienna Museum on Domgasse, which also holds concerts.

## Strauss and Mozart Concerts in the Kursalon

For years, Strauss and Mozart concerts have been held in the Kursalon, the hall where the "Waltz King" himself directed wildly popular concerts 100 years ago (€40-62, concerts generally nightly at 20:15, Johannesgasse 33 at corner of Parkring, tram #2: Weihburggasse or U-4: Stadtpark, tel. 01/512-5790 to check on availability—generally no problem to reserve—or buy online at www.soundofvienna.at). Shows last two hours and are a mix of ballet, waltzes, and  a 15-piece orchestra. It's touristy—tour guides holding up banners with group numbers wait out front after the show. Even so, the performance is playful, visually fun, fine quality for most, and with a tried-and-tested, crowd-pleasing format. The conductor welcomes

## Sightseeing After Dark

Every night in Vienna some sights stay open late. Here's the scoop from Monday through Sunday:

**St. Stephen's Cathedral:** Nightly until 22:00 (but main nave closes earlier). See page 42.

**Kunst Haus Wien:** Nightly until 19:00. See page 79.

**Haus der Musik:** Nightly until 22:00. See page 37.

**Museum of Applied Arts (MAK):** Tuesday until 22:00. See page 76.

**Albertina Museum:** Wednesday until 21:00. See page 53.

**Natural History Museum:** Wednesday until 21:00. See page 58.

**Kunsthistorisches Museum:** Thursday until 21:00. See page 58.

**Leopold Museum:** Thursday until 21:00. See page 59.

**Museum of Modern Art (MUMOK):** Thursday until 21:00. See page 59.

Other late-night activities include: going to an opera or concert (see "Music," earlier in this chapter); a free, open-air cultural event outside City Hall (see next page); or a fun outing at the Prater amusement park (see page 88). Also remember that Vienna's coffee shops (see page 187) and wine gardens (see page 190) are generally open late.

ENTERTAINMENT

the crowd in German (with a wink) and English; after that...it's English only.

## OTHER MUSIC
### Musicals
The Wien Ticket pavilion next to the Opera (near Kärntner Strasse) sells tickets to contemporary American and British musicals performed in German (€10-109). Same-day tickets are available at a 24 percent discount from 14:00 until 18:00 (ticket pavilion open daily 10:00-19:00). Or you can reserve (full-price) tickets for the musicals by phone or online (Wien Ticket, tel. 01/58885, www.wein-ticket. at).

### Films of Concerts
To see free films of great concerts in a lively, outdoor setting near City Hall, see "Nightlife," next.

### Organ Concerts
St. Peter's Church puts on free organ concerts weekdays at 15:00 and weekends at 20:00 (see page 39).

### Classical Music to Go
To bring home Beethoven, Strauss, or the Wiener Philharmonic on a top-quality CD, shop at Gramola on the Graben or EMI on Kärntner Strasse. The Arcadia shop at the Opera is also good.

# Nightlife

If powdered wigs and opera singers in Viking helmets aren't your thing, Vienna has plenty of alternatives.

### The Evening Scene
More than ever, Vienna has become a great place to just be out and about on a balmy evening. While tourists are attracted to the historic central district and its charming, floodlit corners, locals go elsewhere. Depending on your mood and taste, you can join them. Survey and then enjoy lively scenes with bars, cafés, trendy restaurants, and theaters in these areas: **Donaukanal** (the Danube Canal, especially popular in the summer for its imported beaches); **Naschmarkt** (after the produce stalls close up, the bars and eateries bring new life to the place through the evening; see page 67); **MuseumsQuartier** (surrounded by far-out museums, a young scene of bars with local students filling the courtyard; see page 59); and **City Hall** (on the park-like Rathausplatz, where in summer free concerts and a food circus of eateries attract huge local crowds—described next).

### City Hall Open-Air Classical-Music Cinema and Food Circus
A thriving people scene erupts each evening in summer (July-Aug) at the park in front of City Hall (Rathaus, on the Ringstrasse).

Thousands of people keep a food circus of 24 simple stalls busy. There's not a plastic cup anywhere, just real plates and glasses—Vienna wants the quality of eating to be as high as the music that's about to begin. About 2,000 folding chairs face a 60-foot-wide screen up against the City Hall's Neo-Gothic facade. When darkness falls, an announcer explains the program, and then the music starts. The program is different every night—mostly movies of opera and classical concerts, with some films. Ask at the TI or check www.filmfestival-rathausplatz.at for the schedule (programs generally last about 2 hours, starting when it's dark—between 21:30 in July and 20:30 in Aug).

ENTERTAINMENT

Since 1991, the city has paid for 60 of these summer event nights each year. Why? To promote culture. Officials know that the City Hall Music Festival is mostly a "meat market" where young people come to hook up. But they believe many of these people will develop a little appreciation of classical music and high culture on the side.

### Heurigen

Viennese wine gardens, called *Heurigen*, are a great way to enjoy new wine, a light meal, and a festive local atmosphere. Eat and drink in intimate taverns or leafy courtyards, surrounded by antique wine presses, friendly *Wieners*, strolling musicians, and fellow tourists. Most gardens are located on the outskirts of town—in the legendary Vienna Woods—but they're easy to reach by tram, bus, or taxi. For more on the *Heurigen*, including recommendations and transportation information, see page 192.

### English Cinema

Several great theaters offer three or four screens of English movies nightly (€6-9): **Burg Kino,** a block from the Opera, facing the Ring (see below), tapes its weekly schedule to the door—box office opens 30 minutes before each showing; **English Cinema Haydn,** near my recommended hotels on Mariahilfer Strasse (Mariahilfer Strasse 57, tel. 01/587-2262, www.haydnkino.at); and **Artis International Cinema,** right in the town center a few minutes from the cathedral (Schultergasse 5, tel. 01/535-6570).

### The Third Man at Burg Kino

This movie is set in 1949 Vienna—when it was divided, like Berlin, between the four victorious Allies. Reliving the cinematic tale of a divided city about to fall under Soviet rule and rife with smuggling is an enjoyable two-hour experience while in Vienna (€7-9, in English; about 2 showings weekly—usually Sun afternoon and Tue early evening; Opernring 19, tel. 01/587-8406, www.burgkino.at). For more on *The Third Man* (and the museum of the same name), see page 70.

ENTERTAINMENT

# VIENNA CONNECTIONS

This chapter covers Vienna's major train stations and its airport, and includes tips for connections to/from Vienna by car and boat.

## By Train

Vienna has just finished building an impressive new Hauptbahnhof (main train station), and is consolidating most—but not all—train departures there. Multiple rail companies operate out of this station; make sure your ticket is for the train you're getting on. And confirm carefully which station your train uses. Some trains headed west (to Salzburg and Munich) may continue to leave from the Westbahnhof, and regional trains to Krems will probably continue to leave from the Franz-Josefs- Bahnhof. From most of Vienna's stations, the handiest connection to the center is the U-Bahn (subway); line numbers are noted below. For some stations, there's also a handy tram connection. (See the "Vienna's Public Transportation" map on page 28.)

For schedules, check Germany's excellent all-Europe timetable at www.bahn.com. Austria's own timetable at www.oebb.at includes prices, but it's not as user-friendly as the German site—and it doesn't always remind you about discounts or special passes. For general train information in Austria, call 051-717 (to get an operator, dial 2, then 2). For information on types of trains, schedules, passes, and tickets, see "Transportation" on page 499 in Practicalities.

### WIEN HAUPTBAHNHOF

Vienna's new central station (to the south of downtown) opened in early 2014 and is gradually coming online, with twelve pass-through tracks, shopping, and all the services you may need. Besides bringing most of Vienna's train connections under a single roof, the city hopes that the station will inject life into a neighborhood that's been mildly run-down. But with just one U-Bahn line linking to the station, it's often better to reach it by tram or bus.

**Getting into Vienna:** To reach the city center, ride the U-1 for 2-3 stops (direction: Leopoldau) to Karlsplatz or Stephansplatz, or take tram #D (which runs along the Ring). To reach Mariahilfer Strasse, hop on bus #13A. Tram #O runs from the station to Landstrasse and the Wien-Mitte station (for airport trains).

## WESTBAHNHOF (WEST STATION)

This station (at the west end of Mariahilfer Strasse, on the U-3 and U-6 lines) has a modern, user-friendly mall of services, shops, and eateries (including the recommended Buffet Trześniewski—near track 9—with €1.20 finger sandwiches). You can't help but admire how nicely the station's drab, functionalist 1950s shell has been spruced up. From here trains run to/from many points to the west (including **Melk, Hallstatt, Salzburg, Innsbruck,** and **Munich**), though some of these trains may shift to the Hauptbahnhof. You'll find travel agencies, grocery stores, ATMs, change offices, a post office, luggage lockers (€2-4.50, on the ground floor by the WC).

The private **Westbahn** service also leaves from here. It connects Vienna and Salzburg hourly and offers an alternative to the state-run ÖBB trains, including free Wi-Fi and the option to buy your ticket on board for no extra charge (www.westbahn.at). Westbahn's regular fares are half those of ÖBB, but Westbahn doesn't offer the range of money-saving passes that ÖBB does. Eventually Westbahn may move its service to the Hauptbahnhof—check when booking.

**Getting into Vienna:** For the city center, follow orange signs to the U-3 (direction: Simmering). If your hotel is along Mariahilfer Strasse, your stop is on this line, but it may be simpler to walk.

## FRANZ-JOSEFS-BAHNHOF

This small station in the northern part of the city serves **Krems** and other points on the **north bank of the Danube.** Connections from **Český Krumlov** in the Czech Republic sometimes arrive here, too.

**Getting into Vienna:** Although the station doesn't have an U-Bahn stop, convenient tram #D connects it to the city center. Also note that trains coming into town from this direction stop at the Spittelau station (on the U-4 and U-6 lines), one stop before they end at the Franz-Josefs-Bahnhof; consider hopping off your train at Spittelau for a handy connection to other points in Vienna. (Similarly, if you're headed out of town and you're not near the tram #D route, take the U-Bahn to Spittelau and catch your train there.)

## WIEN-MITTE BAHNHOF

This smaller station, just west of the Ring, is the terminus for S-Bahn and CAT trains to the airport. Be aware that its U-Bahn station is called "Landstrasse." From here, take the U-3 to hotels near Stephansplatz or Mariahilfer Strasse, and the U-4 to hotels that are closer to the airport. It's also connected directly to the Hauptbahnhof by tram #O.

## TRAIN CONNECTIONS

Before leaving your hotel, confirm which station your train leaves from.

**From Vienna by Train to: Melk** (2/hour, 1-1.25 hours, some with change in St. Pölten), **Krems** (at least hourly, 1 hour), **Mauthausen** (every 2 hours, 2 hours, change in St. Valentin or Linz), **Bratislava** (2/hour, 1 hour, alternating between Bratislava's main station and Petržalka station, or try going by bus or boat; described on page 257), **Salzburg** (3/hour, 2.5-3 hours), **Hallstatt** (hourly, 3.5-4 hours, last connection leaves around 15:00, change in Attnang-Puchheim), **Innsbruck** (almost hourly, 4-5 hours), **Budapest** (every 2 hours direct, 3 hours, more with transfers; may be cheaper by Orange Ways bus: 2-3/day, 3 hours, www.orangeways. com), **Prague** (6/day direct, 4.75 hours; more with 1 change, 5-6 hours; 1 night train, 6 hours), **Český Krumlov** (7/day with at least one change, 5-6 hours), **Munich** (6/day direct, 4.25 hours; otherwise about hourly, 5-5.75 hours, transfer in Salzburg or Plattling), **Berlin** (9/day, most with 1 change, 9.5 hours, some via Czech Republic; longer on night train), **Dresden** (2/day direct, 7 hours; plus 1 night train/day, 8.75 hours), **Zürich** (nearly hourly, 9-10 hours, 1 with changes in Innsbruck and Feldkirch, night train), **Ljubljana** (1 convenient early-morning train, 6 hours; otherwise 7/day with change in Villach, Maribor, or Graz, 6-7 hours), **Zagreb** (5/day, 6-9 hours, 2 direct, others with 1 change), **Kraków** (5/day, 8-10.5 hours with 1-3 changes, plus a night train), **Warsaw** (2/day direct including 1 night train, 7.75-8.5 hours), **Rome** (3/day, 12-13 hours, plus several overnight options), **Venice** (3/day, 8-9.5 hours with changes—some may involve bus connection; plus 1 direct night train, 12 hours), **Frankfurt** (6/day direct, 7 hours; plus 1 direct night train, 10 hours), **Paris** (7/day, 12-13 hours, 1-3 changes).

**To Prague and Budapest:** Vienna is the springboard for a quick trip to these two magnificent cities—it's three hours by train to Budapest and about five hours to Prague (including a Prague night train, leaves Westbahnhof around 22:00). Purchase tickets at the station or at most travel agencies.

# By Plane

## VIENNA INTERNATIONAL AIRPORT

The airport, 12 miles from the center, is easy to reach from down-town (airport code: VIE, airport tel. 01/700-722-233, www.viennaairport.com). It's freshly renovated, with a striking, black-and-white, "less-is-more" color scheme. The arrivals hall has an array of services: TI (run by a private company called Ruefa), shops, ATMs, eateries, and a handy supermarket. Ramps lead down to the lower-level train station.

### Connecting the Airport and Central Vienna

**By Train:** Trains connect the airport with the Wien-Mitte Bahnhof, on the east side of the Ring (described earlier). Choose between two ways of getting to Wien-Mitte: the regular S-7 **S-Bahn train** (€4.40, 24 minutes), and the express **CAT train** (€12, 16 minutes). Both run twice an hour on the same tracks. The airport tries to steer tourists into taking the CAT train, but it's hard to justify spending almost €8 to save eight minutes of time. I'd take the S-7, unless the CAT is departing first and you're in a big hurry. Trains from downtown start running about 5:00, while the last train from the airport leaves about 23:30.

The **S-Bahn** works just fine and is plenty fast. From the arrivals hall, go down either of the big ramps, follow the red ÖBB signs, then buy a regular two-zone public transport ticket from the multilingual red "Fahrkarten" machines. The €4.40 price includes any transfers to other trams, city buses, S- and U-Bahn lines (see www.wienerlinien.at). Trains to downtown are marked "Floridsdorf." If you'll be using public transportation in Vienna a lot, consider buying a transit pass from the machines instead of a single ticket (see page 27). As these passes are only valid in Vienna's central zone, you'll need to also buy a €2.10 single ticket to cover the stretch between the airport and the limits of the inner zone.

To take the fast **CAT** (which stands for City Airport Train), follow the green signage down the ramp to your right as you come out into the arrivals hall and buy a ticket from the green machines (one-way-€12, or €14 to also cover the connecting link from Wien-Mitte to your final destination by public transit; round-trip ticket valid 30 days-€19, 4 tickets-€38; usually departs both airport and downtown at :06 and :36 past the hour, www.cityairporttrain.com).

**By Bus:** Convenient express airport buses go to various points in Vienna: Morzinplatz/Schwedenplatz U-Bahn station (for city-center hotels, 20 minutes), Westbahnhof (for Mariahilfer Strasse hotels, 45 minutes), and Wien-Meidling Bahnhof (30 minutes). Double check your destination as you board (€8, round-trip-€13,

2/hour, buy ticket from driver, tel. 0810-222-333 for timetable info, www.viennaairportlines.at or www.postbus.at).

**By Taxi:** The 30-minute ride into town costs a fixed €35 from the several companies with desks in the arrivals hall. You can also take a taxi from the taxi rank outside; you'll pay the metered rate (plus a trivial baggage surcharge), which should come out about the same. Save by riding the cheap train/bus downtown, then taking a taxi to your destination.

### Connecting the Airport and Other Cities

There are direct bus connections (from platforms 7, 8, and 9) to **Bratislava** and its airport (1-3/hour, 45-60 minutes, two different companies: Blaguss (www.eurolines.at) and Slovak Lines/Post Bus www.slovaklines.sk or www.postbus.at; see page 257); **Budapest** (5/day, 3-3.5 hours, operated by Blaguss, www.eurolines.at); and **Prague** (8/day, 5.5 hours, www.studentagency.eu, also stops in **Brno**).

### BRATISLAVA AIRPORT

The airport in nearby Bratislava, Slovakia—a hub for some low-cost flights—is just an hour away from Vienna (see page 258 in the Bratislava chapter).

# By Car

### ROUTE TIPS FOR DRIVERS

**Approaching Vienna:** Navigating your way into Vienna is straightforward, but study your map first. Approaching Vienna on the A-1 expressway from **Melk** or **Salzburg,** it's simple: You'll pass Schönbrunn Palace before hitting the Gürtel (the city's outer ring road); turn left onto the Gürtel to reach Mariahilfer Strasse hotels, or continue on to reach hotels inside the Ringstrasse (the city's inner ring; clockwise traffic only).

If you're approaching from **Krems,** stay on A-22 as it follows the Danube, and cross the river at the fourth bridge (Reichsbrücke). At the big roundabout, take the second right onto Praterstrasse, which leads directly to the Ringstrasse. Circle around until you reach the "spoke" street you need.

From **Budapest,** get on A-4 at Nickelsdorf; from there it's a straight shot into Vienna along the Danube Canal. From the canal, turn left at the Aspernbrücke bridge and cross the canal, which puts you directly on the Ringstrasse.

**In Vienna:** The city has deliberately created an expensive hell for cars in the center. Don't even try to drive here. If you must bring a car into Vienna, leave it at an expensive garage.

**Leaving Vienna:** To leave Vienna for points west (such as the Danube Valley and Salzburg), circle the Ringstrasse clock-wise until just past the Opera. Then follow the blue signs past the Westbahnhof to *Schloss Schönbrunn* (Schönbrunn Palace), which is directly on the way to the West A-1 autobahn to Linz. If you stop at the palace for a visit, leave the palace by 15:00 and you should beat rush hour.

# By Boat

High-speed boats connect Vienna to the nearby capitals of Bratislava (Slovakia) and Budapest (Hungary). While it's generally cheaper and faster to take the train—and the boat is less scenic and romantic than you might imagine—some travelers enjoy the Danube riverboat experience.

**To Bratislava:** The **Twin City Liner** runs 3-5 times daily from the terminal at Vienna's Schwedenplatz, where Vienna's town center hits the canal (€30-35 one-way, 1.25-hour trip downstream; U-1 or U-4: Schwedenplatz, mid-April-Oct only, can fill up—reservations smart, Austrian tel. 01/58880, www.twincityliner. com). Their main competitor, **LOD,** is a bit cheaper, but runs only twice a day at most and is less convenient—since it uses Vienna's Reichsbrücke dock on the main river, farther from the city center (€23 one-way, €38 round-trip, 1.5-hour trip downstream; Handelskai 265, U-1: Vorgartenstrasse, tel. from Austria 00-421-2-5293-2226, www.lod.sk).

**To Budapest:** In the summer, the Budapest-based Mahart line runs daily high-speed hydrofoils down the Danube to Budapest (€109 one-way, €125 round-trip, runs Wed, Fri, and Sun, June-Sept only). The boat leaves Vienna at 9:00 and arrives in Budapest at 14:30 (Budapest to Vienna: 9:00-15:30). On any of these boats, you can also stop in Bratislava (explained on page 258). In Vienna, you board at the DDSG Blue Danube dock at the Reichsbrücke (Handelskai 265, U-1: Vorgartenstrasse). To confirm times and prices, and to buy tickets, contact DDSG Blue Danube in Vienna (Austrian tel. 01/58880, www.ddsg-blue-danube.at) or Mahart in Budapest (Hungarian tel. 1/484-4013 or 1/484-4010, www. mahartpassnave.hu).

CONNECTIONS

# NEAR VIENNA

# DANUBE VALLEY

*Melk • The Wachau Valley • Mauthausen*

From the Black Forest in Germany to the Black Sea in Romania, the Danube flows 1,770 miles through 10 countries. Western Europe's longest river (the Rhine is only half as long), it's also the only major river flowing west to east, making it invaluable for commercial transportation. The Danube is at its romantic best just west of Vienna. Mix a cruise with a bike ride through the Danube's Wachau Valley, lined with ruined castles, beautiful abbeys (including the glorious Melk Abbey), small towns, and vineyard upon vineyard.

Much of the valley has a warm fairy-tale glow, but a trip here isn't complete without the chilling contrast of a visit to the Mauthausen concentration camp memorial. Visiting this concentration camp, though a little difficult for non-drivers, is unforgettable and worthwhile even if you've already seen other camps.

## PLANNING YOUR TIME

Allow one day to visit Melk's abbey and to cruise the Wachau Valley by boat or bike; a second day gives you time to get to Mauthausen. It makes sense to see Mauthausen en route to (or from) Salzburg or Hallstatt. For tips on enjoying the nearby riverside sights by boat, bike, bus, and train, see "Getting Around the Wachau Valley" on page 222.

**Day Trip from Vienna:** To day-trip to the Danube, catch an early train to Melk, tour its abbey, eat lunch, and take an afternoon trip along the river from Melk to Krems (it's easier in this direction, as you're going downstream). From Krems, catch the train back to Vienna. The Austrian railway sells a convenient Wachau Kombi-ticket, which includes the train trip from Vienna to Melk, entry to the Melk Abbey, a boat cruise to Krems, and the return train trip to Vienna, for a total of €49 (a decent savings off individual tickets; buy at any Vienna train station). Or, for groups of at least two adults, save yet a few more euros by buying an Einfach-Raus train ticket (see page 503) and taking a regional train (after 9:00 on weekdays) to Melk, then pay for the boat and the abbey separately.

Trains to Melk leave from Vienna's Westbahnhof. Trains from Krems arrive in Vienna at the small Franz-JosefsBahnhof; consider getting off at the previous stop, Spittelau, for better connections (on the U-4 and U-6 subway lines) to other points in Vienna.

**From Vienna by Car and Driver:** Johann Lichtl, based in Vienna, can take you on a day tour of the Danube Valley (see page 30).

**To Hallstatt:** Those heading to Hallstatt by train should avoid arriving there in the evening, when the boat stops running (see "Arrival in Hallstatt" on page 340). Plan a morning or afternoon arrival, even if that means going first to Salzburg and then doubling back to Hallstatt.

# Melk

Sleepy and elegant under its huge abbey, which seems to police the Danube, the town of Melk offers a pleasant stop and is a handy springboard for the beautiful Wachau Valley.

## Orientation to Melk

### TOURIST INFORMATION

The TI is a block off the main square, close to the river, and has info on nearby castles, the latest on bike rental, specifics on bike rides along the river, indoor bike parking, a free WC, a free town map with a self-guided walking tour, and a list of Melk hotels and *Zimmer* in private homes (May-Sept Mon-Sat 9:30-18:00, Sun 9:30-16:00; April and Oct Mon-Sat 9:00-17:00,  closed Sun; very limited hours Nov-March, Kremser Strasse 5, tel. 02752/51160, www.donau.com).

### ARRIVAL IN MELK

Melk is just off the A-1 autobahn that runs between Salzburg and Vienna. The town is also on the main Salzburg-Vienna train line,

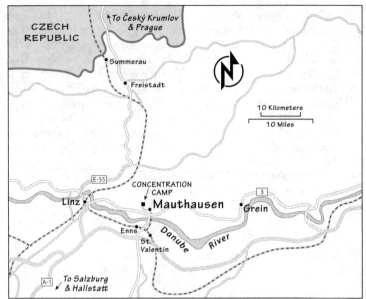

but only slower trains stop here; faster trains bypass the town (so you'll have to transfer in Amstetten or St. Pölten).

**By Train:** Walk straight out of Melk's train station (lockers in station hall-€2-3.50) and continue ahead for several blocks; at the curve, keep straight and go down the stairs, following the cobbled alley that dumps you into the center of the village. Access to Melk Abbey is up on your right (follow signs to *Zum Stift* or *Fussweg Stift Melk*), and the TI is to your left, a block past the square, near the river.

**By Boat:** Turn right as you leave the boat dock and follow the canalside bike path toward the big yellow abbey (the village is beneath its far side). In about five minutes, you'll come to a flashing light (at intersection with bridge); turn left and you're steps from downtown.

To reach the boat dock from Melk, leave the town toward the river, with the abbey on your right. Turn right when you get to the busy road and follow the canal (at the fork just before the gas station, it's quicker to jog left onto the bike path than to follow the main road). Follow signs for *Linienschifffahrt-Scheduled Trips-Wachau*.

**By Car:** If you're just visiting the abbey, you can park there. To park near the old town, head for the free lot just across the canal from the TI, next to Melk's open-air theater (the Wachauarena). To reach it, circle around and cross a small one-lane bridge between the boat docks and gas station, following *Wachauarena* signs.

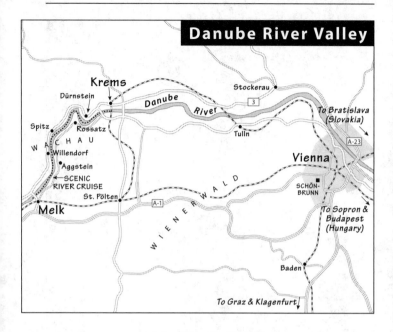

# Danube River Valley

## Sights in Melk

### ▲▲▲MELK ABBEY (BENEDIKTINERSTIFT MELK)

Melk's restored abbey, beaming proudly over the Danube Valley, is one of Europe's great sights. Established as a fortified Benedictine abbey in the 11th century, it was later destroyed by fire. During an 18th-century Baroque building boom, the ruling Habsburgs commissioned architect Jakob Prandtauer to remake the abbey buildings. The abbey church, with its 200-foot-tall dome and symmetrical towers, dominates the complex—emphasizing its sacred purpose.

Freshly painted and gilded throughout, it's a Baroque dream, a lily alone. A grand restoration project was completed by 1996 to celebrate the 1,000th anniversary of the first reference to a country named Österreich (Austria).

**Cost and Hours:** €10, includes entrance to the abbey's park and its bastions; abbey—daily May-Sept 9:00-17:30, April and Oct 9:00-16:30, last entry 30 minutes before closing, Nov-March

DANUBE VALLEY

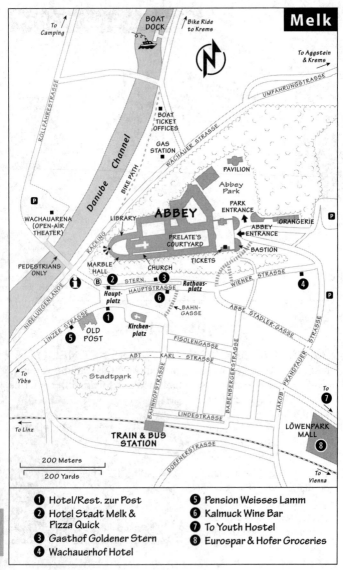

**DANUBE VALLEY**

❶ Hotel/Rest. zur Post
❷ Hotel Stadt Melk &
    Pizza Quick
❸ Gasthof Goldener Stern
❹ Wachauerhof Hotel
❺ Pension Weisses Lamm
❻ Kalmuck Wine Bar
❼ To Youth Hostel
❽ Eurospar & Hofer Groceries

by guided tour only (see below); park—May-Oct daily 9:00-18:00, closed Nov-April; tel. 02752/555-232, www.stiftmelk.at.

**Tours:** One-hour English tours of the abbey are offered daily (April-Oct at 10:55 and 14:55, €12 ticket includes tour and admission). A private guide can be reserved at least one day in advance (€55 plus €10 per-person entrance fee). From Nov-March, the abbey is open only for tours in German with a little English at 11:00 and

14:00. Book guided tours in advance by calling 02752/555-232 or emailing tours@stiftmelk.at.

**Ⓞ Self-Guided Tour:** Although you can take a guided tour, it's easiest just to wander through on your own. Each room is described in English.

• *Go through the first passageway and approach the grand entry to the...*

**East Facade:** Imagine the abbot on the balcony greeting you as he used to greet important guests. Flanking him are statues of Peter and Paul (leaders of the apostles and patron saints of the abbey church) and the monastery's coat of arms (crossed keys). High above are the Latin words "Glory only in the cross" and a huge copy of the Melk Cross (one of the abbey's greatest treasures—the original is hiding in the treasury and viewable only with special permission).

• *Pass into the main courtyard.*

**Prelate's Courtyard:** This is more than a museum. For 900 years, monks of St. Benedict have lived and worked here. Their task: bringing and maintaining Christianity and culture to the region. (Many of the monks live outside the abbey in the community.) They run a high school with about 800 students, a small boarding school, and a busy retreat center.

There have been low points. During the Reformation (1500s), only eight monks held down the theological fort. Napoleon made his headquarters here in 1805 and 1809. And in 1938, when Hitler annexed Austria, the monastery was squeezed into one end of the complex and nearly dissolved. But today, the institution survives—that's the point of the four modern frescoes gracing the courtyard—funded by agriculture (historically, monasteries are big landowners) and your visit.

• *In the far left-hand corner, climb the stairs to the...*

**Imperial Corridor and Abbey Museum:** This 640-foot-long corridor, lined with paintings of Austrian royalty, is the spine of the Abbey Museum. Duck into the first room of the museum (on the left, near beginning of hall). These rooms are filled with art treasures and a recently updated exhibit, with sound-and-light effects meant to convey basic Benedictine precepts. Some English explanations describe the history of the Benedictines in Melk.

• *Continue through the museum—passing through the trippy mirrored room containing gold chalices and monstrances, around a beautifully preserved Northern Renaissance altarpiece, and into the room at the end, with the big rotating model of the abbey.*

**Marble Hall:** While the door frames are real marble, most of this large dining room/ballroom is stucco. The treasure here is the ceiling fresco (by Tirolean Paul Troger, 1731), best appreciated from the center of the room. Notice three themes: 1) The Habsburgs liked to be portrayed as Hercules; 2) Athena, the goddess of wisdom, is included, because the Habsburgs were smart as

**DANUBE VALLEY**

well as strong; and 3) The Habsburgs were into art and culture. This is symbolized by angels figuratively reining in the forces of evil, darkness, and brutality. Through this wise moderation, goodness, beauty, art, and science can rule. Look up again as you leave the room to see how the columns were painted at an angle to give the illusion of a curved ceiling.

**Balcony:** Here you'll enjoy dramatic views of the Danube Valley, the town of Melk, and the facade of the monastery church. The huge statue above everything shows the risen Christ, cross in hand and victorious over death—the central message of the entire place.

**Library:** For the Benedictine monks, the library was—except for the church itself—the most important room in the abbey. Consider how much money they must have invested in its elaborate decor.

In the Middle Ages, monasteries controlled information and hoarded it in their libraries. At a time when most everyone else was illiterate, monks were Europe's educated elite, and had the power to dictate what was true... and what wasn't.

The inlaid bookshelves, matching bindings, and another fine Troger fresco combine harmoniously to create a thematic counterpart to the Marble Hall. This room celebrates not wise politics, but faith. The ceiling shows a woman surrounded by the four cardinal virtues (wisdom, justice, fortitude, and recycling)—natural traits that lead to a supernatural faith. The statues flanking the doors represent the four traditional university faculties (law, medicine, philosophy, and theology).

There would be a Gutenberg Bible in this room...but the abbey sold it in 1925 (it was later donated to Yale University).

**Church:** The finale is the church, with its architecture, ceiling frescoes, stucco marble, grand pipe organ, and sumptuous chapels adorned with chubby cherubs (how many can you count?). All of these elements combine in full Baroque style to make the theological point: A just battle leads to victory. The ceiling shows St. Benedict's triumphant entry into heaven (on a fancy carpet). In the front, below the huge papal crown, the saints Peter and Paul shake hands before departing for their final battles, martyrdom, and ultimate victory. And, high above, the painting in the dome shows that victory: the Holy Trinity, surrounded by saints of particular importance to Melk, happily in heaven.

*Other Abbey Sights:* Near the entrance (and exit) to the abbey, you'll find the abbey's park and bastions (included in your abbey ticket, otherwise €4 for both). The park is home to a picturesque Baroque pavilion housing some fine frescoes by Johann Wenzel Bergel and a café. The bastions offer some decent views from the top terrace, and exhibits by students at the abbey's school are displayed on the second floor. Nearby, in the former orangerie, is the abbey's expensive restaurant.

## Sleeping in Melk

Melk makes a fine and inexpensive overnight stop and has plentiful, usually free parking. Except during August, you shouldn't have any trouble finding a good room at a reasonable rate.

**$$$ Hotel zur Post** is Melk's most modern-feeling hotel—professional and well-run by the Ebner family, with 28 comfy and tidy rooms over a good restaurant (Sb-€65-76, Db-€108-125 depending on size, Db suite-€155, bigger suites that sleep 3-5 people available; 8 percent discount when you book directly with the hotel, pay with cash, and show this book; closed Jan-mid-Feb, elevator, Wi-Fi, free loaner bikes, sauna, Linzer Strasse 1, tel. 02752/52345, www.post-melk.at, info@hotelpost-melk.at).

**$$$ Hotel Stadt Melk,** with 13 bright, straightforward rooms on the town's main square, has helpful new owners and is freshly renovated (Sb-€60, Db-€90-108, lots of stairs, Wi-Fi, sauna, free private parking, Hauptplatz 1, tel. 02752/524-750, www.hotelstadtmelk.at, office@hotelstadtmelk.at, Philippe and Pascal).

**$$ Gasthof Goldener Stern**'s 11 colorful, elegant rooms are each different, with flowers on every pillow. The pricier canopy-bed rooms are very romantic. This lively, homey place—my favorite address in town—buzzes with guests in the atmospheric old restaurant (evenings only) and with Regina and Kurt Schmidt's creativity. It's on a narrow lane that veers up from the main square above the twin turrets (D-€50-62, Db-€58-94, Db suite-€116, price depends on room size, ask about triples and family rooms for up to 6 people, cash only, non-smoking, Wi-Fi, free boat ticket to Spitz with 3-night stay, gluten- and lactose-free breakfasts available,

## Sleep Code

**Abbreviations**    €1 = about $1.40, country code: 43, area code: 02752
**S** = Single, **D** = Double/Twin, **T** = Triple, **Q** = Quad, **b** = bathroom, **s** = shower only.
**Price Rankings**
  **$$$  Higher Priced**—Most rooms €95 or more.
   **$$  Moderately Priced**—Most rooms between €60-95.
    **$  Lower Priced**—Most rooms €60 or less.
Unless otherwise noted, breakfast is included, credit cards are accepted, Wi-Fi is generally free, and everyone speaks some English. Prices change; verify current rates online or by email. For the best prices, always book directly with the hotel.

Sterngasse 17, tel. 02752/52214, www.sternmelk.at, goldenerstern.melk@aon.at).

**$$ Wachauerhof** is a big, dull, traditional 72-room hotel, but it gets the job done in a good location with free private parking—try here if other options are full (Sb-€60, Db-€90, lots of stairs, Wi-Fi, Wiener Strasse 30, tel. 02752/52235, www.wachauerhof.eu, wachauerhof@pgv.at).

**$ Pension Weisses Lamm** is a bit dark and low on atmosphere, but has the cheapest beds in the center. Its 14 rooms, above a lackluster restaurant, are basic (Sb-€40, Db-€58, Tb-€87, cash only, non-smoking, Wi-Fi, Linzer Strasse 7, look for namesake white lamb on sign, mobile 0664-231-5297, www.pension-weisses-lamm-melk.at, pension.weisses.lamm@hotmail.com, Kumus).

**$ *Hostel:*** The modern, institutional, 92-bed youth hostel is a 10-minute walk from the station. Go straight out from the station down Bahnhofstrasse, then turn right at the next corner onto Abt-Karl-Strasse; the hostel is just past the Löwenpark shopping mall (mostly 2- and 4-bed rooms, plus one 8-bed room, all with sink and shower—doubles have private toilets; dorm bed-€23, Sb-€35, Db-€58, €2 less with 3-night stay, includes sheets and breakfast, Wi-Fi, no curfew but reception closes at 21:00, closed Nov-March, Abt-Karl-Strasse 42, tel. 02752/52681, http://melk.noejhw.at, melk@noejhw.at).

***Sleeping near Melk:*** If you have a car, you could stay in a nearby farm or village. The TI has a list of people renting rooms to travelers for about €30 per person, most a few miles from the center. Also consider the good guesthouse in Willendorf, a 20-minute drive from Melk (see page 224).

# Eating in Melk

**Gasthof Goldener Stern** serves fine, inexpensive local cuisine in a relaxed, informal atmosphere (€10-15 main courses, Tue-Sat 17:00-23:00, closed Sun-Mon, Sterngasse 17, tel. 02752/52214).

**Hotel Restaurant zur Post,** classier and pricier, can be worth the few extra euros. Downstairs is a fun and atmospheric wine cellar, with both local and international wines (€12-25 main dishes, €40-50 four-course fixed-price meals, daily 11:30-21:30, closed Jan-mid-Feb, courtyard and fine streetside seating with an abbey view, Linzer Strasse 1, tel. 02752/52345).

**Kalmuck,** a popular wine bar on the main street, is the one place in Melk that stays lively until the wee hours. It also has good lunches (May-Sept only) and serves inexpensive light meals and pub food in the evening (daily 10:00-late, Oct-April from 16:00, Hauptstrasse 10, tel. 02752/517-950).

**Pizza Quick,** on the main square, is takeout-only, but has a full Italian menu and will make you a pie for €7 (daily 11:00-22:00, Hauptplatz 2, tel. 02752/54222).

**Melk Abbey** has a couple of different eateries, which are extremely touristy and full of large groups, but a potential time-saver at lunch for those itching to get on the river.

*Supermarket:* Pick up picnic supplies at either the midrange **Eurospar** or the budget **Hofer,** both in the big Löwenpark mall a 10-minute walk from downtown (Eurospar—Mon-Fri 7:00-19:00, Sat 7:00-18:00, closed Sun; Hofer—same hours but from 8:00, Abt-Karl-Strasse).

# Melk Connections

**From Melk by Train to: Vienna's Westbahnhof** (about 2/hour, 1-1.25 hours, some with transfer in St. Pölten), **Salzburg** (almost hourly, 2.5 hours, transfer in Amstetten), **Mauthausen** (every 2 hours, 1.5-2.5 hours, usually 2 changes—some with significant layovers). Train info: tel. 051-717 (to get an operator, dial 2, then 2), www.oebb.at.

**By Car to/from the Danube Valley:** See "Route Tips for Drivers," page 226.

# The Wachau Valley

The 24-mile stretch of the Danube between Melk and Krems is as pretty as they come—worth ▲▲. This region, called the Wachau,

is blanketed with vineyards and ornamented with cute villages. Keep an eye out for wreaths of straw or greenery, hung out as an invitation to come in and taste. (Why do they call it the Blue Danube? Maybe because in local slang, someone who's feeling his wine is "blue.") Note that in German, Danube is *Donau* (DOH-now), as you'll see by the signs. Austrians know the region for its apricots, made into the jam that fills all that Viennese Sacher-Torte.

## GETTING AROUND THE WACHAU VALLEY

Biking and boating are the most enjoyable ways to experience the stretch from Melk to Krems. Your transportation options for the return trip, however, require some advance thought. You can ride the boat in both directions, but because of the river current, it takes almost twice as long coming back upstream (from Krems to Melk). You can ride a bike in both directions, but given that it's 48 miles round-trip and slightly uphill all the way back, returning via bus or train may be the better option. Also, keep in mind that you can bring bikes on boats and trains—but not on buses.

The following assumes that you're starting in Melk, biking or boating to Krems, and returning by bus or train. You can mix and match options, or stop off at villages in between (such as Spitz). A half-and-half option is cruising by boat from Melk to Spitz—a good midway point—and then biking from Spitz on to Krems (or vice versa).

However you travel, pick up a copy of the free *Wanderkarte Wachau* (technically a hiking map) from the Melk TI so you can trace the route.

### From Melk to Krems

**By Boat:** Five boats per day sail from Melk to Krems (May-Sept; 2/day late April and Oct, no boats off-season). They're run by two different companies: **Brandner** (tel. 07433/259-021, www.brandner.at) and **DDSG** (tel. 01/58880, www.ddsg-blue-danube.

at). They have similar timings, use adjacent boat docks, and charge the same amount (€24 one-way, €28 round-trip, round-trip allows stopovers, bikes ride for €2; rail pass-holders get a 20 percent discount on DDSG sightseeing cruises).

In peak season (May-Sept), boats leave from Melk daily at 8:25 (Brandner), 11:00 (DDSG), 13:50 (both companies), and 16:25 (DDSG, requires change in Spitz). The trip to Krems takes 1.75 hours; because of the six-knot flow of the Danube, the same ride back upstream takes three hours. Both companies also offer longer cruises that start or end in Vienna (check their websites for details).

**By Bike:** It's a three- to four-hour, gently downhill pedal from Melk to Krems. Bicyclists rule here, and you'll find all the amenities that make this valley so popular with Austrians on two wheels. Bike routes are clearly marked with green *Donau-Radweg* signs. (Note: The bike-in-a-red-border signs mean "no biking.") The local TIs give out a *Donauradweg* brochure with a helpful if basic route map.

You can bike either the south or the north side of the river. The advantage of the south side is that there's a dedicated, paved bike path the whole way; at worst you ride next to—but never on—the road (which has less traffic than the north side). The south side is much quieter and more rural, but there are still plenty of vineyards and small *Gasthöfe* in the villages along the way. The north side has more attractions (Willendorf, Spitz, and Dürnstein), but also heavier traffic and arguably poorer views. Inexpensive ferries carry people, bikes, and cars regularly across the river at three points (Spitz, Weissenkirchen, and Dürnstein), so you can also change sides midstream.

In Melk, ask your hotel or the TI for the latest on **bike-rental** options. Some hotels rent or loan bikes. You'll also see automated stands for **Nextbike** throughout the region (including several in Melk, including at the train station, TI, and youth hostel). Their rental system works best for locals, but if you have a mobile phone, you can give it a try. Register online first; when you want to borrow a bike, go to one of the stands, call Nextbike, enter the number of the bike you want, and receive a code to unlock it; you'll call again when you return the bike (€1/hour, €8/24 hours, call center open 24 hours, tel. 02742/229-901, www.nextbike.at).

## From Krems Back to Melk

By **boat**, it's a three-hour ride back to Melk—take train or bus instead.

The last transport of the day from Krems back to Melk leaves around 20:00. If you have a bike, your only option is the **train** back

DANUBE VALLEY

to Melk with a change in St. Pölten (€12, about 1.75 hours, last train at 20:20, no river views).

Otherwise, the **bus** back to Melk is cheaper, quicker, and more scenic (€7; €10 round-trip with day pass, no bikes, www.vor.at). Again, choose between the north and south sides. The north-side bus (#WL1) runs more frequently (almost hourly) than the south-side bus (#WL2, about every two hours). Both cost €8, take an hour to reach Melk, and leave from the platforms on the side of the Krems train station. When you arrive in Melk, ask the bus driver to let you off at Hauptplatz, which is more convenient to my recommended hotels than the station.

## Route Tips for Drivers

With a car, you can drive from Melk to Krems on one side of the river and return on the other side. On the north side, stop at Willendorf (Venus Museum) and Dürnstein (for a glimpse at the town and perhaps a walk up to the ruined castle; use pay lots outside walls). On the south side, consider the villages of Rossatz and Rührsdorf (near Krems), which have many small *Heurigen* winery/restaurants. Closer to Melk is the signposted five-minute detour up a steep, narrow road to the well-preserved ruins of Burg Aggstein, which towers over the valley with magnificent views (free overlook near parking lot, or pay €6.50/person to enter, open daily mid-March-Nov, www.ruineaggstein.at).

# Sights in the Wachau Valley

## Willendorf

This is known among prehistorians as the town where the oldest piece of European art was found—the well-endowed, 25,000-year-old, four-inch statuette known as the *Venus of Willendorf.* (The original is now in Vienna's Natural History Museum—see page 58.) The village is worth a visit for its two-room, smartly designed museum, the **Venusium,** which tells the figure's story and compares it with similar statues found in other parts of Europe (€2, good English descriptions; Easter-late Oct Tue-Sat 10:00-12:00 & 14:00-16:00, Sun 10:00-12:00 & 13:00-16:00; closed off-season; mobile 0664-590-0752, www.willendorf.info). Above the museum, the *Zur Fundstelle* sign leads you to the point where the statue was actually found during railway construction in 1908, and you can see where the hillside has been cut away to reveal the layers of sediment deposited over the millennia.

Consider eating, or even (best with a car) overnighting in Willendorf at **Schneider's Gasthof zur Venus,** steps from the museum. It serves reasonably priced Austrian meals (restaurant closed Mon) and has six good rooms (Sb-€38, Db-€60, Wi-Fi, free parking, tel.

02712/202-020, www.gasthof-zur-venus.at, schneiders@gasthof-zur-venus.at).

**Getting to Willendorf:** Riverboats don't stop here, but the #WL1 bus does (roughly hourly, 20-minute trip from Melk, 40-minute trip from Krems). It's a five-minute walk from the bus stop to the village center.

## Dürnstein

This touristic flypaper of a town lures hordes of tour-bus and cruise-ship visitors with its traffic-free quaintness and its one claim to fame (and fortune): Richard the Lionhearted was imprisoned here in 1193. You can probably sleep in his bedroom. Still, the town is a delight—almost like a Disney movie (but hop with stores selling over-priced ice cream and apricot jam). The ruined castle above (*Burgruine*), where Richard was kept, can be reached by a fairly steep 30-minute hike with great river views. Take Anzuggasse from the riverside promenade up to the downstream town gate, then follow *Weinbau Familie Pölz* signs up the street, which turns into a broad dirt lane lined with informative signposts, and goes all the way up to the castle. There are no services up top, so bring water. Beware: Nonvenomous Aesculapian snakes, up to eight feet long, live in the ruin; they're harmless but best left alone.

## Krems

This town is much bigger than Melk, and home to a small university. Boats from Melk stop about a mile from Krems town center (technically in the adjacent town of Stein). It's a 20-minute walk in, or you can pay €7 to ride a little hop-on, hop-off choo-choo shuttle that connects the dock with the old town and the station.

To walk, go inland from the boat dock to the second roundabout, turn right on Steiner Donaulände, go under the railroad

bridge, walk three blocks farther to a park, then cross through the park and turn left on Utzstrasse. The **TI** is on your right (pick up a map; mid-April-Oct Mon-Fri 9:00-18:00, Sat 11:00-18:00, Sun 11:00-16:00; Nov-mid-April shorter hours and closed Sat-Sun; free Wi-Fi, Utzstrasse 1, tel. 02732/82676, www.krems.info).

The old Krems city gate is a few doors up Utzstrasse from the TI. Stroll the large, traffic-free old town, a shopper's wonderland with a lively restaurant scene. When you're done, find Krems' rail and bus station between the old town and the river. In addition to its hourly train and bus connections to Melk (described earlier), Krems is connected to Vienna's Franz-Josefs-Bahnhof by hourly trains (1 hour).

## Wachau Valley Connections

**BY TRAIN**
For train connections from **Melk,** see page 221.

**ROUTE TIPS FOR DRIVERS**
**Vienna to Hallstatt, via the Wachau Valley, Melk, and Mauthausen (210 miles):** Leave Vienna by crossing the Danube to reach the A-22 autobahn. Head north (following *Praha/Prague* signs) to Stockerau, then take exit #30 to the S-5 highway, which leads to Krems. After Krems, take Route 3 along the river until just after Schallemmersdorf (and just before Emmersdorf), where a bridge leads across the river to Melk. In Melk, signs to *Stift Melk* lead to the Benediktinerstift (Benedictine Abbey).

From Melk, it's a speedy hour to Mauthausen via the autobahn, but the curvy and scenic Route 3 along the river is worth the nausea. At Mauthausen, follow *Ehemaliges KZ-Gedenkstätte Lager* signs to the concentration camp memorial. Leaving Mauthausen, cross the Danube and follow signs to *Enns* (five minutes from Mauthausen town), and join the autobahn there (heading west). Leave the autobahn at exit #224 and follow scenic Route 145 past Gmunden to Stambach, then to road 166, which leads to Hallstatt.

For tips on going from Hallstatt to Vienna with a stop in the Wachau, see "Hallstatt Connections" on page 359.

# Mauthausen Concentration Camp

On top of one of the rolling hills flanking the Danube River, halfway between Vienna and Salzburg, stands the notorious former concentration camp at Mauthausen (MOWT-how-zehn), worth ▲▲▲.  This slave-labor and death camp is the most powerful concentration-camp experience that a traveler can have in Western Europe. The camp functioned from 1938 to 1945, initially to detain and exploit Hitler's domestic political opponents, and then (after 1943) primarily to house Jews and prisoners of war from Eastern Europe. Mauthausen also spawned a network of satellite camps (the nearby one at Gusen has also been turned into a memorial).

Some of the Nazis' camps, such as Auschwitz in Poland, were designed to exterminate people en masse in gas chambers. At others, such as Mauthausen, inmates were essentially worked to death. In these camps, your ability to endure forced labor amounted to a stay of execution. Mauthausen is located above a granite quarry—the region has long supplied building stone to Vienna and Budapest—and the hard labor here was hacking and hauling rocks.

Among Mauthausen's most famous prisoners was Simon Wiesenthal, who dedicated himself after the war to hunting down Nazis and making sure they paid for their crimes. He was one of the lucky survivors—about half of Mauthausen's 200,000 prisoners died, mostly from starvation or exhaustion. Mauthausen was the last concentration camp to be liberated—on May 5, 1945, a week after Hitler's death.

Today enough of Mauthausen's buildings survive to give a gripping sense of the camp's history. You can easily spend the whole day here. At the least, allow two hours to visit the camp itself, or three if you watch the film at the visitors center.

## GETTING TO MAUTHAUSEN

If you have a car, you can visit Mauthausen on the way between Salzburg (or Hallstatt) and Vienna (or Melk). You can also day-trip by car (easy from Melk, doable from Hallstatt or Salzburg, a long day out from Vienna). By train, Mauthausen works best as a day trip from Salzburg or Vienna.

**By Train:** Take the train to Mauthausen from Salzburg (1.75 hours each way, change in Linz) or Vienna (2 hours, change in St. Valentin); connections work about every two hours on both routes. From Melk, there are only a couple of workable connections each day and you usually need to change twice (with lengthy layovers). It's not impossible, but takes longer than from Salzburg or Vienna; check schedules carefully (www.oebb.at).

The Mauthausen train station is three miles from the camp, on the other side of town. There's no bus from the station to the camp. Taxis run about €10-13 (share cost with other tourists, minibus taxis available). Call the Mauthausen-based **Taxi Brixner** (tel. 07238/2439, mobile 0664-462-3699); the station attendant may call for you if you ask politely. Arrange a return pickup with your driver, or ask the camp ticket office to call a taxi for you when you are ready. Budget in time for the taxi trip between the station and the camp (and for the fact that taxis may take a few minutes to arrive).

Visiting Mauthausen with luggage in tow—that is, by public transportation en route between other destinations (for example, on the way between Salzburg and Melk or Vienna)—is only for the dedicated. There are no lockers at Mauthausen station. Inexplica-

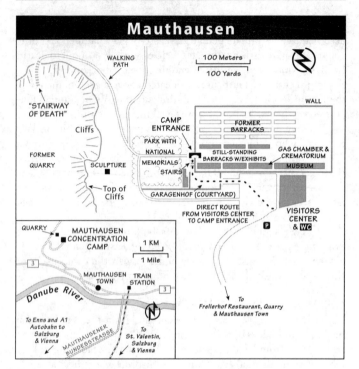

bly, you can't store anything bigger than a daypack at the camp's visitors center—only at the museum. To reach it, you'll need to roll your bags a half-mile uphill from where taxis drop you off. (There's a shortcut, but it involves 30 steps.)

**By Car:** From the main B-3 highway along the Danube, the road up to the camp starts a little west of the actual town of Mauthausen. Look for and follow *KZ-Memorial* or *KZ-Mauthausen* signs. As you arrive at the camp, bear right to reach the parking lot (take ticket; up to 4 hours free). Having a car lets you see the quarry without making the steep hike from the camp grounds: Leave the main parking lot, head down the hill to the first intersection, turn right (following *Gasthaus Kreuzmühle* signs), and look for the quarry on your right and a small unpaved parking area to your left.

## Orientation to Mauthausen

**Cost and Hours:** Free to enter; March-early July daily 9:00-17:30; early July-Oct Tue-Sun 9:00-17:30, closed Mon; Nov-Feb Tue-Sun 9:00-15:45, closed Mon.

**Information:** Pick up a free map either at the information desk or the camp entrance, or consider the excellent €2.60 English guidebook. Tel. 07238/2269, www.mauthausen-memorial.at.

DANUBE VALLEY

**Tours:** Although not essential, a 45-minute **audioguide** is available for €3 at the information desk (leave ID as deposit).

**Services:** The information desk has a bookstore and small lockers for daypacks.

**Eating:** Next door to the visitors center is a **café** serving drinks, snacks, and sandwiches (but no hot meals; open April-Sept Tue-Sun 9:00-17:30, closed Mon; March and Oct Tue-Fri 10:00-16:00, closed Sat-Mon; closed Nov-Feb; tel. 07238/29184). A **farmhouse** below the parking lot also serves meals—see page 231.

**Layout:** Confusingly, the camp has two important areas for visitors. The information desk, café, and visitors center are in the **modern complex** near the parking lot. The museum is within the **camp walls;** to reach it, you'll need to walk all the way around to the left (where you'll also find the path to the quarry and "Stairway of Death") and through the camp entrance. When the visitors center was planned, a tunnel was supposed to lead from it into the camp, bringing you right to the museum. But after the center was built, officials decided that breaching the old camp walls would disturb the historical accuracy of the site.

## Visiting the Camp

Stop briefly at the modern complex (near the parking lot) to glance at the bookstore, use the WC, check daypacks, and—if you'd like to watch the 45-minute film in the visitors center—confirm screening times (generally at the top of each hour; last showing at 16:00). But save a long visit here until after you've seen the camp itself— the most worthwhile sightseeing is inside the camp walls.

Exiting the visitors center complex, circle all the way around to the camp entrance at the left side of the building. You can either walk along the road, or go through the gateway (across the aptly named Garagenhof courtyard and up the stairs).

In the park-like area outside the camp entrance are gripping **memorials** to those who perished here, erected by each home country of the camp's victims. Many yellowed photos have fresh flowers to honor loved ones who are still not forgotten.

Entering the camp brings you onto a long, open area, which was used for roll call several times a day. To either side are some original **barracks** (the others have been torn down) with exhibits. On the left, the second barracks show inmates' housing quarters, while the third is an exhibit of photographs from the days after the camp was liberated.

On the right, the fourth (farthest) barracks is a recently renovated, absorbing **museum** that presents camp's history in English, and shows you its crematoriums and small gas chamber. I'd start here.

The museum's upper floor presents the camp's history chronologically. The central aisle gives wider historical context, while displays on the left explain how the Nazi period and WWII played out in Austria and at Mauthausen specifically. Displays on the right, including many fine, brief audio and video clips of survivors, tell the stories of Mauthausen inmates—how they came to be imprisoned here, the arbitrary rules they suffered under, and the numbers they had to wear. The museum is unusual in providing biographies of many of the Nazi officers who ran the camp, and detailing their postwar fates; some committed suicide, some were sentenced to death by Allied tribunals, and others received long prison terms.

Downstairs, exhibits focus on the documents that camp officers and inmates left behind. Registers of admissions and deaths, drawings and written accounts by survivors, newspaper reports, and many other items testify to the camp's inhumanity.

At the end of this room, you can walk through the **crematorium,** used to burn the bodies of those who died at Mauthausen, and a room listing the names of 81,000 inmates known to have died here. Finally you pass the small **gas chamber,** where about 3,500 inmates were killed. Afterward, you can see a few more exhibits in the adjoining barrack.

Back outside the camp (right in front of you as you exit), find the huge, black **menorah-like sculpture** overlooking the quarry. To your right, a rough cobbled path leads a couple of hundred yards down to the **"Stairway of Death"** (inmates had a much rougher ascent before it was rebuilt in 1942). Connecting the quarry with the camp and its stone depot, the long stairway earned its name for good reason. Inmates were fed the bare minimum to continue working. If they couldn't carry slabs of rocks on their back up the stairway all day long—under the harshest of conditions and on a starvation diet—they were shot on the spot. Most died within a year of their arrival. (Toward the end of the war, the work shifted to making aircraft parts in a factory.) Hike down to the ground level of the vast quarry and ponder the scene; you'll be left with a lasting and poignant impression.

Before you leave, duck back into the visitors center. It has computer screens with more survivor interviews, an exhibit on the camp crematorium, and a graphic 45-minute film. There are several screening rooms—ask the staff which room has the English version.

By visiting a concentration camp and putting ourselves through this emotional wringer, we heed and respect the fervent wish of the victims—that we never forget.

## Sleeping and Eating near Mauthausen

I'd try to overnight in Vienna, Melk, or Salzburg instead of around Mauthausen. But if you're driving and have a special reason to stay near the camp, **$$ Hotel zum Goldenen Schiff,** in the town of Enns across the river (just off the autobahn, less than four miles southwest of Mauthausen), is a solid value. It has 25 comfy rooms and a quaint location right on Enns' delightful main square (Sb-€55, Db-€80-100 depending on size, family rooms, elevator, Wi-Fi, free parking, Hauptplatz 23, tel. 07223/86086, www.hotel-brunner.at, office@hotel-brunner.at). The hotel also rents one €169 honeymoon double halfway up the town hall tower—reached by a stairway with 72 giant steps. This used to be the bell-ringer's apartment before the town bells were automated (reserve on website—and repack into a day bag).

A good option for a refreshing, peaceful meal before or after your visit to Mauthausen is the **Moststube Frellerhof,** a farmhouse 50 yards below the Mauthausen parking lot. Their specialty is apple-and-pear wine (called *Most* in this part of Austria—not the same as the Viennese *Most* made from grapes) and homemade schnapps, and they serve light, farm-fresh lunches and dinners in a fine modern dining room and shady back patio (limited warm food but sandwiches always available, May-Aug Tue-Fri 13:00-22:00, Sat-Sun 11:00-22:00, closed Mon; Sept-April Thu-Sun 11:00-22:00, closed Mon-Wed; playground, tel. 07238/2789).

## Mauthausen Connections

**From Mauthausen by Train:** Trains leave Mauthausen station for **Vienna** (every 2 hours, 2 hours, change in Linz), **Salzburg** (every 2 hours, 1.75 hours, change in St. Valentin or Linz), **Melk** (every 2 hours, 1.5-2.5 hours, usually 2 changes—some with significant layovers), **Hallstatt** (every 2 hours, 2.5 hours, tight transfer at St. Valentin or Linz and another at Attnang-Puchheim—you'll need to leave Mauthausen surprisingly early to be sure to arrive in Hallstatt in time for the last boat, explained on page 340).

DANUBE VALLEY

# BRATISLAVA, SLOVAKIA

Bratislava (brah-tee-SLAH-vah), long a drab lesson in the failings of the communist system, has become downright charming. Its old town bursts with colorfully restored facades, lively outdoor cafés, swanky boutiques, in-love-with-life locals, and (on sunny days) an almost Mediterranean ambience.

The rejuvenation doesn't end in the old town. The ramshackle quarter to the east is gradually being flattened and redeveloped into a new forest of skyscrapers. The hilltop castle is getting a facelift. And even the glum commie suburb of Petržalka is undergoing a Technicolor makeover. Bratislava and Vienna have forged a new twin-city alliance for trade and commerce, bridging Eastern and Western Europe.

You sometimes get the feeling that workaday Bratislavans—who strike some visitors as gruff—are being pulled to the cutting edge of the 21st century kicking and screaming. But many Slovaks embrace the changes and fancy themselves as the yang to Vienna's yin: If Vienna is a staid, elderly aristocrat sipping coffee, then Bratislava is a vivacious young professional jet-setting around Europe. Bratislava at night is a lively place; its very youthful center thrives. While it has tens of thousands of university students, there are no campuses as such—so the old town is the place where students go to play.

Bratislava's priceless location—on the Danube (and the tourist circuit) smack-dab between Budapest and Vienna—makes it a very worthwhile "on the way" destination. Frankly, Bratislava used to leave me cold. But all the changes are positively inspiring.

## PLANNING YOUR TIME

A few hours are plenty to get the gist of Bratislava. Head straight to the old town and follow my self-guided walk, finishing with a stroll along the Danube riverbank to the thriving, modern Eurovea development. With more time, take advantage of one or more of the city's fine viewpoints: Ascend to the "UFO" observation deck atop the funky bridge, ride the elevator up to the Sky Bar for a peek (and maybe a drink), or hike up to the castle for the views (but skip the ho-hum museum inside). If you spend the evening in Bratislava, you'll find it lively with students, busy cafés, and nightlife.

Note that all museums and galleries are closed on Monday.

## Day-Tripping from Vienna to Bratislava

Bratislava is perfect for a day trip from Vienna, or as a stopover on the way from Vienna to Budapest. You have three transportation options: train, bus, or riverboat. It's prudent to bring your passport if crossing over to Bratislava for the day (though it's unlikely anyone will ask for it).

**Trains** connect Vienna and Bratislava easily and quickly (1 hour), leaving twice an hour from Vienna's Hauptbahnhof (main station). This is the most straightforward approach, as a €15 "EU Regio" day pass covers your round-trip as well as public transportation in Bratislava (all for less than the cost of a one-way ticket). Buy the EU Regio ticket from any of the red ÖBB ticket machines in Vienna (choosing "EU Regio" or "Bratislava" makes the option pop up). Pay careful attention to arrival/departure stations, as the Vienna connection alternates between Bratislava's two train stations (Hlavná Stanica and Petržalka). If checking your bag at the station, be sure that your return or onward connection will depart from there. The return portion of the day pass (but not the public transit benefit) is valid for four days.

The **bus** is slightly cheaper, but runs less frequently and departs from less central points in Vienna. The cheapest one-way trip is on the **Blaguss/Eurolines** bus, which connects the Eurolines terminal in Vienna (Erdbergstrasse 200A, U-3: Erdberg) with the convenient Most SNP bus stop underneath the SNP Bridge in Bratislava (runs every 1-2 hours, 1 hour, €7.20 one-way, €12 round-trip, pay driver, www.eurolines.at or www.blaguss.sk). **Slovak Lines/Postbus** buses run more frequently but more slowly (€7.70 one-way, €14.30 round-trip, 1-2/hour, 1.5 hours, tel. 0810-222-3336, www.postbus.at or www.slovaklines.sk) from Vienna's Hauptbahnhof to Bratislava's inconvenient official bus station (Autobusová Stanica Mlynské Nivy, about a 15-minute walk east of the old town). These buses also stop at the Vienna and Bratislava airports.

You can also shuttle between Vienna and Bratislava on the Danube by **riverboat**—it's relaxing, and only a little slower than the bus or train (but more expensive). The fast **Twin City Liner** runs 3-5 times daily between Vienna's Schwedenplatz (where Vienna's town center hits the canal) and a dock at the edge of Bratislava's old town, along Fajnorovo nábrežie (€30-35 each way, 1.25-hour trip; can fill up—reservations smart, Austrian tel. 00-43-1-58880, www.twincityliner.com). A competing line, **LOD**, is a bit cheaper but runs just twice a day and leaves from Vienna's less-convenient Reichsbrücke dock on the main river, farther from the city center (€23 one-way, €38 round-trip, 1.5-hour trip, tel. 02/5293-2226, www.lod.sk).

# Orientation to Bratislava

Bratislava, with 430,000 residents, is Slovakia's capital and biggest city. It has a small, colorful old town *(staré mesto)*, with the castle on the hill above. This small area is surrounded by a vast construction zone of new buildings, rotting residential districts desperately in need of beautification, and some colorized communist suburbs (including Petržalka, across the river). The northern and western parts of the city are hilly and cool (these "Little Carpathians" are draped with vineyards), while the southern and eastern areas are flat and warmer.

## TOURIST INFORMATION

The helpful TI is at Klobučnícka 2, on Primate's Square behind the Old Town Hall (daily May-Sept 9:00-19:00, Oct-April 9:00-18:00, tel. 02/16186, www.visitbratislava.eu). Pick up the free *Bratislava Guide* (with map) and browse their brochures; they can help you find a room in town for a small fee. They also have a branch at the airport.

**Discount Card:** The TI sells the €10 Bratislava City Card, which includes free transit and sightseeing discounts for a full day—but it's worthwhile only if you're doing the old town walking tour (€14 without the card—see "Tours in Bratislava," later; also available for €12/2 days, €15/3 days).

## ARRIVAL IN BRATISLAVA
### By Train

Trains from Vienna stop at one (but never both) of Bratislava's two train stations: Hlavná Stanica or Petržalka. If you're choosing which train (and which station) to use, consider this: Hlavná Stanica is far from welcoming, but it's walkable to some accommodations and the old town; Petržalka (in a suburban shopping area) is small, clean, and modern, but you'll have to take a bus into town. Frequent bus #93 connects the two stations (5-12/hour, 10 minutes; take bus #N93 after about 23:00). For **public transit** info and maps, see http://imhd.zoznam.sk.

**Hlavná Stanica (Main Train Station):** This decrepit and

demoralizing station is about a half-mile north of the old town. It was still standing on my last visit...but barely. The city hopes to tear it down and start from scratch. If those plans go forward, these arrival instructions could also become obsolete.

As you emerge from the tracks, the left-luggage desk is to your right (€2-2.50, depending on weight; look for *úschovňa batožín;* reconfirm open hours at the desk so you'll be able to get your bags when you need them). There are also a few €2 lockers along track 1.

*Getting from the Station to Downtown:* It's a 15-minute **walk** to the town center. Walk out the station's front door and follow the covered walkway next to the looped bus drive; it will bend right and lead to a double pedestrian overpass. Cross the near arch and head downhill on the busy main drag, Štefánikova (named for politician Milan Štefánik, who worked for the post-WWI creation of Czechoslovakia). This once-elegant old boulevard is lined with Habsburg-era facades—some renovated, some rotting. In a few minutes, you'll pass the nicely manicured presidential gardens on your left. Next comes the Grassalkovich Palace, Slovakia's "White House" (with soldiers at guard out front), which faces the busy intersection called Hodžovo Námestie. The old town is just a long block ahead of you now. You can cross the intersection at street level or find the stairs and escalators down to the underground passageway *(podchod).* Head for the green steeple with an onionshaped midsection. This is St. Michael's Gate, at the start of the old town (and the beginning of my self-guided walk, described later).

To shave a few minutes off the trip, go part of the way by **bus** #93 or #X13 (after 23:00, use bus #N93). Walk out the station's front door to the line of bus stops to the right. If your train ticket doesn't cover public transit in Bratislava, buy a 15-minute ticket from the machines for €0.70 (select *základný lístok—platí 15 minút,* then insert coins—change given). Ride two stops to Hodžovo Námestie, across from Grassalkovich Palace, then walk straight ahead toward the green steeple, passing a pink-and-white church.

**Tram** #13 is another option from the station, if it's running again (the tracks have been closed for construction). Trams *(električky)* use the same tickets as buses; ride to the Poštová stop, then walk straight down Obchodná street toward St. Michael's Gate.

**Petržalka Train Station (ŽST Petržalka):** Half of the trains from Vienna arrive at this small, quiet train station, across the river in the modern suburb of Petržalka (PET-ur-ZHAL-kuh). From this station, ride bus #93 (direction: Hlavná Stanica) or #94 (direction: STU) four stops to Zochova (the first stop after the bridge, near St. Michael's Gate); after 23:00, use bus #N93. If you don't have a Vienna-Bratislava train day pass, buy a €0.70/15-minute *základný lístok* ticket (described earlier).

# Welcome to Slovakia

In many ways, Slovakia is the "West Virginia of Europe"—relatively poor and undeveloped, but spectacularly beautiful in its own rustic way. Sitting quietly in the very center of Central Europe, wedged between bigger and stronger nations (Hungary, Austria, the Czech Republic, and Poland), Slovakia was brutally disfigured by the communists, then over-shadowed by the Czechs. But in recent years, this fledgling re-public has found its wings.

With about 5.5 million peo-ple in a country of 19,000 square miles (similar to Massachusetts and New Hampshire combined), Slovakia is one of Europe's small-est nations. Recent economic reforms have caused two very dif-ferent Slovakias to emerge: the modern, industrialized, flat, afflu-ent west, centered on the capital of Bratislava; and the remote, poorer, mountainous, "backward" east, with high unemployment and traditional lifestyles. Slovakia is ethnically diverse: In addition to the Slavic Slovaks, there are Hungarians (about 10 percent of the population, "stranded" here when Hungary lost this land after World War I) and Roma (Gypsies, also about 10 percent). Slova-kia has struggled to incorporate both of these large and often-mistreated minority groups.

Slovakia has spent most of its history as someone else's backyard. For centuries, Slovakia was ruled from Budapest and known as "Upper Hungary." At other times, it was an important chunk of the Habsburg Empire, ruled from neighboring Vienna. But most people think first of another era: the 75 years that Slovakia was joined with the Czech Republic as the country of "Czechoslovakia." From its start in the aftermath of World War I, this union of the Czechs and Slovaks was troubled; some Slovaks chafed at being ruled from Prague, while many Czechs resented the financial burden of their poorer neighbors to the east.

After they gained their freedom from the communists dur-ing 1989's peaceful "Velvet Revolution," the Czechs and Slovaks began to think of the future. The Slovaks wanted to rename the

## By Bus, Boat, or Plane

Buses from Vienna arrive at the Most SNP stop, beneath the old town side of the SNP Bridge. Riverboats use a dock a short walk downstream from the bridge, just below the old town. Walking from either into the old town takes just five minutes. For more on bus and boat connections, see "Day-Tripping from Vienna to Bratislava," earlier. For information on Bratislava's airport, see "Bratislava Connections," at the end of this chapter.

country Czecho-Slovakia, and to redistribute power to give themselves more autonomy within the union. The Czechs balked, relations gradually deteriorated, and the Slovak nationalist candidate Vladimír Mečiar fared surprisingly well in the 1992 elections. Taking it as a sign that the two peoples wanted to part ways, politicians pushed through (in just three months) the peaceful separation of the now-independent Czech and Slovak Republics. (The people in both countries never actually voted on the change, and most opposed it.) The "Velvet Divorce" became official on January 1, 1993.

At first the Slovaks struggled. Communist rule had been particularly unkind to them, and their economy was in a shambles. Visionary leaders set forth bold solutions, including the 2003 implementation of a flat tax (19 percent), followed by EU membership in 2004. Before long, major international corporations began to notice the same thing the communists had: This is a great place to build stuff, thanks to a strategic location (300 million consumers live within a day's truck drive), low labor costs, and a well-trained workforce. Not surprisingly, multiple foreign automakers have plants here. Today Slovakia produces one million cars a year, making the country the world's biggest car producer (per capita) and leading the *New York Times* to dub Slovakia "the European Detroit."

The flat tax and other aggressively pro-business policies have not been without their critics—especially in the very impoverished eastern half of the country, where poor people feel they're becoming even poorer. With the rollback of social services and the proverbial cracks widening, many seem to have been left behind by Slovakia's bold new economy.

Even so, particularly if you zoom in on its success story around Bratislava, the evidence is impressive. Bratislava has only 3 percent unemployment. The standard of living (as it relates to local costs) puts Bratislava in 10th place among European cities. Slovakia joined the EU in 2004; in 2009, it adopted the euro currency. While most of Europe is struggling through difficult economic times, much of Slovakia seems poised for its brightest future yet.

## HELPFUL HINTS

**Money:** Slovakia, like Austria, uses the euro (€1=about $1.40).

**Language:** The official language is Slovak, which is closely related to Czech and Polish—although many Bratislavans also speak English. The local word used informally for both "hi" and "bye" is easy to remember: *ahoj* (pronounced "AH-hoy," like a pirate). "Please" is *prosím* (PROH-seem), "thank you" is *ďakujem* (DYAH-koo-yehm), "good" is *dobrý* (DOH-bree), and "Cheers!" is *Na zdravie!* (nah ZDRAH-vyeh).

**Phone Tips:** To call locally within Bratislava, dial the number without the area code. To make a long-distance call within Slovakia, start with the area code (which begins with 0). To call from Austria to Slovakia, dial 00-421, then the area code minus the initial zero, then the number (from the US, dial 011-421-area code minus zero, then the number). To call from Slovakia to Austria, you'd dial 00-43, then the area code (minus the initial zero) and number.

**Internet Access:** You'll see signs advertising computer terminals around the old town. Free Wi-Fi hotspots are at the three major old town squares (Main Square, Primate's Square, and Hviezdoslav Square).

**Local Guidebook:** For in-depth suggestions on Bratislava sightseeing, dining, and more, look for the excellent and eye-pleasing *Bratislava Active* guidebook by Martin Sloboda (see "Tours in Bratislava," next; around €10, sold at every postcard rack).

# Tours in Bratislava

### Walking Tours

The **TI** offers a one-hour old town walking tour in English every day in the summer at 14:00 (€14, free with €10 Bratislava City Card; book and pay at least two hours in advance). Those arriving by boat will be accosted by guides selling their own 1.5-hour tours (half on foot and half in a little tourist train, €10, in German and English).

### Local Guide

MS Agency, run by **Martin Sloboda** (a can-do entrepreneur and

tireless Bratislava booster, and author of the great local guidebook described earlier), can set you up with a good guide (€130/3 hours, €150/4 hours); he can also help you track down your Slovak roots. Martin, who helped me put this chapter together, is part of the generation that came of age as communism fell and whose energy and leadership are reshaping the city (mobile 0905-627-265, www.msagency.sk, sloboda@msagency.sk).

BRATISLAVA

# Bratislava Old Town Walk

This self-guided orientation walk passes through the heart of delightfully traffic-free old Bratislava and then down to its riverside commercial zone (figure 1.5 hours, not including stops, for this walk). If you're coming from the station, make your way toward the green steeple of St. Michael's Gate (explained in "Arrival in Bratislava," earlier). Before going through the passage into the old town, peek over the railing on your left to the inviting garden below—once part of the city moat.

• *Step through the first, smaller gate, walk along the passageway, and pause as you come through the green-steepled...*

## St. Michael's Gate (Michalská Brána)

This is the last surviving tower of the city wall. Just below the gate, notice the "kilometer zero" plaque in the ground, marking the point from which distances in Slovakia are measured.

• *You're at the head of...*

## Michalská Street

Pretty as it is now, the old center was a decrepit ghost town during the communist era, partly because WWII bombing left Bratislava a damaged husk. The communist regime believed that Bratislavans of the future would live in large, efficient apartment buildings. They saw the old town as a useless relic of the bad old days of poor plumbing, cramped living spaces, social injustice, and German domination—a view which left no room to respect the town's heritage. In the 1950s, they actually sold Bratislava's original medieval cobbles to cute German towns that were rebuilding themselves with elegant Old World character. Locals avoided this desolate corner of the city, preferring to spend time in the Petržalka suburb across the river.

With the fall of communism in 1989, the new government began a nearly decade-long process of restitution—sorting out who had the rights to the buildings, and returning them to their original owners. During this time, little repair or development took place (since there was no point investing in a property until ownership was clearly established). By 1998, most of these property issues had been sorted out, and the old town was made traffic-free. The city replaced all the street cobbles, spruced up the public buildings, and encouraged private owners to restore their property. (If you see any remaining decrepit buildings, it's likely that their ownership is still in dispute.)

# Bratislava

1. Hotel Marrol's
2. Hotel Michalská Brána
3. Hotel Ibis
4. Penzión Virgo
5. Penzión Gremium
6. Downtown Backpackers Hostel
7. 1. Slovak Pub
8. Bratislavský Meštiansky Pivovar
9. Lemon Tree/Sky Bar/Rum Club
10. Shtoor (3)
11. Coffee & Bagel Story; Café Roland; Kaffee Mayer
12. Billa Supermarket

ULICA PALISÁDY

ŠTETINOVA

PANENSKÁ

KOZIA ULICA

LÝCEJNÁ

KONVENTNÁ

PODJAVOR

STAROMESTSKÁ

ZOCHOVA

Župné Nám.

DANKOVSKÉHO

SVORADOVA

KORENIČOVA

ŠKARNICLOVA

ULICA PALISÁDY

ZÁMOCKÁ ULICA

Zochova B

BAŠTOVA

TVARÓŽKOVA

ŽIDOVSKÁ

Fashion Courtyard

KLARISKÁ

KRÁTKA

KAPITULSKÁ

PREPOŠTSKÁ

STRELECKÁ

SUMMER RIDING SCHOOL

CASTLE

ENTRY

KNIGHTS HALL

TICKETS

TREASURE ROOM

PARLIAMENT

VODNÍ

STAROMESTSKÁ

OLD

VENTÚRSKA

ZAM. SCHODY

WALK ENDS

ST. MARTIN'S CATHEDRAL

SCHODY PRI STAREJ VODÁRNI

HOLOCAUST MEMORIAL

NÁBR. ARMÁDNEHO GENERÁLA L. SVOBODU

Most SNP
(Bus stop under bridge) B

RÁZUSOVO NÁBR.

BRATISLAVA

N

100 Meters
100 Yards

SNP BRIDGE

To Petržalka

"UFO" OBSERVATION DECK

TOLSTÉHO

SLÁDKOVIČOVA

To Main Train Station

Presidential Gardens

ŠTEFÁNIKOVA

**6**

Hodžovo Námestie **B**

Hodžovo Nám.

BIG FOUNTAIN

**GRASSALKOVICH PALACE**

**12**

Hodžovo Námestie **B**

TATRACENTROM

NÁM. 1 MÁJA

VYSOKÁ

Kollárovo Nám.

MARIÁNSKA

**7**

OBCHODNÁ

HOLLÉHO

POŠTOVÁ

DREVENÁ

**CROWNE PLAZA HOTEL**

**8**

**10** T Poštová

HEYDUKOVA

KOLÁRSKA

ŠPITÁLSKA

SUCHÉ MÝTO

Hurbanovo Nám.

✝

👣 **WALK BEGINS**

Nám. SNP

**ST. MICHAEL'S GATE**

ZÁMOČNÍCKA

Wine Courtyard

FRANTIŠK.

NEDBALOVA

MICHALSKÁ

CHOCOLATE SHOP

BIELA

**OLD TOWN HALL & CITY HISTORY MUSEUM**

KLOBUČNÍCKA

TESCO DEP'T STORE

Kamenné Nám.

DUNAJSKÁ

SEDLÁRSKA

Františkánske Nám.

NAPOLEONIC SOLDIER STATUE

Primáciálne námestie **i**

**PRIMATE'S PALACE**

**Hlavné námestie**

**11**

**APPONYI PALACE**

LAURINSKÁ

**5**

GORKÉHO

GRÖSSLINGOVÁ

RYBÁRSKA

SCHÖNER NÁCI STATUE

PANSKÁ

ČUMIL STATUE

RYBÁRSKA

DISPLAY CASE

JESENSKÉHO

**TOWN**

**10**

HVIEZDOSLAVOVO NÁM.

FOUNTAIN

**NATIONAL THEATER**

MEDENÁ

**10**

TALLEROVA

ŠTÚROVA

**U.S. EMBASSY**

**9**

TOBRUCKÁ

**1**

**SLOVAK PHILHARMONIC**

**SLOVAK NATIONAL GALLERY**

Nám. L. Štúra

⚓

VAJANSKÉHO NÁBR.

FAJNOROVO NÁBR.

To Eurovea (5 min. walk)

**RIVERBOAT TERMINAL**

**Danube   River**

**BRATISLAVA**

The cafés and restaurants that line this street are inviting, especially in summer. Poke around behind the facades and outdoor tables to experience Bratislava's charm. Courtyards and passageways—most of them open to the public—burrow through the city's buildings. For example, a half-block down Michalská street on the left, the courtyard at #12 was once home to vintners; their former cellars are now coffee shops, massage parlors, crafts boutiques, and cigar shops. Across the street, on the right, the dead-end passage at #5 has an antique shop and small café, while #7 is home to a fashion design shop.

On the left (at #6), the **Cukráreň na Korze** chocolate shop is highly regarded among locals for its delicious hot chocolate and creamy truffles (Mon-Thu 9:00-21:00, Fri-Sat 9:00-22:00, Sun 10:00-21:00, tel. 02/5443-3945).

Above the shop's entrance, the **cannonball** embedded in the wall recalls Napoleon's two sieges of Bratislava (the 1809 siege was 42 days long), which caused massive suffering—even worse than during World War II. Keep an eye out for these cannonballs all over town...somber reminders of one of Bratislava's darkest times.

• *Two blocks down from St. Michael's Gate, where the street jogs slightly right (and its name changes to Ventúrska), detour left along Sedlárska street and head to the...*

## Main Square (Hlavné Námestie)

A modest town hall square that feels too petite for a national capital, this is the centerpiece of Old World Bratislava. Cute little kiosks, with old-time cityscape engravings on their roofs, sell local handicrafts and knick-knacks (Easter through October). Similar stalls fill the square from mid-November until December 23, when the Christmas market here is a big draw (www.vianocnetrhy.sk).

Virtually every building around this square dates from a different architectural period, from Gothic (the yellow tower) to Art Nouveau (the fancy facade facing it from across the square).

Cafés line the square. You can't go wrong here. Choose the ambience you like best (indoors or out) and sip a drink with Slovakia's best urban view. The Art Nouveau **Café Roland,** once a bank, is known for its 1904 Klimt-style mosaics and historic photos of the days when the city was known as Pressburg (Austrian times) or Pozsony (Hungarian times). The barista stands where a different kind of bean counter once did, guarding a vault that now holds coffee (Hlavné Námestie 5; the café may have a new name by the time you visit). The classic choice is the kitty-corner **Kaffee Mayer.** This venerable café, an institution here, has been selling coffee and cakes to a genteel clientele since 1873. You can enjoy your pick-me-up in the swanky old interior or out on the square (€3-3.50 cakes, small selection of expensive-for-Bratislava hot meals, daily 9:30-22:00, Fri-Sat until 23:00, Hlavné Námestie 4, tel. 02/5441-1741).

Peering over one of the benches on the square is a cartoonish statue of a **Napoleonic officer** (notice the French flag marking the embassy right behind him). With bare feet and a hat pulled over his eyes, it's hardly a flattering portrait—you could call it the locals' revenge for Napoleon's sieges. Across the square, another soldier from that period stands at attention.

At the top of the Main Square is the impressive **Old Town Hall** (Stará Radnica), with its bold yellow tower. Near the bottom of the tower (to the left of the window), notice another cannonball embedded in the facade—yet another reminder of Napoleon's impact on Bratislava. Over time, the Old Town Hall grew, annexing the buildings next to it and creating a mishmash of architectural styles along this side of the square. (A few steps down the street to the right are the historic apartments and wine museum at the **Apponyi House**—described later, under "Sights in Bratislava.")

Step through the passageway into the Old Town Hall's gorgeously restored **courtyard,** with its Renaissance arcades. (The **City History Museum**'s entrance is here—described later.)

Then, to see another fine old square, continue through the other end of the courtyard into **Primate's Square** (Primaciálne Námestie). The pink mansion on the right is the **Primate's Palace,** with a fine interior decorated with six English tapestries (described later). At the far end of this square is the **TI.**

• *Backtrack to the Main Square. With your back to the Old Town Hall, go to the end of the square and follow the street to the left (Rybárska Brána). On your way you'll pass a pair of...*

### Whimsical Statues

Playful statues (such as the Napoleonic officer we met earlier) dot Bratislava's old town. Most date from the late 1990s, when city leaders wanted to entice locals back into the newly prettied-up center.

**BRATISLAVA**

## City of Three Cultures:
## Pressburg, Pozsony, Bratislava

Historically more of an Austrian and Hungarian city than a Slovak one, Bratislava has always been a Central European melting pot. Everyone from Hans Christian Andersen to Casanova has sung the wonders of this bustling burg on the Danube.

For most of its history, Bratislava was part of the Austrian Empire and known as Pressburg, with a primarily German-speaking population. (Only the surrounding rural areas were Slovak.) The Hungarians used Pozsony (as they called it) as their capital during the century and a half that Buda and Pest were occupied by Ottoman invaders.

By its turn-of-the-20th-century glory days, the city was a rich intersection of cultures—about 40 percent German, 40 percent Hungarian, and 20 percent Slovak. Shop clerks greeted customers in all three languages. It was said that the mornings belonged to the Slovaks (farmers who came into the city to sell their wares at market), the afternoons to the Hungarians (diplomats and office workers filling the cafés), and the evenings to the Austrians (wine producers who ran convivial neighborhood wine pubs where all three groups would gather). In those wine pubs, the vintner would listen to which language his customers used, then bring them a glass with the serving size expected in their home country: 0.3 liters for Hungarians, 0.25 liters for Austrians, and 0.2 liters for Slovaks (a distinction that still exists today). Jews (one-tenth of the population), and Roma (Gypsies) rounded out the city's ethnic brew.

When the new nation of Czechoslovakia was formed from the rubble of World War I, the city shed its German and Hungarian names, and took the newly created Slavic name of Bratislava. The Slovak population was on the rise, but the city remained tricultural.

World War II changed all of that. With the dissolution of Czechoslovakia, Slovakia became an "independent" country under the thumb of the Nazis—who all but wiped out the Jewish population. Then, at the end of the war, a Czechoslovakia reunited under the Soviet Russian thumb rudely expelled the city's ethnic Germans and Hungarians in retribution for the misdeeds of

Just at the beginning of the street, as you exit the main square, you'll come to a jovial chap doffing his top hat. This is a statue of **Schöner Náci** (see photo, previous page), who lived in Bratislava until the 1960s. This eccentric old man, a poor carpet cleaner, would dress up in his one black suit and top hat, and go strolling through the city, offering gifts to the women he fancied. (He'd often whisper *"schön"*—German for "pretty," which is how he got his nickname.) Schöner Náci now gets to spend eternity greeting

Hitler and Horthy (Hungary's wartime leader).

Bratislava's urban heritage suffered terribly under the communists. The historic city's multilayered charm and delicate cultural fabric were ripped apart, then shrouded in gray. The communists were prouder of their ultramodern SNP Bridge than of the city's historic Jewish quarter—which they razed to make way for the bridge. Now the bridge and its highway slice through the center of the old town, and the heavy traffic rattles the stained-glass windows of St. Martin's Cathedral. Similarly, the city's Germanic heritage was deliberately obscured.

But Bratislava's most recent chapter is one of great success. Since the fall of communism, the city has gone from gloomy victim to thriving economic center and social hub. With a healthy market economy, it now has the chance to re-create itself as Slovakia's national capital. Its population of about 430,000 includes some 60,000 students (at the city's six universities), creating an atmosphere of youthful energy and optimism. Its remarkable position on the Danube, a short commute from Vienna, is prompting its redevelopment as one of Europe's up-and-coming cities.

Bratislava and Vienna have realized that it's mutually beneficial to work together to bring the Slovak capital up to snuff. They're cooperating in a new "twin city" commerce super-zone. In the coming years, foreign investors talk of erecting a Bratislavan skyline of 600-foot-tall skyscrapers and a clutch of glittering new megamalls. Bratislavans also have high hopes for revitalizing the city's transport infrastructure: The highway that barrels between the old town and the castle will be diverted underground (through a tunnel beneath the Danube); a bullet train will swoosh to a stop at a slick new train station; a new six-station subway line will lace the city together; and the entire riverfront will be transformed into a people-friendly park.

As the city pulls funding together, expect lots of construction during your visit. You'd never have guessed it a few years ago, but today calling Bratislava "the next Berlin on a smaller scale" is only a bit of a stretch.

visitors outside his favorite café, Kaffee Mayer. Once he lost an arm: A bunch of drunks broke it off. (It was replaced.) As Prague gets more expensive, Bratislava has become one of the cheaper alternatives for weekend "stag parties," popular with Brits lured here by cheap flights and cheap beer.

• Continue down Rybárska.

At the end of this block, at the intersection with Panská, watch out on the right for Čumil ("the Peeper"), grinning at passersby

BRATISLAVA

from a manhole. This was the first and is still the favorite of Bratislava's statues. There's no story behind this one—the artist simply wanted to create a fun icon and let the townspeople make up their own tales. Čumil has survived being driven over by a truck—twice—and he's still grinning.

• *Keep along Rybárska to reach the long, skinny square called...*

## Hviezdoslav Square (Hviezdoslavovo Námestie)

The landscaping in the center of this square makes it particularly inviting. At the near end is the impressive, silver-topped Slovak National Theater (Slovenské Národné Divadlo). Beyond that, the opulent yellow Neo-Baroque building is the Slovak Philharmonic (Slovenská Filharmónia). When the theater opened in the 1880s, half the shows were in German and half in Hungarian. Today, it's a proud Slovak institution—typical of the ethnic changes that have marked this city's life.

Right in front of the theater (by the Mc-Donald's), look down into the glass **display case** to see the foundation of the one-time Fishermen's Gate into the city. Surrounding the base of the gate is water. This entire square was once a tributary of the Danube, and the Carlton Hotel across the way was a series of inns on different islands. The buildings along the old town side of the square mark where the city wall once stood. Now the square is a lively zone on balmy evenings, with several fine restaurants (including some splurgy steakhouses) offering al fresco tables jammed with visiting European businessmen looking for good-quality, expense-account meals.

Stroll down the long art-and-people-filled square. Each summer, as part of an arts festival, it's ornamented with entertaining modern art. After passing a statue of the square's namesake (Pavol Országh Hviezdoslav, a beloved Slovak poet), you'll come upon an ugly fence and barriers on the left, which mark the fortified US Embassy. Just past the embassy is the low-profile entrance to the **Sky Bar,** an affordable rooftop restaurant with excellent views (ride elevator to seventh floor; see "Eating in Bratislava," later). Farther along, after the giant chessboard, the glass pavilion is a popular venue for summer concerts. On the right near the end of the park, a statue of Hans Christian Andersen is a reminder that the Danish storyteller enjoyed his visit to Bratislava, too.

• *Reaching the end of the square, you run into the barrier for a busy highway. Turn right and walk one block to find the big, black marble slab facing a modern monument—and, likely, a colorful wooden reconstruction of a synagogue.*

## Holocaust Memorial

This was the site of Bratislava's original synagogue. You can see an etching of the building in the big slab.

Turn your attention to the memorial. The word "Remember" carved into the base in Hebrew and Slovak commemorates the 90,000 Slovak Jews who were deported to Nazi death camps. Nearly all were killed. The fact that the town's main synagogue and main church (to the right) were located side by side illustrates the tolerance that characterized Bratislava before Hitler. Ponder the modern statue: The two pages of an open book, faces, hands in the sky, and bullets—all under the Star of David—evoke the fate of 90 percent of the Slovak Jews.

• *Now head toward the adjacent church, up the stairs.*

## St. Martin's Cathedral (Dóm Sv. Martina)

If the highway thundering a few feet in front of this historic

church's door were any closer, the off-ramp would go through the nave. Sad as it is now, the cathedral has been party to some pretty important history. While Buda and Pest were occupied by Ottomans from 1543 to 1689, Bratislava was the capital of Hungary. Nineteen Hungarian kings and queens were crowned in this church—more than have been crowned anywhere in Hungary. In fact, the last Hungarian coronation (not counting the Austrian Franz Josef) was not in Budapest, but in Bratislava. A replica of the Hungarian crown still tops the steeple.

It's worth walking up to the cathedral's entrance to observe some fragments of times past (circle around the building, along the busy road, to the opposite, uphill side). Directly across from the church door is a broken bit of the 15th-century town wall. The church was actually built into the wall, which explains its unusual north-side entry. In fact, notice the fortified watchtower (with a WC drop on its left) built into the corner of the church just above you.

There's relatively little to see inside the cathedral—I'd skip it (€2, Mon-Sat 9:00-11:30 & 13:00-18:00, Sun 13:30-16:00). If you do duck in, you'll find a fairly gloomy interior, some fine carved-wood altarpieces (a Slovak specialty), a dank crypt, a replica of the Hungarian crown, and a treasury in the back with a whimsical wood carving of Jesus blessing Habsburg Emperor Franz Josef.

Head back around the church for a good view (looking toward the river) of the huge bridge called **Most SNP,** the communists' pride and joy (the "SNP" stands for the Slovak National Uprising of 1944 against the Nazis, a typical focus of communist remembrance). As with most Soviet-era landmarks in former communist countries, locals aren't crazy about this structure—not only for the questionable starship *Enterprise* design, but also because

of the oppressive regime it represented. However, the restaurant and observation deck up top has been renovated into a posh eatery called (appropriately enough) "UFO." You can visit it for the views, a drink, or a full meal.

• *You could end the walk here. Two sights (both described later, under "Sights in Bratislava") are nearby. To hike up to the* **castle,** *take the underpass beneath the highway, go up the stairs on the right marked by the* Hrad/Castle *sign, then turn left up the stepped lane marked* Zámocké Schody. *Or hike over the SNP Bridge (pedestrian walkway on lower level) to ride the elevator up the* **UFO** *viewing platform.*

*But to really round out your Bratislava visit, head for the river and stroll downstream (left) to a place where you get a dose of modern development in Bratislava—**Eurovea.** Walk about 10 minutes downstream, past the old town, boat terminals, and iron bridge, until you come to a big, slick complex with a grassy park leading down to the riverbank.*

### Eurovea

Just downstream from the old town is the futuristic Eurovea, with four vibrant layers, each a quarter-mile long: a riverside park, luxu-

ry condos, a thriving modern shopping mall, and an office park. Walking out onto the view piers jutting into the Danube and surveying the scene, it looks like a computer-generated urban dreamscape come true. Exploring the old town gave you a taste of

where this country has been. But wandering this riverside park, enjoying a drink in one of its chic outdoor lounges, and then browsing through the thriving mall, you'll enjoy a glimpse of where Slovakia is heading.

• *Our walk is finished. If you haven't already visited them, consider circling back to some of the sights described next.*

# Sights in Bratislava

If Europe had a prize for "capital city with the most underwhelming museums," I'd cast my vote for Bratislava. You can easily have a great day here without setting foot in a museum. Focus instead on Bratislava's street life and the grand views from the castle and UFO restaurant. If it's rainy or you're in a museum-going mood, the Primate's Palace (with its cheap admission and fine tapestries) ranks slightly above the rest.

## ON OR NEAR THE OLD TOWN'S MAIN SQUARE

All three of these museums are within a few minutes' walk of one another, on or very near the Main Square.

### ▲Primate's Palace (Primaciálny Palác)

Bratislava's most interesting museum, this tastefully restored French-Neoclassical mansion (formerly the residence of the arch-

bishop, or "primate") dates from 1781. The religious counterpart of the castle, it filled in for Esztergom—the Hungarian religious capital—after that city was taken by the Ottomans in 1543. Even after the Ottoman defeat in the 1680s, this remained the winter residence of Hungary's archbishops.

**Cost and Hours:** €3, Tue-Fri 10:00-17:00, Sat-Sun 11:00-18:00, closed Mon, Primaciálne Námestie 1, tel. 02/5935-6394, www.bratislava.sk.

**Visiting the Museum:** The palace, which now serves as a government building, features one fine floor of exhibits. Follow signs for *Expozícia* up the grand staircase to the ticket counter. There are three main attractions: the Mirror Hall, the tapestries, and the archbishop's chapel.

The **Mirror Hall,** used for concerts, city council meetings, and other important events, is to the left as you enter and worth a glance (if it's not closed for an event).

A series of large public rooms, originally designed to impress, are now an art gallery. Distributed through several of these rooms is the museum's pride, and for many its highlight: a series of six English **tapestries,** illustrating the ancient Greek myth of the

BRATISLAVA

tragic love between Hero and Leander. The tapestries were woven in England by Flemish weavers for the court of King Charles I (in the 1630s). They were kept in London's Hampton Court Palace until Charles was deposed and beheaded in 1649. Cromwell sold them to France to help fund his civil war, but after 1650, they disappeared. Centuries later, in 1903, restorers broke through a false wall in this mansion and discovered the six tapestries, neatly folded and perfectly preserved. Nobody knows how they got there (perhaps they were squirreled away during the Napoleonic invasion, and whoever hid them didn't survive). The archbishop—who had just sold the palace to the city, but emptied it of furniture before he left—cried foul and tried to get the tapestries back...but the city said, "A deal's a deal."

After traipsing through the grand rooms, find the hallway that leads through the smaller rooms of the archbishop's private quarters, now decorated with minor Dutch, Flemish, German, and Italian paintings. At the end of this hall, a bay window looks down into the archbishop's own private marble **chapel.** When the archbishop became too ill to walk down to Mass, this window was built for him to take part in the service.

On your way back to the entry, pause at the head of the larger corridor to study a 1900 view of the then much smaller town by Gustáv Keleti. The museum's entry hall also has grand portraits of Maria Theresa and Josef II.

### City History Museum (Mestské Múzeum)

Delving into the bric-a-brac of Bratislava's past, this museum includes ecclesiastical art on the ground floor and a sprawling, chronological look at local history upstairs. The displays occupy rooms once used by the town council—courthouse, council hall, chapel, and so on. Everything is described in English, and the included audioguide tries hard, but nothing quite succeeds in bringing meaning to the place. On your way upstairs, you'll have a chance to climb up into the Old Town Hall's tower, offering so-so views over the square, cathedral, and castle.

**Cost and Hours:** €5, includes audioguide, €6 combo-ticket with Apponyi House, Tue-Fri 10:00-17:00, Sat-Sun 11:00-18:00, closed Mon, last entry 30 minutes before closing, in the Old Town Hall—enter through courtyard, tel. 02/5920-5130, www.muzeum. bratislava.sk.

### Apponyi House (Apponyiho Palác)

This nicely restored mansion of a Hungarian aristocrat is meaningless without the included audioguide (dull but informative). The museum has two parts. The cellar and ground floor feature an interesting exhibit on the vineyards of the nearby "Little Carpathian" hills, with historic presses and barrels, and a replica of an old-time wine-pub table. Upstairs are two floors of urban apartments from old Bratislava, called the Period Rooms Museum. The first floor up shows off the 18th-century Rococo-style rooms of the nobility—fine but not ostentatious, with ceramic stoves. The second floor up (with lower ceilings and simpler wall decorations) illustrates 19th-century bourgeois/middle-class lifestyles, including period clothing and some Empire-style furniture.

**Cost and Hours:** €4, includes audioguide, €6 combo-ticket with City History Museum, Tue-Fri 10:00-17:00, Sat-Sun 11:00-18:00, closed Mon, last entry 30 minutes before closing, Radničná 1, tel. 02/5920-5135, www.muzeum.bratislava.sk.

## BRATISLAVA CASTLE (BRATISLAVSKÝ HRAD)

This imposing fortress, nicknamed the "upside-down table," is the city's most prominent landmark. The oldest surviving chunk is the

13th-century Romanesque watchtower (the one slightly taller than the other three). When Habsburg Empress Maria Theresa took a liking to Bratislava in the 18th century, she transformed the castle from a military fortress to a royal residence suitable for holding court. She added a summer riding school (the U-shaped complex next to the castle), an enclosed winter riding school out back, and lots more. Maria Theresa's favorite daughter, Maria Christina, lived here with her husband, Albert, when they were newlyweds. Locals nicknamed the place "little Schönbrunn," in reference to the Habsburgs' summer palace on the outskirts of Vienna.

Turned into a fortress-garrison during the Napoleonic Wars, the castle burned to the ground in an 1811 fire started by careless soldiers, and was left as a ruin for 150 years before being reconstructed in 1953. Unfortunately, the communist rebuild was drab and uninviting; the inner courtyard feels like a prison exercise yard.

A more recent renovation has done little to improve things, and the museum exhibits inside aren't really worth the cost of admission (described next). The best visit is to simply hike up (it's free to enter the grounds), enjoy the views over town, and take a close-up look at the stately old building (the

big, blocky, modern building next door is the Slovak Parliament).

For details on the best walking route to the castle, see page 247.

## Castle Museum

The newly restored castle has a few sights inside, with more likely to open in the future. Two small exhibits are skippable: the misnamed **Treasure Room** (a sparse collection of items found at the castle site, including coins and fragments of Roman jugs) and the **Knights Hall** (offering a brief history lesson in the castle's construction and reconstruction). You can also enter the **palace** itself. A blinding-white staircase with gold trim leads to the Music Hall, with a prized 18th-century *Assumption* altarpiece by Anton Schmidt (first floor); a collection of historical prints depicting Bratislava and its castle (second floor); and temporary exhibits (third/top floor). From the top floor, a series of very steep, modern staircases take you up to the Crown Tower (the castle's oldest and tallest) for views over town—though the vista from the terrace in front of the castle is much easier to reach and nearly as good.

**Cost and Hours:** €6 for all-inclusive "Road A" ticket, €2 for pointless "Road B" (covers only the less interesting parts of palace—the Treasure Room and Knights Hall); Tue-Sun 10:00-18:00, closed Mon; ticket office is right of main riverfront entrance—enter exhibits from passage into central courtyard, tel. 02/2048-3110, www.snm.sk.

## ▲▲THE SNP BRIDGE AND UFO

Bratislava's bizarre, flying-saucer-capped bridge, completed in 1972 in heavy-handed communist style, has been reclaimed by capitalists. The flying saucer-shaped structure called the UFO (at the Petržalka end of the bridge) is now a spruced-up, overpriced café/restaurant and observation deck, allowing sweeping 360-degree views of Bratislava from about 300 feet above the Danube. Think of it as the Slovak Space Needle.

**Cost and Hours:** €6.50, daily 10:00-23:00, elevator free if you have a meal reservation or order food at the restaurant—main courses steeply priced at €23-28, restaurant opens at 12:00, tel. 02/6252-0300, www.u-f-o.sk.

**Getting There:** The elevator entrance is underneath the tower. Walk across the bridge from the old town (there are pedestrian walkways on the lower level). If you take the downstream (old-town side) walkway, you'll pass historical photos of the bridge's construction, including the demolition of the city's synagogue and other old town buildings.

**◉ Self-Guided Tour:** The "**elevator**" that takes you up is actually a funicular—you'll notice you're moving at an angle. At the top, walk up the stairs to the observation deck.

Begin by viewing the **castle** and **old town**. The area to the right of the old town, between and beyond the skyscrapers, is a massive construction zone.

A time-lapse camera set up here over the next few years would catch skyscrapers popping up like dandelions. International investors are throwing lots of money at Bratislava. (Imagine having so much prime, undeveloped real estate available downtown in the capital of an emerging European economic power...and just an hour down the road from Vienna, no less.) Most of the development is taking place along the banks of the Danube. In a decade, this will be a commercial center.

The huge TV tower caps a forested hill beyond the old town. Below and to the left of it, the pointy monument is **Slavín,** where more than 6,800 Soviet soldiers who fought to liberate Bratislava from the Nazis are buried. Under communist rule, a nearby church was forced to take down its steeple so as not to draw attention away from the huge Soviet soldier on top of the monument.

Now turn 180 degrees and cross the platform to face **Petržalka,** a planned communist suburb that sprouted here in the 1970s. The site was once occupied by a village, and the various districts of modern Petržalka still carry their original names (which now seem ironic): "Meadows" *(Háje),* "Woods" *(Lúky),* and "Courtyards" *(Dvory).* The ambitious communist planners envisioned a city laced with Venetian-style canals to help drain the marshy land, but the plans were abandoned after the harsh crackdown on the 1968 Prague Spring uprising. Without the incentives of private ownership, all they succeeded in creating was a grim and decaying sea of miserable concrete apartment *paneláky* ("panel buildings," so-called because they're made of huge prefab panels).

Today, one in four Bratislavans lives in Petržalka, and things are looking better. Like Dorothy opening the door to Oz, the formerly drab buildings have been splashed with bright new colors. Far from being a slum, Petržalka is a popular neighborhood for Bratislavan yuppies who can't yet afford to build their dream houses. Locals read the Czech-language home-improvement magazine *Panel Plus* for ideas on how to give their *panelák* apartments some style (browse it yourself at www.panelplus.cz).

Petržalka is also a big suburban-style shopping zone (note the supermall down below). But there's still some history here. The **park** called Sad Janka Kráľa (originally, in German, Aupark)—just downriver from the bridge—was technically the first public park in Europe in the 1770s and is still a popular place for locals to relax and court.

Scanning the **horizon** beyond Petržalka, two things stick out: on the left, the old communist oil refinery (which has been fully updated and is now state-of-the-art); and on the right, a sea of modern windmills. These are just over the border, in Austria...and Bratislava is sure to grow in that direction quickly. Austria is about three miles that way, and Hungary is about six miles farther to the left.

Before you leave, consider a drink at the café (€3-4 coffee or beer, €7-20 cocktails). If nothing else, be sure to use the memorable WCs (guys can enjoy a classic urinal photo).

## Sleeping in Bratislava

I'd rather sleep in Vienna—particularly since good-value options in central Bratislava are slim, and service tends to be surly. Business-oriented places charge more on weekdays than on weekends. Expect prices to drop slightly in winter and in the hottest summer months. Hotel Michalská Brána is right in the heart of the old town, while the others are just outside it—but still within a 5-10-minute walk.

**$$$ Hotel Marrol's,** on a quiet street, is the town's most enticing splurge. Although the immediate neighborhood isn't interesting, it's a five-minute walk from the old town, and its 54 rooms are luxurious and tastefully appointed Old World country-style. While pricey, the rates drop on weekends (prices flex, but generally Mon-Thu: Db-€160, Fri-Sun: Db-€120, Sb-€10 less, non-smoking, elevator, air-con, Wi-Fi, loaner laptops, free minibar, gorgeous lounge, Tobrucká 4, tel. 02/5778-4600, www.hotelmarrols.sk, rec@hotelmarrols.sk).

**$$ Hotel Michalská Brána** is a charming boutique hotel just

## Sleep Code

**Abbreviations**    (€1 = about $1.40, country code: 421, area code: 02)
**S** = Single, **D** = Double/Twin, **T** = Triple, **Q** = Quad, **b** = bathroom
**Price Rankings**
  **$$$**  **Higher Priced**—Most rooms €100 or more.
   **$$**  **Moderately Priced**—Most rooms between €50-100.
    **$**  **Lower Priced**—Most rooms €50 or less.
English is spoken at each place. Unless otherwise noted, credit cards are accepted, rooms have no air-conditioning, breakfast is included, and Wi-Fi is generally free. Prices change; verify current rates online or by email. For the best prices, always book directly with the hotel.

inside St. Michael's Gate in the old town. The 14 rooms are sleek, mod, and classy, and the location is ideal—right in the heart of town, but on a relatively sleepy lane just away from the hubbub (Sb-€69-73, Db-€79-83, higher prices are for Mon-Thu nights, extra bed-€20, pricier suites available, non-smoking, air-con, elevator, Wi-Fi, Baštová 4, tel. 02/5930-7200, www.michalskabrana.com, reception@michalskabrana.com).

**$$ Hotel Ibis,** part of the Europe-wide chain, offers 120 nicely appointed rooms just outside the old town, overlooking a busy tram junction—request a quieter room (Mon-Thu: Sb/Db-€85, Fri-Sun: Sb/Db-€69, rates flex with demand, you'll likely save €20 or more with advance booking on their website, breakfast-€10, elevator, air-con, guest computer and Wi-Fi, Zámocká 38, tel. 02/5929-2000, www.ibishotel.com, h3566@accor.com).

**$$ Penzión Virgo** sits on a quiet residential street, an eight-minute walk from the old town. The 11 boutiqueish rooms are classy and well-appointed (Sb-€61, Db-€74—but often discounted to around Sb/Db-€55, extra bed-€13, breakfast-€6, Wi-Fi, inexpensive parking, Panenská 14, tel. 02/3300-6262, www.penzionvirgo.sk, reception@penzionvirgo.sk).

**$$ Penzión Gremium** has six nondescript rooms and three apartments in a very central location, just a block behind the National Theater and a few steps from the old town. It's on a busy street with good windows but no air-conditioning, so it can be noisy on rowdy weekends (Sb-€60, Db-€70, Db apartment-€90, prices soft, breakfast-€7, elevator reaches some rooms, Wi-Fi, Gorkého 11, tel. 02/2070-4874, www.penziongremium.sk, recepcia@penziongremium.sk).

**$ Downtown Backpackers Hostel** is a funky but well-run place located in an old-fashioned townhouse. Rooms are named for famous artists and decorated with reinterpretations of their paint-

BRATISLAVA

ings (45 beds in 7 rooms, D-€54, bunk in 7-8-bed dorm-€18, bunk in 10-bed dorm-€17, breakfast-€3-5, Wi-Fi, free laundry facilities, kitchen, bike rental nearby, Panenská 31—across busy boulevard from Grassalkovich Palace, 10 minutes on foot from main station, tel. 02/5464-1191, mobile 0905/259-714, www.backpackers.sk, info@backpackers.sk).

## Eating in Bratislava

Today's Slovak cooking shows some Hungarian and Austrian influences, but it's closer to Czech—lots of starches and gravy, and plenty of pork, cabbage, potatoes, and dumplings. Keep an eye out for Slovakia's national dish, *bryndzové halušky* (small potato dumplings with sheep's cheese and bits of bacon). For a fun drink and snack that locals love, try a Vinea grape soda and a sweet *Pressburger* bagel in any bar or café.

Like the Czechs, the Slovaks produce excellent beer (*pivo*, PEE-voh). One of the top brands is Zlatý Bažant ("Golden Pheasant"). Bratislava's beer halls are good places to sample Slovak and Czech beers, and to get a hearty, affordable meal of stick-to-your-ribs pub grub. Long a wine-producing area, the Bratislava region makes the same wines that Vienna is famous for. But, as nearly all is consumed locally, most people don't think of Slovakia as wine country.

Bratislava is packed with inviting new eateries. In addition to the heavy Slovak staples, you'll find trendy new bars and bistros, and a smattering of ethnic offerings. The best plan may be to stroll the old town and keep your eyes open for the setting and cuisine that appeals to you most. Or consider one of these options.

**1. Slovak Pub** ("1." as in "the first") attracts a student crowd. Enter from Obchodná, the bustling shopping street just above the old town, and climb the stairs into a vast warren of rustic, old countryside-style pub rooms with uneven floors. Enjoy the lively, loud, almost chaotic ambience while dining on affordable and truly authentic Slovak fare, made with products from the pub's own farm. This is a good place to try the Slovak specialty, *bryndzové halušky* (several varieties for €4-5; €4-12 main courses, Mon 10:00-23:00, Tue-Sat 10:00-24:00, Sun 12:00-24:00, Obchodná 62, tel. 02/5292-6367, www.slovakpub.sk).

**Bratislavský Meštiansky Pivovar** ("Bratislava Town Brewpub"), just above the old town behind the big Crowne Plaza hotel, brews its own beer and also sells a variety of others. Seating stretches over several levels in the new-meets-old interior (€7-15 main courses, Mon-Sat 11:00-24:00, Sun 11:00-23:00, Drevená 8, mobile 0944-512-265, www.mestianskypivovar.sk).

**Lemon Tree/Sky Bar/Rum Club,** a three-in-one place just past the fenced-in US Embassy on the trendy Hviezdoslavovo Námestie, features the same Thai-meets-Mediterranean menu throughout (€8-12 pasta and noodle dishes, €16-19 main courses). But the real reason to come here is for the seventh-floor Sky Bar, with fantastic views of the old town and the SNP Bridge. It's smart to reserve a view table in advance if you want to dine here—or just drop by for a pricey vodka cocktail on the small terrace. You've got the best seat in town, and though prices are expensive for Bratislava, they're no more than what you'd pay for a meal in Vienna (daily 11:00-late, Sun from 12:00, Hviezdoslavovo Námestie 7, mobile 0948-109-400, www.spicy.sk).

At **Eurovea** (the recommended end to my walking tour, 10 minutes downstream from the old town), huge outdoor terraces rollicking with happy eaters line the swanky riverfront residential and shopping-mall complex. You'll pay high prices for the great atmosphere and views at international eateries—French, Italian, Brazilian—and a branch of the Czech beer-hall chain Kolkovna. Or you can head to the food court in the shopping mall, where you'll eat well for €4.

**Shtoor** is a hip, rustic-chic café (named for a revered 19th-century champion of Slovak culture, Ľudovít Štúr) with coffee drinks and €3-5 sandwiches and quiches (takeaway or table service, open long hours daily). They have three locations: in the heart of the old town at Panská 23; just east of the old town (near Eurovea) at Štúrova 8; and inside a Barnes & Noble-type bookstore, Martinus.sk, at Obchodná 26.

**Coffee & Bagel Story** (a chain) sells...coffee and €3 takeout bagel sandwiches. The handiest location is on the town's main square at Hlavné Námestie 8, with picnic tables right out front.

*Supermarket:* Try **Billa,** in the Tatracentrum complex across the street from Grassalkovich Palace (Mon-Sat 7:00-22:00, Sun 8:00-20:00).

# Bratislava Connections

## BY TRAIN
Bratislava has two major train stations: the main station closer to the old town (Hlavná Stanica, abbreviated "Bratislava hl. st." on schedules) and Petržalka station (sometimes called ŽST Petržalka), in the suburb across the river (for full details, see "Arrival in Bratislava," earlier). When checking schedules, pay attention to which station your train uses.

**From Bratislava by Train to: Vienna** (2/hour, 1 hour, buy the €15 round-trip EU Regio day pass, which is cheaper than a one-way fare; departures alternate between the two stations—half from main station, half from Petržalka), **Budapest** (7/day direct, 2.5 hours to Keleti Station, more with transfers; also doable—and possibly cheaper—by Orange Ways bus, 1-4/day, 2.5 hours, www.orangeways.com), **Sopron** (at least hourly, 2.5-3 hours, usually 2 transfers—often at stations in downtown and/or suburban Vienna), **Prague** (5/day direct, 4.25 hours). To reach other Hungarian destinations (including **Eger** and **Pécs**), it's generally easiest to change in Budapest.

## BY BUS
Two companies, **Blaguss/Eurolines** and **Slovak Lines/Postbus,** run buses that connect Bratislava to Vienna (and Vienna Airport) for €7-8 one-way. For details, see "Day-Tripping from Vienna to Bratislava" on page 233. For airport bus connections, see below.

## BY BOAT
Riverboats run on the Danube several times a day, connecting Bratislava to Budapest and Vienna. Conveniently, these boats dock right in front of Bratislava's old town. While they are more expensive, less frequent, and slower than the train, some travelers enjoy getting out on the Danube. For details, see "Day-Tripping from Vienna to Bratislava" on page 233.

## BY PLANE
Bratislava has its own airport, but it's also convenient to fly out from the very nearby Vienna Airport (see page 207).

### Bratislava Airport (Letisko Bratislava)
This airport (airport code: BTS, www.letiskobratislava.sk) is six miles northeast of downtown Bratislava and also easily reached from Vienna. Budget airline Ryanair (www.ryanair.com) has many flights here. Some airlines market it as "Vienna-Bratislava," thanks to its proximity to both capitals. It's compact and manageable, with all the usual amenities (including ATMs).

**From the Airport to Downtown Bratislava:** The airport has easy **public bus** connections to Bratislava's main train station (Hlavná Stanica, €1.30, bus #61, 4-5/hour, 30 minutes). To reach the bus stop, exit straight out of the arrivals hall, cross the street, buy a ticket at the kiosk, and look for the bus stop on your right. For directions from the train station into the old town, see "Arrival in Bratislava," earlier. A **taxi** from the airport into central Bratislava should cost less than €20.

**To Vienna:** Take either the Slovak Lines/Postbus bus, which runs to Vienna's Hauptbahnhof (every 1-2 hours, 2-hour trip, €7.70, www.slovaklines.sk or www.postbus.at) or the Blaguss/Eurolines bus to the Erdberg stop on Vienna's U-3 subway line, on which it's a straight shot to Stephansplatz or Mariahilfer Strasse (every 1-2 hours, 1.5-hour trip, €7.20, www.blaguss.sk or www.eurolines. at). A taxi from Bratislava Airport directly to Vienna costs €60-90 (depending on whether you use a cheaper Slovak or more expensive Austrian cab).

# SALZBURG
## *and the*
## *Salzkammergut*

# SALZBURG

Salzburgers are forever smiling to the tunes of Mozart and *The Sound of Music*. Thanks to its charmingly preserved Old Town, splendid gardens, Baroque churches, and one of Europe's largest intact medieval fortresses, Salzburg feels made for tourism. As a musical mecca, the city puts on a huge annual festival, as well as constant concerts. It's a city with class. Vagabonds visiting here wish they had nicer clothes.

Even without Mozart and the von Trapps, Salzburg is steeped in history. In about A.D. 700, Bavaria gave Salzburg to Bishop Rupert in return for his promise to Christianize the area. Salzburg remained an independent city (belonging to no state) until Napoleon came by in the early 1800s. Thanks in part to its formidable fortress, Salzburg managed to avoid the ravages of war for 1,200 years...until World War II. Allied bombing destroyed many buildings (especially around the train station), but the historic Old Town survived.

Today, eight million tourists crawl Salzburg's cobbles each year. That's a lot of Mozart balls—and all that popularity has led to a glut of businesses hoping to catch the tourist dollar. Still, Salzburg is both a must and a joy.

In the mountains just outside Salzburg is Berchtesgaden (described in the next chapter), a German alpine town that was once a favorite of Adolf Hitler's, but thrills a better class of nature lover today.

## PLANNING YOUR TIME

While Salzburg's museums are, frankly, mediocre, the town itself is a Baroque showpiece of cobbled streets and elegant buildings—simply a touristy stroller's delight. Even if your time is short, consider allowing half a day for the *Sound of Music* tour. The *S.O.M.*

bus tour kills a nest of sightseeing birds with one ticket (city over-view, *S.O.M.* sights, and a fine drive by the lakes).

You'd probably enjoy at least two nights in Salzburg—nights are important for swilling beer in atmospheric local gardens and attending concerts in Baroque halls and chapels. Seriously consider one of Salzburg's many evening musical events (a few are free, some are as low as €22, and most average €40).

To get away from it all, bike down the river or hike across the Mönchsberg cliffs that rise directly from the middle of town. Or consider swinging by Berchtesgaden, just 15 miles away, in Germany. A direct bus gets you there from Salzburg in 45 minutes (see next chapter).

A day trip from Salzburg to Hallstatt (the small-town high-light of the Salzkammergut Lake District—see page 339) is doable by car (1.25 hours each way) but makes for a very long day by public transit (the round trip alone takes five hours). An overnight in Hallstatt is better.

# Orientation to Salzburg

Salzburg, a city of 150,000 (Austria's fourth-largest), is divided into old and new. The Old Town (Alt-stadt), between the Salzach River and Salzburg's mini-mountain (Mönchsberg), holds nearly all the charm and most of the tourists. The New Town (Neustadt), across the river, has the train station, a few sights and museums, and some good accommodations.

## TOURIST INFORMATION

Salzburg has three helpful TIs (main tel. 0662/889-870, www. salzburg.info): at the **train station** (daily 9:00-18:00, May-Sept until 19:00; tel. 0662/8898-7340); on **Mozartplatz** in the old center (daily 9:00-18:00, July-Aug until 19:00, closed Sun Sept-March; tel. 0662/8898-7330); and at the **Alpensied-lung park-and-ride** (May-Sept Thu-Sat 10:00-16:30, generally closed Sun-Wed, closed Oct-April; tel. 0662/8898-7360).

SALZBURG

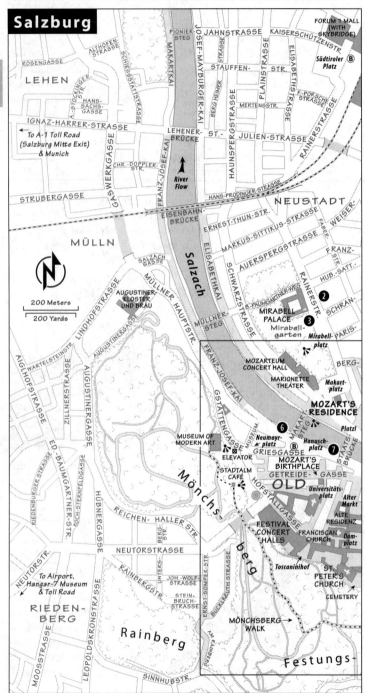

# Salzburg

FORUM 1 MALL
(WITH SKYBRIDGE)

Südtiroler
Platz B

ROSENGASSE

LEHEN

HANS-
SACHS-
GASSE

IGNAZ-HARRER-STRASSE

← To A-1 Toll Road
(Salzburg Mitte Exit)
& Munich

River
Flow

LEHENER-
BRÜCKE

STRUBERGASSE

NEUSTADT

EISENBAHN-
BRÜCKE

MÜLLN

Salzach

200 Meters

200 Yards

AUGUSTINER-
KLOSTER
UND BRÄU

MIRABELL
PALACE 2

Mirabell- 3
garten

Mirabell-
platz

MOZARTEUM
CONCERT HALL

MARIONETTE
THEATER

Makart-
platz

MOZART'S
RESIDENCE

Platzl

MUSEUM OF
MODERN ART

Neumayr- 6
platz

ELEVATOR

STADTALM
CAFÉ

Mönchsberg

Hanusch- B
platz

7

MOZART'S
BIRTHPLACE

GETREIDE-GASSE

OLD

Universitäts-
platz

Alter
Markt

ALTE
RESIDENZ

FESTIVAL
CONCERT
HALLS

Franciscan
Church

Dom-
platz

Toscaninihof

ST.
PETER'S
CHURCH

CEMETERY

To Airport,
Hangar-7 Museum
& Toll Road

RIEDEN-
BERG

Rainberg

MÖNCHSBERG
WALK

Festungs-

SALZBURG

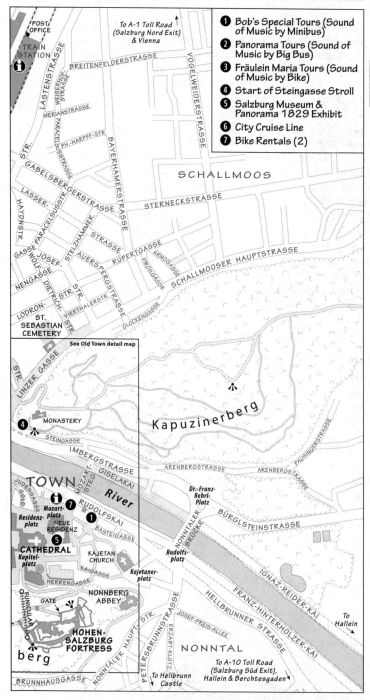

**1** Bob's Special Tours (Sound of Music by Minibus)

**2** Panorama Tours (Sound of Music by Big Bus)

**3** Fräulein Maria Tours (Sound of Music by Bike)

**4** Start of Steingasse Stroll

**5** Salzburg Museum & Panorama 1829 Exhibit

**6** City Cruise Line

**7** Bike Rentals (2)

At any TI, you can pick up a free city-center map (the €0.70 map has a broader coverage and more information on sights, and is particularly worthwhile if biking out of town), the free bus map (*Liniennetz;* shows bus stop names not on the city map), the Salzburg Card brochure (listing sights with current hours and prices), and a bimonthly events guide. The TIs also book rooms (€2.20 fee and 10 percent deposit). Inside the Mozartplatz TI is the privately run Salzburg Ticket Service counter, where you can book concert tickets (see "Music in Salzburg," page 309).

**Salzburg Card:** The TIs sell the Salzburg Card, which covers all your public transportation (including the Mönchsberg elevator and funicular to the fortress) and admission to all the city sights (including Hellbrunn Palace and a river cruise). The card is pricey, but if you'd like to pop into all the sights, it can save money and enhance your experience (€26/24 hours, €35/48 hours, €41/72 hours, www.salzburg.info). To analyze your potential savings, here are the major sights and what you'd pay without the card: Hohensalzburg Fortress and funicular-€11.30; Mozart's Birthplace and Residence-€17; Hellbrunn Palace-€10.50; Salzburg Panorama 1829-€3; DomQuartier Museums-€12; Salzach River cruise-€15; 24-hour transit pass-€3.40. Busy sightseers can save plenty. Get this card, feel the financial pain once, and the city will be all yours.

## ARRIVAL IN SALZBURG

**By Train:** The Salzburg station, gleaming white after a multi-year renovation, has all the services you need: train information, tourist information, luggage lockers (€2-4.50) and a WC (€0.50, both by platform 5), and a handy Spar supermarket (Mon-Sat 6:00-23:00, Sun 8:00-23:00). Ticket counters for both the Austrian and German railways are off the main hall (Mon-Sat 5:30-21:15, Sun 6:30-21:15). If you're looking for the TI, follow the green-

and-white information signs (the blue-and-white ones lead to a railway "InfoPoint"). A transit info desk, down the escalator from the TI or bus platforms, has information on local buses (Mon-Fri 6:00-18:45, Sat 7:30-14:45, closed Sun). Next to the train station is Forum 1, a sizable shopping mall.

Getting downtown from the station is a snap. Simply step outside, find **bus platform C** (labeled *Zentrum-Altstadt*), buy a ticket from the machine, and hop on the next bus. Buses #1, #3, #5, #6, and #25 all do the same route into the city center before diverging. For most sights and Old Town hotels, get off just after the bridge, at the fifth stop (either Rathaus or Hanuschplatz, depending on the bus). For my recommended New Town hotels, get off at Makart-platz (the fourth stop), just before the bridge.

**Taxis** don't make much sense to get from the train station into town, as they're expensive for short rides (€2.50 drop charge, about €8 for most rides in town).

To **walk** downtown (15 minutes), turn left as you leave the station, and walk straight down Rainerstrasse, which leads under the tracks past Mirabellplatz, turning into Dreifaltigkeitsgasse. From here, you can turn left onto Linzer Gasse for many of my recommended hotels, or cross the river to the Old Town. For a slightly longer but more dramatic approach, leave the station the same way but follow the tracks to the river, turn left, and walk the riverside path toward the fortress.

**By Car:** Mozart never drove in Salzburg's Old Town, and neither should you. The best place to park is the **park-and-ride** lot at the Alpensiedlung bus stop, near the Salzburg Süd autobahn exit. Coming on A-8 from Vienna or Munich, take A-10 toward Hallein, and then take the next exit (Salzburg Süd) in the direction of Anif, and look for *P+R* signs. You'll pass Hellbrunn Castle (and the zoo) before arriving at the park-and-ride (€5/24 hours). From the parking lot, catch bus #3 or #8 into town. The TI, in a small building next to the lot, sells bus tickets for less than bus drivers (24-hour transit pass-€3.40 at TI, €5.50 from driver). Alternatively, groups of 2-5 people can buy a combo-ticket from the parking lot attendant, which includes the 24-hour parking fee and a 24-hour transit pass for the whole group (€14, €12 from July-Aug, group must stay together).

If you don't believe in park-and-rides, head to the easiest, cheapest, most central parking lot—the 1,500-car Altstadtgarage, in the tunnel under the Mönchsberg (€18/day, note your slot number and which of the twin lots you're in, tel. 0662/809-900). Your hotel may provide discounted parking passes. If staying in Salzburg's New Town, the Mirabell-Congress garage makes more sense than the Altstadtgarage (see page 311 for directions).

For more info on parking, see www.salzburg.info (under "Arrival and Traffic," choose "Car," then "Parking in Salzburg").

**By Plane:** Salzburg's airport is easily reached by regular city buses #2, #10, and #27 (airport code: SZG, tel. 0662/85800, www.salzburg-airport.com).

## HELPFUL HINTS

**Recommendations Skewed by Kickbacks:** Salzburg is addicted to the tourist dollar, and it can never get enough. Virtually all hotels are on the take when it comes to concert and tour recommendations, influenced more by their potential kickback than by what's best for you. Take any tour or concert advice with a grain of salt. If you book a concert through your hotel, you'll probably lose the discount I've negotiated for my readers who go direct.

**Music Festival:** The Salzburg Festival (Salzburger Festspiele) runs each year from mid-July to the end of August (see page 311).

**Internet Access:** The city has **free Wi-Fi** hotspots at Mirabell Gardens, Mozartplatz, and Kapitelplatz (choose *Salzburg surft* and click *Agree*, info at www.salzburg-surft.at). Travelers with this book can get free Wi-Fi or use a computer for a few minutes (long enough to check email) at the Panorama Tours terminal on Mirabellplatz (daily 8:00-18:00). If you need to print something, the **Ibis Internet Café** is at the train station, right next to the entrance (daily 8:00-22:00, €3/hour, €0.20/page, mobile 0676-8686-2502).

**Post Office:** The one at the train station is open long hours daily. There's another branch in the heart of the Old Town, in the New Residenz (closed Sat-Sun).

**Laundry:** A handy launderette with a few self-serve machines is at Paris-Lodron-Strasse 16, at the corner of Wolf-Dietrich-Strasse, near my recommended Linzer Gasse hotels—or take bus #2, #4, or #21 to the Wolf-Dietrich-Strasse stop (€10 self-service, €15 same-day full-service, Mon-Fri 7:30-18:00, Sat 8:00-12:00, closed Sun, tel. 0662/876-381). On evenings and weekends, head for **Green and Clean,** three stops beyond the train station on the #1 or #2 bus; board from platform D at station, get off at the Gaswerkgasse stop (about €9/load, daily 6:00-22:00, Ignaz-Harrer-Strasse 32, www.greenandclean.at).

**Cinema: Das Kino** is an art-house movie theater that plays films in their original languages (a block off the river and Linzer Gasse on Steingasse, tel. 0662/873-100, www.daskino.at).

**Market Days:** Popular farmers' markets pop up at Universitätsplatz in the Old Town on Saturdays and around the Andräkirche in the New Town on Thursdays. On summer weekends, a string of craft booths with fun goodies for sale stretches along the river.

**Morning Joggers:** Salzburg is a great place for jogging. Within minutes you can be huffing and puffing "The hills are alive..." in green meadows outside of town. The obvious best bets in town are through the Mirabell Gardens along its riverbank pedestrian lanes.

**Updates to This Book:** For updates to this book, check www.ricksteves.com/update.

## GETTING AROUND SALZBURG

**By Bus:** Most visitors take at least a couple of rides on Salzburg's extensive bus system. Everything in this book is within the *Kernzone* (core zone). At *Tabak/Trafik* shops and scarce ticket machines, you can buy €1.70 single-ride tickets or a €3.40 day pass *(24-Stunden-Karte)* good for 24 hours (€2.50 and €5.50 from the driver, respectively). If you'll be in Salzburg for at least five days, the €14.60 *Wochenkarte* makes sense (valid 7 calendar days, starting with the day you validate it). Remember to validate your ticket after purchase (insert it the machines on board).

Get oriented using the free bus map *(Liniennetz)*, available at the TI. Many lines converge at Hanuschplatz, on the Old Town side of the river, in front of the recommended Fisch Krieg Restaurant. To get from the Old Town to the train station, catch bus #1 from the inland side of Hanuschplatz. From the other side of the river, find the Makartplatz/Theatergasse stop and catch bus #1, #3, #5, or #6. Busy stops like Hanuschplatz and Mirabellplatz have several bus shelters; look for your bus number to double-check where exactly you should stand.

For more information, visit www.svv-info.at, call 0662/632-900 (open 24 hours), or visit the office downstairs from bus platform C in front of the train station (Mon-Fri 6:00-18:45, Sat 7:30-14:45, closed Sun).

**By Bike:** Salzburg is great fun for cyclists. The following two bike-rental shops offer 20 percent off to anyone with this book—ask for it: **Top Bike** rents bikes on the river next to the Staatsbrücke (€6/2 hours, €10/4 hours, €15/24 hours, usually daily April-June and Sept-Oct 10:00-17:00, July-Aug 9:00-19:00, closed Nov-March, easy 24/7 return, show this book for 20 percent discount off these prices and free helmet, mobile 0676-476-7259, www.topbike. at, Sabine). **A'Velo Radladen** rents bikes in the Old Town, just outside the TI on Mozartplatz (€4.50/1 hour, €10/4 hours, €16/24 hours, more for electric or mountain bikes; daily 9:00-18:00, until 19:00 July-Aug, but hours unreliable, shorter hours off-season and in bad weather; passport number for security deposit, mobile 0676-435-5950, www.a-velo.at). Some of my recommended hotels and pensions also rent or loan bikes to guests.

**By Funicular and Elevator:** The Old Town is connected to the top of the Mönchsberg mountain (and great views) via funicular and elevator. The **funicular** *(Festungsbahn)* whisks you up into the imposing Hohensalzburg Fortress (included in castle admission, goes every few minutes—for details, see page 292). The **elevator** (Mönchsberg Aufzug) on the west side of the Old Town lifts you to the recommended Stadtalm Café, the Museum of Modern Art and its chic café, wooded paths, and more great views (€2.10

one-way, €3.40 round-trip, normally Mon 8:00-19:00, Tue-Sun 8:00-23:00).

**By Buggy:** The horse buggies *(Fiaker)* that congregate at Residenzplatz charge €40 for a 25-minute trot around the Old Town (www.fiaker-salzburg.at).

# Tours in Salzburg

## Walking Tours

Any day of the week, you can take a one-hour guided walk of the Old Town without a reservation—just show up at the TI on Mozartplatz and pay the guide. The tours are informative. While generally in English only, on slow days you may be listening to everything in both German and English (€9, daily at 12:15, Mon-Sat also at 14:00, tel. 0662/8898-7330). To save money, you can easily do it on your own using this chapter's self-guided walk (or download a free Rick Steves **audio tour** of my walk to your mobile device—see page 10).

## Local Guides

Salzburg is home to over a hundred licensed guides. I have worked with three who are well worth recommending: **Christiana Schnee-weiss** ("Snow White") has been instrumental in both my guidebook research and my TV production in Salzburg, and has her own minibus for private tours outside of town (on foot: €135/2 hours, €165/3 hours; with minibus: €240/4 hours, €350-450/day, up to 6 people; mobile 0664-340-1757, other options explained at www. kultur-tourismus.com, info@kultur-tourismus.com). Two other excellent guides, both a joy to learn from, are **Sabine Rath** (€155/2 hours, €205/4 hours, €310/8 hours, mobile 0664-201-6492, www. tourguide-salzburg.com, info@tourguide-salzburg.com, ask about her creepy witch tours and her Empress Sisi tours) and **Anna Stellnberger** (€150/2 hours, €190/4 hours, €280/8 hours, mobile 0664-787-5177, anna.stellnberger@aon.at). Salzburg has many other good guides (for a list, see www.salzburgguides.at).

## Boat Tours

**City Cruise Line** (a.k.a. Stadt Schiff-Fahrt) runs a basic 40-minute round-trip river cruise with recorded commentary (€15, 9/day July-Aug, 7/day May-June, fewer Sept-Oct and March-April, no boats Nov-Feb). For a longer cruise, ride to Hellbrunn (€18, daily April-Oct at 14:00) and return by bus. Boats leave from the Old Town side of the river just downstream of the Makartsteg bridge (tel. 0662/825-858, www.salzburghighlights.at). While views can be cramped, passengers are treated to a fun finale just before docking, when the captain twirls a fun "waltz."

## ▲▲*The Sound of Music* Tours

Salzburg is the joyful setting of *The Sound of Music*. The Broadway musical and 1965 movie tell the story of a stern captain who hires a governess for his unruly children and ends up marrying her. Though the movie took plenty of Hollywood liberties (see *"The Sound of Music* Debunked"), it's based on the actual von Trapp family from Austria. They really did come from Salzburg. Maria really was a governess who became the captain's wife. They did sing in the Festival Hall, they did escape from the Nazis, and they ended up after the war in Vermont, where Maria passed away in 1987.

Salzburg today has a number of *Sound of Music* sights—mostly locations where the movie was shot, but also some actual places associated with the von Trapps. Some of the main ones are:

• The Mirabell Gardens, with its arbor and Pegasus statue, where the kids sing "Do-Re-Mi."
• Festival Hall, where the real-life von Trapps performed, and where (in the movie) they sing "Edelweiss."
• St. Peter's Cemetery, the inspiration for the scene where the family hides from Nazi guards (it was actually filmed on a Hollywood set).
• Nonnberg Abbey, where the nuns sing "Maria."
• Leopoldskron Palace, which serves as the von Trapps' idyllic lakeside home in the movie (though it wasn't their actual home).
• Hellbrunn Palace gardens, where the famous gazebo in "Sixteen Going on Seventeen" has found a home.

There are many more sights—the horse pond, the wedding church, the fountain in Residenzplatz. Since they're scattered throughout greater Salzburg, taking a tour is the best way to see them efficiently.

I took a *S.O.M.* tour skeptically (as part of my research)—and had a great time. The bus tour version includes a quick but good general city tour, hits the *S.O.M.* spots, and—something that's worthwhile even for non-*S.O.M.* fans—shows you a lovely stretch of the Salzkammergut Lake District. Warning: Many think rolling through the Austrian country-side with 30 Americans singing "Doe, a deer..." is pretty schmaltzy. Local Austrians don't understand all the commotion. (Many have never heard of the movie.) For more on *S.O.M.*, see the sidebar on the next page.

Two companies do *S.O.M.* tours by bus (Bob's and Panorama), while a third company does a bike version. It's best to reserve ahead. Note: Your hotel will be eager to call to reserve for you—to

## *The Sound of Music* **Debunked**

Rather than visit the real-life sights from the life of Maria von Trapp and family, most tourists want to see the places where Hollywood chose to film this fanciful story. Local guides are happy not to burst any *S.O.M.* pilgrim's bubble, but keep these points in mind:

- "Edelweiss" is not a cherished Austrian folk tune or national anthem. Like all the "Austrian" music in *The S.O.M.,* it was composed for Broadway by Rodgers and Hammerstein. It was the last composition that the famed team wrote together, as Hammerstein died in 1960—nine months after the musical opened.
- *The S.O.M.* implies that Maria was devoutly religious throughout her life, but Maria's foster parents raised her as a socialist and atheist. Maria discovered her religious calling while studying to be a teacher. After completing school, she joined the convent not as a nun, but as a novice (that is, she hadn't taken her vows yet).
- Maria's position was not as governess to all the children, as portrayed in the musical, but specifically as governess and teacher for the Captain's second-oldest daughter, also called Maria, who was bedridden with rheumatic fever.
- The Captain didn't run a tight domestic ship. In fact, his seven children were as unruly as most. But he did use a whistle to call them—each kid was trained to respond to a certain pitch.
- Though the von Trapp family did have seven children, the show changed all their names and even their genders. As an adult, Rupert, the eldest child, responded to the often-asked question, "Which one are you?" with a simple, "I'm Liesl!" Maria and the Captain later had three more children together.
- The family didn't escape by hiking to Switzerland (which is a five-hour drive away). Rather, they pretended to go on one of their frequent mountain hikes. With only the possessions in their backpacks, they "hiked" all the way to the train

get their commission—but you won't get the discount I've negotiated.

**Minibus Option:** Most of **Bob's Special Tours** use an eight-seat minibus (and occasionally a 20-seat bus) and therefore have good access to Old Town sights, promote a more casual feel, and spend less time waiting to load and unload. Online bookings close three days prior to the tour date—after that, email, call, or stop by the office to reserve (€48 for adults—€42 with this book if you pay cash and book direct, €42 for kids aged 7-15 and students with ID, €36 for kids 6 and under—includes required car seat but must reserve in advance; daily at 9:00 and 14:00 year-round, tours leave from Bob's office along the river just east of Mozart-

station (it was at the edge of their estate) and took a train to Italy. The movie scene showing them climbing into Switzerland was actually filmed near Berchtesgaden, Germany... home to Hitler's Eagle's Nest, and certainly not a smart place to flee to.

- The actual von Trapp family house exists...but it's not the one in the film. The mansion in the movie is actually two different buildings—one used for the front, the other for the back. The interiors were all filmed on Hollywood sets.

- For the film, Boris Levin designed a reproduction of the Nonnberg Abbey courtyard so faithful to the original (down to its cobblestones and stained-glass windows) that many still believe the cloister scenes were really shot at the abbey. And no matter what you hear in Salzburg, the graveyard scene (in which the von Trapps hide from the Nazis) was also filmed on the Fox lot.

- In 1956, a German film producer offered Maria $10,000 for the rights to her book. She asked for royalties, too, and a share of the profits. The agent claimed that German law forbids film companies from paying royalties to foreigners (Maria had by then become a US citizen). She agreed to the contract and unknowingly signed away all film rights to her story. Only a few weeks later, he offered to pay immediately if she would accept $9,000 in cash. Because it was more money than the family had seen in all of their years of singing, she accepted the deal. Later, she discovered the agent had swindled them—no such law existed.

Rodgers, Hammerstein, and other producers gave the von Trapps a percentage of the royalties, even though they weren't required to—but it was a fraction of what they otherwise would have earned. But Maria wasn't bitter. She said, "The great good the film and the play are doing to individual lives is far beyond money."

platz at Rudolfskai 38, tel. 0662/849-511, mobile 0664-541-7492, office@bobstours.com, www.bobstours.com). Nearly all of Bob's tours stop for a fun luge ride in Fuschl am See when the weather is dry (mountain bobsled-€4.50 extra, generally April-Oct, confirm beforehand).

For a private minibus tour consider **Christina Schneeweiss,** who does an *S.O.M.* tour with more history and fewer jokes (€240, up to 6 people, see "Local Guides," earlier).

**Big-Bus Option: Panorama Tours** depart from their smart kiosk at Mirabellplatz daily at 9:15 and 14:00 year-round (€40, €5 discount for *S.O.M.* tours with this book if you pay in cash and don't need hotel pickup, book by calling 0662/874-029 or

# Salzburg at a Glance

▲▲▲**Salzburg's Old Town Walk** Old Town's best sights in handy orientation walk. **Hours:** Always open. See page 276.

▲▲**Salzburg Cathedral** Glorious, harmonious Baroque main church of Salzburg. **Hours:** May-Sept Mon-Sat 9:00-19:00, Sun 13:00-19:00; March-April, Oct, and Dec closes at 18:00; Jan-Feb and Nov closes at 17:00. See page 280.

▲▲**Getreidegasse** Picturesque old shopping lane with characteristic wrought-iron signs. **Hours:** Always open. See page 286.

▲▲**Hohensalzburg Fortress** Imposing castle capping the mountain overlooking town, with tourable grounds, several mini-museums, commanding views, and good evening concerts. **Hours:** Fortress museums open daily May-Sept 9:00-19:00, Oct-April 9:30-17:00. Concerts nearly nightly. See page 292.

▲▲**Salzburg Museum** Best place to learn more about the city's history. **Hours:** Tue-Sun 9:00-17:00, closed Mon. See page 289.

▲▲*The Sound of Music* **Tour** Cheesy but fun tour through the *S.O.M.* sights of Salzburg and the surrounding Salzkammergut Lake District, by minibus, big bus, or bike. **Hours:** Various options daily at 9:00, 9:15, 9:30, 14:00, and 16:30. See page 271.

▲▲**Mozart's Birthplace** House where Mozart was born in 1756, featuring his instruments and other exhibits. **Hours:** Daily 9:00-17:30, July-Aug until 20:00. See page 290.

▲**DomQuartier Museums** Prince-Archbishop Wolf Dietrich's palace, a cathedral viewpoint, and adjoining buildings covering religious art and Salzburg history. **Hours:** Tue-Sun 10:00-17:00, closed Mon except in July-Aug. See page 288.

▲**Salzburg Panorama 1829** A vivid peek at the city in 1829. **Hours:** Daily 9:00-17:00. See page 290.

0662/883-2110, discount not valid for online reservations, www.panoramatours.com). Many travelers appreciate their more businesslike feel, roomier buses, and higher vantage point.

**Bike Tours by "Fräulein Maria":** For some exercise with your *S.O.M.* tour, you can meet your guide (likely a man) at the Mirabell Gardens (at Mirabellplatz 4, 50 yards to the left of palace entry). The main attractions that you'll pass during the eight-mile pedal include the Mirabell Gardens, the horse pond, St. Peter's Cemetery,

▲**Mozart's Residence** Restored house where the composer lived. **Hours:** Daily 9:00-17:30, July-Aug until 20:00. See page 301.

▲**Mönchsberg Walk** "The hills are alive" stroll you can enjoy right in downtown Salzburg. **Hours:** Doable anytime during daylight hours. See page 299.

▲**Mirabell Gardens and Palace** Beautiful palace complex with fine views, Salzburg's best concert venue, and *Sound of Music* memories. **Hours:** Gardens—always open; concerts—free in the park May-Aug Sun at 10:30, in the palace nearly nightly. See page 301.

▲**Steingasse** Historic cobbled lane with trendy pubs—a tranquil, tourist-free section of old Salzburg. **Hours:** Always open. See page 303.

▲**St. Sebastian Cemetery** Baroque cemetery with graves of Mozart's wife and father, and other Salzburg VIPs. **Hours:** Daily April-Oct 9:00-18:00, Nov-March 9:00-16:00. See page 304.

▲▲**Hellbrunn Palace** Lavish palace on the outskirts of town featuring gardens with trick fountains. **Hours:** Daily May-Sept 9:00-17:30, July-Aug until 21:00, April and Oct 9:00-16:30, closed Nov-March. See page 305.

**St. Peter's Cemetery** Atmospheric old cemetery with mini-gardens overlooked by cliff face with monks' caves. **Hours:** Cemetery—daily June-Aug 6:30-21:30, April-May 6:30-20:00, Sept 6:30-19:00, Oct-March 6:30-18:00. See page 283.

**St. Peter's Church** Romanesque church with Rococo decor. **Hours:** Daily April-Oct 8:00-21:00, Nov-March 8:00-19:00. See page 284.

Nonnberg Abbey, Leopoldskron Palace, and, of course, the gazebo. The tour is very family-friendly, and you'll get lots of stops for goofy photo ops (€26 includes bike, €18 for kids ages 13-18, €12 for kids under age 13, €2 discount for adults and kids with this book, daily May-Sept at 9:30, June-Aug also at 16:30, allow 3.5 hours, reservations required for afternoon tours and recommended for morning tours, mobile 0650-342-6297, www.mariasbicycletours.com). For €8 extra (€20 per family), you're welcome to keep the bike all day.

## BEYOND SALZBURG

Both Bob's and Panorama Tours also offer an extensive array of other day trips from Salzburg (e.g., Berchtesgaden/Eagle's Nest, salt mines, Hallstatt, and Salzkammergut lakes and mountains). One efficient tour worth considering is Bob's full-day *Sound of Music*/**Hallstatt Tour,** which first covers everything in the standard four-hour *S.O.M.* tour, then continues for a four-hour look at the scenic, lake-speckled Salzkammergut, with free time to explore charming Hallstatt (€96, €12 discount if you show this book, pay cash, and book direct; doesn't include entrance fees to optional Hallstatt sights such as salt mine; departs daily at 9:00; Rudolfskai 38, tel. 0662/849-511, mobile 0664-541-7492, office@bobstours. com, www.bobstours.com).

# Salzburg's Old Town Walk

I've linked the best sights in the Old Town into this handy self-guided orientation walk (rated ▲▲▲). You can download a free Rick Steves **audio tour** of this walk; see page 10.

• *Begin at the Mozartsteg, the pedestrian bridge over the Salzach River.*

## ❶ Mozartsteg

Get your bearings: The river flows west to east. On the north bank is the New Town. The south side is the Old Town, dominated by a castle on a hill.

Take in the charming, well-preserved, historic core of Salzburg's Old Town. The skyline bristles with Baroque steeples and green, copper domes. Salzburg has 38 Catholic churches, plus two Protestant churches and a synagogue. The biggest green dome is the cathedral, which we'll visit shortly. Overlooking it all is the castle called the Hohensalzburg Fortress. Far to the right of the fortress, find the Museum of Modern Art—it looks like a mini-castle, but that's actually a water reservoir alongside the modern building.

The milky-green Salzach River thunders under your feet. It's called "salt river" not because it's salty, but because of the precious cargo it once carried. The salt mines of Hallein are just nine miles upstream. For 2,000 years, barges carried the precious salt from here to the wider world—to the Danube, the Black Sea, and on to the Mediterranean. As barges passed through here, they had to pay a toll on their salt. The city was born from the trading of salt *(salz)* defended by a castle *(burg)*—"Salz-burg."

• *Now let's plunge into Salzburg's Old Town. From the bridge, walk one block toward the hill-capping castle into the Old Town. Pass the traffic barriers (that keep this quiet town free of too much traffic) and turn right into a big square—Mozartplatz.*

## ❷ Mozartplatz

All the tourists around you probably wouldn't be here if not for the man honored by this statue—Wolfgang Amadeus Mozart. The

great composer spent most of his first 25 years (1756-1781) in Salzburg. He was born just a few blocks from here. He and his father both served Salzburg's rulers before Wolfgang went on to seek his fortune in Vienna. The statue (considered a poor likeness) was erected in 1842, just after the 50th anniversary of Mozart's death. The music festival of that year planted the seed for what would become the now world-renowned Salzburg Festival.

Mozart stands atop the spot where the first Salzburgers settled. Two thousand years ago, the Romans had a salt-trading town here called Juvavum. In the year 800, Salzburg—by then Christian and home to an important abbey—joined Charlemagne's Holy Roman Empire as an independent city. The Church of St. Michael (whose tower overlooks the square) dates from that time. It's Salzburg's oldest, if not biggest, church.

You may see lots of conservative Muslim families vacationing here. While there are plenty of Muslims in Austria, many of the conservatively dressed women you'll see here are from the United Arab Emirates. Lots of wealthy families from the Middle East come here in the summer to escape the heat back home, to enjoy a break from their very controlled societies, or for medical treatment. Nearby Munich is a popular destination for hospital visits, and the entire family usually joins in for sightseeing and shopping.

• *Before moving on, note the TI (which also sells concert tickets). Also, looking back past Mozart's statue, you may catch a glimpse of a TV tower. This stands atop the 4,220-foot-high Gaisberg hill. The summit is a favorite destination for local nature lovers and strong bikers. Now walk toward the cathedral and into the big square with the huge fountain.*

## ❸ Residenzplatz

As Salzburg's governing center, this square has long been ringed with important buildings. The cathedral borders the south side. The Residenz—the former palace of Salzburg's rulers—is to the right (as you face the cathedral). To the left is the New Residenz, with its bell tower.

In the 1600s, this square got a makeover in the then-fashionable Italian Baroque style. The rebuilding started under energetic Prince-Archbishop Wolf Dietrich, who ruled from 1587 to 1612.

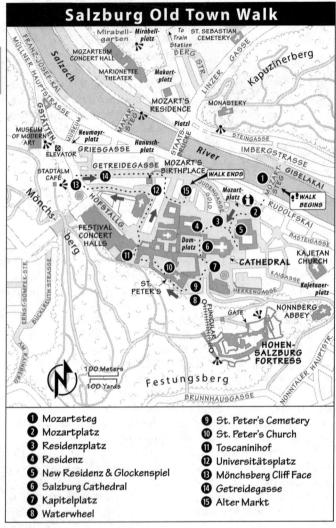

# Salzburg Old Town Walk

1. Mozartsteg
2. Mozartplatz
3. Residenzplatz
4. Residenz
5. New Residenz & Glockenspiel
6. Salzburg Cathedral
7. Kapitelplatz
8. Waterwheel
9. St. Peter's Cemetery
10. St. Peter's Church
11. Toscaninihof
12. Universitätsplatz
13. Mönchsberg Cliff Face
14. Getreidegasse
15. Alter Markt

Dietrich had been raised in Rome. He counted the Medicis as his cousins, and had grandiose Italian ambitions for Salzburg. Fortunately for him, the cathedral conveniently burned down in 1598. Dietrich set about rebuilding it as part of his grand vision to make Salzburg the "Rome of the North."

The fountain is as Italian as can be, an over-the-top version of Bernini's famous Triton Fountain in Rome. It shows Triton on top blowing his conch-shell horn. The water cascades down the basins and sprays playfully in the wind.

Notice that Salzburg's buildings are made from three distinctly different types of stone. Most common is the chunky gray conglomerate (like the cathedral's side walls), quarried from the nearby cliffs. There's also white marble (like the cathedral's towers and windows) and red marble (best seen in monuments inside buildings), both from the Alps near Berchtesgaden.

• *Turn your attention to...*

## ❹ The Residenz

This was the palace of Salzburg's powerful ruler, the prince-archbishop—that is, a ruler with both the political powers of a prince and the religious authority of an archbishop. The ornate Baroque entrance attests to the connections these rulers had with Rome. You can step inside the Residenz courtyard to get a glimpse of the impressive digs.

To see the Residenz interior you must buy a DomQuartier ticket (see page 288). This admits you to the fancy chandeliered staterooms and an impressive collection of paintings.

Notice that the Residenz has a white-stone structure (called the Cathedral Terrace) connecting it with the cathedral. This skyway gave the prince-archbishops an easy commute to church and a chance to worship while avoiding the public.

• *At the opposite end of Residenzplatz from the Residenz is the...*

## ❺ New (Neue) Residenz

In the days of the prince-archbishops, this building hosted parties in its lavish rooms. These days, the New Residenz houses two im-

portant sights: the Salzburg Museum and the Salzburg Panorama 1829 (see page 290). It's also home to the Heimatwerk, a fine shop showing off local handicrafts like dirndls and locally made jelly.

The New Residenz bell tower has a famous glockenspiel. This 17th-century carillon has 35 bells (cast in Antwerp) and chimes daily at 7:00, 11:00, and 18:00. It also plays little tunes appropriate to the season. The mechanism is a big barrel with adjustable tabs that turns like a giant music box, pulling the right bells in the right rhythm. (Twice-weekly tours let you get up close to watch the glockenspiel action: €3, April-Oct Thu at 17:30 and Fri at 10:30, no tours Nov-March, meet at Salzburg Panorama 1829, no reservations needed—just show up).

Notice the tower's ornamental top: an upside-down heart in

flames surrounds the solar system, representing how God loves all of creation.

Residenzplatz sets the tone for the whole town. From here, a series of interconnecting squares—like you'll see nowhere else—make a grand procession through the Old Town. Everywhere you go, you'll see similar Italian architecture. As you walk from square to square, notice how easily you slip from noisy and commercial to peaceful and reflective.

• *Exit the square by walking under the prince-archbishop's skyway. You'll step into the Cathedral Square or Domplatz. A good place to view the cathedral facade is from the far end of the square.*

## ❻ Salzburg Cathedral (Salzburger Dom)

Salzburg's cathedral (rated ▲▲) was one of the first Italian Baroque buildings north of the Alps. The dome stands 230 feet high. Two domed towers flank the entrance. Between them is a false-front roofline. The windows are flanked with classical half-columns and topped with heavy pediments. The facade is ringed with a Baroque balustrade, decorated with garlands and masks, and studded with statues. The whole look reminded visitors that Salzburg was the "Rome of the North."

The church, rebuilt under Wolf Dietrich, was consecrated in 1628. Experts differ on what motivated the builders. As it dates from the years of Catholic-Protestant warfare, it may have been meant to emphasize Salzburg's commitment to the Roman Catholic cause. Or it may have represented a peaceful alternative to the religious strife. Regardless, Salzburg's archbishop was the top papal official north of the Alps, and the city was the pope's northern outpost. With its rich salt production, Salzburg had enough money to stay out of the conflict and earn the nickname "The Fortified Island of Peace."

The cathedral was the center of power for the prince-archbishop in his religious role, and the cathedral square is surrounded by government buildings for his role as secular prince. (You visit some of these rooms as part of the DomQuartier Museums tour; see page 288.)

In the square, the **statue of Mary** (1771) is looking away from the church, welcoming visitors. Photo tip: Try looking at the statue while standing in the rear of the square, immediately under the middle arch. From the right perspective, you'll see that she's positioned to be crowned Queen of Heaven by the two angels on the church facade.

As you approach the church, pause at the iron entrance doors.

The dates on the doors are milestones in the church's history. In the year 774, the first church was consecrated by St. Virgil (see his statue), an Irish monk who became Salzburg's bishop. In 1598, the original church burned. It was replaced in 1628 by the church you see today. The year 1959 marks a modern milestone: The cathedral had been severely damaged by a WWII bomb that blew through the dome. In 1959, the renovation was complete.

• *Go inside. Take some time to let your eyes adjust.*

## The Cathedral Interior

The interior is clean and white, without excess decoration. Because it was built in just 14 years (from 1614 to 1628), the church boasts

harmonious architecture. And it's big—330 feet long, 230 feet tall—built with sturdy pillars and broad arches. When Pope John Paul II visited in 1998, some 5,000 people packed the place.

**Cost and Hours:** Free, but donation prominently requested; May-Sept Mon-Sat 9:00-19:00, Sun 13:00-19:00; March-April, Oct, and Dec until 18:00; Jan-Feb and Nov until 17:00; www.salzburger-dom.at.

**Visiting the Cathedral:** At the back pew, black-and-white photos show the bomb damage of October 16, 1944, which left a gaping hole where the dome once was. In the first chapel on the left is a dark bronze baptismal font. It dates from 1320—a rare survivor from the medieval cathedral. In 1756, little Wolfgang Amadeus Mozart was baptized here. For the next 25 years, this would be his home church. Amadeus, by the way, means "beloved by God."

As you make your way slowly up the nave, notice how you're drawn toward the light. Imagine being part of a sacred procession, passing from the relatively dim entrance to the bright altar with its painting of Christ's resurrection, bathed in light from the dome overhead. The church never had stained glass, just clear windows to let light power the message.

Under the soaring dome, look up and admire the exceptional stucco work, by an artist from Milan. It's molded into elaborate garlands, angels, and picture frames, some of it brightly painted. You're surrounded by the tombs (and portraits) of 10 archbishops.

You're also surrounded by four organs. (Actually, five. Don't forget the biggest organ, over the entrance.) Mozart served as organist here for two years, and he composed several Masses still played today. Salzburg's prince-archbishops were great patrons of music, with a personal orchestra that played religious music in the cathedral and dinner music in the Residenz. The tradition of music continues today. Sunday Mass here can be a musical spectacle—all five organs playing, balconies filled with singers and musicians, creating glorious surround-sound. Think of the altar in Baroque terms, as the center of a stage, with sunrays serving as spotlights in this dramatic and sacred theater.

• *You can visit the underwhelming crypt (downstairs from the left transept, free) with more tombs and a prayer chapel. As you leave the cathedral, check out the concert and Mass schedules posted near the entrance.*

*To learn more about the church, you can visit the **Cathedral Museum** as part of the DomQuartier Museums tour (see page 288). In summer, the **Cathedral Excavations Museum** (Domgrabungsmuseum, outside the church on Residenzplatz and down the stairs) shows off the church's medieval foundations and a few Roman mosaics—worthwhile only for Roman-iacs (€2.50, July-Aug daily 10:00-17:00, closed Sept-June, www.salzburgmuseum.at).*

*Exiting the cathedral, turn left, heading in the direction of the distant fortress on the hill. You'll soon you'll reach a spacious square with a golden orb.*

## ❼ Kapitelplatz

The playful modern sculpture in the square shows a man atop a golden orb. Every year, a foundation commissions a different artist to create a new work of public art somewhere in the city; this one's from 2007. Kapitelplatz is a pleasant square—notice the giant chessboard that often draws a crowd.

Follow the orb-man's gaze up the hill to **Hohensalzburg Fortress.** (I think he's trying to decide whether to shell out €11 for the funicular or save a few euros by hiking up.) Construction of the fortress began in 1077. Over the centuries, the small castle grew into a mighty, whitewashed fortress—so impressive that no army even tried attacking for over 800 years. These days, you can tour the castle grounds, visit some interior rooms and museums, and enjoy incredible views (see page 292). You can hike up (Festungsgasse leads up from Kapitelplatz) or, for €3 more, take the funicular. The funicular's rails actually date from as far back as the 1500s, when animals pulled cargo up to the fortress. Today's electric-powered funicular is from 1910.

Now walk across the square to the pond surrounded by a balustrade and adorned with a Trevi-fountain-like statue of Neptune. It looks fancy, but the pond was built as a horse bath, the 18th-century equivalent of a car wash. Notice the gold lettering above Neptune. It reads, "Leopold the Prince Built Me." But the artist added a clever twist. The inscription uses the letters "LLDVI," and

so on. Those are also Roman numerals—add 'em up: L is 50, D is 500, and so on. It all adds up to 1732—the year the pond was built.
• *With your back to the cathedral, leave the square, exiting through the right corner. You'll pass by a sign on a building that reads* zum Peter-skeller—*to St. Peter's Cemetery. But first, you reach a waterwheel.*

## ❽ Waterwheel

The waterwheel—overlooked by a statue of St. Peter—is part of a clever canal system that brings water to Salzburg from the foot-hills of the Alps, 10 miles away. The canal was built in the 13th century and is still used today. When the stream reached Salz-burg, it was divided into five smaller canals for the citizens' use. The rushing water was harnessed to waterwheels, which powered factories. There were more than 100 watermill-powered firms as late as the 19th century. The water also was used to fight fires, and every Thursday morning they flushed the streets. Hygienic Sal-zburg never suffered from a plague...it's probably the only major town in Austria with no plague monument. For more on the canal system, you might want to visit the nearby Alm River Canal exhibit (which you enter after exiting the funicular on the way down, see page 299).

This particular waterwheel (actually, it's a modern replace-ment) once ground grain into flour to make bread for the monks of St. Peter's Abbey. Nowadays, you can pop into the adjacent bak-ery—fragrant and traditional—and buy a fresh-baked roll for about a euro (Mon-Tue 8:00-17:30, Thu-Fri 7:00-17:30, Sat 7:00-13:00, closed Wed and Sun).
• *You've entered the borders of the former St. Peter's Abbey, a monastic complex of churches, courtyards, businesses (like the bakery), and a cem-etery. Find the* Katakomben *sign and step through the wrought-iron gates into...*

## ❾ St. Peter's Cemetery

This collection of lovingly tended graves abuts the sheer rock face of the Mönchsberg (free, silence requested; open daily June-Aug 6:30-21:30, April-May 6:30-20:00, Sept 6:30-19:00, Oct-March 6:30-18:00; www.stift-stpeter.at). Walk in about 30 yards to the middle of the cemetery. You're surrounded by three churches, each founded in the early Middle Ages atop a pagan Celtic holy site. The biggest church, St. Peter's, sticks its big Romanesque apse into the cemetery.

The graves surrounding you are tended by descendants of the deceased. In Austria (and many other European countries), gravesites are rented, not owned. Rent bills are sent out every 10 years. If no one cares enough to make the payment, your tombstone is removed.

The cemetery plays a role in *The Sound of Music*. The Captain and his large family were well-known in Salzburg for their musical talents. But when Nazi Germany annexed Austria in 1938, the von Trapps decided to flee so that the father would not be pressed into service again. In the movie, they hid here as they made their daring escape. The scene was actually filmed on a Hollywood set, inspired by St. Peter's Cemetery.

Look up the cliff, which has a few buildings attached—called (not quite accurately) "catacombs." Legendary medieval hermit monks are said to have lived in the hillside here. For a small fee, you can enter the *Katakomben* and climb lots of steps to see a few old caves, a chapel, and some fine city views (entrance at the base of the cliff, under the arcade; €2, visit takes 10 minutes; daily 10:00-12:00 & 13:00-18:00, Oct-April until 17:00).

Explore the arcade at the base of the cliff with its various burial chapels. Alcove #XXI has the tomb of the cathedral architect—forever facing his creation. #LIV (which is also the catacombs entry) has two interesting tombs marked by plaques on the floor. "Marianne" is Mozart's sister, nicknamed Nannerl. As children, Mozart and his sister performed together on grand tours of Europe's palaces. Michael Haydn was the brother of Joseph Haydn. He succeeded Mozart as church cathedral organist.

• *Exit the cemetery at the opposite end. Just outside, you enter a large courtyard anchored by...*

## ⓫ St. Peter's Church (Stiftskirche St. Peter)

You're standing at the birthplace of Christianity in Salzburg. St. Peter's Abbey—the monastery that surrounds this courtyard—was founded in 696, barely two centuries after the fall of Rome. The recommended Stiftskeller St. Peter restaurant in the courtyard (known these days for its Mozart Dinner Concert) brags that Charlemagne ate here in the year 803, making it (perhaps) the oldest restaurant in Europe. St. Peter's Church dates from 1147.

**Cost and Hours:** Free, daily April-Oct 8:00-21:00, Nov-March 8:00-19:00, www.stift-stpeter.at.

**Visiting the Church:** Enter the church, pausing in the atrium to admire the Romanesque tympanum (from 1250) over the inner doorway. Jesus sits on a rainbow, flanked by Peter and Paul. Beneath them is a stylized Tree of Life, and overhead, a Latin inscription reading, "I am the door to life, and only through me can you find eternal life."

Enter the nave. The once purely Romanesque interior (you may find a few surviving bits of faded 13th-century frescos) now lies hidden under a sugary Rococo finish. It's Salzburg's only Rococo interior—all whitewashed, with highlights of pastel green, gold, and red. If it feels Bavarian, it's because it was done by Bavarian artists. The ceiling paintings feature St. Peter receiving the keys from Christ (center painting), walking on water, and joining the angels in heaven.

The monastery was founded by St. Rupert (c. 650-718). Find his statue at the main altar—he's the second gold statue from the left. Rupert arrived as a Christian missionary in what was then a largely pagan land. He preached the gospel, reopened the Roman salt mines, and established the city. It was he who named it "Salzburg."

Rupert's tomb is midway up the right aisle. It's adorned with a painting of him praying for his city. Beneath him is a depiction of Salzburg circa 1750 (when this was painted): one bridge, salt ships sailing the river, and angels hoisting barrels of salt to heaven.

• *Exit the courtyard at the opposite side from where you entered. The passageway takes you past dorms still used for student monks. At the T-intersection (where you bump into the Franziskanerkirche), turn left. Pass beneath the archway painted with a modern Lamentation scene (1926). You'll enter a square (Max-Reinhardt-Platz). Pause to admire the line of impressive Salzburg Festival concert halls ahead of you. Then turn left, through an arch, into a small square called...*

## ⓫ Toscaninihof

In this small courtyard, you get a peek at the back end of the large Festival Hall complex. The Festival Hall, built in 1925, has three theaters and seats 5,000 people. It's very busy during the Salzburg Music Festival each summer. As the festival was started in the 1920s (an austere time after World War I), Salzburg couldn't afford a new concert hall, so they remodeled what were once the prince-archbishop's stables and riding school.

The tunnel you see (behind the *Felsenkeller* sign) leads to the actual concert hall. It's generally closed, but occasionally, you can look through nearby doorways and see carpenters building stage sets for an upcoming show.

The von Trapp family performed in the Festival Hall. In the movie, this courtyard is where Captain von Trapp nervously waited before walking onstage to sing "Edelweiss." Then the family slipped away to begin their escape from the Nazis.

The Toscaninihof also has the entrance to the city's huge, 1,500-space, inside-the-mountain parking lot. The stone stairway in the courtyard leads a few flights up to a panoramic view. Continuing up farther you reach the recommended Stadtalm Café.

• *Return to Max-Reinhardt-Platz. Continue straight, heading downhill, along the right side of the big church. As you stroll, you'll pass by popular sausage stands, offering the best of the wurst. You'll pass by a public toilet, and enter Universitätsplatz.*

## ⓬ Universitätsplatz

This square hosts Salzburg's liveliest open-air produce market. It generally runs mornings, Monday through Saturday. It's at its best early Saturday mornings, when the farmers are in town. The fancy yellow facade overlooking the square marks the back end of Mozart's Birthplace, which we'll see shortly.

Find the fountain—it's about 30 yards along. As with public marketplaces elsewhere, it's for washing fruit and vegetables. This fountain—though modern in design—is still part of a medieval-era water system. The water plummets down a hole and on to the river. The sundial over the water hole shows both the time (easy to decipher) and the date (less obvious).

• *Continue toward the end of the square. Along the way, you'll pass several nicely arcaded medieval passageways (on the right), which lead to Salzburg's old main street, Getreidegasse. (Try weaving back and forth through some.)*

## ⓭ Mönchsberg Cliff Face

Rising 200 feet above you is the Mönchsberg, Salzburg's mountain. Today you see the remains of an aborted attempt in the 1600s to cut through the Mönchsberg. It proved too big a job, and when new tunneling technology arrived, the project was abandoned. The stones cut did serve as a quarry for the city's 17th-century growth spurt—the bulk of the cathedral, for example, is built of this economical and local conglomerate stone.

Early one morning in 1669, a huge landslide killed more than 200 townspeople who lived close to where the elevator is now (to the right). Since then the cliffs have been carefully checked each spring and fall. Even today, you might see crews on the cliff, monitoring its stability.

At the base of the cliff are giant horse troughs, for the prince-archbishops' former stables. Paintings show the various breeds and temperaments of horses in the stable. Like Vienna, Salzburg had a passion for the equestrian arts.

• *From here, turn right. You'll pass by the elevator up the Mönchsberg (see page 299). Turn right again, entering a long pedestrian street.*

## ⓮ Getreidegasse

Old Salzburg's colorful main drag, Getreidegasse (rated ▲▲) has been a center of trade since Roman times. Check out all the old wrought-iron signs that advertise what's sold inside. This was the Salzburg of prosperous medieval burghers, or businessmen. These days it bustles with the tourist trade. The buildings date mainly from the 15th century. They're tall and narrow, because this neighborhood was prime real estate, and there was nowhere to build but up. Space was always tight, as the town was squeezed between the river and the mountain, and lots of land was set aside for the church. The architecture still looks much as it did in Mozart's day—though many of the buildings are now inhabited by chain outlets.

Enjoy the traditional signs, and try to guess what they sold. There are signs advertising spirits, a bookmaker, and a horn indi-

cating a place for the postal coach. A brewery has a star for the name of the beer, "Sternbrau." There's a window maker, a key maker, a pastry shop, a tailor, a pretzel maker, a pharmacy, a hat maker, and...ye olde hamburger shoppe, McDonald's.

On the right at #39, **Sporer** serves up homemade spirits (about €2/shot, Mon-Fri 9:30-19:00, Sat 8:30-17:00, closed Sun). This has been a family-run show for a century —fun-loving, proud, and English-speaking. *Nuss* is nut, *Marille* is apricot (typical of Austria), the *Kletzen* cocktail is like a super-thick Baileys with pear, and *Edle Brande* are the stronger schnapps. The many homemade firewaters are in jugs at the end of the bar.

After noticing the building's old doorbells—one per floor—continue down Getreidegasse. At #40, **Eisgrotte** serves good ice cream (€1/scoop). Across from Eisgrotte, a tunnel leads to the recommended **Balkan Grill** (signed as *Bosna Grill*), the local choice for the very best wurst in town. At #28 (a blacksmith shop since the 1400s), Herr Wieber, the iron- and locksmith, welcomes the curious. Farther along, you'll pass McDonald's (required to keep its arches Baroque and low-key).

At Getreidegasse #9, the knot of excited tourists marks the home of Salzburg's most famous resident. Mozart was born here in 1756. It was here that he composed most of his boy-genius works. Inside you see paintings of his family, letters, personal items (a lock of his hair, a clavichord he may have played), all trying to bring life to the Mozart story (see the description on page 290).

• *At Getreidegasse #3, turn right, into the passageway. You'll walk under a whale bone (likely symbolizing the wares of an exotic import shop) and reach the venerable Schatz Konditorei (worth a stop for coffee and pastry). At Schatz, turn left, through the passage. When you reach Sigmund-Haffner-Gasse, glance to the left (for a nice view of the city hall tower), then turn right. Walk along Sigmund-Haffner-Gasse and take your first left, to reach a square called...*

## ⑮ Alter Markt

This is Salzburg's old marketplace. Here you'll find a sausage stand, the venerable and recommended Café Tomaselli, and a fun candy shop at #7. Next door is the beautifully old-fashioned Alte F. E. Hofapotheke pharmacy—duck in discreetly to peek at the Baroque shelves and containers (be polite—the people in line are here for medicine; no photography).

• *Our walk is over. If you're up for more sightseeing, most everything's a short walk from here. You can head up to the Hohensalzburg Fortress. Or visit sights across the river in the New Town—there's a pedestrian bridge nearby.*

# Sights in Salzburg

## IN THE OLD TOWN
### ▲DomQuartier Museums
The DomQuartier ticket admits you to a circular, indoor route through the Residenz (the ornate former palace), the cathedral (which you view from the organ loft), and a couple of adjoining buildings. These sights—largely (but not entirely) focused on religious art and the history of Salzburg's prince-archbishops—were felt to be too minor to stand on their own, but worthwhile when knitted into one whole. The tour includes a good audioguide. On the map, you can see how the interconnected museums ring the Domplatz.

**Cost and Hours:** €12, Tue-Sun 10:00-17:00, closed Mon except in July-Aug, last tickets sold at 16:00, includes audioguide, Residenzplatz 1, tel. 0662/8042-2109, www.domquartier.at.

**Visiting the DomQuartier Museums:** If you enter at the Residenz (you can also enter at the cathedral), signs will guide you along the following circuit:

Once Salzburg's center of power, the **Residenz State Rooms** were the home of the prince-archbishop. Walking through these 15 chandeliered, stuccoed, and frescoed "stately rooms" *(Prunkräume),* you'll see elements of Renaissance, Baroque, and Classicist styles—200 years of let-them-eat-cake splendor.

The painting collection in the **Residenz Gallery**—not surprisingly in this bastion of Catholicism—is strongest in Baroque paintings. Rubens' *Allegory on Charles V* shows the pope's great champion with a sword in one hand and a scepter in the other. Rembrandt's teeny-tiny *Old Woman Praying* glows, despite her wrinkled face and broken teeth (the model was probably his mother). Other highlights include Federico Barocci's intense *Self-Portrait,* Bernardo Strozzi's *Sleeping Child,* and Boucher's rosy-cheeked *Dreaming Shepherdess.* Austria is represented by F. G. Waldmüller's cheery, sun-drenched *Children at the Window* and (Salzburg's own) Hans Makart's honest portrait of his first wife, *Amalie.*

In good weather, you can cross over to the cathedral the same way the prince-archbishops did—walking across their marble sky-way (the **Cathedral Terrace**), high above the unwashed masses. (If it's raining, you'll be sent one floor down to the indoor walkway.)

Though you don't actually tour the **Cathedral** interior, you do glance down on the nave from high above. On this level you can visit two small museums: the Nordoratorium, with modern religious art, and the **Cathedral Museum,** with rich religious objects from the cathedral's long history.

The next section, **St. Peter's Abbey Museum,** introduces you to work and life at the abbey (which claims to be the oldest monastery north of the Alps), and displays curiosities from its collections. Your final stop is a peek inside the **Franciscan Church** (Franziskanerkirche), a Gothic oddity in Baroque Salzburg. Admire the tall (conglomerate-stone) columns supporting an elaborate fan-vaulted ceiling. The altar area is surrounded by exuberantly decorated chapels. Find the unicorn.

### ▲▲Salzburg Museum

This is your best look at Salzburg's history. As the building was once the prince-archbishop's New Residence, many exhibits are in the lavish rooms where Salzburg's rulers entertained.

**Cost and Hours:** €7, €8.50 combo-ticket with Salzburg Panorama 1829; open Tue-Sun 9:00-17:00, closed Mon; includes so-so audioguide, tel. 0662/620-8080, www.salzburgmuseum.at.

**Visiting the Museum:** The centerpiece of the museum is the permanent exhibit called **The Salzburg Myth,** on the second floor. You'll learn how the town's physical beauty—nestled among the Alps, near a river—attracted 19th-century Romantics who made it one of Europe's first tourist destinations, an "Alpine Arcadia." When the music festival began in the 1920s, Salzburg's status grew still more, drawing high-class visitors from across the globe.

After that prelude, the exhibit focuses on the glory days of the prince-archbishops (1500-1800), with displays housed in the impressive ceremonial rooms. Portraits of the prince-archbishops (in Room 2.07) show them to be cultured men, with sensitive eyes, soft hands, and carrying books. But they were also powerful secular rulers of an independent state that extended far beyond today's Salzburg (see the map in Room 2.08).

The heart of the exhibit is Room 2.11—a big, colorful hall where the Salzburg Diet (the legislature) met. The elaborate painted ceiling depicts heroic Romans who sacrificed for their country. Spend some time here with the grab bag of interesting displays, including old guns, rock crystals, and medallions. A portrait shows the prince-archbishop who sums up Salzburg's golden age—Wolf Dietrich von Raitenau (1559-1617). Here he is at age 28, having just assumed power. Educated, well-traveled, a military strategist, and fluent in several languages, Wolf Dietrich epitomized the kind of Renaissance Man who could lead both church and state. He largely created the city we see today—the rebuilt cathedral, Residenz, Residenzplatz, and Mirabell Palace—done in the Italian Baroque style. Nearby exhibits flesh out Wolf Dietrich the man (his shoes and gloves) and the city he created with Italian architect Vincenzo Scamozzi. That city inspired visits and depictions by countless artists, who helped to create what the museum calls the "Salzburg Myth."

The first floor and the *Kunsthalle* in the basement house temporary exhibits.

### ▲Salzburg Panorama 1829

Also in the New Residence, the Salzburg Panorama 1829 displays a wrap-around painting of the city, giving a 360-degree look at Salzburg in the year 1829. From the Salzburg Museum entryway, find the underground "Panorama Passage" that leads to this unique exhibit. The passage itself is lined with archaeological finds (Roman and early medieval), helping set the stage for the Salzburg you're about to see.

In the early 19th century, before the advent of photography, 360-degree "panorama" paintings of great cities or events were popular. These creations were even taken on extended road trips. When this one was created, the 1815 Treaty of Vienna had just divvied up post-Napoleonic Europe, and Salzburg had become part of the Habsburg realm. This photo-realistic painting served as a town portrait done at the emperor's request. The circular view, painted by Johann Michael Sattler, shows the city as seen from the top of its castle. When complete, it spent 10 years touring the great cities of Europe, showing off Salzburg's breathtaking setting.

Today the exquisitely restored painting, hung in a circular room, offers a fascinating look at the city as it was in 1829. The river was slower and had beaches. The Old Town looks essentially as it does today. Your ticket also lets you see the temporary exhibitions in the room that surrounds the Panorama.

**Cost and Hours:** €3, €8.50 combo-ticket with Salzburg Museum, open daily 9:00-17:00, Residenzplatz 9, tel. 0662/620-808-730, www.salzburgmuseum.at.

### ▲▲Mozart's Birthplace (Geburtshaus)

In 1747, Leopold Mozart—a musician in the prince-archbishop's band—moved into this small rental unit with his new bride. Soon they had a baby girl (Nannerl) and, in 1756, a little boy was born—Wolf-

## Mozart's Salzburg

Salzburg was Mozart's home for the first 25 years of his brief, 35-year life. He was born on Getreidegasse and baptized in the cathedral. He played his first big concert, at age six, at the Residenz. He was the organist for the Cathedral, conducted the prince-archbishop's orchestra, and dined at (what's now called) Café Tomaselli. It was from Salzburg that he gained Europe-wide fame, touring the continent with his talented performing family. At age 17, Mozart and his family moved into lavish digs at (today's) Mozart's Residence.

As his fame and ambitions grew, Mozart eventually left Salzburg to pursue his dreams in Vienna. His departure from Salzburg's royal court in 1781 is the stuff of legend. Mozart, full of himself, announced that he was quitting. The prince-archbishop essentially said, "You can't quit; you're fired!" and as Mozart walked out, he was literally kicked in the ass.

gang Amadeus Mozart. It was here that Mozart learned to play piano and violin and composed his first boy-genius works. Even after the family gained fame, touring Europe's palaces and becoming the toast of Salzburg, they continued living in this rather cramped apartment.

Today this is the most popular Mozart sight in town—for fans, it's almost a pilgrimage. Shuffling through with the crowds, you'll peruse three floors of rooms with exhibits displaying paintings, letters, personal items, and lots of facsimiles, all attempting to bring life to the Mozart story. There's no audioguide, but everything's described in English.

Both Mozart sights in Salzburg—the Birthplace and the Residence—are equally good. If I had to choose, I'd go with the Birthplace as the best overall introduction (though it's more crowded), and consider the Residence extra credit. If you're truly interested in Mozart and his times, take advantage of the combi-ticket and see both. If Mozart isn't important to you, skip both museums and concentrate on the city's other sights and glorious natural surroundings.

**Cost and Hours**: €10, €17 combo-ticket with Mozart's Residence in New Town—see page 301, daily 9:00-17:30, July-Aug until 20:00, Getreidegasse 9, tel. 0662/844-313, www.mozarteum. at. Avoid the shoulder-to-shoulder crowds by visiting right when it opens or late in the day.

**Visiting Mozart's Birthplace**: You'll begin on the top floor in the actual apartment—five small rooms, including the bedroom where Mozart was born. The rooms are bare of any furnishings. Instead, you see portraits of the famous family and some memorabilia: Mozart's small-size childhood violin, some (possible) locks of his hair, buttons from his jacket, and a letter to his wife, whom he calls his "little rascal, pussy-pussy."

After leaving the actual apartments, you'll enter the museum portion. First up is an exhibition on Mozart's life after he left Salzburg and moved to Vienna: He jams with Haydn and wows the Viennese with electrifying concerts and new compositions (see a "square piano" which may have been his). Despite his fame, Mozart fell on hard times and died young and poor. But, as the museum shows, his legacy lived on. Computer terminals let you hear his music while following along on his handwritten scores.

Downstairs, the focus is on the operas he wrote (*Don Giovanni, The Magic Flute, The Marriage of Figaro*), with stage sets and video clips. The finale is an old clavichord on which Mozart supposedly composed his final work—the *Requiem*, which was played for his own funeral. (A predecessor of the more complicated piano, the clavichord's keys hit the strings with a simple teeter-totter motion that allows you to play very softly—ideal for composers living in tight apartment quarters.)

The lower-floor exhibit takes you on the road with the child prodigy, and gives a slice-of-life portrait of Salzburg during Mozart's time, including a bourgeois living room furnished much as the Mozart family's would have been.

## ATOP THE CLIFFS ABOVE THE OLD TOWN

Atop the Mönchsberg—the mini-mountain that rises behind the Old Town—is a tangle of paved walking paths with great views, a hostel with a pleasant café/restaurant, a modern art museum, a neighborhood of very fancy homes, and one major sight (the Hohensalzburg Fortress, perched on the Festungsberg, the Mönchsberg's southern arm). You can walk up from several points in town, including Festungsgasse (near the cathedral), Toscaninihof, and the recommended Augustiner Bräustübl beer garden. At the west end of the Old Town, the Mönchsberg elevator whisks you up to the top for a couple euros. The funicular directly up to the fortress is expensive, and worthwhile only if you plan to visit the fortress, which is included in the funicular ticket.

### ▲▲Hohensalzburg Fortress (Festung)

Construction of Hohensalzburg Fortress was begun by Archbishop Gebhard of Salzburg as a show of the Catholic Church's power (see sidebar). Built on a rock (called Festungsberg) 400 feet above the Salzach River, this fortress was never really used. That was the idea. It was a good investment—so foreboding, nobody attacked the town for over 800 years. The city was never taken by force, but when Napoleon stopped by, Salzburg wisely surrendered. After a stint as a military barracks, the fortress was opened to the public in the 1860s by Habsburg Emperor Franz Josef. Today, it remains one of Europe's mightiest castles, dominating Salzburg's skyline and offering incredible views, cafés, and a handful of mediocre museums. It's a pleasant place to grab an ice-cream cone and wander the white-washed maze of buildings while soaking up medieval ambience.

**Cost:** Your cost to enter the fortress depends on whether you get there on foot (the walk is easier than it looks), or, for €3 more, by funicular. Either way, your ticket includes all of the interior sights at the fortress: the Regency Rooms with audioguide (Tour A), the Fortress and Rainer Regiments museums (Tour B), the Marionette Exhibit, and a few minor sights.

**On Foot:** It's a steep but quick walk from Kapitelplatz (next to the cathedral), up Festungsgasse. (Alternatively, you can go up the Mönchsberg at the other end of the Old Town, then take the "Mönchsberg Walk," described on page 299, to the fortress; this is a much longer walk, but the Mönchsberg elevator takes care of some of the altitude gain).

Arriving on foot, you'll pay €8 to enter (at the fortress gate), which includes all of the fortress sights plus the funicular ride down—whether you want it or not. Within one hour of the museums' closing time, the entry price is reduced to €4. After the museums close, you can't enter on foot, but you can exit (the door will lock behind you) and walk down.

**Via Funicular:** Most visitors opt for the one-minute trip on the funicular *(Festungsbahn)*. It starts from Festungsgasse (just off Kapitelplatz, by the cathedral) and comes up inside the for-

tress complex. The round-trip funicular ticket, which includes all the fortress sights, is €11.30 (family ticket-€26.20). If you board the funicular up within one hour of the museums' closing time (i.e., May-Sept after 18:00 or Oct-April after 16:00), you pay only €8, or €6.50 if you don't want to take the funicular down; this is a good deal if you only want a glimpse of the museums. After the museums have closed, the funicular continues to run until about 21:30 or 22:00 (later if there's a concert) and costs €4 round-trip, or €2.50 one-way.

**Hours:** The museums in the fortress are open daily year-round (May-Sept 9:00-19:00, Oct-April 9:30-17:00). The grounds of the fortress stay open and the funicular continues to run even after the museums close, especially when there's a concert (300 nights a year).

**Avoiding Crowds:** You can avoid waits for the funicular ascent with the Salzburg Card (which lets you skip to the head of the line)

SALZBURG

# Hohensalzburg Fortress

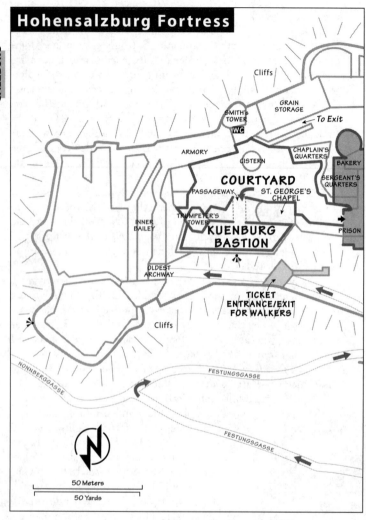

or by walking up. In summer, there are often long waits to get into Tour A (only 60 people are admitted at a time). To avoid crowds in general, visit early in the morning or late in the day.

**Information:** Tel. 0662/8424-3011, www.salzburg-burgen.at.

**Concerts:** The fortress serves as a venue for evening concerts (the Festungskonzerte), which are held in the old banquet rooms on the upper floor of the palace museum. A concert is a good way to see the fortress without noisy crowds. To visit the fortress in the evening for a concert, you'll need to take the funicular (see funicular info described earlier).

For concert details, see page 309.

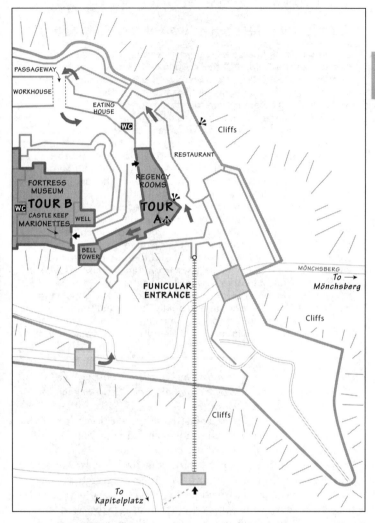

**Café:** The cafés to either side of the upper funicular station

are a great place to nibble on apple strudel while taking in the jaw-dropping view.

**➲ Self-Guided Tour:** The fortress is an eight-acre complex of some 50 buildings, with multiple courtyards and multiple rings of protective walls. Your ticket admits you to all of the interior exhibits.

• *At the top of the funicular, turn right, and bask in the **view** to the*

## Battlefield Salzburg: Popes vs. Emperors

Salzburg is so architecturally impressive today to a great degree because of the Roman Catholic Church. This town was on the frontline of a centuries-long power struggle between Church and emperor. The town's mighty Hohensalzburg Fortress—a symbol of the Church's determination to assert its power here—was built around 1100, just as the conflict was heating up.

The medieval church-state argument, called the "Lay Investiture Controversy," was a classic tug-of-war between a series of popes and Holy Roman Emperors. The prize: the right to appoint (or "invest") church officials in the Holy Roman Emperor's domain. (Although called "Holy," the empire was headed not by priests, but by secular—or "lay"—rulers.)

The Church impinged on the power of secular leaders in several ways: Their subjects' generous tithes went to Rome, leaving less for the emperor to tax. In many areas, the Church was the biggest landowner (people willed their land to the Church in return for prayers for their salvation). And the pope's appointees weren't subject to secular local laws. Holy Roman Emperors were plenty powerful, but not as powerful as the Church.

In 1075, Emperor Henry IV bucked the system, appointing his own set of church officials and boldly renouncing Gregory VII as pope. In retaliation, Gregory excommunicated both Henry and the bishops he'd appointed. One of Henry's chief detractors was

*south (away from town) toward the Alps. Continue up through the fortress gates—two defensive rings for double protection. Emerging into the light, go left (uphill) to find the entrance to....*

**Tour A—The Regency Rooms:** Here you see a few (mostly bare) rooms, following an audioguide included with your ticket. The Stable Rooms highlight various prince-archbishops and models showing the fortress' growth, starting in 1077. The last model (1810) shows it at its peak. The fortress was never overthrown, but it did make a negotiated surrender with Napoleon, and never saw action again. Your tour includes a room dedicated to the art of "enhanced interrogation" (to use American military jargon)—filled with tools of that gruesome trade.

One of the most esteemed prisoners held here was Prince-Archbishop Wolf Dietrich, who lost favor with the pope, was captured by a Bavarian duke, and spent his last seven years in Hohensalzburg. It's a complicated story—basically, the pope counted on Salzburg to hold the line against the Protestants for several generations following the Reformation. Wolf Dietrich was a good Catholic, as were most Salzburgers. But the town's important businessmen and the region's salt miners were Protestant, and for Salzburg's financial good, Wolf Dietrich dealt with them in a tolerant and

Salzburg's pope-appointed archbishop, Gebhard, who started construction of Hohensalzburg Fortress in a face-off with the defiant emperor.

The German nobility seized on the conflict as an opportunity to rebel, seizing royal property and threatening to elect a new emperor. To placate the nobles, Henry sought to regain the Church's favor. In January of 1077, Henry traveled south to Italy—supposedly crossing the Alps barefoot and in a monk's hair shirt—to Canossa, where the pope was holed up. The emperor knelt in the snow outside the castle gate for three days, begging the pope's forgiveness. (To this day, the phrase "go to Canossa" is used to refer to any act of humility.)

But the German princes continued their revolt, electing their own king (Henry's brother-in-law, Rudolf of Rheinfelden). Henry's reconciliation with the Church was brief: In short order he named an antipope (Clement III), killed Rudolf in battle, and invaded Rome. Archbishop Gebhard was forced out of Salzburg and spent a decade in exile, raising forces against Henry in an attempt to reclaim the Salzburg archdiocese.

The back-and-forth continued until 1122, when a power-sharing accord was finally reached between Henry's son, Emperor Henry V, and Pope Calistus II.

pragmatic way. Eventually the pope—who allowed zero tolerance for Protestants in those heady Counter-Reformation days—had Wolf Dietrich locked up and replaced.

The highlight of Tour A is the commanding city view from the top of a tower. To the north is the city. To the south are Salzburg's suburbs in a flat valley, from which rises the majestic 6,000-foot Untersberg massif of the Berchtesgaden Alps. To the east, you can look down into the castle complex to see the palace where the prince-archbishops lived. As you exit, pause at the "Salzburger Bull," a mechanical barrel organ used to wake the citizens every morning.

**Tour B—The Fortress Museum (Festungsmuseum):** This extensive museum covers the history of the fortress (including models of how it was constructed), everyday objects (dishes, beds, ovens), weapons (pikes, swords, pistols, cannons), old musical instruments, and more torture devices (including a chastity belt).

On the top floor are three pretty ceremonial rooms, including the one where the evening concerts are held. (Check out the colorfully painted tile stove in the far room.) The rest of the top floor is given over to the Rainer Regiments Museum, dedicated to the

Salzburg soldiers who fought mountain-to-mountain on the Italian front during World War I.

**Marionette Exhibit:** Marionette shows are a Salzburg tradition (think of the "Lonely Goatherd" scene in *The Sound of Music*). Two fun rooms show off various puppets and scenery backdrops. Videos show glimpses of the Marionette Theater performances of Mozart classics (see page 310). Give the hands-on marionette a whirl, and find Wolf Dietrich in a Box.

**Fortress Courtyard:** The courtyard was the main square for the medieval fortress's 1,000-some residents, who could be self-sufficient when necessary. The square was ringed by the shops of craftsmen, blacksmiths, bakers, and so on. The well dipped into a rain-fed cistern. The church is dedicated to St. George, the protector of horses (logical for an army church) and decorated by fine red marble reliefs (1512). Behind the church is the top of the old lift (still in use) that helped supply the fortress. Under the archway next to it are the steps that lead back into the city, or to the paths across the Mönchsberg.

• *Just downhill from the chapel, find an opening in the wall that leads to a balcony with a view of Salzburg—the Kuenburg Bastion.*

**Kuenburg Bastion:** Survey Salzburg from here and think about fortifying an important city by using nature. The fortress sits atop a ridgeline with sheer cliffs on three sides, giving it a huge defensive advantage. Meanwhile, the town of Salzburg sits between the natural defenses of the Salzach River and the ridge. (The ridgeline consists of the Mönchsberg— the cliffs to the left—and Festungsberg—the little mountain

you're on. The fortress itself has three concentric rings of defense: the original keep in the center (where Tour B is located), the vast whitewashed walls (near you), and still more beefed-up fortifications (on the hillside below you, added against an expected Ottoman invasion). With all these defenses, the city only required a few more touches: the New Town across the river needed a bit of a wall arcing from the river to its hill. Back then, only one bridge crossed the Salzach into town, and it had a fortified gate. Cradled amid the security of its defenses—both natural and man-made— independent Salzburg thrived for nearly a thousand years.

• *Our tour is over. To **walk**—either down to Salzburg or across the Mönchsberg (see "Mönchsberg Walk," next)—you'll want to take the exit at the east end of the complex. Get out your fortress-issued map and locate the route that leads to that exit.*

*To reach the **funicular**, just backtrack. If you take the funicular down, don't miss (at the bottom of the lift) the...*

**Alm River Canal Exhibit:** At the base of the funicular, below the fortress, is this fine little exhibit on how the river was broken into five smaller streams—powering the city until steam took up the energy-supply baton. Pretend it's the year 1200 and follow (by video) the flow of the water from the river through the canals, into the mills, and as it's finally dumped into the Salzach River. (The exhibit technically requires a funicular ticket—but you can see it unofficially by slipping through the exit at the back of the amber shop, next door to the funicular terminal.)

## Mönchsberg Sights
### ▲Mönchsberg Walk

The paved, wooded walking path along the narrow ridgeline between the Mönchsberg elevator and the fortress is less than a mile long and makes for a great 30-minute hike. There's some up and down, but the total elevation gain is about equal going in either direction.

The mountain is small, and frequent signposts direct you between all the key points, so it's hard to get lost. *(Festung Hohensalzburg* and *Museum der Moderne Salzburg* refer to the fortress and elevator ends of the mountain, respectively. The spots where you can go down the stairs into town are signed *Altstadt.)* The views of Salzburg are the main draw, but there's also a modern art museum, mansions to ogle, and a couple of places to eat or enjoy a scenic drink. Along the way, you'll see stunning views of Salzburg, rustic homes, a few unique little castle-like homes, occasional modern art sculptures in yards, a snack shack, the sheer cliff face with its layers of sediment, parts of the medieval wall, and information plaques on Salzburg's first settlers and on quarrying the cliffs.

You can do this walk in either direction. If you're planning to visit the fortress, do the walk first and the fortress last, saving €3 by skipping the funicular up: Take the Mönchsberg elevator, walk across to the fortress, pay the €8 entry price at the fortress gate, see the fortress, then take the funicular down—included in your fortress ticket.

The Mönchsberg **elevator** *(Aufzug)* starts from Gstättengasse/Griesgasse on the west side of the Old Town (€2.10 one-way, €3.40 round-trip, normally Mon 8:00-19:00, Tue-Sun 8:00-23:00).

You can also **climb** up and down under your own power; this saves a few more euros (no matter which direction you go). Paths or stairs lead up from the Augustiner beer hall (see page 325), Toscaninihof (near the Salzburg Festival concert halls), and Festungsgasse (at the base of the fortress).

**Cafés:** The elevator deposits you right at Mönchsberg 32, a

SALZBURG

sleek modern café/bar/restaurant adjacent to the modern art museum and a fine place for a drink or splurge meal (see page 324 for details). From there, it's a five-minute walk to the rustic, recommended Stadtalm Café, with wooden picnic tables and a one-with-nature allure. Next to the Stadtalm is a surviving section of Salzburg's medieval wall with an info plaque showing how the wall once looked.

## Museum of Modern Art on Mönchsberg

The modern-art museum—a stark concrete-and-glass exhibition space—features temporary exhibits. It's located right at the top of the Mönchsberg elevator. Next to the museum is the "Sky Space," a cylindrical stone tower intended to let you contemplate the sky.

**Cost and Hours:** €8, Tue-Sun 10:00-18:00, Wed until 20:00, closed Mon.

## IN THE NEW TOWN, NORTH OF THE RIVER

The following sights are across the river from the Old Town. I've connected them with walking instructions.
• *Begin at the Makartsteg pedestrian bridge, where you can survey the...*

## Salzach River

Salzburg's river is called "salt river" not because it's salty, but because of the precious cargo it once carried—the salt mines of Hallein are just nine miles upstream. Salt could be transported from here all the way to the Danube, and on to the Mediterranean via the Black Sea. The riverbanks and roads were built when the river was regulated in the 1850s. Before that, the Salzach was much wider and slower moving. Houses opposite the Old Town fronted the river with docks and "garages" for boats. The grand buildings just past the bridge (with their elegant promenades and cafés) were built on reclaimed land in the late 19th century.

Scan the cityscape. Notice all the churches. Salzburg, nicknamed the "Rome of the North," has 38 Catholic churches (plus two Protestant churches and a synagogue). Find the five streams gushing into the river. These date from the 13th century, when the river was split into five canals running through the town to power its mills. The Stein Hotel (upstream, just left of next bridge) has a popular roof-terrace café (see page 304). Downstream, notice the Museum of Modern Art atop the Mönchsberg, with a view restaurant and a faux castle (actually a water reservoir). The Romanesque bell tower with the green copper dome in the distance is the Augustine church, site of the best beer hall in town (the Augustiner Bräustübl).
• *Cross the bridge, pass the recommended Café Bazar (a fine place for a*

*drink), walk two blocks inland, and take a left past the heroic statues into...*

## ▲Mirabell Gardens and Palace (Schloss)

These bubbly gardens, laid out in 1730 for the prince-archbishop, have been open to the public since 1850 (thanks to Emperor Franz  Josef, who was rattled by the popular revolutions of 1848). The gardens are free and open until dusk. The palace is open only as a concert venue (explained later). The statues and the arbor (far left) were featured in *The Sound of Music*.

Walk through the gardens to the palace and find the statue of the horse (on the river side of the palace). Look back, enjoy the garden/cathedral/castle view, and imagine how the prince-archbishop must have reveled in a vista that reminded him of all his secular and religious power.

The rearing **Pegasus statue** (rare and very well-balanced) is the site of a famous *Sound of Music* scene where the kids all danced before lining up on the stairs with Maria (30 yards farther along). The steps lead to a small mound in the park (made of rubble from a former theater).

Nearest the horse, stairs lead between two lions to a pair of tough dwarves (early volleyball players with spiked mittens) welcoming you to Salzburg's **Dwarf Park.** Cross the elevated walk (noticing the city's fortified walls) to meet statues of a dozen dwarves who served the prince-archbishop—modeled after real people with real fashions in about 1600. This was Mannerist art, from the hyper-realistic age that followed the Renaissance.

There's plenty of **music** here, both in the park and in the palace. A brass band plays free park concerts (May-Aug Sun at 10:30). To properly enjoy the lavish Mirabell Palace—once the prince-archbishop's summer palace and now the seat of the mayor—get a ticket to a Schlosskonzerte (my favorite venue for a classical concert—see page 309).

• *Now go a long block southeast to Makartplatz, where, opposite the big and bright Hotel Bristol, you'll find...*

## ▲Mozart's Residence (Wohnhaus)

In the fall of 1773, when Wolfgang was 17—and his family was flush with money from years of touring—the Mozarts moved here from their cramped apartment on Getreidegasse. The exhibits are aimed a bit more toward the Mozart connoisseur than those at Mozart's Birthplace, but the place comes with a good introductory video, is less crowded, and includes an informative audioguide. The building itself, bombed in World War II, is a reconstruction.

**Cost and Hours:** €10, €17 combo-ticket with Mozart's Birthplace in Old Town—see page 290, daily 9:00-17:30, July-Aug until 20:00, allow an hour for visit, Makartplatz 8, tel. 0662/8742-2740, www.mozarteum.at. Behind the ticket desk is the free Mozart Sound and Film Collection, an archive of historic concerts on video (Mon-Tue and Fri 9:00-13:00, Wed-Thu 13:00-17:00, closed Sat-Sun).

**Visiting Mozart's Residence:** The exhibit—seven rooms on one floor—starts in the main hall, which was used by the Mozarts to entertain Salzburg's high society. Here, you can see the museum's prize possession—Mozart's very own piano, as well as his violin. The family portrait on the wall (from around 1780) shows Mozart with his sister Nannerl at the piano, their father on violin, and their mother—who'd died two years earlier in Paris. A display

of air guns and targets shows Mozart's fascination with a popular game of the time that they played in the garden. (Known crudely as licking an "arse," it speaks of Wolfgang's disdain for the rigors of high society.) Before moving on, consider spending time with the good introductory video in this room.

Room 2 trumpets the successes the Mozart family enjoyed while living here: portraits of Salzburg bigwigs they hung out with, letters from Mozart bragging about his musical successes, and the publication of Leopold's treatise on playing violin.

Room 3 is dedicated to father Leopold—*Kapellmeister* of the prince-a member of the archbishop's orchestra, musician, and composer in his own right. Was Leopold a loving nurturer of young Wolfgang or an exploiting Svengali?

Room 4 stars "Nannerl" (Maria Anna), Mozart's sister, who was five years older. Though both were child prodigies, playing four-hand showpieces for Europe's crowned heads, Nannerl went on to lead a stable life as wife and mother.

Room 5 boasts "Mozart's first printed work"—a sonata for clavichord and violin he wrote when he was eight. Room 6 shows many portraits of Mozart, some authentic, some not, but all a testament to his long legacy. By the time Mozart was 25, he'd grown tired of his father, this house, and Salzburg, and he went on to Vienna—to more triumphs, but ultimately, a sad end.

• *From here, you can walk a few blocks back to the main bridge (Staatsbrücke), where you'll find the Platzl, a square once used as a hay market. Pause to enjoy the kid-pleasing little fountain. Look down handsome*

*Linzer Gasse (once the road to Linz and Vienna), with its attractive small shops. Near the fountain (with your back to the river), Steingasse leads darkly to the right.*

## ▲Steingasse Stroll

Heading up dim, narrow Steingasse, you get a rare glimpse of medieval Salzburg. It's not the church's Salzburg of grand squares and Baroque facades, but the people's Salzburg, of cramped quarters and humble cobbled lanes. Inviting cocktail bars along here come alive at night (see "Steingasse Pub Crawl" on page 326).

Stop at #9 and look across the river into the Old Town; the city's original bridge once connected Salzburg's two halves right here. According to the plaque (of questionable veracity) at #9, this is where Joseph Mohr, who wrote the words to "Silent Night," was born—poor and illegitimate—in 1792. There is no doubt, however, that the popular Christmas carol was composed and first sung in the village of Oberndorf, just outside of Salzburg, in 1818. Stairs lead from near here up to a 17th-century Capuchin monastery.

On the next corner, the wall is gouged out. This scar was left even after the building was restored, to serve as a reminder of the American GI who tried to get a tank down this road during a visit to the town brothel—two blocks farther up Steingasse. Within steps of here is the art cinema (showing movies in their original language) and four recommended bars (described on page 326).

At #19, find the carvings on the old door. Some say these are notices from beggars to the begging community (more numerous after post-Reformation religious wars, which forced many people out of their homes and towns)—a kind of "hobo code" indicating whether the residents would give or not. Trace the wires of the old-fashioned doorbells to the highest floors.

Farther on, you step through the old fortified gate (at #20) and find a commanding Salzburg view across the river. Notice the red dome marking the oldest nunnery in the German-speaking world (established in 712) under the fortress and to the left. The real Maria, who inspired *The Sound of Music*, taught in this nunnery's school. In 1927, she and Captain von Trapp were married in the church you see here (not the church filmed in the movie). He was 47. She was 22. Hmmmm.

From here look back, above the arch you just passed through, and up at part of the town's medieval fortification. The coat of arms on the arch is of the prince-archbishop who paid Bavaria a huge ransom to stay out of the Thirty Years' War (smart move). He then built this fortification (in 1634) in anticipation of rampaging armies from both sides.

Today, this street is for making love, not war. The Maison de

Plaisir (a few doors down, at #24) has for centuries been a Salzburg brothel. But the climax of this walk is more touristic.

• *For a grand view, head back to the Platzl and the bridge, enter the Stein Hotel (left corner, overlooking the river), and ride the elevator to...*

## Stein Terrasse

This café offers one of the best views in town. Hidden from the tourist crush, it's a trendy, professional, local scene. You can discreetly peek at the view, enjoy a drink or light meal, or come back later to gaze into the eyes of your travel partner as you sip a nightcap (small snacks, indoor/outdoor seating, daily 7:00-24:00).

• *Back at the Platzl and the bridge, you can head straight up Linzer Gasse (away from the river) into a neighborhood packed with recommended accommodations, as well as our final New Town sight, the...*

## ▲St. Sebastian Cemetery

Wander through this quiet oasis. Mozart is buried in Vienna, his mom's in Paris, and his sister is in Salzburg's Old Town (St. Peter's)—but Wolfgang's wife Constanze ("Constantia") and his father Leopold are buried here (from the black iron gate entrance on Linzer Gasse, walk 19 paces and look left). When Prince-Archbishop Wolf Dietrich had the cemetery moved from around the cathedral and put here, across the river, people didn't like it. To help popularize it, he had his own mausoleum built as its centerpiece. Continue straight past the Mozart tomb to this circular building (English description at door). In the corner to the left of the entrance is the tomb of the Renaissance scientist and physician Paracelsus, best known for developing laudanum as a painkiller.

**Cost and Hours:** Free, daily April-Oct 9:00-18:00, Nov-March 9:00-16:00, entry at Linzer Gasse 43 in summer; in winter go around the corner to the right, through the arch at #37, and around the building to the doorway under the blue seal.

## NEAR SALZBURG
### ▲▲Hellbrunn Palace and Gardens

In about 1610, Prince-Archbishop Sittikus decided he needed a lavish palace with a vast and ornate garden purely for pleasure

(I imagine after meditating on stewardship and Christ-like values). He built this summer palace and hunting lodge, and just loved inviting his VIP guests from throughout Europe for fun with his trick fountains. Today, Hellbrunn is a popular sight for its formal garden (one of the oldest in Europe, with a gazebo made famous by *The Sound of Music*), amazing fountains, palace exhibits, and the excuse it offers to simply get out of the city.

**Cost and Hours:** €10.50 ticket includes fountain tour and palace audioguide, daily May-Sept 9:00-17:30, July-Aug until 21:00—but tours from 18:00 on don't include the castle (which closes in the evening), April and Oct 9:00-16:30, these are last tour times, closed Nov-March, tel. 0662/820-3720, www.hellbrunn.at.

**Getting There:** Hellbrunn is nearly four miles south of Salzburg.

*By Bus:* Take bus #25 from the train station or the Rathaus stop by the Staatsbrücke bridge (2-3/hour, 20 minutes). Get off at the Schloss Hellbrunn stop.

*By Bike:* In good weather, the trip out to Hellbrunn makes for a pleasant 30-minute bike excursion (see "Riverside or Meadow Bike Ride," later, and ask for a map when you rent your bike).

**Visiting the Palace:** Upon arrival, buy your **fountain tour** ticket and get a tour time. Tours generally go on the half-hour. The 40-minute English/German tours take you laughing and scrambling through a series of amazing 17th-century garden settings with lots of splashy fun and a guide who seems almost sadistic in the joy he has in soaking his group. (Hint: When you see a wet place, cover your camera.) If there's a wait until your tour, you can see the palace first.

With the help of the included audioguide, wander through the modest **palace** exhibit to the sounds of shrieking fountain-taunted tourists below. The palace was built in a style inspired by the Venetian architect Palladio, who was particularly popular around 1600, and it quickly became a cultural destination. This was the era when the aristocratic ritual was to go hunting in the morning (hence the wildlife-themed decor) and enjoy an opera in the evening. The first opera north of the Alps, imported from Italy, was performed here.

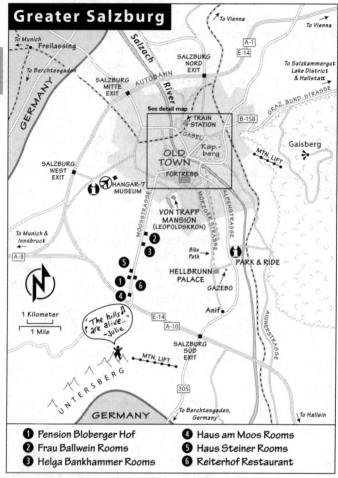

# Greater Salzburg

**1** Pension Bloberger Hof
**2** Frau Ballwein Rooms
**3** Helga Bankhammer Rooms
**4** Haus am Moos Rooms
**5** Haus Steiner Rooms
**6** Reiterhof Restaurant

The decor is Mannerist (between Renaissance and Baroque), with faux antiquities and lots of surprising moments—intentional irregularities were in vogue after the strict logic, balance, and Greek-inspired symmetry of the Renaissance. (For example, the main hall is not in the palace's center, but at the far end.) The palace exhibit also explains the impressive 17th-century hydraulic engineering that let gravity power the intricate fountains.

After the fountain tour you're also free to wander the delightful **garden.** Pop out to see the **gazebo** made famous by the "Sixteen Going On Seventeen" song from *The Sound of Music* (relocated here in the 1990s; look for *Sound-of-Music Pavilion* signs).

SALZBURG

### ▲▲Riverside or Meadow Bike Ride

The Salzach River has smooth, flat, and scenic bike lanes along each side (thanks to medieval tow paths—cargo boats would float downstream and be dragged back up by horses). On a sunny day, I can think of no more shout-worthy escape from the city.

Perhaps the most pristine, meadow-filled farm-country route is the nearly four-mile path along Hellbrunner Allee; it's an easy ride with a worthy destination (Hellbrunn Palace, listed earlier): From the middle of town, head along the river on Rudolfskai, with the river on your left and the fortress on your right. After passing the last bridge at the edge of the Old Town (Nonntaler Brücke), cut inland along Petersbrunnstrasse, until you reach the university and Akademiestrasse. Beyond it find the start of Freisaalweg, which becomes the delightful Hellbrunner Allee bike path...which leads directly to the palace (paralleling Morzgerstrasse; see map on page 306). For a nine-mile ride, continue on to Hallein (where you can tour a salt mine—see next listing; if heading to Hallein directly from Salzburg, head out from the north bank of the river, i.e. the New Town side, which is more scenic).

Even a quickie ride across town is a great Salzburg experience. In the evening, the riverbanks are a world of floodlit spires. For bike rental information, see "Getting Around Salzburg—By Bike," earlier.

### ▲Hallein Salt Mine (Salzbergwerke)

You'll be pitched plenty of different salt-mine excursions from Salzburg, all of which cost substantial time and money. One's plenty. This salt-mine tour (in Bad Dürrnberg, just above the town of Hallein, 9 miles from Salzburg) is a good choice. Wearing white overalls and sliding down the sleek wooden chutes, you'll cross underground from Austria into Germany while learning about the old-time salt-mining process. The tour entails lots of time on your feet as you walk from cavern to cavern, learning the history of the mine by watching a series of video skits with an actor channeling Prince-Archbishop Wolf Dietrich. The visit also includes a "Celtic Village" open-air museum.

**Cost and Hours:** €19, €17 if purchased online, allow 2.5 hours for the visit, daily April-Oct 9:00-17:00, Nov-Dec and Feb-March 10:00-15:00—these are last tour times, closed Jan, English-speaking guides—but let your linguistic needs be known loud and clear, tel. 06132/200-8511, www.salzwelten.at.

**Getting There:** The convenient *Salz Erlebnis* ticket from Salzburg's train station covers your transport and admission in one money-saving round-trip ticket (€29, buy ticket at train station, no discount with railpass; covers train to Hallein, then 11-minute ride on bus #41 to salt mines in Bad Dürrnberg, runs hourly, check schedules when buying tickets).

## Hangar-7

This purpose-built hangar at the Salzburg airport (on the other side of the runways from the terminal) houses the car-and-aircraft collection of Dietrich Mateschitz, the flamboyant founder of the Red Bull energy-drink empire. Under the hangar's modern steel-and-glass dome are 20 or so glittering planes and racecars, plus three pretentious eateries, all designed to brandish the Red Bull "culture." To learn about the machines, you can borrow an iPod Touch with English information, or get information on the iPads posted by each exhibit.

Mateschitz (now in his 70s) remains Salzburg's big personality: He has a mysterious mansion at the edge of town, sponsors the local "Red Bull" soccer and hockey teams, owns several chic Salzburg eateries and cocktail bars, and employs 6,000 mostly good-looking people. He seems much like the energy drink that made him rich and powerful—a high-energy, anything's-possible cultural Terminator.

**Cost and Hours:** Free, daily 9:00-22:00, bus #10 from Hanuschplatz to the Pressezentrum/Kuglhof stop—don't get off at the airport terminal, Wilhelm-Spazier-Strasse 7a, tel. 0662/2197, www.hangar-7.com.

**Eating:** Two floors up, the Mayday Bar has light meals and an unusual, experimental menu (€10-15 dishes). On the first floor, you'll probably want to skip the Ikarus Restaurant—all it offers is a €160 fixed-price meal. On the ground floor, the Carpe Diem bar serves drinks (it's an outpost of the larger Carpe Diem bar in the Old Town, also owned by Mateschitz).

## ▲▲Hallstatt and Berchtesgaden

Rustic Hallstatt, crammed like a swallow's nest into the narrow shore between a lake and a steep mountainside, is a 2.5-hour bus or train ride from Salzburg. It's my favorite town in the scenic Salzkammergut Lake District (see the Hallstatt chapter). Berchtesgaden (covered in the next chapter) is equally scenic, and home to Hitler's Eagle's Nest and other interesting sights. Both of these towns make for busy but worthwhile side-trips from Salzburg, and both are easy enough to do on your own. But if you're on a tight schedule, taking a bus tour can be a good use of your time and money (for details, see page 276).

# Music in Salzburg

Music lovers come to Salzburg in late July and August for the Salzburg Festival, but there are also smaller, less expensive festivals at other times of year. The regular programs at the city's theaters and concert halls are often accessible to visitors. And all year long, you can enjoy pleasant, if touristy concerts held in historic venues around town—or a musical Mass on Sunday morning. To help case out your options, pick up the events calendar brochure at the TI (free, bimonthly) or check www.salzburg.info (under "Art & Culture," click on "Music"). I've never planned in advance, and I've enjoyed great concerts with every visit.

## NIGHTLY MUSICAL EVENTS
The following concerts are mostly geared to tourists and can have a crank-'em-out feel, but still provide good value, especially outside festival times.

### Concerts at Hohensalzburg Fortress (Festungskonzerte)
Nearly nightly concerts—Mozart's greatest hits for beginners—are held in the "prince's chamber" of the fortress atop the hill, featuring small chamber groups (€32-40 plus €4 for the funicular, open seating after the first six more expensive rows; at 19:30, 20:00, or 20:30; doors open 30 minutes early, reserve at tel. 0662/825-858 or via www.salzburghighlights.at, pick up tickets at the door). The medieval-feeling chamber has windows overlooking the city, and the concert gives you a chance to enjoy the grand city view and a stroll through the castle courtyard. For €52, you can combine the concert with a four-course dinner (starts 2 hours before concert). Purists may object to hearing Baroque music in an incongruously Gothic setting.

### Concerts at the Mirabell Palace (Schlosskonzerte)
The nearly nightly chamber music concerts at the Mirabell Palace are performed in a lavish Baroque setting. They come with more sophisticated programs and better musicians than the fortress concerts...and Baroque music flying around a Baroque hall is a happy bird in the right cage (open seating after the first five pricier rows, €31-37, usually at 20:00—but check flier for times, doors open one hour ahead, tel. 0662/848-586, www.salzburger-schlosskonzerte.at).

### Mozart Dinner Concert
For those who'd like some classical music but would rather not sit through a concert, the elegant Stiftskeller St. Peter restaurant (see page 321) offers a traditional candlelit meal with Mozart's greatest hits performed by a string quartet and singers in historic cos-

tumes gavotting among the tables. In this elegant Baroque setting, tourists clap between movements and get three courses of food (from Mozart-era recipes) mixed with three 20-minute courses of crowd-pleasing music—structured much as such evenings were in Baroque-era times (€56, €9 discount for Mozart lovers who reserve direct and mention this book, music starts nightly May-Sept at 20:00, Oct-April at 19:00, arrive 30 minutes before that, dress is "smart casual," to reserve call 0662/828-695 or email office@skg.co.at, www.mozart-dinner-concert-salzburg.com).

## WEEKLY MUSICAL EVENTS
### Friday and Saturday: Mozart Piano Sonatas
These short (45-minute) and fairly inexpensive concerts in St. Peter's Abbey are ideal for families (€22, €11 for kids, €55 for a family of four, almost every Fri and Sat at 19:00 year-round, in the abbey's Romanesque Hall—a.k.a. Romanischer Saal, enter from inner courtyard 20 yards left of St. Peter's Church, mobile 0664-423-5645, www.agenturorpheus.at, then click on "Konzerte" and "Salzburg—Mozart Klaviersonaten").

### Sunday Morning: Free Brass Band Concerts
Traditional brass bands play in the Mirabell Gardens (May-Aug Sun at 10:30).

### Sunday Morning: Music at Mass
Each Sunday morning, three great churches offer a Mass, generally with glorious music. The **Salzburg Cathedral** is likely your best bet for fine music to worship by. The 10:00 service generally features a Mass written by a well-known composer performed by choir, organist, or other musicians. The worship service is often followed at 11:30 by a free organ concert (music program at www.kirchen.net/dommusik). Nearby (just outside Domplatz, with the pointy green spire), the **Franciscan Church** is the locals' choice and is enthusiastic about its musical Masses (at 9:00, www.franziskanerkirche-salzburg.at—click on "Programm"). **St. Peter's Church** sometimes has music (at 10:15, www.stift-stpeter.at—click on "Kirchen-musik," then "Jahresprogramm").

### Marionette Theater
Salzburg's much-loved marionette theater offers operas with spellbinding marionettes and recorded music. A troupe of 10 puppeteers brings to life the artfully created puppets at the end of their five-foot strings. The 180 performances a year alternate between *The Sound of Music* and various German-language operas (with handy superscripts in English). While the 300-plus-seat venue is forgettable, the marionettes enchant adults and children alike.

   **Cost and Hours:** €20-35, kids-€15, May-Sept nearly nightly at 19:30 plus some matinees, a few shows in Dec, none Oct-Nov or Jan-April, near Mozart's Residence at Schwarzstrasse 24, tel. 0662/872-406, www.marionetten.at.

### Salzburg Festival (Salzburger Festspiele)

From mid-July to the end of August, Salzburg hosts its famous Salzburg Festival, founded in 1920 to employ Vienna's musicians in the summer. This fun and festive time is crowded—a total of 200,000 tickets are sold annually—but there are usually plenty of beds (except for a few Aug weekends). Events take place primarily in three big halls: the Opera and Orchestra venues in the Festival House, and the Landestheater, where German-language plays are performed. Tickets for the big events are generally expensive (€50-600) and sell out well in advance (bookable from Jan). But many "go to the Salzburg Festival" by seeing smaller, non-festival events during the festival weeks. For these unofficial events, same-day tickets are normally available—ask at the TI. For specifics on this year's festival, visit www.salzburgfestival.at.

Music lovers in town during the festival without tickets (or money) can still enjoy **Festival Nights,** free videos of previous festival performances projected on a big screen on Kapitelplatz (behind the cathedral). It's a fun scene, with plenty of folding chairs and a food circus of temporary eateries (schedule at www.salzburg. info; search for "Festival Nights").

# Sleeping in Salzburg

I've listed the rates you'll typically find in May, June, the first half of July, September, and October. Rates rise significantly (20-30 percent) during the music festival (mid-July-Aug), during Advent (the four weeks leading up to Christmas, when street markets are at full blast), and around Easter. Rates are lower in the off-season. Many places charge 10 percent extra for a one-night stay.

## IN THE NEW TOWN, NORTH OF THE RIVER

These listings cluster around Linzer Gasse, a lively pedestrian shopping street that's a 15-minute walk or quick bus ride from the train station (for directions, see "Arrival in Salzburg," earlier) and a 10-minute walk to the Old Town. If you're coming from the Old Town, simply cross the main bridge (Staatsbrücke). Linzer Gasse is straight ahead. If driving, exit the highway at Salzburg-Nord, follow Vogelweiderstrasse straight to its end, and turn right. Parking is easy at the nearby Mirabell-Congress garage (€15/day, your hotel may be able to get you a €1-2 discount, Mirabellplatz).

**$$$ Altstadthotel Wolf-Dietrich,** around the corner from Linzer Gasse on pedestrians-only Wolf-Dietrich-Strasse, has 40

---

## Sleep Code

**Abbreviations**   (€1 = about $1.40, country code: 43, area code: 0662)
**S** = Single, **D** = Double/Twin, **T** = Triple, **Q** = Quad, **b** = bath-
room, **s** = shower only
**Price Rankings**
  **$$$**  **Higher Priced**—Most rooms €125 or more.
   **$$**  **Moderately Priced**—Most rooms between €75-125.
    **$**  **Lower Priced**—Most rooms €75 or less.
Unless otherwise noted, credit cards are accepted, break-
fast is included, Wi-Fi is generally free, and English is spoken.
Salzburg levies a hotel tax of €1 per person, per night, which
is generally not included in the rates I've quoted. Prices can
change without notice; verify current rates online or by email.
For the best prices, always book directly with the hotel.

---

well-located, tastefully plush rooms (half of them overlook St. Sebastian Cemetery; a third are in an annex across the street). Prices
include a huge breakfast spread and an afternoon *Kaffee-und-
Kuchen* snack (roughly Sb-€90, Db-€150, Tb-€175, rates vary with
demand, family deals, readers of this book who reserve direct get
a 10 percent discount on prevailing price—insist on this discount
deducted from whatever price is offered that day; non-smoking,
elevator, guest computer and Wi-Fi, annex rooms have air-con,
pool with loaner swimsuits, sauna, free DVD library, Wolf-Dietrich-Strasse 7, tel. 0662/871-275, www.salzburg-hotel.at, office@
salzburg-hotel.at).

**$$ Hotel Trumer Stube,** well-located three blocks from the
river just off Linzer Gasse, has 20 small, attractive rooms (Sb-
€72.50, Db-€120, Tb-€151, Qb-€177; email and ask for the best
Rick Steves cash-only rate, €7.50/person less if you skip breakfast;
non-smoking, elevator, Wi-Fi, look for the flower boxes at Berg-
strasse 6, tel. 0662/874-776, www.trumer-stube.at, info@trumer-
stube.at, Vivienne).

**$$ Hotel Krone 1512,** about five blocks from the river, offers
23 decent, simply furnished rooms in a building that dates to medi-
eval times. Back-facing rooms are quieter than the streetside ones.
Cheapskates can save by requesting the near-windowless "student"
double. Stay a while in their pleasant cliffside garden (Sb-€79,
Db-€108-122, Tb-€152, Qb-€198, €14/person less if you skip
breakfast—bakeries and cafés nearby, family deals, guests with this
book who reserve direct get about 8 percent off—plus another 4
percent if you pay with cash, elevator, guest computer and Wi-Fi,
Linzer Gasse 48, tel. 0662/872-300, www.krone1512.at, hotel@
krone1512.at, run by Ukrainian-Austrian-Canadian Niko).

**$$ Gästehaus im Priesterseminar Salzburg** occupies two

floors of a dormitory for theological students that have been turned into a superbly located hotel. The 47 high-ceilinged rooms ring the stately Baroque courtyard of a grand building. Each room has a Bible and a cross (and no TV), but guests are not required to be in a contemplative frame of mind (Sb-€60, Db-€106-120 depending on size, Db suite-€138, one-night stay-€4/person extra, 3-night minimum in July-Aug, elevator; guest computer, cable Internet, and Wi-Fi—must borrow router and leave deposit; kitchen, laundry facilities; reception closes Mon-Sat at 18:00, Sun at 15:00—arrange ahead if arriving later; Dreifaltigkeitsgasse 14, tel. 0662/8774-9510, www.gaestehaus-priesterseminar-salzburg.at, gaestehaus@priesterseminar.kirchen.net).

**$$ Hotel Schwarzes Rössl** is a university dorm that becomes a student-run hotel each July, August, and September. The location couldn't be handier. It looks like a normal hotel from the outside, and its 56 rooms, while a bit spartan, are as comfortable as a hotel on the inside (S-€60, Sb-€70, D-€88, Db-€106, Tb-€135, ask for Rick Steves discount, good breakfast, guest computer, Wi-Fi in common areas, no rooms rented Oct-June, just off Linzer Gasse at Priesterhausgasse 6, tel. 0662/874-426, www.academiahotels.at, schwarzes.roessl@academiahotels.at).

**$$ Institute St. Sebastian** is in a somewhat sterile but very clean historic building next to St. Sebastian Cemetery. From October through June, the institute houses female students from various Salzburg colleges and also rents 40 beds for travelers (men and women). From July through September, the students are gone, and they rent all 118 beds (including 20 twin rooms) to travelers. The building has spacious public areas, a roof garden, a piano that guests are welcome to play, and some of the best rooms and dorm beds in town for the money. The immaculate doubles come with modern baths and head-to-toe twin beds (S-€48, Sb-€53, D-€68, Db-€85, Tb-€105, Qb-€118, one-night stay-€3/person extra, elevator, non-smoking, Wi-Fi, self-service laundry-€4/load; reception closes at 21:00 or in the afternoon off-season; Linzer Gasse 41, enter through arch at #37, tel. 0662/871-386, www.st-sebastian-salzburg.at, office@st-sebastian-salzburg.at). Students like the €24 bunks in 4- to 10-bed dorms (free lockers). You'll find self-service kitchens on each floor (fridge space is free; request a key). If you need parking, request it when you book.

## On Rupertgasse

These two similar hotels are about five blocks farther from the river on Rupertgasse—a breeze for drivers but with more street noise than the places on Linzer Gasse. They're both modern and well-run, with free on-site parking, making them good values if you don't mind being a 15-20-minute walk or quick bus ride from the

SALZBURG

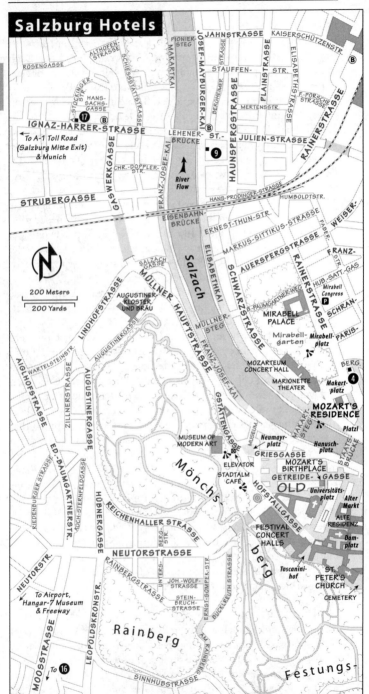

# Salzburg Hotels

JAHNSTRASSE

KAISERSCHÜTZENSTR.

ALTHOFENSTRASSE

ROSENGASSE

SCHIESSSTÄTTENSTRASSE

MAKARTKAI

PIONIER-STEG

JOSEF-MAYBURGER-KAI

STAUFFEN-STR.

BERGHEIMER

PLAINSTRASSE

ELISABETHSTRASSE

F.-PORSCHE-STRASSE

(B)

HANS-SACHS-GASSE

STOCKINGER GASSE

**17**

(B)

IGNAZ-HARRER-STRASSE

LEHENER-BRÜCKE

(B)

ST.-

MERTENSSTR.

RAINERSTRASSE

← A-1 Toll Road
(Salzburg Mitte Exit)
& Munich

CHR.-DOPPLER-STR.

FRANZ-JOSEF-KAI

■ **9**

HAUNSPERGSTRASSE

JULIEN-STRASSE

GASWERKGASSE

River
Flow

STRUBERGASSE

EISENBAHN-BRÜCKE

HANS-PRODINGER-STRASSE

HUMBOLDTSTR.

ERNEST-THUN-STR.

WEIBER-

N

SALZACH GASSE

MÜLLNER HAUPTSTRASSE

LINDHOFSTRASSE

ELISABETHKAI

Salzach

SCHWARZSTRASSE

MARKUS-SITTIKUS-STRASSE

AUERSPERGSTRASSE

RAINERSTRASSE

FABER-

FRANZ-

HUB.-SATT.-GAS.

200 Meters

200 Yards

AUGUSTINER-KLOSTER UND BRÄU

AUGUSTINERGASSE

E.-BAUMGARTNERWEG

Mirabell
Congress

P

SCHRAN-

PARIS-

AIGLHOFSTRASSE

WARTELSTEINSTR.

ZILLNERSTRASSE

AUGUSTINERGASSE

MÜLLNER-STEG

FRANZ-JOSEF-KAI

GSTÄTTENGASSE

MIRABELL
PALACE

Mirabell-garten

Mirabell-platz

MOZARTEUM
CONCERT HALL

MARIONETTE
THEATER

BERG.

Makart-platz

**4** ■

RIEDENBURGER STRASSE

ED.-BAUMGARTNERSTR.

HÜBNERGASSE

REICHENHALLER STRASSE

HOCH-STERNFELDGASSE

Mönchs-

MUSEUM OF
MODERN ART

MUSEUM STR.

Neumayr-platz

ELEVATOR

STADTALM
CAFÉ

GRIESGASSE

HOFSTALLGASSE

MAKART STEG

MOZART'S
RESIDENCE

Platzl

Hanusch-platz

STAATS-BRÜCKE

MOZART'S
BIRTHPLACE

GETREIDE- GASSE

OLD

Universitäts-platz

Alter
Markt

ALTE
RESIDENZ

NEUTORSTRASSE

RAINBERGSTRASSE

UNTERS-

JOH.-WOLF-STRASSE

STEIN-BRUCH-STRASSE

ERNST-SOMPEK-STR.

BUCKLREUTH STRASSE

AM RAINBER.

berg

FESTIVAL
CONCERT
HALLS

Toscanini-hof

Dom-platz

ST.
PETER'S
CHURCH

CEMETERY

NEUTORSTR.

← To Airport,
Hangar-7 Museum
& Freeway

MOOSSTRASSE

LEOPOLDSKRONSTR.

Rainberg

SINNHUBSTRASSE

To **16**

Festungs-

SALZBURG

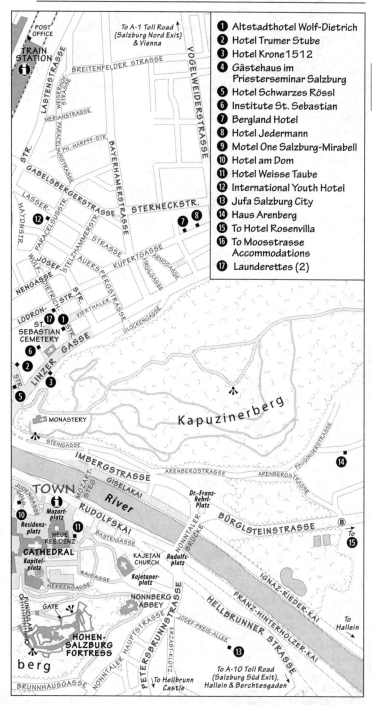

1 Altstadthotel Wolf-Dietrich
2 Hotel Trumer Stube
3 Hotel Krone 1512
4 Gästehaus im Priesterseminar Salzburg
5 Hotel Schwarzes Rössl
6 Institute St. Sebastian
7 Bergland Hotel
8 Hotel Jedermann
9 Motel One Salzburg-Mirabell
10 Hotel am Dom
11 Hotel Weisse Taube
12 International Youth Hotel
13 Jufa Salzburg City
14 Haus Arenberg
15 To Hotel Rosenvilla
16 To Moosstrasse Accommodations
17 Launderettes (2)

Old Town. From the station, take bus #2 to the Vogelweiderstrasse stop; from Hanuschplatz, take #4 to Grillparzerstrasse.

**$$ Bergland Hotel** is charming and classy, with 18 comfortable neo-rustic rooms. It's a modern building, spacious and solid (Sb-€65, Db-€95-105 depending on size, big Db suites-€130, non-smoking, elevator, pay guest computer, Wi-Fi, Rupertgasse 15, tel. 0662/872-318, www.berglandhotel.at, office@berglandhotel.at, Kuhn family).

**$$ Hotel Jedermann,** a few doors down, is simpler and larger. It's tastefully done and comfortable, with an artsy painted-concrete ambience, a backyard garden, and 30 rooms (Sb-€75, Db-€95, Tb-€120, Qb-€160, non-smoking, elevator, pay guest computer, cable Internet and Wi-Fi, Rupertgasse 25, tel. 0662/873-2410, www.hotel-jedermann.com, office@hotel-jedermann.com, Herr und Frau Gmachl).

### Near the Train Station

**$$ Motel One Salzburg-Mirabell** is an inexpensive chain hotel right along the river with 119 cookie-cutter rooms. It's six blocks (or a two-stop bus ride) from the train station, and a 15-minute riverside walk or short bus ride from the Old Town (Sb-€78, Db-€101, €7.50/person less if you skip breakfast, elevator, Wi-Fi, parking-€12/day, Elisabethkai 58, bus #1 or #2 from platform D at station to St.-Julien-Strasse—use underpass to cross road safely, tel. 0662/885-200, www.motel-one.com, salzburg-mirabell@motel-one.com).

### IN THE OLD TOWN

These two hotels are nicely located near Mozartplatz. While this area is car-restricted, your hotel can give you a code that lets you drive in to unload, pick up a map and parking instructions, and head for the €18-per-day garage in the mountain (punch the code into the gate near Mozartplatz). You can't drive into the narrow Goldgasse, but you can park to unload at the end of the street.

**$$$ Hotel am Dom,** on the narrow Goldgasse pedestrian street, offers 15 chic, upscale rooms, some with their original wood-beam ceilings. Manager Josef promises his best rates to readers of this book who reserve direct and pay cash (Sb-€110-130, standard Db-€130-180, "superior" Db-€150-200, rates vary with demand, air-con, non-smoking, elevator; guest computer, cable Internet, and Wi-Fi; Goldgasse 17, tel. 0662/842-765, www.hotelamdom.at, office@hotelamdom.at).

**$$$ Hotel Weisse Taube** has 30 comfortable rooms in a quiet dark-wood 14th-century building, well-located about a block off Mozartplatz (typically Sb-€99, Db with shower-€129-139, bigger Db with bath-€159, extra bed-€30-35, 10 percent discount with this book if you reserve directly with hotel and pay cash, elevator, Wi-Fi, tel. 0662/842-404, Kaigasse 9, www.weissetaube.at, hotel@weissetaube.at).

## HOSTELS

The Institute St. Sebastian, listed earlier, also has cheap dorm beds.

**$ International Youth Hotel,** a.k.a. the "Yo-Ho," is the most lively, handy, and American of Salzburg's hostels. This backpacker haven is a youthful and easygoing place that speaks English first; has cheap meals, 186 beds, lockers, tour discounts, and no curfew; plays *The Sound of Music* free daily at 19:00; runs a lively bar; and welcomes anyone of any age. The noisy atmosphere and lack of a curfew can make it hard to sleep (€18-21/person in 4- to 8-bed dorms, €21-22 in dorms with bathrooms, S-€40, D-€65, Ds-€75, T-€72, Q-€88, Qs-€93, includes sheets, breakfast-€3.50, pay guest computer, Wi-Fi, laundry-€4/load, 6 blocks from station toward Linzer Gasse and 6 blocks from river at Paracelsusstrasse 9, tel. 0662/879-649, www.yoho.at, office@yoho.at).

**$ Jufa Salzburg City,** quietly set amidst modern university buildings a short walk from the Old Town, is an upscale, privately run, 132-room "hostel" that actually has mostly double and quad rooms with very spartan furnishings. It has pleasant public spaces and offers lots of extras—including Ping-Pong, foosball, and a cafeteria with inexpensive meals—but the hotel-style rooms cost as much as those at better-located lodgings (bed in 8-person dorm-€22, Db-€110, Qb-€172, higher prices during festival, includes sheets, guest computer, Wi-Fi in common areas only, *The Sound of Music* plays daily at 20:00, laundry-€5/load, limited parking-€5/day, just around the east side of the castle hill at Josef-Preis-Allee 18; from train station, take bus #5 or #25 to the Justizgebäude stop, then continue one block past the bushy wall, cross Petersbrunnstrasse, find shady Josef-Preis-Allee, and walk a few minutes to the end—the hostel is the big orange/green building on the right; tel. 05/708-3613, www.jufa.eu/en, salzburg@jufa.eu).

## FOUR-STAR HOTELS IN RESIDENTIAL NEIGHBORHOODS AWAY FROM THE CENTER

If you want to pay a little extra for plush furnishings, spacious public spaces, generous balconies, gardens, and free parking—and don't mind a longish walk or bus ride to the Old Town—consider the following places. These two modern hotels are set near each other in a residential area. While not ideal for train travelers, drivers in need of no-stress comfort for a home base should consider these (see map on page 314).

**$$$ Haus Arenberg** rents 16 big, breezy rooms—most with generous balconies—in a modern, ranch-style mansion with a quiet garden. Though in one of Salzburg's toniest neighborhoods, with Porsches lining the narrow hillside lanes, it's relaxed and unpretentious. Figure a 15-minute downhill walk to the center of town (along atmospheric Steingasse) and 20 minutes back up, or take bus #6, #7, or #10 to the Volksgarten stop and hike five minutes uphill (Sb-€85, Db-€135, Tb-€159, Qb-€165, no elevator, Wi-Fi, library, electric bikes-€12/day, Blumensteinstrasse 8, tel. 0662/640-097, www.arenberg-salzburg.at, info@arenberg-salzburg.at, Leobacher family). If driving here, get detailed directions.

**$$$ Hotel Rosenvilla,** farther out than Haus Arenberg, offers 15 bright, attentively furnished rooms surrounded by a leafy garden, around the corner from a stop for the bus into town (Sb-€79, Db-€135, bigger Db-€145, Db suite-€168, no elevator, Wi-Fi, electric bikes-€12/day, Höfelgasse 4, tel. 0662/621-765, www.rosenvilla.com, hotel@rosenvilla.com, take bus #7 from Hanuschplatz to the Finanzamt stop, Stefanie).

## PENSIONS ON MOOSSTRASSE

These are generally roomy and comfortable, and come with a good breakfast, free parking, farm-fresh scents, and mountains in the distance. They offer much more for your money than lodgings in town. Each is mere steps from a bus stop and the 15-minute ride from town is easy: with a €3.40 24-hour transit pass *(24-Stunden-Karte)* and frequent service, it shouldn't keep you away (see map on page 314). I've listed prices for two nights or more—if staying only one night, expect a small surcharge.

Moosstrasse runs southwest from the Old Town (behind the Mönchsberg). It was laid out a century ago through reclaimed marshland and lined with farm lots on each side. Some farm families continue to work the land, while others concentrate on offering rooms.

Handy bus #21 connects Moosstrasse to the center frequently (Mon-Fri 4/hour until 19:00, Sat 4/hour until 17:00, evenings and Sun 2/hour, last bus leaves downtown around 23:00). To get to these pensions from the train station, take any bus heading toward the center to Makartplatz, where you'll change to #21. If you're coming from the Old Town, catch bus #21 from Hanuschplatz, just downstream of the Staatsbrücke bridge, by the Fisch Krieg Restaurant. Buy your ticket from the streetside machine and punch it when you board the bus. The stop you get off at for each place is included in the listings below. Follow along with the stops on the map in the bus and press the button as soon as you hear yours announced—the bus only stops when requested.

If you're driving from the center, go through the tunnel, continue straight on Neutorstrasse, and take the fourth left onto

Moosstrasse. Drivers exit the autobahn at *Süd* and then head in the direction of *Grodig*.

Reiterhof, at Moosstrasse 151 by the Hammerauer Strasse bus stop, is a popular, reasonably priced restaurant near these listings.

**$$ Pension Bloberger Hof,** more a hotel than a pension, is comfortable and friendly, with a peaceful, rural location and 20 farmer-plush, good-value rooms. Inge and her daughter Sylvia offer a 10 percent discount to those who have this book, reserve direct, and pay cash (Sb-€70-80, Db-€85, big new Db with balcony-€110, Db suite-€140, extra bed-€20, 10 percent extra for one-night stays, dinner for guests available Mon-Sat 18:00-21:00, no dinner on Sun, family apartment with kitchen, non-smoking, guest computer and Wi-Fi, free loaner bikes, free station pickup if staying 3 nights, Hammerauer Strasse 4, bus stop: Hammerauer Strasse, tel. 0662/830-227, www.bloberger hof.at, office@blobergerhof.at).

**$ Frau Ballwein** offers eleven cozy, charming, and fresh rooms in a delightful, family-friendly farmhouse. Some rooms have balconies with an intoxicating view (Sb-€47, Db-€63, Tb-€85, Qb-€95, 2-bedroom apartment for up to 5 people-€115, no surcharge for one-night stays, cash only, farm-fresh breakfasts amid her hanging teapot collection, non-smoking, Wi-Fi, 2 free loaner bikes, Moosstrasse 69a, bus stop: Gsengerweg, tel. 0662/824-029, www.haus-ballwein.at, haus.ballwein@gmx.net).

**$ Helga Bankhammer** rents four inexpensive, nondescript rooms in a farmhouse, with a real dairy farm out back (D-€52, Db-€54, no surcharge for one-night stays, family deals, non-smoking, Wi-Fi, laundry-about €7/load, Moosstrasse 77, bus stop: Marienbad, tel. 0662/830-067, www.privatzimmer.at/helga.bankhammer, bankhammer@aon.at).

**$ Haus am Moos** has nine nicely furnished rooms in a relaxed country atmosphere, with a garden, swimming pool, breakfast buffet with mountain views, and a tiny private chapel (Sb-€32, Db-€60, extra bed-€15, family rooms, no surcharge for one-night stays, non-smoking, guest computer and Wi-Fi, Moosstrasse 186a, bus stop: Lehrbauhof, tel. 0662/824-921, www.ammoos.at, ammoos186a@yahoo.de, Strasser family).

**$ Haus Steiner**'s six rooms are straightforward and quiet, with older modern furnishings; there's a minimum two-night stay (Sb-€36, Db-€60, Tb-€90, non-smoking, guest computer and Wi-Fi, Moosstrasse 156c, bus stop: Hammerauer Strasse, tel. 0662/830-031, www.haussteiner.com, info@haussteiner.com, Rosemarie Steiner).

# Eating in Salzburg

**SALZBURG**

## IN THE OLD TOWN

**Gasthaus zum Wilden Mann** is *the* place if the weather's bad and you're in the mood for a hearty, cheap meal at a shared table in one well-antlered (and non-smoking) room. Notice the century-old flood photos on the wall. For a quick lunch, get the *Bauernschmaus,* a mountain of dumplings, kraut, and peasant's meats (€13). While they have a few outdoor tables, the atmosphere is all indoors, and the menu is more geared to cold weather. Owner Robert—who runs the restaurant with Schwarzenegger-like energy—enjoys fostering a convivial ambience and encouraging strangers to share tables. I simply love this place (€10-14 main courses, specials posted on the wall, kitchen open Mon-Sat 11:00-21:00, closed Sun, 2 minutes from Mozart's Birthplace, enter from Getreidegasse 22 or Griesgasse 17, tel. 0662/841-787, www.wildermann.co.at).

**St. Paul's Stub'n Beer Garden** is tucked secretly away under the fortress with a decidedly untouristy atmosphere. The food is better than at beer halls, and a young, bohemian-chic clientele fills its two troll-like rooms and its idyllic tree-shaded garden. *Kasnock'n* is a tasty dish of *Spätzle* with cheese served in an iron pan. It includes a side salad for €9 (€10 with ham)—it's enough for two. Reservations are smart (€9-17 main courses, Mon-Sat 17:00-22:00, open later for drinks only, closed Sun, Herrengasse 16, tel. 0662/843-220, http://paulstubm.blogspot.com, Bernard).

**Zirkelwirt** serves reasonably priced Austrian standards (schnitzel, goulash, *Spätzle* with kraut) and big €8-9 salads in an updated *Gasthaus* dining room and exotic plant-screened terrace. Just a block off Mozartplatz, it's a world away from the tourism of Old Town (€9-13 main courses, daily 11:00-24:00, Pfeifergasse 14, tel. 0662/842-796, www.zumzirkelwirt.at).

**Saran Essbar,** in the middle of Old Town, is the product of hardworking Mr. Saran (from the Punjab), who cooks and serves with his heart. This delightful little eatery casts a rich orange glow under medieval vaults. Its fun menu is small (Mr. Saran is committed to both freshness and value), mixing Austrian (great schnitzel and strudel) and South Asian cuisine (€12-17 main courses, vegetarian options, cash only, no reservations, daily 11:00-15:00 & 17:00-22:00, longer hours during festival, a block off Mozartplatz at Judengasse 10, tel. 0662/846-628, www.saranessbar.at).

**Café Tomaselli** (with its Kiosk annex and terrace seating across the way) has long been Salzburg's top place to see and be seen. While pricey, it is good for lingering and people-watching. Tomaselli serves light meals and lots of drinks, keeps long hours daily, and has fine seating on the square, a view terrace upstairs, and indoor tables. Despite its fancy inlaid wood paneling, 19th-century portraits, and chandeliers, it's surprisingly low-key (€4-8 light meals, daily 7:00-20:00, until 22:00 during festival, Alter Markt 9, tel. 0662/844-488, www.tomaselli.at).

**Vietnam Pho 18,** fragrant with fresh cilantro, is where the Nguyen family dishes up Vietnamese noodle soups and other Asian standards in a six-table restaurant a long block from the cathedral (€7-9 main courses, eat in or take out, Sat-Thu 11:30-15:00 & 17:00-20:00, Fri 11:30-15:00, Kapitelgasse 11, mobile 0660-257-5588).

**Stiftskeller St. Peter** has been in business for more than 1,000 years—it was mentioned in the biography of Charlemagne. These days it's classy and high-end touristy, serving uninspired traditional Austrian cuisine (€18-27 main courses, kitchen open daily 11:30-22:00 or later, indoor/outdoor seating, next to St. Peter's Church at foot of Mönchsberg, tel. 0662/841-268, www.haslauer.at). They host the Mozart Dinner Concert described on page 309.

## Youthful Cafés at the West End of the Old Town

**Bar Club Café Republic,** a hip hangout for local young people opposite the base of the Mönchsberg elevator, feels like a theater lobby during intermission. It serves good food both outdoors and in (with both smoking- and non-smoking rooms inside). It's ideal if you want something mod, untouristy, and un-wursty (Asian and international menu, €10-16 main courses, lots of hard drinks, open daily 8:00-late, trendy breakfasts served 8:00-18:00, Sun brunch with live music 10:00-13:00, music with a DJ Fri and Sat from 23:00, salsa dance club Tue night from 21:00—no cover, Anton-Neumayr-Platz 2, tel. 0662/841-613, www.republic-cafe.at).

**Afro Cafe,** between Getreidegasse and the Mönchsberg elevator, is non-smoking and a hit with local students. It serves tea, coffee, cocktails, and tasty food with a dose of '70s funk and a healthy sense of humor. The food isn't really African, but does give a nod to the continent, as do the murals and the leopard-spot menus (€8.20 weekday lunches, €12-19 main courses, Mon-Sat 9:00-24:00, closed Sun, between Getreidegasse and cliff face at Bürgerspitalplatz 5, tel. 0662/844-888, www.afrocafe.at).

**Carpe Diem** is a project by the local Donald Trump, Red Bull tycoon Dietrich Mateschitz. Salzburg's beautiful people, fueled by Red Bull, present themselves here in the chic ground-floor café and trendy "lifestyle bar" (smoking allowed), which serves quality cocktails and fine finger food in cones (café open daily 8:30-24:00). Upstairs is an expensive, non-smoking restaurant boasting a Michelin star (€26-37 main courses, €4.50 cover charge, €19.50 lunch special, restaurant open Mon-Sat 12:00-14:00 & 18:30-22:00, closed Sun; Getreidegasse 50, tel. 0662/848-800, www. carpediemfinestfingerfood.com).

SALZBURG

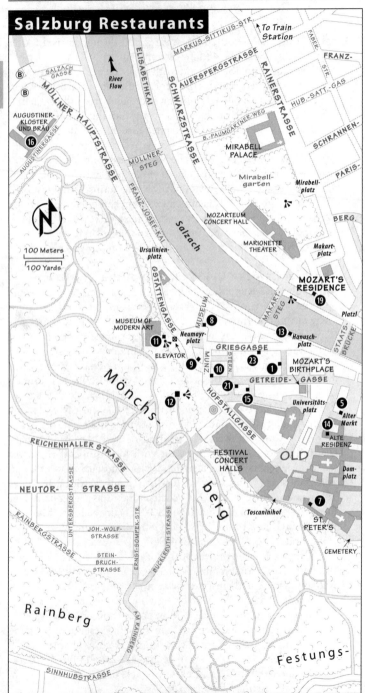

# Salzburg Restaurants

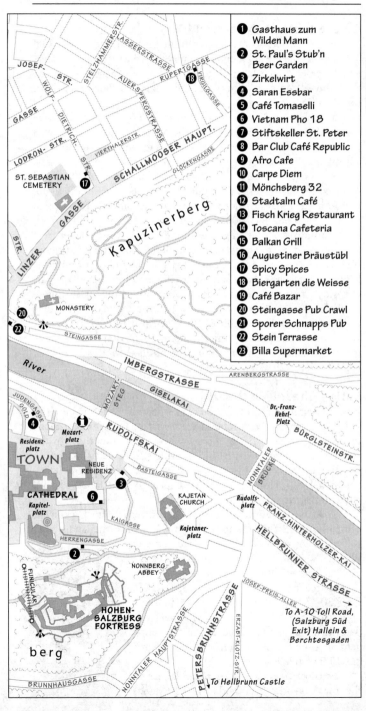

1. Gasthaus zum Wilden Mann
2. St. Paul's Stub'n Beer Garden
3. Zirkelwirt
4. Saran Essbar
5. Café Tomaselli
6. Vietnam Pho 18
7. Stiftskeller St. Peter
8. Bar Club Café Republic
9. Afro Cafe
10. Carpe Diem
11. Mönchsberg 32
12. Stadtalm Café
13. Fisch Krieg Restaurant
14. Toscana Cafeteria
15. Balkan Grill
16. Augustiner Bräustübl
17. Spicy Spices
18. Biergarten die Weisse
19. Café Bazar
20. Steingasse Pub Crawl
21. Sporer Schnapps Pub
22. Stein Terrasse
23. Billa Supermarket

SALZBURG

## On the Cliffs Above the Old Town

Riding the Mönchsberg elevator from the west end of the Old Town up to the clifftop deposits you near two very different eateries: the chic Mönchsberg 32 at the modern art museum, and the Stadtalm Café at the funky old mountaineers' hut—each with commanding city views.

**Mönchsberg 32** is a sleek, modern café/bar/restaurant overlooking Salzburg from the top of the Mönchsberg elevator. Even if you're not hiking anywhere, this makes for a great place to enjoy a drink and the view (€5 coffee or ice cream, €22-32 main courses, €3 cover charge, €14 lunch special, Tue-Sun 9:00-24:00, closed Mon except during festival, popular breakfasts served until 16:00, buy a one-way elevator ticket—they give customers a free pass to descend, tel. 0662/841-000. www.m32.at).

**Stadtalm Café** sits high above the Old Town on the edge of the cliff, with cheap prices, good traditional food, and great views. Nearby are the remnants of the old city wall. If hiking across the Mönchsberg, make this a stop (€10-12 main dishes, €9-10 salads, cliff-side garden seating or cozy-mountain-hut indoor seating—one indoor view table is booked for a decade of New Year's celebrations, daily May-Sept 10:00-22:00, Oct-April 10:00-18:00, hours are weather-dependent, 5 minutes from top of Mönchsberg elevator, also reachable by stairs from Toscaninihof, Mönchsberg 19C, tel. 0662/841-729, www.stadtalm.at, Peter).

## Eating Cheaply in the Old Town

**Fisch Krieg Restaurant,** on the river where the fishermen used to sell their catch, is a great value. They serve fast, fresh, and inexpensive fish in a casual dining room—where trees grow through the ceiling—as well as great riverside seating (€2.50-€3 fishwiches to go, €8-9 self-serve main courses, salad bar, Mon-Fri 8:30-18:30, Sat 8:30-13:00, closed Sun, Hanuschplatz 4, tel. 0662/843-732, www.fisch-krieg.at).

**Toscana Cafeteria Mensa** is the university lunch canteen, very basic but fast and cheap—with drab indoor seating and a great courtyard for good weather. Choose between two daily soup- and main-course specials, each around €5-6 and one always meatless; there's free tap water (Mon-Thu 8:30-17:00, Fri 8:30-15:00, hot meals served 11:30-13:30 only, closed Sat-Sun, closed early Aug-mid-Sept, behind the Old Residenz, in the courtyard opposite Sigmund-Haffner-Gasse 16, tel. 0662/8044-6909).

**Sausage stands** *(Würstelstände)* serve the town's favorite "fast food." The best stands (like those on Universitätsplatz) use the same boiling water all day, which gives the weenies more flavor. For a list of helpful terms, see page 485. The 60-year-old **Balkan Grill,** run by chatty Frau Ebner, is a Salzburg institution, selling just one type of spicy sausage—*Bosna*—with your choice of toppings (€3.40; survey the five options—described in English—and choose a number; takeout only, steady and sturdy local crowd, Mon-Sat 11:00-19:00, Sun 15:00-19:00, hours vary with demand, Jan-Feb closed Sun, hiding down the tunnel at Getreidegasse 33 across from Eisgrotte).

*Picnics:* Picnickers will appreciate the well-stocked **Billa supermarket** at Griesgasse 19a, next to the Hanuschplatz bus stop (Mon-Fri 7:15-19:30, Sat 7:15-18:00, Sun 11:00-15:00). The smaller **Spar supermarket** in the train station is open long hours (Mon-Sat 6:00-23:00, Sun 8:00-23:00). The bustling morning **produce market** (Mon-Sat, closed Sun) on Universitätsplatz, behind Mozart's Birthplace, is fun, but expensive.

## AWAY FROM THE CENTER

**Augustiner Bräustübl,** a huge 1,000-seat beer garden within a monk-run brewery in the Kloster Mülln, is rustic and raw. On busy nights, it's like a Munich beer hall with no music but the volume turned up. When it's cool outside, enjoy a historic indoor setting in any of several beer-sloshed and smoke-stained halls (one of which is still for smokers). On balmy evenings, it's like a Renoir painting—but with beer breath and cigarette smoke—outdoors under chestnut trees. Local students mix with tourists eating hearty slabs of grilled meat with their fingers or cold meals from the self-serve picnic counter, while children frolic on the playground kegs. For your beer: Pick up a half-liter or full-liter mug, pay the lady (*schank* means self-serve price, *bedienung* is the price with waiter service), wash your mug, give Mr. Keg your receipt and empty mug, and you will be made happy. Waiters only bring beer; they don't bring food—instead, go up the stairs, survey the hallway of deli counters, grab a tray, and assemble your own meal (or, as long as you buy a drink, you can bring in a picnic—many do). Classic pretzels from the bakery and spiraled, salty radishes make great beer even better. Locals agree that the hot food here is not as good as the beer. Stick with the freshly cooked meat dishes: I made the mistake of choosing schnitzel which was reheated in the microwave. For dessert—after a visit to the strudel kiosk—enjoy the incomparable floodlit view of old Salzburg from the nearby Müllnersteg pedestrian bridge and a riverside stroll home (daily 15:00-23:00, Augustinergasse 4, tel. 0662/431-246, www.augustinerbier.at).

**Getting There:** It's about a 15-minute walk along the river (with the river on your right) from the Old Town side of the Staatsbrücke bridge. After passing the Müllnersteg pedestrian bridge, just after Café am Kai, follow the stairs up to a busy street, and cross it. From here, either continue up more stairs into the trees and around the small church (for a scenic approach to the monastery), or stick to the sidewalk as it curves around to Augustinergasse. Either way, your goal is the huge yellow building. Don't be fooled by second-rate gardens serving the same beer nearby. You can also take a bus from Hanuschplatz (#7, #8, #21, #24, #27, or #28) two stops to the Landeskrankenhaus stop, right in front of the beer garden.

## NORTH OF THE RIVER, NEAR LINZER GASSE HOTELS

**Spicy Spices** is a trippy vegetarian-Indian restaurant where Suresh Syal (a.k.a. "Mr. Spicy") serves tasty curry and rice, samosas, organic salads, vegan soups, and fresh juices. It's a *namaste* kind of place, where everything's proudly organic (€7.50 specials served all day, €9 with soup or salad, €0.50 extra for takeout—refunded if you return the container, Mon-Fri 10:30-21:30, Sat-Sun 12:00-21:30, Wolf-Dietrich-Strasse 1, tel. 0662/870-712).

**Biergarten die Weisse,** close to the hotels on Rupertgasse and away from the tourists, is a longtime hit with the natives. If a beer hall can be happening, this one—modern yet with antlers—is it. Their famously good beer is made right there; favorites include their fizzy wheat beer (Die Weisse Original) and their seasonal beers (ask what's on offer). Enjoy the beer with their good, cheap traditional food in the great garden seating, or in the wide variety of indoor rooms—sports bar, young and noisy, or older and more elegant (€10-14 main courses, Mon-Sat 10:00-24:00, closed Sun, Rupertgasse 10, bus #2 to Bayerhamerstrasse or #4 to Grillparzerstrasse, tel. 0662/872-246, www.dieweisse.at).

**Café Bazar,** overlooking the river between the Mirabell Gardens and the Staatsbrücke bridge, is as close as you'll get to a Vienna coffee house in Salzburg. Their outdoor terrace is a classy spot for a drink with an Old-Town-and-castle view (reasonable prices, light meals, Mon-Sat 7:30-23:00, Sun 9:00-18:00, Oct-May closes Mon-Sat at 19:30, Schwarzstrasse 3, tel. 0662/874-278).

## Steingasse Pub Crawl

For a fun post-concert activity, drop in on a couple of atmospheric bars along medieval Steingasse (described on page 303). This is a local and hip scene—yet is accessible to older tourists: dark bars filled with well-dressed Salzburgers lazily smoking cigarettes and talking philosophy to laid-back tunes (no hip-hop). These four places are all within about 100 yards of each other. Start at the Linzer Gasse end of Steingasse. As they are quite different, survey all before choosing your spot (all open until the wee hours). Most don't serve food, but **Reyna,** a convenient four-table pizzeria and Döner Kebab shop at #3, stays open late.

**Pepe Cocktail Bar,** with Mexican decor and Latin music, serves cocktails and nachos (Wed-Sun 19:00-until late, closed Mon-Tue, live DJs on Sat, Steingasse 3, tel. 0662/873-662, www. pepe-cocktailbar.at).

**Saiten Sprung** wins the "Best Atmosphere" award. The door is kept closed to keep out the crude and rowdy. Just ring the bell and enter its hellish interior—lots of stone and red decor, with mountains of melted wax beneath age-old candlesticks and an ambience of classic '70s and '80s music. Stelios, who speaks English with Greek charm, serves cocktails and fine wine, though no food (Mon-Sat 21:00-until late, closed Sun except in Dec, Steingasse 11, tel. 0662/881-377).

**Fridrich,** two doors down, is an intimate little place under an 11th-century vault, with lots of mirrors and a silver ceiling fan. Bernd Fridrich is famous for his martinis and passionate about Austrian wines, and has a tattered collection of vinyl that seems hell-bent on keeping the 1970s alive. Their Yolanda cocktail (grapefruit and vodka) is a favorite. He and his partner Ferdinand serve little dishes designed to complement the focus on socializing and drinking, though their €13 "little of everything dish" can be a meal for two (€6-13 appetizers, Thu-Tue from 18:00, closed Wed except during festival, Steingasse 15, tel. 0662/876-218, www. gastlokal-fridrich.at).

**Selim's Bar,** with cozy seating both inside and out, has a cool, conversation-friendly atmosphere with mellow music. A few years back, Tom Cruise and Cameron Diaz filmed a movie scene here. Gentlemanly Selim, who came here long ago from Algeria, also works as a dance instructor (no food, Mon-Sat 18:00-late, also open Sun in July-Aug and Dec, across street from cinema at Steingasse 10, mobile 0664-433-8447).

# Salzburg Connections

## BY TRAIN

Salzburg's train station, located so close to the German border, is covered not just by Austrian railpasses, but German ones as well—including the Bayern-Ticket (see page 388). Deutsche Bahn (German Railway) ticket machines at the Salzburg train station make it easy to buy tickets to German destinations.

**From Salzburg by Train to: Berchtesgaden** (roughly hourly, 1.5 hours, change in Freilassing, faster and prettier by bus—see "Getting There" in the Berchtesgaden chapter), **Füssen** (roughly hourly, 4 hours on fast trains, 5 hours on slow trains eligible for Bayern-Ticket, change in Munich and sometimes in Buchloe), **Re-**

utte (hourly, 5 hours, change in Augsburg and Kempten, or in Munich and Garmisch), **Hallstatt** (every 30-90 minutes, 50 minutes to Attnang-Puchheim, short wait, then 1.5 hours to Hallstatt; also works well by bus—see below), **Innsbruck** (hourly, 2 hours), **Vienna** (3/hour, 2.5-3 hours), **Melk** (almost hourly, 2.5 hours, transfer in Amstetten), **Munich** (2/hour, 1.5 hours on fast trains, 2 hours on slower trains eligible for Bayern-Ticket), **Frankfurt** (4/day direct, 5.75 hours), **Ljubljana** (3/day, 4.5 hours, some with change in Villach), **Prague** (4/day, 6.25 hours with change in Linz or 7.5 hours with change in Landshut), **Venice** (5/day, 6-8 hours, change in Innsbruck or Villach, short night train option). Austrian train info: tel. 051-717 (to get an operator, dial 2, then 2), from Germany call 00-43-51-717, www.oebb.at. German train info: tel. 0180-599-6633, from Austria call 00-49-180-599-6633, www.bahn.com.

## BY BUS

To reach **Berchtesgaden,** bus #840 is easier than the train (about hourly Mon-Fri, 6-8/day Sat-Sun, 45 minutes, buses leave from platform G across street from Salzburg train station and also stop in Mirabellplatz and near Mozartplatz).

The bus trip to **Hallstatt** via Bad Ischl is cheaper, more scenic (with views of the Wolfgangsee), and only slightly slower than the train via Attnang-Puchheim—but the bus trip isn't covered by rail passes (bus #150 to Bad Ischl—Mon-Fri nearly hourly, Sat-Sun every 1-2 hours, 1.5 hours, leaves from platform F outside Salzburg train station, also stops at Mirabellplatz and Hofwirt, tel. 0810-222-333, www.postbus.at; at Bad Ischl station, change to the train—20-minute ride to Hallstatt, then ride the boat across the lake—or continue by bus to the Lahn section of Hallstatt with a change in Gosaumühle).

## ROUTE TIPS FOR DRIVERS

**From Salzburg to Innsbruck:** To leave town driving west, go through the Mönchsberg tunnel and follow blue *A-1* signs for Munich. It's 1.5 hours from Salzburg to Innsbruck.

**From Salzburg to Hallstatt:** To avoid tolls, stick to the most direct route (B-158 via St. Gilgen). If you're in a hurry, get on the Munich-Vienna autobahn (follow blue A-1 signs, toll sticker required), head for Vienna, exit at Thalgau (#274), and follow signs to Hof, Fuschl, and St. Gilgen. The Salzburg-Hallstatt road passes two luge rides (see Hallstatt chapter), St. Gilgen (pleasant but touristy), and Bad Ischl (the center of the Salzkammergut, with a spa, the emperor's villa if you need a Habsburg history fix, and a good TI, tel. 06132/277-570).

# BERCHTESGADEN, GERMANY

This alpine ski region, just across the border from Salzburg in a finger of German territory that pokes south into Austria, is famous for its fjord-like lake and its mountaintop Nazi retreat. Long before its association with Hitler, Berchtesgaden (BERKH-tehs-gah-dehn) was one of the classic Romantic corners of Germany. In fact, Hitler's propagandists capitalized on the Führer's love of this region to establish the notion that the native Austrian was truly German at heart. Today visitors cruise up the romantic Königssee to get in touch with the soul of Bavarian Romanticism; ride a bus up to Hitler's mountain retreat (5,500 feet); see the remains of the Nazis' elaborate last-ditch bunkers; ride an old miners' train into the mountain to learn all about salt mining; and hike along a secluded gorge to a high waterfall.

Remote little Berchtesgaden (pop. 7,500) can be inundated with Germans during peak season, when you may find yourself in a traffic jam of tourists desperately trying to turn their money into fun.

## GETTING THERE

Berchtesgaden is only 15 miles from Salzburg. The quickest way there from Salzburg is by bus #840 from the Salzburg train station (runs about hourly Mon-Fri, 6-8/day Sat-Sun, usually at :15 past the hour, 45 minutes, buy tickets from driver, €9.80 *Tageskarte* day pass covers your round trip plus most local buses in Berchtesgaden—except bus #849 up to the Eagle's Nest, last bus back leaves Berchtesgaden at 18:15; check schedules at www.svv-info.at—click "Timetables," then under "Find a timetable" select "Timetable book page," then enter "840"). On my last visit, bus #840 left from platform G across the street from the Salzburg train station (alongside the building with the H&M and Müller shops; as you exit the station's front door, go right). You can also catch bus #840 from the middle of Salzburg—after leaving the station, it stops a few minutes later on Mirabellplatz, and then in Salzburg's Old Town (on Rudolfskai, near Mozartplatz).

You can also get to Berchtesgaden from Salzburg by train via Freilassing, but it takes twice as long as the bus and isn't as scenic. The train is an option, though, if you need to get between Salzburg and Berchtesgaden in the evening or early morning, when no buses run.

## PLANNING YOUR TIME

The Nazi and Hitler-related sites outside Berchtesgaden are the town's main draw and merit a half-day to see. David and Christine Harper's tour of the sites is a good value and worth planning around (afternoons only, see "Tours in Berchtesgaden").

To do the Nazi sites on your own by bus, try this plan (confirm times in advance): 9:15—depart Salzburg on bus #840; 10:00—arrive Berchtesgaden station, look at murals in main hall; 10:15—bus #838 departs for Obersalzberg Documentation Center, arrives 10:27, visit bunkers and museum; 11:50—ride bus #849 from Documentation Center up to Eagle's Nest, look around and eat lunch; 13:30—take bus #849 down from Eagle's Nest; 14:14—ride bus #838 from Documentation Center to Berchtesgaden station. You could return to Salzburg on the 15:15 bus, or stay in Berchtesgaden to visit other attractions. On weekdays, consider an earlier start, leaving Salzburg on the 8:15 bus.

If you have time for more than the Nazi sites, Berchtesgaden also has tourable salt mines (similar to the ones at Hallein—see page 307) and a romantic, pristine lake called Königssee (extremely popular with less-adventurous Germans). Visiting either can take up to a half-day. While combining either of these with the Nazi sites is easy for drivers, it's challenging for those coming by public transport. Bus travelers wanting to fill up the rest of the day might be happier spending an hour walking through Berchtesgaden's Old Town, or going for a short hike in the Almbach Gorge (described later).

If you're visiting Berchtesgaden on your way between Salzburg and points in Germany, you can leave luggage in lockers at the Berchtesgaden train station during your visit.

# Orientation to Berchtesgaden

Berchtesgaden's train station is worth a stop for its luggage lockers (along the train platform), WC (free, also near platform), and history (specifically, its vintage 1937 Nazi architecture and the murals in the main hall). The oversized station was built to accommodate (and intimidate) the hordes of Hitler fans who flocked here in hopes of seeing the Führer. The building next to the station, just beyond the round tower, was Hitler's own V.I.P. reception area.

Berchtesgaden's central bus terminal (ZOB) is just in front of the train station. There are bakeries and a few forgettable restaurants nearby (consider bringing a picnic). The old center of Berchtesgaden, bypassed by most tourists, is up the hill behind the station (use the bridge over the tracks).

## TOURIST INFORMATION

The TI is on the other side of the roundabout from the train station, in the yellow building with green shutters (mid-June-Sept Mon-Fri 8:30-18:00, Sat 9:00-17:00, Sun 9:00-15:00; Oct-mid-June Mon-Fri 8:30-17:00, Sat 9:00-12:00, closed Sun; German tel. 08652/9670, from Austria call 00-49-8652-9670, www.berchtesgadener-land.info). Pick up a local map, and consider the 30-page local-bus schedule *(Fahrplan,* €0.30) if you'll be hopping more than one bus.

## GETTING AROUND BERCHTESGADEN

None of the sights I list are within easy walking distance from the station, but they're all connected by convenient local buses, which use the station as a hub (all these buses—except the special bus #849 between the Obersalzberg Documentation Center and the Eagle's Nest chalet—are free with the *Tageskarte* day pass from Salzburg; timetables at www.rvo-bus.de, or call 08652/94480). You'll want to note departure times and frequencies while still at the station, or pick up a schedule at the TI.

From the train station, buses #840 (the same line as the bus from Salzburg) and #837 go to the salt mines (a 20-minute walk otherwise). Bus #840 also goes to the Almbach Gorge. Bus #838 goes to the Obersalzberg Documentation Center, and bus #841 goes to the Königssee.

# Tours in Berchtesgaden

### Eagle's Nest Historical Tours

For 20 years, David and Christine Harper—who rightly consider this visit more an educational opportunity than simple sightseeing—have organized thoughtful tours of the Hitler-related sites near Berchtesgaden. Their bus tours, usually led by native English speakers, depart from the TI, opposite the Berchtesgaden train station. Tours start by driving through the remains of the Nazis' Obersalzberg complex, then visit the bunkers underneath the Documentation Center, and end with a guided visit to the Eagle's Nest (€53/person, €1 discount with this book, English only, daily

# Berchtesgaden and Nearby

To Vienna

To Vienna

AUTOBAHN  A-1

To Munich

Freilassing

2 Kilometers

2 Miles

TRAIN STATION

A-1

158

A-8

Salzburg

To Salzkammergut & Hallstatt

20

AUSTRIA

HELLBRUNN CASTLE

Untersberg

A-10

SALZBURG SÜD EXIT

Bad Reichenhall

21

305

Bus #840 Between Salzburg & Berchtesgaden

Hallein

GERMANY

Dürrnberg

ALMBACH GORGE

SALT MINE

20

Oberau

305

Bus #840 / 837 to Salt Mines

SALT MINES

Unterau

Ober-salzberg

NAZI DOCUMENTATION CENTER

Berchtesgaden

Bus #838

Kehlstein

A-10

Bus #841

Königssee

Shuttle Bus #849 Only

HITLER'S EAGLE'S NEST

Watzmann

Königssee

To Villach (Austria), Italy & Slovenia

St. Bartholomä

at 13:15 mid-May–late Oct, 4 hours, 30 people maximum, reservations strongly recommended, private tours available, German tel. 08652/64971, from Austria call 00-49-8652-64971, www.eagles-nest-tours.com). While the price is €53, your actual cost for the guiding is only about €26, as the tour takes care of your transport and admissions, not to mention relieving you of having to figure out the local buses up to Obersalzberg. Coming from Salzburg, you can take the 10:15 or 11:15 bus to Berchtesgaden, eat a picnic lunch, take the tour, then return on the 18:15 bus from Berchtesgaden, which gets you back to Salzburg 45 minutes later. If you're visiting near the beginning or end of the season, be aware that tours will be canceled if it's snowing at the Eagle's Nest (as that makes the twisty, precipitous mountain road too dangerous to drive). David and Christine also arrange off-season tours, though the Eagle's Nest isn't open for visitors in winter (€120/up to 4 people; see website for details).

If you'd like to use the morning (before the tour) to sightsee in and around Berchtesgaden, here are two good plans. One is to leave Salzburg on the 8:15 bus (Mon-Fri only), arrive at the salt mines as they open at 9:00 (when there's no line), see the mines, then take the bus or walk (either along the river or through the old town) up to the TI, where the Harpers' tour begins. The other is to leave Salzburg on the 8:15 or 9:15 bus, get off at the Kugelmühle stop to hike the Almbachklamm, then continue on a later bus, arriving in Berchtesgaden at 12:00 or 13:00. Bringing a picnic isn't essential, but it beats a rushed restaurant lunch.

### Bus Tours from Salzburg

While Salzburg-based tour companies (including Bob's Special Tours, www.bobstours.com, and Panorama tours, www.panoramatours.com) offer half- and full-day tours to Berchtesgaden, I don't recommend them except as a last resort. They take you to (but not into) the sights described here—meaning that you pay the tour price of €48-96 for the same transport that you can buy yourself for €9.50. Even on the full-day tours, you cannot see both the Eagle's Nest and the Obersalzberg Documentation Center—you have to choose between them. Take David and Christine Harper's tour instead, or visit the Documentation Center and Eagle's Nest on your own by bus, using the plan suggested earlier (under "Planning Your Time").

## Sights in Berchtesgaden

### ▲▲▲NAZI SITES NEAR BERCHTESGADEN

Early in his career as a wannabe tyrant, Adolf Hitler had a radical friend who liked to vacation in Berchtesgaden, and through him

Hitler came to know and love this dramatic corner of Bavaria. Berchtesgaden's part-Bavarian, part-Austrian character held a special appeal to the Austrian-German Hitler. In the 1920s, just out of prison, he checked into an alpine hotel in Obersalzberg, three miles uphill from Berchtesgaden, to finish work on his memoir and Nazi primer, *Mein Kampf.* Because it was here that he claimed to be inspired and laid out his vision, some call Obersalzberg the "cradle of the Third Reich."

In the 1930s, after becoming the German Chancellor, Hitler chose Obersalzberg to build his mountain retreat, a supersized alpine farmhouse called the Berghof. His handlers crafted Hitler's image here—surrounded by nature, gently receiving alpine flowers from adoring little children, lounging around with farmers in lederhosen...no modern arms industry, no big-time industrialists, no ugly extermination camps. In reality, Obersalzberg was home to much more than Hitler's alpine chalet. It was a huge compound of 80 buildings—fenced off from the public after 1936—where the major decisions leading up to World War II were hatched. Hitler himself spent about a third of his time at the Berghof, hosted world leaders in the compound, and later had it prepared for his last stand.

Some mistakenly call the entire area "Hitler's Eagle's Nest." But that name actually belongs only to the Kehlsteinhaus, a small mountaintop chalet on a 6,000-foot peak that juts up two miles south of Obersalzberg. (A visiting diplomat humorously dubbed it the "Eagle's Nest," and the name stuck.) In 1939, it was given to the Führer for his 50th birthday. While a fortune was spent building this perch and the road up to it, Hitler, who was afraid of heights, visited only 14 times. Hitler's mistress, Eva Braun, though, liked to hike up to the Eagle's Nest to sunbathe.

In April of 1945, Britain's Royal Air Force bombed the Obersalzberg compound nearly flat, but missed the difficult-to-target Eagle's Nest entirely. Almost all of what survived the bombing at Obersalzberg was blown up in 1952 by the Allies—who wanted to leave nothing as a magnet for future neo-Nazi pilgrims—before they turned the site over to the German government. The most extensive surviving remains are of the Nazis' bunker system, intended to serve as a last resort for the regime as the Allies closed in. In the 1990s, a museum, the Obersalzberg Documentation Center, was built on top of one of the bunkers. The museum and bunker, plus the never-destroyed Eagle's Nest, are the two Nazi sites worth seeing near Berchtesgaden.

## Obersalzberg Documentation Center and Bunker

To reach the most interesting part of this site, walk through the museum and down the stairs into the vast and complex bunker system. Construction began in 1943, after the Battle of Stalingrad ended the Nazi aura of invincibility. This is a professionally engineered underground town, which held meeting rooms, offices, archives for the government, and lavish living quarters for Hitler— all connected by four miles of tunnels cut through solid rock by slave

labor. You can't visit all of it, and what you can see was stripped and looted bare after the war. But enough is left that you can wander among the concrete and marvel at megalomania gone mad.

The museum above, which has almost no actual artifacts, is designed primarily for German students and others who want to learn and understand their still-recent history. There's little English, but you can rent the €2 English audioguide.

**Cost and Hours:** €3 covers both museum and bunker; April-Oct daily 9:00-17:00; Nov-March Tue-Sun 10:00-15:00, closed Mon; last entry one hour before closing, allow 1.5 hours for visit, German tel. 08652/947-960, from Austria tel. 00-49-8652-947-960, www.obersalzberg.de.

**Getting There:** Hop on bus #838 from Berchtesgaden's train station (daily, roughly hourly, 12 minutes, 5-minute walk from Obersalzberg stop).

### Eagle's Nest (Kehlsteinhaus)

Today, the chalet that Hitler ignored is basically a three-room, reasonably priced restaurant with a scenic terrace, 100 yards below  the summit of a mountain. You could say it's like any alpine hiking hut, just more massively built. On a nice day, the views are magnificent. If it's fogged in (which it often is), most people won't find it worth coming up here (except on David and Christine Harper's tours—described earlier—which can make the building come to life even without a view). Bring a jacket, and prepare for crowds in summer (less crowded if you go early or late in the day).

From the upper bus stop, a finely crafted tunnel (which will have you humming the *Get Smart* TV theme song) leads to the original polished-brass elevator, which takes you the last 400 feet up to the Eagle's Nest. Wander into the fancy back dining room (the best-preserved from Hitler's time), where you can see the once-sleek marble fireplace chipped up by souvenir-seeking troops in 1945.

**Cost and Hours:** Free, generally open mid-May-late Oct, snowfall sometimes forces a later opening or earlier closing.

**Getting There:** The only way to reach the Eagle's Nest—even if you have your own car—is by specially equipped bus #849, which leaves from the Documentation Center and climbs steeply up the one-way, private road—Germany's highest (every 25 minutes, 15 minutes, €16.10 round-trip, *Tageskarte* day passes not valid, buy ticket from windows, last bus up 16:00, last bus down 16:25, free parking at Documentation Center).

## ▲SALT MINES (SALZBERGWERK BERCHTESGADEN)

At the Berchtesgaden salt mines, you put on traditional miners' outfits, get on funny little trains, and zip deep into the mountain. For two hours (which includes time to get into and back out of your miner's gear), you'll cruise subterranean lakes; slide speedily down two long, slick, wooden banisters; and learn how they mined salt so long ago. Call ahead for crowd-avoidance advice; when the weather gets bad, this place is mobbed with a two-hour wait for the next open tour. Tours are in German, but English-speakers get audioguides.

**Cost and Hours:** €16, daily May-Oct 9:00-17:00, Nov-April 11:00-15:00—these are last-entry times, German tel. 08652/600-20, from Austria dial 00-49-8652-600-20, www.salzzeitreise.de.

**Getting There:** The mines are a 20-minute walk or quick bus ride (#837 or #840) from the Berchtesgaden station; ask the driver to let you off at the Salzbergwerk stop. (Since buses coming from Salzburg pass here on the way into Berchtesgaden, you can also simply hop off at the mines before getting into town, instead of backtracking from the station.) If you have extra time, you can take a longer, more interesting 35-minute walk from the station to the mines through Berchtesgaden's Old Town.

## ▲KÖNIGSSEE

Three miles south of Berchtesgaden, the idyllic Königssee stretches like a fjord through pristine mountain scenery to the dramatically situated Church of St. Bartholomä and beyond. To get to the lake from Berchtesgaden, hop on bus #841 (about hourly from train station to boat dock, 10 minutes), or take the scenically woodsy, reasonably flat 1.25-hour walk (well-signed). Drivers pay €4 to park.

Most visitors simply glide scenically for 35 minutes on the silent, electronically propelled **boat** to the church, enjoy that peaceful setting, then glide back. Boats, going at a sedate Bavarian speed and filled with Germans chuckling at the captain's commentary, leave with demand—generally 2-4 per hour (late April-mid-Oct, no boats off-season, €14 round-trip, German tel. 08652/96360, from Austria dial 00-49-8652-96360, www.seenschifffahrt.de). At a rock cliff midway through the journey, your captain stops, and the first mate pulls out a trumpet to demonstrate the fine echo.

The remote, red-onion-domed **Church of St. Bartholomä**

(once home of a monastery, then a hunting lodge of the Bavarian royal family) is surrounded by a fine beer garden, rustic fishermen's pub, and inviting lakeside trails. The family next to St. Bartholomä's lives in the middle of this national park and has a license to fish—so very fresh trout is the lunchtime favorite.

While the Königssee is lovely once you're on the water, all the preliminaries are a bit tedious. The bus from Berchtesgaden drops you next to a complex with WCs, ATMs, and a TI; across the parking lot rise the golden arches of McDonald's. From there, a brick path leads five minutes downhill to the lakeshore through a thicket of souvenir stores selling marmot-fat ointment, quartz chunks, carved birdhouses, and "superpretzels." At the ticket windows, you'll get a set departure time (expect a wait, as boats fill up). Rowboat rental is also an option (€7-10/hour), but the church is too far up the lake to reach easily by muscle power alone.

## ALMBACH GORGE (ALMBACHKLAMM)

This short, popular hike is a good option for nature lovers who come to see Berchtesgaden's Nazi sites, then want to fill up the rest of the day hiking along a stream-filled gorge with a minimum of fuss and crowds. Though not a world-class attraction (and not for children, due to drop-offs), it can easily make for an enjoyable two or three hours. Most visitors do it as roughly a four-mile roundtrip, though you can go farther if you wish.

Leave bus #840 at the Kugelmühle stop (12 minutes towards Salzburg from Berchtesgaden) and check the next bus times—two hours between buses is enough for a quick visit, three hours for a leisurely one. Walk five minutes along Kugelmühlweg (following the *Almbachklamm* signs) to the trailhead. First you'll see the **Gasthaus zur Kugelmühle,** which serves reasonably priced meals (daily 11:30-19:30, tel. 08650/461, from Austria dial 00-49-8650-461, www.gasthaus-kugelmuehle. de). In front of the restaurant is an old wooden apparatus for shaping marble blocks into round toy spheres (hence the name—*Kugel* means ball, *Mühle* means mill). Just beyond is a gate where you pay €3 to enter the gorge; pick up a map and get hiking advice here (daily May-Oct 9:00-18:00; gorge closed in winter).

A rushing stream cascades through the gorge, which the trail crosses and recrosses on numbered steel bridges. The trail is well-maintained and exciting, and accessible to anyone who is reasonably fit, sure-footed, and wearing sturdy shoes. However, it's not safe or appropriate for young children because the path has some steep, unguarded drop-offs that could land kids into the cold water. Expect some narrow and slippery parts, and take advantage of the handrails and steel cables strung along some portions for support. You can just walk up as far as you have time for, but the high Sulzer waterfall by bridge #19 is a traditional turn-around point. The walk there and back can be done in two hours at a good clip, but allowing three makes for a more pleasant visit.

# HALLSTATT
## AND THE
## SALZKAMMERGUT

Commune with nature in the Salzkammergut, Austria's Lake District. "The hills are alive," and you're surrounded by the loveliness that has turned on everyone from Emperor Franz Josef to Julie Andrews. This is *Sound of Music* country. Idyllic and majestic, but not rugged, it's a gentle land of lakes, forested mountains, and storybook villages, rich in hiking opportunities and inexpensive lodging. Settle down in the postcard-pretty, lake-cuddling town of Hallstatt. While there are plenty of lakes and charming villages in the Salzkammergut, Hallstatt is really the only one that matters.

## PLANNING YOUR TIME
Hallstatt serves as a relaxing break between Vienna and Salzburg. One night and a few hours to browse are all you'll need to fall in love. To relax or take a hike in the surroundings, give it two nights and a day.

## Orientation to Hallstatt

Lovable Hallstatt (HAHL-shtaht) is a tiny town bullied onto a ledge between a selfish mountain and a swan-ruled lake, with a waterfall ripping furiously through its middle. It can be toured on foot in about 15 minutes. Salt veins in the mountain rock drew people here centuries before Christ. The symbol of Hallstatt, which you'll see all over town, consists of two adjacent spirals—a design based on jewelry found in Bronze Age Celtic graves high in the nearby mountains.

Hallstatt has two parts: the tightly packed medieval town center (which locals call the Markt) and the newer, more car-friendly Lahn, a few minutes' walk to the south. A lakeside promenade connects the old center to the Lahn. The tiny "main" boat dock (a.k.a.

Market Dock), where boats from the train station arrive, is in the old center of town. Another boat dock is in the Lahn, next to Hallstatt's bus stop and grocery store.

The charms of Hallstatt are its village and its lakeside setting. Come here to relax, nibble, wander, and paddle. While tourist crowds can trample much of Hallstatt's charm in August, the place is almost dead in the off-season. The lake is famous for its good fishing and pure water.

## TOURIST INFORMATION

At the helpful TI, in the Lahn by the boat dock and bus stop, Teresa and Stefanie can explain hikes and excursions, and find you a room (July-Aug Mon-Fri 9:00-16:00, Sat-Sun 9:00-15:00; Sept-June Mon-Fri 9:00-13:00 & 14:00-17:00, closed Sat-Sun; Seestrasse 99, tel. 06134/8208, www.dachstein-salzkammergut.at).

On Mondays in high season, the TI offers 1.5-hour **walking tours** of the town in English and German (€8, mid-May-Oct at 17:00). They can also arrange private tours (€105), or you can use an audioguide to explore (€5, €50 deposit).

## ARRIVAL IN HALLSTATT

**By Train:** If you're coming on the main train line that runs between Salzburg and Vienna, you'll change trains at Attnang-Puchheim to get to Hallstatt (you won't see Hallstatt on the schedules, but any train to Ebensee and Bad Ischl will stop at Hallstatt). Day-trippers can check their bags at the Attnang-Puchheim station (follow signs for *Schliessfächer,* coin-op lockers are at the street, curbside near  track 1, €2-3.50/24 hours). Note: Connections can be tight—check the TV monitor.

Hallstatt's train station is a wide spot on the tracks across the lake from town. *Stefanie* (a boat) meets you at the station and glides scenically across the lake to the old town center (€2.40, meets each train until 18:50—don't arrive after that, www.hallstattschifffahrt. at). The last departing boat-train connection leaves Hallstatt at 18:15, and the first boat goes in the morning at 6:50 (Sat-Sun at 8:10 in summer, 8:45 off-season).

Once in Hallstatt, you're steps away from the hotels in the old center and a 15-minute walk from accommodations (and the TI) in the Lahn.

**By Bus:** Hallstatt's bus stop is by the boat dock and TI in the

Lahn. It takes 15 minutes to walk from the bus stop into the old center along the lakeside path.

**By Car:** The main road skirts the old center via a long tunnel above the town; you'll emerge in the Lahn. If you're staying at one of my recommended accommodations in the Lahn, you can park right at the hotel—all have free parking.

Gates close the old center to traffic during the day (10:00-17:00), and it's illegal to park here at any time. As you approach town, electronic signs direct you to available parking. If you are staying at a hotel in the old town, follow signs to lot P1 (€9/day, reserved for hotel guests). Choose "Hotelticket" at the gate when you enter and hang onto your ticket—you'll need it when you leave. To reach your hotel, go to the Hotel-Shuttle Info-Point in the lot, tell the attendant (or the intercom) where you're staying, and hop on the free shuttle, which will drop you at or near your hotel. You can also use this shuttle when you depart; ask your hotelier for details. When you leave the lot, pay at the machine.

Day-trippers should head to lot P2, which is closer to the old town center (€7.50/3-12 hours; not served by hotel shuttle).

For more parking tips, see www.hallstatt.net/parking-in-hallstatt/cars.

## HELPFUL HINTS

**Internet Access:** For free Wi-Fi, drop by the café at the recommended **Heritage Hotel.** If you need a computer, try **Hallstatt Umbrella Bar** (summers only, weather permitting—since it's literally under a big umbrella, halfway between the old center and the Lahn along the lake at Seestrasse 145).

**Laundry:** The old town's "general store," the **Gemischtwarenhandlung am See,** has a coin-operated washer and dryer (€5 each, daily May-Oct 7:00-21:30, shorter hours Nov-April, across from the Protestant church, mobile 0664-917-9001). The staff of the **campground** in the Lahn will wash and dry your clothes for €8/load (drop off daily mid-April-mid-Oct 8:00-10:00 & 16:00-18:00, pick up in afternoon or next morning, closed off-season, tel. 06134/8322).

**Boat Rental:** Two outfits rent electric boats in high season. **Krumböck** has locales next to the main boat dock and 75 yards past Bräugasthof (€13/hour, tel. 06134/20619). **Hemetsberger** rents from near Gasthof Simony as well as by the Lahn boat dock (€12/hour, tel. 06134/8228). Both are open daily until 19:00 in peak season and in good weather. Boats have two speeds: slow and stop. Spending an extra €3/hour gets you a faster, 500-watt boat; you can pay a bit more for a boat with a roof (nice in hot weather). Both places also rent rowboats and paddleboats (slightly cheaper).

HALLSTATT

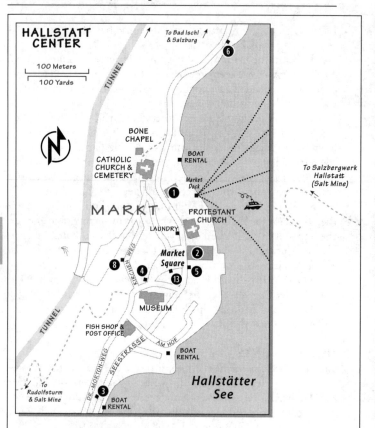

**HALLSTATT CENTER**

100 Meters
100 Yards

TO Bad Ischl & Salzburg

TUNNEL

BONE CHAPEL

CATHOLIC CHURCH & CEMETERY

BOAT RENTAL

Market Dock

To Salzbergwerk Hallstatt (Salt Mine)

MARKT

PROTESTANT CHURCH

LAUNDRY

Market Square

KIRCHEN WEG

MUSEUM

FISH SHOP & POST OFFICE

DR.-MORTON-WEG

SEESTRASSE

AM HOF

BOAT RENTAL

TUNNEL

To Rudolfsturm & Salt Mine

BOAT RENTAL

*Hallstätter See*

ECHERNTAL

ECHERNTALWEG

1 Heritage Hotel
2 Hotel/Rest. Grüner Baum
3 Bräugasthof Hallstatt
4 Gasthof Zauner
5 Gasthof Simony & Rest. Am See
6 Pension Sarstein
7 Helga Lenz Rooms
8 Gasthaus zur Mühle Hostel
9 Gasthof Pension Grüner Anger
10 Haus Trausner
11 Herta Höll Rooms
12 Pizzeria Bella Milano
13 Marktbeisl zur Ruth Pub
14 Internet Access
15 Campground (Laundry Service)

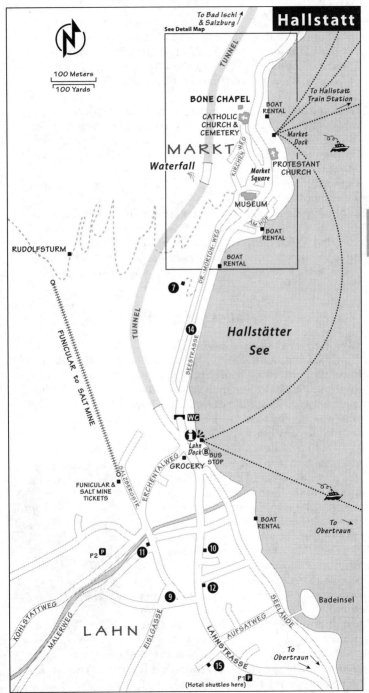

**Hallstatt**

To Bad Ischl & Salzburg

See Detail Map

N

100 Meters
100 Yards

TUNNEL

To Hallstatt Train Station

BONE CHAPEL

BOAT RENTAL

CATHOLIC CHURCH & CEMETERY

Market Dock

M A R K T

KIRCHEN WEG

Waterfall

Market Square

PROTESTANT CHURCH

MUSEUM

AM HOF

BOAT RENTAL

RUDOLFSTURM

DR. MORTON-WEG

BOAT RENTAL

**7**

**14**

SEESTRASSE

*Hallstätter See*

FUNICULAR to SALT MINE

TUNNEL

WC

**1**

Lahn Dock

**B**

BUS STOP

GROCERY

ERCHENTALWEG

SALZBERGSTR.

FUNICULAR & SALT MINE TICKETS

BOAT RENTAL

To Obertraun

P2 **P**

**11**

**10**

**12**

**9**

Badeinsel

KOHLSTATTWEG

MALERWEG

L A H N

EISLGASSE

LAHNSTRASSE

AUFSATWEG

SEELÄNDE

To Obertraun

**15**

P1 **P**

(Hotel shuttles here)

HALLSTATT

**Dirndl Rental:** If you feel compelled to re-enact *The Sound of Music,* **Dirndl to Go** rents authentic versions of these traditional dresses by the hour (€22/first hour, €6/hour after that, daily May-Oct 11:00-17:00, Nov-April by arrangement, in Gasthof Simony, Wolfengasse 105, mobile 0650-366-6503, www.dirndl-to-go.at, Claudia).

**Parks and Swimming:** Green and peaceful lakeside parks line the south end of Lake Hallstatt. If you walk 15 minutes south of the old center to the Lahn, you'll find a grassy public park, playground, mini-golf, and swimming area *(Badestrand)* with the fun Badeinsel play-island.

**Views:** For a great view over Hallstatt, hike above the recommended Helga Lenz B&B as far as you like, or climb any path leading up the hill. The 40-minute steep hike down from the salt-mine tour gives the best views (see "Sights in Hallstatt," later). While most visitors stroll the lakeside drag between the old and new parts of town, make a point to do the trip once by taking the more higgledy-piggledy high lane called Dr.-Morton-Weg.

## Hallstatt Walk

• *This short, self-guided walk starts at the dock.*

**Boat Landing:** There was a Hallstatt before there was a Rome. In fact, because of the importance of salt mining here, an entire epoch—the Hallstatt Era, from 800 to 400 B.C.—is named for this important spot. Through the centuries, salt was traded and people came and went by boat. You'll still see the traditional *Fuhr* boats, designed to carry heavy loads in shallow water.

Tiny Hallstatt has two big churches: **Protestant** (bordering the square on the left, with a grassy lakeside playground) and **Catholic** (towering up above, with its fascinating bone chapel). Its faded St. Christopher—patron saint of travelers, with his cane and baby Jesus on his shoulder—watched over those sailing in and out.

Until 1875, the town was extremely remote...then came a real road and the train. The good ship *Stefanie* shuttles travelers back and forth from here to the Hallstatt train station, immediately across the lake. The *Bootverleih* sign advertises boat rentals. By the way, *Schmuck* is not an insult...it means jewelry.

Notice the one-lane road out of town (below the church). Until 1966, when a bigger tunnel was built above Hallstatt, all the traffic crept single-file right through the town.

Look down the shore at the huge homes. Several families lived in each of these houses, back when Hallstatt's population was about double its present 1,000. Today, the population continues to shrink, and many of these generally underused houses rent rooms to visitors.

Hallstatt gets about three months of snow each winter, but the lake hasn't frozen over since 1981. See any swans? They've patrolled the lake like they own it since the 1860s, when Emperor Franz Josef and Empress Sisi—the Princess Diana of her day (see page 137)—made this region their annual holiday retreat. Sisi loved swans, so locals made sure she'd see them here. During this period, the Romantics discovered Hallstatt, many top painters worked here, and the town got its first hotel (now the Heritage Hotel).

Recently, local divers discovered that the lake also served as Hallstatt's garbage can. For centuries, if something was *kaputt*, locals would just toss it into the lake. In 1945, Nazi medals decorating German and Austrian war heroes suddenly became dangerous to own. Throughout the former Third Reich, hard-earned medals floated down to lonely lake beds, including Hallstatt's.

• *Walk over the town's stream, and pop into the...*

**Protestant Church:** The Catholic Counter-Reformation was very strong in Austria, but pockets of Protestantism survived, especially in mining towns like Hallstatt. In 1860, Emperor Franz Josef finally allowed non-Catholic Christians to build churches. Before that, they were allowed to worship only in low-key "houses of prayer." In 1863, Hallstatt's miners pooled their humble resources and built this fine church. Step inside (free and often open). It's very plain, emphasizing the pulpit and organ rather than fancy art and saints. Check out the portraits: Martin Luther (left of altar), the town in about 1865 with its new church (left wall), and a century of pastors.

• *Continue past the church to the...*

**Market Square (Marktplatz):** In 1750, a fire leveled this part of town. The buildings you see now are all late 18th-century structures built of stone rather than flammable wood. The three big buildings on the left are government-subsidized housing (mostly for seniors and people with health problems). Take a close look at the two-dimensional, up-against-the-wall pear tree (it likes the sun-warmed wall). The statue features the Holy Trinity.

• *Continue a block past Gasthof Simony. At the first corner, just before the* Gemeindeamt *(City Hall), jog left across the little square and then right down the tiny lane marked* Am Hof, *which leads through an intimate bit of domestic town architecture, boat houses, lots of firewood, and maybe a couple of swans hanging out. The lane circles back to the main drag and the...*

**Museum Square:** Because 20th-century Hallstatt was of no industrial importance, it was untouched by World War II. But once upon a time, its salt was worth defending. High above, peeking out of the trees, is Rudolfsturm (Rudolf's Tower). Originally a 13th-century watchtower protecting the salt mines, and later the mansion of a salt-mine boss, it's now a restaurant with a great view. A zigzag trail connects the town with Rudolfsturm and the salt mines just beyond. The big, white houses by the waterfall were water-powered mills that once ground Hallstatt's grain. (If you hike up a few blocks, you'll see the river raging through town.)

Around you are the town's post office, museum, City Hall, and Dachstein Sport Shop. A statue recalls the mine manager who excavated prehistoric graves in about 1850. Much of the *Schmuck* sold locally is inspired by the jewelry found in the area's Bronze Age tombs.

The memorial wooden stairs in front of the museum are a copy of those found in Hallstatt's prehistoric mine—the original stairs are more than 2,500 years old. For thousands of years, people have been leaching salt out of this mountain. A brine spring sprung here, attracting Bronze Age people in about 1600 B.C. Later, they dug tunnels to mine the rock (which was 70 percent salt), dissolved it into a brine, and distilled out the salt—precious for preserving meat. For a look at early salt-mining implements and the town's story, visit the museum (described later).

The post office is actually a "Post Partner"—a government-funded attempt to turn low-profit post offices into something more viable (selling souvenirs, renting bikes, and employing people with disabilities who otherwise wouldn't work). The *Fischerei* provides the town with its cherished fresh lake fish. The county allows two commercial fishermen on the lake. They spread their nets each morning and sell their catch here to town restaurants, or to any locals cooking up a special dinner.

• *Nearby, still on Museum Square, find the...*

**Dachstein Sport Shop:** During a renovation project, the builders dug down and hit a Celtic and ancient Roman settlement. Peek through the glass pavement on the covered porch to see where the Roman street level was. If the shop is open, pop in and go downstairs (free). You'll walk on Roman flagstones and see the small gutter that channeled water to power an ancient hammer mill (used to pound iron into usable shapes). In prehistoric times, people lived near the mines. Romans were the first Hallstatt lakeside settlers. The store's owners are committed to sharing Hallstatt's fascinating history and often display old town paintings and folk art.

• *From this square, the first right (after the bank) leads up a few stairs to the street called...*

**Dr.-Morton-Weg:** House #26A dates from 1597. Follow the lane uphill to the left past more old houses. Until 1890, this was the town's main drag, and the lake lapped at the lower doors of these houses. Therefore, many main entrances were via the attic, from this level. Enjoy this back-street view of town. Just after the arch, near #133, check out the old tools hanging outside the workshop, and the piece of wooden piping. It's a section taken from the 25-mile wooden pipeline that carried salt brine from Hallstatt to Ebensee. This was in place from 1595 until the last generation, when the last stretch of wood was replaced by plastic piping. At the pipe, enjoy the lake view and climb down the stairs. From lake level, look back up at the striking traditional architecture (the fine woodwork on the left was recently rebuilt after a fire; parts of the old house on the right date to medieval times).

• *Your tour is finished. From here, you have boat rentals, the salt-mine tour, the town museum, and the Catholic church (with its bone chapel) all within a few minutes' walk.*

## Sights in Hallstatt

### ▲▲Catholic Church and Bone Chapel

Hallstatt's Catholic church overlooks the town from above. The lovely church has twin altars. The one on the left was made by town artists in 1897. The one on the right is more historic—dedicated in 1515 to Mary, who's flanked by St. Barbara (on right, patron of miners) and St. Catherine (on  left, patron of foresters—a lot of wood was needed to fortify the many miles of tunnels, and to boil the brine to distill the salt).

Behind the church, in the well-tended graveyard, is the 12th-century Chapel of St. Michael (even older than the church). Its bone chapel—or charnel house *(Beinhaus)*—contains more than 600 skulls. Each has been lovingly decorated and marked with the deceased's name and date of death. (Skulls with dark, thick garlands are oldest—18th century; those with flowers are more recent—19th century.) Space was so limited in this cemetery that bones had only 12 peaceful, buried years here before making way for the freshly dead. Many of the dug-up bones and skulls ended up in this chapel. They stopped this practice in the 1960s, about the same time the Catholic Church began permitting cremation. But one woman (who died in 1983) managed to sneak her skull in later (dated 1995, under the cross, with the gold tooth). The skulls on the books are those of priests.

**Cost and Hours:** Free to enter church, bone chapel-€1.50, daily May-Sept 10:00-18:00, Oct 10:00-16:00, closed Nov-April, free English flier, tel. 06134/8279.

**Getting There:** From near the main boat dock, hike up the covered wooden stairway and follow the *Kath. Kirche* signs.

## ▲Hallstatt Museum

This high-quality museum tells the story of Hallstatt. It focuses on the Hallstatt Era (800-400 B.C.), when this village was the salt-mining hub of a culture that spread from France to the Balkans. Back then, Celtic tribes dug for precious salt, and Hallstatt was, as its name means, the "place of salt." The highlight of the museum is the countless number of artifacts excavated from prehistoric gravesites around the mine. The museum also offers a five-minute 3-D movie and 26 displays on everything from the region's flora and fauna to local artists and the surge in Hallstatt tourism during the Romantic Age. Everything is labeled in English, and the ring binders have translations of the longer texts.

**Cost and Hours:** €8; May-Sept daily 10:00-18:00; April and Oct daily 10:00-16:00; Nov-March Wed-Sun 11:00-15:00, closed Mon-Tue; Seestrasse 56, tel. 06134/828-015, www.museum-hallstatt.at.

## ▲Lake Trip

For a quick boat trip, you can ride the *Stefanie* across the lake and back for €4.80. It stops at the tiny Hallstatt train station for 30 minutes (note return time in the boat's window), giving you time to walk to a hanging bridge (ask the captain to point you to the *Hängebrücke*—HENG-eh-brick-eh—a 10-minute lakeside stroll to the left). For a longer tour, take a round-trip ride to Obertraun

(€9, 4-5/day June-Sept only, 50 minutes) or Steeg (€10, 3/day mid-July-Aug only, 1.25 hours); check the posted schedule or www.hallstattschifffahrt.at for departure times. Those into relaxation can rent a sleepy electric motorboat to enjoy town views from the water.

## ▲Salt-Mine Tour

If you have yet to tour a salt mine, consider visiting Hallstatt's, which claims to be the oldest in the world. The presentation is very

low-tech, as the mining company owns all three mine tours in the area and sees little reason to invest in the experience when they can simply mine the tourists. Still, it gives an interesting look at mining through the centuries and culminates with a fun banister slide.

**Cost and Hours:** €26 combo-ticket includes mine and round-trip funicular, €19 for mine tour only, buy all tickets at funicular station—note the time and tour number on your ticket; open daily late April-mid-Sept 9:00-16:00, mid-Sept-Oct 9:00-14:30, closed Nov-late April; €2 audioguide (leave ID as deposit), no children under age 4, arrive early or late to avoid summer crowds, tel. 06132/200-2400, www.salzwelten.at.

**Funicular:** You can also just take the funicular without going on the mine tour (€7 one-way, €13 round-trip, 4/hour, daily late April-mid-Sept 9:00-18:00, mid-Sept-Oct 9:00-16:30, closed Nov-late April). Note that the later funicular departures miss the last mine tour of the day. The funicular starts in the Lahn, close to the bus stop, Lahn boat dock, and P2 parking lot.

**Visiting the Mine:** Allow about three hours total; the tour itself takes one hour. After riding the funicular above town and enjoying the view, you'll hike 10 minutes to the mine (past excavation sites of many prehistoric tombs and a glass case with 2,500-year-old bones—but there's little to actually see). As you wait for the next tour departure, you'll check your bag and put on old miners' clothes, then hike 200 yards higher in your funny outfit to meet your guide, who escorts your group down a tunnel that was dug in 1719.

Inside the mountain, you'll watch a slide show, follow your guide through several caverns as you learn about mining techniques over the last 7,000 years, see a silly laser show on a glassy subterranean lake, peek at a few waxy cavemen with pickaxes, and ride

HALLSTATT

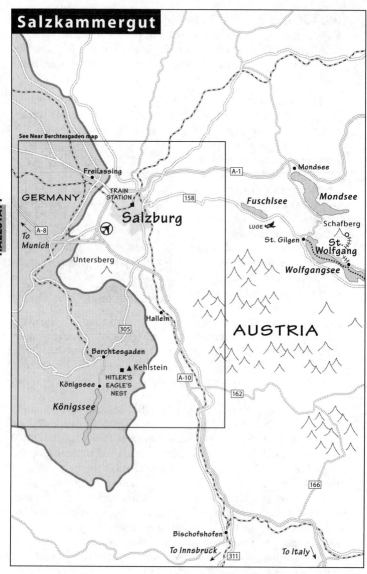

# Salzkammergut

See Near Berchtesgaden map

GERMANY

Freilassing

TRAIN STATION

Salzburg

A-8

To Munich

Untersberg

305

Hallein

Berchtesgaden

▲ Kehlstein

Königssee

HITLER'S EAGLE'S NEST

Königssee

A-1

Mondsee

Fuschlsee

Mondsee

LUGE

St. Gilgen

Schafberg

St. Wolfgang

Wolfgangsee

AUSTRIA

158

A-10

162

166

Bischofshofen

To Innsbruck  311

To Italy

the train out. The highlight for most is sliding down two banisters (the second one is longer and ends with a flash for an automatic souvenir photo that clocks your speed—see how you did compared to the rest of your group after the tour).

While the tour is mostly in German, the guide is required to speak English if you ask...so ask. Be sure to dress for the constant 47-degree temperature.

**Returning to Hallstatt:** If you skip the funicular down, the steep and scenic 40-minute hike back into town is (with strong knees) a joy. At the base of the funicular, notice the train tracks leading to the Erbstollen tunnel entrance. This lowest of the salt tunnels goes many miles into the mountain, where a shaft connects it to the tunnels you just explored. Today, the salty brine from these tunnels flows 25 miles through the world's oldest pipeline—made of wood until quite recently—to the huge modern salt works (next to the highway) at Ebensee.

## ▲Local Hikes

Mountain lovers, hikers, and spelunkers who use Hallstatt as their home base keep busy for days (ask the TI for ideas). A good, short, and easy walk is the two-hour round-trip up the Echern Valley to the Waldbachstrub waterfall and back: From the parking lot, follow signs to the salt mines, then follow the little wooden signs marked *Echerntalweg*. With a car, consider hiking around nearby Altaussee (flat, 3-hour hike) or along Grundlsee to Toplitzsee. Regular buses connect Hallstatt with Gosausee for a pleasant hour-long walk around that lake. Or consider walking nine miles halfway around Lake Hallstatt via the town of Steeg (boat to train station, walk left along lake and past idyllic farmsteads, returning to Hallstatt along the old salt trail, *Soleleitungsweg*); for a shorter hike, walk to Steeg along either side of the lake, and catch the train from Steeg back to Hallstatt's station. The TI can also recommend a great two-day hike with an overnight in a nearby mountain hut.

## Biking

The best two bike rides take nearly the same routes as the hikes listed previously: up the Echern Valley and around the lake (bikers do better going via Obertraun along the lakeside bike path—start with a ride on the *Stefanie*). There's no public bike rental in Hallstatt, but some hotels have loaner bikes for guests.

## NEAR HALLSTATT
### ▲▲Dachstein Mountain Cable Car and Caves

A few miles up the lake beyond Hallstatt, a cable car glides up to the high, barren Dachstein mountain plateau. Along the way, you can hop off to tour two different caves: the refreshingly chilly Giant Ice Caves and the less-impressive Mammoth Caves.

**Getting to the Cable Car:** To drive to the valley station for the cable car to Dachstein, continue along the main road south of Hallstatt about three miles; just before reaching the village of Obertraun, turn right up a side road for a mile, following the Dachstein signs. Without a car, the handiest and cheapest option is the bus (€1.70, 7-9/day, 15 minutes, leaves from bus stop in the Lahn, drops you directly at cable-car station). Romantics could take the boat from Hallstatt's main boat dock to Obertraun (€5.50, 4-5/day June-Sept only, 30 minutes, www.hallstattschifffahrt.at)—but it's a 40-minute hike from there to the lift station.

    **Returning to Hallstatt:** Plan to leave by mid-afternoon. The last bus from the cable-car station back to Hallstatt leaves at 17:20. If you miss the bus, try getting a ride from a fellow cable-car passenger. Otherwise, you can either call a taxi (€13, ask cable-car staff for help) or walk back along the lakefront (about one hour).

## Dachstein Cable Car

This mighty gondola leaves every 15 minutes, rising in three stages high up to the Dachstein Plateau—crowned by Dachstein, the highest mountain in the Salzkammergut (9,800 ft). The first segment stops at **Schönbergalm** (4,500 ft, runs May-late Oct), which has a mountain restaurant and two huge caves (described next). The second segment goes to the summit of **Krippenstein** (6,600 ft, runs May-late Oct). The third segment descends to **Gjaidalm** (5,800 ft, runs mid-June-late Oct), where several hikes begin.

    For a quick high-country experience, Krippenstein is better than Gjaidalm. Its "five-fingers" viewpoint features metal walkways that extend out from the mountain (not for the faint of heart). From Krippenstein, you get 360-degree views of the surrounding mountains and a good look at the scrubby, limestone, karstic landscape (which absorbs, through its many cracks, the rainfall that ultimately carves all those caves). You can eat here, and even stay overnight. An easy half-hour walk from the Krippenstein lift station takes you to the Dachstein Shark, another good viewpoint.

    **Cost and Hours:** €28, includes all three stages whether you use them or not, last cable car back down usually at about 17:00—30 minutes later in high summer, all stations have free Wi-Fi, tel. 050140, www.dachstein-salzkammergut.com.

    **Cable Car and Caves Combo-Tickets:** Several combo-tickets are available for the cable car and caves. The round-trip cable-car ride to Schönbergalm, including entrance to one of the caves, is €29. The €35 combo-ticket includes the cable car and entry to both caves. If you're gung-ho enough to visit both caves and ride the cable car farther up the mountain, the €41 same-day, all-inclusive ticket makes sense (covers the cable car all the way to Gjaidalm and back, as well as entry to both caves). Cheaper family rates are available.

## Giant Ice Caves (Riesen-Eishöhle)

These caves, near the Schönbergalm cable-car stop (4,500 ft), were discovered in 1910. Today, guides lead tours in German and English on a 50-minute, half-mile hike through an eerie, icy, subterranean world, passing limestone canyons the size of subway stations. The temperature is just around freezing, and although the many steps help keep you warm, aim to dress as the guides do, in a jacket and hat. If you just do this cave visit, allow at least 2.5 hours round-trip from the valley station.

At the Schönbergalm lift station, report to the ticket window to get your tour time. Behind the station is a free little museum—in a local-style wood cabin designed to support 200 tons of snow—with exhibits about the caves (mostly in German only; save it for the way back). It's a steep 10-minute hike from the station up to the cave entry, along a paved path with switchbacks. Allow time to pause for breath. The limestone caverns, carved by rushing water, are named for scenes from Wagner's operas—the favorite of the mountaineers who first came here. If you're nervous, note that the iron oxide covering the ceiling takes 5,000 years to form. Things are very stable.

**Cost and Hours:** €29 includes cable car, various combo-tickets available (described earlier), open May-late Oct, 50-minute tours start at 9:20, last tour at 16:00—16:30 in high summer.

### Mammoth Caves (Mammuthöhle)

While huge and well-promoted, these are much less interesting than the ice caves and—for most—not worth the time. Of the 30-mile limestone labyrinth excavated so far, you'll walk a half-mile.

**Cost and Hours:** €29 includes cable car, various combo-tickets available (described earlier), open mid-May-late Oct, hour-long tours 10:30-14:30—until 15:00 in high summer, entrance a 10-minute hike from lift station.

### Summer Luge Rides (Sommerrodelbahnen) on the Hallstatt-Salzburg Road

If you're driving between Salzburg and Hallstatt, you'll pass two luge rides operated by the same company. Each is a ski lift that drags you backward up the hill as you sit on your go-cart. At the top, you ride the cart down the winding metal course. It's easy: Push to go, pull to stop, take your hands off your stick and you get hurt. For more details, see "Luge Lesson" on page 445.

Each course is just off the road with easy parking. The ride up and down takes about 10 minutes. The one in **Fuschl am See** (closest to Salzburg, look for *Sommerrodelbahn* sign) is half as long and cheaper (1,970 ft). The one in **Strobl** near Wolfgangsee (look for *Riesen-schutzbahn* sign) is a double course, and more scenic with grand lake views (4,265 ft, each track is the same speed). These are fun, but the concrete courses near Reutte are better (see page 445).

**Cost and Hours:** Fuschl am See—€4.50/ride, €31.50/10 rides, tel. 06226/8452; Strobl—€6.70/ride, €47/10 rides, tel.

06137/7085, www.rodelbahnen.at; courses open May-Oct 10:00-18:00 but generally closed in bad weather.

# Nightlife in Hallstatt

Locals would laugh at the thought. But if you want some action after dinner, you do have a few options: **Gasthaus zur Mühle** is a youth hostel that serves pizza in its smoky restaurant; later, when drinks replace food, it has a rustic sports-bar ambience (open late, closed Tue and Nov, run by Ferdinand). Or, for your late-night drink, savor the Market Square from the trendy little pub called **Marktbeisl zur Ruth,** where locals congregate with soft music, a good selection of drinks, two small rooms, and tables on the square (daily 11:00-late, tel. 06134/20017, www.marktbeisl.at).

# Sleeping in Hallstatt

Hallstatt's TI can almost always find you a room (either in town or at B&Bs and small hotels outside of town—which are more likely to have rooms available and come with easy parking). If you are arriving by car and have a reservation for a place in the old town, head directly to parking lot P1, where you'll catch a shuttle to your hotel (see page 341).

I've listed prices for high season (generally May-Oct). Mid-July and August can be tight. Early August is worst. Hallstatt is not the place to splurge—some of the best rooms are in *Gästezimmer,* just as nice and modern as rooms in bigger hotels, at half the cost. In summer, a double bed in a private home costs about €60 with breakfast. It's hard to get an advance reservation for a one-night stay (try calling the TI for help). But if you drop in and they have a spot, one-nighters are welcome. Prices include breakfast, lots of stairs, and a silent night. *"Zimmer mit Aussicht?"* (TSIM-mer mit OWS-zeekt) means "Room with view?"—worth asking for. Unlike many businesses in town, the cheaper places don't take credit cards.

As most rooms here are in old buildings with well-cared-for wooden interiors, dripping laundry is a no-no at Hallstatt pensions. Be especially considerate when hanging laundry over anything but tile—if you must hand-wash larger clothing items here, ask your host about using their clothesline.

### IN THE OLD CENTER
**$$$ Heritage Hotel,** next to the main boat dock, is the town's fanciest place to stay. It has 34 rooms with modern furnishings in a lakeside main building with an elevator; uphill are another 20 rooms in two separate buildings for those willing to climb stairs for better views (Sb-€150, Db-€209, these prices with this book when

HALLSTATT

you book directly with hotel, free sauna, cable Internet and Wi-Fi, laundry service-€15, Landungsplatz 101, tel. 06134/20036, www. hotel-hallstatt.com, info@hotel-hallstatt.com).

**$$$ Hotel Grüner Baum,** on the other side of the church from the main boat dock, has a great location, fronting Market Square and overlooking the lake in back. The owner, Monika, moved here from Vienna and renovated this stately—but still a bit creaky—old hotel with urban taste. Its 30 rooms have classy furnishings and new hardwood floors (Db-€158-213, price depends on view, 8 percent discount with this book when you book directly with hotel, extra bed-€52, family rooms, elevator, Wi-Fi,

laundry service-€16, closed Nov, 20 yards from boat dock, tel. 06134/82630, www.gruenerbaum.cc, contact@gruenerbaum.cc).

**$$$ Gasthof Zauner** is run by a friendly mountaineer, Herr Zauner, whose family has owned it since 1893. Recently renovated, the 13 pricey, pine-flavored rooms near the inland end of Market Square are decorated with sturdy alpine-inspired furniture (sealed not with lacquer but with beeswax, to let the wood breathe out its calming scent). Lederhosen-clad Herr Zauner recounts tales of local mountaineering lore, including his own impressive ascents (Sb-€83, Db-€135, lakeview Db-€165, elevator, Wi-Fi, closed Nov-early Dec, Marktplatz 51, tel. 06134/8246, www.zauner. hallstatt.net, zauner@hallstatt.at).

**$$ Bräugasthof Hallstatt** is like a museum filled with antique furniture and ancient family portraits. This former brewery, now a good restaurant, rents eight clean, cozy upstairs rooms. It's run by Verena and her daughter, Verena. Five of the rooms have gorgeous little lakeview balconies (Sb-€70, Db-€105, Tb-€155, Wi-Fi, along lake at Seestrasse 120, tel. 06134/8221, www.brauhaus-lobisser.com, info@brauhaus-lobisser.com, Lobisser family).

**$$ Gasthof Simony** is a well-worn, grandmotherly, 12-room place on the square, with a lake view, balconies, ancient beds, creaky wood floors, slippery rag rugs, antique furniture, and a lakefront garden for swimming (S-€45, D-€80, Ds-€90, Db-€105, Tb-€150, Qb-€180, cash only, Wi-Fi in lobby, Marktplatz 105, tel. 06134/8231, gasthof-simony.at, info@gasthof-simony.at).

**$$ Pension Sarstein** is a big, flower-bedecked house right on the water on the edge of the old center. Its four renovated rooms and three apartments are bright, and all have lakeview balconies. You can swim from its plush and inviting lakeside garden (rooms with breakfast: D-€64, Db-€80, Tb-€100; apartments with kitch-

## Sleep Code

**Abbreviations** (€1 = about $1.40, country code: 43, area code: 06134)
**S** = Single, **D** = Double/Twin, **T** = Triple, **Q** = Quad, **b** = bathroom, **s** = shower only.
**Price Rankings**
 **$$$**  **Higher Priced**—Most rooms €110 or more.
 **$$**  **Moderately Priced**—Most rooms between €70-110.
 **$**  **Lower Priced**—Most rooms €70 or less.
Unless otherwise noted, credit cards are accepted, English is spoken, Wi-Fi is generally free, and breakfast is included. Prices change; verify current rates online or by email. For the best prices, always book directly with the hotel.

en and no breakfast: Db-€80, Tb-€100, Qb-€120; €5/person extra for 1-night stay, cash preferred, Wi-Fi in lobby, a few loaner bikes, 200 yards to the right of the main boat dock at Gosaumühlstrasse 83, tel. 06134/8217, www.hallstatt.net/accommodation/boarding-houses/house-sarstein-hallstatt, pension.sarstein@aon.at, helpful Isabelle and Klaus Fischer).

**$ Helga Lenz** rents two fine *Zimmer* a steep five-minute climb above Dr.-Morton-Weg (look for the green *Zimmer* sign). This large, sprawling, woodsy house has a nifty garden perch, wins the "Best View" award, and is ideal for those who sleep well in tree houses and don't mind the steps up from town (Db-€60, Tb-€90, €2/person extra for 1-night stay, cash only, family room, no Internet access, closed Nov-March, Hallberg 17, tel. 06134/8508, www.hallstatt.net/lenz, haus-lenz@aon.at).

**$ *Hostel*: Gasthaus zur Mühle Jugendherberge,** below the waterfall and along the gushing town stream, has 46 of the cheapest good beds in town (bed in 3- to 8-bed coed dorms-€18, twin D-€36, family quads, sheets-€5, breakfast-€6, big lockers with a €15 deposit, Wi-Fi, closed Nov, reception closed Tue Sept-mid-May—arrange in advance if arriving on Tue, Kirchenweg 36, tel. 06134/8318, www.hallstatturlaub.at, toeroe-f@hallstatturlaub.at, Ferdinand Törö). The smoky restaurant here is active late into the evening (see "Nightlife in Hallstatt," earlier).

### IN THE LAHN

**$$ Gasthof Pension Grüner Anger,** near the bus station and base of the funicular, is practical and modern. It's big and quiet, with 11 rooms and no creaks or squeaks. There are mountain views, but none of

the lake (Sb-€60, Db-€88-94, non-smoking, guest computer and Wi-Fi, free loaner bikes, free parking, Lahn 10, tel. 06134/8397, www.anger.hallstatt.net, anger@aon.at, Sulzbacher family). If arriving by train, have the boat captain call Herr Sulzbacher, who will pick you up at the dock. Frau Sulzbacher cooks good-value three-course dinners for guests (served Tue-Sun, reserve in afternoon).

$ Two good *Gästezimmer* are just past the bus stop/parking lot and over the bridge. **Haus Trausner** has three clean, bright, new-feeling rooms adjacent to the Trausner family home (Ds/Db-€56, 2-night minimum for reservations, cash only, breakfast in garden or your room, showers are in-room, no Internet access, free parking, Lahnstrasse 27, tel. 06134/8710, www.hallstatt.net/accommodation/bed-and-breakfast/family-trausner-steinboeck, trausner1@aon.at, charming Maria Trausner makes you want to settle right in). **Herta Höll** rents two spacious, modern rooms on the ground floor of her riverside house (Db-€60-65, €2/person extra for 1-night stay, extra beds possible, 2- to 3-night minimum in summer, cash only, cable Internet and Wi-Fi, free parking, Salzbergstrasse 45, tel. 06134/8531, www.hallstatt.net/accommodation/bed-and-breakfast/guesthouse-hoell, frank.hoell@aon.at).

## Eating in Hallstatt

In this town, when someone is happy to see you, they'll often say, "Can I cook you a fish?" While everyone cooks the typical Austrian fare, fish is your best bet here. *Reinanke* (whitefish) is caught wild out of Lake Hallstatt and served the same day. *Saibling* (lake trout) is also tasty and costs less. You can enjoy good food inexpensively, with delightful lakeside settings. Restaurants in Hallstatt tend to have unreliable hours and close early on slow nights, so don't wait too long to get dinner. Most of the eateries listed here are run by recommended hotels.

**Restaurant Bräugasthof,** on the edge of the old center, is a good value. The indoor dining room is cozy in cool weather. On a balmy evening, its great lakeside tables offer the best ambience in town—you can feed the swans while your trout is being cooked (€11-15 main courses, daily 11:30-late, closed Nov and March, closed one day per week Dec-Feb, Seestrasse 120, tel. 06134/8221, www.brauhaus-lobisser.com).

**Hotel Grüner Baum** is a more upscale option, with elegant (and often slow) service at tables overlooking the lake inside and out (€16-26 main courses, daily 11:30-21:00, closed Nov, at bottom of Market Square, tel. 06134/8263, www.gruenerbaum.cc).

**Gasthof Simony's Restaurant am See** serves Austrian cuisine on yet another gorgeous lakeside terrace, as well as indoors (€11-15 main courses, daily 11:30-20:00, closed Nov-April, tel. 06134/8231, gasthof-simony.at).

**Pizzeria Bella Milano,** in the Lahn, is a local favorite and a good option after visiting the salt mines or going swimming. The outdoor tables have mountain views, and to-go meals are available if you want to eat by the lake or in your room. They serve both pizza and Italian standards, along with some Austrian options (€7-10 main courses and pizzas, daily 11:00-22:00, in winter may open evenings only, Lahn 41, tel. 06134/20037, www.bella-milano.at).

*Picnics and Cheap Eats:* The **Zauner** bakery/butcher/grocer, great for picnickers, makes fresh sandwiches to go (Mon-Sat 7:30-12:00, also 15:00-18:00 on Tue and Thu-Fri, closed Sun; uphill to the left from Market Square). The only supermarket is the small **Nah und Frisch,** in the Lahn at the bus stop (Mon-Fri 8:00-18:00, Sat 8:00-17:00, shorter hours off-season and closed Sun year-round). **Snack stands** near the main boat dock and the Lahn boat dock sell *Döner Kebab* and so on for €4 (tables and fine lakeside picnic options nearby).

# Hallstatt Connections

## BY TRAIN

Most travelers leaving Hallstatt are going to Salzburg or Vienna. In either case, you need to catch the shuttle boat (€2.40, departs 15 minutes before every train) to the little Hallstatt train station across the lake, and then ride 1.5 hours to **Attnang-Puchheim** (trains depart every 30-90 minutes from about 7:00 to 18:00). Trains are synchronized, so after a short wait in Attnang-Puchheim, you'll catch your  onward connection to **Salzburg** (50 minutes) or **Vienna** (2.5 hours; allow 3.5-4 hours total). The Hallstatt station has a ticket machine, or you can buy tickets online. In town, your hotel or the TI can help you find schedule information, or check www.oebb.at. Train info: tel. 051-717 (to get an operator, dial 2, then 2).

## BY BUS

The bus ride from Hallstatt to **Salzburg** is cheaper and more scenic than the train, and only slightly slower. You can still start off from Hallstatt by rail, taking the boat across the lake to the station and then the train toward Attnang-Puchheim—but get off after about 20 minutes in **Bad Ischl,** where you catch bus #150 to Salzburg (€10, Mon-Fri nearly hourly, Sat-Sun every 1-2 hours, 1.5 hours, www.postbus.at).

Alternatively, you can reach Bad Ischl on bus #542/543 from the Hallstatt bus stop (€4.30, 6-8/day, easy change in Gosaumühle) and then catch bus #150 to Salzburg. The Hallstatt TI has a schedule.

In Salzburg, bus #150 stops at Hofwirt and Mirabellplatz (convenient to Linzergasse hotels) before ending at the Salzburg train station.

## BY CAR

### Route Tips for Drivers

**Hallstatt to Vienna, via Mauthausen, Melk, and Wachau Valley** (210 miles): Leave Hallstatt early. Follow the scenic Route 145 through Gmunden to the autobahn and head east. After Linz, take exit #155 at Enns, and follow the signs for *Mauthausen* (five miles from the freeway). Go through Mauthausen town and follow the *Ehemaliges KZ-Gedenkstätte Lager* signs. When leaving Mauthausen for Melk, enjoy the riverside drive along scenic Route 3 (or take the autobahn if you're in a hurry or prone to carsickness). At Melk, signs to *Stift Melk* lead to the abbey. Other *Melk* signs lead into the town.

From Melk (get a Vienna map at the TI), cross the river again (signs to *Donaubrücke*) and stay on Route 3. After Krems, the riverside route (now the S-5) hits the autobahn (A-22), and you'll barrel right into Vienna's traffic. (See "By Car—Route Tips for Drivers" in the Vienna Connections chapter for details, page 208.)

**Vice Versa:** For tips on doing the above trip in reverse (Vienna to Wachau to Mauthausen to Hallstatt), see "Wachau Valley Connections" on page 226.

**From Salzburg:** For tips on driving here from Salzburg, see the end of the Salzburg chapter.

# TIROL

# INNSBRUCK AND HALL

Tirol—in Austria's panhandle, south of Bavaria—is a winter sports mecca known for its mountainous panoramas. In the region's capital, Innsbruck, the Golden Roof glitters and an alpine peak is in every view—but drivers strike it rich by staying in neighboring Hall, which has twice the charm and none of the tourist crowds. This region makes a fine stop for those en route from Germany to Italy, or Vienna to Switzerland.

# Innsbruck

Innsbruck is famous as a ski resort and a hiking haven...but when compared to the music and architecture of Salzburg and Vienna, it's stale strudel. The city's most-promoted sights are a ski jump and a gilded porch roof. Still, a quick look is easy and interesting. And the setting is impressive, along the fast-flowing Inn River with high peaks towering on both sides.

## Orientation to Innsbruck

Many sights, hotels, and restaurants are in Innsbruck's small, traffic-free medieval center. The old main street has handsome pedestrian arcades like those in Bolzano, Bern, and other alpine towns. Where the old town abuts the river is the original *Brücke* (bridge) over the Inn. Directly south of the old center, the broad Maria-Theresien-Strasse leads through a handsome neighborhood of 18th- and 19th-century buildings, bounded by the train station to the east. Suburbs climb up the foothills to the north and south.

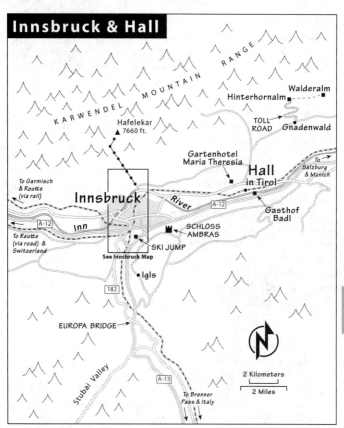

# Innsbruck & Hall

TOLL ROAD

KARWENDEL MOUNTAIN RANGE

Walderalm

Hinterhornalm

Hafelekar
▲ 7660 ft.

Gnadenwald

Gartenhotel
Maria Theresia

**Hall**
in Tirol

To
Salzburg
& Munich

To Garmisch
& Reutte
(via rail)

**Innsbruck**

River

A-12

Gasthof
Badl

To Reutte
(via road) &
Switzerland

A-12

Inn

SCHLOSS
AMBRAS

SKI JUMP

See Innsbruck Map

• Igls

182

EUROPA BRIDGE →

Stubai Valley

A-13

To Brenner
Pass & Italy

2 Kilometers

2 Miles

INNSBRUCK & HALL

## TOURIST INFORMATION

Innsbruck's main TI is at the edge of the old town (daily 9:00-18:00, Burggraben 3, three blocks in front of Golden Roof, tel. 0512/5356, www.innsbruck.info). There's also a mini-office at the **train station,** inside the bookstore (July-Aug daily 9:00-19:00; Sept-June Mon-Sat 10:00-18:00, closed Sun; tel. 0512/583-766). Both offices sell €1 maps and can help you find a room.

**Innsbruck Card:** The €33, 24-hour Innsbruck Card includes free local transport as far as Hall and entry to most of the attractions I've listed. It pays for itself if you ride the lifts to the top of the Hafelekar and back, and see one major sight. If you don't go up the mountain, the card is only worth it if you visit three or four major sights and connect them with the bus or Sightseer minibus. (You could validate it in the early afternoon, visit two sights, climb the Stadtturm tower, and do two more the next day before your 24 hours expire.) In Innsbruck, the card is sold at the TI and most participating sights. The card also covers Hall's Mint Museum (but not the Mint Tower) and is available from Hall's TI. There are also versions valid for 48 and 72 hours (€41 and €47).

**Walking Tours:** The TI offers a basic one-hour city walk of Innsbruck (€10, free with Innsbruck Card, daily at 14:00, July-Sept also daily at 11:00).

## ARRIVAL IN INNSBRUCK

**By Train:** Some trains stop at Innsbruck's Westbahnhof, but stay on the train until you reach the main train station (Hauptbahnhof). The main station has lockers (€2-4.50), a large supermarket, a TI (inside the bookstore—see earlier), and a *Reisezentrum,* where you can get rail information and tickets (daily 6:30-20:45). Local buses stop out front.

From the station, it's a 10-minute walk to the old town center. As you exit, walk to the right end of the square in front of the station. Turn left on Brixnerstrasse, and follow it past the fountain at Boznerplatz, where it turns into Meranerstrasse. Go straight until it dead-ends into Maria-Theresien-Strasse, then turn right and head 300 yards into the old town. You'll pass the TI on Burggraben (on your right), and then Hotel Weisses Kreuz and the Golden Roof.

## HELPFUL HINTS

**Laundry: Bubblepoint** is a handy self-service launderette (€4/load plus €1/10 minutes for dryer, coin-op Internet access-€2/hour, Mon-Fri 8:00-21:00, Sat-Sun 8:00-20:00, a block toward Golden Roof from train station at Brixnerstrasse 1, tel. 0512/5650-0750, www.bubblepoint.com).

**Internet Access:** Most hotels have guest computers or Wi-Fi. McDonald's (at the train station, or on the main street in the old town at Herzog-Friedrich-Strasse 35) has free Wi-Fi for the price of an ice cream.

**Bike Rental: Die Börse** bike shop has a range of choices, from city cruisers (€17/9 hours) to mountain bikes (€25/9 hours; daily 9:00-18:00, closes on Sun between 12:00 and 14:00 and if the weather is bad; in the back courtyard at Leopoldstrasse 4, tel. 0512/581-742, www.dieboerse.at). The local transport company, IVB, offers automated bike rentals around town, but the system is in German only and not geared toward tourists.

## GETTING AROUND INNSBRUCK

You won't need public transportation if you're sticking to Innsbruck's compact medieval center and the Hafelekar lift, but you'll take **trams** or **buses** to the museums and ski jump at Bergisel, to Schloss Ambras, or to Hall.

A single ticket within Innsbruck costs €1.80 from machines

(€2 from the driver); a day pass is €4.50. Tickets to Hall cost more, and there's a confusing array of family and group tickets. Sort out your options at the IVB office *(Kundencenter),* near the old town (Mon-Fri 7:30-18:00, closed Sat-Sun, Stainerstrasse 2, tel. 0512/53070, www.ivb.at or www.vvt.at).

A made-for-tourists minibus called the **Sightseer** (part of the public transit system; also known as bus #TS) follows a circular route around town, connecting the key sights. Buy tickets at the TI, the IVB office, or from the driver (€10.90/24-hour pass, covered by Innsbruck Card, no single-ride tickets). Your Sightseer ticket also covers other buses and trams within Innsbruck. The Sightseer is pricey—more than twice the cost of a regular day pass on public transit—and runs less frequently, but some find it more convenient (minimal headphone commentary in English, departs every 40 minutes from stop near Congress Center 9:00-17:40, frequency drops off-season, www.sightseer.at).

# Sights in Innsbruck

## IN THE OLD TOWN
### ▲▲The Golden Roof (Goldenes Dachl) and Herzog-Friedrich-Strasse

The three-block pedestrian street (Herzog-Friedrich-Strasse) in front of the much-ogled Golden Roof is Innsbruck's tourism central.

Stand in front of the Roof to get oriented. Emperor Maximilian I loved Innsbruck, and he built a palace here—including the balcony topped with 2,657 gilded copper tiles. The **Golden Roof** (1494) offered Maximilian an impressive spot from which to view his medieval spectacles.

Most buildings along this street are Gothic (notice the entry arches), but across the street from the Golden Roof (to the left as you face the Roof) is the frilly Baroque-style **Helblinghaus** façade. The arcades, common in Tirol, offer shelter from both sun and snow.

Above you is the bulbous **city tower** *(Stadtturm),* with 148 steps that you can climb for a great view (€3, daily June-Sept 10:00-20:00, Oct-May 10:00-17:00, tel. 0512/561-500, www.innsbruck. info). This was the old town watchtower; a prison was on the second floor. Like many Austrian buildings (including the nearby

## Innsbruck

1. Hotel Weisses Kreuz & Martin/Reformhaus Veg. Deli
2. Ibis Innsbruck Hauptbahnhof
3. Pension Stoi
4. Nepomuk Hostel
5. Weisses Rössl Restaurant
6. Weinhaus Happ Restaurant
7. Die Wilderin Restaurant
8. Mamma Mia Restaurant
9. Launderette
10. Bike Rental

Karwendel

500 Meters
500 Yards

SCHNEEBURGGASSE

### OLD TOWN DETAIL

CONGRESS INNSBRUCK (CONF. CENTER)

HOFGARTEN

SONNENSTR.

HERREN

INNSTRASSE

ST. JAKOB'S

Inn River

HERZOG-OTTO-STR.

GOLDEN ROOF

HOF-BURG

RENNWEG

UNIVERSITÄTS

BACHLECHNER

HERZOG-

8

6

FRIEDRICH-STRASSE

CITY TOWER

STIFT

FOLK ART MUSEUM

7

HOF-KIRCHE

To Zürich

5

SEILER

EGGER

4

SCHLOSSER.

1

BURG

MUSEUMSTR.

EXIT INNSBRUCK/ WEST

INNRAIN

MARKT.

URSULINENPASSAGE

GRABEN

ERLERSTR.

IVB TRANSIT CENTER

100 Meters
100 Yards

To Triumphal Arch

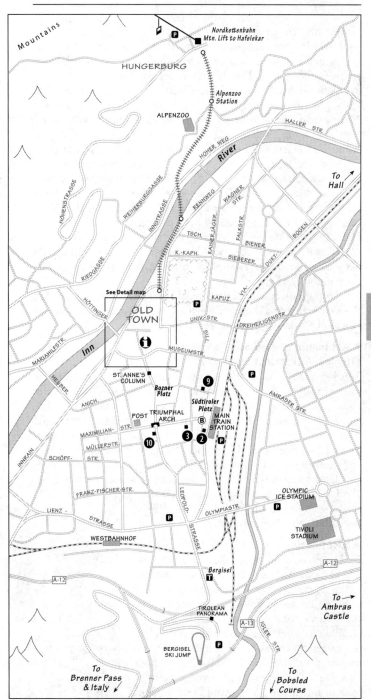

Hofkirche), the tower originally had a pointy Gothic spire—replaced with this onion-shaped one when Baroque was in vogue.

A block in front of the Golden Roof—next to the McDonald's—is the historic **Hotel Weisses Kreuz.** It's built on Roman foundations, but has only been hosting guests for the last 500 years. The white cross *(weisses Kreuz)* is the symbol of the Order of Malta—knights who opened up guesthouses for Holy Land-bound pilgrims during the Crusades. In 1769, a 13-year-old Wolfgang Amadeus Mozart and his father stayed here on their way to Italy. A generation later, this hotel was one of the centers of resistance against Napoleon, and later still, against the Nazis (giving shelter to Jewish refugees). When American soldiers moved in from Italy, they made the hotel their headquarters. Today, it's still a functioning—and recommended—hotel. It recently hosted Otto von Habsburg, the Man Who Would Be Emperor, if his great-great-uncle hadn't started—and lost—World War I. Though Otto could have stayed in the fanciest place in town, he chose this historic, comfortable inn instead.

If you walk down the shop-lined Hofgasse (facing the Golden Roof, go right), you'll reach the Museum of Tirolean Folk Art, the Hofkirche, and Hofburg palace.

### ▲▲Museum of Tirolean Folk Art (Tiroler Volkskunstmuseum)

This big museum offers the best look anywhere at traditional Tirolean lifestyles. Fascinating exhibits range from wedding dresses and gaily painted cribs and nativity scenes, to maternity clothes and babies' trousers. My favorite part is the carefully reconstructed interiors of several Tirolean homes through the ages. The free electronic text guide (leave ID as deposit) is worthwhile. Scan the barcode near most exhibits, and a description pops up on your device.

**Cost and Hours:** €10, includes admission to the Hofkirche, Tirol Panorama, and several lesser museums; daily 9:00-17:00, Universitätsstrasse 2, tel. 0512/5948-9510, www.tiroler-landesmuseen.at.

### ▲▲Hofkirche

Emperor Maximilian I liked Innsbruck so much, he wanted to be buried here, surrounded by 28 larger-than-life cast-bronze statues of his ancestors, relatives, in-laws...and his favorite heroes of the dying Middle Ages (such as King Arthur). They stand like giant chess pieces on the black-and-white-checkerboard marble floor. The good €1.50 English book tells you who everyone is, but you have to go back to the museum entrance to buy it. Don't

# Emperor Maximilian I (1459-1519)

The big name in Innsbruck is Emperor Maximilian I, who made this city a regional capital and built the Golden Roof. This Habsburg emperor was a dynamic, larger-than-life Renaissance man—soldier, sculptor, and statesman (though not very good at any of those pursuits). At the same time, he clung to the last romantic fantasies of the Middle Ages; for example, he was the last Habsburg who personally led his troops into battle. (To see where he fits in among other Habsburgs, see the family tree on page 455.)

Most people associate the Habsburg Empire with Vienna, which was the capital of the empire's Eastern European holdings during its peak in the 17th and 18th centuries. But during Maximilian's time, two centuries earlier, the focus was on Italy—he took the "Roman" part of "Holy Roman Emperor" very seriously. This made Innsbruck very important, since it was the capital of Tirol (which then included much of today's northern Italy and was on the Italian frontier).

This visionary emperor hoped that once all of Italy was his, Innsbruck would become the permanent capital of his empire. In reality, he was unlucky at war and ran up huge debts. But his strategic marriage to Mary of Burgundy set the stage for the large-scale expansion of the empire. Though he wanted to be a war hero, as with most Habsburgs, his biggest victory came with a trip to the altar.

miss King Arthur (as you face the altar, he's the fifth from the front on the right, next to the heavy-metal dude) and Mary of Burgundy, Maximilian's first—and favorite—wife (third from the front on the left). Some of these sculptures, including that of König Artur, were designed by German Renaissance painter Albrecht Dürer.

That's Maximilian himself, kneeling on top of the huge sarcophagus. Sadly, the real Max isn't inside. By the time he died, Maximilian had become notorious for running up debts, and his men weren't allowed to bring his body here.

Just inside the door to the church, you'll find the tomb of the popular Tirolean soldier Andreas Hofer, who fought against Napoleon.

**Cost and Hours:** €5, €10 combo-ticket with Museum of Tirolean Folk Art; open Mon-Sat 9:00-17:00, Sun 12:30-17:00; ticket includes audioguide, Universitätsstrasse 2—enter through museum, www.tiroler-landesmuseen.at.

## Hofburg

This 18th-century Baroque palace, built by Maria Theresa and full of her family portraits, is only worth a visit if you aren't going to the much bigger and better palaces in Vienna. The lone advantage is that, unlike the more famous Habsburg palaces, you'll have this one virtually to yourself. You get to see the empress' reception rooms, her private apartment, and a few rooms of exhibits.

**Cost and Hours:** €8, daily 9:00-17:00, last entry 30 minutes before closing, tel. 0512/587-186, www.hofburg-innsbruck.at.

**Nearby:** Should you need a **Sacher-Torte** fix, opposite the Hofburg entrance you'll find the local outpost of the venerable Viennese institution, Café Sacher (daily 8:30-24:00).

### St. James' Cathedral (Dom zu St. Jakob)

Innsbruck's own cathedral is your typical Baroque pastry: pink, frilly, and lots of gold. What makes it unique is the centerpiece of the high altar: one of Lucas Cranach's best-known Madonna and Childs, the *Mariahilf.*

**Cost and Hours:** Free, Mon-Sat 10:30-18:30, Sun 12:30-18:30, Domplatz 6, tel. 0512/583-902, www.dibk.at.

### Maria-Theresien-Strasse

The broad, Baroque Maria-Theresien-Strasse stretches south from the medieval center. It's a fine, traffic-free shopping street (though some of the action has moved to the indoor Rathaus Galerien mall, which you can enter partway down). Along the street are two monuments:

**St. Anne's Column (Annasäule)** marks the middle of the old marketplace. This was erected in the 18th century by townspeople thankful that their army had defeated an invading Bavarian army and saved the town (it's the same idea as the plague columns throughout Central Europe).

At the far end of the street, the **Triumphal Arch** is a gate Maria Theresa built to commemorate a happy and a sad occasion. The happy: Her son Leopold II, archduke of Tuscany, met and married a Spanish princess here in Innsbruck—and Maria Theresa and her husband Franz came for the ceremony. But Franz partied a little too hard and died the day after the wedding. (Maria Theresa wore black for the rest of her life.) The south-facing side of the arch—what you see as you  approach the center—shows the interlocked rings of the happy couple. But the flipside, visible as you leave town, features mournful statuary.

### ▲Slap-Dancing (Tiroler Abend)

The Gundolf family offers an entertaining evening of slap-dancing and yodeling nightly at 20:30 from April through October (€29 includes a drink with 2-hour show, dinner-€17 extra, pick-up/ drop-off service-€4, tickets and info at TI or your hotel; located far from the center at Gasthaus Sandwirt, Reichenauerstrasse 151, near Jugendherberge stop of bus #O; reservations tel. 0512/263-263, www.tirolerabend.info). On Thursday evenings in summer, the city puts on a free outdoor folk show under the Golden Roof (July-Sept, weather permitting).

## OUTER INNSBRUCK

These sights are within a tram ride of the old town.

### ▲Ambras Castle (Schloss Ambras)

Just southeast of town is the Renaissance palace Archduke Ferdinand II (1529-1595) renovated for his wife (it was originally a medieval castle). Its extensive grounds are replete with manicured gardens, a 17th-century fake waterfall, and resident peacocks. Visit the armory and the "curiosities" collection, containing the archduke's assortment of the beautiful and bizarre (*Kunst- und Wunderkammer*, ranging from stuffed sharks to ancient Portuguese frocks). The beautiful Spanish Hall (built 1569-1572) is clearly the prize of the whole complex, but it's closed in winter. Its intricate wooden ceiling and 27 life-size portraits of Tirolean princes make this a popular venue for classical music concerts.

**Cost and Hours:** €10, discounted to €7 Dec-March, open daily 10:00-17:00, closed Nov, audioguide-€3, Schlossstrasse 20; take tram #3 to last stop and then walk 15 minutes, or go direct on the Sightseer; tel. 01/525-244-802, www.schlossambras-innsbruck.at.

### ▲Ski Jump Stadium (Bergisel)

The ski jump here was used for the 1964 and 1976 Olympics. The original ramp (which wasn't up to modern standards) was torn down in 2000 and rebuilt from scratch. The jump is interesting and the views over the city are superb, but for mountain thrills, you're better off riding up to the ridge on the other side of the valley (see "Nordkettenbahn up to Hafelekar," later).

**Cost and Hours:** €9.50 whether you take funicular or not, €13 combo-ticket with Tirol Panorama; June-Oct daily 9:00-18:00; Dec-May Wed-Mon 10:00-17:00, closed Tue; closed Nov, last entry 30 minutes before closing, funicular back down runs until

15 minutes after closing, Bergiselweg 3, tel. 0512/589-259, www. bergisel.info.

**Visiting the Jump:** For the best view of the jump itself, go to the right just after you pass through the ticket gate and climb the steps (following *Olympisches Feuer* signs) to the Olympic rings and the dishes that held the Olympic flame. The plaques here honor Dorothy Hamill and a host of others who brought home the gold.

To get to the top of the ski jump, you can zip up in a funicular (2-minute ride), or walk up the 455 steps. At the top, an elevator takes you up the tower to great views from an outdoor viewing platform. One level below, a panoramic restaurant serves pricey meals. As you ride the funicular down alongside the jump, imagine yourself speeding down the ramp, then flying into the air...gulp. Note the cemetery, thoughtfully placed just below the jump.

**Getting There: Drivers** find it just off the Brenner Pass road on the south side of town (follow signs to *Bergisel*). Using **public transportation**, it's an easy tram ride from the center (tram #1 to the Bergisel stop, 6/hour) and then a 10-minute uphill walk following *Bergisel* signs; near the top of the woodsy path, bear left past the wooden pavilions for the Tirol Panorama (described next), or continue uphill for the ski jump. You can avoid most of the walk by taking the pricier Sightseer bus, which drops you near the Tirol Panorama.

### ▲▲Tirol Panorama

This worthwhile museum, right by the ski jump, houses a giant panoramic painting created in 1896 to memorialize Tirol's 1809 victory over Napoleon's forces. Other exhibits trace the political and military history of Tirol. Be sure to pick up the free audioguide, which is essential for understanding the mostly German-captioned exhibits.

**Cost and Hours:** €7, €10 combo-ticket with Museum of Tirolean Folk Art, €13 combo-ticket with ski jump; Wed-Mon 9:00-17:00, closed Tue; mandatory bag check with €1 deposit, Bergisel 1 (for directions, see ski jump listing, above), tel. 0512/5948-9611, www.tiroler-landesmuseen.at.

**Visiting the Panorama:** The first exhibit is the *Cyclorama*, a huge 360-degree painting of Napoleon's defeat at the hands of a ragtag Tirolean army right here at Bergisel. Napoleon had given Tirol to Bavaria, and Bavarian troops had occupied Innsbruck, but the local army managed to surprise and rout them, attacking early Sunday morning on a holiday weekend. Much like Salzburg's similar panorama painting, this one also toured Europe more than a century ago, giving the wider world a view of Innsbruck's mountain setting. The audioguide explains the battle's background in detail.

The next part of the museum (in an underground passageway) is a good general exhibit on Tirolean culture and politics. Through the passageway is the formerly separate Kaiserjäger Museum, dedicated to the Tirolean regiment in the Habsburg army, and in particular their sacrifices during World War I. Military-history buffs will be in their groove here, but most will find it skippable—except for the room dedicated to Andreas Hofer, the leader of the 1809 uprising (he's the guy with the beard, and you get to see his sword). Alas, the Bavarians retook Innsbruck a few months later. Hofer was captured and executed, but remains Tirol's great hero.

## INTO THE MOUNTAINS
A popular mountain-sports center and host of the 1964 and 1976 Winter Olympics, Innsbruck is surrounded by 150 mountain lifts, 1,250 miles of trails, and 250 hikers' huts. Ask your hotel or hostel for a free Club Innsbruck card (different from the Innsbruck Card sold by the TI), which offers overnight guests various discounts, bike tours, and free guided hikes in summer. Hikers meet in front of Congress Innsbruck daily at 8:45; each day, it's a different hike in the surrounding mountains and valleys (bring only lunch and water; boots, rucksack, and transport are provided; confirm with TI).

### ▲▲▲Nordkettenbahn up to Hafelekar
Right from the center of town, a series of three lifts—collectively called the Nordkettenbahn—whisk you above the tree line to the

ridge perched thousands of feet directly above the Golden Roof. This is the fastest and easiest way to get your Tirolean mountain high. It's not cheap, but on a clear day, the trip is worth every euro. If you're going to the top (€29.50 round-trip), it makes sense to get the Innsbruck Card for €33, which covers your trip, the Alpenzoo (described next), and much more; see page 363.

The first stage, the Hungerburgbahn **funicular,** leaves from the *Star Trek*-esque station outside Congress Innsbruck (the conference center right behind the Hofburg). It stops at the Alpenzoo station before reaching the Hungerburg hillside viewpoint (€7.40 round-trip, €11 combo-ticket with Alpenzoo, prices slightly higher in winter, Mon-Fri 7:15-19:30, Sat-Sun 8:00-19:30, every 15 minutes, tel. 0512/293-344, www.nordkette.com).

From the Hungerburg viewpoint, you'll catch the first of two **cable cars** that lead up into the mountains. The first one gets you to the Seegrube perch (with a reasonably priced self-serve cafeteria—no picnicking allowed); you'll change there for the highest station, Hafelekar, which has a café (round-trip: €29.50 from Innsbruck, €25.10 from Hungerburg; last lift down from Hafelekar at 17:00, from Seegrube at 17:30; both run every 15 minutes).

Cable-car tickets and Alpenzoo combo-tickets (but not funicular tickets) include free parking in the underground Congress garage.

If you've lucked out on weather, you'll see Innsbruck stretching across the valley to the Bergisel ski jump and, just to its right, the graceful Europa Bridge that leads up the Brenner Pass to Italy, beyond the peaks. Looking down the valley to the left, see if you can spot the town of Hall and its Mint Tower. Hike the 10-minute trail up to the Hafelekar peak (7,657 feet, no hiking boots needed), or choose from a range of longer hiking/walking options (well-explained in lift brochures). Serious mountain bikers will thrill at the steep trails—some of Europe's toughest (see page 364 for bike-rental information). At a minimum, walk the short path behind the lift station to peer over the ridge into the Karwendel Alps, jutting up between you and the German border. Take time to relax and soak in the view before returning to earth.

### ▲Alpenzoo

This zoo is one of Innsbruck's most popular attractions (not hard when the competition is the Golden Roof). You'll see all of the animals that hide out in the Alps, including bears, wolves, chamois, elk, marmots, and at least one gigantic vulture.

**Cost and Hours:** €9, €11 combo-ticket with Hungerburg-bahn funicular, daily April-Oct 9:00-18:00, Nov-March 9:00-17:00, Weiherburggasse 37, tel. 0512/292-323, www.alpenzoo.at.

**Getting There:** The easiest way up is with the funicular (described earlier). It's OK to stop off on a round-trip ticket to Hungerburg and continue up or down (follow signs 5 minutes from Alpenzoo station to the zoo itself). Or you could take the local #W bus, or just walk (following *Fussweg Alpenzoo* signs from the river).

## Olympic Bobsled

For those who envy Olympic bobsled teams whooshing down curvy chutes (who doesn't?), Innsbruck offers the chance to ride an actual Olympic course. In the summer, you'll ride with a pilot and three others down the 4,000-foot-long course in a sled-on-wheels; in the winter it's the real thing on ice.

**Cost and Hours:** Summer—€28, July-Aug only, Wed-Fri at 16:00; winter—€30, Jan-March only, Tue at 10:00 and 19:00, Thu at 19:00; in both seasons call ahead, no kids under 12, tel. 05275/51220, mobile 0664-357-8607, www.knauseder-event.at—select "Events," then *"Gästebob"* or *"Sommerbob."*

**Getting There:** From the city center, take bus #J from Marktgraben (near Maria-Theresien-Strasse and the TI) to the Olympia express stop (2/hour, 25 minutes)—it's a short walk along Römerstrasse to the building with the silver *Zielhaus* sign. Drivers coming from the A-12 autobahn should take the Innsbruck Mitte exit, and follow signs to *Igls* and then to *Olympia Bobbahn*.

## NEAR INNSBRUCK
### ▲▲Alpine Side-Trip by Car to Hinterhornalm

In Gnadenwald, a village sandwiched between Hall and its Alps, pay a €4.50 toll, pick up a brochure, then corkscrew your way up the mountain. Marveling at the crazy amount of energy put into such a remote road project, you'll finally end up at the rustic Hinterhornalm restaurant (generally daily mid-May-Oct 10:00-18:00, open later in summer—but entirely weather-dependent and often closed, closed Nov-mid-May, mobile 0664-211-2745). Hinterhornalm is a hang-gliding springboard. On good days, it's a butterfly nest. From there, it's a level 20-minute walk to Walderalm, a cluster of three dairy farms with 70 cows that share their meadow with the clouds. The cows ramble along ridge-top lanes surrounded by cut-glass peaks. The ladies of the farms serve soup, sandwiches, and drinks (very fresh milk in the afternoon) on rough plank tables. Below you spreads the Inn River Valley and, in the distance, tourist-filled Innsbruck.

# Sleeping in Innsbruck

The prices listed here include city tax and are for high season (generally May-Sept and Dec). Expect them to drop slightly at other times.

**$$ Hotel Weisses Kreuz,** near the Golden Roof, has been housing visitors for 500 years (see page 365). While its common

INNSBRUCK & HALL

---

# Sleep Code

**Abbreviations**  (€1 = about $1.40, country code: 43, area code: 0512)
**S** = Single, **D** = Double/Twin, **T** = Triple, **Q** = Quad, **b** = bathroom, **s** = shower only.

**Price Rankings**

To help you sort easily through these listings, I've divided the rooms into two categories, based on the price for a standard double room with bath:

  **$$  Higher Priced**—Most rooms €85 or more.

  **$  Lower Priced**—Most rooms less than €85.

Unless otherwise noted, credit cards are accepted, English is spoken, Wi-Fi is generally free, and breakfast is included. Prices change; verify current rates online or by email. For the best prices, always book directly with the hotel.

---

spaces still have an old-inn feel—with an airy atrium stairway, antique Tirolean furniture, and big wood beams—its 40 rooms are recently renovated and comfortable, and a good value for the location (S-€46, Sb-€78, D-€78, small Db-€124, big Db-€138-149, extra bed-€22, non-smoking, elevator, guest computer and Wi-Fi, parking €14/day—reserve ahead, 50 yards in front of Golden Roof, as central as can be in the old town at Herzog-Friedrich-Strasse 31, tel. 0512/594-790, www.weisseskreuz.at, hotel@weisseskreuz.at). If it's full, two nearby hotels have similar profiles and prices (Weinhaus Happ and the Weisses Rössl, both with recommended restaurants listed under "Eating in Innsbruck," later).

**$$ Ibis Innsbruck Hauptbahnhof** lacks character but has 75 predictable, acceptably priced rooms right next to the train station. Reach the hotel through the underground passageway (by the luggage lockers), or exit the station's main doors and then go up the escalator of the black modern building that's at the left end of the square as you emerge (Sb-€75, Db-€94, breakfast-€11, non-smoking, elevator, guest computer and Wi-Fi, parking-€12/day, Sterzinger Strasse 1, tel. 0512/570-3000, www.ibishotel.com, h5174@accor.com).

**$ Pension Stoi** rents 17 inexpensive, basic rooms 200 yards from the train station and a 10-minute walk from the old town center. The entranceway and oddly located reception are a bit off-putting, but the rooms are fine (S-€46, Sb-€49, D-€68, Db-€75, T-€86, Tb-€100, Q-€105, Qb-€120, no breakfast, Wi-Fi, four free parking spaces—no guarantees, reception open daily 8:00-21:00; walk left as you leave the station and head down Salurnerstrasse, take first left on Adamgasse, then watch for signs in the courtyard on the right, Salurnerstrasse 7; tel. 0512/585-434, www.pensionstoi.at, pensionstoi@aon.at).

**$ Nepomuk's** offers 18 backpacker beds in two well-worn, well-located apartments above Café Munding, a pastry shop in the old town. The reception and breakfast are in the café. They only accept reservations by telephone (bed in 4- to 6-bed dorms: €24-26, D-€58; prices include breakfast, sheets, and towels; Wi-Fi, kitchen, Kiebachgasse 16, tel. 0512/584-118, mobile 0664/787-9197, www.nepomuks.at).

## Eating in Innsbruck

**Weisses Rössl** is in the old town, but a little off the tourist track. For culinary adventurers, it features traditional Tirolean treats such as oven-roasted liver and calf's head. Fear not: Schnitzels and steaks abound, or try the tasty *Grillteller* (an assortment of grilled meats) or *Hauspfandl*—meat, potatoes, and veggies served up in a cast-iron skillet (€10-18 main courses, Mon-Sat 11:45-15:00 & 18:00-23:00, closed Sun; facing the Roof, go one block left to Kiebachgasse and turn left to #8; tel. 0512/583-057, www.roessl.at).

**Weinhaus Happ** is another good option, on the left as you face the Golden Roof. It offers standards like Wiener schnitzel, but also game, fish, and salads, in a labyrinth of cozy, traditional *Stuben.* You can order smaller, lower-priced portions of most dishes (€10-19 main courses, daily 11:00-22:30, Herzog-Friedrich-Strasse 14, tel. 0512/582-980, www.weinhaus-happ.at).

**Die Wilderin,** a block and a half from the Golden Roof, is a small dinner-only eatery, with a big bar, tables on two levels, and a commitment to serving only dishes made with locally sourced ingredients. They'll explain the modern, German-only menu (€16-18 main courses, €9 vegetarian plates, Tue-Sun 17:00-24:00, closed Mon, Seilergasse 5, tel. 0512/562-728, www.diewilderin.at).

**Mamma Mia,** a cheaper escape from traditional fare, dishes up hearty €8 portions of pizza and pasta. They have indoor and outdoor seating, or you can get it to go (pizza by the slice-€3, daily 10:30-24:00, Kiebachgasse 2, tel. 0512/562-902).

**Martin/Reformhaus** is a health-food store with an eat-in or takeout deli where vegetarians can feast on tasty organic meals (daily soups and salads, €7 weekday lunch specials; open Mon-Fri 8:30-18:30, Sat 8:30-17:00, closed Sun; Herzog-Friedrich-Strasse 29, tel. 0512/565-099).

*Supermarkets:* **MPreis,** in the train station, is large and has long hours (daily 6:00-21:00). There's also a small MPreis in the old town and a **Spar** by the TI.

## Innsbruck Connections

**From Innsbruck to Hall:** Trains and buses both use Innsbruck's main station (buses leave from platform A) and cost €3.40 (covered by Innsbruck Card; €6.80 day pass, €9.60 day pass includes Innsbruck city transport). The **train** is a bit more scenic (4/hour, 9 minutes, plus 10-minute walk from Hall station into town) than the **bus** (#4, 4/hour, 2/hour on Sun, 25 minutes), which goes through industrial suburbs before dropping you right in Hall's town center (see "Arrival in Hall" on page 379). Don't take bus #D, which is slow and stops on the far side of Hall's old town.

From Innsbruck by Train to: Salzburg (hourly, 2 hours), **Vienna** (nearly hourly, 4-5 hours), **Reutte** (every 2 hours, 2.5 hours, change in Garmisch), **Füssen,** Germany (3/day, 4 hours, fastest via train to Reutte and then bus #4258/#74 to Füssen, last easy connection leaves Innsbruck around 14:30), **Munich** (every 2 hours, 2 hours), **Zürich** (every 2 hours, 3.5 hours), **Milan** (every 2 hours, 5.5 hours, change in Verona, seat reservation required), **Venice** (2/day direct, more with changes in Verona, 4.5-5.5 hours). There are also night trains to **Vienna** (it's a short night, though), **Milan,** and **Rome.** Train info: tel. 051-717 (to get an operator, dial 2, then 2), www.oebb.at.

For driving directions to Reutte, Switzerland, and Italy, see page 384.

# Hall

Hall—a rich salt-mining center when Innsbruck was just a humble bridge *(Brücke)* town on the Inn River—has a larger and more attractive old town than its sprawling neighbor. Its main square is the scene of a brisk farmers' market on Saturday mornings. Hall closes down tight for its afternoon siesta and sleeps on Sunday—but Innsbruck's sights are a short drive, bus trip, or bike ride away. Drivers get more value for their money by staying in Hall instead of Innsbruck.

## Orientation to Hall

### TOURIST INFORMATION

Hall's helpful TI offers lots of information, sells Innsbruck Cards, and can help you find a room (Mon-Fri 9:00-18:00, Sat 9:00-13:00, closed Sun, near bus stop at Unterer Stadtplatz 19, tel. 05223/455-440, www.hall-wattens.at).

The TI organizes one-hour town walking tours in English at 10:00 on Monday, Thursday, and Saturday (€6, includes admissions, €8 also includes tour of Mining Museum).

## ARRIVAL IN HALL

For directions to my two recommended hotels in Hall, see page 382.

**By Bus:** Coming from Innsbruck, get off at the Unterer Stadtplatz stop, just below downtown Hall. From the bus stop, the Mint Museum is to your right; the town square is five minutes uphill to your left (use the underpass to cross the street).

**By Train:** Hall's train station is a 10-minute walk from the town center (exit straight ahead up Bahnhofstrasse, turn right at the busy road, and you'll soon reach the fountain that marks the bottom of town).

**By Car:** Drivers approaching on the autobahn take the Hall-Mitte exit. You'll cross a big bridge over the river; just after it, the small P5 lot on the right has a three-hour maximum (€1/hour, buy ticket from machine, Mon-Fri 8:30-18:00 except free 12:00-14:00, Sat 8:30-12:00, free at other times and all day Sun). Or, continue straight through the intersection and turn left to the underground P2 parking garage (5-minute walk from old town center, first hour free, €1.70/hour after that, €10.20/24 hours).

**On Foot or by Bike:** Hall and Innsbruck are connected by a pleasant bike path along the Inn River and through some parks. From Innsbruck, cross the Inn River, then simply follow the river downstream along the Inntal Radweg, minding signs to Hall. A comfortable 30-minute pedal will get you there.

# Sights in Hall

### Main Square (Oberer Stadtplatz)

Hall's quaint main square is worth a visit. In the next square over (Pfarrplatz) is the Town Hall (Rathaus) and St. Nicholas Parish Church (Pfarrkirche St. Nikolaus). This much-appended Gothic church is decorated Baroque, with fine altars, a twisted apse, and a north wall lined with bony relics.

### Hall Mint Museum and Mint Tower (Münze Hall und Münzerturm)

Beginning in the 15th century, Hall began minting coins—most notably the *Taler* (which eventually became

"dollar" in English). The former town mint, housed in Hasegg Castle, is near the Unterer Stadtplatz bus stop, just below the old town. Inside, the **Hall Mint Museum** shows off the town's proud minting heritage. The centerpiece is a huge, fully functioning replica of a 16th-century minting press—powered by water and made almost entirely of wood. The renovated **Mint Tower** provides a workout (185 steps, or 202 if you go medieval and take the narrow original stairs) and a great view. Your tower ticket lets you check out the world's largest silver coin, worth roughly $40,000 (and weighing 44 pounds—suddenly the change in my pocket doesn't feel so heavy). It was made in 2008 to commemorate the 500th anniversary of Maximilian I's coronation and another event, apparently equally momentous: Austria's co-hosting of the 2008 European soccer championships.

**Cost and Hours:** Museum—€6, includes excellent audioguide, tower—€4, €8 combo-ticket for both; open Tue-Sun 10:00-17:00, closed Mon; shorter hours and closed Sun-Mon off-season, closed mid-Jan-March; last entry one hour before closing, tel. 05223/585-5165, www.muenze-hall.at.

**Getting There:** The bus from Innsbruck drops you off right by the castle (stop: Unterer Stadtplatz, go through door marked *#17* and *Burg Hasegg*); from the recommended Gasthof Badl, it's the first big building you'll see after crossing the old wooden pedestrian bridge.

### Mining Museum (Bergbaumuseum)

Back when salt was money, Hall was loaded. Try catching a tour at this museum, where the town has reconstructed one of its original salt mines, complete with pits, shafts, drills, tools, and a tiny-but-slippery wooden slide.

**Cost and Hours:** €5, €8 town walk includes museum; English tours Mon, Thu, and Sat at 11:30; no need to reserve—but punctuality is crucial; one block south of main square, at corner of Fürstengasse and Eugenstrasse; tel. 05223/455-440, www.hall-wattens.at.

### Biking

If you're here for a few days, consider enjoying the valley on two wheels. The riverside bike path (7 miles from Hall to Volders) is a treat. Rent bikes at **Die Bike-Box** (€14/half-day, €18/day, electric bikes-€22/day, Mon-Fri 9:00-14:00 & 15:00-19:00, Sat 9:00-13:00, closed Sun, across street and 75 yards down from Unterer Stadtplatz bus stop at Unterer Stadtplatz 10, 05223/55944, www.diebikebox.com).

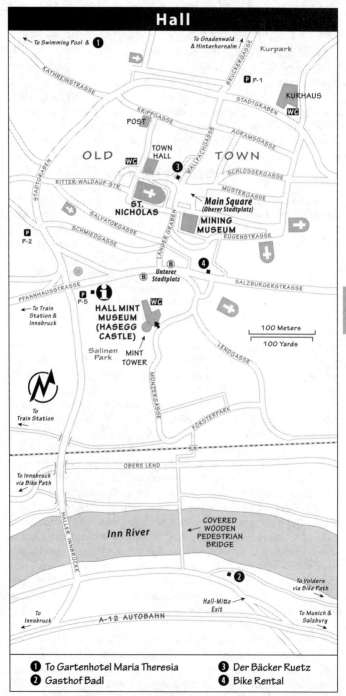

# Hall

← To Swimming Pool & ①

To Gnadenwald & Hinterhornalm ↗

Kurpark

KATHREINSTRASSE

BRUCKERGASSE

P P-1

STADTGRABEN

KURHAUS

WC

KRIPPGASSE

POST

OLD

TOWN

AGRAMSGASSE

TOWN HALL

WALPACHGASSE

SCHLOSSERGASSE

WC

③

MUSTERGASSE

STADTGRABEN

RITTER-WALDAUF-STR.

ST. NICHOLAS

Main Square (Oberer Stadtplatz) ←

P P-2

SALVATORGASSE

MINING MUSEUM

EUGENSTRASSE

SCHMIEDGASSE

LANGER GRABEN

④

B

B Unterer Stadtplatz

SALZBURGERSTRASSE

PFANNHAUSSTRASSE

P P-5

i

← To Train Station & Innsbruck

HALL MINT MUSEUM (HASEGG CASTLE)

WC

100 Meters

100 Yards

Salinen Park

MINT TOWER

MÜNZERGASSE

LENDGASSE

To Train Station ←

FÖRSTERPARK

OBERE LEND

← To Innsbruck via Bike Path

HALLER INNBRÜCKE

Inn River

COVERED WOODEN PEDESTRIAN BRIDGE

To Volders via Bike Path →

② 

Hall-Mitte Exit →

To Munich & Salzburg →

← To Innsbruck

A-12 AUTOBAHN

① To Gartenhotel Maria Theresia

② Gasthof Badl

③ Der Bäcker Ruetz

④ Bike Rental

**INNSBRUCK & HALL**

## Swimming Pool

To really make a splash, check out Hall's magnificent *Freis-chwimmbad*, a huge outdoor pool complex with four diving boards, giant lap pool, big slide, and kiddies' pool, all surrounded by a lush garden, sauna, mini-golf, and lounging locals.

**Cost and Hours:** €4, €2.30 after 16:00, open daily early May-early Sept 9:00-19:00, closed off-season, at campground northwest of Hall near Gartenhotel Maria Theresia, follow *Schwimmbad* signs from downtown to Scheidensteinstrasse 24, tel. 05223/45464.

# Sleeping in Hall

**(area code: 05223)**

Lovable towns that specialize in lowering the pulse of local vacationers line the Inn River Valley. I like Hall best, but up the hill on either side of the river are more towns strewn with fine farmhouse hotels, pensions, and private rooms, all with free parking.

**$$ Gartenhotel Maria Theresia** is just a 15-minute walk from Hall's center, next to a village church and across from a farm. You'll feel a little bit like landed Tirolean gentry, at prices that would get you only a commoner's lodgings in Innsbruck. This spacious, elegantly comfortable, 27-room family-run place is a good-value splurge and makes a great hub from which to explore the Inn Valley (Sb-€72-77, Db-€124-134, Tb-€186, price depends on room size, family deals, elevator, Wi-Fi, beautiful garden patio, restaurant, fine-dining room in wine cellar, free parking, bike rentals-€18/day, playground, petting zoo, parrots and macaques, ask about mountain-bike tours, Reimmichlstrasse 25—see map on page 363, tel. 05223/56313, www.gartenhotel.at, info@gartenhotel.at).

**Getting to Gartenhotel Maria Theresia:** If you arrive by **car** from Innsbruck, take the Hall-Mitte exit, and go over the bridge and through the light. At the roundabout, veer left (you'll already see signs) onto Speckbacherstrasse. Go left on Scheidenstein-strasse, right on Badgasse, and left on Reimmichelstrasse. If you arrive by **bus** or **train,** it's a long walk (especially from the train station)—take a taxi instead (about €10 from station or main bus stop). To shorten the walk, ride the bus three stops past the Unterer Stadtplatz stop to the Kurhaus stop, then follow Stadtgraben (with the town on your left) until it turns downhill, and go right onto Kathreinstrasse, which feeds into Scheidensteinstrasse (20-minute walk from Kurhaus stop to hotel).

**$ Gasthof Badl** is a big, comfortable, friendly, riverside place with 26 rooms run by Sonja and her family, with help from Leo, their enormous, easygoing dog. I like its convenience (right off the expressway but a short and scenic walk from the old town), peace, big breakfast, and warm welcome (Sb-€51-54, Db-€79-89,

Tb-€120, Qb-€142, family deals, elevator, Wi-Fi, laundry ser-
vice-€9.50, recommended restaurant; bike rentals-€5/12 hours,
€7/24 hours; Innbrücke 4, tel. 05223/56784, www.badl.at, info@
badl.at).

**Getting to Gasthof Badl:** It's easy for **drivers** to find—from
the east, it's immediately off the Hall-Mitte freeway exit; you'll
see the orange-lit *Bed* sign. From Innsbruck, take the Hall-Mitte
exit, and rather than turning left over the big bridge into town, go
straight. To reach Gasthof Badl from the Unterer Stadtplatz **bus
stop,** go through the door next to the bus stop (marked *#17* and
*Burg Hasegg*), cut through a couple of courtyards until you're under
the castle tower, then follow Münzergasse (marked by red-and-
blue no-parking signs) across the creek. Go straight until you hit
the train tracks, then turn left to use the railroad underpass, which
is about 10 yards away. Coming out of the underpass, go right up
the ramp and, from there, cross the old wooden bridge to the hotel.
From the **train station,** leave the station to the right, follow the
tracks straight ahead, and as the street curves left, veer right on the
footpath that follows the tracks to access the railroad underpass,
then head straight across the old wooden bridge.

# Eating in Hall

The restaurant at the recommended **Gasthof Badl** serves excellent
dinners until 21:30 (€10-15 main courses, closed Sun).

**Der Bäcker Ruetz,** on the main square just behind the fountain, is a big branch of a chain bakery and a solid place for a quick
lunch (with self-serve seating indoors and out). It offers good and
filling sandwiches for €3-5—along with pretzels, rolls, and pastries. Enjoy a coffee and *Erdbeerstrudel* (strawberry strudel) while
people-watching in the sun, or get your food to go for a picnic
(Mon-Fri 7:00-18:30, Sat-Sun 7:00-17:00, Sparkassengasse 1, tel.
05223/54828).

# Hall Connections

## BY TRAIN AND BUS

Hall and Innsbruck are connected by train (4/hour, 9 minutes) and
bus (#4, 4/hour, 2/hour on Sun, 25 minutes). Drivers staying in
freeway-handy Hall can leave the car parked there and side-trip
into Innsbruck on the bus.

## BY CAR
### Route Tips for Drivers
**From Hall into Innsbruck:** For old Innsbruck, take the autobahn from Hall to the Innsbruck Ost exit and follow the signs to

*Zentrum,* then *Kongresshaus,* and park as close as you can to the old center on the river *(Hofgarten).* If you'll be riding up the cable-car section of the Nordkettenbahn (see page 373), you can park for free at the Congress garage (8:00-18:00).

Just south of Innsbruck is the ski jump (see page 371; from the autobahn take the Innsbruck Süd exit and follow signs to *Bergisel).* Park at the end of the road near the Andreas Hofer Memorial, and climb to the empty, grassy stands for a picnic.

**From Hall or Innsbruck to Reutte:** Head west (direction Bregenz/Switzerland) and leave the freeway at Telfs, where signs direct you to Reutte (a 1.5-hour drive).

**From Innsbruck to Switzerland:** Head west on the autobahn, as above. (If you're coming directly from Innsbruck's ski jump, go down into town along the huge cemetery and follow blue *A-12/ Garmisch/Arlberg* signs). The eight-mile-long Arlberg tunnel saves you 30 minutes on your way to Switzerland, but costs you lots of scenery and €8.50 (Swiss francs and credit cards accepted). For a joyride and to save a few bucks, skip the tunnel, exit at St. Anton, and go via Stuben.

After the speedy Arlberg tunnel, you're 30 minutes from Switzerland. Bludenz, with its characteristic medieval quarter, makes a good rest stop. Pass Feldkirch (and another long tunnel) and exit the autobahn at Rankweil/Feldkirch Nord, following signs for *Altstätten* and *Meiningen (CH).* Crossing the baby Rhine River, you've left Austria.

**Side-Trip over Brenner Pass into Italy:** A short swing into Italy is fast and easy from Innsbruck or Hall (45-minute drive, easy border crossing). To get to Italy, take the A-13/E-45 expressway, which heads across the great Europa Bridge over Brenner Pass. It costs €8, but in 30 minutes you'll be at the border. (Note: Traffic can be heavy on summer weekends.)

In Italy, drive to the colorful market town of Vipiteno/Sterzing. **Reifenstein Castle** gives one of Europe's most intimate looks at medieval castle life. Let the friendly lady of Reifenstein (Frau Steiner) show you around her wonderfully preserved castle. Its layout and even its decor have changed little since the 15th century, when the castle passed into the hands of the Teutonic Knights. Since 1813, a branch of the noble Thurn and Taxis family has owned the castle. You can only visit it on Frau Steiner's one-hour tours, given in German, Italian, and English, as needed (€7; tours run mid-April-Oct Sun-Fri at 10:30, 14:00, and 15:00; late July-early Sept also at 16:00; always closed Sat, meet at drawbridge and be punctual, ideally call ahead to confirm tour, minimum of 4 people—or €28—needed for tour to run, mobile 339-264-3752, www. sterzing.com—click on "Culture" and then "Castles").

# BAVARIA AND WESTERN TIROL

*Germany: Füssen • King's Castles
• Wieskirche • Oberammergau
• Linderhof Castle • Ettal Monastery
• Zugspitze • Austria: Reutte*

---

In this picturesque corner of the Alps (2.5 hours west of Innsbruck), you'll find a timeless land of fairy-tale castles, painted buildings shared by cows and farmers, and locals who still dress in dirndls and lederhosen and yodel when they're happy.

This area straddles the border between Bavaria (part of Germany) and Tirol (part of Austria). On the German side, you can

tour "Mad" King Ludwig II's ornate Neuschwanstein Castle, Europe's most spectacular. Stop by the Wieskirche, an ornately decorated Baroque church that puts the faithful in a heavenly mood, and browse through Oberammergau, Germany's woodcarving capital and home of the famous Passion Play (next performed in 2020). Yet another impressive castle (Linderhof), another fancy church (Ettal), and a sky-high viewpoint (the Zugspitze) round out southern Bavaria's top attractions. Then, just over the border in Austria, you can explore the ruined Ehrenberg Castle and scream down a mountain on an oversized skateboard at one of the area's many luge runs. In this chapter, I'll first cover the German side (with the most sights), then the Austrian side (around Reutte in Tirol).

## CHOOSING A HOME BASE

My hotel recommendations in this chapter cluster in three areas: Füssen and Oberammergau (in Germany), and Reutte (in Austria). When selecting a home base, here are a few factors to consider:

**Füssen** offers the easiest access to the region's biggest attraction, the "King's Castles" (Neuschwanstein and Hohenschwangau), and is the handiest base for train travelers. The town itself is a mix of real-world and cutesy-cobbled, and has some of the glitziest hotels in the area (as well as more affordable options).

**Oberammergau** is the best-known, most touristy, and cutest town of the bunch. World-famous for its once-per-decade Passion Play, it's much sleepier the other nine years. It's a long bus ride or a 45-minute drive from Oberammergau to the King's Castles. But three lesser, yet still worthwhile sights are close by: Ettal Monastery, Linderhof Castle, and the German lift to the Zugspitze.

**Reutte** is the least appealing town, and is less practical for train travelers, but the villages around it are home to some of the coziest, most pleasant rural accommodations in the region—making it a particularly good option for drivers. Reutte butts up against the ruined Ehrenberg Castle, and the King's Castles, Linderhof, and the Austrian approach to the Zugspitze are all within a 30-minute drive.

For specifics on public-transit logistics from each town, see "By Public Transportation," later.

## PLANNING YOUR TIME AND GETTING AROUND BAVARIA

While Germans and Austrians vacation here for a week or two at a time, the typical speedy American traveler will find two days' worth of sightseeing. With a car and more time, you could enjoy three or four days, but the basic visit ranges anywhere from a long day trip from Munich to a three-night, two-day stay. If the weather's good and you're not going to Switzerland, be sure to ride a lift to an alpine peak.

### By Car

This region is best by car, and all the sights are within an easy 60-mile loop from Füssen or Reutte. Even if you're doing the rest of your trip by train, consider renting a car for your time here (for local rental offices, see page 392).

Here's a good plan for a one-day circular drive from **Reutte** (from **Füssen,** you can start about 30 minutes later):

| | |
|---|---|
| 7:00 | Breakfast |
| 7:30 | Depart hotel |
| 8:00 | Arrive at Neuschwanstein to pick up tickets for the two castles (Neuschwanstein and Hohenschwangau) |
| 9:00 | Tour Hohenschwangau |
| 11:00 | Tour Neuschwanstein |
| 13:00 | Drive to Oberammergau (with a 15-minute stop at the |

BAVARIA

Füssen & Reutte Area

Wieskirche), and spend an hour there browsing the carving shops and grabbing a quick lunch

15:00   Drive to Ettal Monastery for a half-hour stop, then on to Linderhof Castle

16:00   Tour Linderhof

18:00   Drive along scenic Plansee Lake back to your hotel

19:00   Back at hotel

20:00   Dinner

Off-season (Oct-March), start your day an hour later, since Neuschwanstein and Hohenschwangau tours don't depart until 10:00; and skip Linderhof, which closes at 16:00.

The next morning, you could stroll through Reutte, hike to the Ehrenberg ruins, and ride a mountain luge on your way to Munich, Innsbruck, Switzerland, Venice, or wherever.

If you're based in **Oberammergau** instead, get an early start and hit Neuschwanstein and Hohenschwangau first. If the weather's good, hike to the top of Ehrenberg Castle (in Reutte). Drive along the Plansee and tour Linderhof and Ettal Monastery on your way back home.

## By Public Transportation

Where you stay determines which sights you can see most easily. Train travelers use **Füssen** as a base, and bus or bike the three miles to the King's Castles and the Tegelberg luge or gondola. Staying in **Oberammergau** gives you easy access to Linderhof and Ettal Monastery, and you can day-trip to the top of the Zugspitze via Garmisch. **Reutte** is the least convenient base if you're carless, but travelers staying there can easily bike or hike to the Ehrenberg ruins, and can reach Neuschwanstein by bus (via Füssen), bike (1.5 hours), or taxi if available (ask your hotelier); if you stay at the recommended Gutshof zum Schluxen hotel (between Reutte and Füssen, in Pinswang, Austria) it's a 1- to 1.5-hour hike through the woods to Neuschwanstein.

Visiting sights farther from your home base is not impossible by local bus, but requires planning. The Deutsche Bahn (German Railway) journey planner at www.bahn.com does a great job of finding bus connections that work, on both sides of the border. (Schedules for each route are available at www.rvo-bus.de, but only in German.) Those staying in **Füssen** can day-trip by bus to Reutte and the Ehrenberg ruins, to the Wieskirche, or, with some effort, to Oberammergau. From **Oberammergau,** you can reach Neuschwanstein and Füssen by bus if you plan ahead. From **Reutte,** you can take the train to Ehrwald to reach the Zugspitze from the Austrian side, but side-trips to Oberammergau and Linderhof are impractical. More transport details are provided later, under each individual destination.

Hitchhiking, though always risky, is a slow-but-doable way to connect the public-transportation gaps. For example, even reluctant hitchhikers can catch a ride from Linderhof back to Oberammergau, as virtually everyone leaving there is a tourist like you and heading that way.

If you'll be taking a lot of trains in Bavaria (for example, day-tripping to Munich), consider the **Bayern-Ticket:** It covers buses and slower regional trains throughout Bavaria for up to five people at a very low price (€23/day for the first person plus €4 for each additional person).

## By Bike

This is great biking country. Many hotels loan bikes to guests, and shops in Reutte and at the Füssen train station rent bikes for €10-15 per day. The ride from Reutte to Neuschwanstein and the Tegelberg luge (1.5 hours) is a natural.

## Bavarian Craftsmanship

The scenes you'll see painted on the sides of houses in Bavaria are called *Lüftlmalerei*. The term came from the name of the house ("Zum Lüftl") owned by a man from Oberammergau who pioneered the practice in the 18th century. As the paintings became popular during the Counter-Reformation Baroque age, themes tended to involve Christian symbols, saints, and stories (such as scenes from the life of Jesus), to reinforce the Catholic Church's authority in the region. Some scenes also depicted an important historical event that took place in that house or town.

Especially in the northern part of this region (for example, in Rothenburg), you'll see *Fachwerkhäuser*—half-timbered houses. A timber frame outlines the wall, which was traditionally filled in with a mixture of wicker and clay. These are most often found inside fortified cities that were once strong and semi-independent (such as Rothenberg, Nürnberg, and Dinkelsbühl). Farther south, you'll see sturdy, white-walled masonry houses with woodwork on the upper stories and an overhanging roof. Many Bavarian homes and hotels have elaborate wooden paneling and furniture, often beautifully carved or made from special sweet-smelling wood.

## HELPFUL HINTS

**Welcome to Germany:** Most of the destinations in this chapter (except for the Reutte area and the Austrian side of the Zugspitze) are in a different country. While Germans use the same euro currency as Austrians, postage stamps and phone cards only work in the country where you buy them. To call from Austria to Germany, dial 00-49 and then the number listed in this section (omitting the initial zero). To telephone from Germany to Austria, dial 00-43 and then the number (again, omitting the initial zero).

**Sightseeing Pass:** The Bavarian Palace Department offers a **14-day ticket** (called *Mehrtagesticket*) that covers admission to Neuschwanstein (but not Hohenschwangau) and Linderhof, as well as many other castles not described in this book (including ones in Munich, Nürnberg, and Würzburg). If your travels will take you deeper into Germany, this might be worth considering (one-person pass-€24, family/partner version for up to two adults plus children-€40, www.schloesser.bayern.de).

**Local Guest Tax:** Hotels and B&Bs in the region are required to collect a local tax (called a *Kurtax*) of about €2 per person per night. This is usually included in the rates I've listed, but may be listed separately on your bill. Usually, this tax funds a card that provides discounts on attractions and free public transportation; details are in each city's "Tourist Information" sections.

**Visiting Churches:** At any type of church, if you'd like to attend a service, look for the *Gottesdienst* schedule. In every small German town in the very Catholic south, when you pass the big town church, look for a sign that says *Heilige Messe.* This is the schedule for holy Mass, usually on Saturday *(Sa.)* or Sunday *(So.).*

# Füssen, Germany

Dramatically situated under a renovated castle on the lively Lech River, Füssen (FEW-sehn) has been a strategic stop since ancient times. Its main street was once part of the Via Claudia Augusta, which crossed the Alps in Roman times. Going north, early travelers could follow the Lech River downstream to the Danube, and then cross over to the Main and Rhine valleys—

a route now known to modern travelers as the "Romantic Road." Today, while Füssen is overrun by tourists in the summer, few venture to the back streets...which is where you'll find the real charm. Apart from my self-guided walk and the Füssen Heritage Museum, there's little to do here—but it's a fine base for visiting the King's Castles and the other surrounding attractions.

BAVARIA

## Orientation to Füssen

Füssen's roughly circular old town huddles around its castle and monastery, along the Lech River. The train station, TI, and many shops are at the north end of town, and my recommended hotels and eateries are within easy walking distance. Roads spin off in all directions (to the lake, to Neuschwanstein, to Austria). Halfway between Füssen and the German border (as you drive, or a woodsy walk from town) is the **Lechfall,** a thunderous waterfall (with a handy WC).

### TOURIST INFORMATION

The TI is in the center of town (July-mid-Sept Mon-Fri 9:00-18:00, Sat 10:00-14:00, Sun 10:00-12:00; mid-Sept-June Mon-Fri 9:00-17:00, Sat 10:00-14:00, closed Sun; one Internet terminal, free with Füssen Card—described next, 3 blocks down Bahnhofstras-se from station at Kaiser-Maximilian-Platz 1, tel. 08362/93850, www.fuessen.de). If necessary, the TI can help you find a room. After hours, the little self-service info pavilion near the front of the TI features an automated room-finding service with a phone to call hotels.

Be sure to ask your hotel for a **Füssen Card,** an electronic pass that your hotel tax entitles you to. The card gives you free use of public transit in the immediate region (including the bus to Neuschwanstein), as well as discounts at major attractions: €1 each on Neuschwanstein, Hohenschwangau, the Museum of the Bavar-ian Kings, and the Forggensee boat trip, and €2 on the Füssen Heritage Museum (plus discounts on the Tegelberg gondola, the Royal Crystal Baths, and the Hahnenkammbahn cable car near Reutte). Some accommodations won't tell you about the card un-less you request it. You may be asked for a €3-5 deposit; be sure to return the card before you leave town. After the hotel activates the card, it can take an hour or two before it actually works at sights and on buses.

## ARRIVAL IN FÜSSEN

**By Train:** From the unstaffed train station (lockers available, €2-3), continue two blocks in the same direction as the tracks to reach the center of town and the TI. Buses to Neuschwanstein, Reutte, and elsewhere leave from a parking lot next to the station. Plans are afoot to tear down and replace the old station building, so specifics may change.

**By Car:** Füssen is known for its traffic jams, and you can't drive into the old town. The most convenient lots (follow signs) are the underground P-5 (across street from old town entrance, €7/day) and the aboveground P-3 (off Kemptener Strasse, €9/day).

## HELPFUL HINTS

**Internet Access: ICS Internet Café** has four computers, a print-er...and a betting salon in back (€2.50/hour, daily 9:00-24:00, Luitpoldstrasse 8, tel. 08362/883-7073). The **city library** (Stadtbibliothek), inside the monastery complex that houses the Füssen Heritage Museum, has computers and Wi-Fi but limited hours (€1/30 minutes, free with Füssen Card; Tue-Wed 13:00-17:00, Thu 13:00-19:00, Fri 10:00-17:00, closed Mon, Lechhalde 3, tel. 08362/903-144).

**Bike Rental: Fahrrad-Station,** sitting right where the train tracks end, outfits sightseers with good bikes and tips on two-wheeled fun in the area (prices per 24 hours: €10-city bike, €15-sport bike, €20-electric bike; March-Oct Mon-Fri 9:00-12:00 & 14:00-18:00, Sat 9:00-13:00, Sun 10:00-12:00, closed Nov-

Feb, tel. 08362/505-9155, mobile 0176-2205-3080, www. ski-sport-luggi.de). For a strenuous but enjoyable 20-mile loop trip, see page 414.

**Car Rental:** Two rental agencies are about an €8 taxi ride from the center: **Schlichtling** (Mon-Fri 8:00-18:00, Sat 9:00-12:00, closed Sun, Hiebeler Strasse 49, tel. 08362/922-122, www. schlichtling.de) and **Auto Osterried/Europcar** (daily 8:00-19:00, past waterfall on road to Austria, Tiroler Strasse 65, tel. 08362/6381).

**Local Guide: Silvia Beyer** speaks English, knows the region very well, and can even drive you to sights that are hard to reach by train (€30/hour, mobile 0160-9011-3431, silliby@web.de).

# Füssen Walk

For most, Füssen is just a home base for visiting Ludwig's famous castles. But the town has a rich history and hides some evocative corners, as you'll see when you follow this self-guided orientation walk. This 45-minute stroll is designed to get you out of the cutesy old cobbled core where most tourists spend their time. Throughout the town, "City Tour" information plaques explain points of interest in English (in more detail than I've provided).

• *Begin at the square in front of the TI, three blocks from the train station.*

BAVARIA

## Ⓐ Kaiser-Maximilian-Platz

The entertaining "Seven Stones" fountain on this square, by sculptor Christian Tobin, was built in 1995 to celebrate Füssen's 700th birthday. The stones symbolize community, groups of people gathering, conviviality...each is different, with "heads" nodding and talking. It's granite on granite. The moving heads are not connected, and nod only with waterpower. While frozen in winter, it's a popular and splashy play zone for kids on hot summer days.

• *Walk half a block down the busy street (to the left, with the TI at your back). You'll soon see...*

## Ⓑ Hotel Hirsch and Medieval Towers

Recent renovations have restored some of the original Art Nouveau flavor to Hotel Hirsch, which opened in 1904. In those days, aristocratic tourists came here to appreciate the castles and natural wonders of the Alps. Across the busy street stands one of two surviving towers from Füssen's medieval town wall (c. 1515), and next to it is a passageway into the old town.

• *Walk 50 yards farther down the busy street to another tower. Just before it, you'll see an information plaque and an archway where a small street called Klosterstrasse emerges through a surviving piece of the old town wall. Step through the smaller pedestrian archway, walk along Klosterstrasse for a few yards, and turn left through the gate into the...*

### ❸ Historic Cemetery of St. Sebastian (Alter Friedhof)

This peaceful oasis of Füssen history, established in the 16th century, fills a corner between the town wall and the Franciscan monastery. It's technically full, and only members of great and venerable Füssen families (who already own plots here) can join those who are buried (free, daily April-Sept 7:30-19:00, Oct-March 8:00-17:00).

Immediately inside the gate and on the right is the tomb of Domenico Quaglio, who painted the Romantic scenes decorating the walls of Hohenschwangau Castle in 1835. Across the cemetery, on the old city wall (beyond the church), is the World War I memorial, listing all the names of men from this small town killed in that devastating conflict (along with each one's rank and place of death). A bit to the right, also along the old wall, is a statue of the hand of God holding a fetus—a place to remember babies who died before being born. And in the corner, farther to the right, is a gated area with the simple wooden crosses of Franciscans who lived just over the wall in the monastery. Strolling the rest of the grounds, note the fine tomb art from many ages collected here, and the loving care this community gives its cemetery.

• *Exit on the far side, just past the dead Franciscans, and continue toward the big church.*

### ❹ Town View from Franciscan Monastery (Franziskaner-kloster)

From the Franciscan Monastery (which still has big responsibilities, but only a handful of monks in residence), there's a fine view over the medieval town with an alpine backdrop. The Church of St. Magnus and the High Castle (the former summer residence of the Bishops of Augsburg) break the horizon. The tall, skinny smokestack (c. 1886) and workers' housing on the left are reminders that when Ludwig built Neuschwanstein, the textile industry (linen and flax) was very big here. Walk all the way to the far end of the monastery chapel and peek around the corner, where you'll see a gate that proclaims the *Ende der romantischen Strasse* (end of the Romantic Road).

BAVARIA

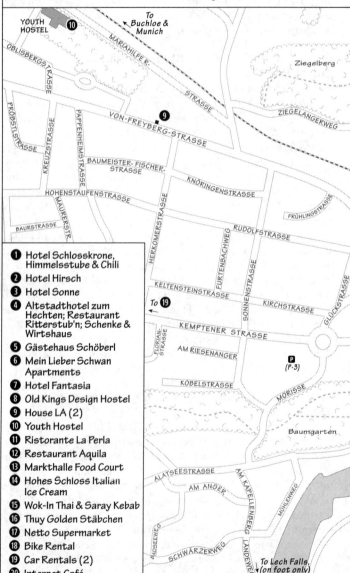

## SELF-GUIDED WALK

- **A** Kaiser-Maximilian-Platz
- **B** Medieval Towers (2)
- **C** Historic Cemetery of St. Sebastian
- **D** Town View
- **E** Lech Riverbank
- **F** Church of the Holy Spirit, Bread Market & Lute-Makers (2)
- **G** Benedictine Monastery
- **H** Füssen Heritage Museum
- **I** St. Magnus Basilica
- **J** High Castle

- **1** Hotel Schlosskrone, Himmelsstube & Chili
- **2** Hotel Hirsch
- **3** Hotel Sonne
- **4** Altstadthotel zum Hechten; Restaurant Ritterstub'n; Schenke & Wirtshaus
- **5** Gästehaus Schöberl
- **6** Mein Lieber Schwan Apartments
- **7** Hotel Fantasia
- **8** Old Kings Design Hostel
- **9** House LA (2)
- **10** Youth Hostel
- **11** Ristorante La Perla
- **12** Restaurant Aquila
- **13** Markthalle Food Court
- **14** Hohes Schloss Italian Ice Cream
- **15** Wok-In Thai & Saray Kebab
- **16** Thuy Golden Stäbchen
- **17** Netto Supermarket
- **18** Bike Rental
- **19** Car Rentals (2)
- **20** Internet Café

BAVARIA

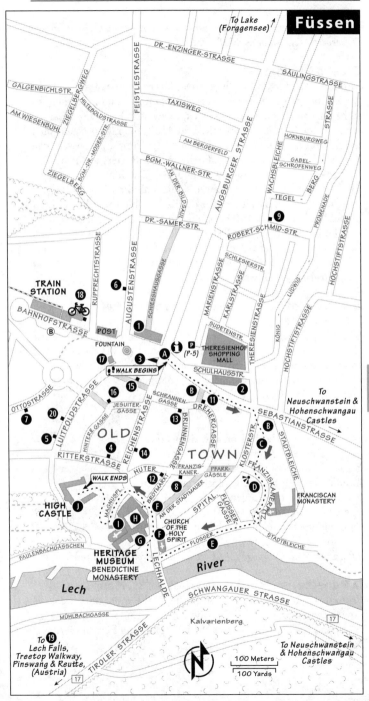

Füssen

To Lake (Forggensee)

DR.-ENZINGER-STRASSE

SÄULINGSTRASSE

STRASSE

GALGENBICHLSTR.

AM WIESENBÜHL

ZIEGELBERGWEG

HILTEBOLDSTRASSE

BGM.-DR.-MOSER-STR.

FEISTLESTRASSE

TAXISWEG

AM BERGERFELD

HORNBURGWEG

GABEL-SCHROFENWEG

BGM.-WALLNER-STR.

ZIEGELBERG

AN DER BILDSÄUL

DR.-SAMER-STR.

AUGSBURGER STRASSE

TEGEL

BERG

PROMENADE

ROBERT-SCHMID-STR.

❾

SCHLESIERSTR.

HOCHSTIFTSTRASSE

RUPPRECHTSTRASSE

AUGUSTENSTRASSE

SCHIESSHAUSGASSE

MARIENSTRASSE

KARLSTRASSE

THERESIENSTRASSE

LUDWIG

KÖNIG

HOCHSTIFTSTRASSE

TRAIN STATION

❶⑧

BAHNHOFSTRASSE

Ⓑ

POST

❻

❶

SUDETENSTR.

THERESIENHOF SHOPPING MALL

FOUNTAIN

❶⑦

Ⓐ

Ⓟ (P-5)

❸

WALK BEGINS

SCHULHAUSSTR.

To Neuschwanstein & Hohenschwangau Castles

BAVARIA

OTTOSTRASSE

❼

LUITPOLDSTRASSE

HINTERE GASSE

JESUITER-GASSE

❶⑥ ❶⑤

SCHRANNEN-GASSE

REICHENSTRASSE

Ⓑ

❷

❶①

DREHERGASSE

SEBASTIANSTRASSE

Ⓑ

❷⓪

OLD

BRUNNENGASSE

❶③

TOWN

KLOSTERSTR.

Ⓒ

STADTBLEICHE

❺

❹

RITTERSTRASSE

❶④

HUTER

FRANZIS-KANER.

PFARR-GASSLE

FRANZISKANERPL.

❶②

BROTMARKT

❽

AN DER STADTMAUER

SPITAL

FLOSSER-GASSE

Ⓓ

FRANCISCAN MONASTERY

WALK ENDS

MAGNUSPL.

Ⓘ

Ⓗ

Ⓕ

CHURCH OF THE HOLY SPIRIT

Ⓕ

FLOSSER

STADTBLEICHE

HIGH CASTLE

Ⓙ

Ⓖ

Ⓔ

FAULENBACHGÄSSCHEN

LECHHALDE

HERITAGE MUSEUM

BENEDICTINE MONASTERY

River

Lech

SCHWANGAUER STRASSE

MÜHLBACHGASSE

TIROLER STRASSE

Kalvarienberg

17

To ❶❾ Lech Falls, Treetop Walkway, Pinswang & Reutte, (Austria)

17

To Neuschwanstein & Hohenschwangau Castles

N

100 Meters

100 Yards

• *Now go down the stairway and turn left, through the medieval "Bleachers' Gate" (marked 5½) to the...*

## ❶ Lech Riverbank

This low end of town, the flood zone, was the home of those whose work depended on the river—bleachers, rafters, and fishermen. In its heyday, the Lech River was an expressway to Augsburg (about 70 miles to the north). Around the year 1500, the rafters established the first professional guild in Füssen. Cargo from Italy passed here en route to big German cities farther north. Rafters would assemble rafts and pile them high with goods—or with people needing a lift. If the water was high, they could float all the way to Augsburg in as little as one day. There they'd disassemble their raft and sell off the lumber along with the goods they'd carried, then make their way home to raft again. Today you'll see no modern-day rafters here, as there's a hydroelectric plant just downstream.

• *Walk upstream a bit, appreciating the river's milky color, and head inland (turn right) immediately after crossing under the bridge.*

## ❻ Church of the Holy Spirit, Bread Market, and Lute-Makers

Climbing uphill, you pass the colorful Church of the Holy Spirit (Heilig-Geist-Spitalkirche) on the right. As this was the church of the rafters, their patron, St. Christopher (with the Baby Jesus on his shoulder), is prominent on the facade. Today it's the church of Füssen's old folks' home (it's adjacent—notice the easy-access skyway).

Farther up the hill on the right (almost opposite an archway into a big courtyard) is Bread Market Square (Brotmarkt), with a fountain honoring a famous 16th-century lute-making family, the Tieffenbruckers. In its day, Füssen (surrounded by forests) was a huge center of violin- and lute-making, with about 200 workshops. Today only three survive.

• *Backtrack and go through the archway into the courtyard of the former...*

## ❼ Benedictine Monastery (Kloster St. Mang)

From 1717 until secularization in 1802, the monastery was the power center of town. Today the courtyard is popular for concerts, and the building houses the City Hall and Füssen Heritage Museum.

## ⑧ Füssen Heritage Museum

This is Füssen's one must-see sight (€6, €7 combo-ticket includes painting gallery and castle tower; April-Oct Tue-Sun 11:00-17:00, closed Mon; shorter hours and closed Mon-Thu Nov-March; tel. 08362/903-146, www.museum.fuessen.de).

Pick up the loaner English translations and follow the one-way route. In the St. Anna Chapel, you'll see the famous *Dance of Death*. This was painted shortly after a plague devastated the community in 1590. It shows 20 social classes, each dancing with the Grim Reaper—starting with the pope and the emperor. The words above say, essentially, "You can say yes or you can say no, but you must ultimately dance with death." Leaving the chapel, you walk over the metal lid of the crypt. Upstairs, exhibits illustrate the rafting trade and violin- and lute-making (with a complete workshop). The museum also includes an exquisite *Kaisersaal* (main festival hall), an old library, an exhibition on textile production, and a King Ludwig-style "castle dream room."

• *Leaving the courtyard, hook left around the old monastery and go uphill. The square tower marks...*

## ⑨ St. Magnus Basilica (Basilika St. Mang)

St. Mang (or Magnus) is Füssen's favorite saint. In the eighth century, he worked miracles all over the area with his holy rod. For centuries, pilgrims came from far and wide to enjoy art depicting the great works of St. Magnus. Above the altar dangles a glass cross containing his relics (including that holy stick). Just inside the door is a chapel remembering a much more modern saint—Franz Seelos (1819-1867), the local boy who went to America (Pittsburgh and New Orleans) and lived such a righteous life that in 2000 he was beatified by Pope John Paul II. If you're in need of a miracle, fill out a request card next to the candles.

• *From the church, a lane leads high above, into the courtyard of the...*

## ⑩ High Castle (Hohes Schloss)

This castle, long the summer residence of the Bishop of Augsburg, houses a painting gallery (the upper floor is labeled in English) and a tower with a view over the town and lake (included in the €7 Füssen Heritage Museum combo-ticket, otherwise €6, same hours as museum). Its courtyard is interesting for the striking perspective tricks painted onto its flat walls.

From below the castle, the city's main drag (once the Roman Via Claudia, and now Reichenstrasse) leads from a grand statue of St. Magnus past lots of shops, cafés, and strolling people to Kaiser-Maximilian-Platz and the TI...where you began.

## Sleeping in Füssen

**(country code: 49, area code: 08362)**
Convenient Füssen is just three miles from Ludwig's castles and offers a cobbled, riverside retreat. All recommended accommodations are within a few handy blocks of the train station and the town center. Parking is easy, and some hotels also have their own lot or garage. Prices listed are for one-night stays in high season (mid-June-Sept). Most hotels give about 5-10 percent off for two-night stays—always request this discount—and prices drop by 10-20 percent off-season. Competition is fierce, so shop around. Be sure to ask your hotelier for a Füssen Card (see page 391).

Remember, to call Füssen from Austria, dial 00-49- and then the number (minus the initial zero).

### BIG, FANCY HOTELS IN THE CENTER OF TOWN
**$$$ Hotel Schlosskrone,** with 64 rooms and all the amenities, is just a block from the station. It also runs two restaurants and a fine pastry shop—you'll notice at breakfast (Sb-€111, standard Db-€153, bigger Db-€173, Db with balcony-€179, Tb-€192, Qb-€208, various pricey suites also available, air-con in a few expensive rooms only, elevator, Wi-Fi, free sauna and fitness center, parking-€10/day, Prinzregentenplatz 2-4, tel. 08362/930-180, www.schlosskrone.de, rezeption@schlosskrone.de, Norbert Schöll and family).

**$$$ Hotel Hirsch** is a romantic, well-maintained, family-run, 53-room, old-style hotel that takes pride in tradition. Their standard rooms are fine, and their rooms with historical and landscape themes are a fun splurge (typical rates: Sb-€122, standard Db-€139-154, theme Db-€174-184, book direct on their website for best prices, family rooms, elevator, Wi-Fi, free parking, Kaiser-Maximilian-Platz 7, tel. 08362/93980, www.hotelfuessen.de, info@hotelhirsch.de).

**$$$ Hotel Sonne,** in the heart of town, has a modern lobby and takes pride in decorating (some would say overdecorating) its 50 stylish rooms (Sb-€109, Db-€135, fancier Db-€145-195, Tb-€149, bigger Tb-€199, Qb-€219, 5 percent discount if you book on their website, elevator, guest computer, Wi-Fi; free laundry

---

# Sleep Code

**Abbreviations**                                    **(€1 = about $1.40)**
**S** = Single, **D** = Double/Twin, **T** = Triple, **Q** = Quad, **b** = bath-room, **s** = shower only.
**Price Rankings**
  **$$$**  **Higher Priced**—Most rooms €130 or more.
  **$$**  **Moderately Priced**—Most rooms between €70-130.
  **$**  **Lower Priced**—Most rooms €70 or less.
Unless otherwise noted, credit cards are accepted, English is spoken, Wi-Fi is generally free, and breakfast is included. The prices listed here include local tax. Prices change; verify current rates online or by email. For the best prices, always book directly with the hotel.

---

machine, €3 if you need soap; free sauna and fitness center, park-ing-€6-8/day, kitty-corner from TI at Prinzregentenplatz 1, on GPS you may need to enter Reichenstrasse 37, tel. 08362/9080, www.hotel-sonne.de, info@hotel-sonne.de).

## SMALLER, MID-PRICED HOTELS AND PENSIONS

**$$ Altstadthotel zum Hechten** offers 34 modern and nicely reno-vated rooms in a friendly, traditional building right under Füssen Castle in the old-town pedestrian zone. It's a good value, with lots of extras (laundry-€10-20/load, travel resource/game room with maps and books, borrowable hiking gear, fun miniature bowling alley in basement, recommended restaurant), a family-run feel, and borderline-kitschy decor (Sb-€74, Db-€108, bigger Db-€125, Tb-€148, Qb-€178, often less if you stay 3 nights, ask when you reserve for 5 percent off these prices with this book, also mention if you're very tall as most beds can be short, non-smoking, lots of stairs, guest computer, Wi-Fi, parking-€4/day on-site—or free a 5-min-ute walk away, in the heart of the old town at Ritterstrasse 6, tel. 08362/91600, www.hotel-hechten.com, info@hotel-hechten.com, Pfeiffer and Tramp families).

**$$ Gästehaus Schöberl,** run by the head cook at Altstadthotel zum Hechten, rents six attentively furnished, modern rooms a five-minute walk from the train station. One room is in the owners' house, and the rest are in the building next door (Sb-€55, Db-€80, Tb-€105, two-room Qb-€140, cash only, Wi-Fi, free parking, Lu-itpoldstrasse 14-16, tel. 08362/922-411, www.schoeberl-fuessen.de, info@schoeberl-fuessen.de, Pia and Georg Schöberl).

**$$ Mein Lieber Schwan,** a block from the train station, is a former private house with four superbly outfitted apartments, each with a double bed, sofa bed, kitchen, and antique furnishings. The catch is the three-night minimum stay in high season (Sb-€77-88,

Db-€89-100, Tb-€107-116, Qb-€124-133, price depends on apartment size, cash or PayPal only, no breakfast, Wi-Fi, free parking, laundry facilities, garden, from station turn left at traffic circle to Augustenstrasse 3, tel. 08362/509-980, www.meinlieberschwan. de, fewo@meinlieberschwan.de, Herr Bletschacher). Herr Bletschacher also has two slightly larger, more expensive apartments at Klosterstrasse 10, near the cemetery.

**$$ Hotel Fantasia,** recently converted from a home for nuns, has 16 rooms a short walk through the park from the train station (Sb-€69-89, Db-€99-129, Tb-€120-150, Qb-€160-170, Quint/b-€180-190, price depends on room size, 5 percent discount if you book on their website, Wi-Fi, parking-€5/day, Ottostrasse 1, tel. 08362/9080, www.hotel-fantasia.de, info@hotel-fantasia.de).

## BUDGET BEDS

**$ Old Kings Design Hostel** shoehorns two eight-person dorms and three doubles into an old townhouse buried deep in the pedestrian zone. While the quarters are tight (all the rooms share two bathrooms), the Old World location, creative decor, and reasonable prices are enticing (dorm bed-€24, D-€57-60, breakfast-€5, Wi-Fi, kitchen, laundry-€4/load, reception open daily 7:30-12:00 & 16:00-21:00, Franziskanergasse 2, tel. 08362/883-7385, www. oldkingshostel.com, info@oldkingshostel.com).

**$ House LA,** run by energetic mason Lahdo Algül and hardworking Agata, has two branches. The backpacker house has 11 basic, clean, mostly four-bed dorm rooms at rock-bottom prices about a 10-minute walk from the station (dorm bed-€18, D-€46, breakfast-€3, pay guest computer, Wi-Fi, free parking, Wachsbleiche 2). A second building has five family apartments with kitchen and bath, each sleeping four to six people (apartment-€60-90, depends on number of people and season—mention Rick Steves for best price, breakfast-€3, Wi-Fi, free parking, 6-minute walk back along tracks from station to von Freybergstrasse 26; contact info for both: tel. 08362/607-366, mobile 0170-624-8610, www.housela. de, info@housela.de). Both branches rent bikes (€8/day) and have laundry facilities (€7/load).

**$ Füssen Youth Hostel,** with 138 beds in 32 institutional rooms, occupies a pleasant modern building in a grassy setting an easy walk from the center. There are ping-pong tables and a basketball net out front, but few other extras (bed in 2- to 6-bed dorm rooms-€23, bunk-bed Db-€51, €3 more for nonmembers, €2 extra for one-night stays, €4 extra for those over age 26, includes breakfast and sheets, laundry-€5/load, dinner-€5.50, lockers, Wi-Fi, free parking, office open daily 8:00-12:00 & 17:00-22:00, from station backtrack 10 minutes along tracks, Mariahilfer Strasse

5, tel. 08362/7754, www.fuessen.jugendherberge.de, fuessen@
jugendherberge.de).

# Eating in Füssen

**Restaurant Ritterstub'n** offers delicious, reasonably priced German grub, fish, salads, veggie plates, gluten-free options, and a
fun kids' menu. They have three eating zones: modern decor in
front, traditional Bavarian in back, and a courtyard. Demure Gabi
serves while her husband cooks standard Bavarian fare (€8-16 main
courses, smaller portions available for less, €6.50 lunch specials,
€19 three-course fixed-price dinners, Tue-Sun 11:30-14:30 &
17:30-23:00, closed Mon, Ritterstrasse 4, tel. 08362/7759, www.
restaurant-ritterstuben.de).

**Schenke & Wirtshaus** (inside the recommended Altstadthotel zum Hechten) dishes up hearty, traditional Bavarian dishes
in a cozy setting. They specialize in pike *(Hecht)* pulled from the
Lech River, served with a tasty fresh-herb sauce (€8-16 main courses, salad bar, daily 11:00-22:00, Ritterstrasse 6, tel. 0836/91600,
www.hotel-hechten.com).

**Ristorante La Perla** is an Italian restaurant with fair prices,
along a passageway through Füssen's town wall. Sit either in the
classic interior, at streetside tables on a quiet Old Town lane, or in
a back courtyard (€8-11 pizzas and pastas, €12-22 meat and fish
dishes, daily 11:00-22:00, in winter closed 14:30-17:30 and all day
Mon, Drehergasse 44, tel. 08362/7155).

The **Himmelsstube** is the restaurant inside Hotel Schlosskrone, right on Füssen's main traffic circle. It offers a €10 weekday lunch buffet and live Bavarian zither music most Fridays and
Saturdays during dinner (€10-20 main courses). Choose between
a traditional dining room and a pastel winter garden (both feel
quite formal). If your hotel doesn't offer breakfast, consider their
€13.50 breakfast or huge €17 Sunday brunch buffet (open Mon-
Sat 7:30-10:30 & 11:30-14:30 & 18:00-22:00, Sun 7:30-13:00 &
18:00-22:00, Prinzregentenplatz 2-4, tel. 08362/930-180, www.
schlosskrone.de). The hotel's second restaurant, **Chili,** serves Mediterranean dishes.

**Restaurant Aquila** serves modern German and Italian-influ-
enced dishes in a simple indoor setting and at outdoor tables on
the delightful little Brotmarkt square (€10-18 main courses, serious
€10-11 salads, Wed-Mon 11:30-21:30, closed Tue, Brotmarkt 9,
tel. 08362/6253, www.aquila-fuessen.de).

*Food Court:* The fun **Markthalle** offers a wide selection of reasonably priced, wurst-free food. Located in an old warehouse from
1483, it's now home to a fishmonger, deli counters, a fruit stand,
a bakery, and a wine bar. Buy your food from one of the vendors,

BAVARIA

park yourself at any one of the tables, then look up and admire the Renaissance ceiling (Mon-Fri 8:00-20:00, Sat 8:00-15:00, closed Sun, corner of Schrannengasse and Brunnengasse).

*Brewpub near the Castles:* If you have a car, consider heading to **Schloss Brauhaus,** in the village of Schwangau (described on page 416).

*Gelato:* **Hohes Schloss Italian Ice Cream** is a good *gelateria* on the main drag with a huge menu of elaborate sundaes and an inviting people-watching perch (Reichenstrasse 14).

*Cheap Eats:* **Wok-In,** in the Luitpold-Passage at Reichenstrasse 33, has little atmosphere but serves good Thai food to eat in or take out (Mon-Sat 11:00-22:00, Sun 12:00-21:00, tel. 08362/924-905). At the outer end of the passage, **Saray Kebab** is the town's favorite Middle Eastern takeaway joint (Luitpoldstrasse 1). The Vietnamese **Thuy Golden Stäbchen,** on a deserted back street, has low prices and outdoor tables with a castle view (Hinteregasse 29).

*Picnic Supplies:* Bakeries and butcher shops (*Metzger*) abound and frequently have ready-made sandwiches. For groceries, try the discount **Netto** supermarket, underground at Prinzregentenplatz, the roundabout on your way into town from the train station, or the midrange **REWE** in the Theresienhof shopping complex behind Hotel Hirsch (both supermarkets open Mon-Sat 7:00-20:00, closed Sun).

## Füssen Connections

Bus schedules from Füssen can be very confusing. The website www.bahn.com is good for figuring out your options for a particular day and route.

**From Füssen to: Neuschwanstein** (bus #73 or #78, departs from train station, most continue to Tegelberg lift station after castles, 1/hour, 10 minutes, €2.10 one-way, buses #9606 and #9651 also make the trip; taxis cost €10 one-way); **Wieskirche** (bus #73, #9606, or #9651; 4-6 buses/day, 45-60 minutes); **Oberammergau** (bus #9606, 4-5/day, 1.5 hours, bus sometimes starts as #73 and changes number to #9606 en route—confirm with driver that bus is bound for Oberammergau); **Reutte** (bus #74 in Germany, changes number to #4258 in Austria, Mon-Fri 6/day, Sat-Sun 4/day, last bus 19:00, 30-50 minutes, €4.30 one-way); **Zugspitze** (possible as day trip via bus #74 to Reutte, then train to Ehrwald or Garmisch-Partenkirchen, allow up to 3.5 hours total to reach the top); **Munich** (hourly, 2 hours, some change in Buchloe); **Innsbruck** (fastest via bus #4258/#74 to Reutte, then train from Reutte to Innsbruck via Garmisch, 3/day, 4 hours; otherwise via Munich); **Salzburg** (roughly hourly, 4 hours on fast trains, 5 hours on slow trains eligible for Bayern-Ticket, change in Munich and sometimes in Buchloe); **Rothenburg ob der Tauber** (hourly, 5-6 hours, look for connections with only 3 changes—often in Augsburg, Treuchtlingen, and Steinach); **Frankfurt** (hourly, 5-6 hours, 1-2 changes). Train info: tel. 0180-599-6633, www.bahn.com.

# The Best of Bavaria

Within a short drive of Füssen and Reutte, you'll find some of the most enjoyable—and most tourist-filled—sights in Germany. The otherworldly "King's Castles" of Neuschwanstein and Hohenschwangau capture romantics' imaginations, the ornately decorated Wieskirche puts the faithful in a heavenly mood, and the little town of Oberammergau overwhelms visitors with cuteness. Yet another remarkable castle (Linderhof), another fancy church (Ettal), and a sky-high viewpoint (the Zugspitze) round out southern Bavaria's top attractions.

# The King's Castles: Neuschwanstein and Hohenschwangau

The most popular tourist destinations in southern Bavaria are the two "King's Castles" (Königsschlösser) near Füssen. The older Hohenschwangau, King Ludwig's boyhood home, is less famous but more historic. The more dramatic Neuschwanstein, which inspired Walt Disney, is the one everyone visits. I'd recommend visiting both and hiking above Neuschwanstein to Mary's Bridge. If you enjoy romantic hikes, also plan to walk down through the gorge below. Reservations are a magic wand that smooths out your visit. With fairy-tale turrets in a fairy-tale alpine setting built by a fairy-tale king, these castles are understandably a huge hit.

## GETTING THERE

If arriving by **car,** note that road signs in the region refer to the sight as *Königsschlösser,* not Neuschwanstein. There's plenty of parking (all lots-€5). The first lots require more walking. The most convenient lot, by the lake (#4, *Parkplatz am Alpsee*), is up the small road past the souvenir shops and ticket center.

From **Füssen,** those without cars can catch **bus** #73 or #78 (hourly, generally departs Füssen's train station at :05 past the hour, €2.10 each way, 10 minutes, extra buses often run when crowded; a few departures of #9606 and #9651 also make this trip). A Bayern-Ticket (see page 388) or the local guest card available from your hotel (see page 391) lets you ride for free. You can also take a **taxi** (€10 one-way), ride a rental **bike** (two level miles), or—if you're in a pinch—**walk** (less than an hour). The bus drops you at the tourist office; it's a one-minute walk from there to the ticket office. When returning, note that buses #73 and #78 pointing left (with your back to the TI) are headed to Füssen, while the same numbers pointing right are going elsewhere.

From **Reutte,** take bus #4258 (number changes to #74 in Germany) to the Füssen train station, then hop on bus #73 or #78 to the castles. Or take a taxi right to the castles if available.

# Orientation to the King's Castles

**Cost:** Neuschwanstein and Hohenschwangau cost €12 apiece. A "Königsticket" combo-ticket for both castles costs €23, and a "Schwanenticket," which also covers the Museum of the Bavarian Kings—described on page 412—costs €29.50. Children under age 18 (accompanied by an adult) are admitted free. Neuschwanstein, but not Hohenschwangau, is covered by Bavaria's 14-day ticket (Mehrtagesticket).

**Hours:** The ticket center, located at street level between the two castles, is open daily April-Sept 8:00-17:30, Oct-March 9:00-15:30. The first castle tour of the day departs an hour after the ticket office opens and the last normally departs 30 minutes after it closes: April-Sept at 9:00 and 18:00, Oct-March at 10:00 and 16:00.

**Getting Tickets for the Castles:** Every tour bus in Bavaria converges on Neuschwanstein, and tourists flush in each morning from Munich. A handy reservation system sorts out the chaos for smart travelers. (One out of every three castle tickets is reserved. Look left. Look right. If you want to be smarter than these two people, prebook.) Tickets, whether reserved in advance or bought on the spot, come with admission times. If you miss your appointed tour time, you can't get in. To tour both castles, you must do Hohenschwangau first (logical, since this gives a better introduction to King Ludwig's short life). You'll get two tour times: Hohenschwangau and then, two hours later, Neuschwanstein.

**Arrival:** Make the **ticket center** your first stop. If you have a reservation, stand in the short line for picking up tickets. If you don't have a reservation...welcome to the very long line. Arrive by 8:00 in summer, and you'll likely be touring at 9:00. During August, the busiest month, tickets for English tours can run out by around noon. Because day-trippers from Munich tend to take the morning train—with a bus connection arriving at the castles by about 11:15—if you need to buy a ticket on the

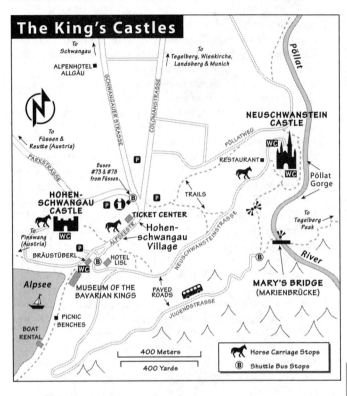

**The King's Castles**

To
Schwangau

ALPENHOTEL
ALLGÄU

SCHWANGAUER STRASSE

COLOMANSTRASSE

To
Tegelberg, Wieskirche,
Landsberg & Munich

Pöllat

NEUSCHWANSTEIN
CASTLE

WC

PÖLLATWEG

RESTAURANT

WC

Pöllat
Gorge

To
Füssen &
Reute (Austria)

PARKSTRASSE

P

Buses
#73 & #78
from Füssen

P

HOHEN-
SCHWANGAU
CASTLE

To
Pinswang
(Austria)

WC

B

P

TICKET CENTER

Hohen-
schwangau
Village

ALPSEESTR.

TRAILS

To
Tegelberg
Peak

NEUSCHWANSTEINSTRASSE

BRÄUSTÜBERL

P

B

HOTEL
LISL

WC

B

MARY'S BRIDGE
(MARIENBRÜCKE)

River

Alpsee

MUSEUM OF THE
BAVARIAN KINGS

PAVED
ROADS

JUGENDSTRASSE

PICNIC
BENCHES

BOAT
RENTAL

400 Meters

400 Yards

🐎 Horse Carriage Stops

Ⓑ  Shuttle Bus Stops

spot, you'll be wise to try to make it here by 11:00 to beat this crowd.

**Reservations:** It's smart to reserve in peak season (June-Oct—especially in July-Aug, when slots can book up several days in advance). Reservations cost €1.80 per person per castle, and must be made no later than 17:00 on the previous day. It works best to book online (www.ticket-center-hohenschwangau.de); you can also reserve by phone (tel. 08362/930-830) or email (info@ticket-center-hohenschwangau.de). A few hotels can book these tickets for you with enough notice (ask). You must pick up reserved tickets an hour before the appointed entry time, as it takes a while to walk up to the castles. (It doesn't usually take an hour, though—so this might be a good time to pull out a sandwich or a snack.) Show up late and they may have given your slot to someone else (but then they'll likely help you make another reservation). If you know a couple of hours in advance that you're running late and can call the office, they'll likely rebook you at no charge.

**Getting Up to the Castles:** From the ticket booth, Hohenschwangau is an easy 10-minute climb (just zigzag up to the big yellow castle, following the signs), while Neuschwanstein is a moderately steep 30-minute hike in the other direction (also well-signed—the most direct and least steep approach begins across the street from the ticket center).

To minimize hiking to Neuschwanstein, you can take a **shuttle bus** (generally leaves every few minutes from in front of Hotel Lisl, just above ticket office and to the left, but occasionally full or on break) or a horse-drawn carriage (in front of Hotel Müller, just above ticket office and to the right), but neither gets you to the castle doorstep. The shuttle bus drops you off near Mary's Bridge (Marienbrücke), leaving you a steep, 10-minute downhill walk to the castle—so be sure to see the view from Mary's Bridge *before* hiking down (€1.80 one-way, €2.60 round-trip not worth it since you have to hike uphill to the bus stop for your return trip). **Horse-drawn carriages** (€6 up, €3 down) are slower than walking and stop below Neuschwanstein, leaving you a five-minute uphill hike. Here's the most economical and least strenuous plan: Ride the bus to Mary's Bridge for the view, hike down to Neuschwanstein, and then catch the horse carriage from the castle back down to the parking lot (total round-trip cost: €4.80). Carriages also run to Hohenschwangau (€4.50 up, €2 down).

Warning: Both the shuttle bus and the carriage can have long lines at peak times—especially if it's raining. You might wait up to 45 minutes for the bus, making it slower than walking. If you're cutting it close to your appointed time, you may need to hoof it.

**Entry Procedure:** For each castle, tourists jumble at the entry, waiting for their ticket number to light up on the board. When it does, power through the mob (most waiting there are holding higher numbers) and go to the turnstile. Warning: You must use your ticket while your number is still on the board. If you space out while waiting for a polite welcome, you'll miss your entry window and never get in.

**Services:** A TI (run by helpful Thomas), bus stop, ATM, WC (€0.50), lockers (€1), coin-op Internet terminal, and telephones cluster around the main intersection a couple hundred yards before you get to the ticket office (TI open daily April-Sept 10:00-17:30, Oct-March 10:00-16:00, tel. 08362/819-765, www.schwangau.de). While bathrooms inside the castles themselves are free, you'll pay €0.30-0.50 to use the WCs elsewhere.

**Best Views:** In the morning, the light comes in just above the mountains—making your initial view of Neuschwanstein hazy and disappointing (though views from the ticket center up to Hohenschwangau are nice). Later in the day, the sun

## "Mad" King Ludwig (1845-1886)

A tragic figure, Ludwig II (a.k.a. "Mad" King Ludwig) ruled Bavaria for 22 years until his death in 1886 at the age of 40. Bavaria was weak. Politically, Ludwig's reality was to "rule" either as a pawn of Prussia or a pawn of Austria. Rather than deal with politics in Bavaria's capital, Munich, Ludwig frittered away most of his time at his family's hunting palace, Hohenschwangau. He spent much of his adult life constructing his fanciful Neuschwanstein Castle—like a kid builds a tree house—on a neighboring hill upon the scant ruins of a medieval castle. Here and in his other projects (such as Linderhof Castle and the never-built Falkenstein Castle), even as he strove to evoke medieval grandeur, he embraced the state-of-the-art technology of the Industrial Age in which he lived. Neuschwanstein had electricity, running water, and a telephone (but no Wi-Fi).

Ludwig was a true romantic living in a Romantic age. His best friends were artists, poets, and composers such as Richard Wagner. His palaces are wallpapered with misty medieval themes—especially those from Wagnerian operas.

Although Ludwig spent 17 years building Neuschwanstein, he lived in it only 172 days. Soon after he moved in (and before his vision for the castle was completed), Ludwig was declared mentally unfit to rule Bavaria and taken away. Two days after this eviction, Ludwig was found dead in a lake. To this day, people debate whether the king was murdered or committed suicide.

**BAVARIA**

drops down into the pasture, lighting up Neuschwanstein magnificently. Regardless of time of day, the best accessible Neuschwanstein view is from Mary's Bridge (or, for the bold, from the little bluff just above it)—an easy 10-minute hike from the castle. (Many of the postcards and posters you'll see are photographed from high in the hills, best left to avid hikers.)

**Eating:** Bring a packed lunch. The park by the Alpsee (the nearby lake) is ideal for a picnic, although you're not allowed to sit on the grass—only on the benches (you could also eat out on the lake in one of the old-fashioned rowboats, rented by the hour in summer). The restaurants in the "village" at the foot of Europe's Disney castle are mediocre and overpriced, feeding off the endless droves of hungry, shop-happy tourists. There are no grocery shops near the castles, but you can buy sandwiches and hot dogs across from the TI, and at the *Imbiss* (takeout window) next to Hotel Alpenstuben (between the TI and ticket center). For a sit-down meal, the yellow **Bräustüberl cafeteria** serves the cheapest grub, but isn't likely to be a highlight of your visit (€6-7 gut-bomb grill meals, often with live folk music, daily 11:00-17:00, close to end of road and lake). Up near Neuschwanstein itself (near the horse carriage drop-off) is another cluster of overpriced eateries.

**After Your Castle Visit:** If you follow my advice, you could be done with your castle tours in the early afternoon. With a car, you could try to squeeze in a nearby sight (such as Linderhof Castle, Ehrenberg Castle ruins, or Wieskirche). If you'd rather stick closer to this area, here are some ideas: The hike from Neuschwanstein up to **Mary's Bridge** is easy and rewarding; the hike back down to the valley through the **Pöllät Gorge** is also highly recommended. With a **bike,** you could pedal through the mostly flat countryside that spreads out in front of Neuschwanstein (perhaps partway around Forggensee). And nearby—an easy drive or bus ride away—the Tegelberg area has both a high-mountain **cable car** and a fun **luge** ride. All of these options are described later in this chapter. Yet another option is to walk all the way around **Alpsee,** the lake below Hohenschwangau (about 1.5 hours, some steps).

## Sights at the King's Castles

The two castles complement each other perfectly. But if you have to choose one, Neuschwanstein's wow factor—inside and out—is undeniable.

### ▲▲▲HOHENSCHWANGAU CASTLE

Standing quietly below Neuschwanstein, the big, yellow Ho-henschwangau Castle was Ludwig's boyhood home. Originally

built in the 12th century, it was ru-ined by Napoleon. Ludwig's father, King Maximilian II, rebuilt it in 1830. Hohenschwangau (hoh-en-SHVAHN-gow, loosely translated as "High Swanland") was used by the royal family as a summer hunt-ing lodge until 1912. The Wittels-bach family (which ruled Bavaria for nearly seven centuries) still owns the place (and lived in the annex—today's shop—until the 1970s).

The interior decor (mostly Neo-Gothic, like the castle itself) is harmonious, cohesive, and original—all done in 1835, with paint-ings inspired by Romantic themes. As you tour the castle, imagine how the paintings must have inspired young Ludwig. For 17 years, he lived here at his dad's place and followed the construction of his dream castle across the way—you'll see the telescope still set up and directed at Neuschwanstein.

The excellent 30-minute tours give a better glimpse of Ludwig's life than the more-visited and famous Neuschwanstein Castle tour. Tours here are smaller (35 people rather than 60) and more relaxed. You'll explore rooms on two floors—the queen's rooms, and then, upstairs, the king's. (Conveniently, their bedrooms were connected by a secret passage.) You'll see photos and busts of Ludwig and his little brother, Otto; some Turkish-style flourishes (to please the king, who had been impressed after a visit to the Orient); more than 25 different depictions of swans (honoring the Knights of Schwangau, whose legacy the Wittelsbachs inherited); over-the-top gifts the Wittelsbachs received from their adoring subjects; and paintings of VIGs (very important Germans, including Martin Luther—who may or may not have visited here—and an infant Charlemagne).

One of the most impressive rooms is the Banquet Hall (also known as the Hall of Heroes); one vivid wall mural depicts a savage, yet bloodless, fifth-century barbarian battle. Just as the castle itself had running water and electricity despite its historic appearance, its Romantic decor presents a sanitized version of the medieval past, glossing over inconvenient details. You'll also see Ludwig's bedroom, which he inherited from his father. He kept most of the decor (including the nude nymphs frolicking over his bed), but painted the ceiling black and installed transparent stars that could be lit from the floor above to create the illusion of a night sky.

## ▲▲▲NEUSCHWANSTEIN CASTLE

Imagine "Mad" King Ludwig as a boy, climbing the hills above his dad's castle, Hohenschwangau, dreaming up the ultimate fairy-

tale castle. Inheriting the throne at the young age of 18, he had the power to make his dream concrete and stucco. Neuschwanstein (noy-SHVAHN-shtine, roughly "New Swanstone") was designed first by a theater-set designer...then by an architect. While it was built upon the ruins of an old castle and looks medieval, Neuschwanstein is modern iron-and-brick construction with a sandstone veneer—only about as old as the Eiffel Tower. It feels like something you'd see at a home show for 19th-century royalty. Built from 1869 to 1886, it's the epitome of the Romanticism popular in 19th-century Europe. Construction stopped with Ludwig's death (only a third of the interior was finished), and within six weeks, tourists were paying to go through it.

During World War II, the castle took on a sinister role. The Nazis used Neuschwanstein as one of their primary secret storehouses for stolen art. After the war, Allied authorities spent a year sorting through and redistributing the art, which filled 49 rail cars from this one location alone. It was the only time the unfinished rooms were put to use.

Today, guides herd groups of 60 through the castle, giving an interesting—if rushed—30-minute tour. (While you're waiting for your tour time to pop up on the board, climb the stairs up to the upper courtyard to see more of the exterior, which isn't covered on your tour.) Once inside, you'll go up and down more than 300 steps, visiting 15 lavish rooms with their original furnishings and fanciful wall paintings—mostly based on Wagnerian opera themes.

Ludwig's extravagant throne room, modeled in a Neo-Byzantine style to emphasize his royal status, celebrates six valiant Christian kings (whose mantle Ludwig clearly believed he had donned) under a huge gilded-bronze chandelier. The exquisite two-million-stone mosaic floor is a visual encyclopedia of animals and plant life. The most memorable stop may be the king's gilded-lily bedroom, with his elaborately carved canopy bed (with a forest of Gothic church spires on top), washstand (filled with water piped in from the Alps), and personal chapel. After passing through Ludwig's living room (decorated with more than 150 swans) and a faux grotto, you'll climb to the fourth floor for the grand finale: the Singers' Hall, an ornately decorated space filled with murals depicting the story of Parzival, the legendary medieval figure with whom Ludwig identified.

After the tour, before you descend to the king's kitchen, see the 13-minute video (runs continuously, English subtitles). This uses historical drawings and modern digital modeling to tell the story of how the castle was built, and illustrates all of the unfinished parts of Ludwig's vision (more prickly towers, a central chapel, a fancy view terrace, an ornate bathhouse, and more). Finally you'll see a digital model of Falkenstein—a whimsical, over-the-top, never-built castle that makes Neuschwanstein look stubby. Falkenstein occupied Ludwig's fantasies the year he died.

After the kitchen (state of the art for this high-tech king in its day), you'll see a room lined with fascinating drawings (described in English) of the castle plans, as well as a large castle model.

## NEAR THE CASTLES

These activities are right around the castles—an easy way to round out your day if you have extra time.

### ▲▲Mary's Bridge (Marienbrücke)

Before or after the Neuschwanstein tour, climb up to Mary's Bridge to marvel at Ludwig's castle, just as Ludwig did. Jockey with a

United Nations of tourists for the best angle. This bridge was quite an engineering accomplishment 100 years ago. (Access to the bridge is closed in bad winter weather, but many travelers walk around the barriers to get there—at their own risk, of course.)

For an even more glorious castle view, the frisky can hike even higher: After crossing the bridge, you'll see very rough, steep, unofficial trails crisscrossing the hillside on your left. If you're willing to ignore the *Lebensgefahr* (danger of death) signs, you can scamper up to the bluff just over the bridge.

The trail connecting Neuschwanstein to Mary's Bridge is also scenic, with views back on Neuschwanstein's facade in one direction, and classic views of Hohenschwangau—perched on its little hill between lakes, with cut-glass peaks on the horizon—in the other.

### ▲Pöllat Gorge (Pöllatschlucht)

The river gorge that slices into the rock just behind Neuschwanstein's lofty perch is a more interesting and scenic—and less crowded—alternative to shuffling back down the main road. While it takes an extra 15 minutes or so, it's well worth it. You'll find the trailhead just above the Neuschwanstein exit, on the path toward Mary's Bridge (look for *Pöllatschlucht* signs; gorge trail closed in winter).

You'll begin by walking down a steep, well-maintained set of concrete stairs, with Germany's finest castle looming through the trees. Then you'll pop out along the river, passing a little beach (with neatly stacked stones) offering a view up at the grand waterfall that gushes beneath Mary's Bridge. From here, follow the river as it goes over several smaller waterfalls—and for a while stroll along steel walkways and railings that help make this slippery area safer. After passing an old wooden channel used to harness the power of all that water, you'll hit level ground; turn left and walk through a pleasantly untouristy residential settlement back toward the TI.

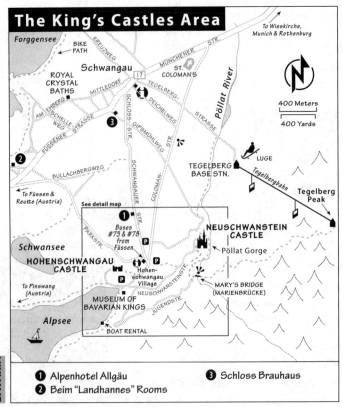

The King's Castles Area

To Wieskirche, Munich & Rothenburg

Forggensee

BIKE PATH

KREUZWEG

MÜNCHENER STR.

Schwangau

ST. COLOMAN'S

17

Pöllat River

ROYAL CRYSTAL BATHS

MITTLEDORF

TEGELBERG-DEICHELWEG

AM EHBERG

SCHELLE-WEG

SCHLOSS-STR.

400 Meters

400 Yards

FÜSSENER STRASSE

❸

GIPSMÜHLWEG STR.

STRASSE

BULLACHBERGWEG

❷

To Füssen & Reutte (Austria)

SCHWANGAUER STR.

COLOMAN-STR.

LUGE

TEGELBERG BASE STN.

Tegelbergbahn

TEGELBERG PEAK

See detail map

❶

PARKSTR.

Buses #73 & #78 from Füssen

P

NEUSCHWANSTEIN CASTLE

Pöllat Gorge

Schwansee

HOHENSCHWANGAU CASTLE

P

Hohen-schwangau Village

P

NEUSCHWANSTEINSTR.

MARY'S BRIDGE (MARIENBRÜCKE)

To Pinswang (Austria)

MUSEUM OF BAVARIAN KINGS

JUGENDSTR.

Alpsee

BOAT RENTAL

❶ Alpenhotel Allgäu     ❸ Schloss Brauhaus
❷ Beim "Landhannes" Rooms

**BAVARIA**

## Museum of the Bavarian Kings
## (Museum der Bayerischen Könige)

About a five-minute walk from the castles' ticket center, in a former grand hotel on the shore of the Alpsee, this modern, well-presented exhibit documents the history of the Wittelsbachs, Bavaria's former royal family. On display are plenty of family portraits and busts, as well as treasures including Ludwig II's outlandish royal robe and elaborately decorated fairy-tale sword, and the impressive dining set given as a golden-anniversary present to his cousin Ludwig III and his wife, the last reigning Wittelsbachs. After losing the throne, the family spoke out against the Nazis, and some were sent to concentration camps as a result. A free, dry audioguide lends some context to the family's history, in more detail than most casual visitors want. The museum is worth the price only if you're captivated by this clan and have some time to kill. (But trying to squeeze it between your two castle visits is a bit too brief—especially if you like to linger.)

**Cost and Hours:** €9.50; combo-ticket with Hohenschwangau-€20.50, with Neuschwanstein-€20, with both castles-€29.50; daily April-Sept 9:00-19:00, Oct-March 10:00-18:00; no reservations required, includes audioguide, mandatory lockers with refundable €1 deposit, Alpseestrasse 27, tel. 08362/926-4640, www.museumderbayerischenkoenige.de.

## NEAR FÜSSEN AND THE CASTLES
Here are a few attractions that lie within a few miles of Füssen or Neuschwanstein. All can be reached by car, bike, or bus.

### ▲Tegelberg Gondola (Tegelbergbahn)
Just north of Neuschwanstein is a fun play zone around the mighty Tegelberg Gondola, a scenic ride to the mountain's 5,500-foot

summit. At the top on a clear day, you get great views of the Alps and Bavaria and the vicarious thrill of watching hang gliders and paragliders leap into airborne ecstasy. Weather permitting, scores of adventurous Germans line up and leap from the launch ramp at the top of the lift. With someone leaving every two or three minutes, it's great for spectators. Thrill seekers with exceptional social skills may talk themselves into a tandem ride with a paraglider. From the top of Tegelberg, it's a steep and demanding 2.5-hour hike down to Ludwig's castle. (Avoid the treacherous trail directly below the gondola.) Around the gondola's valley station, you'll find a playground, a cheery eatery, the stubby remains of an ancient Roman villa, and a summer luge ride (described next).

**Cost and Hours:** €19 round-trip, €12.20 one-way; first ascent daily at 9:00; last descent April-Oct at 17:00, mid-Dec-March at 16:00, closed Nov-mid-Dec; 4/hour, 5-minute ride to the top, in bad weather call first to confirm, tel. 08362/98360, www.tegelbergbahn.de.

**Getting There:** From the castles, most #73 and #78 buses from Füssen continue to the Tegelbergbahn valley station (5-minute ride). It's a 30-minute walk or 10-minute bike ride from the castles.

### ▲Tegelberg Luge
Next to the gondola's valley station is a summer luge course (*Sommerrodelbahn*). A summer luge is like a bobsled on wheels (for more details, see "Luge Lesson" on page 445). This course's stainless-steel track is heated, so it's often dry and open even when drizzly weather shuts down the concrete luges. A funky cable system pulls riders (in their sleds) to the top without a ski lift. It's not as long,

fast, or scenic as Austria's Biberwier luge (described on page 445), but it's handy, harder to get hurt on, and half the price.

**Cost and Hours:** €3.50/ride, shareable 6-ride card-€15; hours vary but typically April-June Mon-Fri 13:00-17:00, Sat-Sun 10:00-17:00; July-Sept daily 10:00-18:00; may open for season earlier in spring or stay open later in fall if weather is good; in bad weather call first to confirm, waits can be long in good weather, no children under age 3, ages 3-8 may ride with an adult, tel. 08362/98360, www.tegelbergbahn.de.

## ▲Royal Crystal Baths (Königliche Kristall-Therme)

This pool/sauna complex just outside Füssen is the perfect way to relax on a rainy day, or to cool off on a hot one. The main part of the complex (downstairs), called the *Therme*, contains two heated indoor pools and a café; outside you'll find a shallow kiddie pool, a lap pool, a heated *Kristallbad* with massage jets and a whirlpool, and a salty mineral bath. The extensive saunas upstairs are well worth the few extra euros, as long as you're OK with nudity. (Swimsuits are required in the downstairs pools, but *verboten* in the upstairs saunas.) You'll see pool and sauna rules in German all over, but don't worry—just follow the locals' lead.

To enter the baths, first choose the length of your visit and your focus (big outdoor pool only, all ground-floor pools but not the saunas, or the whole enchilada—a flier explains all the prices in English). You'll get a wristband and a credit-card-sized ticket with a bar code. Insert that ticket into the entry gate, and keep it—you'll need it to get out. Enter through the yellow changing stalls—where you'll change into your bathing suit—then choose a storage locker (€1 coin deposit). When it's time to leave, reinsert your ticket in the gate—if you've gone over the time limit, feed extra euros into the machine.

**Cost and Hours:** Baths only-€11/2 hours, €17/4 hours, €21/all day; saunas-about €5-6 extra, towel rental-€3, bathrobe rental-€5, bathing suits sold but not rented; daily 9:00-22:00, Fri-Sat until 23:00; nude swimming everywhere Tue and Fri after 19:00; from Füssen, drive, bike, or walk across the river, turn left toward Schwangau, and then, about a mile later, turn left at signs for *Kristall-Therme*, Am Ehberg 16; tel. 08362/819-630, www.kristalltherme-schwangau.de.

## Bike or Boat Around the Forggensee

On a beautiful day, nothing beats a bike ride around the bright-turquoise Forggensee, a nearby lake. This 20-mile ride is exclusively on bike paths (give it a half-day; it's tight to squeeze it in the afternoon after a morning of castle visits, but possible with an early start). Locals swear that going clockwise is less work, but either way has a couple of strenuous uphill parts. Still, the amazing views of the surrounding Alps will distract you from your churning legs—so this is still a great way to spend the afternoon. Rent a bike, pack a picnic lunch, and figure about a three-hour round-trip. From Füssen, follow *Festspielhaus* signs; once you reach the theater, follow *Forggensee Rundweg* signs.

You can also take a **boat ride** on the Forggensee, leaving either from the Füssen "harbor" (*Bootshafen*) or the theater (*Festspielhaus*), a 20- to 30-minute walk north of town (€8/50-minute cruise, 6/day; €11/2-hour cruise, 3/day; runs daily June-mid-Oct, no boats off-season, tel. 08362/921-363, www.stadt-fuessen.de—click on "*Forggensee-Schiffahrt*"). Unless it's very crowded in the summer, you can bring your bike onto the boat and get off across the lake—shortening the total loop.

### Treetop Walkway (Bumkronenweg Ziegelwies)
This elevated wooden "treetop path" lets you stroll for a third of a mile, high in the trees on a graceful yet sturdy suspension-bridge-like structure 60 feet in the air. The

walkway crosses the Austria-Germany border and offers views of the surrounding mountains and the "wild" alpine Lech River, which can be a smooth glacier-blue mirror one day and a muddy torrent the next. Located east of Füssen, just past Lech Falls on the road to Reutte, the walkway can be accessed at either end. The Austrian end (closer to Reutte) has a large parking lot, a tiny ticket booth, and no WC. At the German end (closer to Füssen), parking is scarce and you enter/exit the walkway via a small museum about local flora and fauna. Stairs (kids can take the slide) lead down to a riverside trail that loops about a mile through a kid-friendly park, with a log raft to cross a little creek, a wonky little bridge, and a sandy stream great for wading. Those with more energy to burn can try the slightly longer mountain loop trail, accessed by a tunnel under the road.

**Cost and Hours:** €4, free for kids under age 16, daily May-Oct 10:00-17:00, closed Nov-April and in bad weather, last entry at 16:30, Tiroler Strasse 10, tel. 08362/938-7550, www.baumkronenweg.eu.

## Sleeping near the King's Castles

**(Germany country code: 49, area code: 08362)**
These two places are in Schwangau, very near the castles. Though best for drivers, both are a quick taxi ride from the Füssen train

station and also close to bus stops. In return for paying the Schwangau hotel tax, you get a card with the same benefits as the Füssen Card (see page 391).

**$$ Alpenhotel Allgäu** is a small, family-run hotel with 18 rooms in a bucolic setting. It's a 15-minute walk from the castle ticket office, not far beyond the humongous parking lot (small Sb without balcony-€54, Sb-€60, perfectly fine older Db-€89, newer Db-€97, Tb-€141, book directly with hotel and ask about discount with cash and this book, all but one room have porches or balconies—some with castle views, family rooms, Wi-Fi, elevator, free parking, just before tennis courts at Schwangauer Strasse 37 in the town of Schwangau—don't let your GPS take you to Schwangauer Strasse 37 in Füssen, tel. 08362/81152, www.alpenhotel-allgaeu. de, info@alpenhotel-allgaeu.de, Frau Reiss).

**$ Beim "Landhannes,"** a 200-year-old working dairy farm run by Conny Schön, is a great value for drivers. They rent three creaky but sunny rooms, and keep flowers on the balconies, big bells and antlers in the halls, and cows in the yard (Sb-€35, Db-€70, €5 less per person for 3 or more nights, also rents apartments with kitchen with a 5-night minimum, cash only, Wi-Fi, free parking, nearby bike rental, poorly signed in the village of Horn on the Füssen side of Schwangau, look for the farm down a tiny lane through the grass 100 yards in front of Hotel Kleiner König, Am Lechrain 22, tel. 08362/8349, www.landhannes.de, info@landhannes.de).

# Eating near the King's Castles

For pointers on quick, functional eateries in the immediate castle area, see "Orientation to the King's Castles," earlier.

If you have a car and want to eat at a good-value, non-touristy place without going into Füssen, consider **Schloss Brauhaus,** a sprawling microbrewery restaurant in the village of Schwangau, about 1.5 miles from the castles. They brew five types of beer (dark, light, wheat, and two seasonal brews) and serve classic German fare (€11-19 hearty meals). Choose between the woody-industrial interior—with big copper vats and a miniature bowling alley—or the outdoor *Biergarten,* with distant views of Neuschwanstein (food served Mon-Thu 14:00-21:00, Fri-Sun 11:00-21:00; beer served until 23:00; Gipsmühlweg 5 in Schwangau—watch for signs on the main street, Füssener Strasse, coming in from Füssen; tel. 08362/926-4680, www.schlossbrauhaus.de).

# Wieskirche

Germany's greatest Rococo-style church, this "Church in the Meadow"—worth ▲▲—looks as brilliant as the day it floated down from heaven. Overripe with decoration but bright and bursting with beauty, this church is a divine droplet, a curly curlicue, the final flowering of the Baroque movement.

## ORIENTATION

**Cost and Hours:** Donation requested, daily April-Oct 8:00-20:00, Nov-March 8:00-18:00. The interior is closed to sightseers for about an hour during services: Sun at 8:30 and 11:00; Tue, Wed, and Sat at 10:00; and Fri at 19:00 (17:00 in winter). Tel. 08862/932-930, www.wieskirche.de.

**Getting There:** By car, the Wieskirche is a 30-minute drive north of Neuschwanstein or Füssen. Head north, turn right at Steingaden, and follow the brown signs (parking-€2/2 hours minimum). With careful attention to schedules, you can day-trip here from Füssen by bus (4-6/day, 45-60 minutes), but it's a long round-trip for a church that most see in 10-15 minutes. Trinket shops and snack stands (one sells freshly made doughnuts—look for *Wieskücherl* sign) clog the parking area in front of the church; take a commune-with-nature-and-smell-the-farm detour back through the meadow to the parking lot.

## VISITING THE CHURCH

This pilgrimage church is built around the much-venerated statue of a scourged (or whipped) Christ, which supposedly wept in 1738. The carving—too graphic to be accepted by that generation's Church—was the focus of worship in a peasant's barn. Miraculous-

ly, it shed tears—empathizing with all those who suffer. Pilgrims came from all around. A tiny and humble chapel was built to house the statue in 1739. (You can see it where the lane to the church leaves the parking lot.) Bigger and bigger crowds came. Two of Bavaria's top Rococo architects, the Zimmermann brothers (Johann Baptist and Dominikus), were commissioned to build the Wieskirche that stands here today.

Follow the theological sweep from the

altar to the ceiling: Jesus whipped, chained, and then killed (notice the pelican above the altar—recalling a pre-Christian story of a bird that opened its breast to feed its young with its own blood); the painting of Baby Jesus posed as if on the cross; the golden sacrificial lamb; and finally, high on the ceiling, the resurrected Christ before the Last Judgment. This is the most positive depiction of the Last Judgment around. Jesus, rather than sitting on the throne to judge, rides high on a rainbow—a symbol of forgiveness—giving any sinner the feeling that there is still time to repent, with plenty of mercy on hand. In the back, above the pipe organ, notice the closed door to paradise, and at the opposite end (above the main altar), the empty throne—waiting for Judgment Day.

Above the doors flanking the altar are murky glass cases with 18th-century handkerchiefs. People wept, came here, were healed, and no longer needed their hankies. Walk through either of these doors and up an aisle flanking the high altar to see votives—requests and thanks to God (for happy, healthy babies, and so on). Notice how the kneelers are positioned so that worshippers can meditate on scenes of biblical miracles painted high on the ceiling and visible through the ornate tunnel frames. A priest here once told me that faith, architecture, light, and music all combine to create the harmony of the Wieskirche.

Two paintings flank the door at the rear of the church. The one on the right shows the ceremonial parade in 1749 when the white-clad monks of Steingaden carried the carved statue of Christ from the tiny church to its new big one. The second painting (on the left), from 1757, is a votive from one of the Zimmermann brothers, the artists and architects who built this church. He is giving thanks for the successful construction of the new church.

If you can't visit the Wieskirche, visit one of the other churches that came out of the same heavenly spray can: Oberammergau's church, Munich's Asamkirche, Würzburg's Hofkirche Chapel (at the Residenz), the splendid Ettal Monastery (free and near Oberammergau), and, on a lesser scale, Füssen's basilica.

**Driving from Wieskirche to Oberammergau:** If doing this drive, you'll cross the **Echelsbacher Bridge,** which arches 230 feet over the Pöllat Gorge. Thoughtful drivers let their passengers walk across to enjoy the views, then meet them at the other side. Any kayakers? Notice the painting of the traditional village woodcarver (who used to walk from town to town with his art on his back) on the first big house on the Oberammergau side. It holds the Alm-dorf Ammertal shop, with a huge selection of overpriced carvings and commission-hungry tour guides.

# Oberammergau

The Shirley Temple of Bavarian villages, and exploited to the hilt by the tourist trade, Oberammergau wears too much makeup. During

its famous Passion Play (every 10 years, next in 2020), the crush is unbearable—and the prices at the hotels and restaurants can be as well. The village has about 1,200 beds for the 5,000 play-goers coming daily. But the rest of the time, Oberammergau—while hardly "undiscovered"—is a pleasant, and at times even sleepy, Bavarian village.

If you're passing through, Oberammergau is a ▲ sight—worth a wander among the half-timbered *Lüftlmalerei* houses frescoed with biblical scenes and famous fairy-tale characters. It's also a relatively convenient home base for visiting Linderhof Castle, Ettal Monastery, and the Zugspitze (via Garmisch). A smaller (and less conveniently located) alternative to Füssen and Reutte, it's worth considering for drivers who want to linger in the area. A day trip to Neuschwanstein from Oberammergau is manageable if you have a car, but train travelers do better to stay in Füssen.

## GETTING THERE

**Trains** run from Munich to Oberammergau (nearly hourly, 1.75 hours, change in Murnau). From Füssen, you can take the **bus** (#9606, 4-5/day, 1.5 hours). **Drivers** can get here from Reutte in less than 30 minutes via the pretty Plansee Lake, or from Munich in about an hour.

# Orientation to Oberammergau

This village of about 5,000 feels even smaller, thanks to its remote location. The downtown core, huddled around the onion-domed church, is compact and invites strolling; all of my recommended sights, hotels, and restaurants are within about a 10-minute walk of each other. While the town's name sounds like a mouthful, it's based on the name of the local river (the Ammer) and means, roughly, "Upper Ammerland."

**Tourist Information:** The helpful, well-organized TI provides a wide range of glossy brochures, including maps and English information on area hikes (mid-July-mid-Sept Mon-Fri 9:00-18:00, Sat-Sun 9:00-13:00; mid-Sept-mid-July same hours but

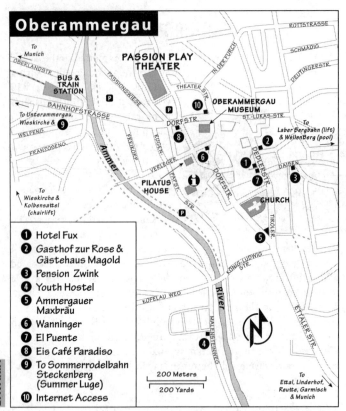

# Oberammergau

**To Munich**
ROTTSTRASSE
SCHMADIG
OBERLANDSTR.
DEUTINGERSTR.

**PASSION PLAY THEATER**

**BUS & TRAIN STATION**

BAHNHOFSTRASSE

**To Unterammergau, Wieskirche &** ❾

WELFENG.

THEATER STR.

**OBERAMMERGAU MUSEUM**

ST.-LUKAS-STR.

DORFSTR.

**To Laber Bergbahn (lift) & WellenBerg (pool)**

FRANZOSENG.

❿

❽

Ammer

EUGEN-

FREIKORP.

VERLEGER-

❻

DEDLERSTR.

DAISEN-

❷

❶

❸

**To Wieskirche & Kolbensattel (chairlift)**

**PILATUS HOUSE**

ℹ️

DORFSTR.

❼

PAPST-

STR.

**CHURCH**

TIROLER-

❺

KÖNIG-LUDWIG-STR.

KOFELAU WEG

River

MALENSTEINWEG

❹

ETTALER STR.

- ❶ Hotel Fux
- ❷ Gasthof zur Rose & Gästehaus Magold
- ❸ Pension Zwink
- ❹ Youth Hostel
- ❺ Ammergauer Maxbräu
- ❻ Wanninger
- ❼ El Puente
- ❽ Eis Café Paradiso
- ❾ To Sommerrodelbahn Steckenberg (Summer Luge)
- ❿ Internet Access

200 Meters
200 Yards

**To Ettal, Linderhof, Reutte, Garmisch & Munich**

closed Sun; Nov-Dec also closed Sat; Eugen-Papst-Strasse 9A, tel. 08822/922-740, www.ammergauer-alpen.de).

**Internet Access: Hotel Alte Post,** right in the heart of town, offers access to the public. Pay at the hotel reception, then either use Wi-Fi or the terminals in the little room at the right end of the building (€3/hour, €5/day, daily 7:00-21:00, Dorfstrasse 19, tel. 08822/9100).

## ARRIVAL IN OBERAMMERGAU

The town's **train** station is a short walk from the center: Turn left, cross the bridge, and you're already downtown.

If you're **driving,** you'll find that there are two exits from the main road into Oberammergau—at the north and south ends. Either way, make your way to the free lot between the TI and the river. While there's ample street parking in town, most is time-limited and/or requires payment—be sure to read signs carefully. Hotels and sights are well-signed in the town.

## Woodcarving in Oberammergau

The Ammergau region is relatively poor, with no appreciable industry and no agriculture, save for some dairy farming. What they *do* have is wood. Carving religious and secular themes became a lucrative way for the locals to make some money, especially when confined to the house during the long, cold winter. And with a major pilgrimage site—Ettal Monastery—just down the road, there was a built-in consumer base eager to buy hand-carved crucifixes and other souvenirs. Carvers from Oberammergau peddled their wares across Europe, carrying them on their backs (on distinctive wooden backpack-racks called *Kraxe*) as far away as Rome.

Today, the Oberammergau Carving School (founded in 1887) is a famous institution that takes only 20 students per year out of 450 applicants. Their graduates do important restoration work throughout Europe. For example, much of the work on Dresden's Frauenkirche was done by these artists.

# Sights in Oberammergau

### ▲Local Arts and Crafts

The town's best sight is its woodcarving shops *(Holzschnitzerei)*. Browse through these small art galleries filled with very expensive whittled works. The beautifully frescoed **Pilatus House** at Ludwig-Thoma-Strasse 10 has an open workshop where you can watch woodcarvers and painters at work on summer afternoons (free; late May-mid-Oct Tue-Sat 13:00-18:00, closed Sun-Mon; open weekends in Dec, closed rest of year, tel. 08822/949-511). Upstairs in the Pilatus House is a small exhibit of "reverse glass" paintings *(verre églomisé)* that's worth a quick glance.

### ▲Oberammergau Museum

This museum showcases local woodcarving, with good English explanations. The ground floor has a small exhibit of nativity scenes *(Krippe*—mostly made of wood, but some of paper or wax). In the back, find the small theater, where you can watch an interesting film in English about the 2010 Passion Play. Upstairs is a much more extensive collection of the wood carvings that helped put Oberammergau on the map, including a room of old woodcarving tools, plus a small exhibit on Roman archaeological finds in the region. Your ticket also lets you into the lobby of the Passion Play Theater, described next.

**Cost and Hours:** €6, includes museum and theater lobby; Easter-Oct and Dec-mid-Jan Tue-Sun 10:00-17:00; closed Mon, Nov, and mid-Jan-Easter; Dorfstrasse 8, tel. 08822/94136, www. oberammergaumuseum.de.

## Passion Play Theater (Festspielhaus)

Back in 1633, in the midst of the bloody Thirty Years' War and with horrifying plagues devastating entire cities, the people of Oberammergau promised God that if they were spared from extinction, they'd "perform a play depicting the suffering, death, and resurrection of our Lord Jesus Christ" every decade thereafter. The town survived, and, heading into its 41st decade, the people of Oberammergau are still making good on the deal. For 100 days every 10 years (most recently

in 2010), about half of the town's population (a cast of 2,000) are involved in the production of this extravagant five-hour Passion Play—telling the story of Jesus' entry into Jerusalem, Crucifixion, and Resurrection.

Until the next show in 2020, you'll have to settle for reading the book, seeing Nicodemus tool around town in his VW, or taking a quick look at the theater, a block from the center of town.

**Visiting the Theater:** With a ticket for the Oberammergau Museum (described earlier), you can enter the theater lobby, where there's a modest exhibit on the history of the performances. A long wall of photographs of past performers shows the many generations of Oberammergauers who have participated in this tradition. Climb the stairs and peek into the theater itself, which has an unusual indoor/outdoor design and a real-life alpine backdrop.

To learn more, you can take a 45-minute guided tour of the theater, organized by the museum (€6, or €8 if you also want to visit the museum; tours run Easter-Oct only, Tue-Sun at 11:00 in English, at 10:00 and 14:00 in German; tel. 08822/94136, www.oberammergaumuseum.de).

## Oberammergau Church

The town church is typically Bavarian Baroque, but a poor cousin of the one at Wies. Being in a woodcarving center, it's only logical that all the statues are made of wood, and then stuccoed and gilded to look like marble or gold. Saints Peter and Paul flank the altar, where the central painting can be raised to reveal a small stage decorated to celebrate special times during the church calendar. In the central dome, a touching painting shows Peter and Paul bidding each other farewell (with the city of Rome as a backdrop) on the day of their execution—the same day, in the year A.D. 67. On the left, Peter is crucified upside-down. On the right, Paul is beheaded with a sword (open daily 8:00-19:30; a fine little €3 booklet explains it all).

Wander through the lovingly maintained **graveyard,** noticing the wide variety in headstones. A towering stone WWI memorial at the gate has an imposing look and sternly worded celebrations of the "heroes" of that war. But around the other side, below it on the outer fence, find the newer glass panel that modifies the sentiment: "We honor and remember the victims of the violence that our land gave the world."

## NEAR OBERAMMERGAU

These attractions are a long walk from town, but easy to reach by car or bike.

### Mountain Lifts

Oberammergau has two mountain lifts of its own. At the east end of town is the **Laber Bergbahn,** a gondola that lifts you up to fine views over the town (www.laber-bergbahn.de). Across town to the west is the **Kolbensattel** chairlift—popular for skiers in winter and hikers in summer (www.kolbensattel.de). From the top, you can hike along the ridge to a series of mountain huts: In about 1.5 hours, you'll reach Pürschling; two hours later is Brunnenkopf (from which you could hike down to Linderhof Castle). Get tips and maps from the TI before doing any of these hikes. Also at Kolbensattel is the 1.5-mile-long Alpine Coaster—similar to a luge, but fixed to a track.

### WellenBerg Swimming Pool

Near the Laber Bergbahn lift and a 25-minute walk from town is this sprawling complex of indoor and outdoor pools and saunas.

**Cost and Hours:** €7/3 hours, €12/day, €4 extra for sauna, daily 10:00-21:00, Himmelreich 52, tel. 08822/92360, www.wellenberg-oberammergau.de.

### Sommerrodelbahn Steckenberg

The next town over, Unterammergau, hosts a stainless-steel summer luge track that's faster than the Tegelberg luge, but not nearly as wicked as the one in Biberwier. This one has double seats (allowing a parent to accompany kids) and two sticks—one for each hand; be careful of your elbows. Unlike other luges, children under age three are allowed, and you only pay one fare when a parent and child ride together.

**Cost and Hours:** €3/ride, €12/6 rides; daily May-early Oct 10:00-17:00, Sat-Sun until 18:00, closed off-season and when wet; Liftweg 1 in Unterammergau, clearly marked and easy 2.5-mile bike ride to Unterammergau along Bahnhofstrasse/Rottenbucherstrasse, take the first left when entering Unterammergau, tel. 08822/4027, www.steckenberg.de.

# Sleeping in Oberammergau

**(country code: 49, area code: 08822)**

Accommodations in Oberammergau tend to be affordable (compared to Füssen or Reutte) and friendly. All offer free parking. Prices listed are for summer (generally May-Oct) and include the €1.80 local tax.

**$$ Hotel Fux**—quiet, romantic, and well-run—rents eight large rooms decorated in the Bavarian *Landhaus* style (Sb-€67, Db-€93, extra bed-€22, guest computer and Wi-Fi, Mannagasse 2a, tel. 08822/93093, www.hotel-in-oberammergau.de, info@firmafux.de). They also have six apartments for stays of at least 3-4 days.

**$$ Gasthof zur Rose** is a big, central, classic, family-run place with 19 mostly small but comfortable rooms, with tiny bathrooms. At the reception desk, look at the several decades' worth of photos showing the family performing in the Passion Play (Sb-€62, Db-€84, Tb-€96, Qb-€108, guest computer and Wi-Fi, Dedlerstrasse 9, tel. 08822/4706, www.rose-oberammergau.de, info@rose-oberammergau.de, Frank family).

**$$ Pension Zwink** offers 10 small, quiet, woody rooms in a residential-feeling neighborhood just across the street from the town center (Sb-€40, Db-€70, Wi-Fi, Daisenbergerstrasse 10, tel. 08822/923-753, www.pension-oberammergau.de, info@pension-oberammergau.de).

**$ Gästehaus Magold,** homey and family-friendly, has three bright and spacious rooms—twice as nice as the cheap hotel rooms in town, and for much less money (Db-€60, cash only, non-smoking, cable Internet, also has two family apartments—minimum stay in summer, immediately behind Gasthof zur Rose at Kleppergasse 1, tel. 08822/4340, www.gaestehaus-magold.de, info@gaestehaus-magold.de, Christine).

**$ Oberammergau Youth Hostel,** on the river, was recently remodeled and is just a short walk from the center (€23/bed, includes breakfast and sheets, €3 extra for nonmembers, €2 extra for one-night stays, €4 extra for those over age 26, reception open 8:00-10:00 & 17:00-19:00, closed mid-Nov-Dec, Malensteinweg 10, tel. 08822/4114, www.oberammergau.jugendherberge.de, oberammergau@jugendherberge.de).

## Eating in Oberammergau

**Ammergauer Maxbräu,** in the Hotel Maximilian on the edge of downtown, serves high-quality, thoughtfully presented Bavarian fare with a modern, international twist. The rustic-yet-mod interior—with big copper vats where they brew their own beer—is cozy on a rainy day. And in nice weather, locals fill the beer garden out front (€12-19 main courses, daily 11:00-22:00, right behind the church, Ettaler Strasse 5, tel. 08822/948-740, www.maximilian-oberammergau.de).

**Gasthof zur Rose,** a couple of blocks off the main drag, serves reasonably priced Bavarian food in its dining room and at a few outdoor tables (€10-15 main courses, Tue-Sun 12:00-14:00 & 17:00-21:00, closed Mon, Dedlerstrasse 9, tel. 08822/4706, www.rose-oberammergau.de).

**Wanninger** is a café by day (coffee, cakes, €7-9 budget weekday lunches, €9-10 main courses) and a steakhouse by night (€18-26 steaks, €13-18 main courses; food served daily 12:00-22:00, Dorfstrasse 22, tel. 08822/836).

**El Puente** may vex Mexican food purists, but it's the most hopping place in town, with €7.50 cocktails attracting young locals and tourists alike. Come not for the burritos and enchiladas, but for the bustling energy (€11-15 burgers and Mexican standards, €20-24 steaks, Mon-Sat 18:00-23:30, closed Sun, Daisenbergerstrasse 3, tel. 08822/945-777, www.elpuente-oberammergau.de).

*Dessert:* **Eis Café Paradiso** serves up good Italian-style gelato along the main street; in nice weather, Germans sunbathe with their big sundaes on the generous patio out front (daily until 22:00 in summer, Dorfstrasse 4, tel. 08822/6279).

## Oberammergau Connections

**From Oberammergau to: Linderhof Castle** (bus #9622, 8/day Mon-Fri, 5/day Sat-Sun, 30 minutes; many of these also stop at **Ettal Monastery**), **Hohenschwangau** (for Neuschwanstein) and **Füssen** (bus #9606, 3-4/day, 1.5 hours, some transfer or change number to #73 at Echelsbacher Brücke), **Garmisch** (bus #9606, nearly hourly, better frequency in morning, 40 minutes; also possible—but much longer—by train with a transfer in Murnau, 1.5 hours; from Garmisch, you can ascend the **Zugspitze**), **Munich** (nearly hourly trains, 1.75 hours, change in Murnau). Train info: tel. 0180-599-6633, www.bahn.com.

# Linderhof Castle

This homiest of "Mad" King Ludwig's castles is a small, comfortably exquisite mini-Versailles—good enough for a minor god, and worth ▲▲. Set in the woods 15 minutes from Oberammergau and surrounded by fountains and sculpted, Italian-style gardens, it's the only palace I've toured that actually had me feeling envious.

## ORIENTATION

**Cost:** €8.50, €5 for grotto only.

**Hours:** Daily April-mid-Oct 9:00-18:00, mid-Oct-March 10:00-16:00 (grotto closed mid-Oct-March); last tour 30 minutes before closing, tel. 08822/92030, www.linderhof.de.

**Crowd-Beating Tips:** July and August crowds can mean an hour's wait between when you buy your ticket and when you start your tour. It's most crowded in the late morning. During this period, you're wise to arrive after 15:00. Any other time of year, you should get your palace tour time shortly after you arrive. If you do wind up with time to kill, consider it a blessing—the gardens are fun to explore, and some of the smaller buildings can be seen quickly while you're waiting for your appointment. While it's possible to reserve ahead by fax or email for 10 percent extra (see the website for details), it's generally not necessary.

**Getting There:** Without a car, getting to (and back from) Linderhof is a royal headache, unless you're staying in Oberammergau. Buses from Oberammergau take 30 minutes (#9622, 8/day Mon-Fri, 5/day Sat-Sun). If you're driving, park near the ticket office (€2.50). Driving from Reutte, take the scenic Plansee route.

**Sightseeing Tips and Procedure:** The complex sits isolated in natural splendor. Plan for lots of walking and a two-hour stop to fully enjoy this royal park. Bring raingear in iffy weather. Your ticket comes with an entry time to tour the palace, which is a 10-minute walk from the ticket office. At the palace entrance, wait in line at the turnstile listed on your ticket (A through D) to take the required 30-minute English tour. Afterwards, explore the rest of the park; be sure not to miss the grotto (10-minute uphill hike from palace, brief but interesting free tour in English, no appointments—the board out front lists the time of the next tour). Then see the other royal buildings dotting the king's playground if you like. You can eat lunch at a café across from the ticket office.

## VISITING THE CASTLE

The main attraction here is the **palace** itself. While Neuschwanstein is Neo-Gothic—romanticizing the medieval glory days of Bavaria—Linderhof is Baroque and Rococo, the frilly, overly ornamented styles more associated with Louis XIV, the "Sun King" of France. And, while Neuschwanstein is full of swans, here you'll see fleur-de-lis (the symbol of French royalty) and multiple portraits of Louis XIV, Louis XV, Madame Pompadour, and other pre-Revolutionary French elites. Though they lived a century apart, Ludwig and Louis were spiritual contemporaries: Both clung to the notion of absolute monarchy, despite the realities of the changing world around them. Capping the palace roofline is one of Ludwig's favorite symbols: Atlas, with the weight of the world literally on his shoulders. Oh, those poor, overburdened, misunderstood absolute monarchs!

Ludwig was king for 22 of his 40 years. He lived much of his last eight years here—the only one of his castles that was finished in his lifetime. Frustrated by the limits of being a "constitutional monarch," he retreated to Linderhof, inhabiting a private fantasy world where extravagant castles glorified his otherwise weakened kingship. You'll notice that the castle is small—designed for a single occupant. Ludwig, who never married or had children, lived here as a royal hermit.

The castle tour includes 10 rooms on the upper floor. (The downstairs, where the servants lived and worked, now houses the gift shop.) You'll see room after room exquisitely carved with Rococo curlicues, wrapped in gold leaf. Up above, the ceiling paintings have 3-D legs sticking out of the frame. Clearly inspired by Versailles, Linderhof even has its own (much smaller) hall of mirrors—decorated with over a hundred Nymphenburg porcelain vases and a priceless ivory chandelier. The bedroom features an oversized crystal chandelier, delicate Meissen porcelain flowers framing the mirrors, and a literally king-size bed—a two-story canopy affair draped in blue velvet. Perhaps the most poignant sight, a sad commentary on Ludwig's tragically solitary lifestyle, is his dinner table—preset with dishes and food—which could rise from the kitchen below into his dining room so he could eat alone. (Examine the incredibly delicate flowers in the Meissen porcelain centerpiece.)

The palace is flanked on both sides with grand, terraced **fountains** (peopled by gleaming golden gods) that erupt at the top and bottom of each hour. If you're waiting for your palace tour to begin, hike up to the top of either of these terraces for a fine photo-op.

(The green gazebo, on the hillside between the grotto and the palace, provides Linderhof's best view.)

The other must-see sight at Linderhof is Ludwig's **grotto.** Exiting the gift shop behind the palace, turn right, then cut left through the garden to climb up the hill. You'll wait out front for the next tour (the time is posted on the board), then head inside. Inspired by Wagner's *Tannhäuser* opera, this artificial cave (300 feet long and 70 feet tall) is actually a performance space. Its rocky walls are made of cement poured over an iron frame. (While Ludwig exalted the distant past, he took full advantage of then-cutting-edge technology to bring his fantasies to life.) The grotto provided a private theater for the reclusive king to enjoy his beloved Wagnerian operas—he was usually the sole member of the audience. The grotto features a waterfall, fake stalactites, and a swan boat floating on an artificial lake (which could be heated for swimming). Brick ovens hidden in the walls could be used to heat the huge space. The first electricity in Bavaria was generated here, to change the colors of the stage lights and to power Ludwig's fountain and wave machine.

**Other Sights at Linderhof:** Several other smaller buildings are scattered around the grounds; look for posted maps and directional signs to track them down. Most interesting are the **Moroccan House** and **Moorish Kiosk.** With over-the-top decor seemingly designed by a sultan's decorator on acid, these allowed Ludwig to "travel" to exotic lands without leaving the comfort of Bavaria. (The Moorish Kiosk is more interesting; look for its gilded dome in the woods beyond the grotto.) At the far edge of the property is **Hunding's Hut,** inspired by Wagner's *The Valkyrie*—a rustic-cottage stage-set with a giant fake "tree" growing inside of it. And closer to the entrance—along the path between the ticket booth and the palace—is the **King's Cottage,** used for special exhibitions (often with an extra charge).

# Ettal Monastery

In 1328, the Holy Roman Emperor was returning from Rome with what was considered a miraculous statue of Mary and Jesus. He was in political and financial trouble, so to please God, he founded a monastery with this statue as its centerpiece. The monastery, located here because it was suitably off

the beaten path, became important as a place of pilgrimage and today, Ettal is on one of the most-traveled tourist routes in Bavaria. Stopping here (free and easy for drivers) offers a convenient peek at a splendid Baroque church. Restaurants across the road serve lunch. A visit is worth ▲.

## ORIENTATION

**Cost and Hours:** The church is free and open daily 8:00-19:45 in summer, until 18:00 off-season, tel. 08822/740, www.kloster-ettal.de. It's best not to visit during Mass (usually Sun at 9:30 and 11:00). If you're moved to make a donation, you can use the self-serve credit-card machine (to the right as you enter)... or drop a coin in one of the old-fashioned collection boxes.

**Getting There:** Ettal Monastery dominates the village of Ettal— you can't miss it. Ettal is a few minutes' **drive** (or a delightful **bike** ride) from Oberammergau. Just park (€1/4 hours in larger lots; free in small, crowded lot near the *Klosterladen*, alongside the building) and wander in. Some Oberammergau-to-Linderhof **buses** stop here (see "Oberammergau Connections," earlier).

## VISITING THE MONASTERY

As you enter the more than 1,000-square-foot **courtyard,** imagine the 14th-century Benedictine abbey, an independent religious

community. It produced everything it needed right here. In the late Middle Ages, abbeys like this had jurisdiction over the legal system, administration, and taxation of their district. Since then, the monastery has had its ups and downs. Secularized during the French Revolution and Napoleonic age, the Benedictines' property was confiscated by the state and sold. Religious life returned a century later. Today the abbey survives, with 50 or 60 monks. It remains a self-contained community, with living quarters for the monks, workshops, and guests' quarters. Along with their religious responsibilities, the brothers make their famous liqueur, brew beer, run a hotel, and educate 380 students in their private high school. The monks' wares are for sale at two shops (look for the *Klosterladen* by the courtyard or the *Kloster-Markt* across the street).

After entering the outer door, notice the **tympanum** over the inner door dating from 1350. It shows the founding couple, Emperor Louis the Bavarian and his wife Margaret, directing our attention to the crucified Lord and inviting us to enter the church contemplatively.

BAVARIA

## 20 + C + M + B + 14

All over Germany (and much of Catholic Europe), you'll likely see written on doorways a mysterious message: "20 + C + M + B + 14." This is marked in chalk on Epiphany (Jan 6), the Christian holiday celebrating the arrival of the Magi to adore the newborn Baby Jesus. In addition to being the initials of the three wise men (Caspar, Melchior, and Balthazar), the letters also stand for the Latin phrase *Christus mansionem benedicat*—"May Christ bless the house." The little crosses separating the letters remind all who enter that the house has been blessed in this year (20+14). Epiphany is a bigger deal in Catholic Europe than in the US. The holiday includes gift-giving, feasting, and caroling door to door—often collecting for a charity organization. Those who donate get their doors chalked up in thanks, and these marks are left on the door through the year.

Stepping inside, the light draws our eyes to the **dome** (it's a double-shell design, 230 feet high) rather than to the high altar. Illusions—with the dome opening right to the sky—merge heaven and earth. The dome fresco shows hundreds of Benedictines worshipping the Holy Trinity...the glory of the Benedictine Order. This is classic "south-German Baroque."

Statues of the **saints** on the altars are either engaged in a holy conversation with each other or singing the praises of God. Broken shell-style patterns seem to create constant movement, with cherubs adding to the energy. Side altars and confessionals seem to grow out of the architectural structure; its decorations and furnishings become part of an organic whole. Imagine how 18th-century farmers and woodcutters, who never traveled, would step in here on Sunday and be inspired to praise their God.

The origin of the monastery is shown over the **choir arch:** An angel wearing the robe of a Benedictine monk presents the emperor with a marble Madonna and commissions him to found this monastery. (In reality, the statue was made in Pisa, circa 1300, and given to the emperor in Italy.)

Dwarfed by all the magnificence and framed by a monumental tabernacle is that tiny, most precious statue of the abbey—the miraculous **statue of Mary and the Baby Jesus.**

**Nearby:** The fragrant **demonstration dairy** *(Schaukäserei)* about a five-minute walk behind the monastery is worth a quick

BAVARIA

look. The farmhouse displays all the steps in the production line, starting with the cows themselves (next to the house), to the factory staff hard at work, and through to the end products, which you can sample in the shop (try the beer cheese). Better yet, enjoy a snack on the deck while listening to the sweet music/incessant clanging of cowbells (free; daily 10:00-17:00—but to see the most cheese-making action, come in the morning, ideally between 10:00-11:00; Mandlweg 1, tel. 08822/923-926, www.schaukaeserei-ettal.de). To walk there from the monastery's exit, take a left and go through the passageway; take another left when you get to the road, then yet another left at the first street (you'll see it up the road, directly behind the abbey).

# Zugspitze

The tallest point in Germany, worth ▲▲ in clear weather, is also a border crossing. Lifts from both Austria and Germany meet at the 9,700-foot summit of the Zugspitze (TSOOG-shpit-seh). You can straddle the border between two  great nations while enjoying an incredible view. Restaurants, shops, and telescopes await you at the summit.

BAVARIA

## SUMMITING THE ZUGSPITZE

**German Approach:** There are several ways to ascend from this side, but they all cost the same (€51 round-trip, €42 in winter, tel. 08821/7970, www.zugspitze.de).

If relying on **public transit,** you'll first head to Garmisch (for details on getting there from Füssen, see page 402; from Oberammergau, see page 425). From there, you'll ride a train to Eibsee (30 minutes, hourly departures daily 8:15-14:15), at which point you can choose: Walk across the parking lot and zip up to the top in a cable car (10 minutes, daily 8:00-16:15, departs at least every 30 minutes; in busy times departs every 10 minutes, but since each car fits only 35—which the electronic board suspensefully counts down as each passenger goes through the turnstile—you may have to wait to board), or transfer to a cogwheel train (45 minutes to the top, departs about hourly—coordinated with Garmisch train; once up top, you'll transfer from the train to a short cable car for the quick, 3-minute ascent to the summit).

**Drivers** can go straight to Eibsee (about 10 minutes beyond Garmisch—head through town following signs for *Fernpass/*

*Reutte,* and watch for the Zugspitze turnoff on the left); once there, you have the same cable car vs. cog railway choice. (Even though they're not taking the train from Garmisch, drivers pay the same—€50 round-trip, plus another €3 for parking.)

You can choose how you want to go up and down at the spur of the moment: both ways by cable car, both by cog train, or mix and match. Although the train ride takes longer, many travelers enjoy the more involved cog-railway experience—at least one way. The disadvantage of the train is that more than half of the trip is through dark tunnels deep in the mountains; aside from a few fleeting glimpses of the Eibsee sparkling below, it's not very scenic.

Arriving at the top, you'll want to head up to the third floor (elevators recommended, given the high altitude)—follow signs for *Gipfel* (summit).

To get back down to Eibsee, the last cable car departs the summit at 16:45, and the last cogwheel train at 16:30. On busy days, you may have to reserve a return time once you reach the top—if it's crowded, look for signs and prebook your return to avoid getting stuck up top longer than you want. In general, allow plenty of time for afternoon descents: If bad weather hits in the late afternoon, cable cars can be delayed at the summit, causing tourists to miss their train connection from Eibsee back to Garmisch.

Hikers can enjoy the easy six-mile walk around the lovely Eibsee Lake (start 5 minutes downhill from cable-car station).

**Austrian Approach:** The Tiroler Zugspitzbahn ascent is less crowded and cheaper than the Bavarian one. Departing from above the village of Ehrwald (a 30-minute train trip from Reutte, train runs every 2 hours), the lift zips you to the top in 10 minutes (€39 round-trip, departures in each direction at :00, :20, and :40 past the hour, daily 8:40-16:40 except closed mid-April-late May and most of Nov, last ascent at 16:00, drivers follow signs for *Tiroler Zugspitzbahn,* free parking, Austrian  tel. 05673/2309, www.zugspitze.at). While those without a car will find the German ascent from Garmisch easier, the Austrian ascent is also doable: Either hop the bus from the Ehrwald train station to the Austrian lift (departures nearly hourly), or pay €8 for the five-minute taxi ride from Ehrwald train station.

## SELF-GUIDED TOUR

Whether you've ascended from the Austrian or German side, you're high enough now to enjoy a little tour of the summit. The two terraces—Bavarian and Tirolean—are connected by a narrow walkway, which was the border station before Germany and Austria opened their borders. The Austrian (Tirolean) side was higher until the Germans blew its top off in World War II to make a flak tower, so let's start there.

**Tirolean Terrace:** Before you stretches the Zugspitzplatt glacier. Each summer, a 65,000-square-foot reflector is spread over the ice to try to slow the shrinking. Since metal ski-lift towers collect heat, they, too, are wrapped to try to save the glacier. Many ski lifts fan out here, as if reaching for a ridge that defines the border between Germany and Austria. The circular metal building is the top of the cog-railway line that the Germans cut through the mountains in 1931. Just above that, find a small square building—the *Hochzeitskapelle* (wedding chapel) consecrated in 1981 by Cardinal Joseph Ratzinger (now Pope Benedict XVI).

Both Germany and Austria use this rocky pinnacle for communication purposes. The square box on the Tirolean Terrace provides the Innsbruck airport with air-traffic control, and a tower nearby is for the German *Katastrophenfunk* (civil defense network).

This highest point in Germany (there are many higher points in Austria) was first climbed in 1820. The Austrians built a cable car that nearly reached the summit in 1926. (You can see it just over the ridge on the Austrian side—look for the ghostly, abandoned concrete station.) In 1964, the final leg, a new lift, was built connecting that 1926 station to the actual summit, where you stand now. Before then, people needed to hike the last 650 feet to the top. Today's lift dates from 1980, but was renovated after a 2003 fire. The Austrian station, which is much nicer than the German station, has a fine little museum—free with Austrian ticket, €2.50 if you came up from Germany—that shows three interesting videos (6-minute 3-D mountain show, 30-minute making-of-the-lift documentary, and 45-minute look at the nature, sport, and culture of the region).

Looking up the valley from the Tirolean Terrace, you can see the towns of Ehrwald and Lermoos in the distance, and the valley that leads to Reutte. Looking farther clockwise, you'll see Eibsee Lake below. Hell's Valley, stretching to the right of Eibsee, seems to merit its name.

**Bavarian Terrace:** The narrow passage connecting the two terraces used to be a big deal—you'd show your passport here at the little blue house and shift from Austrian shillings to German marks. Notice the regional pride here: no German or Austrian national banners, but regional ones instead—*Freistaat Bayern* (Bavaria) and *Land Tirol*.

The German side features a golden cross marking the summit...the highest point in Germany. A priest and his friends hauled it up in 1851. The historic original was shot up by American soldiers using it for target practice in the late 1940s, so what you see today is a modern replacement. In the summer, it's easy to "summit" the Zugspitze, as there are steps and handholds all the way to the top. Or you can just stay behind and feed the birds. The yellow-beaked ravens get chummy with those who share a little pretzel or bread. Below the terrace, notice the restaurant that claims—irrefutably—to be the "highest Biergarten in Deustchland."

The oldest building up here is the rustic tin-and-wood weather tower near the border crossing, erected in 1900 by the *Deutscher Wetterdienst* (German weather service). The first mountaineers' hut, built in 1897, didn't last. The existing one—entwined with mighty cables that cinch it down—dates from 1914. In 1985, observers clocked 200-mph winds up here—those cables were necessary. Step inside the restaurant to enjoy museum-like photos and paintings on the wall (including a look at the team who hiked up with the golden cross in 1851).

Near the waiting area for the cable cars and cogwheel train is a little museum (in German only) that's worth a look if you have some time to kill before heading back down. If you're going down on the German side, remember you must choose between the cable car (look for the *Eibsee* signs) or cog railway (look for *Talfahrt/Descent*, with a picture of a train; you'll board a smaller cable car for the quick trip to the train station).

**BAVARIA**

# Reutte, Austria

Reutte (ROY-teh, with a rolled *r*), a relaxed Austrian town of 6,000, is a 20-minute drive across the border from Füssen. While over-

looked by the international tourist crowd, it's popular with Germans and Austrians for its climate. Doctors recommend its "grade 1" air.

Although its setting—surrounded by alpine peaks—is striking, the town itself is pretty unexceptional. But that's the point. I enjoy Reutte for the opportunity it offers to simply be in a real

community. As an example of how the town is committed to its character, real estate can be sold only to those using it as a primary residence. (Many formerly vibrant alpine towns made a pile of money but lost their sense of community by becoming resorts. They allowed wealthy foreigners—who just drop in for a week or two a year—to buy up all the land, and are now shuttered up and dead most of the time.)

Reutte has one claim to fame among Americans: As Nazi Germany was falling in 1945, Hitler's top rocket scientist, Werner von Braun, joined the Americans (rather than the Russians) in Reutte. You could say that the American space program began here.

Reutte isn't featured in any other American guidebook. The town center can be congested and confusing, and its charms are subtle. It was never rich or important. Its castle is ruined, its buildings have painted-on "carvings," its churches are full, its men yodel for each other on birthdays, and its energy is spent soaking its Austrian and German guests in *Gemütlichkeit*. Most guests stay for a week, so the town's attractions are more time-consuming than thrilling.

Some travelers tell me this town is over-Reutte-d. Füssen's tidy pedestrian core and glitzy hotels make it an easier home base. But in my view, Reutte's two big trump cards are its fine countryside accommodations (the farther from the town center, the more rustic, authentic, and relaxing) and its proximity to one of my favorite ruined castles, Ehrenberg. Since you need a car to take best advantage of these pluses (as well as to reach the King's Castles quickly), Reutte is a good place for drivers to spend the night.

## Orientation to Reutte

Reutte feels spread out, because it's really a web of several villages that fill a basin hemmed in by mountains and cut through by the Lech River. Drivers find its tangle of crisscrossing roads bewildering at first; know where you're going and follow signs (to your point of interest, hotel, or neighboring village) to stay on track.

**Reutte** proper, near the train station, has a one-street downtown where you'll find the TI, museum, and a couple of hotels and eateries. The area's real charm lies in the abutting hamlets, and that's where my favorite hotels and restaurants are located: **Breitenwang,** flowing directly from Reutte to the east, marked by its pointy steeple; **Ehenbichl,** a farming village cuddled up against the mountains to the south; **Höfen,** squeezed between an airstrip and a cable-car station, just across the river from Ehenbichl; and remote **Pinswang,** stranded in a forgotten valley halfway to Germany, just over the mountain from Neuschwanstein. Watching over it all to the south are the **Ehrenberg Castle** ruins—viewable from just about everywhere and evocatively floodlit at night—two miles out of town on the main Innsbruck road.

## TOURIST INFORMATION

Reutte's TI is a block in front of the train station (Mon-Fri 8:00-12:00 & 14:00-17:00, no midday break July-Aug, Sat 8:30-12:00, closed Sun, Untermarkt 34, tel. 05672/62336, www.reutte.com). Go over your sightseeing plans, ask about a folk evening, and pick up city and biking/hiking maps, bus schedules, the *Sommerprogramm* events schedule (in German only), and a free town info booklet (with a good self-guided walk).

Guests staying in the Reutte area (and, therefore, paying local hotel tax) are entitled to an **Aktiv-Card**—be sure to ask your hotel for one. The TI has a brochure explaining all of the perks of this card, including free travel on local buses (including the Reutte-Füssen route—but not Füssen-Neuschwanstein) and free admission to some otherwise very pricey attractions, including the recommended museum below Ehrenberg Castle, the Hahnenkammbahn mountain lift (summer only), and the Alpentherme bath complex (2 hours free each day). Also included are various guided hikes in the surrounding mountains (get schedule from TI), and discounts on mountain-bike tours, rafting trips, and paragliding.

## ARRIVAL IN REUTTE

**By Car:** From the expressway, always take the south *(Süd)* exit into town (even if you pass the *Nord* exit first). For parking in town, blue lines denote pay-and-display spots (if you're staying more than 30 minutes, pay at the meter, then put the receipt in your windshield). There are a few spaces just outside the TI that are free for up to 30 minutes—handy for stopping by with a few questions en route to your out-of-town hotel. For longer stays, there's a free lot (P-1) just past the train station on Muhlerstrasse (about a 10-minute walk from the town center and TI).

**By Train or Bus:** From Reutte's tidy little train and bus station (no baggage storage, usually unstaffed), exit straight ahead and walk three minutes straight up Bahnhofstrasse. After the park on your left, you'll see the TI; my recommended town-center hotels are down the street just beyond the TI and its parking lot.

## HELPFUL HINTS

**Laundry:** There isn't an actual launderette in town, but the recommended Hotel Maximilian lets non-guests use its laundry service (wash, dry, and fold-€16/load; hotel guests pay €12).

**Bike Rental:** Try **Intersport** (€15/day, Mon-Fri 9:00-18:00, Sat 9:00-17:00, closed Sun, Lindenstrasse 25, tel. 05672/62352), or check at the recommended Hotel Maximilian.

**Taxi:** Taxi service is in flux; ask your hotelier about options with an Aktiv-Card.

**"Nightlife":** Reutte is pretty quiet. For any action at all, there's a strip of bars, dance clubs, and Italian restaurants on Linden-strasse.

## Sights in and near Reutte

### ▲▲EHRENBERG CASTLE ENSEMBLE (FESTUNGSENSEMBLE EHRENBERG)

If Neuschwanstein was the medieval castle dream, Ehrenberg is the medieval castle reality. Once the largest fortification in

Tirol, its brooding ruins lie about two miles outside Reutte. What's here is actually an "ensemble" of four castles, built to defend against the Bavarians and to bottle up the strategic Via Claudia trade route, which cut through the Alps as it con-

nected Italy and Germany. Half-forgotten and overgrown only a decade ago, they've been transformed into a fine attraction with hiking paths, a museum, guesthouse, and—soon—the longest pedestrian suspension bridge in the world. The European Union helps fund the project because it promotes the heritage of a multinational region—Tirol—rather than a country.

In Roman times, the Via Claudia—the road below Ehrenberg—was the main route between northern Italy (Verona) and southern Germany (Augsburg), and was broad enough for wheeled traffic. In medieval times, historians estimate that about 10,000 tons of precious salt passed through this valley each year, so it's no wonder the locals built this complex of fortresses and castles to control traffic and levy tolls on all who passed.

The complex has four parts: the old toll buildings on the valley floor, where you park (the Klause); the oldest castle, on the hilltop directly above (Ehrenberg); a mightier castle on a slightly higher peak of the same hill (Schlosskopf); and a smaller fortification across the valley (Fort Claudia). All four were once a single complex connected by walls. Signs posted throughout the site help visitors find their way and explain some background on the region's history, geology, flora, and fauna, and colorful, fun boards relate local folktales.

**Cost and Hours:** The castle ruins themselves are free and always open, but the museum and suspension bridge charge admission (for details, see individual listings).

**Getting There:** The castles are on the road to Lermoos and Innsbruck, just five minutes by car from Reutte (parking-€2/day). It's also a pleasant 30- to 45-minute walk or a short bike ride; bikers

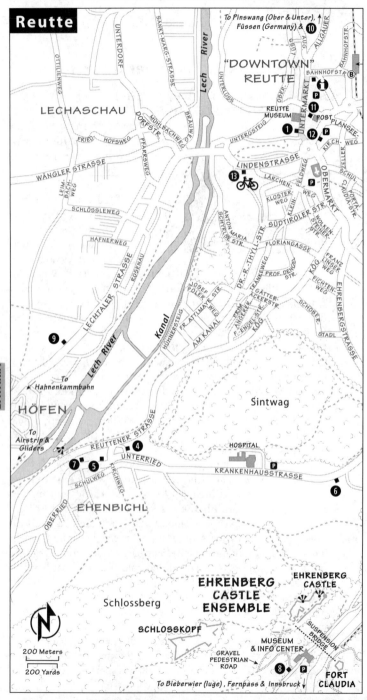

# Reutte

BAVARIA

**LECHASCHAU**

To Pinswang (Ober & Unter), ↑
Füssen (Germany) & ⑩

"DOWNTOWN" REUTTE

ⓑ

BAHNHOFSTR.
AUG. ALLGÄUER
BAHNHOFSTR.

ℹ
Ⓟ
⑪

REUTTE MUSEUM
①

UNTERMARKT
⑫
POST
PLANSEE-

UNTERGASSE
KIRCH- WEG

LINDENSTRASSE
⑬ 🚲

LÄRCHEN- WEG
FELDWEG
OBERMARKT
Ⓟ

POSTA CLAUDIA STR.
SCHUL-

KLOSTER- WEG
WOLKEN- STEINER- STR.
KLEIN- WEG

SÜDTIROLER STR.

ANTON MARIA SCHMID STR.
DR.-R.-THYLL-STR.

FLORIANGASSE
FRANZ LINDER WEG

PROF. DENGL- STR.
KÖG
FICHTEN- WEG

JOSEF POLER WEG
FR. ATTLMAYR WEG
AM KANAL
FRANKEWEG
GÄTTER-ACKERSTR.
PAM ANGER

EHRENBERGSTRASSE

SCHÖBE-
STADL

HÜHNERSTEIG
F. ENGELSTR.
KÖG

**Sintwag**

Kanal

Lech River

To ⑨
← Hahnenkammbahn

**HÖFEN**

To
← Airstrip & Gliders

REUTTENER STRASSE

HOSPITAL
Ⓟ
KRANKENHAUSSTRASSE
⑥

🪂 ④
⑦ ⑤
UNTERRIED
SCHULWEG  KIRCHWEG

OBERRIED

**EHENBICHL**

**Schlossberg**

**EHRENBERG CASTLE ENSEMBLE**

**EHRENBERG CASTLE**
↯

**SCHLOSSKOPF**

SUSPENSION BRIDGE

MUSEUM & INFO CENTER
⑧ Ⓟ

GRAVEL PEDESTRIAN ROAD

**FORT CLAUDIA**

To Bieberwier (luge), Fernpass & Innsbruck →

N

200 Meters
200 Yards

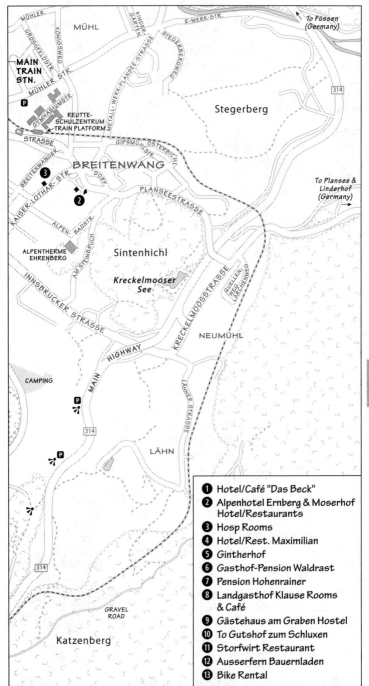

BAVARIA

1. Hotel/Café "Das Beck"
2. Alpenhotel Ernberg & Moserhof Hotel/Restaurants
3. Hosp Rooms
4. Hotel/Rest. Maximilian
5. Gintherhof
6. Gasthof-Pension Waldrast
7. Pension Hohenrainer
8. Landgasthof Klause Rooms & Café
9. Gästehaus am Graben Hostel
10. To Gutshof zum Schluxen
11. Storfwirt Restaurant
12. Ausserfern Bauernladen
13. Bike Rental

can use the *Radwanderweg* along the Lech River (the TI has a good map).

Local bus #4250 runs sporadically from Reutte's main train station to Ehrenberg (5-7/day Mon-Sat, 1/day Sun, 10 minutes, €2.80; see www.vvt.at for schedules—the stop name is "Ehrenberger Klause"). However, no buses run directly *back* to Reutte from the castle.

## ▲Museum

While there are no real artifacts here (other than the sword used in A.D. 2014 to make me the honorary First Knight of Ehrenberg), the clever, kid-friendly museum is hands-on and well-described in English. The focus is on castles, knights, and medieval warcraft. Some of the exhibits trace the fictional journey of a knight named Heinrich to Jerusalem in the late 1300s. You can try on a set of armor (and then weigh yourself), see the limited vision knights had to put up with when wearing helmets, learn about everyday medieval life, empathize with victims of the plague, join a Crusade, and pretend to play soccer with gigantic stone balls once tossed by a catapult. In the armory section, you can heft replica weapons from the period. Several videos and soundtracks spring to life if you press a button (select *E* for English).

A smaller exhibit (with separate entry fee) focuses on local plants and animals and the still-wild Lech River (on other side of info desk and gift shop). The info desk and gift shop themselves are worth a stop even if you skip the museum, and have maps of the trails leading up to the castles.

**Cost and Hours:** Museum-€8, nature exhibit-€5.50, combo-ticket for both-€10.80, family discounts, daily 10:00-17:00, closed Nov-mid-Dec, tel. 05672/62007, www.ehrenberg.at.

**Eating:** Next to the museum, the **Landgasthof Klause** serves typical Tirolean meals (€7-10 pastas and vegetarian meals, €11-17 main courses, daily 8:00-23:00, hot food served until 20:30, tel. 05672/62213, www.gasthof-klause.com). They also rent a few rooms if you'd like to stay right at Ehrenberg (see page 449).

## ▲▲Ehrenberg Ruins

Ehrenberg, a 13th-century rock pile, provides a super opportunity to let your imagination off its leash. Hike up 30 minutes from the parking lot in the valley for a great view from your own private ruins. The trail is well-marked and has well-groomed gravel, but it's quite steep, and once you reach the castle itself, you'll want good shoes to scramble over the uneven stairs. The castle is always open.

**❷ Self-Guided Tour:** From the parking

lot, follow yellow signs up into the woods, tracking *Ruine Ehrenberg* or *Bergruine Ehrenberg*. At the top of the first switchback, notice the option to turn left and hike 45 minutes up to Schlosskopf, the higher castle (described next; this is an easier ascent than the very steep route you can take from closer to Ehrenberg). But we'll head right and continue up the path through the lower entrance bastion of Ehrenberg.

Emerging from the woods, you'll pop out at a saddle between two steep hills. As you face Reutte, the hill on the left is Schlosskopf (notice the steeper ascent here to reach the top), and to the right is Ehrenberg. Ehrenberg is the older of the two, built around 1290. Thirteenth-century castles were designed to stand boastfully tall. Later, with the advent of gunpowder, castles dug in. (Notice the 18th-century ramparts around the castle.)

Now continue twisting up the path to Ehrenberg Castle. As you approach its outer gate, look for the small **door** to the left. It's the night entrance (tight and awkward, and therefore safer against a surprise attack). But we'll head through the **main gate**—actually, two of them. Castles were designed with layered defenses—outer bastion down below, outer gate here, inner gate deeper within—which allowed step-by-step retreat, giving defenders time to regroup and fight back against invading forces.

After you pass through the outer gate, but before climbing to the top of the castle, follow the path around to the right to a big, grassy courtyard with commanding views and a fat, restored **turret.** This stored gunpowder and held a big cannon that enjoyed a clear view of the valley below. In medieval times, all the trees approaching the castle were cleared to keep an unobstructed view.

Look out over the valley. The pointy spire marks the village of **Breitenwang,** which was the site of a Roman camp in A.D. 46. In 1489, after a bridge was built across the Lech River at Reutte (marked by the onion-domed church), Reutte was made a market town and eclipsed Breitenwang in importance. Any gliders circling? They launch from just over the river in Höfen.

For centuries, this castle was the seat of government—ruling an area called the "judgment of Ehrenberg" (roughly the same as today's "district of Reutte"). When the emperor came by, he stayed here. In 1604, the ruler moved downtown into more comfortable quarters, and the castle was no longer a palace.

Now climb to the top of Ehrenberg Castle. Take the high ground. There was no water supply here—just kegs of wine, beer, and a cistern to collect rain. Up at the top, appreciate how strategic this lofty position is—with commanding views over Reutte and its broad valley, as well as the narrow side-valley where the highway to the south runs. But also notice that you're sandwiched between two higher hilltops: Schlosskopf in one direction and Falkenberg (across the narrow valley) in the other. In the days before gunpowder, those higher positions offered no real threat. But in the age of cannonballs, Ehrenberg was suddenly very vulnerable...and very obsolete.

Still, Ehrenberg repelled 16,000 Swedish soldiers in the defense of Catholicism in 1632. But once the Schlosskopf was fortified a few decades later, Ehrenberg's days were numbered, and its end was not glorious. In the 1780s, a local businessman bought the castle in order to sell off its parts. Later, in the late 19th century, when vagabonds moved in, the roof was removed to make squatting miserable. With the roof gone, deterioration quickened, leaving only this evocative shell and a whiff of history.

Scramble around the ruined walls a bit—nocking imaginary arrows—and head back down through the main gate, returning to the valley the way you came. If you have more energy and castle curiosity, you could try conquering the next castle over: Schlosskopf.

## ▲Schlosskopf

When Bavarian troops captured Ehrenberg in 1703, the Tiroleans climbed up to the bluff above it to rain cannonballs down on their former fortress. In 1740, a mighty new castle—designed to defend against modern artillery—was built on this sky-high strategic location: Schlosskopf ("Castle Head"). But it, too, fell into ruin and by the end of the 20th century, the castle was completely overgrown with trees—you literally couldn't see it from Reutte. But today the trees have been shaved away, and the castle has been excavated. In 2008, the Castle Ensemble project, led by local architect Armin Walch, opened the site with English descriptions and view platforms. One spot gives spectacular views of the strategic valley. The other looks down on the older Ehrenberg Castle ruins, illustrating the strategic problems presented with the advent of cannon.

**Getting There:** There are two routes to Schlosskopf, both steep and time-consuming. The steeper of the two (about 30 minutes straight up) starts at the little saddle of land between the two castles (described earlier). The second, which curls around the back of the hill, is less steep but takes longer (45-60 minutes); this one begins from partway down the gravel switchbacks between Ehrenberg and the valley floor—just watch for *Schlosskopf* signs.

## Suspension Bridge

At more than 1,200 feet, this suspended pedestrian bridge is set to be the longest of its type in the world (and should be completed by the time you visit). Plans call for it to hang more than 300 feet above the valley floor, connecting Ehrenberg with the previously difficult-to-reach Fort Claudia across the valley.

**Cost and Hours:** Likely €8, daily 8:00-22:00, tel. 05672/62007, www.highline179.com.

## IN THE TOWN
### Reutte Museum (Museum Grünes Haus)
Reutte's cute city museum offers a quick look at the local folk culture and the story of the castles. There are exhibits on Ehrenberg and the Via Claudia, local painters, and more—ask to borrow the English translations.

**Cost and Hours:** €3; May-Oct Tue-Sat 13:00-17:00, closed Sun-Mon; shorter hours and closed Sun-Tue off-season; closes Easter-end of April and Nov-early Dec; in the bright-green building at Untermarkt 25, around corner from Hotel Goldener Hirsch, tel. 05672/72304, www.museum-reutte.at.

### ▲▲Tirolean Folk Evening
Ask the TI or your hotel if there's a Tirolean folk evening scheduled. During the summer (July-Aug), nearby towns (such as Höfen on Tue) occasionally put on an evening of yodeling, slap dancing, and Tirolean frolic. These are generally free and worth the short drive. Off-season, you'll have to do your own yodeling. There are also weekly folk concerts featuring the local choir or brass band in Reutte's Zeiller Platz, as well as various groups in the surrounding communities (free, July-Aug only, ask at TI). For listings of these and other local events, pick up a copy of the German-only *Sommer-programm* schedule at the TI.

### Alpentherme Ehrenberg
This new, extensive swimming pool and sauna complex, a 15-minute walk from downtown Reutte, is a tempting retreat. The Badewelt section features two indoor pools and a big outdoor saltwater pool, as well as two waterslides. The all-nude Saunaparadies section (no kids under age 16) consists of three indoor saunas, three freestanding outdoor saunas, and a big outdoor swimming pool. They'll issue you a wristband that lets you access your locker and buy snacks on credit without needing a key or money. Those staying in the Reutte area can access the pools for two hours free with an Aktiv-Card (see "Tourist Information," earlier); it's a nice way to relax after hiking around castles all day.

**Cost and Hours:** Pools only-€9.50/2 hours, €11.50/4 hours, €13.50/day; sauna and pools-€19.50/3 hours, €25.50/day; towel rental-€3, robe rental-€5, swimsuits sold but not rented; daily 10:00-21:00, sauna until 22:00, closes for one week every May; Thermenstrasse 10, tel. 05672/72222, www.alpentherme-ehrenberg.at.

## ACROSS THE RIVER, IN HÖFEN
Just over the Lech River are two very different ways to reach high-altitude views. To get here from Reutte, head up Lindenstrasse

(where the cobbled Obermarkt ends), cross the bridge, and turn left down Lechtaler Strasse; as you enter the village of Höfen, you'll see the cable car to your right and the airstrip to your left.

## ▲Scenic Flights

For a major thrill on a sunny day, drop by the tiny airport in Höfen, where small single-prop planes and gliders take passengers on scenic flights. Although I've listed contact information below, your best bet is to show up at the airstrip on a good-weather afternoon and ask around. Prop planes can buzz the Zugspitze and Ludwig's castles and give you a bird's-eye peek at Reutte's Ehrenberg ruins (tel. 05672/632-0729 or mobile 0664-221-2233, www.flugsportverein-reutte.at). Or, to try something more angelic, how about gliding *(Segelfliegen)?* For a modest price, you and a pilot get 30 minutes in a two-seat glider. Just watching the towrope launch the graceful glider like a giant slow-motion rubber-band gun is exhilarating (mobile 0676-945-1288, www.segelflugverein-ausserfern.at, Adrian Eberhardt).

**Getting There:** The prop planes and gliders are based out of two different restaurants that face the airstrip. From the main road, watch for the big building marked *Flugplatz* down below. The contact for the prop-plane pilots is the Fliegerklause café (closed Mon); for the gliders, head 100 yards farther down the road to the Thermic Ranch.

## Hahnenkammbahn

This mountain lift swoops you in small enclosed cars high above the tree line to an attractive restaurant and starting point for several hikes. In the alpine flower park, special paths lead you past countless varieties of local flora. Unique to this lift is a barefoot hiking trail *(Barfusswanderweg),* designed to be walked without shoes—no joke.

**Cost and Hours:** €12 one-way, €17.50 round-trip, runs June-Sept daily 9:00-16:30, also in good weather late May and Oct-early Nov, flowers best in late July, base station across the river in Höfen, tel. 05672/62420, www.reuttener-seilbahnen.at.

## NEAR REUTTE
### Sights Along the Lech River

The Lech River begins high in the Alps and meanders 75 miles (including right past Reutte) on its way to the Lechfall, where it becomes navigable, near Füssen. This stretch of the Lech River Valley (Lechtal) has been developed as a popular hiking trail, called the **Lechweg,** divided into 15 stages *(Strecken);* part of the area has also been designated as a nature park. A variety of glossy brochures—mostly in German and available at local TIs and hotels—explain

# Luge Lesson

Taking a wild ride on a summer luge (pronounced "loozh") is a quintessential alpine experience. In German, it's called a *Sommerrodelbahn* ("summer toboggan run"). To try one of Europe's great accessible thrills (€3-8), take the lift up to the top of a mountain, grab a wheeled sled-like go-cart, and scream back down the mountainside on a banked course. Then take the lift back up and start all over again.

Luge courses are highly weather-dependent, and can close at the slightest hint of rain. If the weather's questionable, call ahead to confirm that your preferred luge is open. Stainless-steel courses are more likely than concrete ones to stay open in drizzly weather.

Operating the sled is simple: Push the stick forward to go faster, pull back to apply brakes. Even a novice can go very, very fast. Most are cautious on their first run, speed demons on their second...and bruised and bloody on their third. A woman once showed me her travel journal illustrated with her husband's dried five-inch-long luge scab. He had disobeyed the only essential rule of luging: Keep both hands on your stick. To avoid a bumper-to-bumper traffic jam, let the person in front of you get as far ahead as possible before you start. You'll emerge from the course with a windblown hairdo and a smile-creased face.

Here are a few key luge terms:

| | |
|---|---|
| *Lenkstange* | lever |
| *drücken / schneller fahren* | push / go faster |
| *ziehen / bremsen* | pull / brake |
| *Schürfwunde* | scrape |
| *Schorf* | scab |

the importance of the Lech to local culture and outline some enticing hikes.

Within the pristine Tiroler Lech Nature Park, a little outside Reutte, is an impressive wooden **lookout tower** from which you can observe the vibrant bird life in the wetlands along the Lech River (110 different species of birds nest here). Look for *Vogelerlebnispfad* signs as you're driving through the village of Pflach (on the road between Reutte and Füssen; www.naturpark-tiroler-lech.at).

### ▲▲Biberwier Luge Course

Near Lermoos, on the road between Reutte and Innsbruck, you'll find the Biberwier *Sommerrodelbahn*. At 4,250 feet, it's the longest summer luge in Tirol. The only drawbacks are its brief season, short hours, and a proclivity for shutting down sporadically—even at the slightest bit of rain. If you don't have a car, this is not worth the trouble; consider the luge near Neuschwanstein instead (see "Tegelberg Luge" on page 413). The ugly cube-shaped building marring the countryside near the luge course is a hotel for outdoor adventure enthusiasts. You can ride your mountain bike right into your room, or skip the elevator by using its indoor climbing wall.

**Cost and Hours:** €7.70/ride, cheaper with multi-ride tickets; daily early May-early Oct 9:00-16:30, closed off-season; tel. 05673/2323, www.bergbahnen-langes.at.

**Getting There:** It's 20 minutes from Reutte on the main road toward Innsbruck; Biberwier is the first exit after a long tunnel.

## ▲Fallerschein

Easy for drivers and a special treat for those who may have been Kit Carson in a previous life, this extremely remote log-cabin village, south of Reutte, is a 4,000-foot-high flower-speckled world of serene slopes and cowbells. Thunderstorms roll down the valley like it's God's bowling alley, but the pint-size church on the high ground, blissfully simple in a land of Baroque, seems to promise that this huddle of houses will survive, and the river and breeze will just keep flowing. The couples sitting on benches are mostly Austrian vacationers who've rented cabins here. Some of them, appreciating the remoteness of Fallerschein, are having affairs.

**Getting There:** From Reutte, it's a 45-minute drive. Take road 198 to Stanzach (passing Weisenbach am Loch, then Forchach), then turn left toward Namlos. Follow the L-21 Berwang road for about five miles to a parking lot. From there, it's a two-mile walk down a drivable but technically closed one-lane road. Those driving in do so at their own risk.

*Sleeping in Fallerschein:* **$ Michl's Fallerscheiner Stube** is a family-friendly mountain-hut restaurant with a low-ceilinged attic space that has basic beds for up to 17 sleepy hikers. The accommodations aren't fancy, but if you're looking for remote, this is it (dorm bed-€20, cheaper without breakfast, dinner-€11, sheets-€4, open May-Oct only, wildlife viewing deck, mobile 0676-727-9681, www.alpe-fallerschein.com, michaelknitel@alpe-fallerschein.com, Knitel family).

# Sleeping in and near Reutte

**(country code: 43, area code: 05672)**

While it's not impossible by public transport, staying here makes most sense for those with a car. Reutte is popular with Austrians and Germans, who visit year after year for one- or two-week vacations. Prices stay fairly even throughout the year and include a guest tax of €2 per person per day. Remember to ask for the Aktiv-Card, which is covered by your guest tax and includes lots of free-bies (for details, see page 436). All of my recommendations have free parking and a great breakfast.

Most of my listings are in the "villages" around Reutte (such as Breitenwang, Ehenbichl, and Höfen), which basically feel like the suburbs. For locations, see the Reutte map. For even more options, check www.reutte.com (or ask the Reutte TI) for their list of pri-vate homes that rent out rooms. These average about €30 per person per night in a room with breakfast and facilities down the hall.

## IN CENTRAL REUTTE

**$$ Hotel "Das Beck"** offers 17 clean, sunny rooms (many with balconies) filling a modern building in the heart of town close to the train station. This is the most practical option for those coming by train or bus. It's a great value, and guests are personally taken care of by Hans, Inge, Tamara, and Birgit. Their small café offers tasty snacks and specializes in Austrian and Mediterranean wines. Expect good conversation overseen by Hans (Sb-€48-55, Db-€72-78, Tb-€96-99, price depends on room size—more for a balcony; family suites: Db-€90, Tb-€108, Qb-€125; these prices with this book in 2015 if you book direct, non-smoking, guest computer and Wi-Fi, Untermarkt 11, tel. 05672/62522, www.hotel-das-beck.at, info@hotel-das-beck.at).

## IN BREITENWANG

Now basically a part of Reutte, the older and quieter village of Bre-itenwang has good *Zimmer* and a fine bakery. It's a 20-minute walk from the Reutte train station: From the post office, follow Plan-seestrasse past the onion-dome church to the pointy straight-dome church near the two hotels. The Hosps—as well as some other families renting private rooms—are along Kaiser-Lothar-Strasse, the first right past this church. Reutte's Alpentherme indoor pool complex, free for two hours a day with your Aktiv-Card, is just around the block.

If staying in Breitenwang and traveling by train, take advan-tage of the tiny Reutte-Schulzentrum Station, just a five-minute walk from these listings. All trains on the Garmisch-Reutte line stop here, but only on demand—which means you have to let the conductor know in advance where you want to get off. To board at Reutte-Schulzentrum, stand on the platform and flag the train down; you'll be able to buy a ticket from the conductor with no penalty.

**$$ Alpenhotel Ernberg**'s 26 fresh wood-paneled rooms (most with terraces) are run with great care by friendly Hermann, who combines Old World elegance with modern touches. Nestle in for some serious coziness among the carved-wood eating nooks, tiled stoves, and family-friendly backyard (Sb-€55-65, Db-€90-100, price depends on demand, less for 2 nights, Wi-Fi, popular restaurant, Planseestrasse 50, tel. 05672/71912, www.ernberg.at, info@ernberg.at).

**$$ Moserhof Hotel** has 40 new-feeling rooms plus an elegant dining room (Sb-€61, Db-€100, larger Db-€110, these special rates promised in 2015 if you ask for the Rick Steves discount when you reserve and pay cash, extra bed-€35, most rooms have balconies, elevator, Wi-Fi, restaurant, sauna and whirlpool, Planseestrasse 44, tel. 05672/62020, www.hotel-moserhof.at, info@hotel-moserhof.at, Hosp family).

**$ Walter and Emilie Hosp** rent three simple rooms sharing one bathroom in a comfortable, quiet, and modern house two blocks from the Breitenwang church steeple. You'll feel like you're staying at Grandma's (S-€30, D-€60, less if you stay 2 nights, cash only, Kaiser-Lothar-Strasse 29, tel. 05672/65377).

## IN EHENBICHL, NEAR THE EHRENBERG RUINS

These listings are a bit farther from central Reutte, a couple of miles upriver in the village of Ehenbichl. From central Reutte, go south on Obermarkt and turn right on Kög, which becomes Reuttener Strasse, following signs to *Ehenbichl*. These places are inconvenient by public transit (ask your hotelier if a taxi is available or brave infrequent local buses; see www.vvt.at for schedules).

**$$ Hotel Maximilian** offers 30 rooms at a great value. It includes table tennis, play areas for children (indoors and out), a pool table, and the friendly service of Gabi, Monika, and the rest of the Koch family. They host many special events, and their hotel has extras such as a sauna and a piano (Sb-€60, Db-€85-99 depending on demand—weekends usually more expensive, reserve directly with hotel by email and mention this book for best prices, family deals, elevator, guest computer, free Wi-Fi in common areas, pay Wi-Fi in rooms, laundry service-€12/load—non-guests pay €16, good restaurant open evenings only, Reuttener Strasse 1 in Ehenbichl—don't let your GPS take you to Reuttener Strasse in Pflach, tel. 05672/62585, www.maxihotel.com, info@hotelmaximilian.at). They rent cars to guests only (€0.72/km, automatic transmission, book in advance) and bikes to anyone (€5/half-day, €10/day; or, for non-guests, €6/half-day, €12/day).

**$$ Gintherhof** is a working dairy farm that provides its guests with fresh milk, butter, and bacon. Kind, hardworking Annelies Paulweber offers a warm welcome, geranium-covered balconies, six cozy and well-appointed rooms with carved-wood ceilings, and a Madonna in every corner (Db-€77, Db suite-€81, €5/person less for 3 nights, cash only, family rooms, Wi-Fi, Unterried 7, just up the road behind Hotel Maximilian, tel. 05672/67697, www. gintherhof.com, info@gintherhof.com).

**$$ Gasthof-Pension Waldrast,** separating a forest and a meadow, is run by the farming Huter family and their dog, Picasso. The place feels hauntingly quiet and has no restaurant, but it's inexpensive and offers 10 pleasant, spacious rooms with generous sitting areas, castle-view balconies, and well-preserved furniture from the 1960s and '70s. They've restored a nearly 500-year-old mill on their property and happily show it to interested guests. This is my only listing within easy walking distance of the Ehrenberg Castle ruins (Sb-€45, Db-€77, Tb-€96, Qb-€115, 5 percent off second night or longer with this book if you reserve directly with hotel, cash only, non-smoking, Wi-Fi, Krankenhausstrasse 16, tel. 05672/62443, www.waldrasttirol.com, info@waldrasttirol.com, Gerd).

**$$ Pension Hohenrainer,** a quiet, no-frills place, has 12 rooms past their prime, with some castle-view balconies (Sb-€38-40, Db-€76-80, €5/person less for 3 nights, cash only, family rooms, guest computer, Wi-Fi, reception in Gasthof Schlosswirt across the street and through the field, follow signs up the road behind Hotel Maximilian into village of Ehenbichl, Unterried 3, tel. 05672/62544 or 05672/63262, mobile 0676-799-6902, www. hohenrainer.at, hohenrainer@aon.at).

## AT THE EHRENBERG RUINS

**$$ Landgasthof Klause** café, just below the Ehrenberg ruins and next to the castle museum, rents 14 non-smoking, sleek, and modern rooms with balconies, as well as six apartments. You'll need a car to get anywhere besides Ehrenberg (Sb-€47, Db-€86, Tb-€111, ask for Rick Steves discount when you book, Wi-Fi, tel. 05672/62213, www.gasthof-klause.com, gasthof-klause@gmx.at).

## ACROSS THE RIVER, IN HÖFEN

**$$ Gästehaus am Graben,** with 13 rooms, is a good value less than two miles from Reutte, with fine castle views and family rooms sleeping four to six (Db-€60-80, Qb-€120-140, price depends on room size and amenities, less if you stay 3 nights, non-smoking, Wi-Fi, closed April and Nov-mid-Dec; from downtown Reutte, cross bridge and follow main road left along river, or take bus #4268 to the Graben stop; Graben 1, tel. 05672/626-440, www.hoefen.at, info@hoefen.at, Reyman family).

## IN PINSWANG

The village of Pinswang is closer to Füssen (and Ludwig's castles), but still in Austria. While this hotel works best for drivers, about half of the departures of yellow post bus #4258/#74, which runs between the Reutte and Füssen train stations, stop here (3-4/day, get off at Pinswang Gemeindeamt stop, verify details with hotel or at www.postbus.at, or use www.bahn.com and plug in "Pinswang Gemeindeamt" to find a workable train-bus connection).

**$$ Gutshof zum Schluxen** gets the "Remote Old Hotel in an Idyllic Setting" award. This family-friendly farm, with 34 rooms, offers rustic elegance. Its picturesque meadow setting will turn you into a dandelion-picker, and its proximity to Neuschwanstein will turn you into a hiker—the castle is just an hour's walk away. The hotel has new owners, and prices and services may change (Sb-€56, Db-€106, extra bed-€32, bike rental, restaurant, bar, between Reutte and Füssen in village of Pinswang, tel. 05677/89030, www.schluxen.at, info@schluxen.at).

To reach Neuschwanstein from this hotel by foot or bike, follow the dirt road up the hill behind the hotel. When the road forks at the top of the hill, go right (downhill), cross the Austria-Germany border (marked by a sign and deserted hut), and follow the narrow paved path to the castles. It's a 1- to 1.5-hour hike or a great circular bike trip (allow 30 minutes; cyclists can return to Schluxen from the castles on a different 30-minute bike route via Füssen).

## Eating in Reutte

The nicer restaurants in Reutte are all in hotels. **Alpenhotel Ernberg,** the **Moserhof Hotel,** and **Hotel Maximilian** (evenings only) all have fine restaurants. On weekdays, Alpenhotel Ernberg serves good three-course business lunches for €11.

**Storfwirt** is a great place for a quick and cheap weekday lunch. This rustic cafeteria in downtown Reutte serves some 300 happy eaters every day. There's a salad bar, €6 pastas, and daily soup-and-main-course specials for €7-8 (always something for vegetarians, Mon-Fri 9:00-14:00, closed Sat-Sun). Their adjacent **deli** is a great place to shop for a Tirolean picnic; choose from the local meats, cheeses, and prepared salads in the glass case, pick up a schnitzel with potato salad (€4-6), or ask them to make you a sandwich to order. You can take your food away or eat at informal tables (deli open Mon-Fri 7:00-18:00, Sat 7:30-12:00, closed Sun; Schrettergasse 15 but facing Tauschergasse—roughly next door to the big Müller pharmacy and post office, tel. 05672/62640, www.storfwirt.at, helpful manager Rainer).

*Picnic Supplies:* Along Mühlerstrasse near the intersection with Untermarkt, is the **Ausserfern Bauernladen** (farmer's shop), which sells only locally produced products. You can buy picnic fixings here (cheeses, spreads, and *Heuwürstchen* or *Cabanossi* sausages are good), or ask them to make you a rustic sandwich to eat at one of the tables (Wed-Fri 9:00-18:00, Sat 9:00-12:00, closed Sun-Tue, Obermarkt 3, mobile 0676-575-4588).

**Billa** supermarket also has everything you'll need for a picnic (across from TI, Mon-Fri 7:15-19:30, Sat 7:15-18:00, closed Sun).

# Reutte Connections

**From Reutte by Train to: Ehrwald** (at base of Zugspitze lift, every 2 hours, 30 minutes), **Garmisch** (same train, every 2 hours, 1 hour), **Innsbruck** (every 2 hours, 2.5 hours, change in Garmisch), **Munich** (every 2 hours, 2.5 hours, change in Garmisch), **Salzburg** (every 2 hours, 5 hours, change in Garmisch and Munich). Austrian train info: tel. 051-717 (to get an operator, dial 2, then 2), www.oebb.at; German train info: tel. 0180-599-6633, www.bahn.com.

**By Bus to: Füssen** (#4258—but known as #74 in Germany, Mon-Fri 6/day, Sat-Sun 4/day, last bus at 17:30, 30-50 minutes, €4.30 one-way, buses depart from train station, pay driver).

Ask your hotelier about **taxis** to Füssen or the King's Castles.

## ROUTE TIPS FOR DRIVERS
From downtown Reutte, *Fernpass* signs lead you out to the main Innsbruck road, which is also the best way to reach the Ehrenberg ruins. To reach the Ehrenberg Castle ruins, the Biberwier luge, the Zugspitze (either the Austrian ascent at Ehrwald or the German ascent at Garmisch), or Innsbruck, turn right for the on-ramp (marked Fernpass and Innsbruck) to highway 179. But if you're headed for Germany via the scenic Plansee Lake, Linderhof Castle, Ettal Monastery, or Oberammergau, continue straight (bypassing the highway on-ramp).

BAVARIA

# VIENNA: PAST AND PRESENT

## Timeline

**c. A.D. 1**   The Romans occupy and defend the "crossroads of Europe," where the west-east Danube River crosses the north-south Brenner Pass through the Alps. Their settlement in Vienna, called Vindobona, was centered on the site of today's cathedral.

**c. 500**   Lombard "barbarians"—following on the heels of the Vandals and Huns—drive the last Romans out, claiming this prime location as their own.

**c. 800**   Charlemagne designates Austria—as one boundary of his European empire—the "Eastern Empire," or *Österreich*. Charlemagne is crowned Holy Roman Emperor, a title Austria's rulers would later claim for themselves. Vienna (now called Wenia) develops further as a thriving trade city.

**1147**   St. Stephen's Cathedral is begun in the Romanesque style (still seen today in the facade). The church would take more than 300 years to complete.

**1200**   Vienna's city wall is completed, financed with ransom money paid to liberate the kidnapped King Richard the Lionheart of England.

**1273**   An Austrian noble from the Habsburg family (Rudolf I) is elected Holy Roman Emperor, ruling Austria, Germany, and northern Italy. From 1438 until 1806, every emperor but one is a Habsburg. The Habsburgs arrange strategic marriages for their children with other prominent royalty around

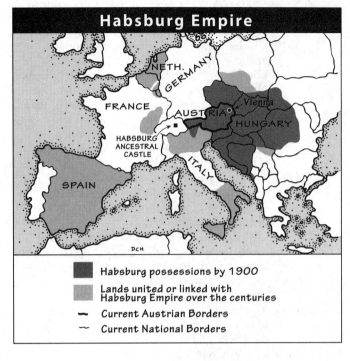

# Habsburg Empire

NETH.

GERMANY

FRANCE

AUSTRIA

Vienna

HUNGARY

HABSBURG
ANCESTRAL
CASTLE

ITALY

SPAIN

DCH

Habsburg possessions by 1900

Lands united or linked with
Habsburg Empire over the centuries

Current Austrian Borders

Current National Borders

Europe, gaining power through international connections.

**c. 1450** Vienna flourishes under Holy Roman Emperor Frederick III, considered the "father" of Vienna for turning the small village into a royal town with a cosmopolitan feel. Frederick makes the city his capital, and the Hofburg his home. St. Stephen's soaring 450-foot spire is completed (1433), the north tower is begun (1450), and the church is given a bishopric (1469), becoming a cathedral. Frederick's impressive tomb stands in the cathedral today.

**1493** Maximilian I is crowned emperor, donning the stunning, jeweled Imperial Crown (c. 960) now displayed in the Hofburg Treasury. His marriage to Mary of Burgundy weds two kingdoms together, and their grandson, Charles V, inherits a vast empire. The combined lands instantly make the Habsburg Empire a major player in European politics. In 1498, Maximilian establishes the Vienna Boys' Choir to sing for him at Mass.

**c. 1500**   The elaborately carved pulpit is erected in the nave at St. Stephen's Cathedral.

**1519**   Charles V (r. 1519-1556) is the most powerful man in Europe, ruling Austria, Germany, the Low Countries, parts of Italy, and Spain (with its New World possessions). Charles is responsible for trying to solve the problems of all those lands, including battling Ottomans in Vienna and Lutherans in Germany. While many lands north of the Danube turn Protestant, Austria remains Catholic.

**1522**   Charles V gives Austria (and the Ottoman problem) to his little brother, Ferdinand, who, four years later, marries into the Bohemian and Hungarian crowns.

**1529**   Ottoman invaders from today's Turkey besiege Vienna, beginning almost two centuries of battles between Austria and the Ottoman Empire. In the course of the wars, Austria gains possession of Hungary and much of Eastern Europe.

**1533**   Vienna—with 50,000 inhabitants and a long history as the major city of the region—becomes the official capital of the Habsburg Empire.

**1556**   Charles V retires from the throne to enter a monastery, leaving his kingdom to his son (King Philip II of Spain), and the crown of Holy Roman Emperor to his brother, Ferdinand I of Austria. From now on, Austria's rulers would concentrate on ruling their eastern empire, which includes part or all of present-day Austria, Hungary, the Czech Republic, Slovakia, Romania, Slovenia, Croatia, Bosnia-Herzegovina, Serbia, northern Italy (Venice), and, later, parts of Poland and Ukraine.

**1648**   The Thirty Years' War—a bitter struggle between Catholic and Protestant forces—finally comes to an end, leaving the Holy Roman Empire an empire in name only. Its figurehead emperor oversees a scattered group of German-speaking people, mainly in Austria and (what is now) Germany.

**1679**   A disastrous bubonic plague kills 75,000 Viennese (remembered today by the plague monument on the Graben).

**1683**   Almost 200,000 Muslims from Ottoman Turkey surround the city of Vienna once again. The Ottomans are driven off, leaving behind bags

# Habsburg Family Tree

| | |
|---|---|
| **RUDOLF IV** (1339–1365) | Founded Habsburg dynasty—for the next six centuries, descendants ruled Austria; many were elected Holy Roman Emperors as well. |

*Two Generations* ↓

| | |
|---|---|
| **MAXIMILIAN I** (1459–1519) | By war and marriage, extended realm in all directions—making the Habsburgs a major European power. |

*One Generation* ↓

| | |
|---|---|
| **CHARLES V** (1500–1558) | Ruled as the most powerful man in Europe, when Habsburg Empire reached its pinnacle, stretching from Bohemia to Bolivia. |

*Five Generations* ↓

| | |
|---|---|
| **MARIA THERESA (& FRANZ I)** (1717–1780) | Defended Austria against France. Had 16 children, most of whom she married off to Europe's royalty, including Marie-Antoinette, who became Mrs. Louis XVI, the (last) Queen of France. |

↓ *Son*

| | |
|---|---|
| **JOSEF II** (1741–1790) | Enlightened rule abolished serfdom and brought about other democratic reforms. Patron of Mozart. |

↓ *Nephew*

| | |
|---|---|
| **FRANZ II** (1768–1835) | Demoted from HRE to Emperor of Austria after being defeated by (future son-in-law) Napoleon. |

*One Generation* ↓

| | |
|---|---|
| **FRANZ JOSEF (& SISI)** (1830–1916) | The last Habsburg with any real power, his long reign saw the decline of his out-of-date empire. |

*Great- Nephew* ↓          *Nephew* ↘

| | |
|---|---|
| **KARL I (& ZITA)** (1887–1922) | **FRANZ FERDINAND** (1863–1914) |
| At the tail end of his ancestors' dynasty, ruled for two wartime years before renouncing political power. | Heir to the throne—until his assassination in 1914, which sparked World War I and the end of Habsburgs' rule...and Europe as they knew it. |

of coffee that help fuel a beverage craze around Europe. Vienna's first coffeehouse opens.

**1672-1714**  Three wars with Louis XIV of France (including the War of the Spanish Succession) drain Austria.

**1703-1711**  The Habsburgs put down the Hungarian War of Independence, led by Transylvanian prince Ferenc Rákóczi.

**1735**  The Spanish Riding School is built at the Hofburg.

**1740**  Maria Theresa (r. 1740-1780) ascends to the throne. She eventually has 16 children and still finds time to fight two wars in 25 years, defending her right to rule. Adored by her subjects for her down-to-earth personality, she brings Austria international prestige by marrying her daughters to Europe's royalty. Under Maria Theresa, Schönbrunn Palace reaches its peak of luxury.

**1781**  Maria Theresa's son Josef II, who frees the serfs and takes piano lessons from Mozart, rules Austria as an "enlightened despot."

**1791**  Mozart's comic opera *The Magic Flute* debuts. Vienna is the world capital of classical music, home to Haydn (1732-1809), Mozart (1756-1791), and Beethoven (1770-1827). Mozart was married in St. Stephen's Cathedral, and, after his death, his Requiem Mass is played there.

**1792**  When the French queen, the Habsburg's Marie-Antoinette, is imprisoned and (later) beheaded by revolutionaries in Paris, her nephew, Austria's Emperor Franz II, seeks revenge, beginning two decades of wars between revolutionary France and monarchist Austria.

**1805**  Napoleon defeats Austria at Austerlitz, his greatest triumph over the forces of monarchy. Napoleon occupies Vienna, moves into Schönbrunn Palace, and forces Holy Roman Emperor Franz II to hand over the imperial crown (1806), ending a thousand years of empire. Napoleon even marries Franz II's daughter, Marie-Louise.

**1814-1815**  After Napoleon is defeated once and for all, an Austrian, Chancellor Metternich, heads the Congress of Vienna—reinstalling kings and nobles recently deposed by Napoleon. Metternich's politics sets the tone for Vienna's conservative, bourgeois-dominated society.

**Early 1800s**  Throughout the Habsburgs' Central and Eastern European holdings, a gradual cultural revival takes place. Natives of Habsburg lands such as Hungary, the Czech Republic, Slovakia, and Slovenia enjoy a renewed appreciation for their unique, traditional, non-Austrian culture and language—setting the stage for a rocky century that will culminate in the fall of the empire.

**1832** Franz Sacher invents Vienna's signature dessert, the Sacher-Torte.

**1848** Emperor Franz Josef (emperor of Austria, but not the "Holy Roman Emperor") rules for the next 68 years, maintaining white-gloved tradition while overseeing great change—Austria's decline as an empire and entrance into the modern industrial world. During his first year on the throne, a wave of revolution sweeps Europe, endangering many of his holdings.

**1849** Almost 100,000 Viennese attend the funeral of violinist Johann Strauss, responsible for the dance craze called the waltz. His son, Johann Strauss II (1825-1899), takes the baton of the Strauss Orchestra and waltzes on.

**c. 1850** Vienna's Golden Age occupies the latter half of the 19th century. The city is the epicenter of European culture: fine music, exquisite art, coffee and chocolates, dress-up balls, enlightened city planning, and cutting-edge science.

**1854** Franz Josef marries the beautiful/neurotic Elisabeth ("Sisi"), and they settle into their lavish home in the Hofburg's Imperial Apartments.

**1857** Vienna—population 450,000—is bursting at the seams. The city embarks on a massive urban renewal project. The old city wall is torn down and turned into a wide, circular boulevard called the Ringstrasse, lined with grand buildings including the Opera, City Hall, and Kunsthistorisches Museum. The buildings are state-of-the-art, but decorated in styles that echo the past: Neoclassical, Neo-Gothic, and so on. Vienna's incredible transformation is overseen by Emperor Franz Josef, Mayor Karl Ludwig, and chief architect Otto Wagner.

**1866** Prussia provokes war and defeats Austria, effectively freezing Austria out of any involvement in a modern German nation.

**1867** *The Blue Danube*, a waltz by Johann Strauss II, debuts. But Austria—while at its cultural peak—is beginning its slow political decline. To better suppress the huge Slavic population in its sprawling empire, and facing a low-morale moment after the war with Prussia, Austria gives partial control over its territories to Hungary. This creates the "Dual Monarchy" of the Austro-Hungarian Empire. In a symbolic compromise, Franz Josef, "emperor" of Austria, is crowned "king" of Hungary (the origin of the royal boast "K+K"—*kaiserlich und königlich*, imperial and royal).

**1869** The Vienna Opera House opens. Vienna in the late 19th century is home to composers Johannes Brahms, Richard Strauss, and Gustav Mahler.

**1897** The Secession building opens, displaying works by Vienna's exciting young generation of artists who vow to "secede" from academic tradition.

**1898** The Ringstrasse's horse-drawn trams give way to electric-powered streetcars.

**1899** Viennese psychiatrist Sigmund Freud publishes *The Interpretation of Dreams,* launching psychoanalysis and the 20th-century obsession with repressed sexual desires, the unconscious mind, and couches.

**c. 1900** As the century turns, Vienna is the globe's fifth-largest city (population 2.2 million)—bigger than it is today. It's balanced on the cusp between traditional Old World elegance and subversive modern trends. Stalin and Trotsky are rattling around Vienna. Women are smoking, riding bikes, and demanding the right to vote. In 1900, Adolf Loos builds his controversial, minimalist Loos House across from the old-school Hofburg.

**1907** Gustav Klimt's painting *The Kiss*—sensual, daring, semi-abstract, and slightly decadent—epitomizes the Viennese *Jugendstil* (Art Nouveau) movement.

**1908** A young aspiring artist named Adolf Hitler is rejected by Vienna's Academy of Fine Arts for the second time—one of many rejections and frustrations that will lead him to embrace his violent, anti-Semitic worldview.

**1914** Austria fires the opening shots of World War I to avenge the assassination of its heir to the throne, Archduke Franz Ferdinand.

**1919** After its defeat in World War I, the Austro-Hungarian Empire is divided into separate democratic nations, with Austria assigned the small, landlocked borders that it has today.

**1927** Riots in the streets of Vienna between liberals and fascists leave dozens dead and hundreds wounded; they show the deep rift in Austrian society. By the time the global Depression reaches Austria, the country is a powder keg of extreme ideologies.

**1932** Mirroring events in Germany, a totalitarian government (headed by Engelbert Dollfuss) replaces a weak democracy floundering in economic depression.

**1938** Led by Austrian-born Chancellor Adolf Hitler, Nazi Germany—using the threat of force and riding a surge of Germanic nationalism—annexes Austria in the *Anschluss,* and leads it into World War II. Hitler returns to Vienna in triumph, stands on the New Palace balcony at the Hofburg, and addresses his adoring throngs.

**1939-45** During World War II, Austria is part of Nazi Germany and suffers the consequences. Of Vienna's 200,000 Jews, about a third die in death camps. Nearly 100,000 Jews, criminals, and political dissidents die at Mauthausen Concentration Camp, just up the Danube from Vienna.

**1943** The first Allied bombs strike Vienna. Over the next two years, half of the historic center is destroyed in Allied air raids. St. Stephen's Cathedral catches fire, collapsing the wooden roof. Many of the city's top art treasures are stowed safely in cellars and salt mines.

**1945** As the war ends, Vienna is liberated by Soviet troops. The city is in ruins. Like Germany, a defeated Austria is divided by the victors into occupied zones, but the country's occupation is short-lived.

**1949** The movie *The Third Man* premieres, showing Vienna as a shady, espionage-laced city caught between Cold War superpowers.

**1952** A new cathedral roof, rebuilt with local donations, is dedicated.

**1955** Modern Austria (with Vienna as its capital) is born as a neutral nation, with the blessing of the international community. The treaty is signed at Belvedere Palace.

**1961** Kennedy meets Khrushchev in Vienna for peace talks. As neutral territory between East and West, Vienna is a natural choice for summits between the Cold War superpowers. It also becomes home to several UN organizations. The OPEC nations make Vienna its seat in 1965.

**1974** The Graben is pedestrianized, signaling the city's determination to modernize while preserving its historic core.

**1978** The subway system (U-Bahn) opens its first line (U-1).

**1990s** Vienna absorbs tens of thousands of war refugees during the breakup of Yugoslavia.

**1995** Austria joins the European Union.

**2000** The European Union places sanctions on Austria (lifted a few months later) when the far-right Freedom Party—campaigning under the slogan *Überfremdung* ("Too many foreigners")—gains seats in Austria's parliament.

**2002** The Freedom Party does badly in elections.

**2003** Vienna's first Starbucks boldly opens—directly across from one of Vienna's oldest, best-loved coffee shops. *Gott in Himmel!*

**2004** Heinz Fischer, a center-left career politician, is elected president. He is re-elected in 2010.

**2008** In September, the revived far-right parties win 29 percent of the popular vote. But a month later, their leader Jörg Haider is killed in a car crash.

**2014** Just after midnight on January 1, 50 million people around the world welcome the New Year by watching a broadcast of the Vienna Philharmonic playing a waltz by Strauss.

**Today** You arrive in Vienna and make your own history.

# Notable Austrians

### Charles V (1500-1558)

Through a series of marriages and unexpected deaths, Charles V inherited not only the Habsburg properties in Austria, but also the Netherlands and the Spanish Empire, including its colonies in the Americas. He said that he ruled an empire "upon which the sun never sets" (a phrase the British stole for their own dominions in the 19th century). But even the most powerful ruler on earth couldn't stop the spread of Protestantism. Charles' vision of a unified, Catholic, European empire was thwarted by Martin Luther, German Protestant princes, and their allies, the French.

### Maria Theresa (1717-1780)

The first and only female head of the Habsburg dynasty, Maria Theresa consolidated the power of the throne but also reformed

Austria by banning torture, funding schools and universities, and allowing some religious freedom for Protestants. Her changes, and those of her son, Josef II, allowed Austria to withstand the upheavals of the French Revolution. Her apartments at Vienna's Schönbrunn Palace are tourable today (see page 133; for more on the empress, see page 55).

## Marie-Antoinette (1755-1793)
The youngest daughter of Maria Theresa, Marie-Antoinette's marriage to the heir to the French throne was supposed to cement the alliance between France and Austria. But she was not popular; even before the revolution, pamphleteers called her hopelessly stupid, accusing her of adultery, sexual deviance, and treason. During the Reign of Terror, she lost her head to the guillotine, inspiring countless romantic novels and two Hollywood movies.

## Wolfgang Amadeus Mozart (1756-1791)
The ultimate child prodigy, Mozart started composing when he was five and performed for Empress Maria Theresa when he was eight. A giant of classical music, he wrote masterpieces in every genre he touched—operas, symphonies, chamber music, piano sonatas, and string quartets. Fans flock to visit his childhood homes in Salzburg (see pages 290 and 301).

## Johann Strauss II (1825-1899)
Vienna was the hometown of many great composers, such as Josef Haydn and Franz Schubert, but Johann Strauss II (the Younger) best captured its spirit. "The Waltz King" helped popularize this musical genre in the 19th century and wrote the most famous waltz of all, "The Blue Danube," as well as the operetta *Die Fledermaus*. These musical achievements came despite the objections of his father—also a famous composer—who wanted his son to be a banker.

## Franz Josef (1831-1916)
At the age of 18, Franz Josef became emperor—beginning a 68-year reign surpassed in European history only by France's Louis XIV and a Liechtenstein prince. Franz Josef, a staunch conservative but a terrible general, presided over—and likely contributed to—the decline of the Austro-Hungarian Empire. His family life was similarly troubled; his estranged wife, "Sisi," was assassinated by an Italian anarchist, and his only son, Crown Prince Rudolf, committed suicide (or did he?) in the arms of a mistress. The end of the Habsburg dynasty came two years after Franz Josef's death. His Hofburg Imperial Apartments in Vienna are open to the public (see page 133; for more on the emperor, see page 142).

PAST & PRESENT

## Sigmund Freud (1856-1939)

The Austrian physician and psychoanalyst revolutionized the study of human behavior. According to Freud, repressed desires—sexual desires in particular—explained why humans behave the way we do. Although he was a world figure of immense influence, the Nazis despised his Jewish roots and burned his books. After they took over Austria in 1938, Freud left for London, where he died a year later. His office in Vienna has been turned into the Sigmund Freud Museum (see page 80).

## Gustav Klimt (1862-1918)

Erotic, symbolic, Byzantine, radical—the turn-of-the-century paintings of Gustav Klimt shook Viennese society. A leader of the Vienna Secession movement, Klimt was criticized at one point for "pornographic" art—years before the gold-wrapped lovers of *The Kiss* became an art school icon. His portrait *The Golden Adele* set a record when American billionaire Ronald Lauder bought it in 2006 for $135 million—at that time the most expensive painting ever sold. Klimt's art is displayed in museums throughout Vienna; *The Kiss,* for example, is in Belvedere Palace (for more on the artist, see page 74).

## Franz Ferdinand (1863-1914)

No one expected Archduke Franz Ferdinand to be the heir to the Habsburg dynasty. But when Crown Prince Rudolf killed himself in 1889 and Franz Ferdinand's father died in 1896, the young archduke suddenly became the hope of the Habsburgs. As inspector general of the army, he was invited to Sarajevo to review Austrian troops. On June 28, 1914, after his chauffeur took a wrong turn on the city's streets, Franz Ferdinand and his wife were assassinated by a Serbian nationalist, triggering World War I and the eventual end of the dynasty.

## Adolf Loos (1870-1933)

The man who said "decoration is a crime" was one of the most influential architects of the modern era. Born in what is now the Czech Republic, he trained in Germany and even spent three years tramping around America as a dishwasher and a mason. But it was in Vienna where he made his name. Excessive ornamentation was criminal, he declared, because it wasted labor and materials; the modern era deserved stripped-down facades. Examples of Loos' architecture—a bookstore, bar, and even WCs—are in downtown Vienna (see page 100).

## Ferdinand Porsche (1875-1951)

This Austrian automotive engineer is best known as the father of the Volkswagen Beetle. Hitler demanded that Germany build a cheap "people's car," so Porsche began working on his world-famous design in 1934. Three years later, Hitler gave him one of Germany's highest awards. This automotive genius is also known for launching (with the help of his son) the Porsche sports car. But he was a century too soon with another one of his inventions: the world's first electric/gasoline hybrid car, the Mixte, created in 1901 in Vienna.

### Adolf Hitler (1889-1945)

The future dictator—directly responsible for the deaths of more than 43 million people during World War II—was born in Brau-nau am Inn, north of Salzburg. After dropping out of high school at age 16, he spent eight years in prewar Vienna trying to make his way as an artist. (He was rejected twice by Vienna's Academy of Fine Arts.) Although Hitler served in the German army during World War I, he didn't become a German citizen until 1932, just one year before becoming the nation's chancellor and *der Führer*.

### Maria von Trapp (1905-1987)

An orphan by age seven, Maria Augusta Kitschier was raised in Tirol by an anti-Catholic socialist. When she mistakenly attended a religious lecture (she had thought it would be a Bach concert), she was so moved that she became a staunch Catholic. Her memoir of life as a novice at a Salzburg convent and later as governess for the von Trapp family was the basis for *The Sound of Music* (see page 272). Salzburg remains the epicenter for *S.O.M.* sights and tours.

### Billy Wilder (1906-2002)

Born in Austria, Hollywood legend Billy Wilder won Oscars for directing *The Lost Weekend* and *The Apartment*. He also wrote and/or directed such Hollywood classics as *Some Like It Hot, The Seven Year Itch, Ball of Fire, Sunset Boulevard, Stalag 17, Sabrina,* and the dark and brooding *Double Indemnity*. He lost his mother in the Holocaust and was often bitter about his native country. "The Aus-trians are brilliant people," he once said. "They made the world believe that Hitler was a German and Beethoven an Austrian."

### Otto Preminger (1906-1986)

Like Wilder, Otto Preminger grew up in Vienna's Jewish commu-nity. His success in Viennese theater eventually led to Hollywood, where Preminger hit the big time directing the 1944 mystery *Laura*. Twice nominated for a best-director Oscar (for *Laura* and *The Cardinal)*, Preminger made films that challenged Hollywood taboos of the time, such as rape *(Anatomy of a Murder)*, drug addiction *(The Man with the Golden Arm)*, and homosexuality *(Advise and Consent)*.

## Arnold Schwarzenegger (b. 1947)

Born in a village near Graz, Arnold Schwarzenegger was obsessed with bodybuilding even as a teenager. After winning international bodybuilding contests, Schwarzenegger got his big break as *Conan the Barbarian,* a role that spawned a string of blockbuster action movies, including the *Terminator* series. In 2003, Ah-nold switched careers and was elected the Republican governor of California; the "Governator" was re-elected to a second term in 2006. After leaving office in 2011, news broke that Schwarzenegger had fathered a son more than 14 years earlier with the family housekeeper—prompting his wife, Maria Shriver, to file for divorce.

## Felix Baumgartner (b. 1969)

After learning to parachute in the Austrian military, daredevil skydiver Felix Baumgartner, who was born in Salzburg, has made a career of high-profile, wildly dangerous jumps off buildings, bridges, and mountains. All of Austria (and millions around the world) watched on October 14, 2012, when he plummeted 24 miles to earth in a heart-stopping supersonic jump from a helium-balloon capsule. Baumgartner simultaneously set three world records: highest-altitude manned balloon flight (24 miles up), highest-altitude parachute jump (128,100 feet), and greatest free-fall velocity (834 mph).

For more on Austrian history, consider *Europe 101: History and Art for the Traveler,* written by Rick Steves and Gene Openshaw (available at www.ricksteves.com).

# PRACTICALITIES

## Contents

This chapter covers the practical skills of European travel: how to get tourist information, pay for purchases, sightsee efficiently, find good-value accommodations, eat affordably but well, use technology wisely, and get between destinations smoothly. To study ahead and round out your knowledge, check out "Resources" for a summary of recommended books and films.

## Tourist Information

Austria's national tourist office **in the US** can be a wealth of information. They have maps and information on festivals, hiking, the wine country, and more. Call 212/944-6880 or visit www.austria.info.

**In Austria:** The local tourist information office (abbreviated **TI** in this book) is your best first stop in any new town or city. Try to arrive, or at least telephone, before it closes. Throughout Austria, you'll find TIs are usually well-organized and have English-speaking staff.

TIs are good places to get a city map and information on public transit (including bus and train schedules), walking tours, special events, and nightlife. Many TIs have information on the entire country or at least the region, so try to pick up maps for destinations you'll be visiting later in your trip. If you're arriving in town after the TI closes, call ahead or pick up a map in a neighboring town.

As national budgets tighten, many TIs have been privatized. This means they have become sales agents for big tours and hotels, and their "information" becomes unavoidably colored. While TIs are eager to book you a room, use their room-finding service only as a last resort. They are unable to give hard opinions on the relative value of one place over another. The accommodations stakes are too high to go potluck through the TI. Even if there's no "fee," you'll save yourself and your host money by going direct with the listings in this book.

## Travel Tips

**Emergency and Medical Help:** In Austria (and Germany), dial 112 for police or medical emergencies. If you get sick, do as the locals do and go to a pharmacist for advice (*Apotheke;* look for the stylized red *A*). If the pharmacy is closed, a sign near the door indicates the closest pharmacy that's open. Or ask at your hotel for help—they'll know the nearest medical and emergency services.

**Theft or Loss:** To replace a passport, you'll need to go in person to an embassy (see page 515). If your credit and debit cards disappear, cancel and replace them (see "Damage Control for Lost Cards" on page 471). File a police report, either on the spot or within a day or two; you'll need it to submit an insurance claim for lost or stolen rail passes or travel gear, and can help with replacing your passport or credit and debit cards. For more information, see www.ricksteves.com/help. Precautionary measures can minimize the effects of loss—back up your digital photos and other files frequently.

**Time Zones:** Austria, like most of continental Europe, is generally six/nine hours ahead of the East/West Coasts of the US. The exceptions are the beginning and end of Daylight Saving Time: Europe "springs forward" the last Sunday in March (two weeks after most of North America), and "falls back" the last Sunday in October (one week before North America). For a handy online time converter, try www.timeanddate.com/worldclock.

**Business Hours:** Most shops throughout Austria are open from about 9:00 until 18:00-20:00 on weekdays, but close earlier on Saturday (as early as 12:00 in towns and as late as 17:00 in cities), and are almost always closed on Sunday. Grocery stores in train stations are generally open daily until late. Banks in Vienna are open weekdays roughly from 8:00 until 15:00 (until 17:30 on Thu), but elsewhere in Austria, banks often close for lunch (open Mon-Fri 8:00-12:00 and 14:00-16:00). Many museums and sights are closed on Monday, and most regions, including Bavaria, shut down during religious holidays.

Sundays have the same pros and cons as they do for travelers in the US: Special events pop up, sights may have limited hours, shops and banks are closed, public transportation options are fewer, and there's no rush hour. Popular destinations are even more crowded on weekends.

**Watt's Up?** Europe's electrical system is 220 volts, instead of North America's 110 volts. Most newer electronics (such as laptops, battery chargers, and hair dryers) convert automatically, so you won't need a converter, but you will need an adapter plug with two round prongs, sold inexpensively at travel stores in the US. Avoid bringing older appliances that don't automatically convert voltage; instead, buy a cheap replacement in Europe.

**Discounts:** Discounts aren't listed in this book. However, many sights offer discounts for seniors, groups of 10 or more, families, and students or teachers with proper identification cards (www.isic.org). Always ask. Some discounts are available only for citizens of the European Union (EU).

**Online Translation Tip:** You can use Google's Chrome browser (available free at www.google.com/chrome) to instantly translate websites. With one click, the page appears in (very rough) English translation. You can also paste the URL of the site into the translation window at www.google.com/translate.

# Money

This section offers advice on how to pay for purchases on your trip (including getting cash from ATMs and paying with plastic), dealing with lost or stolen cards, VAT (sales tax) refunds, and tipping.

## WHAT TO BRING
Bring both a credit card and a debit card. You'll use the debit card at cash machines (ATMs) to withdraw local cash for most purchases, and the credit card to pay for larger items. Some travelers carry a third card, in case one gets demagnetized or eaten by a temperamental machine.

For an emergency stash, bring several hundred dollars in hard cash in $20 bills. If you need to exchange the bills, go to a bank;

**PRACTICALITIES**

avoid using currency exchange booths because of their lousy rates and/or outrageous fees.

## CASH

Cash is just as desirable in Europe as it is at home. Small businesses (B&Bs, mom-and-pop cafés, shops, etc.) prefer that you pay your bills with cash. Some vendors will charge you extra for using a credit card, and some won't take credit cards at all. Cash is the best—and sometimes only—way to pay for cheap food, bus fare, taxis, and local guides.

Throughout Europe, ATMs are the standard way for travelers to get cash. To withdraw money from an ATM (known as a *Bankomat* in Austria and a *Geldautomat* in Germany), you'll need a debit card (ideally with a Visa or MasterCard logo for maximum usability), plus a PIN code. Know your PIN code in numbers; there are only numbers—no letters—on European keypads. For increased security, shield the keypad when entering your PIN code, and don't use an ATM if anything on the front of the machine looks loose or damaged (a sign that someone may have attached a "skimming" device to capture account information). Try to withdraw large sums of money to reduce the number of per-transaction bank fees you'll pay.

When possible, use ATMs located outside banks—a thief is less likely to target a cash machine near surveillance cameras, and if your card is munched by a machine, you can go inside for help. Stay away from "independent" ATMs such as Travelex, Euronet, Moneybox, Cardpoint, and Cashzone, which charge huge commissions, have terrible exchange rates, and may try to trick users with "dynamic currency conversion" (described at the end of "Credit and Debit Cards," next).

Although you can use a credit card for an ATM transaction, it only makes sense in an emergency, because it's considered a cash advance (borrowed at a high interest rate) rather than a withdrawal.

While traveling, if you want to monitor your accounts online to detect any unauthorized transactions, be sure to use a secure connection (see page 498).

Pickpockets target tourists. To safeguard your cash, wear a money belt—a pouch with a strap that you buckle around your waist like a belt and tuck under your clothes. Keep your cash, credit cards, and passport secure in your money belt, and carry only a day's spending money in your front pocket.

## CREDIT AND DEBIT CARDS

For purchases, Visa and MasterCard are more commonly accepted than American Express. Just like at home, credit or debit cards work easily at larger hotels, restaurants, and shops. I typically use

PRACTICALITIES

---

# Exchange Rate

### 1 euro (€) = about $1.40

To convert prices in euros to dollars, add about 40 percent: €20 = about $28, €50 = about $70. (Check www.oanda.com for the latest exchange rates.) Just like the dollar, one euro (€) is broken down into 100 cents. Coins range from €0.01 to €2, and bills from €5 to €500.

---

my debit card to withdraw cash to pay for most purchases. I use my credit card only in a few specific situations: to book hotel reservations by phone, to cover major expenses (such as car rentals, plane tickets, and hotel stays), and to pay for things near the end of my trip (to avoid another visit to the ATM). While you could use a debit card to make most large purchases, using a credit card offers a greater degree of fraud protection (because debit cards draw funds directly from your account).

**Ask Your Credit- or Debit-Card Company:** Before your trip, contact the company that issued your debit or credit cards.

• Confirm that your **card will work overseas,** and alert them that you'll be using it in Europe; otherwise, they may deny transactions if they perceive unusual spending patterns.

• Ask for the specifics on transaction **fees.** When you use your credit or debit card—either for purchases or ATM withdrawals— you'll often be charged additional "international transaction" fees of up to 3 percent (1 percent is normal) plus $5 per transaction. If your card's fees seem high, consider getting a different card just for your trip: Capital One (www.capitalone.com) and most credit unions have low-to-no international fees.

• If you plan to withdraw cash from ATMs, confirm your daily **withdrawal limit,** and if necessary, ask your bank to adjust it. Some travelers prefer a high limit that allows them to take out more cash at each ATM stop (saving on bank fees), while others prefer to set a lower limit in case their card is stolen. Note that foreign banks also set maximum withdrawal amounts for their ATMs. Also, remember that you're withdrawing euros, not dollars—so if your daily limit is $300, withdraw just €200. Many frustrated travelers walk away from ATMs thinking their cards have been rejected, when actually they were asking for more cash in euros than their daily limit allowed.

• Get your bank's emergency **phone number** in the US (but not its 800 number, which isn't accessible from overseas) to call collect if you have a problem.

• Ask for your credit card's **PIN** in case you need to make an

PRACTICALITIES

emergency cash withdrawal or encounter Europe's "chip-and-PIN" system; the bank won't tell you your PIN over the phone, so allow time for it to be mailed to you.

**Chip and PIN:** Europeans are increasingly using chip-and-PIN cards, which are embedded with an electronic chip (in addition to the magnetic stripe found on American-style cards). To make a purchase with a chip-and-PIN card, the cardholder inserts the card into a slot in the payment machine, then enters a PIN (like using a debit card in the US) while the card stays in the slot. The chip inside the card authorizes the transaction; the cardholder doesn't sign a receipt. Your American-style card might not work at payment machines using this system, such as those at train and subway stations, toll roads, parking garages, luggage lockers, bike-rental kiosks, and self-serve gas pumps.

If you have problems using your American card in a chip-and-PIN machine, here are some suggestions: For either a debit card or a credit card, try entering that card's PIN when prompted. (Note that your credit-card PIN may not be the same as your debit-card PIN; you'll need to ask your bank for your credit-card PIN.) If your cards still don't work, look for a machine that takes cash, seek out a clerk who might be able to process the transaction manually, or ask a local if you can pay them cash to run the transaction on their card.

And don't panic. Most travelers who use only magnetic-stripe cards don't run into problems. Still, it pays to carry plenty of euros; remember, you can always use an ATM to withdraw cash with your magnetic-stripe debit card.

If you're still concerned, you can apply for a chip card in the US (though I think it's overkill). One option is the no-annual-fee GlobeTrek Visa, offered by Andrews Federal Credit Union in Maryland (open to all US residents; see www.andrewsfcu.org). In the future, chip cards should become standard issue in the US: Visa and MasterCard have asked US banks and merchants to use chip-based cards by late 2015.

**Dynamic Currency Conversion:** If merchants offer to convert your purchase price into dollars (called dynamic currency conversion, or DCC), refuse this "service." You'll pay even more in fees for the expensive convenience of seeing your charge in dollars. "Independent" ATMs (such as Travelex and Moneybox) may try to confuse customers by presenting DCC in misleading terms. If an ATM offers to "lock in" or "guarantee" your conversion rate, choose "proceed without conversion." Other prompts might state, "You can be charged in dollars: Press YES for dollars, NO for euros." Always choose the local currency in these situations.

## DAMAGE CONTROL FOR LOST CARDS

If you lose your credit, debit, or ATM card, you can stop people from using it by reporting the loss immediately to the respective global customer-assistance centers. Call these 24-hour US numbers collect: Visa (tel. 303/967-1096), MasterCard (tel. 636/722-7111), and American Express (tel. 336/393-1111). In Austria, to make a collect call to the US, dial 0800-200-288. Press zero or stay on the line for an English-speaking operator. In Germany, dial 0800-225-5288. European toll-free numbers (listed by country) can be found at the websites for Visa and MasterCard.

Providing the following information will allow for a quicker cancellation of your missing card: full card number, whether you are the primary or secondary cardholder, the cardholder's name exactly as printed on the card, billing address, home phone number, circumstances of the loss or theft, and identification verification (your birth date, your mother's maiden name, or your Social Security number—memorize this, don't carry a copy). If you are the secondary cardholder, you'll also need to provide the primary cardholder's identification-verification details. You can generally receive a temporary card within two or three business days in Europe (see www.ricksteves.com/help for more).

If you report your loss within two days, you typically won't be responsible for any unauthorized transactions on your account, although many banks charge a liability fee of $50.

## TIPPING

Tipping in Austria isn't as automatic and generous as it is in the US. For special service, tips are appreciated, but not expected. As in the US, the proper amount depends on your resources, tipping philosophy, and the circumstances, but some general guidelines apply.

**Restaurants:** Tipping is an issue only at restaurants that have table service. If you order your food at a counter, don't tip.

At Austrian restaurants that have a waitstaff, a service charge is generally included in the bill, although it's common to round up after a good meal (usually 5-10 percent; so, for an €18.50 meal, pay €20). Give the tip directly to your server. Rather than leaving coins, Austrians usually pay with paper, saying how much they'd like the bill to be (for example, for an €8.10 meal, give a €20 bill and say "*Neun Euro*"—"Nine euros"—to get €11 change).

**Taxis:** For a typical ride, round up your fare about 5-10 percent (for instance, if the fare is €4.50, pay €5; for a €28 fare, pay €30). If the cabbie hauls your bags and zips you to the airport to help you catch your flight, you might want to toss in a little more. But if you feel like you're being driven in circles or otherwise ripped off, skip the tip.

**Services:** In general, if someone in the service industry does

PRACTICALITIES

a super job for you, a small tip of a euro or two is appropriate...but not required. If you're not sure whether (or how much) to tip for a service, ask your hotelier or the TI.

## GETTING A VAT REFUND

Wrapped into the purchase price of your Austrian souvenirs is a Value-Added Tax (VAT) of 20 percent. You're entitled to get most of that tax back if you purchase more than €75.01 (about $105) worth of goods at a store that participates in the VAT-refund scheme. Typically, you must ring up the minimum at a single re-tailer—you can't add up your purchases from various shops to reach the required amount.

Getting your refund is usually straightforward and, if you buy a substantial amount of souvenirs, well worth the hassle. If you're lucky, the merchant will subtract the tax when you make your purchase. (This is more likely to occur if the store ships the goods to your home.) Otherwise, you'll need to:

**Get the paperwork.** Have the merchant completely fill out the necessary refund document. You'll have to present your passport. Get the paperwork done before you leave the store to ensure you'll have everything you need (including your original sales receipt).

**Get your stamp at the border or airport.** Process your VAT document at your last stop in the European Union (such as at the airport) with the customs agent who deals with VAT refunds. Arrive an additional hour early before you need to check in for your flight, to allow time to find the local customs office—and to stand in line. It's best to keep your purchases in your carry-on. If they're too large or dangerous to carry on (such as knives), pack them in your checked bags and alert the check-in agent. You'll be sent (with your tagged bag) to a customs desk outside security, which will examine your bag, stamp your paperwork, and put your bag on the belt. You're not supposed to use your purchased goods before you leave. If you show up at customs wearing your new lederhosen, officials might look the other way—or deny you a refund.

**Collect your refund.** You'll need to return your stamped document to the retailer or its representative. Many merchants work with a service, such as Global Blue or Premier Tax Free, that has offices at major airports, ports, or border crossings (either before or after security, probably strategically located near a duty-free shop). These services, which extract a 4 percent fee, can refund your money immediately in cash or credit your card (within two billing cycles). If the retailer handles VAT refunds directly, it's up to you to contact the merchant for your refund. You can mail the documents from home, or more quickly, from your point of departure (using an envelope you've prepared in advance or one that's been provided by the merchant). You'll have to wait—it can take months.

## CUSTOMS FOR AMERICAN SHOPPERS

You are allowed to take home $800 worth of items per person duty-free, once every 30 days. You can take home many processed and packaged foods: vacuum-packed cheeses, dried herbs, jams, baked goods, candy, chocolate, oil, vinegar, mustard, and honey. Fresh fruits and vegetables and most meats are not allowed. However, canned meat is allowed if it doesn't contain any beef, veal, lamb, or mutton. As for alcohol, you can bring in one liter duty-free (it can be packed securely in your checked luggage, along with any other liquid-containing items).

To bring alcohol (or liquid-packed foods) in your carry-on bag on your flight home, buy it at a duty-free shop at the airport. You'll increase your odds of getting it onto a connecting flight if it's packaged in a "STEB"—a secure, tamper-evident bag. But stay away from liquids in opaque, ceramic, or metallic containers, which usually cannot be successfully screened (STEB or no STEB).

To check customs rules and duty rates, visit www.cbp.gov.

# Sightseeing

Sightseeing can be hard work. Use these tips to make your visits to Austria's finest sights meaningful, fun, efficient, and painless.

## PLAN AHEAD

Set up an itinerary that allows you to fit in all your must-see sights. For a one-stop look at opening hours in Vienna and Salzburg, see the "At a Glance" sidebars on page 44 and page 274. Most sights keep stable hours, but you can easily confirm the latest by checking with the TI or visiting museum websites.

Don't put off visiting a must-see sight—you never know when a place will close unexpectedly for a holiday, strike, or restoration. Many museums are closed or have reduced hours at least a few days a year, especially on holidays such as Christmas, New Year's, and Labor Day (May 1). A list of holidays is on page 516; check museum websites for possible closures during your trip. In summer, some sights may stay open late. Off-season, many museums have shorter hours.

Going at the right time helps avoid crowds. This book offers tips on the best times to see specific sights, such as Schönbrunn Palace in Vienna and Neuschwanstein Castle in Bavaria. Try visiting popular sights very early, at lunch, or very late. Evening visits are usually peaceful, with fewer crowds.

Study up. To get the most out of the self-guided tours and sight descriptions in this book, read them before you visit. Schönbrunn Palace is much more fascinating if you've polished your knowledge of the Habsburg dynasty in advance.

## AT SIGHTS

Here's what you can typically expect:

**Entering:** Be warned that you may not be allowed to enter if you arrive 30 to 60 minutes before closing time. And guards start ushering people out well before the actual closing time, so don't save the best for last.

Some important sights have a security check, where you must open your bag or send it through a metal detector. Some sights require you to check daypacks and coats. (If you'd rather not check your daypack, try carrying it tucked under your arm like a purse as you enter.)

At churches—which often offer interesting art (usually free) and a cool, welcome seat—a modest dress code (no bare shoulders or shorts) is encouraged though rarely enforced.

**Photography:** If the museum's photo policy isn't clearly posted, ask a guard. Generally, taking photos without a flash or tripod is allowed. Some sights ban photos altogether.

**Temporary Exhibits:** Museums may show special exhibits in addition to their permanent collection. Some exhibits are included in the entry price, while others come at an extra cost (which you may have to pay even if you don't want to see the exhibit).

**Expect Changes:** Artwork can be on tour, on loan, out sick, or shifted at the whim of the curator. To adapt, pick up a floor plan as you enter, and ask museum staff if you can't find a particular item.

**Audioguides:** Many sights rent audioguides, which generally offer excellent recorded descriptions in English (generally included in admission, otherwise about $5). If you bring your own earbuds, you can enjoy better sound and avoid holding the device to your ear. To save money, bring a Y-jack and share one audioguide with your travel partner. Increasingly, museums are offering apps (often free) that you can download to your mobile device. I've produced free downloadable audio tours of the major sights in Vienna and Salzburg; see page 10.

**Services:** Important sights may have an on-site café or cafeteria (usually a handy place to rejuvenate during a long visit). The WCs at sights are generally free and clean.

**Before Leaving:** At the gift shop, scan the postcard rack or thumb through a guidebook to be sure that you haven't overlooked something that you'd like to see.

Every sight or museum offers more than what is covered in this book. Use the information in this book as an introduction—not the final word.

PRACTICALITIES

# Sleeping

I favor hotels and restaurants that are handy to your sightseeing activities. Rather than list hotels scattered throughout a city, I describe two or three favorite neighborhoods and recommend the best accommodations values in each, from dorm beds to fancy doubles with all of the comforts.

While accommodations in Austria are fairly expensive, they are normally very comfortable and usually come with breakfast.

A triple is much cheaper than a double and a single. Single travelers get the best value at B&B-type lodgings, where the single price is often little more than half the double-room price. Hotels, in contrast, charge almost as much for a single room as for a double. Hostels and dorms always charge per person.

A major feature of this book is its extensive and opinionated listing of good-value rooms. I like places that are clean, central, relatively quiet at night, reasonably priced, friendly, small enough to have a hands-on owner and stable staff, run with a respect for Austrian traditions, and not listed in other guidebooks. (In Austria, for me, meeting six out of these eight criteria means it's a keeper.) I'm more impressed by a convenient location and a fun-loving philosophy than flat-screen TVs and a pricey laundry service.

Book your accommodations well in advance, especially if you'll be traveling during busy times. See page 516 for a list of major holidays and festivals in Austria; for tips on making reservations, see page 478.

Some people make reservations as they travel, calling hotels a few days to a week before their arrival. If you'd rather travel without any reservations at all, you'll have greater success snaring rooms if you arrive at your destination early in the day. If you anticipate crowds (weekends are worst), on the day you want to check in, call hotels at about 9:00 or 10:00, when the receptionist knows who'll be checking out and which rooms will be available. If you encounter a language barrier, ask the fluent receptionist at your current hotel to call for you.

## RATES AND DEALS

I've described my recommended accommodations using a Sleep Code (see sidebar). Prices listed are for one-night stays in peak season, breakfast is generally included (sometimes continental, but often buffet), and assume you're booking directly with the hotel

PRACTICALITIES

# Sleep Code

(€1 = about $1.40, country code: 43)

## Price Rankings

To help you sort easily through my listings, I've divided the accommodations into three categories, based on the highest price for a standard double room with bath during high season:

**$$$**  Higher Priced

**$$**  Moderately Priced

**$**  Lower Priced

I always rate hostels as $, whether or not they have double rooms, because they have the cheapest beds in town.

Prices can change without notice; verify the hotel's current rates online or by email. For the best prices, always book directly with the hotel.

## Abbreviations

To pack maximum information into minimum space, I use the following code to describe accommodations in this book. Prices listed are per room, not per person. When a price range is given for a type of room (such as double rooms listing for €100-150), it means the price fluctuates with the season, size of room, or length of stay; expect to pay the upper end for peak-season stays.

**S**  = Single room (or price for one person in a double).

**D**  = Double or twin. "Double beds" can be two twins sheeted together and are usually big enough for nonromantic couples.

**T**  = Triple (generally a double bed with a single).

**Q**  = Quad (usually two double beds; adding an extra child's bed to a T is usually cheaper).

**b**  = Private bathroom with toilet and shower or tub.

**s**  = Private shower or tub only (the toilet is down the hall).

According to this code, a couple staying at a "Db-€90" hotel would pay a total of €90 (about $126) for a double room with a private bathroom. Unless otherwise noted, breakfast is included, hotel staff speak basic English, and credit cards are accepted. If the city adds a room tax, it generally isn't included in the rates I list. There's almost always Wi-Fi and/or a guest computer available, either free or for a fee.

(not through an online hotel-booking engine or TI). Booking services extract a commission from the hotel, which logically closes the door on special deals. Book direct.

For most of the hotels I list, I provide a website (which often has a built-in booking form) and an email address; you can expect a response in English within a day (and often sooner).

If you're on a budget, it's smart to email several hotels to ask for their best price. Comparison-shop and make your choice. This is especially helpful when dealing with the larger hotels that use "dynamic pricing," a computer-generated system that predicts the demand for particular days and sets prices accordingly: High-demand days will often be more than double the price of low-demand days. This makes it impossible for a guidebook to list anything more accurate than a wide range of prices. I regret this trend. While you can assume that hotels listed in this book are good, it's very difficult to say which ones are the better value unless you email to confirm the price.

As you look over the listings, you'll notice that some accommodations promise special prices to Rick Steves readers. To get these rates, you must book direct (that is, not through a booking site like TripAdvisor or Booking.com), mention this book when you reserve, and then show the book upon arrival. Rick Steves discounts apply to readers with ebooks as well as printed books. Because I trust hotels to honor this, please let me know if you don't receive a listed discount. Note, though, that discounts understandably may not be applied to promotional rates.

In general, prices can soften if you do any of the following: offer to pay cash, stay at least three nights, or mention this book. You can also try asking for a cheaper room or a discount, or offer to skip breakfast.

## TYPES OF ACCOMMODATIONS
### Hotels
In this book, the price for a double room in a hotel ranges from €45 (very simple, toilet and shower down the hall) to €200-plus (maximum plumbing and the works). In small towns such as Hallstatt or Innsbruck, you can find a good double with a private bath for around €75; in more expensive cities like Vienna or Salzburg, you'll usually pay at least €90.

Room prices depend on the season and the day of the week, but peak times vary from one town to the next. In Vienna, business hotels have their highest rates in September and October, and rates are also high around New Year's Eve. In Salzburg, rates always rise significantly during the music festival (mid-July-Aug), during the four weeks leading up to Christmas, and usually around Easter. High season in Füssen and Reutte is June-September.

Many hotels have gone completely non-smoking, though smokers can still light up outdoors. Some hotels have non-smoking rooms or floors—let them know your preference when you book.

Bigger hotels commonly have elevators. When you're inside an elevator, press "E" if you want to descend to the "ground floor" *(Erdgeschoss)*. Hotel elevators, while becoming more common, are

**PRACTICALITIES**

# Making Hotel Reservations

Reserve your rooms several weeks in advance—or as soon as you've pinned down your travel dates. Note that some national holidays merit your making reservations far in advance (see page 516).

**Requesting a Reservation:** It's easiest to book your room through the hotel's website. (For the best rates, always use the hotel's official site and not a booking agency's site.) If there's no reservation form, or for complicated requests, send an email (see below for a sample request). Most recommended hotels take reservations in English.

The hotelier wants to know:

- the number and type of rooms you need
- the number of nights you'll stay
- your date of arrival (use the European style for writing dates: day/month/year)
- your date of departure
- any special needs (such as bathroom in the room or down the hall, cheapest room, twin beds vs. double bed, and so on)

Mention any discounts—for Rick Steves readers or otherwise—when you make the reservation.

**Confirming a Reservation:** Most places will request a credit-card number to hold your room. If they don't have a secure online reservation form—look for the *https*—you can email it (I do), but it's safer to share that confidential info via a phone call or two emails (splitting your number between them).

**Canceling a Reservation:** If you must cancel, it's courteous—and smart—to do so with as much notice as possible, especially

often very small—pack light, or you may need to take your bags up one at a time.

If you're arriving early in the morning, your room probably won't be ready. You can drop your bag safely at the hotel and dive right into sightseeing.

Hoteliers can be a great help and source of advice. Most know their city well, and can assist you with everything from public transit and airport connections to finding a good restaurant, the nearest launderette, or a Wi-Fi hot spot.

Even at the best places, mechanical breakdowns occur: Air-conditioning malfunctions, sinks leak, hot water turns cold, and toilets gurgle and smell. Report your concerns clearly and calmly at the front desk. For more complicated problems, don't expect instant results.

If you suspect night noise will be a problem (if, for instance, your room is over a café), ask for a quieter room in the back or on

| From: | rick@ricksteves.com |
|---|---|
| Sent: | Today |
| To: | info@hotelcentral.com |
| Subject: | Reservation request for 19-22 July |

Dear Hotel Central,

I would like to reserve a room for 2 people for 3 nights, arriving 19 July and departing 22 July. If possible, I would like a quiet room with a double bed and a bathroom inside the room.

Please let me know if you have a room available and the price.

Thank you!
Rick Steves

for smaller family-run places. Be warned that cancellation policies can be strict; read the fine print or ask about these before you book. Internet deals may require prepayment, with no refunds for cancellations.

**Reconfirming a Reservation:** Always call to reconfirm your room reservation a few days in advance. For smaller hotels and pensions, I call again on my day of arrival to tell my host what time I expect to get there (especially important if arriving late—after 17:00).

**Phoning:** For tips on how to call hotels overseas, see page 488.

an upper floor. To guard against theft in your room, keep valuables out of sight. Some rooms come with a safe, and other hotels have safes at the front desk. I've never bothered using one.

Checkout can pose problems if surprise charges pop up on your bill. If you settle your bill the afternoon before you leave, you'll have time to discuss and address any points of contention (before 19:00, when the night shift usually arrives).

Above all, keep a positive attitude. Remember, you're on vacation. If your hotel is a disappointment, spend more time out enjoying the city you came to see.

## B&Bs (Pensions) and Private Rooms

Compared to hotels, a pension gives you double the cultural intimacy for half the price (and usually includes a hearty breakfast). While you may lose some of the conveniences of a hotel—such as in-room phones, frequent bed-sheet changes, and the ease of paying with a credit card—I happily make the trade-off for the lower rates and personal touches. Similarly priced, a *Gasthof* is a small, family-run hotel.

Private rooms *(Zimmer)* are simply rooms rented out to travelers in private homes. These are inexpensive—as little as €25 per person with a hearty breakfast—and very common in areas popular with travelers (such as the Salzkammergut Lake District and Germany's Bavaria). Look for *Zimmer Frei* or *Privatzimmer* signs (green signs indicate that rooms are available; orange means they're booked/*belegt*). TIs often have a list of private rooms; use the list to book rooms yourself to avoid having the TI take a cut from you and your host. Especially in private homes, where the boss changes the sheets, people staying several nights are most desirable. One-night stays are quite often charged extra.

You'll get your own key to a private room that's clean, comfortable, and simple, though usually homey. Some private rooms are like mini-guesthouses, with a separate entrance and several rooms, each with a private bath. Others are family homes with spare bedrooms (the rooms sometimes lack sinks, but you have free access to the bathroom and shower in the home). Be considerate: Avoid excessively long showers and turn off lights when you leave.

## Hostels

You'll pay about $30 per bed to stay at a hostel. Follow signs marked *Jugendherberge* (with triangles) or with the logo showing a tree next to a house. Travelers of  any age are welcome if they don't mind dorm-style accommodations and meeting other travelers. Most hostels offer kitchen facilities, guest computers, Wi-Fi, and a self-service laundry. Nowadays, concerned about bedbugs, hostels are likely to provide all bedding, including sheets. Family and private rooms may be available on request.

**Independent hostels** tend to be easygoing, colorful, and informal (no membership required); www.hostelworld.com is the standard way backpackers search and book hostels, but also try www.hostelz.com and www.hostels.com.

**Official hostels** are part of Hostelling International (HI) and share an online booking site (www.hihostels.com). HI hostels typically require that you either have a membership card or pay extra per night.

# The Good and Bad of Online Reviews

User-generated travel review websites—such as TripAdvisor, Booking.com, and Yelp—have quickly become a huge player in the travel industry. These sites give you access to actual reports—good and bad—from travelers who have experienced the hotel, restaurant, tour, or attraction.

My hotelier friends in Europe are in awe of these sites' influence. Small hoteliers who want to stay in business have no choice but to work with review sites—which often charge fees for good placement or photos, and tack on commissions if users book through the site instead of directly with the hotel.

While these sites work hard to weed out bogus users, my hunch is that a significant percentage of reviews are posted by friends or enemies of the business being reviewed. I've even seen hotels "bribe" guests (for example, offer a free break-fast) in exchange for a positive review. Also, review sites can become an echo chamber, with one or two flashy businesses camped out atop the ratings, while better, more affordable, and more authentic alternatives sit ignored farther down the list. (For example, I find review sites' restaurant recommendations skew to very touristy, obvious options.)

Remember that a user-generated review is based on the experience of one person. That person likely stayed at one hotel and ate at a few restaurants, and doesn't have much of a basis for comparison. A guidebook is the work of a trained researcher who has exhaustively visited many alternatives to assess their relative value. I recently checked out some top-rated TripAdvisor listings in various towns; when stacked up against their competitors, some are gems, while just as many are duds.

Both types of information have their place, and in many ways, they're complementary. If a hotel or restaurant is well-reviewed in a guidebook or two, and also gets good ratings on one of these sites, it's likely a winner.

## OTHER ACCOMMODATION OPTIONS

Whether you're in a city or the countryside, renting an apartment, house, or villa can be a fun and cost-effective way to delve into Europe. Websites such as HomeAway and its sister sites VRBO and GreatRentals let you correspond directly with European property owners or managers.

Airbnb and Roomorama make it reasonably easy to find a place to sleep in someone's home. Beds range from air-mattress-in-living-room basic to plush-B&B-suite posh. If you want a place to sleep that's free, Couchsurfing.org is a vagabond's alternative to Airbnb. It lists millions of outgoing members, who host fellow "surfers" in their homes.

**PRACTICALITIES**

# Eating

Traditional Austrian cuisine is heavy and hearty, and borrows much from the cuisines of neighboring Hungary, Bohemia, and Germany. Food here is tasty and inexpensive, but can get monotonous if you fall into a schnitzel-filled rut. Be adventurous. For variety, keep in mind that all but the smallest towns have a restaurant serving non-Austrian cuisine.

For breakfast, expect fresh-baked bread and jam, plus cereal, cold cuts, and cheese. Austrians eat lunch and dinner about when we do, though they tend to eat a bigger lunch and smaller dinner.

Austrians are health-conscious, but many starchy, high-fat, high-calorie traditional foods remain staples on restaurant menus. As a new generation takes over their grandparents' restaurants and inns, however, it's becoming easier to find lighter versions of the meaty standards—and organic ingredients are getting more popular. Order house specials whenever possible.

The classic dish, a stand-by on menus across Austria, is Wiener schnitzel (a veal cutlet that's been pounded flat with a mallet, breaded, and fried; some restaurants offer only cheaper pork cutlets, and others give you a choice). Variations include Cordon bleu (filled with ham and cheese), and *Naturschnitzel* (not breaded, and served with rice and sauce). The Austrian version of *Gulasch*—a thick, meaty stew spiced with onion and paprika, somewhat different from the soupier Hungarian dish—is another traditional favorite. Chicken *(Huhn)* is usually served grilled or breaded and baked. Pork *(Schwein)* comes in all forms, including *Schweinsbraten* (roasted and served with dumplings and sauerkraut). Beef appears in goulash, as schnitzel, and in the Viennese *Tafelspitz* (boiled and served with vegetables). Fish dishes are very popular in this landlocked country and generally very good.

Vegetarians can make a meal out of starchy dishes like *Eiernockerl* (egg gnocchi), *Geröstete Knödel* (roasted dumplings) and *Spätzle* (little noodles often served with cheese and onions). Noodles, potatoes, rice, and salads are standard side dishes, often ordered and paid for separately. *Spargel* (giant white asparagus) is a must in early summer. For a meal-sized salad, order a *Salatteller.*

Like the Czechs (and other neighbors), Austrians are fond of soup. Lunch specials at restaurants often include soup and a main course. Dumplings in soup are common (*Speckknödel* have ham mixed with the dough; *Leberknödel* are filled with liver), as is "pancake soup," made with crepes that have been cut into strips.

While you're sure to have *Apfelstrudel,* try *Topfenstrudel,* too (wafer-thin strudel pastry filled with sweet cheese and raisins). *Palatschinken* (sweet filled crepes) are another borrowing from Hungarian cuisine. The very Austrian *Kaiserschmarr'n* consists of

## Mozart Balls *(Mozartkugeln)*

The Mozart ball is a chocolate confection with a marzipan, hazelnut, and pistachio-cream center that's become practically a symbol of Austria. Mozart balls make fun gifts and souvenirs, but aren't all created equal—there are several producers at different price and quality levels. For the absolutely most authentic, handmade Mozart balls (perfectly round and made of just pistachio and chocolate), visit one of the Fürst confectionery shops in Salzburg, which invented the Mozart ball in 1890 (there's one at Getreidegasse 47).

Most Mozart balls today are made by machine. The flat-bottomed ones made by Reber (whose factory in actually in Germany, just across the border from Salzburg) are made with pure cocoa butter and milk powder, and cost correspondingly more (at least €3 per 100 grams). Mirabell, the largest Austrian producer, is based in Salzburg and produces perfectly round balls using cheaper palm oil (€1.50 per 100 grams). You'll see a few off-brands, too, with prices as low as €1 per 100 grams. Supermarkets have the lowest prices. You'll pay more to buy the treats in a decorative box than in a plastic sack.

fluffy, caramelized, shredded pancake strips, usually served with jam or raisins and nuts (the name is a pun, meaning both "Emperor's shreds" and "Emperor's nonsense"). Delectable, fancy specialty desserts, like Sacher-Torte, Vienna's famous chocolate cake, are plentiful in city cafés.

Ethnic restaurants provide a welcome break from Austrian fare. Most foreign cuisine is newly arrived to feed recent immigrants. (Asian and Turkish food are good values.) It's easy to find Italian restaurants and pizzerias. Of course, much "Austrian" cooking is actually the legacy of a crumbled empire (which included Hungary and Bohemia—where Austrian cuisine gets its goulash and dumplings).

Hotels often serve fine food. A *Gaststätte* is a simple, less-expensive restaurant. For smaller portions, order from the *kleine Hunger* (small hunger) section of the menu.

When restaurant-hunting, choose a spot filled with locals, not the place with the big neon signs boasting, "We Speak English and Accept Credit Cards." Venturing even a block or two off the main drag leads to higher-quality food for less than half the price of the tourist-oriented places. Locals eat better at lower-rent locales.

Most restaurants tack a menu onto their door for browsers and have an English menu inside. Only a rude waiter will rush you. Good service is relaxed (slow to an American). You might be charged for bread you've eaten from the basket on the table; have the waiter take it away if you don't want it. To wish others "Happy

**PRACTICALITIES**

eating!" offer a cheery *"Guten Appetit!"* When you want the bill, say, *"Rechnung* (REKH-nung), *bitte."* For tips on tipping, see page 471.

## CHEAP MEALS

In Austria, you're never far from a *Würstelstand* (sausage stand)—for details, see the sidebar. Most bakeries and supermarkets sell cheap sandwiches; look for *Leberkäsesemmel* (roll filled with Austrian meatloaf) as well as *Schnitzelsemmel* (schnitzel sandwich). Supermarkets have a range of prepared foods that are good for picnics. *Stehcafés* (food counters) usually offer open-face finger sandwiches *(belegte Brote)* with a wide array of toppings. Other cheap eateries include department-store cafeterias, *Schnell-Imbiss* (fast-food) stands, university cafeterias *(Mensas)*, hostels, and—especially in big cities—*Döner Kebab* kiosks (serving either sliced meat and vegetables, or falafel, in pita bread, as well as other Middle Eastern fast-food options). For a quick, cheap bite, have a deli make you a *Wurstsemmel*—a basic sausage sandwich.

## BEVERAGES

For most visitors, it's not only the rich pastries that provide the fondest memories of Austrian cuisine, but the wine and the beer as well.

**Wine:** The wine (85 percent white) from the Danube River Valley and eastern Austria is particularly good.

The Austrian wine industry specializes in fine boutique wines (generally not exported, and therefore not well-known) rather than focusing on mass production. Locals order white or red Austrian wines expecting quality equal to French and Italian wines. When in Austria, I go for the better local wines when dining—well worth the cost (generally about €4 per small glass).

Some menus list wine prices by the tenth of a liter, or deciliter (dl); keep in mind that a normal-sized glass of wine (2 deciliters, often listed as "0,2 l") will cost twice what's listed. You can also order your wine by the *Viertel* (quarter-liter, 8 oz) or *Achtel* (eighth-liter, 4 oz).

When sampling Austrian wine, some vocabulary helps. You can say, *"Ein Viertel Weisswein* (white wine), *bitte* (please)." Order it *süss* (sweet), *halb trocken* (medium), or *trocken* (dry). *Rotwein* is red wine and *Sekt* is sparkling wine.

Try *Grüner Veltliner* if you like a dry white wine. *Traubenmost* is a heavenly grape juice—alcohol-free but on the verge of wine. *Most* is the same thing, but lightly alcoholic. *Sturm* is "new wine," stronger than *Most*, available only in autumn and part of the *Heuriger* phenomenon (described on page 192). Many locals claim it takes several years of practice to distinguish between *Sturm* wine and vinegar. The local red wine, called *Portugieser*, is pretty good.

## Best of the Wurst

Sausage (wurst) is a staple of the Germanic diet. Most restaurants offer it (often as the cheapest thing on the menu), but it's more commonly eaten at take-out fast-food stands and counters. Sausage is fast, tasty, very local—and even a chance for culinary adventure, as your options go far beyond the hometown hot dog. Some sausages are boiled *(gekocht)*, and some are grilled *(gegrillt)*. Most are pork-based. Generally, the darker the weenie, the spicier it is.

The generic term Bratwurst simply means "grilled sausage," as opposed to boiled *Brühwurst*. Regional variations of both abound. While some types of wurst can be found all over, others are unique to a particular area. Here are some key words:

**Blutwurst, Blunzn:** Made from congealed blood.

**Bosna:** With onions and sometimes curry.

**Burenwurst:** Pork sausage similar to what we'd call "kielbasa."

**Debreziner:** Boiled, thin, and spicy, with paprika.

**Frankfurter:** A boiled sausage, like our hot dog (also called *Wiener Würstchen*).

**Käsekrainer:** Boiled, with melted cheese inside.

**Thüringer:** Long, skinny, peppery, and wedged into a much shorter roll.

**Waldviertler:** Smoked sausage.

**Weisswurst:** Boiled white sausage (peel off the casing before you eat it), served with sweet mustard and a pretzel.

Sauces and sides include *Senf* (mustard; ask for *süss*—sweet; or *scharf*—sharp), *Ketchup, Curry-Ketchup* (a tasty curry-infused ketchup), Kraut (sauerkraut), and sometimes horseradish (called *Kren* in Austria and southern Germany).

At sausage stands, you'll most commonly get a roll with your wurst (which won't resemble an American hot-dog bun). Sometimes the sausage is inside the roll; sometimes you get it on a plate with a fork and the roll to the side. You might be given the choice of a slice of bread *(Brot)*, a pretzel *(Breze)*, or (in restaurants) potato salad instead of a roll. Traditionally, if the wurst is *frisch* (fresh), you're supposed to "eat it before the noon bell tolls."

In fall, try the red "new" wine, *roter Sturm;* it's so fruity that locals say "Eat up!" when toasting with it. If you ask for a *gespritzter Wein* (or *gespritzte Weisse*), you'll get a spritzer—white wine pepped up with a little sparkling water. Locals find this refreshing in the summer.

**Beer:** While better known for its wine than its beer, Austria offers plenty of fun for beer drinkers. Each region is proud of its local breweries—in Vienna, try Ottakringer; in Salzburg, look for Stiegl and Augustiner Bräu; and in Tirol, check out Frastanzer and

## Smoke Free? We'll See.

While many of its neighbors (including Italy, France, and many German states) have passed strict, extensive bans on smoking in public places, Austria has remained a haven for cigarette smokers. Austrian restaurants and cafés are only required to set aside at least half their space for non-smokers. Smaller establishments (under 50 square meters, or 540 square feet) that physically can't accommodate two viable zones can go all-smoking or entirely non-smoking. Restaurant and café owners who ignore the law can be fined up to €10,000 (and the smokers themselves can be fined up to €1,000).

But a host of exemptions and exceptions means that many establishments have escaped making any real changes. The law was toughened a bit in 2010, but it remains to be seen whether it will have much effect. In general, you should expect the possibility of some smoke in any restaurant (unless I've noted that it's "non-smoking"). Even "non-smoking" sections can be inundated with secondhand smoke. Fortunately for non-smokers, many eateries offer plenty of outdoor seating.

Fohrenburger. Lager (called *Märzen* here) is popular, as are *Pils* (barley-based), *Weissbier* (yeasty and wheat-based), and *Bock* (hoppy seasonal ale). A few more terms: *Flaschenbier* is bottled, *vom Fass* is on tap, and *Malzbier* is the malted soft drink that children learn on. *Radler* is half beer and half lemon soda. Dark beer *(Dunkles)* is uncommon in Austria, but easy to find if you make a foray into Bavaria. Designated drivers can try Ottakringer's delicious non-alcoholic beer, called "Null Komma Josef." When you order beer, ask for *ein Pfiff* (a fifth-liter, about 7 oz), *ein Seidel* (third-liter, 10 oz), *ein Krügerl* (half-liter, 17 oz), or *eine Mass* (a whole liter—about a quart).

**Water, Juice, and Soda:** Tap water *(Leitungswasser)* is sometimes served for a nominal fee (about €0.40), but waiters would prefer that you buy *Mineralwasser* (*mit/ohne Gas*, with/without carbonation). Popular soft drinks include *Apfelsaft gespritzt* (half apple juice, half sparkling water), *Spezi* (Coke and orange soda), and the *über*-Austrian Almdudler (a thirst-quenching ginger-ale-like soda). In cafés, look for *Himbeersoda* (raspberry soda) and the refreshing *Holunder gespritzt* (elderberry juice mixed with sparkling water).

Hang on to the half-liter mineral-water bottles (sold everywhere for about €1). Buy juice in cheap liter boxes, then drink some and store the extra in your water bottle.

# Communicating

"How can I stay connected in Europe?"—by phone and Internet—may be the most common question I hear from travelers. You have three basic options:

**1. "Roam" with your US smartphone.** This is the easiest option, but likely the most expensive. It works best for people who won't be making very many calls, and who value the convenience of sticking with what's familiar (and their own phone number). In recent years, as data roaming fees have dropped and free Wi-Fi has become easier to find, the majority of travelers are finding this to be the best all-around option.

**2. Use an unlocked mobile phone with European SIM cards.** This is a much more affordable option if you'll be making lots of calls, since it gives you 24/7 access to cheap European rates. Although remarkably cheap, this option does require a willingness to grapple with the technology and do a bit of shopping around for the right phone and card. Savvy travelers who routinely use SIM cards swear by them.

**3. Use public phones and get online at your hotel or at Internet cafés.** These options can work in a pinch, particularly for travelers who simply don't want to hassle with the technology, or want to be (mostly) untethered from their home life while on the road.

Each of these options is explained in greater detail in the following pages. Mixing and matching works well. For example, I routinely bring along my smartphone for Internet chores and Skyping on Wi-Fi, but also carry an unlocked phone and buy cheap SIM cards for affordable calls on the go.

For an even more in-depth explanation of this complicated topic, see www.ricksteves.com/phoning.

## HOW TO DIAL

Many Americans are intimidated by dialing European phone numbers. You needn't be. It's simple, once you break the code.

### Dialing Within Austria

The following instructions apply whether you're dialing from an Austria mobile phone or a landline (such as a pay phone or your hotel-room phone). If you're roaming with a US phone number, follow the "Dialing Internationally" directions described later.

Austria, like much of the US, uses an area-code dialing system. If you're dialing within an area code, you just dial the local number to be connected; but if you're calling outside your area code, you have to dial both the area code (which starts with 0) and the local number. If you're calling a mobile phone within Austria,

PRACTICALITIES

# Hurdling the Language Barrier

Austrians speak German (though with a distinctly Austrian flair that differs a bit across regional dialects). Most young and/or well-educated Austrians—especially those in larger towns and the tourist trade—speak at least some English. Still, you'll get more smiles by using the German pleasantries (see the "German Survival Phrases for Austria" on page 521). In smaller, non-touristy towns, the language barrier is higher.

German—like English, Dutch, Swedish, and Norwegian—is a Germanic language, making it easier on most American ears than Romance languages (such as Italian and French). These tips will help you pronounce German words: The letter *w* is always pronounced as *v* (e.g., the word for "wonderful" is *wunderbar*, pronounced VOON-der-bar). The letter *j* is always pronounced as *y* (so *Joghurt* is pronounced the same as English "yogurt"), and the letter *v* is pronounced as *f* (so the number *vier*—four—sounds just like "fear"). There are no silent letters.

The rule for pronouncing *ie* and *ei* never changes: Always say the name of the second letter. So *ie* sounds like the letter "e" (as in *hier* and *Bier,* the German words for "here" and "beer"), while *ei* sounds like the letter "i" (as in *nein* and *Wein*, the German words for "no" and "wine"). The vowel combination *au* is pronounced "ow" (as in *Frau*). The vowel combinations *eu* and *äu* are pronounced "oy" (as in *neu, Deutsch,* and *Bräu,* the German words for "new," "German," and "brew"). To pronounce *ö* and *ü,* purse your lips when you say the vowel; the other vowel with an umlaut, *ä,* is pronounced the same as "e" in "men." (In typewritten German, these can be depicted as the vowel followed by an *e*—*oe, ue,* and *ae,* respectively.) The letter *Eszett (ß)* represents "ss."

you must always dial the complete number (which starts with 06). You'll find area codes listed throughout this book, or you can get them from directory assistance (tel. 16).

For example, Vienna's area code is 01 and the number of one of my recommended Vienna hotels is 534-050. To call the hotel within Vienna, you'd dial 534-050. To call it from Salzburg, you'd dial 01/534-050.

## Dialing Internationally to or from Austria

Always start with the **international access code**—011 if you're calling from the US or Canada, 00 from anywhere in Europe. If you're dialing from a mobile phone, simply insert a + instead (by holding the 0 key.)

• Dial the **country code** of the country you're calling (43 for Austria, or 1 for the US or Canada).

• Then dial the area code (without its initial 0) and the local number. (If you're calling a mobile-phone number internationally,

Written German always capitalizes all nouns.

Regional dialects aside, the language spoken by Austrians isn't all that different from the *Deutsch* spoken by Germans—but those small differences are a big deal to Austrians. The most important one is how you say "hello": Austrians will greet you (and each other) with a *Grüss Gott*, or perhaps *Servus*—but never with the German *Guten Tag*, a phrase that sounds oddly uptight to Austrians (and as foreign as being wished a "G'day" in the US). Instead, stick to *Grüss Gott* ("May God greet you"), or a simple *Grüss*, for "hello." You'll get the correct pronunciation after the first volley—listen and copy.

You're likely to run into a few other un-German German words on your trip, such as *Jänner* and *Feber* for January and February (rather than the German *Januar* and *Februar*). A lot of food names are different: In Austria, potatoes are *Erdäpfel* (not *Kartoffeln*), tomatoes are *Paradeiser* (not *Tomaten*), a bread roll is a *Semmel* (not *Brötchen*), corn is *Kukuruz* (not *Mais*), green beans are *Fisolen* (not *grüne Bohnen*), cauliflower is *Karifiol* (not *Blumenkohl*), whipped cream is *Obers* (not *Schlagsahne*), and apricot jam and ice cream will be labeled as *Marille* (not *Aprikose*). Tacking an *-l* or *-erl* on the end of a word makes it a diminutive form—like adding "-ette" or "-ie" to an English word (or *-chen* in standard German).

Austrians appreciate any effort on your part to speak German—even if it's just *ein Bissl* (a little bit)—and if you already speak some German German, they'll understand you just fine. Give it your best shot.

you also drop the 0.) The European calling chart lists specifics per country.

**Calling from the US to Austria:** To call the recommended Vienna hotel from the US, dial 011 (US access code), 43 (Austria's country code), 1 (Vienna's area code without the initial 0), and 534-050.

**Calling from any European Country to the US:** To call my office in Edmonds, Washington, from anywhere in Europe, I dial 00 (Europe's access code), 1 (US country code), 425 (Edmonds' area code), and 771-8303.

## More Dialing Tips

The chart on the next page shows how to dial per country. For online instructions, see www.countrycallingcodes.com or www.howtocallabroad.com.

Remember, if you're using a mobile phone, dial as if you're in that phone's country of origin. So, when roaming with your US phone number in Austria, dial as if you're calling from the US. But if you're using a European SIM card, dial as you would from that European country.

Note that calls to a European mobile phone are substantially more expensive than calls to a fixed line. Off-hour calls are generally cheaper.

In Austria, phone numbers can have varying lengths. For instance, a hotel might have a seven-digit phone number and an eight-digit fax number.

For tips on communicating over the phone with someone who speaks another language, see page 488.

## USING YOUR AMERICAN SMARTPHONE IN EUROPE

Even in this age of email, texting, and near-universal Internet access, smart travelers still use the telephone. I call TIs to smooth out sightseeing plans, hotels to get driving directions, museums to confirm tour schedules, restaurants to check open hours or to book a table, and so on.

Most people enjoy the convenience of bringing their own smartphone. Horror stories about sky-high roaming fees are dated and exaggerated, and major service providers work hard to avoid surprising you with an exorbitant bill. With a little planning, you can use your phone—for voice calls, messaging, and Internet access—without breaking the bank.

Start by figuring out whether your phone works in Europe. Most phones purchased through AT&T and T-Mobile (which use the same technology as Europe) work abroad, while only some phones from Verizon or Sprint do—check your operating manual (look for "tri-band," "quad-band," or "GSM"). If you're not sure, ask your service provider.

### Types of Roaming

"Roaming" with your phone—that is, using it outside of its home region, such as in Europe—generally comes with extra charges, whether you are making voice calls, sending texts, or reading your email. The fees listed here are for the three major American providers—Verizon, AT&T, and T-Mobile; Sprint's roaming rates tend to be much higher. But policies change fast, so get the latest details before your trip. For example, as of mid-2014, T-Mobile waived voice, texting, and data roaming fees for some plans.

**Voice calls** are the most expensive. Most providers charge from $1.29 to $1.99 per minute to make or receive calls in Europe. (As you cross each border, you'll typically get a text message explaining the rates in the new country.) If you plan to make multiple calls, look into a global calling plan to lower the per-minute cost, or buy a package of minutes at a discounted price (such as 30 minutes for $30). Note that you'll be charged for incoming calls whether or not you answer them; to save money ask your friends to stay in contact by texting, and to call you only in case of an emergency.

**Text messaging** costs 20 to 50 cents per text. To cut that cost, you could sign up for an international messaging plan (for example, $10 for 100 texts). Or consider apps that let you text for free (iMessage for Apple, Google Talk for Android, or WhatsApp for any device); however, these require you to use Wi-Fi or data roaming. Be aware that Europeans use the term "SMS" ("short message service") to describe text messaging.

**Data roaming** means accessing an Internet signal that's carried over the cellular telephone network. Prices have dropped dramatically in recent years, making this an affordable way to bridge gaps between Wi-Fi hotspots. You'll pay far less if you set up an international data roaming plan. Most providers charge $25-30 for 100-120 megabytes of data. That's plenty for basic Internet tasks—100 megabytes lets you view 100 websites or send/receive 1,000 text-based emails, but you'll burn through that amount quickly by streaming videos or music. If your data use exceeds your plan amount, most providers will automatically kick in an additional 100- or 120-megabyte block for the same price. (For more on Wi-Fi versus data roaming—including strategies for conserving your data—see "Using Wi-Fi and Data Roaming," later.)

### Setting Up (or Disabling) International Service

With most service providers, international roaming (voice, text, and data) is disabled on your account unless you call to activate it. Before your trip, call your provider (or navigate their website), and cover the following topics:

- Confirm that your phone will work in Europe.
- Verify global roaming rates for voice calls, text messaging, and data roaming.
- Tell them which of those services you'd like to activate.
- Consider any add-on plans to bring down the cost of international calls, texts, or data roaming.

When you get home from Europe, be sure to cancel any add-on plans that you activated for your trip.

Some people would rather use their smartphone exclusively on Wi-Fi, and not worry about either voice or data charges. If that's you, call your provider to be sure that international roaming options are deactivated on your account. To be double-sure, put your phone in "airplane mode," then turn your Wi-Fi back on.

### Using Wi-Fi and Data Roaming

A good approach is to use free Wi-Fi wherever possible, and fill in the gaps with data roaming.

## European Calling Chart

Just smile and dial, using this key:
AC = Area Code, LN = Local Number.

| European Country | Calling long distance within ... | Calling from the US or Canada to ... | Calling from a European country to ... |
|---|---|---|---|
| **Austria** | AC + LN | 011 + 43 + AC (without initial zero) + LN | 00 + 43 + AC (without initial zero) + LN |
| **Belgium** | LN | 011 + 32 + LN (without initial zero) | 00 + 32 + LN (without initial zero) |
| **Bosnia-Herzegovina** | AC + LN | 011 + 387 + AC (without initial zero) + LN | 00 + 387 + AC (without initial zero) + LN |
| **Croatia** | AC + LN | 011 + 385 + AC (without initial zero) + LN | 00 + 385 + AC (without initial zero) + LN |
| **Czech Republic** | LN | 011 + 420 + LN | 00 + 420 + LN |
| **Denmark** | LN | 011 + 45 + LN | 00 + 45 + LN |
| **Estonia** | LN | 011 + 372 + LN | 00 + 372 + LN |
| **Finland** | AC + LN | 011 + 358 + AC (without initial zero) + LN | 999 (or other 900 number) + 358 + AC (without initial zero) + LN |
| **France** | LN | 011 + 33 + LN (without initial zero) | 00 + 33 + LN (without initial zero) |
| **Germany** | AC + LN | 011 + 49 + AC (without initial zero) + LN | 00 + 49 + AC (without initial zero) + LN |
| **Gibraltar** | LN | 011 + 350 + LN | 00 + 350 + LN |
| **Great Britain & N. Ireland** | AC + LN | 011 + 44 + AC (without initial zero) + LN | 00 + 44 + AC (without initial zero) + LN |
| **Greece** | LN | 011 + 30 + LN | 00 + 30 + LN |
| **Hungary** | 06 + AC + LN | 011 + 36 + AC + LN | 00 + 36 + AC + LN |
| **Ireland** | AC + LN | 011 + 353 + AC (without initial zero) + LN | 00 + 353 + AC (without initial zero) + LN |
| **Italy** | LN | 011 + 39 + LN | 00 + 39 + LN |

| European Country | Calling long distance within ... | Calling from the US or Canada to ... | Calling from a European country to ... |
|---|---|---|---|
| **Latvia** | LN | 011 + 371 + LN | 00 + 371 + LN |
| **Montenegro** | AC + LN | 011 + 382 + AC (without initial zero) + LN | 00 + 382 + AC (without initial zero) + LN |
| **Morocco** | LN | 011 + 212 + LN (without initial zero) | 00 + 212 + LN (without initial zero) |
| **Netherlands** | AC + LN | 011 + 31 + AC (without initial zero) + LN | 00 + 31 + AC (without initial zero) + LN |
| **Norway** | LN | 011 + 47 + LN | 00 + 47 + LN |
| **Poland** | LN | 011 + 48 + LN | 00 + 48 + LN |
| **Portugal** | LN | 011 + 351 + LN | 00 + 351 + LN |
| **Russia** | 8 + AC + LN | 011 + 7 + AC + LN | 00 + 7 + AC + LN |
| **Slovakia** | AC + LN | 011 + 421 + AC (without initial zero) + LN | 00 + 421 + AC (without initial zero) + LN |
| **Slovenia** | AC + LN | 011 + 386 + AC (without initial zero) + LN | 00 + 386 + AC (without initial zero) + LN |
| **Spain** | LN | 011 + 34 + LN | 00 + 34 + LN |
| **Sweden** | AC + LN | 011 + 46 + AC (without initial zero) + LN | 00 + 46 + AC (without initial zero) + LN |
| **Switzerland** | LN | 011 + 41 + LN (without initial zero) | 00 + 41 + LN (without initial zero) |
| **Turkey** | AC (if there's no initial zero, add one) + LN | 011 + 90 + AC (without initial zero) + LN | 00 + 90 + AC (without initial zero) + LN |

- The instructions above apply whether you're calling to or from a European landline or mobile phone.

- If calling from any mobile phone, you can replace the international access code with "+" (press and hold 0 to insert it).

- The international access code is 011 if you're calling from the US or Canada.

- To call the US or Canada from Europe, dial 00, then 1 (country code for US and Canada), then the area code and number. In short, 00 + 1 + AC + LN = Hi, Mom!

PRACTICALITIES

**Wi-Fi** (sometimes called "WLAN")—Internet access through a wireless router—is readily available throughout Europe. But just like at home, the quality of the signal may vary. Be patient, and don't get your hopes up. At accommodations, access is often free, but you may have to pay a fee, especially at expensive hotels. At hotels with thick stone walls, the Wi-Fi router in the lobby may not reach every room. If Wi-Fi is important to you, ask about it when you book—and be specific ("in the rooms?"). Get the password and network name at the front desk when you check in.

When you're out and about, your best bet for finding free Wi-Fi is often at a café. They'll usually tell you the password if you buy something. Or you can stroll down a café-lined street, smartphone in hand, checking for unsecured networks every few steps until you find one that works. Some towns have free public Wi-Fi in highly trafficked parks or piazzas. You may have to register before using it, or get a password at the TI.

**Data roaming**—that is, accessing the Internet through the cellular network—is handy when you can't find useable Wi-Fi. Because you'll pay by the megabyte (explained earlier), it's best to limit how much data you use. Save bandwidth-gobbling tasks like Skyping, watching videos, or downloading apps or emails with large attachments until you're on Wi-Fi. Switch your phone's email settings from "push" to "fetch." This means that you can choose to "fetch" (download) your messages when you're on Wi-Fi rather than having them continuously "pushed" to your device. And be aware of apps—such as news, weather, and sports tickers—that automatically update. Check your phone's settings to be sure that none of your apps are set to "use cellular data."

I like the safeguard of manually turning off data roaming on my phone whenever I'm not actively using it. To turn off data and voice roaming, look in your phone's menu—try checking under "cellular" or "network," or ask your service provider how to do it. If you need to get online but can't find Wi-Fi, simply turn on data roaming long enough for the task at hand, then turn it off again.

Figure out how to keep track of how much data you've used (in your phone's menu, look for "cellular data usage"; you may have to reset the counter at the start of your trip). Some companies automatically send you a text message warning if you approach or exceed your limit.

There's yet another option: If you're traveling with an unlocked smartphone (explained later), you can buy a SIM card that also includes data; this can be far, far cheaper than data roaming through your home provider.

PRACTICALITIES

## Internet Calling

To make totally free voice and video calls over the Internet, all you need are a smartphone, tablet, or laptop; a strong Wi-Fi signal; and an account with one of the major Internet calling providers: Skype (www.skype.com), FaceTime (preloaded on most Apple devices), or Google+ Hangouts (www.google.com/hangouts). If the Wi-Fi signal isn't strong enough for video, try sticking with an audio-only call. Or...wait for your next hotel. Many Internet calling programs also work for making calls from your computer to telephones worldwide for a very reasonable fee—generally just a few cents per minute (you'll have to buy some credit before you make your first call).

## USING EUROPEAN SIM CARDS

Using your American phone in Europe is easy, but it's not always cheap. And unreliable Wi-Fi can make keeping in touch frustrating. If you're reasonably technology-savvy, and would like to have the option of making lots of affordable calls, it's worth getting comfortable with European SIM cards.

Here's the basic idea: First you need an unlocked phone that works in Europe. Then, in Europe, shop around for a SIM card—the little data chip that inserts into your phone—to equip it with a European number. Turn on the phone, and bingo! You've got a European phone number (and access to cheaper European rates).

### Getting an Unlocked Phone

Your basic options are getting your existing phone unlocked, or buying a phone (either at home or in Europe).

Some phones are electronically "locked" so that you can't switch SIM cards (keeping you tied to your original service provider). But it's possible to "unlock" your phone—allowing you to replace the original SIM card. An unlocked phone is versatile; not only does it work with any European provider, but many US providers now offer no-contract, prepaid (or "pay-as-you-go") alternatives that work with SIM technology.

You may already have an old, unused mobile phone in a drawer somewhere. Call your service provider and ask if they'll send you the unlock code. Otherwise, you can buy one: Search an online shopping site for an "unlocked quad-band phone," or buy one at a mobile-phone shop in Europe. Either way, a basic model typically costs $40 or less.

### Buying and Using SIM Cards

Once you have an unlocked phone, you'll need to buy a SIM card—a small, fingernail-size chip that stores your phone number and other information. (A smaller variation called "micro-SIM" or "nano-SIM" cards—used in most iPhones—are less widely available.)

SIM cards are sold at mobile-phone shops, department-store electronics counters, and newsstands for $5–10, and usually include about that much prepaid calling credit (making the card itself virtually free). Because SIM cards are prepaid, there's no contract and no commitment; I routinely buy one even if I'm in a country for only a few days.

In Austria, buying a SIM card is as easy as buying a pack of gum (though some European countries require you to register the SIM card with your passport as an antiterrorism measure).

When using a SIM card in its home country, it's free to receive calls and texts, and it's cheap to make calls—domestic calls average 20 cents per minute. You can also use SIM cards to call the US—sometimes very affordably (Lycamobile, which operates in multiple European countries, lets you call a US number for less than 10 cents a minute). Rates are higher if you're roaming in another country. But if you bought the SIM card within the European Union, roaming fees are capped no matter where you travel throughout the EU (about 25 cents/minute to make calls, 7 cents/minute to receive calls, and 8 cents for a text message).

While you can buy SIM cards just about anywhere, I like to seek out a mobile-phone shop, where an English-speaking clerk can help explain my options, get my SIM card inserted and set up, and show me how to use it. When you buy your SIM card, ask about rates for domestic and international calls and texting, and about roaming fees. Also find out how to check your credit balance (usually you'll key in a few digits and hit "Send"). You can top up your credit at any newsstand, tobacco shop, mobile-phone shop, or many other businesses (look for the SIM card's logo in the window).

To insert your SIM card into the phone, locate the slot, which is usually on the side of the phone or behind the battery. Turning on the phone, you'll be prompted to enter the "SIM PIN" (a code number that came with your card).

If you have an unlocked smartphone, you can look for a European SIM card that covers both voice and data. This is often much cheaper than paying for data roaming through your home provider.

## Types of Telephone Cards

Europe uses two different types of telephone cards. Both types are sold at post offices, newsstands, street kiosks, tobacco shops, and train stations.

**Insertable Phone Cards:** These cards can only be used at pay phones: Simply take the phone off the hook, insert the card, wait for a dial tone, and dial away. The phone displays your credit ticking down as you talk. Each European country has its own insertable phone card—so your Austrian card won't work in a German phone.

**International Phone Cards:** These prepaid cards can be used to make inexpensive calls—within Europe, or to the US, for pennies a minute—from nearly any phone, including the one in your hotel room. The cards come with a toll-free number and a scratch-to-reveal PIN code. If the voice prompts aren't in English, experiment: Dial your code, followed by the pound sign (#), then the phone number, then pound again, and so on, until it works.

## LANDLINE TELEPHONES AND INTERNET CAFÉS

If you prefer to travel without a smartphone or tablet, you can still stay in touch using landline telephones, hotel guest computers, and Internet cafés.

### Landline Telephones

Phones in your **hotel room** can be great for local calls and for calls using cheap international phone cards (described in the sidebar). Many hotels charge a fee for local and "toll-free" as well as long-distance or international calls—always ask for the rates before you dial. Since you'll never be charged for receiving calls, it can be more affordable to have someone from the US call you in your room.

While **public pay phones** are on the endangered species list, you'll still see them in post offices and train stations. Pay phones generally come with multilingual instructions. Most public phones work with insertable phone cards (described in the sidebar).

You'll see many cheap **call shops** that advertise low rates to faraway lands, often in train-station neighborhoods. While these target immigrants who want to call home cheaply, tourists can use them, too. Before making your call, be completely clear on the rates.

### Internet Cafés and Public Internet Terminals

Finding public Internet terminals in Europe is no problem. Many hotels have a computer in the lobby for guests to use. Otherwise,

PRACTICALITIES

head for an Internet café, or ask the TI or your hotelier for the nearest place to access the Internet.

European computers typically use non-American keyboards. A few letters are switched around, and command keys are labeled in the local language. Many European keyboards have an "Alt Gr" key (for "Alternate Graphics") to the right of the space bar; press this to insert the extra symbol that appears on some keys. Europeans have different names for, and different ways to type, the @ symbol. On German-language keyboards, to type an @ symbol, press the "Alt Gr" key and Q at the same time. If you can't locate a special character (such as the @ symbol), simply copy it (Ctrl-C) from a Web page and paste it (Ctrl-V) into your email message.

## SECURITY OVER THE INTERNET

Whether you're accessing the Internet with your own device or at a public terminal, using a shared network or computer comes with the potential for increased security risks. Ask the hotel or café for the specific name of their Wi-Fi network, and make sure you log on to that exact one; hackers sometimes create a bogus hotspot with a similar or vague name (such as "Hotel Europa Free Wi-Fi"). It's better if a network uses a password (especially a hard-to-guess one) rather than being open to the world.

While traveling, you may want to check your online banking or credit-card statements, or to take care of other personal-finance chores, but Internet security experts advise against accessing these sites entirely while traveling. Even if you're using your own computer at a password-protected hotspot, any hacker who's logged on to the same network can see what you're up to. If you need to log on to a banking website, try to do so on a hard-wired connection (i.e., using an Ethernet cable in your hotel room), or if that's not possible, use a secure banking app on a cellular telephone connection.

If using a credit card online, make sure that the site is secure. Most browsers display a little padlock icon, and the URL begins with *https* instead of *http*. Never send a credit-card number over a website that doesn't begin with *https*.

If you're not convinced a connection is secure, avoid accessing any sites (such as your bank's) that could be vulnerable to fraud.

## MAIL

You can mail one package per day to yourself worth up to $200 duty-free from Europe to the US (mark it "personal purchases"). If you're sending a gift to someone, mark it "unsolicited gift." For details, visit www.cbp.gov and search for "Know Before You Go."

The Austrian postal service works fine, but for quick transatlantic delivery (in either direction), consider services such as DHL (www.dhl.com).

# Transportation

If you're debating between public transportation and car rental, consider these factors: Cars are best for three or more traveling together (especially families with small kids), those packing heavy, and those scouring the countryside. Trains and buses are best for solo travelers, blitz tourists, city-to-city travelers, those with an ambitious, multi-country itinerary, and those who don't want to drive in Europe. While a car gives you more freedom, trains and buses zip you effortlessly and scenically from city to city, usually dropping you in the center, often near a TI. Cars are an expensive headache in places like Vienna and Salzburg.

## TRAINS

Austrian trains are generally slick, speedy, and fairly punctual, with synchronized connections. They cover cities well, but some frustrating schedules make a few out-of-the-way recommendations (such as the Mauthausen concentration camp memorial) not worth the time and trouble for the less determined. Note that it's illegal to smoke on Austria's trains and most of its buses.

### Types of Trains

The Austrian Railways (a.k.a. Österreichische Bundesbahn, or ÖBB) operates several classes of trains, which differ substantially in speed, comfort, and price.

Austria's newest, fastest, and reddest train, the Railjet, streaks between Budapest, Vienna, Munich (or Innsbruck), and Zürich.

Red regional trains (labeled R and REX on schedules) are the slowest—the milk-run R trains stop at every small station—but cost much less. Mid-level, usually white IC and EC trains are air-conditioned, but are older than the Railjets and ICEs (and don't always have electrical outlets for your laptop).

### Schedules

Schedules change by season and vary between weekdays and weekends. To verify train times shown in this book, visit www.oebb. at (Austrian Railways, with full price information included) or www. bahn.com (Germany's excellent Europe-wide timetable site, without most Austrian prices but easier to navigate). At staffed train stations, attendants will print out a step-by-step itinerary for you, free

# Public Transportation in Austria

Rail
Bus
Boat

of charge. Schedules are also posted at stations. The computerized trackside machines marked *Fahrkarten* show prices but do not, unfortunately, give schedule information.

If you're changing trains en route and have a tight connection, note the numbers of the platforms (*Bahnsteig* or *Gleis*) where you will arrive and depart (listed on printed and online itineraries). This will save you precious time hunting for your connecting train.

You can call Austria's train information number from anywhere in the country: toll tel. 051-717 (to get an operator, dial 2, then 2). Ask for an English speaker.

## Rail Passes

The easy-to-use Austria Pass can be a good value for rail travel within the country if you are taking several longer trips. If you're traveling in a neighboring country as well, consider a two-country Eurail Pass, which allows you to pair Austria with Germany, Switzerland, the Czech Republic, or Hungary. The Austria-Croatia-Slovenia Pass covers travel in those three countries, and the Euro-

pean East Pass covers Austria and the Czech Republic, Slovakia, and Hungary (cheaper than most two-country combos). Another option is the Eurail Select Pass, which gives you up to 10 travel days (within a two-month period) in four adjacent countries of your choice. If you're planning a whirlwind tour of Europe, another possibility is the comprehensive Eurail Global Pass. Most passes are available in a saverpass version, which gives you a 15 percent discount on rail passes for two or more companions traveling together.

Rail pass travelers should know what extras are covered by their pass, such as discounts on Danube boats. Flexipass holders should note that discounted trips don't use up a flexi-day, but fully covered ("free") trips do. The "used" flexipass day can also cover your train travel on that day (but if you're not planning to travel more that day, it makes sense to pay for, say, the S-Bahn to Vienna's airport rather than use up a day of your pass for it).

Seat reservations are not required on daytime trains except in the ritzy Railjet business compartment. Optional seat reservations

# Rail Passes

Prices listed are for 2014 and are subject to change. For the latest prices, details, train schedules (and easy online ordering), see www.ricksteves.com/rail.

"Saver" prices are per person for two or more people traveling together. "Youth" means under age 26. The fare for children 4–11 is half the adult individual fare or Saver fare. Kids under age 4 travel free.

## AUSTRIA PASS

|  | Indiv. 1st Cl. | Indiv. 2nd Cl. | Saver 1st Cl. | Saver 2nd Cl. | Youth 2nd Cl. |
|---|---|---|---|---|---|
| 3 days in 1 month | $258 | $182 | $220 | $155 | $120 |
| Extra rail days (max. 5) | 27 | 19 | 23 | 16 | 13 |

## AUSTRIA–GERMANY PASS

|  | Indiv. 1st Cl. | Indiv. 2nd Cl. | Saver 1st Cl. | Saver 2nd Cl. | Youth 2nd Cl. |
|---|---|---|---|---|---|
| 5 days in 2 months | $459 | $394 | $394 | $338 | $338 |
| 6 days in 2 months | 506 | 433 | 433 | 370 | 370 |
| 8 days in 2 months | 604 | 514 | 514 | 441 | 441 |
| 10 days in 2 months | 702 | 597 | 597 | 576 | 576 |

## AUSTRIA–SWITZERLAND PASS

|  | Individual 1st Class | Saver 1st Class | Youth 2nd Class |
|---|---|---|---|
| 4 days in 2 months | $386 | $329 | $271 |
| Extra rail days (max. 6) | 43 | 36 | 30 |

## AUSTRIA–CZECH or AUSTRIA–HUNGARY PASS

|  | Individual 1st Class | Saver 1st Class | Youth 2nd Class |
|---|---|---|---|
| 4 days in 2 months | $287 | $245 | $188 |
| Extra rail days (max. 6) | 35-39 | 30-33 | 23-25 |

## AUSTRIA–CROATIA–SLOVENIA PASS

|  | Individual 1st Class | Saver 1st Class | Youth 2nd Class |
|---|---|---|---|
| 4 days in 2 months | $305 | $266 | $221 |
| Extra rail days (max. 6) | 44 | 37 | 31 |

## EUROPEAN EAST PASS

|  | 1st Class | 2nd Class |
|---|---|---|
| 5 days in 1 month | $342 | $235 |
| Extra rail days (max. 5) | 38 | 32 |

Covers Austria, Czech Republic, Slovakia, Hungary and Poland.

**Map key:**
Approximate point-to-point one-way second-class rail fares in US dollars. First class costs 50 percent more. Add up the approximate ticket costs for your trip to see if a rail pass will save you money.

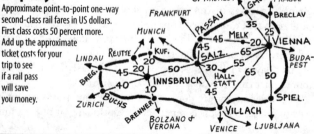

in first or second class cost €3 extra with either a ticket or a rail pass.

For more detailed advice on figuring out the smartest rail pass options for your train trip, visit the Trains & Rail Passes section of my website at www.ricksteves.com/rail.

## Tickets

When buying individual tickets, remember that traveling in second class instead of first class provides the same transportation for 33 percent less. Bikes cost €5-12 extra on EC and IC trains—must reserve in advance—and €5 extra for a day of travel on local trains. Ticket fares are shown on the rail pass chart in this chapter and at www.oebb.at.

**Deals:** If you're not using a rail pass, it's worth knowing about three types of special tickets in Austria, which can save you a lot of money.

**Daypass:** Austrian Railways' **Einfach-Raus-Ticket** ("Just Get Outta Here" ticket) is a cheap way for couples and small groups to travel. It's valid only on slower regional trains: R, REX, S-Bahn, RSB, ER, and EZ (€35, €44 with bikes, covers 2-5 people for a whole day of travel, not valid Mon-Fri before 9:00, cannot be used by solo travelers).

**Discount Card:** Many Austrians have a **Vorteils** card, which knocks 50 percent off all rail fares (adults €99, valid one year). The adult version isn't worth it for most travelers, but the **youth** version (under 26 only, €19) and **senior** version (age 61 and above, €29) pay for themselves with just one trip from Vienna to Innsbruck. The **family** version (€19 per parent) is also a great deal—parents get the 50 percent discount, and with each parent, up to 2 kids aged 6-14 go free (normally they'd pay half the adult fare). To get a Vorteils card, go to any station ticket counter. The plastic card will be sent to your address back home, and you'll get a temporary card on the spot that's valid for two months.

**Advance-Purchase Discounts:** If you book online at www.oebb.at at least three days in advance, Austrian Railways offers **"SparSchiene"** fares that can be as low as €9 domestically and €19 internationally. Availability is limited, and these tickets lock you into a departure time. Either print out your ticket yourself, or get a code that lets you collect it from machines at any train station.

For a whole day of travel on local trains in Bavaria, such as from Salzburg to Munich and Füssen, consider the Bayern-Ticket (€23/day for the first person plus €4 for each additional person).

**Buying Tickets:** Major Austrian stations have a handy *Rei-sezentrum* (Travel Center) where you can ask questions and buy tickets. Many smaller stations, though, are unstaffed, with tickets sold only from machines (marked *Fahrkarten*, which means "tick-

## Driving in Austria

Note: Your times may vary based on traffic, construction, and road conditions.

20 Kilometers
20 Miles

m = miles
h = hours

GERMANY

To Rothenburg

To Prague

150m • 2h

240m • 4h

Munich

80m • 1.25h

80m • 1.25h

Salzburg

70m • 1.5h

100m • 1.5h

15m .5h

Füssen

12m .25h

Berchtesgaden

Lake Constance

Reutte

60m • 1.25h

110m • 2h

Hall

Innsbruck

140m • 3.5h

180m • 3.5h

25m .5h

220m • 3.5h

To Zürich

Brenner Pass

150m • 2.5h

SWITZERLAND

ITALY

To Verona

---

ets"). You can pay with bills, coins, or credit cards (if your credit card isn't accepted, just use cash). Boarding a local train without a ticket can earn you a hefty fine if you could have bought a ticket at the station where you boarded.

## RENTING A CAR

If you're renting a car in Austria, bring your driver's license. You're also required to have an International Driving Permit—an official translation of your driver's license (sold at your local AAA office for $15 plus the cost of two passport-type photos; see www.aaa.com). While that's the letter of the law, I've often rented cars without having this permit. If all goes well, you'll likely never be asked to show the permit—but it's a must if you end up dealing with the police.

Most Austrian car-rental companies require you to be at least 19 years old and to have held your license for one year. Drivers under the age of 24 may incur a young-driver surcharge, and some rental companies do not rent to anyone 75 or older. If you're con-

PRACTICALITIES

sidered too young or old, look into leasing (covered later), which has less-stringent age restrictions.

Research car rentals before you go. It's cheaper to arrange most car rentals from the US. Call several companies or look online to compare rates.

Most of the major US rental agencies (including Avis, Budget, Enterprise, Hertz, and Thrifty) have offices throughout Europe. Also consider the two major Europe-based agencies, Europcar and Sixt. It can be cheaper to use a consolidator, such as Auto Europe/Kemwel (www.autoeurope.com) or Europe by Car (www.europebycar.com), which compares rates at several companies to get you the best deal, but because you're working with a middle-man, it's especially important to ask in advance about add-on fees and restrictions.

Regardless of the car-rental company you choose, always read the fine print carefully for add-on charges—such as one-way drop-off fees, airport surcharges, or mandatory insurance policies—that aren't included in the "total price." You may need to query rental agents pointedly to find out your actual cost.

For the best deal, rent by the week with unlimited mileage. To save money on fuel, ask for a diesel car. I normally rent the smallest, least-expensive model with a stick shift (generally much cheaper than an automatic). Almost all rentals are manual by default, so if you need an automatic, request one in advance; be aware that these cars are usually larger models (not as maneuverable on narrow, winding roads).

Figure on paying roughly $200 for a one-week rental. Allow extra for supplemental insurance, fuel, tolls, and parking. For trips of three weeks or more, look into leasing; you'll save money on insurance and taxes. Be warned that international trips—say, picking up in Vienna and dropping in Budapest—can be expensive (it depends partly on distance).

As a rule, always tell your car-rental company up front exactly which countries you'll be entering. Some companies levy extra insurance fees for trips taken in certain countries with certain types of cars (such as BMWs, Mercedes, and convertibles). Double-check with your rental agent that you have all the documentation you need before you drive off (especially if you're crossing borders into non-Schengen countries, such as Croatia, where you might need to present proof of insurance).

Big companies have offices in most cities; ask whether they can pick you up at your hotel. Small local rental companies can be cheaper but aren't as flexible.

Compare pickup costs (downtown can be less expensive than the airport) and explore drop-off options. Always check the hours of the location you choose: Many rental offices close from midday Saturday until Monday morning and, in smaller towns, at lunchtime.

When selecting a location, don't trust the agency's description of "downtown" or "city center." In some cases, a "downtown" branch can be on the outskirts of the city—a long, costly taxi ride from the center. Before choosing, plug the addresses into a mapping website. You may find that the "train station" location is handier. But returning a car at a big-city train station or downtown agency can be tricky; get precise details on the car drop-off location and hours, and allow ample time to find it.

When you pick up the rental car, check it thoroughly and make sure any damage is noted on your rental agreement. Find out how your car's lights, turn signals, wipers, radio, and fuel cap function, and know what kind of fuel the car takes (diesel vs. unleaded). When you return the car, make sure the agent verifies its condition with you. Some drivers take pictures of the returned vehicle as proof of its condition.

## Navigation Options

When renting a car in Europe, you have several alternatives for your digital navigator: Use your smartphone's online mapping app, download an offline map app, or rent a GPS device with your rental car (or bring your own GPS device from home).

Online mapping apps used to be prohibitively expensive for overseas travelers—but that was before most carriers started offering affordable international data plans. If you're already getting a data plan for your trip, this is probably the way to go (see "Using Your American Smartphone in Europe," earlier).

A number of well-designed apps allow you much of the convenience of online maps without any costly demands on your data plan. City Maps 2Go is one of the most popular of these; OffMaps, Google Maps, and Navfree also all offer good, zoomable offline maps for much of Europe (some are better for driving, while others are better for navigating cities).

Some drivers prefer using a dedicated GPS unit—not only to avoid the data-roaming fees, but because a stand-alone GPS can be easier to operate (important if you're driving solo). The major downside: It's expensive—around $10-30 per day. Also your car's GPS unit may only come loaded with maps for its home country—if you need additional maps, ask. Make sure your device's language is set to English before you drive off. If you have a portable GPS device at home, you can take that instead. Many American GPS devices come loaded with US maps only—you'll need to buy and download European maps before your trip. This option is far less expensive than renting.

## Car Insurance Options

When you rent a car, you are liable for a very high deductible, sometimes equal to the entire value of the car. Limit your financial risk with one of these options: Buy Collision Damage Waiver (CDW) coverage from the car-rental company, get coverage through your credit card (free, if your card automatically includes zero-deductible coverage), or get collision insurance as part of a larger travel-insurance policy.

**CDW** includes a very high deductible (typically $1,000-1,500). Though each rental company has its own variation, basic CDW costs $10-30 a day (figure roughly 30 percent extra) and reduces your liability, but does not eliminate it. When you pick up the car, you'll be offered the chance to "buy down" the basic deductible to zero (for an additional $10-30/day; this is often called "super CDW" or "zero-deductible coverage").

If you opt instead for **credit-card coverage**, there's a catch. You'll technically have to decline all coverage offered by the car-rental company, which means they can place a hold on your card (which can be up to the full value of the car). In case of damage, it can be time-consuming to resolve the charges with your credit-card company. Before you decide on this option, quiz your credit-card company about how it works.

If you're already purchasing a **travel-insurance policy** for your trip, adding collision coverage is an option. For example, Travel Guard (www.travelguard.com) sells affordable renter's collision insurance as an add-on to its other policies; it's valid everywhere in Europe except the Republic of Ireland, and some Italian car-rental companies refuse to honor it, as it doesn't cover you in case of theft.

For more on car-rental insurance, see www.ricksteves.com/cdw.

## Leasing

For trips of three weeks or more, consider leasing (which automatically includes zero-deductible collision and theft insurance). By technically buying and then selling back the car, you save lots of money on tax and insurance. Leasing provides you a brand-new car with unlimited mileage and a 24-hour emergency assistance program. You can lease for as little as 21 days to as long as five and a half months. Car leases must be arranged from the US. One of many companies offering affordable lease packages is Europe by Car (www.europebycar.com/lease).

## DRIVING

Learn the universal road signs (explained in charts in most road atlases and at service stations). Seat belts are required, and two beers under those belts are enough to land you in jail.

**Road Rules:** Be aware of typical European road rules. For example, many countries require headlights to be turned on at all times; in Austria, you're required to use low-beam headlights when driving in urban areas. It's generally illegal to drive while using your mobile phone without a hands-free headset. Austria requires an "emergency corridor" during traffic jams on expressways and toll roads—follow what other drivers are doing and stay out of the cleared lane.

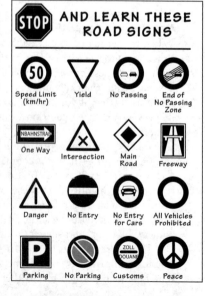

STOP **AND LEARN THESE ROAD SIGNS**

Speed Limit (km/hr) — Yield — No Passing — End of No Passing Zone

One Way — Intersection — Main Road — Freeway

Danger — No Entry — No Entry for Cars — All Vehicles Prohibited

Parking — No Parking — Customs — Peace

In Europe, you're not allowed to turn right on a red light, unless there is a sign or signal specifically authorizing it, and on expressways it's illegal to pass drivers on the right. Ask your car-rental company about these rules, or check the US State Department website (www.travel.state.gov, search for your country in the "Learn about your destination" box, then click on "Travel and Transportation").

**Tolls:** Austria charges drivers who use their major roads. You'll need to have a *Vignette* sticker stuck to the inside of your rental car's windshield (buy at the border crossing, big gas stations near borders, or a rental-car agency). The cost is €8.50 for 10 days, or €24.80 for two months. Not having one earns you a stiff fine. Place it on your windshield exactly as shown on the back of the sticker, and keep the lower tear-off portion—it's your receipt.

**Fuel:** Unleaded gasoline comes in regular (91 octane) and "Euro-Super" (95 octane). If you are also driving in Germany, pumps marked "E10" or "Super E10" mean the gas contains 10 percent ethanol—make sure your rental can run on this mix. You don't have to worry about learning the German word for diesel. Your US credit and debit cards may not work at self-service gas pumps. Pay the attendant or be sure to carry sufficient cash in euros.

**Navigation:** Use good local maps and study them before each drive. Learn which exits you need to look out for, which major cities you'll travel toward, where the ruined castles lurk, and so on. Ring roads go around a city. To get to the center of a city, follow signs for *Zentrum* or *Stadtmitte*. When navigating, you'll see *nord*, *süd*, *ost*, and *west*.

**Autobahn:** Every long drive between my recommended destinations is via the autobahn (super-freeway) and *Schnellstrassen* (expressway) system, and nearly every scenic backcountry drive is paved and comfortable.

The shortest distance between any two points is the autobahn. Blue signs direct you to the autobahn, and in Austria, unlike in Germany, the autobahn has a speed limit (130 km/hour, unless otherwise signed). Learn the signs: *Dreieck* ("three corners") means a Y in the road; *Autobahnkreuz* is an interchange. While all roads seem to lead to the little town of Ausfahrt, that's the German word for exit. Exits are spaced about every 20 miles and often have a gas station, a restaurant, a mini-market, and sometimes a tourist information desk. Exits and intersections refer to the next major city or the nearest small town. Peruse the map and anticipate which town names to look out for. Know what you're looking for—miss it, and you're long autobahn-gone.

**Parking:** For parking on the street, you can pick up a cardboard clock (*Parkscheibe*, available free at gas stations, police stations, and *Tabak* shops). Display your arrival time on the clock and put it on the dashboard, so parking attendants can see you've been there less than the posted maximum stay (blue lines indicate 90-minute zones on Austrian streets). Your US credit and debit cards may not work at automated parking garages; be sure to carry sufficient cash in euros.

**Theft:** Keep your valuables in your hotel room or, if you're between destinations, covered in your trunk. Leave nothing worth stealing in the car, especially overnight. If your car's a hatchback, take the trunk cover off at night so thieves can look in without breaking in. Try to make your car look locally owned by hiding the "tourist-owned" rental-company decals and putting a local newspaper in your front or back window. While you should avoid parking lots with twinkly asphalt, thieves break car windows anywhere, even at stoplights.

## FLIGHTS

The best comparison search engine for both international and intra-European flights is www.kayak.com. For inexpensive flights within Europe, try www.skyscanner.com or www.hipmunk.com; for inexpensive international flights, try www.vayama.com.

**Flying to Europe:** Start looking for international flights four to five months before your trip, especially for peak-season travel. Off-season tickets can be purchased a month or so in advance. Depending on your itinerary, it can be efficient to fly into one city and out of another. If your flight requires a connection in Europe, see our hints on navigating Europe's top hub airports at www.ricksteves.com/hub-airports.

**Flying within Europe:** If you're considering a train ride that's more than five hours long, a flight may save you both time and money. When comparing your options, factor in the time it takes to get to the airport and how early you'll need to arrive to check in.

Well-known cheapo airlines include easyJet (www.easyjet.com), Ryanair (www.ryanair.com), and Austria's own Niki (www.flyniki.com).

Be aware of the potential drawbacks of flying on the cheap: nonrefundable and nonchangeable tickets, minimal or nonexistent customer service, treks to airports far outside town, and stingy baggage allowances with steep overage fees. If you're traveling with lots of luggage, a cheap flight can quickly become a bad deal. To avoid unpleasant surprises, read the small print before you book.

# Resources

## RESOURCES FROM RICK STEVES

*Rick Steves Vienna, Salzburg & Tirol* is one of many books in my series on European travel, which includes country guidebooks,

city guidebooks (Rome, Florence, Paris, London, etc.), Snapshot guides (excerpted chapters from my country guides), Pocket Guides (full-color little books on big cities), and my budget-travel skills handbook, *Rick Steves Europe Through the Back Door*. Most of my titles are available as ebooks. My phrase books—for German, French, Italian, Spanish, and Portuguese—are practical and budget-oriented. My other books include *Europe 101* (a crash course on art and history designed for travelers); *Mediterranean Cruise Ports* and *Northern European Cruise Ports* (how to make the most of your time in port); and *Travel as a Political Act* (a travelogue sprinkled with tips for bringing home a global perspective). A more complete list of my titles appears near the end of this book.

**Video:** My public television series, *Rick Steves' Europe,* covers European destinations in 100 shows, with three episodes on Austria. To watch full episodes online for free, see www.ricksteves.com/tv.

Or to raise your travel I.Q. with video versions of our popular classes, including talks on Germany and Austria, see www.ricksteves.com/travel-talks.

**Audio:** My weekly public radio show, *Travel with Rick Steves,* features interviews with travel experts from around the world. I've also produced free, self-guided **audio tours** of some of the top sights in Vienna and Salzburg. All of this audio content is available for free at Rick Steves Audio Europe, an extensive online library organized by destination. Choose whatever interests you, and download it for free via the Rick Steves Audio Europe app, www.ricksteves.com/audioeurope, iTunes, or Google Play.

## Maps

The black-and-white maps in this book are concise and simple, designed to help you locate recommended places and get to local TIs, where you can pick up more in-depth maps of cities and regions (usually free). Better maps are sold at newsstands and bookstores. Before you buy a map, look at it to be sure it has the level of detail you want.

European bookstores, especially in touristy areas, have good selections of maps. For drivers, I'd recommend a 1:200,000- or

**PRACTICALITIES**

## Begin Your Trip at www.RickSteves.com

My **website** is *the* place to explore Europe. You'll find thousands of fun articles, videos, photos, and radio interviews on European destinations; money-saving tips for planning your dream trip; monthly travel news; my travel talks and travel blog; my latest guidebook updates (www.ricksteves.com/update); and my free Rick Steves Audio Europe app. You can also follow me on Facebook and Twitter.

Our **Travel Forum** is an immense, yet well-groomed collection of message boards, where our travel-savvy community answers questions and shares their personal travel experiences (www.ricksteves.com/forums).

Our **online Travel Store** offers travel bags and accessories that I've designed specifically to help you travel smarter and lighter. These include my popular bags (rolling carry-on and backpack versions), money belts, totes, toiletries kits, adapters, other accessories, and a wide selection of guidebooks, planning maps, and DVDs.

Choosing the right **rail pass** for your trip—amid hundreds of options—can drive you nutty. Our website will help you find the perfect fit for your itinerary and your budget: We offer easy, one-stop shopping for rail passes, seat reservations, and point-to-point tickets.

Want to travel with greater efficiency and less stress? We organize **tours** with more than three dozen itineraries and more than 800 departures reaching the best destinations in this book...and beyond. We offer a 14-day tour of Germany, Austria, and Switzerland; a 12-day My Way: Alpine Europe "unguided" tour; and a 12-day tour of Berlin, Prague, and Vienna. You'll enjoy great guides, a fun bunch of travel partners (with small groups of 24 to 28 travelers), and plenty of room to spread out in a big, comfy bus when touring between towns. You'll find European adventures to fit every vacation length. For all the details, and to get our Tour Catalog and a free Rick Steves Tour Experience DVD (filmed on location during an actual tour), visit www.ricksteves.com or call us at 425/608-4217.

1:300,000-scale map for each country. Train travelers usually manage fine with the freebies they get with the train pass and from the local tourist offices.

## RECOMMENDED BOOKS AND MOVIES

To learn more about Austria past and present, check out a few of these books and films.

## Nonfiction

For an overview of Austrian history, try *The Austrians: A Thousand-Year Odyssey* (Brook-Shepherd), though most of its focus is on the 19th and 20th centuries. Frederic Morton's *A Nervous Splendor* and *Thunder at Twilight* tell the story of the Austro-Hungarian Empire's last years in a light, lively way. *Fin-de-Siècle Vienna: Politics and Culture* (Schorske) is a dense but comprehensive analysis of the birth of modernism through Klimt, Freud, and other Viennese luminaries. *The Spell of the Vienna Woods: Inspiration and Influence from Beethoven to Kafka* (Hofmann) blends personal anecdotes, history, tourist information, and stories about artists who found inspiration in the 540-square-mile area that serves as Vienna's playground. *Beethoven: The Music and the Life* (Lockwood) includes details about the musician's life in Vienna and his contributions to its culture.

**Memoirs:** *The Story of the Trapp Family Singers,* written by Maria von Trapp, tells the true story behind the musical phenomenon. Stefan Zweig's *World of Yesterday* looks at how he became a successful writer in the "lost world" of prewar Vienna. In *The Hare with the Amber Eyes,* Edmund de Waal insightfully recounts the rise and fall of his storied family, whose Vienna home, the Palais Ephrussi on the Ringstrasse, was confiscated by the Nazis in the *Anschluss.*

## Fiction

Much fiction set in Vienna concerns the imagined lives of famous artists. *The Painted Kiss* (Hickey) reflects the lush elegance of fin-de-siècle Vienna and the relationship between painter Gustav Klimt and his pupil Emilie Flöge, who posed for Klimt's masterpiece *The Kiss.* In *The Seven-Per-Cent Solution* (Meyer), Sherlock Holmes travels to Vienna to meet with Sigmund Freud and gets involved in a case. *Henry James' Midnight Song* (Hill) is another literary mystery with a cast of famous historical characters. Mystery fans could also consider *Airs Above the Ground* (Stewart), with Lipizzaner stallions and the Austrian Alps as a backdrop, as well as *A Death in Vienna* (Tallis), which involves a cover-up by the Catholic Church.

Austrian feminist Elfriede Jelinek, known for exploring dark themes, won the 2004 Nobel Prize in Literature. Her most famous novel, *Die Klavierspielerin* (*The Piano Teacher,* made into a movie) is about a troubled piano teacher who messes up the lives of her students. Robert Schneider's *Brother of Sleep,* set in an Austrian mountain village in the early 19th century, tells the story of a musical prodigy who goes unappreciated by the locals. Viennese writer Joseph Roth's classic novel *Radetzky March* follows four generations of a family during the decline and fall of the Habsburgs.

## Films

*The Great Waltz* (1938) portrays the life of composer Johann Strauss. Orson Welles infuses *The Third Man* (1949, actually shot in bombed-out Vienna) with noir foreboding. In *Miracle of the White Stallions* (1963), the Lipizzaner stallions are the stars in this true story of how the horses were liberated by General Patton after World War II. The beloved musical *The Sound of Music* (1965), also partially set in World War II, helped turn Julie Andrews into a star. *Mayerling* (1968) is about the suicide of Habsburg heir Archduke Rudolf (played by Omar Sharif), which played a pivotal role in Austrian history.

*Mahler* (1974) describes the man behind the music, and *Amadeus* (1984) made Mozart into a flesh-and-blood man (who giggles), as did *Immortal Beloved* (1994) for Beethoven. To familiarize yourself with Sisi (a.k.a. Austria's Empress Elisabeth, a 19th-century Princess Diana), look for the series of 1950s films starring Romy Schneider.

In *Before Sunrise* (1995), Ethan Hawke sightsees, talks, romances, and talks some more with Julie Delpy in Vienna. *The Illusionist* (2006) set in circa-1900 Vienna, is about a magician who uses his abilities to gain the love of a woman engaged to the crown prince.

# APPENDIX

## Contents

## Useful Contacts

### Emergency Needs
**Emergency (police and ambulance):** Tel. 112

### Embassies
**US Embassy in Vienna:** Boltzmanngasse 16, tel. 01/313-390, embassy@usembassy.at; consular services at Parkring 12, daily 8:00-11:30, tel. 01/313-397-535, www.usembassy.at, consulatevienna@state.gov

**Canadian Embassy in Vienna:** Laurenzerberg 2, 3rd floor, Mon-Fri 8:00-12:30 & 13:30-15:30, tel. 01/531-383-000, after-hours emergencies call collect Canadian tel. 613/996-8885, www.austria.gc.ca, vienn@international.gc.ca

### Directory Assistance
**Directory Assistance Within Austria:** Tel. 16
**International Directory Assistance:** Tel. 08

# Holidays and Festivals

This list includes selected festivals in major cities, plus national holidays observed throughout Austria. Vienna and Salzburg have music festivals nearly every month, and many sights and banks close on national holidays—keep this in mind when planning your itinerary. Before planning a trip around a festival, verify its dates by checking the festival's website or TI sites (www.austria.info).

| | |
|---|---|
| **Jan 1** | New Year's Day |
| **Jan** | Perchtenlaufen (winter festival, parades), Salzburg |
| **Jan-mid Feb** | Vienna Ball Season (2,000 hours of dancing, www.wien.info, click on "Dance" tab) |
| **Jan-Feb** | Fasnacht (carnival season, balls, parades), western Austria |
| **Good Friday** | Karfreitag, April 3 in 2015, March 25 in 2016 |
| **Easter & Easter Monday** | Ostersonntag & Ostermontag, April 5-6 in 2015, March 27-28 in 2016; Easter Festival, Salzburg |
| **May-June** | Vienna Festival of Arts and Music (www.festwochen.or.at) |
| **May 1** | May Day with maypole dances, throughout Austria |
| **Ascension** | Christi Himmelfahrt, May 14 in 2015, May 5 in 2016 |
| **Pentecost Monday** | Pfingstmontag, May 25 in 2015, May 16 in 2016 |
| **Corpus Christi** | Fronleichnam, June 4 in 2015, May 26 in 2016 |
| **Late June** | Midsummer Eve celebrations, throughout Austria |
| **Mid-July-Aug** | Salzburg Festival (www.salzburgfestival.at) |
| **Aug 15** | Assumption (Mariä Himmelfahrt), parts of Austria |
| **Sept 24** | St. Rupert's Day (Ruperti-Kirtag), Salzburg |
| **Mid-Sept-early Oct** | Fall beer festivals, throughout Bavaria |
| **Oct 26** | Austrian National Day (Nationalfeiertag) |

| | |
|---|---|
| **Nov 1** | All Saints' Day (Allerheiligen) |
| **Nov 11** | St. Martin's Day celebrations (feasts), Austria and Bavaria |
| **Dec 6** | St. Nicholas Day (Nikolaustag, parades), throughout Austria |
| **Dec 8** | Feast of the Immaculate Conception (Mariä Empfängnis) |
| **Dec 24** | Christmas Eve (Heilige Abend), when Austrians celebrate Christmas |
| **Dec 25** | Christmas |
| **Dec 26** | St. Stephen's Day (Stefanitag) |
| **Dec 31** | New Year's Eve (Silvester, a.k.a. Altjahrstag; fireworks), throughout Austria, particularly Vienna |

# Conversions and Climate

## NUMBERS AND STUMBLERS

- Europeans write a few of their numbers differently than we do. 1 = 1, 4 = 4, 7 = 7.
- In Europe, dates appear as day/month/year, so Christmas 2016 is 25/12/16.
- Commas are decimal points and decimals are commas. A dollar and a half is $1,50, one thousand is 1.000, and there are 5.280 feet in a mile.
- When counting with fingers, start with your thumb. If you hold up your first finger to request one item, you'll probably get two.
- What Americans call the second floor of a building is the first floor in Europe.
- On escalators and moving sidewalks, Europeans keep the left "lane" open for passing. Keep to the right.

## METRIC CONVERSIONS

A kilogram is 2.2 pounds, and 1 liter is about a quart, or almost four to a gallon. A kilometer is six-tenths of a mile. I figure kilometers to miles by cutting them in half and adding back 10 percent of the original (120 km: 60 + 12 = 72 miles, 300 km: 150 + 30 = 180 miles).

| | |
|---|---|
| 1 foot = 0.3 meter | 1 square yard = 0.8 square meter |
| 1 yard = 0.9 meter | 1 square mile = 2.6 square kilometers |
| 1 mile = 1.6 kilometers | 1 ounce = 28 grams |
| 1 centimeter = 0.4 inch | 1 quart = 0.95 liter |
| 1 meter = 39.4 inches | 1 kilogram = 2.2 pounds |
| 1 kilometer = 0.62 mile | 32°F = 0°C |

APPENDIX

## CLOTHING SIZES

When shopping for clothing, use these US-to-European comparisons as general guidelines (but note that no conversion is perfect).

- Women's dresses and blouses: Add 30
  (US size 10 = European size 40)
- Men's suits and jackets: Add 10
  (US size 40 regular = European size 50)
- Men's shirts: Multiply by 2 and add about 8
  (US size 15 collar = European size 38)
- Women's shoes: Add about 30
  (US size 8 = European size 38-39)
- Men's shoes: Add 32-34
  (US size 9 = European size 41; US size 11 = European size 45)

## VIENNA'S CLIMATE

The first line is the average daily high; the second line, the average daily low. The third line shows the average number of days without rain. For more detailed weather statistics for destinations throughout Austria (as well as the rest of the world), check www.wunderground.com.

| J | F | M | A | M | J | J | A | S | O | N | D |
|---|---|---|---|---|---|---|---|---|---|---|---|
| **Vienna** | | | | | | | | | | | |
| 34° | 38° | 47° | 58° | 67° | 73° | 76° | 75° | 68° | 56° | 45° | 37° |
| 25° | 28° | 30° | 42° | 50° | 56° | 60° | 59° | 53° | 44° | 37° | 30° |
| 16 | 17 | 18 | 17 | 18 | 16 | 18 | 18 | 20 | 18 | 16 | 16 |

## FAHRENHEIT AND CELSIUS CONVERSION

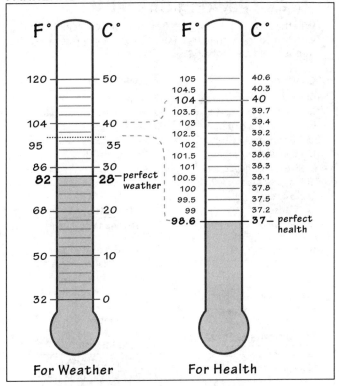

*Europe takes its temperature using the Celsius scale, while we opt for Fahrenheit. For a rough conversion from Celsius to Fahrenheit, double the number and add 30. For weather, remember that 28°C is 82°F— perfect. For health, 37°C is just right. At a launderette, 30°C is cold, 40°C is warm (usually the default setting), 60°C is hot, and 95°C is boiling.*

# Packing Checklist

Whether you're traveling for five days or five weeks, you won't need more than this. Pack light to enjoy the sweet freedom of true mobility.

## Clothing

- ☐ 5 shirts: long- & short-sleeve
- ☐ 2 pairs pants or skirt
- ☐ 1 pair shorts or capris
- ☐ 5 pairs underwear & socks
- ☐ 1 pair walking shoes
- ☐ Sweater or fleece top
- ☐ Rainproof jacket with hood
- ☐ Tie or scarf
- ☐ Swimsuit
- ☐ Sleepwear

## Money

- ☐ Debit card
- ☐ Credit card(s)
- ☐ Hard cash ($20 bills)
- ☐ Money belt or neck wallet

## Documents & Travel Info

- ☐ Passport
- ☐ Airline reservations
- ☐ Rail pass/train reservations
- ☐ Car-rental voucher
- ☐ Driver's license
- ☐ Student ID, hostel card, etc.
- ☐ Photocopies of all the above
- ☐ Hotel confirmations
- ☐ Insurance details
- ☐ Guidebooks & maps
- ☐ Notepad & pen
- ☐ Journal

## Toiletries Kit

- ☐ Toiletries
- ☐ Medicines & vitamins
- ☐ First-aid kit
- ☐ Glasses/contacts/sunglasses (with prescriptions)
- ☐ Earplugs
- ☐ Packet of tissues (for WC)

## Miscellaneous

- ☐ Daypack
- ☐ Sealable plastic baggies
- ☐ Laundry soap
- ☐ Spot remover
- ☐ Clothesline
- ☐ Sewing kit
- ☐ Travel alarm/watch

## Electronics

- ☐ Smartphone or mobile phone
- ☐ Camera & related gear
- ☐ Tablet/ereader/media player
- ☐ Laptop & flash drive
- ☐ Earbuds or headphones
- ☐ Chargers
- ☐ Plug adapters

## Optional Extras

- ☐ Flipflops or slippers
- ☐ Mini-umbrella or poncho
- ☐ Travel hairdryer
- ☐ Belt
- ☐ Hat (for sun or cold)
- ☐ Picnic supplies
- ☐ Water bottle
- ☐ Fold-up tote bag
- ☐ Small flashlight
- ☐ Small binoculars
- ☐ Insect repellent
- ☐ Small towel or washcloth
- ☐ Inflatable pillow
- ☐ Some duct tape (for repairs)
- ☐ Tiny lock
- ☐ Address list (to mail postcards)
- ☐ Postcards/photos from home
- ☐ Extra passport photos
- ☐ Good book

# German Survival Phrases for Austria

When using the phonetics, pronounce ī as the long I sound in "light."

| English | German | Pronunciation |
|---|---|---|
| Good day. | *Grüss Gott.* | **grews** gote |
| Do you speak English? | *Sprechen Sie Englisch?* | **shprehkh**-ehn zee **ehgn**-lish |
| Yes. / No. | *Ja. / Nein.* | yah / nīn |
| I (don't) understand. | *Ich verstehe (nicht).* | ikh fehr-**shtay**-heh (nikht) |
| Please. | *Bitte.* | **bit**-teh |
| Thank you. | *Danke.* | **dahng**-keh |
| I'm sorry. | *Es tut mir leid.* | ehs toot meer līt |
| Excuse me. | *Entschuldigung.* | ehnt-**shool**-dig-oong |
| (No) problem. | *(Kein) Problem.* | (kīn) proh-**blaym** |
| (Very) good. | *(Sehr) gut.* | (zehr) goot |
| Goodbye. | *Auf Wiedersehen.* | owf **vee**-der-zayn |
| one / two | *eins / zwei* | īns / tsvī |
| three / four | *drei / vier* | drī / feer |
| five / six | *fünf / sechs* | fewnf / zehkhs |
| seven / eight | *sieben / acht* | **zee**-behn / ahkht |
| nine / ten | *neun / zehn* | noyn / tsayn |
| How much is it? | *Wieviel kostet das?* | **vee**-feel **kohs**-teht dahs |
| Write it? | *Schreiben?* | **shrī**-behn |
| Is it free? | *Ist es umsonst?* | ist ehs oom-**zohnst** |
| Included? | *Inklusive?* | in-kloo-**zee**-veh |
| Where can I buy / find...? | *Wo kann ich kaufen / finden...?* | voh kahn ikh **kow**-fehn / **fin**-dehn |
| I'd like / We'd like... | *Ich hätte gern / Wir hätten gern...* | ikh **heh**-teh gehrn / veer **heh**-tehn gehrn |
| ...a room. | *...ein Zimmer.* | īn **tsim**-mer |
| ...a ticket to ___. | *...eine Fahrkarte nach ___.* | ī-neh **far**-kar-teh nahkh |
| Is it possible? | *Ist es möglich?* | ist ehs **mur**-glikh |
| Where is...? | *Wo ist...?* | voh ist |
| ...the train station | *...der Bahnhof* | dehr **bahn**-hohf |
| ...the bus station | *...der Busbahnhof* | dehr **boos**-bahn-hohf |
| ...the tourist information office | *...das Touristen- informations- büro* | dahs too-**ris**-tehn-in-for-maht-see-**ohns**-**bew**-roh |
| ...the toilet | *...die Toilette* | dee toh-**leh**-teh |
| men | *Herren* | **hehr**-rehn |
| women | *Damen* | **dah**-mehn |
| left / right | *links / rechts* | links / rehkhts |
| straight | *geradeaus* | geh-**rah**-deh-**ows** |
| What time does this open / close? | *Um wieviel Uhr wird hier geöffnet / geschlossen?* | oom **vee**-feel oor veerd heer geh-**urf**-neht / geh-**shloh**-sehn |
| At what time? | *Um wieviel Uhr?* | oom **vee**-feel oor |
| Just a moment. | *Moment.* | moh-**mehnt** |
| now / soon / later | *jetzt / bald / später* | yehtst / bahld / **shpay**-ter |
| today / tomorrow | *heute / morgen* | **hoy**-teh / **mor**-gehn |

## In a German Restaurant

| English | German | Pronunciation |
|---|---|---|
| I'd like / We'd like... | Ich hätte gern / Wir hätten gern... | ikh **heh**-teh gehrn / veer **heh**-tehn gehrn |
| ...a reservation for... | ...eine Reservierung für... | **ī**-neh reh-zer-**feer**-oong fewr |
| ...a table for one / two. | ...einen Tisch für eine Person / zwei Personen. | **ī**-nehn tish fewr **ī**-neh pehr- zohn / tsvī pehr-zohnehn |
| Non-smoking. | Nichtraucher. | **nikht**-rowkh-er |
| Is this seat free? | Ist hier frei? | ist heer frī |
| Menu (in English), please. | Speisekarte (auf Englisch), bitte. | **shpī**-zeh-kar-teh (owf **ehng**-lish) **bit**-teh |
| service (not) included | Trinkgeld (nicht) inklusive | **trink**-gehlt (nikht) in-kloo-**zee**-veh |
| cover charge | Eintritt | **īn**-trit |
| to go | zum Mitnehmen | tsoom **mit**-nay-mehn |
| with / without | mit / ohne | mit / **oh**-neh |
| and / or | und / oder | oont / **oh**-der |
| menu (of the day) | (Tages-) Karte | (**tah**-gehs-) **kar**-teh |
| set meal for tourists | Touristenmenü | too-**ris**-tehn-meh-**new** |
| specialty of the house | Spezialität des Hauses | **shpayt**-see-ah-lee-**tayt** dehs **how**-zehs |
| appetizers | Vorspeise | **for**-shpī-zeh |
| bread / cheese | Brot / Käse | broht / **kay**-zeh |
| sandwich | Sandwich | **zahnd**-vich |
| soup | Suppe | **zup**-peh |
| salad | Salat | zah-**laht** |
| meat | Fleisch | flīsh |
| poultry | Geflügel | geh-**flew**-gehl |
| fish | Fisch | fish |
| seafood | Meeresfrüchte | **meh**-rehs-**frewkh**-teh |
| fruit | Obst | ohpst |
| vegetables | Gemüse | geh-**mew**-zeh |
| dessert | Nachspeise | **nahkh**-shpī-zeh |
| mineral water | Mineralwasser | min-eh-**rahl**-vah-ser |
| tap water | Leitungswasser | **lī**-toongs-vah-ser |
| milk | Milch | milkh |
| (orange) juice | (Orangen-) Saft | (oh-**rahn**-zhehn-) zahft |
| coffee / tea | Kaffee / Tee | kah-**fay** / tay |
| wine | Wein | vīn |
| red / white | rot / weiß | roht / vīs |
| glass / bottle | Glas / Flasche | glahs / **flah**-sheh |
| beer | Bier | beer |
| Cheers! | Prost! | prohst |
| More. / Another. | Mehr. / Noch eins. | mehr / nohkh īns |
| The same. | Das gleiche. | dahs **glīkh**-eh |
| Bill, please. | Rechnung, bitte. | **rehkh**-noong **bit**-teh |
| tip | Trinkgeld | **trink**-gehlt |
| Delicious! | Lecker! | **lehk**-er |

For more user-friendly German phrases, check out *Rick Steves' German Phrase Book and Dictionary* or *Rick Steves' French, Italian & German Phrase Book.*

# INDEX

INDEX

INDEX

**INDEX**

# MAP INDEX

### Explore Europe

At ricksteves.com you can browse through thousands of articles, videos, photos and radio interviews, plus find a wealth of money-saving travel tips for planning your dream trip. And with our mobile-friendly website, you can easily access all this great travel information anywhere you go.

### TV Shows

Preview the places you'll visit by watching entire half-hour episodes of Rick Steves' Europe (choose from all 100 shows) on-demand, for free.

# ricksteves.com

*your travel dreams into affordable reality*

## Radio Interviews

Enjoy ready access to Rick's vast library of radio interviews covering travel

tips and cultural insights that relate specifically to your Europe travel plans.

## Travel Forums

Learn, ask, share! Our online community of savvy travelers is a great resource

for first-time travelers to Europe, as well as seasoned pros. You'll find forums on each country, plus travel tips and restaurant/hotel reviews. You can even ask one of our well-traveled staff to chime in with an opinion.

## Travel News

Subscribe to our free Travel News e-newsletter, and get monthly updates from Rick on what's happening in Europe.

# Audio Europe™

# Pack Light and Right

*Gear up for your next adventure at ricksteves.com*

### Light Luggage

Pack light and right with Rick Steves' affordable, custom-designed rolling carry-on bags, backpacks, day packs and shoulder bags.

### Accessories

From packing cubes to moneybelts and beyond, Rick has personally selected the travel goodies that will help your trip go smoother.

## Shop at ricksteves.com

# Rick Steves has

*Experience maximum Europe*

### Save time and energy

This guidebook is your independent-travel toolkit. But for all it delivers, it's still up to you to devote the time and energy it takes to manage the preparation and logistics that are essential for a happy trip. If that's a hassle, there's a solution.

### Rick Steves Tours

A Rick Steves tour takes you to Europe's most interesting places with great

# great tours, too!

## *with minimum stress*

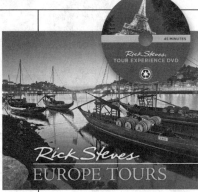

guides and small groups of 28 or less. We follow Rick's favorite itineraries, ride in comfy buses, stay in family-run hotels, and bring you intimately close to the Europe you've traveled so far to see. Most importantly, we take away the logistical headaches so you can focus on the fun.

### Join the fun

This year we'll take 18,000 free-spirited travelers— nearly half of them repeat customers—along with us on 40 different itineraries, from Ireland to Italy to Istanbul. Is a Rick Steves tour the right fit for your travel dreams? Find out at ricksteves.com, where you can also get Rick's latest tour catalog and free Tour Experience DVD.

Europe is best experienced with happy travel partners. We hope you can join us.

---

## See our itineraries at ricksteves.com

Rick Steves guidebooks are published by Avalon Travel,
a member of the Perseus Books Group.

# NOW AVAILABLE:
# eBOOKS, DVD & BLU-RAY

## TRAVEL CULTURE

Europe 101
European Christmas
Postcards from Europe
Travel as a Political Act

### eBOOKS

*Nearly all Rick Steves guides are available as ebooks. Check with your favorite bookseller.*

### *RICK STEVES' EUROPE* DVDs

11 New Shows 2013–2014
Austria & the Alps
Eastern Europe
England & Wales
European Christmas
European Travel Skills & Specials
France
Germany, BeNeLux & More
Greece, Turkey & Portugal
Iran
Ireland & Scotland
Italy's Cities
Italy's Countryside
Scandinavia
Spain
Travel Extras

## BLU-RAY

Celtic Charms
Eastern Europe Favorites
European Christmas
Italy Through the Back Door
Mediterranean Mosaic
Surprising Cities of Europe

### PHRASE BOOKS & DICTIONARIES

French
French, Italian & German
German
Italian
Portuguese
Spanish

### JOURNALS

Rick Steves Pocket Travel Journal
Rick Steves Travel Journal

### PLANNING MAPS

Britain, Ireland & London
Europe
France & Paris
Germany, Austria & Switzerland
Ireland
Italy
Spain & Portugal

**RickSteves.com** 🇫 🇹 **@RickSteves**

Rick Steves books and DVDs are available at bookstores
and through online booksellers.

Photo © Patricia Feaster

# Credits

## RESEARCHER
To help update this book, Rick relied on...

### Ian Watson
Ian has worked on Rick's guidebooks since 1993, after starting out with Let's Go and Frommer's guides. Originally from upstate New York, Ian speaks several European languages, including German, and makes his home in Reykjavík, Iceland.

## CONTRIBUTOR
### Gene Openshaw

Gene is a writer, composer, and lecturer on art and history. Specializing in writing tours of Europe's cultural sights, Gene has co-authored a dozen of Rick's books and contributes to Rick's public television series. As a composer, Gene has written a full-length opera *(Matter)*, a violin sonata, and dozens of songs. He lives near Seattle with his daughter, and roots for the Mariners in good times and bad.

## ACKNOWLEDGMENTS
Rick and his staff extend sincere thanks to tour guides Ursula Klaus, Wolfgang Höfler, Lisa Zeiler, and Martin Sloboda for their help with this book.

Avalon Travel
a member of the Perseus Books Group
1700 Fourth Street
Berkeley, CA 94710

Printed in Canada by Friesens. First printing October 2014.

ISBN 978-1-63121-056-3
ISSN 1946-617X

For the latest on Rick's lectures, guidebooks, tours, public radio show, and public television series, contact Rick Steves' Europe, 130 Fourth Avenue North, Edmonds, WA 98020, tel. 425/771-8303, www.ricksteves.com, rick@ricksteves.com.

**Rick Steves' Europe**
**Managing Editor:** Risa Laib
**Editorial & Production Manager:** Jennifer Madison Davis
**Editors:** Glenn Eriksen, Tom Griffin, Cameron Hewitt, Suzanne Kotz, Cathy Lu, Carrie Shepherd
**Editorial & Production Assistant:** Jessica Shaw
**Editorial Intern:** Mallory Presho-Dunne
**Researchers:** Gene Openshaw, Ian Watson
**Maps & Graphics:** David C. Hoerlein, Sandra Hundacker, Lauren Mills, Mary Rostad

**Avalon Travel**
**Senior Editor and Series Manager:** Madhu Prasher
**Editor:** Jamie Andrade
**Associate Editor:** Maggie Ryan
**Copy Editor:** Denise Silva
**Proofreader:** Kelly Lydick
**Indexer:** Beatrice Wikander
**Production:** Tabitha Lahr and Jane Musser
**Cover Design:** Kimberly Glyder Design
**Maps & Graphics:** Kat Bennett, Mike Morgenfeld

**Photo Credits**
**Front Cover:** Strauss Statue © Cameron Hewitt
**Page i:** National Theater at Night © Rick Steves
**Additional Photography:** Dominic Bonuccelli, Brandner Schiffahrt GmbH, Ben Cameron, Cameron Hewitt, David C. Hoerlein, K&T Boarding House, Debi Jo Michael, Gene Openshaw, Rick Steves, Gretchen Strauch, Karoline Vass, Ian Watson (photos are used by permission and are the property of the original copyright owners)

# ABOUT THE AUTHOR

## RICK STEVES

 Since 1973, Rick Steves has spent 100 days every year exploring Europe. Along with writing and researching a bestselling series of guidebooks, Rick produces a public television series *(Rick Steves' Europe)*, a public radio show *(Travel with Rick Steves)*, a blog on Facebook, and an app and podcast *(Rick Steves Audio Europe)*; writes a nationally syndicated newspaper column; organizes guided tours that take over 15,000 travelers to Europe annually; and offers an information-packed website (www.ricksteves.com). With the help of his hardworking staff of 90 at Rick Steves' Europe—in Edmonds, Washington, just north of Seattle—Rick's mission is to make European travel fun, affordable, and culturally enlightening for Americans.

Connect with Rick:

facebook.com/RickSteves          twitter: @RickSteves